Cognitive Development and Learning in Instructional Contexts

SECOND EDITION

James P. Byrnes

University of Maryland

Allyn and Bacon

Boston • London • Toronto • Sydney • Tokyo • Singapore

For Julia and Tommy—
whose development inspires me
and whose affection sustains me

Vice President: Paul A. Smith
Editorial Assistant: Lauren Finn
Marketing Managers: Brad Parkins and Kathleen Morgan
Editorial Production Service: Marbern House
Manufacturing Buyer: Suzanne Lareau
Cover Administrator: Kristina Mose-Libon
Electronic Composition: Omegatype Typography, Inc.

Internet: www.ablongman.com

Between the time Website information is gathered and published, some sites may have closed.
Also, the transcription of URLs can result in typographical errors. The publisher would appreciate
notification where these occur so that they may be corrected in subsequent editions.

ISBN: 0-205-30858-9

Printed in the United States of America

10   9   8   7   6   5   4   3   RRD-VA   05   04   03   02

Contents

4 *Higher-Order Thinking* **70**

PART TWO • *Age Changes in Specific Subject Areas*   **121**

Preface

In 1989, I developed a course at the University of Maryland called *Cognitive Development in School Contexts* in which I organized the psychological literature on reading, writing, math, science, and social studies into a developmental perspective. I believed at that time and I believe even more strongly now that teacher preparation programs should be **centered on** developmental theory and research. In other words, instead of spending lots of time explaining instructional techniques and spending very little time thinking about developmental trends in school-related learning and motivation, I think equal time (at least) should be given to methods and educationally relevant developmental research. The goal of that original course was to give preservice and practicing teachers insight into age changes in specific subject areas and developmental mechanisms that could explain these changes. In addition, I wanted them to become familiar with contemporary theories of learning, higher-order thinking, and motivation. Finally, I wanted teachers to become aware of persistent and puzzling gender and ethnic differences in school achievement. Because no one book covered all these topics in 1989, I was motivated to write this book. As far as I can tell, the present edition is still the only book that considers all these traditional educational psychology topics from a developmental perspective.

Goals of This Book

I want to equip teachers, principals, policy-makers, parents, and students with the knowledge they need to be effective problem-solvers about educational issues. I say more about this in Chapter 1, but my premise is that one can solve a learning or motivation problem (e.g., too few children in your school perform at grade level) only if one knows the cause of this problem. Informing readers of this book about the inner workings of the mind is identical to teaching a car mechanic about the inner workings of car engines or teaching physicians about the inner workings of the body. Car mechanics need to be intimately familiar with the workings of an engine in order to know how to fix a problem when it occurs. Physicians cannot cure an ailment if they do not know how various organs and tissues work. In the same way, a teacher could not solve a learning or motivation problem without knowledge of how the mind works. Presenting an instructional method to a teacher without giving him or her knowledge of the mind is like presenting a drug therapy to a physician without explaining how the drug operates within the body. The more mysterious a therapy or instructional program is (e.g., "It works but I don't know why"), the more likely it is to be used ineffectively or inappropriately.

Of course, there are many other students and professionals who would benefit from the information contained in this book. For example, most developmental psychologists are generally unfamiliar with the research that has examined development in school subjects such as math or reading. Relatedly, most cognitive development books devote a single chapter (if that) to school-related learning. The opposite can be said about traditional books in educational psychology. Although many of the ideas contained in this book also appear in traditional educational psychology texts (e.g., theories of memory and motivation), developmental ideas are relegated to a single chapter. Thus, the present book serves as a useful complement or an alternative to traditional cognitive development and educational psychology texts. In addition, undergraduates, graduate students, and parents can benefit from the information presented here because it is intended to enhance their metacognition about school-related learning and motivation. Knowing how the mind works is useful information for students who face their own problems in school (e.g., why do I find it hard to learn calculus?) and useful for parents as they try to help their children solve school-related problems.

Scientific Basis of the Work

The view of the mind presented in this book is grounded firmly in research; that is, I have included only claims about the mind that are supported by sound, empirical studies conducted by developmental, educational, or cognitive psychologists. Too often, educators are swayed by approaches that "sound good" but are not supported by credible data. In fact, officials in the federal government are now moving toward funding programs in the schools that have a scientific basis only. My emphasis on data led me sometimes to go against the prevailing consensus in some educational circles. In other words, I decided to omit a popular approach or topic from my book when it had no data to support it. In most cases, however, the educational community has created important reforms that are based on the research that I describe in my book.

Changes in the Second Edition

Several new features of this edition are worth noting. First, close to 300 new references have been added (a 60-percent increase) to reflect multiple, burgeoning areas in developmental, educational, and cognitive psychology. Second, the chapters have been reorganized into two main sections: (a) Part I: foundations (theories of learning, higher-order thinking, and motivation that apply to any subject area) and (b) Part II: age changes in specific subject areas. Third, I moved the motivation chapter from the end of the book to the foundations section to facilitate activities described in the next change. Fourth, additional case studies are added to all chapters in Part II to allow students to apply what they have learned to the evaluation of each case. The cases are now simply described without an evaluation. Instructors who use this book are encouraged to ask students to take what they learn in the foundations portion of the book and the first part of each chapter to identify the strengths and weaknesses of popular instructional approaches. Fifth, the utility of a developmental approach is explained more fully in Chapter 1 and discussions of developmental mechanisms of age changes now appear in every chapter. Sixth, brain research relevant to theories of learning, memory, reading, writing, math, and individual differences is reviewed in appropriate chapters.

Acknowledgments

I have the good fortune of working in a college of education that is filled with talented individuals. I owe intellectual debts to Patricia Alexander, Nathan Fox, John Guthrie, Jamie Metsala, Steve Porges, Saundra Nettles, Judith Torney-Purta, Allan Wigfield, and Kathy Wentzel in my own Human Development department. They have taught me much about learning, reading, brain development, emotional development, the development of minority children, social studies learning, and motivation. In the rest of the college of education, I have benefitted from my discussions with colleagues in math education (Jim Fey, Pat Campbell, Anna Graeber), science education (Bill Holliday, John Layman), social studies education (Joe Cirrincione, Bruce Van Sledright), reading (Peter Afflerbach, Jean Dreher, Marilyn Chambliss), and special education (Steve Graham, Karen Harris). I also want to thank Nancy Forsyth and Paul Smith at Allyn and Bacon for their encouragement and feedback, and also for securing excellent advice from the reviewers of the first edition: Karen K. Block, University of Pittsburgh; Harold Jones, Lander University; Michael Piburn, Arizona State University; Alice J. Corkhill, University of Nevada; Shari Tishman, Harvard University; Jay Blanchard, Arizona State University; Dale H. Schunk, Purdue University; and Peter Oliver, University of Hartford.

I am grateful, as well, to the reviewers of the second edition for their helpful comments: Julianne C. Turner, University of Notre Dame; Nora Newcombe, Temple University; Linda Baker, The University of Maryland, Baltimore County; Linda Metzke, Lyndon State College; Elisabeth L. McFalls, University of South Florida–Tampa; Sandra Katz, University of Pittsburgh; and Helena P. Osana, University of Missouri–Columbia.

Finally, I want to thank my wife Barbara for many hours of discussion about educational issues and for her support while I wrote this book.

1

Introduction

The goal of this introductory chapter is to give you a sense of what this book is about. To accomplish this goal, this chapter is divided into four sections. In the first section, you will be told the reasons why this book was written and also learn about the "diagnosis" approach to problem-solving. In the second section, you will learn about two constructs that are used to organize the studies reported in this book: cognitive development and individual differences. In the third section, you will be told about the importance of developmental and individual differences in cognition. In the final section, you will be presented with the themes that emerge from nearly every chapter in this book.

Why This Book Was Written

There are four reasons why this book was written:

1. to help successful graduate and undergraduate students understand why they are so successful;
2. to help students who are dissatisfied with their performance in school understand how they can improve their performance;
3. to help teachers or teachers-in-training understand the nature of learning and motivation; and
4. to give educators, principals, and parents the knowledge they need to evaluate current instructional practices and have a clear sense of how things should change when ineffective practices are discovered.

For the readers of this book who are interested in learning or motivation problems, this book can be thought of as either a "self-help" book or "how to" book (depending on whether you, or someone else, is experiencing the problems related to classroom learning or motivation). The approach taken here, however, is not one in which the readers of this book will be given a series of prescriptions or recipes for success. Instead, readers will be given the information they need to effectively diagnose the causes of learning problems on their own and figure out how to solve these problems on their own.

To help you appreciate the utility of this "diagnosis" approach to problem-solving, consider the following analogy. A car mechanic would not be in business very long if he or she engaged in a "try this/try that" approach to engine repair. Usually, the same engine problem (e.g., stalling) can have two or more possible causes such as insufficient air getting to the carburetor, water in the fuel line, etc. The mechanic will only be able to repair the problem if he or she can identify which possible cause is the culprit (e.g., insufficient air) and then somehow deal with this cause (e.g., turns a screw on the carburetor which lets in more air).

Implicit in this analogy is the idea that effective problem-solving begins with a firm understanding of the domain in question. Good car mechanics know all of the parts of the car and how these parts work. This knowledge helps them comprehend failures because they understand how things disrupt the normal functioning of the part in question. By the end of this book, you will learn a lot about the components of the mind and how these work when people learn information. This knowledge will help you understand how things can interfere with the optimal functioning of the mind and give you an idea of how to deal with these interferences.

To get a sense of some of the diagnoses that you will be able to make after reading this book, consider the following list of questions:

1. Why are some school subjects so difficult for young children to understand? Why is it that older children learn the same material more easily?
2. Why do people seem to forget so much of what they learn in school? Why do younger children forget more than older children?
3. Why are so many high school graduates unable to apply what they learned in school to the real world?
4. Why is it that not all students in the same grade learn the same material equally well?
5. Why do so many students lose their motivation to do well in school as they grow older?
6. In any given grade, why are some students more motivated than others?

Regardless of whether you are a teacher, parent, policy-maker, or student, you are probably interested in finding answers to these questions. The goal of this book is to provide the best possible answers to them. You will note that whenever this book provides an answer to one of these questions, you will be given a diagnosis.

A related way to understand the information in this book is to refer to the distinction between **conceptual** and **procedural knowledge** (see Chapters 2, 3, and 8). Procedural knowledge, or "knowing how," is knowledge of goal-directed actions (Byrnes, 1999). When people know how to tie their shoes, compute answers to math problems, or drive a car, they have procedural knowledge. In each case, there are a set of actions that are performed to accomplish some goal. For example, people drive cars in order to get to work, go to the store, and so on. Experienced teachers have an important kind of procedural knowledge that many non-teachers lack. In particular, they know how to teach different topics using specific instructional techniques and lessons. Teachers know, however, that there are many different ways to teach the same topic. For example, to teach math facts, a teacher could either use flash cards or have children incidentally learn these facts as they play games on the computer. In the real world, some instructional techniques work better than others. This book was written to give teachers the conceptual knowledge they need to understand *why* some techniques work better than others. In this sense, the information in this book is like the conceptual knowledge that teachers now give to children to help them stop performing math procedures in a mindless way (see Chapter 8).

Two Central Constructs

As a third way of coming to know the content of this book, let's next examine two central constructs that organize many of the ideas that you will learn about. As the title of this book implies, the primary focus of this book is cognitive development in instructional contexts. To get a clearer understanding of this focus, we first need to define what is meant by the phrase **cognitive development.** The word "cognitive" is used to imply that we shall be focusing on mental processes such as thinking, learning, remembering, and problem-solving (as opposed to other psychological constructs such as emotions, friendships, and personality traits). Unlike the behaviorist who focuses exclusively on children's actions (e.g., responding "true" to some question on a test), we will be considering the cognitive events that subtend or cause these behaviors (e.g., their conceptual understanding of the test question).

The word "development" is used to imply two things: (a) cognitive processes *change* with age or experience, and (b) this change is *for the better.* Sometimes children are more likely to do maladaptive things with age (e.g., smoke cigarettes). In this book, we shall be concerned primarily with alterations that help children do better in school and in the world of adults. A developmental focus, however, is not simply limited to a recounting of adaptive age trends (e.g., many children change from being non-readers at age one to fluent readers by age nine). It also involves a consideration of the factors and processes that *produce* these age trends. In the developmental literature, these factors and processes are collectively called **developmental mechanisms** (Klahr & MacWhinney, 1998). As we shall see in Chapter 2, Jean Piaget became famous for his claim that many age trends can be explained using a developmental mechanism called **equilibration.** Other examples of developmental mechanisms include instruction (e.g., older children have more math knowledge than younger children because this knowledge was provided to them by teachers) and maturation (e.g., older children respond faster than younger children because the former have more myelinated neurons in their brain than the latter).

In sum, then, we shall examine how cognitive processes such as thinking improve with age. However, we shall limit our literature review to the research which has examined school-related learning (e.g., children's learning of math, science, and social studies). This limitation explains the second part of the title and makes this present book distinct from other cognitive development texts that devote little attention to school subjects (e.g., Flavell, Miller, & Miller, 1993; Siegler, 1998).

In addition to examining developmental differences in cognitive performance, this book also examines so-called **individual differences.** To get a good sense of the meaning of this construct, it is helpful to compare it to the notion of developmental differences. When researchers examine developmental differences in performance, they usually compare the average student in a grade to the average student in another grade (e.g., the average sixth grader compared to the average third grader). By considering the average or typical student in a grade, developmental researchers intentionally ignore differences that might exist among children in the same grade. In contrast, researchers who study individual differences try to reveal differences between one child in a grade and another child in that same grade (e.g., one sixth grader compared to another sixth grader). So, if you return to the questions posed in the first section of this chapter, you will see that whereas questions 1, 2, and 5 focus on developmental differences, questions 4 and 6 focus on individual differences. In nearly every chapter, we shall examine both developmental and individual differences in cognitive performance on school-related tasks.

Why Study Developmental and Individual Differences?

Any experienced teacher will tell you that there is no such thing as an instructional technique that works well for all students in all grade levels. There are always groups of students who benefit more from a certain technique than others. Research has consistently confirmed this experience-based conviction (Pressley et al., 1994; Snow, 1994). Similarly, successful teachers would tell you that you should not teach a topic to first graders the same way that you would teach it to sixth graders. One of the main goals of this book is to help readers understand *why* instruction has to be catered to the needs of different groups of students. Such information will not only help teachers become more flexible, adaptive problem-solvers in the classroom, but it will also help consumers of instruction (e.g., parents and students) pose counter-arguments to an instructor's claim that a student's learning problems could not be due to the way a particular instructional technique was implemented because the technique is "known to work."

In addition, as Vygotsky noted a long time ago, the best way to understand the current state of a group of learners is to know where they have come from and where they seem to be going (Wertsch, 1985). An unfortunate aspect of much of the work in educational psychology is that researchers do not always take a developmental perspective. It can be quite informative for a high school teacher to know how his or her students used to think when they were in middle school. Similarly, it can be equally useful for this teacher to think about what his or her students are capable of so that instruction can help them get there.

Relatedly, a developmental perspective suggests a rather different role for teachers than that implied by a more traditional, "stand and deliver" perspective. When children are viewed from a developmental perspective, teachers tend to view themselves as **facilitators of directed, progressive change.** In other words, they ask themselves, "How did my students get this way, where are they supposed to be going, and how can I get them there?"

In effect, they stop being concerned with getting a particular set of facts or ideas in their students' heads and start thinking about being agents of positive change. In addition, a fundamental assumption of a developmental perspective is that there are nearly always factors that **constrain** the extent to which children can change. Sometimes children have so little knowledge about a subject that this knowledge cannot serve as a foundation for new learning. In this way, lack of knowledge constrains new learning. Other times children have too little processing capacity to perform complex mental processes in their heads (in the same way that a computer with too little RAM cannot run a complex game on a CD-ROM). In such situations, limited processing capacity constrains new learning and performance. Finally, as noted above, a developmental perspective helps teachers appreciate the role of developmental mechanisms. If developmental mechanisms explain or cause age changes, then it stands to reason that teachers have to become familiar with developmental mechanisms and figure out how to manipulate them to produce a desired change.

Common Themes Across Chapters

The final way to provide an overview of the contents of this book is to present the issues or themes that seem to arise in almost every chapter. Six themes stand out:

1. *The contrast between rote learning and meaningful learning.* In every subject area (e.g., math, science, social studies), there are a whole host of facts to be learned and skills to be acquired. For example, students are asked to learn facts such as "$6 \times 7 = 42$" and "water is made up of hydrogen and oxygen," as well as skills such as knowing how to add fractions and knowing how to conduct a good experiment. Most educators and students recognize that these facts and skills could be learned in either a meaningless, rote way or a meaningful way. We shall see in the chapters on math, science, reading, and social studies that there is a strong push these days to engage students in meaningful as opposed to rote learning. In addition, the contrast between rote and meaningful learning plays an important role in the discussions of higher order thinking in Chapter 3 and in discussions of memory in Chapter 4. Finally, the contrast between Thorndike's theory and other theories of learning (e.g., Schema theory) also hinges on the distinction between rote and meaningful learning (see Chapter 2).

2. *The emphasis on the Constructivist view of learning.* The Constructivist view of learning stands in sharp contrast to what can be called the Objectivist view of learning (Cobb, Yackel, & Wood, 1992; Pirie & Kieren, 1992; Roth, 1994; Stofflett, 1994). Objectivists believe that knowledge can exist outside the mind of the knower and that learning is simply the process by which this externally-real knowledge is transferred rather directly to the knower's mind. In this "immediate acquisition" conception, there is no reason why students should have trouble learning anything. Moreover, it is assumed that what students get out of a lecture or lab is what is contained in the lecture or lab (fact for fact) and that all students will acquire the same information (Pressley et al., 1994). In other words, the relationship among ideas (e.g., that between money and base-ten arithmetic) exists in real objects, is obvious, and can be immediately seen by all students.

In contrast, Constructivists believe that knowledge has no existence outside of someone's mind and that students always **interpret** what is presented to them using their pre-existing knowledge, histories, and typical ways of perceiving and acting (Pirie & Kieren, 1992). Because students often have unique experiences and histories, Constructivists expect that students will develop idiosyncratic understandings of the same material which differs from the understandings of experts in a field. For example, it is conceivable that in a class of fifteen students, fifteen different interpretations of the same lecture on gravity could ensue. Moreover, it is likely that each of these "alternative conceptions" of gravity would differ from that of someone who has a doctorate in physics. Finally, Constructivists believe that students take what they can from a lecture or experience and use the partial understandings that are gleaned to build more complete and accurate understandings over time with repeated encounters with the same material.

The first place Constructivism appears in later chapters of this book is in the discussion of Piagetian and Schema theory in Chapter 2. But Constructivist themes emerge repeatedly in the chapters on math, science, social studies, and reading. It is fair to say that among leading educators in each of these fields (i.e., math educators, science educators, etc.), the Constructivist approach is widely accepted and advocated. As we shall see, Constructivists and Objectivists teach very differently.

3. *The existence of developmental and individual differences in cognitive performance.* In addition to recognizing a recurrent emphasis on meaningful learning and Constructivism, you will also see that important developmental and individual differences exist for all subject areas. In particular, you will see that certain topics or skills are quite difficult for children to learn before they have first mastered other ideas (e.g., ideas such as "rational number," "freedom of speech," or "atomic structure"). The existence of developmental differences in the ability to comprehend ideas or express a skill confirm the impression of experienced teachers that you cannot teach the same topic the same way to all different age groups.

In addition, you will see that for all subject areas, there are gender differences or ethnic differences in performance as well as motivational differences among students in the same class. Such findings support the contention that not all students benefit from "standard" instruction and that every classroom contains students who are not having their needs met. The last chapter in this book attempts to diagnose the causes of gender and ethnic differences so that problem-solvers could get clues as to how to eliminate these differences. The other chapters report the nature and extent of these and other individual differences in specific subject areas.

4. *Student achievement is disappointing in nearly every subject area.* When one looks at national achievement data for the existence of developmental or individual differences in performance, it is easy to miss the point that most students perform at levels far below what is desirable. On many National Assessments of Educational Progress, for example, whereas students can score as high as 500, the top scorers on the math, science, reading, social studies, or writing tests get scores of only 350. Thus, even the top scorers (who represent only a small fraction of students and who often are high school seniors) only obtain mediocre scores. What is equally disturbing is the fact that most students score below that mediocre level. It is possible to dismiss such data based on a general suspicion of standardized tests, but something seems to be amiss when so many different types of standardized and experimenter-made tests imply low levels of knowledge and skill in many students. Moreover, even if some readers of this book believe that scoring at the 350 level is not so bad, few would disagree with the claim that there is room for improvement in the way we teach.

In nearly every chapter, suggestions are made as to how best to teach children given what we know about the nature of the mind. It will be important to compare these suggestions to the "standard" approach to teaching a subject that is described in the same chapter to begin to diagnose the reasons why few students attain the top levels of performance on a variety of tests.

5. *There are a number of constraints on cognitive development that affect the rate at which improvements can occur.* In all of the school subjects covered in this book (i.e., reading, math, etc.), change does not come easily or quickly. Minimally, this finding implies that there can be no "quick fixes" to the educational problems that plague the United States and other countries. Moreover, a developmental analysis suggests that the rate of change slows with age, presumably because the cognitive systems associated with specific skills have grown in size and complexity. As such, one would expect that it would be easier to bring a faltering first grader up to speed than a fifth grader.

6. *We still do not fully understand the causes of success and failure in school.* Although, as you will see, a great deal of research has been conducted with respect to children's learning of school subjects, we still have a long way to go in order to fully understand why some students succeed and others do not. Part of the reason for this slow pace of progress is that we have been applying well-founded psychological models of cognition and research to educational subject matters for just thirty years. As a result, the fields of development and educational psychology are still in their infancies relative to fields such as medicine, chemistry, or physics. Moreover, every time we conduct a new experiment, the data may help us answer one question, but also cause us to ask five more. In addition, developmentalists have spent more time revealing age trends than they have exposing the developmental mechanisms responsible for these age trends. Nevertheless, the fact that it is possible to find six common themes across most chapters is quite telling because it means that we are probably moving in the right direction.

As you read the rest of this book, set the goal of using the information you learn about the nature of learning and motivation to form your own diagnoses of what is right and wrong with our educational system. In addition, keep an eye out for the themes of meaningfulness, Constructivism, and the importance of developmental and individual differences. Finally, come back to this chapter when you finish this book to see if you can answer the questions posed earlier.

2

Theories of Cognitive Development and Learning

Summary

1. Thorndike described knowledge in terms of neurally-based associations between situations and responses; knowledge grows according to the laws of exercise and effect; students are viewed more as "other regulated" than "self-regulated."

2. Piaget pioneered the notion of constructivism and described knowledge in terms of schemes, concepts, and structures; knowledge is manifested in four levels of thought and grows through processes of abstraction and equilibration; equilibration is the manifestation of self-regulated thinking for Piaget.

3. Schema theorists argue that although schemata sometimes cause students to misunderstand or misremember things, they usually help us solve problems, categorize efficiently, understand, and remember main ideas; schemata are formed through an abstraction process and can change in response to experience.

4. Information Processing theorists posit the existence of two forms of knowledge: declarative and procedural; knowledge acquisition is described as passing information through three memory stores; self-regulated students use strategies to create permanent memories, plan, and monitor their performance.

5. Vygotsky described knowledge in terms of concepts and functions; knowledge acquisition is described as a process of internalizing the words and actions of teachers, parents, and more capable peers; self-regulated students use egocentric and inner speech to help themselves stay on track.

6. Connectionists create "brain-style" systems to model cognition; these systems involve units that are linked to each other at various associate strengths (or weights); knowledge change consists of altering the weights between units.

7. Three themes emerge from the theories: (a) practice is important, (b) learning should be meaningful and goal-directed, and (c) the knowledge children bring to the classroom can greatly affect what they learn.

We will begin our exploration of the conceptual knowledge needed for instructional procedures (see Chapter 1) by considering several influential theories of cognitive development and learning. Over the last 100 years, many such theories have been proposed by scholars in the field of psychology. We obviously cannot examine all these views in a single chapter, so we need to limit the selection in some way. Given the goals of this book, we shall examine those theories that have shaped contemporary research in the areas of math learning, scientific reasoning, social studies learning, reading comprehension, or writing. By "shaped" we mean that educational researchers have recently used the theories to (a) interpret developmental or individual differences among students or (b) design new experiments.

The two requirements that the theories be educationally relevant and currently driving research limit the selection to just five theories. Whereas two of these theories are associated with individuals (Piaget, Vygotsky), the other three represent groups of researchers who share certain assumptions about the nature of the mind (Information Processing theory, Schema theory, Connectionism). For contrastive purposes, we shall also examine Thorndike's theory to see how the newer approaches differ from older approaches. There are also two other theories that should be addressed in this book, but they have only indirect links to education (i.e., the Expert-Novice approach and "Theory" theory). As a result, they are discussed in subsequent chapters (i.e., the Novice-Expert approach in Chapter 4 and Theory theory in Chapter 10).

The six theories of the present chapter shall be described in an order that largely mirrors the order in which they historically influenced educational and developmental researchers: Thorndike, Piaget, Schema theory, Information Processing theory, Vygotsky, and Connectionism. For each theory, we shall see how it provides answers to five questions:

1. *The "Nature of Knowledge" Question:* What form does knowledge take in a student's mind?
2. *The "Learning and Knowledge Growth" Question:* How do students acquire knowledge and how does this knowledge grow?
3. *The "Self-Regulation" Question:* How do students help themselves "stay on track" and adapt to the demands of the classroom?
4. *The "Educational Applications" Question:* How might the theory explain student successes and failures or help teachers provide more effective forms of instruction?
5. *The "Neuroscience" Question:* How does the theory relate to the field of cognitive neuroscience?

As will become clear, these questions allow us to compare and contrast theories in an effective way. At a general level, the six theories differ with respect to (a) whether they even try to answer specific questions and (b) the answers they provide if an attempt is made. The neuroscience question has been included to allow us to consider the extent to which theories have something to say about the important connections between the brain and the mind. It has been recently argued that theories should be evaluated in terms of whether they are biologically plausible and whether they make predictions consistent with findings in cognitive neuroscience (Byrnes & Fox, 1998).

Thorndike's Theory

Although Thorndike's (1913) classic theory is out of favor (and has been since at least the 1960s), it is still useful to examine it for two reasons: (a) many teachers seem to implicitly rely on Thorndike's principles when they teach, and (b) many contemporary theories can explain aspects of learning that Thorndike's theory cannot explain. By comparing the newer approaches to Thorndike's view, we get a better sense of the value of the newer approaches.

In what follows, Thorndike's theory shall be summarized in five subsections. Each subsection corresponds to one of the five questions listed earlier.

The Nature of Knowledge

What form does knowledge take in a student's mind? If we could somehow open up a student's head and "see" his or her knowledge, what would it look like? Thorndike felt that all knowledge consisted of a network of associative *bonds* between situations and responses. Some examples of pairings between situations and responses are shown in Figure 2.1.

Thorndike assumed that a student's brain could encode and store mental traces of individual aspects of a situation (e.g., the blackboard, the desks, the teacher, etc. in Situation 1). When these aspects are perceived, they activate the mental traces corresponding to them. The mental traces in turn are collectively associated with a specific response. When the association is very strong, every time a student is in Situation 1, he or she responds with Response 1. Every time he or she is in Situation 2, he or she responds with Response 2 (not Response 1 or 3).

For Thorndike, all knowledge, no matter how complex, consists of associative bonds between situations and responses. Thus, whether we are talking about answering a question with a simple multiplication fact or solving calculus word problems, students know what to do or say in a given situation by virtue of having a response (e.g., a formula for a derivative) associated with that situation (e.g., seeing a calculus word problem).

FIGURE 2.1   *Thorndike's Theory: Examples of Situation-Response Pairings*

Situation 1: A student is in Mrs. Jones' classroom with his classmates;
Mrs. Jones says, "3 × 3 = ?" (with rising intonation)

Response 1: The student responds, "9!"

Situation 2: A student is in the first seat of a row; Mr. Johnson says, "Class, this is your seat work for today" as he hands a pile of papers to the student.

Response 2: The student takes one and passes the pile to the student behind her.

Situation 3: A student is walking home and approaches a crosswalk; she looks up and sees that the traffic light is red.

Response 3: She stands at the corner and does not try to cross.

Learning and Knowledge Growth

The learning and knowledge growth question pertains to a theorist's beliefs about developmental mechanisms (see Chapter 1). If a child has more knowledge at some later point than at an earlier point, how would Thorndike explain this developmental change? The answer lies in his three laws of associative learning. The first two, the law of exercise and the law of effect, are discussed next. The third, the law of readiness, is discussed in a later section because of its neuroscientific overtones.

The Law of Exercise is actually comprised of two sub-laws: the Law of Use and the Law of Disuse. The Law of Use states that "When a modifiable connection is made between a situation and a response, that connection's strength is, all other things being equal, increased (Thorndike, 1913, Vol. 2, p. 2)." The Law of Disuse, by contrast, states that "When a modifiable connection is *not* made between a situation and response during a length of time, that connection's strength is decreased" (Thorndike, 1913, Vol. 2, p. 4). Hence, the more two events co-occur, the stronger the association between them. In Chapter 3, we shall see how this idea is very similar to claims made by contemporary memory researchers.

As for **The Law of Effect,** it states that "When a modifiable connection between a situation and response is made and is accompanied or followed by a satisfying state of affairs, that connection's strength is increased; when made and accompanied or followed by an annoying state of affairs, its strength is decreased" (Thorndike, 1913, Vol. 2, p. 4). The difference between the Laws of Exercise and Effect relates to the speed with which strength is increased. The bond between a situation and response is said to be "stamped in" (i.e., dramatically increased and "hard-wired" in the brain) when the response is followed by a satisfying state of affairs; when it is followed by an annoying state of affairs, it is "stamped out." Unlike B. F. Skinner who argued that there is no such thing as reinforcement-less learning (Skinner, 1974), Thorndike's Law of Exercise suggests that simple pairings can create associations that grow slowly in strength with each successive co-occurrence.

The strength of an associative bond refers to the speed and regularity with which a response comes to mind when a student is in a particular situation. For example, a weak bond would be in evidence when nothing comes to mind when the teacher says, "3 × 3 = ?" in Situation 1 (see Figure 2.1). Similarly, if the response "9" comes to the student's mind on only three out of the ten days in which the teacher asks the question, we would have further evidence of a weak bond.

Self-Regulation

How do students help themselves "stay on track" and adapt to the demands of the classroom? Thorndike did not have much to say about how students regulate themselves as much as how *teachers* can regulate students. As suggested above, Thorndike's views are rather similar to those of B. F. Skinner. Thorndike preceded Skinner in time and Skinner used Thorndike's theory as a starting point for his own. Both tended to emphasize "other-regulation" or "stimulus-regulation" over self-regulation, but it is important to note that there are behaviorists who have developed theories of self-regulation (e.g., Belfiore & Hornyak, 1998).

Educational Applications

Thorndike wrote several books in the areas of educational psychology and arithmetic learning. Given his laws of learning, he had three main suggestions for teachers:

1. Use lots of repetition in order to build up associative bonds between situations and responses (e.g., flashcards, choral responding, etc.).
2. Be sure to follow correct responses with rewards (e.g., stickers, praise) and incorrect responses with punishments (e.g., low grades, public corrections).
3. Be sure to keep instructional units on related subjects separated in time. When two topics share stimulus features (e.g., the 3, 4, and = in $3 + 4 = 7$ and $3 \times 4 = 12$), the bonds for individual associations will not increase in strength in the manner intended. In fact, wrong answers will be regularly retrieved (e.g., answering "7" when asked, "What is 3 times 4?").

There are many teachers who even today rely heavily on rote repetition and reward systems to build up factual knowledge in their students. As we will see later in this chapter and throughout the rest of this book, many people dispute the idea that students should engage in large amounts of fact-learning when they are in school.

Relation to Neuroscience

Thorndike felt that associations were realized in the brain by way of connections among neurons. In particular, he felt that there were neurons corresponding to perceived aspects of the situation and other neurons corresponding to responses. When an association is created, these two groups of neurons (one group for the situation and one for the response) become connected to each other through an additional neuronal pathway. This form of "connectionism" is the forerunner to modern day connectionism (see later in this chapter and Chapter 6 for a description of modern connectionism).

Thorndike called the pathway of neurons connected by synapses a **conduction unit** and argued that satisfying states of affairs " . . . stimulate, or at least permit, the action of neural connections and neural conductions that are in readiness to act. . . . The essential satisfyingness in these cases is then the conduction along neuron[s] and across synapses that are ready for conduction [as opposed to their state during a refractory period in which they cannot fire] and the essential annoyingness in these cases is the absence of such conduction" (Thorndike, 1913, Vol. 1, p. 127). This line of argumentation eventually led to his third law of learning:

The Law of Readiness says that, when any conduction unit is in readiness to conduct, for it to do so is satisfying. When any conduction unit is not in readiness to conduct, for it to conduct is annoying (Thorndike, Vol. 2, p. 1–2).

Thus, Thorndike attempted to explain the operation of all three laws by appealing to the actions of neurons in the brain. Although his claims regarding the neural basis of reinforcement and punishment have proven to be incorrect (i.e., he suggests that *any* neural connection ready to conduct could provide a neural basis for reinforcement), the idea that learning is grounded in synaptic connections is surprisingly consistent with contemporary thinking in brain science (e.g., Squire, 1987).

Piaget's Theory

During the 1960s and early 1970s, Piaget's theory was the dominant theory of cognitive development in the fields of developmental psychology and education. Whereas interest in and acceptance of Piagetian theory has decreased sharply since that time for developmental psychologists, a number of educational researchers still advocate many of Piaget's core views (but disagree with certain claims). Let's examine how Piaget would answer our five questions.

The Nature of Knowledge

What form does knowledge take for Piaget? When Piaget referred to children's knowledge, he used one of three terms: scheme (plural = schemata), concept, and structure. A **scheme** can be either physical or mental and may be described as actions or processes that are used repeatedly by a child to attain goals or solve problems (Piaget, 1952). An example of a physical scheme would be the "grasping" scheme that infants use to pick up and familiarize themselves with the physical properties of objects (e.g., Is it hard? Does it make noise? etc.). An example of a mental scheme would be the "isolation of variables" scheme (see Chapter 10) that adolescents use to figure out such things as what factors cause a pendulum to swing fast or slow (e.g., Is it the length of the string? Is it how hard I push?).

Schemata are enduring action sequences that a child or adolescent uses across a wide range of objects and situations. In describing this quality, Piaget (1952) said that schemata are "transposable" and "generalizable." Thus, an infant might use the "grasping" scheme in two completely different situations involving two completely different objects for the very same purpose: to see what the objects are like. The tendency to use schemes across situations and stimuli makes them different than the singular, situation-bound responses described by Thorndike. A second important difference is that schemata are used to accomplish goals; Thorndike did not believe that actions were driven by goals.

In addition to studying the role of schemes in development, Piaget also focused on a variety of **concepts** such as time, space, causality, number, conservation, and classes. Classes are categories of things such as "dog" and "triangle." Concepts differ from schemata in that concepts are not goal-directed procedures as much as forms of understanding that involve **relations** among things or aspects of things (Byrnes, 1992b). For example, the concept of time involves understanding the relation between speed and distance (Piaget, 1969). Causality involves understanding the relation between causes and effects (Piaget & Garcia, 1974). Classes involve both the membership relation between things and the categories to which they belong (e.g., "Rover" is a "dog") and the class-inclusion relation between one category and another (e.g., "dogs" are kinds of "animals") (Inhelder & Piaget, 1964).

For Piaget, a second difference between schemata and concepts concerns the fact that whereas children at all age levels possess schemata of one form or another (physical or mental), only older children, adolescents, and adults possess concepts. Concepts are formed by way of abstraction across different objects and situations. For example, the category of "dog" describes what is true of all dogs despite subtle differences in appearance or differences in location. Similarly, the five-minute gap between 12:05 and 12:10 is true for all clocks not just some clocks. This gap is also identical to that between 12:13 and 12:18. Finally, the number "5" is an abstraction across all sets of objects that have five objects in them no matter what these objects look like or where they can be found. For Piaget, the abstraction process takes some time and requires lots of experience with objects in many different situations. It is for this reason that Piaget argued that concepts emerge slowly over time. In his studies, he found "true" concepts (as he defined them) only in older children, adolescents, and adults. He called the ideas in younger children "pseudo-concepts."

This emphasis on the abstract and relational quality of concepts makes for another difference between the views of Piaget and Thorndike. Whereas Piaget spoke of many different types of mental relations (e.g., before/after; in front of/behind; caused/not caused; greater than/less than; is a kind of; etc.), Thorndike spoke of only one kind: associations. For Piaget, temporal, spatial, causal, numerical, and categorical relations are imposed on the world of objects by children in order to imbue it with meaning (i.e., make it make sense). Associations are devoid of meaning.

Besides "scheme" and "concept," the third term that Piaget used to describe knowledge was **structure.** A structure is something that has both form and content (Piaget, 1970). The form of a knowledge structure is the organization of ideas (Byrnes, 1992a). Piaget endeavored to show how many different knowledge domains have the same form (i.e., organization) despite having different content. For example, the class-inclusion relation can be found in domains as different as biology ("the pancreas is an organ . . ."), math ("a square is a parallelogram . . ."), and social studies ("a republic is a form of government . . ."). Piaget liked to describe such recurrent structures using formulas. For the class-inclusion relation, he used the formula "A + A' = B" where "A" stands for a subordinate class (e.g., "pancreas"), "B" stands for the superordinate class (e.g., "organ") and "A'" stands for the rest of the subordinate categories that make up the superordinate class (e.g., all other organs besides the pancreas). Inasmuch as many concepts and schemata can be described in terms of form and content, they too are structures.

Learning and Knowledge Growth

How do students acquire schemata and concepts? What is Piaget's developmental mechanism? When Piaget first started out in the 1920s, there were only two possible explanations of where knowledge comes from: empiricism and nativism. **Empiricists** like philosopher John Locke and psychologist Edward Thorndike believed that people's minds are "blank slates" when they are born (though Thorndike also attributed a number of inborn tendencies as well). Children's natural biological endowment allows them to form associations between things that they perceive through their senses. Thus, most empiricists are happy with Thorndike's two laws of association for explaining how students acquire knowledge.

The world has a natural regularity to it that imposes itself on our minds (e.g., the cycle of day followed by night). Thus, empiricists would argue that we could develop a concept of time by merely observing the cycles of days, months, seasons, and so forth (Byrnes, 1992a).

Nativism is the polar opposite of empiricism. Nativists like Immanuel Kant and Noam Chomsky believe that the world is not terribly regular or organized. In addition, they argue that conceptual relations (e.g., causality, time, etc.) could not be sensed in the same way that color or temperature could be sensed. Together, these two beliefs imply that concepts could not be acquired through exposure to the world. If the latter proposition is true, then it follows that the vast majority of important concepts must be inborn. As such, one could either observe them in a newborn or see them unfold over time as a child's brain matures. Nativists suggest that we are born with concepts of causality, time, space, and so on in order to make sense of stimulation that makes no inherent sense.

After much reflection, Piaget found problems with both empiricism and nativism. As a result, he created a third alternative: **constructivism.** He agreed with the nativistic view that people have concepts that they impose on the world to make sense of it but disagreed with the claim that these ideas were inborn. He agreed with the empiricist view that the world has a certain regularity and structure to it that children come to know through experience but disagreed with the idea that concepts are learned immediately through exposure to the world. His middle-ground stance was that exposure to the world and children's activities cause them to create mental precursors to more fully-developed ideas. He felt that children's minds take these precursor components and continually build more sophisticated ideas out of them.

For example, when children are born, they lack voluntary control over their arm and hand movements. Everything is reflexive. Soon, however, they gain some voluntary control and begin creating "grasping" and "pushing" schemes out of reflexes (hence, reflexes serve as precursors to the schemes). Early on, the "grasping" and "pushing" schemes are not interconnected. By around eight to twelve months, however, a child who wants an attractive toy hidden behind a barrier can combine the "grasping" and "pushing" scheme together in order to retrieve the toy. Children are not born with this knowledge of how to put the two schemes together, nor can they be taught this earlier in the first year even though they have the two schemes. Children *themselves* think of putting the two schemes together to attain a goal (i.e., get the toy). Later on, the act of counting objects will serve as a precursor to the mathematical idea of sets, and grouping actions will serve as a precursor to mental addition and subtraction. Still later, children will combine addition and subtraction together with the insight that subtraction is the opposite of addition. In effect, actions have a certain logical structure to them that serve as a template for conceptual relations.

Perhaps an analogy will help clarify the differences between empiricism, nativism, and constructivism. Imagine that a student's knowledge is like a brick wall and that each brick is a piece of information that is interconnected to other pieces of information. Empiricists think that a child's mind is merely a receptacle for a teacher who builds the wall inside the child's head. As they teach something, they metaphorically lay another brick in just the right spot. In contrast, nativists think that the wall is already built when children are born. All teachers do is help students "turn inward" and see what they already know. Or, they can wait for the wall to build up by itself in children's minds as their brains mature.

Constructivists think that teachers provide the "bricks," but they merely toss the bricks to students who try to lay the bricks themselves. Sometimes students do not understand a "brick," so they drop it, lay it in the wrong place, or let it sail over their heads. The latter occurs when they have not built the wall up high enough to be able to lay a certain kind of brick (e.g., a really abstract idea).

A problem with empiricism is that it cannot explain student misunderstandings. If a teacher explains things properly, there is nothing that should interfere with the brick being properly laid in a student's mind. Moreover, ideas could be learned at any age in a fairly direct manner. In contrast, nativism could account for children's failure to understand by saying that certain ideas have not "unfolded" yet. However, nativists would have a hard time explaining interesting errors on the part of children in which they seem to put existing ideas together on their own in a creative way. Moreover, nativism could not explain misconceptions and distortions in fully mature individuals (i.e., adults).

Piaget's theory can explain the slow progression of understanding that we find with many educational concepts as well as misconceptions. He used the notion of **assimilation** to describe the process of a student taking some experience or piece of information and finding a home for it in his or her existing knowledge structure (i.e., finding a spot in the wall for a brick that was just tossed). Sometimes an idea is so discrepant from what a child believes that it cannot be assimilated. He used the notion of **accommodation** to describe the process of changing the existing configuration of knowledge in order that the troublesome idea can be assimilated (Piaget, 1952). Keeping with our wall analogy, accommodation would be like rearranging the bricks in the wall so that a new brick can find a home. In most cases, assimilation is always partial in the sense that children only assimilate that portion of an experience that is consistent with their current understanding.

In his discussion of the role of play, dreams, and imitation in cognitive development, Piaget (1962, p. 104) argued that " . . . imitation is a continuation of accommodation, play is a continuation of assimilation, and intelligence is a harmonious combination of the two." He was suggesting that when one assimilates, one inserts one's own ideas into reality; when one accommodates, one's schemes and ideas come into closer conformity with reality and tend to be fairly direct copies of it. Play and fantasy, moreover, are examples of over-assimilation (i.e., putting too much of one's ideas into reality). In contrast, children engage in over-accommodation when they try to directly copy the actions of someone (without putting their own "spin" on the actions). His analysis of imitation further suggests that a child could not imitate someone (e.g., reproduce the actions of a teacher or coach) unless his or her schemes were sufficiently developed to be able to perform the requisite actions or operations.

To illustrate assimilation and accommodation further, let's examine a few examples. Young preschoolers who are driving at night with their parents often think that the moon is following them (it certainly looks that way!). The physics of the explanation are too abstract for them to comprehend, so they could not assimilate this explanation if it were provided. Ultimately, this knowledge of the physical world will change enough that they will understand such ideas (see Chapter 10). Similarly, somewhat older students think that numbers are positive amounts derived from counting. The idea that numbers can be negative quantities or various configurations of components (e.g., 3 = 1 + 1 + 1 or 1 + 2 or 3 + 0;

etc.) is discrepant from their current ideas so such ideas are not easily assimilated (see Chapter 9). Eventually, children can grasp such ideas because their knowledge has accommodated.

Piaget argued that confronting discrepant ideas is absolutely essential for knowledge growth (Piaget, 1980). If children never had experiences or heard information which contradicted the erroneous ideas that they construct by themselves, they would never develop the correct conceptions. Thus, the "readiness" idea of waiting until a child's mind matures enough is actually an implication of nativism, not Piaget's constructivism.

Moreover, Piaget argued that assimilation and accommodation work in opposition to each other. When we assimilate something, our mind metaphorically says "The current organization and accuracy of my ideas is fine. Find a place for this new information somewhere." When we accommodate, our mind says "The current organization is not fine. Reorganize things and create new space." You cannot keep things the same and change them at the same time. Thus, only one of assimilation or accommodation "wins out" in any given situation. This "battle" between these processes means that change in children's misconceptions can be frustratingly slow for teachers. Once again, empiricists would have a hard time explaining the slow change in wrong ideas (though they could appeal to the notion that wrong ideas were somehow repeatedly reinforced). When the battle is resolved over some idea and a balance is restored between assimilation and accommodation (Piaget called this resolution **equilibration**), children's understanding usually moves to a higher plane, a higher level of insight. It often becomes more abstract as well. For example, in order for a child to come to understand that dogs and people are both animals, they have to change their concept of "animal" in such a way that it is more abstract (e.g., "a living thing that can move itself" from "furry four-legged things"). In sum, then, equilibration is Piaget's developmental mechanism.

When he conducted his experiments with many children ranging from infants to adolescents, Piaget observed that children's experience and the process of equilibration seemed to promote the emergence of four levels of thought: the sensori-motor level, the preoperational level, the concrete operational level, and the formal operational level. Each level is characterized by how children view the world.

When the world is viewed from the standpoint of **sensori-motor** thinking (birth to about eighteen months of age), things are understood with respect to what actions can be performed on them. For example, a bottle, a toy, and a finger are all the same because they are "suckables." In addition, sensori-motor thinking is limited to the here-and-now. Children who can only reason at the sensori-motor level (e.g., infants or severely retarded older students) cannot think about the past or things that might happen in the future. They simply perceive things in current view and try to use a motoric scheme to interact with these things.

After motoric schemes have been repeated many times to attain goals, children's minds form abstract, mental versions of these schemes. As a result, children can imagine themselves doing something before they do it. Once children can think in this representational way, they have moved into the **preoperations** level (begins around eighteen to twenty-four months of age). In addition to being able to imagine future events, children can also think about things that happened to them in the past. Thus, preoperational children are freed from the here-and-now. Piaget called this kind of thought representational in the sense that children can re-present absent objects to their consciousness for consideration (Piaget, 1962).

Although preoperational thinking is more advanced and more adaptive than sensorimotor thought, it is limited in four ways. First, it has overly strong ties to perception, perceptual similarity, and spatial relations. For example, the author's daughter, when she was three, believed that a family exists only when the family members hug. When they are spatially separated, the family no longer exists! Similarly, many preschoolers think that an arrangement of five pennies spread out in a row contains more pennies than a pile of five pennies.

When they mentally group things, preschoolers rely heavily on perceptual similarity. For example, they think that "dogs" and "horses" are both "doggies" and that "goldfish" and "whales" are both "fishies." Grouping things by perceptual similarity, of course, is not a good idea because few categories are defined this way. Do we define the category of "doctor" by how doctors look? How about "country," "dictator," "polynomial," or "acid?" Most categories in fields such as science, mathematics, and social studies are defined in a non-perceptual, abstract way. As a result, a Piagetian perspective predicts that these categories would be hard for preschoolers to grasp.

The second limitation of preoperational thinking is that it is **unidimensional;** that is, children can think about only one aspect of something at a time. For example, when they are asked to sort objects into categories, they use just one dimension (e.g., size) rather than multiple dimensions (e.g., size and color). In addition to studies of categorization, Piaget revealed unidimensionality in his many studies of conservation. **Conservation** is the belief that the amount of something stays the same despite superficial changes in appearance. In his classic "beaker" task, for example, preschoolers only attended to the height of the glasses and not the width in judging which of two glasses has more juice in it. It is easy to show how many concepts in school are multi-dimensional (e.g., the definition of a "square" or a "republic"), so this second limitation would cause problems for students if it persisted after preschool. The tendency to focus on just one dimension or view things only from one's own perspective has been called **centration** (Piaget & Inhelder, 1969).

The third limitation of preoperational thought is that it is **irreversible;** that is, preschoolers often cannot mentally imagine something that has just been done (e.g., a ball of clay being rolled into a sausage) being "undone" (e.g., the sausage being rolled back into a ball). Piaget (1962) likened this limitation to a movie projector that cannot play movies in reverse. Again, most subjects in school contain ideas that involve reversibility. In math, for example, we have the fact that addition is the opposite of subtraction and that "–5" is the opposite of "5." In history classes, it is common to speculate whether some trend could ever be reversed (e.g., Russian citizens going back to repressive communism after tasting freedom and capitalism). Hence, preoperational children tend to think of things in terms of their static configuration instead of thinking of them in terms of a reversible transformation (Inhelder & Piaget, 1958).

The fourth limitation of preoperational thinking, according to some early works of Piaget, is that children *have difficulty distinguishing between reality and fantasy.* For example, they sometimes have difficulty telling the difference between real people and TV characters (so do many soap opera fans!) and also are bothered by nightmares that seem awfully real.

These four limitations of preoperational thinking are overcome when children develop the concrete operational mode of thought around age five or six. In particular, concrete operational children are no longer limited to using perceptual similarity when they group things. However, although children can understand somewhat more abstract properties, these properties still must be something one can point to or concretely describe (e.g., "warm-blooded" for "mammals"). In addition to going beyond mere perceptual similarity, concrete operational children also do not confuse spatial arrangements with actual quantities (e.g., a squashed clay ball has the same amount of clay as a ball that has been rolled into a sausage). In addition, children can think about two dimensions at once and can also mentally "undo" a real event that has happened. Finally, concrete operational children do not confuse reality with fantasy and are more concerned with playing games by the rules than with assimilating the world to their own fanciful desires. In fact, they seem to be overly concerned with "the way things are."

In some cultures, thinking that is (a) freed from perceptual relations, (b) reversible, (c) two dimensional, and (d) realistic would be sufficient for full adaptation to that culture. In most industrialized cultures, however, people apparently need more than that. For example, many things in school require comprehension of more than two dimensions and the ability to go beyond reality to think about hypothetical possibilities (e.g., Would the Vietnam war have ended earlier if Kennedy had not be assassinated?). Moreover, some ideas cannot be defined by pointing to something or using concrete descriptions (e.g., the fourth dimension; conservatism; the "limit" of a function; etc.). Students who can think about multiple dimensions, hypothetical possibilities, and abstract properties have entered Piaget's **formal operations** level of thinking (begins usually around age ten or eleven).

The idea that children are limited to a particular type of thought when they are in a particular age range has prompted many researchers to criticize Piaget's theory and conduct a number of studies to refute the notion of stages (see Brainerd, 1978). Children have been shown to grasp ideas earlier than Piaget found and many studies have shown that students rarely demonstrate the same level of thought (e.g., concrete operations) across a range of tasks (Gelman & Baillargeon, 1983). Thus, most of us are preoperational for some topics (e.g., computers), concrete operational for others (e.g., economics), and formal operational for others (e.g., math). Recent findings also suggest that four- and five-year-olds have less trouble with the fantasy-reality distinction than Piaget found in his early studies (Wellman, 1992). These and other problems with the theory led many developmental psychologists to lose interest in Piaget's theory. What these researchers look for now are forms of constructivism that lack the idea of stages and attribute greater skills to young children (e.g., Schema theory—see below; and so-called "Theory-Theory"; see Chapter 10).

Self-Regulation

How do students help themselves "stay on track" and adapt to the demands of the classroom? For Piaget, the mind is naturally predisposed toward self-regulation (or "autoregulation" as he called it). In particular, he felt that it is maladaptive for the mind to be "out of sync" with reality. When students try out an idea on the world and find that it is wrong, it is natural for their minds to modify this idea so that it becomes more in line with reality. This tendency for the mind to be self-modifying and self-correcting is, of course, what Piaget had in mind when he described the relation between assimilation and accommodation. Piaget (1952) wrote that the mind's tendency to be adaptive is embodied in the form of equilibration. Note that this claim makes Piaget different from radical constructivists who argue that there is no reality "out there" independent of all of our minds (e.g., Cobb, Yackel, & Wood, 1992).

To see the adaptive value of the schemata and concepts that Piaget described, consider what would happen if (a) a sixteen-year-old understood numbers the way a five-year-old does; (b) an adult could not tell the difference between things that are caused and things that happen by chance; and (c) a three-year-old did not understand that things continue to exist even when they are not in view. Concepts such as these are fundamental to reality. No one could survive in our culture without them.

Educational Applications

The applications of Piaget's theory to educational practice can be stated in the form of three principles:

Principle 1:   In order for students to create mental structures, they must first internalize action schemes by repeatedly performing them to attain a goal.

This principle derives from Piaget's views about how preoperational thought arises out of the internalization of sensori-motor schemes and how the logic of actions serve as a template for mental logical structures. It implies that if a teacher wants his or her students to be able to read silently or perform mental computations, students need lots of practice performing these actions overtly to reach a goal. Moreover, it is very consistent with the idea of hands-on learning.

Principle 2:   Thinking at each developmental level has unique features to take into consideration when designing educational programs.

Preoperational thought is unidimensional, irreversible, and based on a mixture of concrete reality and fantasy. Concrete operational thought is two-dimensional, reversible, and exclusively based in concrete reality. Formal operational thought is multidimensional, reversible, and can function in both concrete reality and hypothetical possibilities. In making a decision regarding when and how to present some topic, teachers can ask three questions: (1) how many dimensions or issues do students have to consider at once? (2) Does understanding the topic require reversible thought or an understanding of opposites? (3) Are there things I can point to in order to illustrate the idea sufficiently? If a topic seems to require a certain level of thought (e.g., concrete operations), teachers can use the ages of their students as a rough guess as to whether students would be capable of understanding this topic. For example, between age five and nine, children are generally limited to concrete operations. If the topic requires formal operations, teachers may elect to present it when students are about eight or nine in order to challenge their thinking and promote growth. In addition, teachers should distill precursory ideas from the topic which could be grasped and ultimately put together by students. For example, to help students be able to understand algebraic functions later, a teacher could have them form charts in which one value (e.g., the height a ball is dropped) is paired with another (e.g., the height it bounces). Over time, children will get a sense of systematic links between values.

Principle 3:   Children will not progress in their thinking unless they are provided with (a) precursory ideas that serve as the foundation for later ideas; (b) experiences that contradict their current, incorrect understandings; and (c) alternatives that they can grasp and execute.

Once again, the "do nothing until they are ready" approach is not consistent with Piaget's theory.

Relation to Neuroscience

Over the years, it has been common for Piaget's theory to be misconstrued as being maturational in focus. He expected that all children would go through his four stages at roughly the same ages mainly because he assumed that the physical structure of the world was pretty much the same for all children. Hence, children's mental structures would tend to run up against the same reality regardless of whether they lived in Switzerland, the United States, or Africa. However, maturation also plays a role:

> "It is clear that maturation must have a part in the development of intelligence, although we know very little about the relations between the intellectual operations and the brain. In particular, the sequential character of the stages is an important clue to their partly biological nature and thus argues in favor of the constant role of the genotype and epigenesis. But this does not mean that we can assume there exists a hereditary program underlying human intelligence: there are not 'innate ideas' (in spite of what Lorenz maintained about the a priori nature of human thought). Even logic is not innate and only gives rise to progressive epigenetic construction. Thus, the effects of maturation consist essentially of opening new possibilities for development; that is, giving access to structures that could not be evolved before these possibilities were offered. But between possibility and actualization, there must intervene a set of other factors such as exercise, experience, and social interaction" (Piaget, 1983, p.117).

Thus, if children do not interact with the physical and social world, they will not develop the structures associated with Piaget's four stages by the time they reach physical maturity in adolescence. Thus, brain maturation is a necessary but not sufficient condition for the development of knowledge. As for more specific proposals regarding mind-brain relationships, Piaget had very little to say. He did, however, frequently suggest that mental assimilation was analogous to biological assimilation (e.g., he said that we assimilate ideas much like we assimilate nutrients during digestion). Moreover, he regularly noted interesting parallels between (a) biological structures and functions and (b) mental structures and functions (Piaget, 1970), and argued that mental assimilation is the natural extension of more biological assimilations that occur in the body. Thus, the theory has a certain biological "feel" to it, but it did not lend itself to the same kind of specific neuroscientific mappings that are made possible by Thorndike's theory (see above) or connectionism (see below).

Schema Theory

About the same time that Piaget's theory began to decline in popularity among psychologists (i.e., the early 1970s), Schema theory began to rise in popularity. Whereas psychologists liked the interesting memory distortions that Schema theory could explain, educational researchers found Schema theory to be extremely useful for explaining such things as reading comprehension and scientific thinking. Let's now see how Schema theorists would answer our five questions.

The Nature of Knowledge

What form does knowledge take in a student's mind? As might be inferred from its name, Schema theory posits the existence of knowledge structures called **schemata** (singular = schema). Schemata come in two basic forms: one type for objects (e.g., a schema for "dog" or "house") and another type for events. The latter have been commonly called **scripts** (e.g., a "restaurant" script or a "birthday party" script; Nelson, 1986) and also **event representations.** Regardless of whether we are talking about objects or events, a schema can be defined as a mental representation of what all instances of something have in common. For example, your "house" schema represents what is common to all of the houses that you have been in and your "restaurant" script represents the typical sequence of events that occur when you go to a restaurant (Anderson, 1990; Smith, 1989). To illustrate these notions, Figure 2.2 presents the contents of many people's schemata for houses and restaurants.

The "House" schema shown in Figure 2.2 is depicted using the "slot filler" convention. Here, "slots" such as "parts" specify the values that the object has on various attributes (e.g., values = wood, brick, and stone). An alternative and, perhaps, more popular way of depicting someone's knowledge (especially among educational researchers) is to use the

---

FIGURE 2.2   *Contents of Most People's "House" Schema and "Restaurant" Script*

"House" Schema
  Superset: building
  Parts: rooms
  Materials: wood, brick, stone
  Function: human dwelling
  Shape: rectilinear, triangular
  Size: 100–10,000 sq ft

"Restaurant" Script
  Enter → give reservation name → be seated → order drinks → look at
  menu → discuss menu → order meal → talk → eat salad or soup → eat
  food → order dessert → eat dessert → pay bill → leave tip → leave

---

The "house" schema comes from Anderson (1990); the "restaurant" script comes from college student responses in Bower, Black, & Turner (1979).

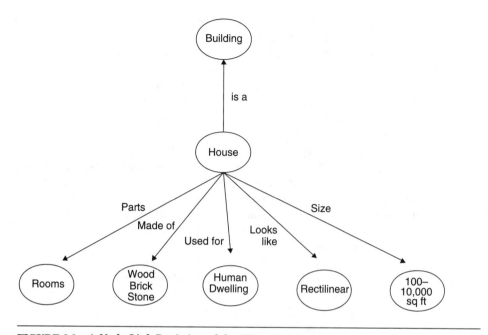

FIGURE 2.3   *A Node-Link Depiction of the "House" Schema*

node-link format. Figure 2.3 provides a node-link depiction of the "House" schema. The node-link convention is useful because it shows the relations among ideas. Each relation is depicted with an arrow (e.g., the "is a" link for the superset relation) and each idea is represented by an oval (the node for "house").

Schemata serve four functions in your mind. First, they **categorize** your experiences (Smith, 1989). Creating categories makes for a more efficient use of your memory capacity than storing each individual experience that you have as a separate memory. To see this, assume that there are exactly 10,000 types of things in the world (e.g., dogs, cats, trees, people, restaurants, etc.) and that you have personally encountered 100 instances of each type of thing (e.g., 100 different dogs in your lifetime). That would make for 1 million separate, specific, and unrelated memories. If your mind were a filing cabinet, you would have 1 million separate folders for each experience! In contrast, if you categorized things as you encountered them (e.g., "Here's another dog"), your experiences would be grouped together in far fewer folders (i.e., 10,000) that could be searched more quickly for relevant information (e.g., a single folder for all of your encounters with dogs).

But schemata improve the efficiency of memory in another way as well. Instead of storing all details of an experience (much the way a videotape does), a schema is more like a sheet of paper that contains your notes about the experience. You only write down what was common to an experience with a specific object (e.g., what happened with "Rover") and other previous experiences with the same type of object (e.g., what happened with "Spot," "Fido," and "Fifi"). All other details are lost and, therefore, do not use up space in your memory.

The other advantage of categorizing things is that your mind set ups expectations (Smith & Medin, 1981). When you have a category for "dogs" for example, you do not say "Oh, what's that!?" when you encounter a dog (expressing surprise and wariness about an unknown thing), your mind says "Oh, its just another dog. He'll probably wag his tail or bark." Similarly, people who have a well-established "restaurant" script do not get intimidated and confused when they enter a restaurant because their script tells them what to expect and what to do when certain things happen (e.g., expect a host or hostess to give you a menu; see Figure 2.2).

The categorizing function of schemata is very much related to two other roles they play in the mind: helping us to **remember** and **comprehend** things. When you create a schema for something and attach a label to it (e.g., "dogs"), you can retrieve what you know about this type of thing using the label. Using the label or hearing someone else use it is like having a label on a folder in your mental filing cabinet that you can use to find and pull out the folder pertaining to that type of thing. Similarly, other aspects of the thing that are stored in memory (e.g., what it looks like; its parts; etc.) can be used to retrieve the entire schema. For example, if you see a wagging tail under a friend's kitchen table, you will probably retrieve your "dog" schema from memory based on that clue.

By "comprehension," it is meant that "you understand what is going on." As we shall see in Chapter 7, schemata help us understand what is happening in a story and what to expect next. When an author writes,

"Mary heard a croaking sound under the bush. She picked up the small creature and felt its bumpy skin . . . ," we use our schema for "frog" (as well as those for "bush," "creature," etc.) to form a mental representation of what just happened in the story. People who have "croaks" and "bumpy skin" as part of their "frog" schema would know immediately that the character has found a frog under the bush.

In addition to helping us to categorize, remember, and comprehend our experiences, schemata are also an important constituent of our **problem-solving** ability. In elementary school, children are presented with four main types of arithmetic word problems (Riley, Greeno, & Heller, 1983). After solving many individual problems of a particular type, children are said to form a schema for that type. Similarly, in high school algebra and physics classes, students encounter repeated cases of the same type of problems and likewise form schemata for these problems (Clement, 1982; Mayer, 1982). Schemata help students know what to do when they encounter specific problems much like the way schemata help people know what to do when they enter a restaurant (see Chapters 7 and 9 for details). Figure 2.4 lists three instances of the same type of problem as well as a schema that might form for this type of problem.

Learning and Knowledge Growth

How do students acquire knowledge according to Schema theorists and how does this knowledge change? There are three ways to answer this question. The first involves explaining how schemata are formed in the first place. The second involves explaining how existing schemata affect the storage of incoming stimulation. The third involves describing three types of schematic change.

FIGURE 2.4   *A Schema for the Same Type of Word Problem*

Individual Problems

1. John had three apples. Mary gave him two more. How many does he have now?

Solution: Add John's amount to Mary's.

2. Bill had two hats. Charley gave him three more. How many does Bill have now?

Solution: Add Bill's amount to Charley's.

3. Jessica has three brothers and sisters. Her mom just had a baby. How many brothers and sisters does she have now?

Solution: Add the two amounts together.

A Schema for Them

Person 1 has a certain amount of things. Person 2 gives Person 1 a certain amount more. How many does Person 1 have now?

Solution: Add the two amounts together.

Schemata are said to be formed through the process of **abstraction** (Adams, 1990; Hintzman, 1986). As alluded to earlier, children find themselves in multiple situations involving the same object. For example, the first time that a child sees a vacuum cleaner, it might be when her mom vacuums her family room. The next time it might be dad using it in her bedroom. The next time it might be grandma at grandma's house. Over time, what is retained in her "vacuum cleaner" schema will be just those aspects of the experience that are common to all situations involving it. She will see that it does not matter who uses it, what room it is used in, or what color it is. What is common is the fact that it is used to clean rugs and that it makes a characteristic noise. The latter information will make up her schema for the object.

The emphasis on abstraction makes Schema theory simultaneously similar to Piaget's theory and distinct from Thorndike's theory. In particular, whereas Thorndike emphasized highly specific memory traces for specific situations, Piagetians and Schema theorists argue that specific details are lost when schemata and concepts are formed. Schema theory is also similar to Piaget's theory in its emphasis on meaningful relationships among ideas (the "links" in a node-link structure) and constructivism (Paris, 1978). However, Schema theory is distinct from Piagetian theory because it does not emphasize the existence of stages, levels of understanding, or levels of abstraction (see Chapter 3 on the latter point).

Once formed, schemata affect what is remembered about an experience through three processes: selection, gist-extraction, and interpretation (Alba & Hasher, 1982). As mentioned earlier, a major tenet of Schema theory is that the mind does not encode and store all aspects of an experience. Rather, it uses schemata to **select** just those aspects of the situation that are schema-relevant. At a baseball game, for example, you will not remember every single aspect of the experience (i.e., all of the sights and sounds at the park), you will only remember those aspects of the experience that are consistent with your "baseball game" script (e.g., who won; important plays; etc.). Similarly, students will not remember all aspects of a class (e.g., the tie Mr. Nelson had on during his history class), they will remember just those aspects that are consistent with their script for that teacher's typical class (e.g., the normal sequence of events that happen during Mr. Nelson's fourth period history class).

According to Schema theorists, those aspects of the experience that are selectively encoded and stored are initially specific, accurate, and verbatim traces of those aspects. For example, on any given day, Mr. Nelson's students may use their script for his class to expect that he will end the class for that day as he usually does: by telling them about the quiz for the next day. This expectation causes students to selectively attend to his description of the quiz (and not attend to his earlier, atypical description of a TV show that he watched). After he informs them about the quiz, his words are stored in their verbatim form.

Soon, however, the second process of **gist-extraction** begins. During gist-extraction, Mr. Nelson's exact wording (i.e., the verbatim trace) is replaced by the "gist" of what he said. For example, if Mr. Nelson actually said "The quiz will cover the sections of the chapter which describe the accomplishments of Louis XIV and Louis XV," the gist-extraction process might leave a student with the memory that they had to "read sections about two kings."

Together, the processes of selection and gist-extraction mean that it would be hard for someone to give an accurate and detailed description of some experience. They could only give a short account of generally what happened. If true, these limitations on memory mean that people could not be very reliable witnesses in trials. Unless they are interviewed almost immediately after they witness a crime, it would be impossible for them to give an accurate description of details such as what people were wearing, what color car they drove, and what exactly was said.

These memory problems could be further compounded by the third process affecting what is retained from an experience: **interpretation.** As alluded to earlier, schemata help the comprehension process by "filling in" things that are not said or seen. For example, the lines above about "Mary" do not say that she picked up a frog, but people would nevertheless **infer** that she did. Similarly, if you read the lines "She spoke to the manager about the meat prices," you might infer that the woman was complaining that the prices were too high (Alba & Hasher, 1982). Although inferences are important to the comprehension process, they are merely probabilistic and could be incorrect. Returning to the legal aspects again, consider the situation in which you saw a man and a woman interacting in front of a parked car. What behaviors would lead you to infer that they were together or knew each other? What would lead you to infer they were unacquainted and that the man might be bothering the woman? If the woman were attacked and you were later questioned by the police about what you saw, you might say "They seemed to know each other." Such a statement might lead the police to limit their pool of suspects to someone who knew the victim. Note, however, that your inference might be incorrect.

The alleged over-emphasis on distorted, non-veridical memories in Schema theory prompted many psychologists to lose interest in it during the 1980s. Studies show that people are quite capable of accurate, verbatim recall when they put their mind to it (Alba &

Hasher, 1982). Moreover, other studies show that sometimes people do not make extremely obvious inferences (Schacter, 1989). Thus, whereas Schema theory can account for some important aspects of memory, categorization, and comprehension, it cannot account for all aspects of learning.

So far we have answered the "learning and knowledge growth" question by considering how schemata are formed and the three processes that affect your memory of experiences (i.e., selection, gist-extraction, and interpretation). We now turn to the issue of how schemata change. Rumelhart (1984) speculated that schemata are modified by one of three processes: accretion, tuning, or restructuring. Both **accretion** and **tuning** involve modifying an existing schema so that it becomes more flexible. Tuning involves a somewhat larger structural change than accretion. An example of accretion would be adding the value "adobe" to the "materials" slot in the "house" schema (see Figure 2.2). In simply adding values, you should note that the basic structure of the schema stays the same.

An example of tuning would be adding a new slot to an existing schema. For example, let's say that early in life, you did not have the slot for "size" in your "house" schema. Over time, however, you soon realized that there are many different kinds of buildings besides houses and that the size of these buildings is one clue that helps you determine what kind of building it is. In response to this environmental feedback, you add the slot for "size" to your "house" schema.

In contrast to accretion and tuning which basically modify portions of existing structures, **restructuring** involves more substantial changes. One such change would be a wholesale modification of the basic relations that comprise a schema. Another would be the process of creating entirely new schemata by way of making analogies to old schemata. A good illustration of the former process is the shift from preoperational categories (based on perceptual similarity) to concrete operational categories (use of more abstract features). When this occurs, all of the "slots" that would make up a preoperational schema for something (e.g., the single slot "looks fishy" for fish) would be replaced by entirely different "slots" (e.g., "lays eggs," "breathes through gills," etc.). A good example of the second type of restructuring would be the case of a college student who transfers to a new university. This student could use his script for registering for courses in his former university to create a new one (by analogy) for registering for courses in his new university.

Note that Rumelhart's description of accretion, tuning, and reorganization is not really a description of a developmental mechanism. Developmental mechanisms specify the factors or processes that transform an earlier state of knowledge into a later state of knowledge. It is interesting to know *that* knowledge can change in several ways, but it would be more useful to know *why* it changes in these ways. For example, why would restructuring happen instead of tuning? Thus, Schema theory is fairly imprecise on the issue of developmental mechanisms.

Self-Regulation

How do students help themselves "stay on track" and adapt to the demands of the classroom? Schema theorists have not had much to say about self-regulation except to say that successful problem-solvers have a large repertoire of flexible, accurate schemata. It can be presumed that they would say that adaptive (i.e., successful) students are more likely to develop such schemata in response to feedback than maladaptive (i.e., unsuccessful) students.

Educational Applications

There are three main implications of Schema theory for educational practice:

1. Teachers should view learning as the acquisition and modification of schemata rather than as the acquisition of rote-learned, isolated facts. To form schemata, teachers should present multiple instances of something (e.g., a particular kind of word problem) and have students identify the common features of the instances. To form scripts, teachers should have students experience the same type of event and have them abstract commonalities across these events (e.g., routines).
2. Teachers should expect that without various study aids (e.g., notes), students will sometimes retain only a small, selective portion of an experience or lesson; they might also elaborate or distort what they have retained using inferences.
3. Meaningful learning occurs when students can incorporate new information into an existing schema or when they can create new schemata by way of analogy to old schemata. To facilitate these processes, teachers should evoke appropriate schemata before presenting a topic in lecture or before students read about the topic. If the topic is new and students lack a schema for the material, teachers can use **advance organizers** to promote analogical reasoning (Mayer, 1979). An advance organizer is a short introductory statement that details the similarities between a new topic and a topic that students already know. For example, a science teacher can use a row of dominos to illustrate how electricity passes through a wire. Similarly, a social studies teacher can use the American congress as an example to help students understand the British parliament.

Relation to Neuroscience

Schema theorists have had very little to say regarding the neuroscientific basis of schemata. Questions that remain unanswered include the following: (1) Are schemata for objects stored in different regions of the brain than schemata for events? (2) Is the neural assembly that underlies a schema different than the neural assembly that underlies an individual fact or specific experience?

Information Processing Theory

Information Processing theory began to influence educational researchers around the same time that Schema theory did (i.e., the mid-1970s) and continues to influence their thinking now. Here's how Information Processing theorists would answer our four questions:

The Nature of Knowledge

What form does knowledge take in a student's mind? Information Processing theory has its roots in the field of Artificial Intelligence (AI). Over the last 40 years, AI researchers have endeavored to create computer systems to simulate human cognitive skills (e.g., mental computations, language comprehension, chess playing, etc.) and have equipped these computer systems with two main types of knowledge structures: one that models human **declarative knowledge** (e.g., Collins & Loftus, 1975; Newell & Simon, 1972) and another that models human **procedural knowledge** (Newell & Simon, 1972). Declarative knowledge or "knowing that" is a compilation of facts such as "A bird can fly," "triangles have three sides," and "Harrisburg is the capital of Pennsylvania." Procedural knowledge or "knowing how to" is a compilation of linear action sequences that people perform to attain goals. Examples of procedural knowledge include knowing how to tie shoes, knowing how to write the alphabet, knowing how to count, knowing how to drive, and so forth. This dichotomy between facts and procedures is similar to Piaget's distinction between concepts and schemes, as well as to the distinction in Schema theory between schemata for objects and schemata for events.

On computers, declarative knowledge has been modeled using **semantic nets** (also called **propositional networks** because facts are often stated in the form of propositions such as "Birds have feathers."). A semantic net is a node-link structure similar to that shown in Figure 2.3 which specifies the relations among facts. In most models, the relations among ideas are associative in nature. The more often you encounter a fact such as "Birds have feathers," the stronger the associative bond between the constituents "Birds" and "feathers" becomes. The label "semantic" is used because words (e.g., "bird") are often associated to facts and these facts give meaning to the words.

Procedural knowledge has primarily been modeled using **productions.** In its original form (e.g., Newell & Simon, 1972), a production was an "if-then" statement in which an action was linked to certain antecedent conditions. Usually these antecedent conditions specify two things: some state of the environment and the goals of the individual. Some examples of productions would be:

1. *Condition:*   IF (the numbers are fractions) AND (the goal is to add), THEN

    Action: (use the least common denominator method).

2. *Condition:*   IF (the shoe is on) AND (the goal is to tie it), THEN

    Action: (make two loops and. . . .).

Productions are said to "fire" when the conditions described in the "IF" part are met (e.g., for the first production above, the person perceives "1/2 + 1/4" and has the goal of wanting to add these fractions). The speed and regularity with which productions fire depends on the strength of an associative bond between conditions and actions. Information Processing theorists call a set of productions a "production system."

The discerning reader will recognize a strong similarity between productions and Thorndike's description of situation-response pairs. The difference between situation-response pairs and productions is that the latter often include more general notions (e.g., concepts like "fractions") as well as goals (Singly & Anderson, 1989).

Before moving on to the issue of learning and knowledge growth, it is important to note that not all researchers who align themselves with Information Processing theory think that semantic nets and production systems are good models of human knowledge. Some think that all knowledge is procedural and suggest dropping declarative knowledge (Winograd, 1975). Others prefer to use flowcharts and rules to describe performance rather than use productions (Siegler, 1998). Still others spend most of their time describing important skills and processes (e.g., intelligence, analogical reasoning) and only occasionally focus on the nature of knowledge (e.g., Sternberg, 1985). Thus, the issues of (a) whether we have one or two kinds of knowledge and (b) how best to model knowledge, are still being worked out.

Learning and Knowledge Growth

How do students acquire knowledge? At the heart of Information Processing theory is an account of how information from the environment becomes stored in memory. The most influential model of this storage process was originally proposed by Atkinson and Shiffrin in 1968. In this model, human memory is conceived of as three *stores.* Information (i.e., stimulation in the environment) is said to pass first through the *sensory store,* then through the *short term store,* and finally ends up in the *long term store.* These stores are characterized by structural characteristics such as how much information they can hold (*capacity*) and how long they can hold it (Siegler, 1998).

When stimulation is detected by sensory receptors, it gets into the sensory store in the form of an *icon.* To get a sense of a visual icon, stare briefly at an object and close your eyes. You will see an image of this object with your eyes closed. Note, however, how quickly it fades. Experiments have shown that the capacity of the sensory store is not terribly large. For example, when a twelve-item matrix is flashed, subjects only retain about 40 percent of the items. It has also been found that icons will form even for stimuli that are exposed for only 1/20 of a second (Siegler, 1998).

Icons, however, will only last for one second, unless you attend to them (Atkinson & Shiffrin, 1968). *Attention* causes information in the sensory store to be passed along to the short term store. Early on, the size of the average person's short term memory was said to be a fixed capacity of about seven "chunks" of information (range five to nine). Thus, when presented with seven pieces or less of information (e.g., seven shopping items, a phone number without the area code, etc.), people are able to retain all items. If more than seven items are presented, some of the items will not enter the short term store and will, therefore, be forgotten. In contemporary thinking, this seven-chunk limitation has been challenged (see Chapter 3).

In earlier formulations, the term "chunk" did not refer to just a single piece of information. Rather, it referred to a meaningful grouping of items. Thus, whereas the list of eight numbers "1 7 9 4 2 8 6 5 0" requires eight chunks, the list of eight letters "N I N E T E E N" only requires one chunk because these eight letters make up a single meaningful grouping. In essence, by clustering the items in any long list into meaningful clusters, one reduces the number of short term memory chunks required to retain this information. In line with Schema theory, the process of forming short term, chunked representations (i.e., **encoding**) is said to be selective in Information Processing theory (Siegler,

1998). The selectivity of encoding is argued to be adaptive in light of the limits of short term memory capacity. That is, one has to selectively encode certain things because it is impossible to encode everything in a situation.

If nothing is done to the information in short term memory within 15 to 30 seconds, it will be lost or forgotten (Siegler, 1998). For example, if someone tells you his or her phone number, you will probably forget it in 15 seconds unless you do something else. Clearly, phone numbers and most of the information presented in school are important to remember for longer than 15 seconds. Ideally, one would like to get information into one's long term memory because storage is permanent there. In order for information to pass from short term memory to long term memory, it is typically necessary to use a memory *strategy*. What would you do in the case of a phone number? Probably rehearse it over and over. Using a strategy like rehearsal is like pressing the "save" button on a personal computer. One's short term memory is like a computer's "buffer" or RAM that temporarily holds textual information and puts it on the screen while you work on it. One's long term memory is like a floppy diskette or a hard disk. Once information is "written" on them by the "save" function, it is there permanently. According to Information Processing theorists, the experience of forgetting really indicates that you are having a problem of **retrieval** (i.e., getting information out of long term memory); it does not indicate that there has been a genuine decay or loss of information.

Besides the assumption of permanence, Information Processing theorists make two other assumptions about long term memory. First, it is assumed that, unlike short term memory, the capacity of long term memory is unlimited. That is, a person's long term memory will never run out of space. Second, it is believed that information about objects is held in a fragmentary way. For example, information such as the name of an object (how it sounds, how to spell it), what the object looks like, the kind of thing it is, and so on are all held in separate places in long term memory. This assumption explains the "tip-of-the-tongue" phenomenon in which one can only recall portions of some information (Siegler, 1998).

Thus, "learning" for Information Processing theorists is all about attending to information in the environment and using strategies to transfer it from short-term storage to long-term storage. These two processes of attention and strategy constitute the primary developmental mechanisms for Information Processing theory. As we shall see in the next chapter, children become more skilled at using their attentional and strategic capacities as they grow older. In effect, they become more efficient and effective "information processors" with age. These increased skills help them overcome the processing limitations imposed by the sensory store and short term store such that they gain knowledge more quickly and efficiently than younger children.

Having answered both the "nature of knowledge" and "learning and knowledge growth" questions, we are now in a position to see how the answers to these questions interface. The statement that people have declarative and procedural knowledge really means that they store factual knowledge and procedures in long term memory. Both kinds of knowledge get into long term memory by way of memory strategies such as rehearsal. The more often information is rehearsed, the stronger the associative bonds between individual segments of knowledge.

Self-Regulation

How do students help themselves "stay on track" and adapt to the demands of the class-room? Information Processing theorists would answer this question by appealing to two aspects of performance: **strategies** and **cognitive monitoring** (Brown, Ferrara, Bransford, & Campione, 1983; Flavell, Miller, & Miller, 1993; Pressley, Borkowski, & Schneider, 1987). Strategies are actions that you perform to attain goals. Two examples of strategies would be (a) using rehearsal to learn a set of vocabulary words and (b) writing a summary of a chapter to make sure that you have all of the main points. Cognitive monitoring involves processes such as deciding which strategies you will use to attain a goal (rehearsal or something else), monitoring how well things are going as you make your way toward the goal (Am I learning this stuff? Do I understand?), and then evaluating how things went after you reach your goal (Could I have learned this a better way?). To see the difference between strategies and cognitive monitoring, consider the following manufacturing example. A strategy is like a worker who tries to make something and cognitive monitoring is like a supervisor who picks a worker for a certain job, tells the worker what to make, wanders by to see how the worker is doing, and then inspects the product after the worker is finished.

We need strategies because the world throws more information at us than our memories can handle. That is, we frequently experience "information overload." Strategies help us retain far more information than we would without them. But we would not acquire, use, or switch strategies without having the ability to plan, monitor, and evaluate our performance. That is why true adaptation to the world requires both strategies and cognitive monitoring.

Educational Applications

Information Processing theory has two main implications for educational practice:

1. Teachers need to recognize that students are naturally limited in the amount of information they can process and remember. One way to circumvent their capacity limitations is to divide information into smaller segments and give them ample time to learn the segments. A second way would be to provide explicit strategy instruction (see Chapter 3). A third way is to organize individual pieces of information so that groups of these items will form "chunks."
2. Building up a large repertoire of declarative and procedural knowledge that can be easily accessed requires lots of exposure and practice. Teachers should provide these opportunities for their students.

Relation to Neuroscience

A basic premise of Information Processing theory is that the human mind is similar to a computer in the sense that both are symbol processors. This suggestion led some to argue that the human brain is analogous to the hardware of a computer. The mind, in contrast, is analogous to the software of a computer. As Neisser (1967, p. 6) wrote,

"The task of a psychologist trying to understand human cognition is analogous to that of a man trying to discover how a computer has been programmed. In particular, if the program seems to store and reuse information, he would like to know by what 'routines' or 'procedures' this is done. Given this purpose, he will not care much whether his particular computer stores information in magnetic codes or in thin films; he wants to understand the program, not the 'hardware'. . . . He wants to understand its utilization, not its incarnation."

In a similar way, Marr (1982) suggested that there are three levels at which some psychological process could be characterized by a theorist: the computational level, the algorithmic level, and the implementation level. The *computational* level describes the primary task to be performed by some system or individual (e.g., find the area under a curve). The *algorithmic* level describes the steps taken by a particular individual when that individual performs the task in question (e.g., uses calculus versus measures the area with a ruler). The *implementation* level describes the mechanisms by which the algorithm is carried out in some physical system (e.g., a brain or a computer). Marr argued that when researchers are trying to create a computer simulation of some cognitive process (e.g., vision), they can temporarily ignore implementation issues when they are working on issues at the computational and algorithmic levels. In other words, they need not worry about such things as whether the program will run on a Macintosh or IBM when they are considering what the task will be and what algorithm will be used to accomplish the task. Information Processing theorists have used Marr's account to argue that psychologists normally operate at the computational and algorithmic levels when they construct theories of mental events. As such, they, too, do not have to be concerned about implementation issues (i.e., how the brain manages to carry out some cognitive process).

The computer analogy is part of a larger and influential paradigm known as the computational theory of mind (Block, 1990; Pylyshyn, 1989). The basic claim of the computational theory is that " . . . the mind is the program of the brain and that the mechanisms of the mind involve the same sorts of computations over representations that occur in computers" (Block, 1990, p. 247). For the present purposes, the details of this claim are less important than the ultimate realization that:

> " . . . the computer model of the mind is profoundly *unbiological.* We are beings who have a useful and interesting biological level of description, but the computer model aims for a level of description of the mind that abstracts away from the biological realizations of cognitive structures. . . . Of course, this is not to say that the computer model is in anyway incompatible with a biological approach. Indeed, cooperation between the biological and computational approaches is vital to *discovering* the program of the brain. . . . Nonetheless, the computer model of mind has a built-in antibiological bias in the following sense. If the computer model is right, we should be able to create intelligent systems in our image. . . . It is an open empirical question whether or not the computer model is correct. Only if it is *not* correct could it be said that psychology, the science of mind, is a biological science" (Block, 1990, p. 261).

Thus, Information Processing theory is rather different than other theories described in this book because of its built-in anti-biological bias.

Vygotsky's Theory

Vygotsky was a Russian psychologist who conducted his most important work during the 1920s and 1930s. Because behaviorism dominated American psychology until the late 1950s, however, Americans did not learn of his ideas until about 1962 when one of his works was translated. Overshadowed first by Piaget's theory and then by Information Processing theory, it was not until interest in both of these theories started to wane (i.e., the late 1970s) that a large number of psychologists and educational researchers used Vygotsky's theory to study learning. Let's see how Vygotsky would answer our five questions.

The Nature of Knowledge

What form does knowledge take in a student's mind? In his writings, Vygotksy (1962, 1978) referred to two kinds of cognitive entities: **concepts** and **functions.** Though we have seen from Piaget's work that there are many different types of concepts (e.g., time, space, causality, etc.), Vygotsky limited himself to studying the type of concepts known as categories. A concept, for Vygotsky, was a class of things that had a label (e.g., "square") and could be defined by a set of criteria (e.g., four sides, equal sides, etc.). In his view, a child demonstrated a mature understanding of a concept when he or she (a) seemed to know all of the defining criteria for that concept (e.g., four sides, equal sides, etc. for squares) and (b) understood that the word for the concept (e.g., "square") is arbitrary and conventional (Vygotsky, 1962). Children who demonstrated a mature understanding of many categories were said to comprehend "true" concepts (also called **scientific concepts** by Vygotsky).

In his studies, Vygotsky found that children did not seem to understand "true" concepts until early adolescence. Prior to that time, children only seemed to be capable of lower-level "pseudoconcepts" and so-called **spontaneous concepts.** A pseudoconcept is in evidence when a child can use the label for the concept correctly (e.g., uses "square" to refer to squares) but seems to be unaware of the defining criteria. A spontaneous concept is a concept constructed by a child that is largely based on his or her own experience. Thus, the definition of "dog" might include criteria such as "brown with white spots" and "grandmother" might include the criteria "has a soft lap" (Vygotsky, 1978).

In contrast to the idiosyncratic, personalized quality of spontaneous concepts, "true" or scientific concepts are marked by their generality. This generality derives from the fact that true concepts are defined in an abstract and context-independent way. For example, unlike the words "that" or "him" which often mean different things in different contexts (e.g., "him" could mean Bill in one context and Fred in another), concepts such as "atom," "democracy," "fraction," and so forth are defined in ways which make the specifics of contexts irrelevant. For example, the definition of "democracy" is meant to apply to all democracies, not just one that someone happens to be talking about in a particular context. The discerning reader will note that in emphasizing the abstract character of "true" concepts, Vygotksy is similar to Piaget and Schema theorists. The connection to Piaget was not accidental in that he borrowed the distinction between spontaneous and scientific concepts from an early work of Piaget. He was, moreover, one of the first people to criticize Thorndike's view that knowledge consists of non-abstract situation-response pairs.

Besides concepts, Vygotsky was also interested in the development of five main cognitive "functions": language, thinking, perception, attention, and memory. He did not, however, describe the nature of these functions in any great detail. Instead, he described them briefly using examples and tried to show how success on problem-solving and memory tasks depended on the **integration** of one or more of these functions in development. For example, when confronted with the task of obtaining a treat from a cabinet that was out of reach, Vygotsky found that successful children used language to plan a strategy and talk themselves through to solution. In Vygotsky's mind, they combined the language, perception, and attention functions together.

Vygotsky (1978) felt that the integrations involving language were particularly important because they separated us from lower animal species. When an animal tries to solve a problem, it relies on genetically-determined responses or on responses that have been reinforced by the environment. Its decisions are either under the control of genetic predispositions or under the control of stimuli in the environment. When humans solve problems, in contrast, they can use their language skills to invent new strategies or get ideas from other humans. The language function, then, helps humans break the "stimulus-response" cycle and gain control over the environment. In Vygotsky's mind, symbols in language "mediate" between stimuli and responses (see Chapter 4).

Learning and Knowledge Growth

How do students acquire knowledge and skills? Vygotsky and his followers have answered this question in three ways. First, they assumed that the tendency to use symbols (e.g., speech) during problem-solving is something that children acquire by way of social interaction. Vygotsky (1978, p. 57) argued that "Every function in the child's cultural development appears twice: first on the social level, and later on the individual level; first *between* people (*interpsychological*) and then *inside* the child (*intrapsychological*)." So, for example, prior to a child using verbal rehearsal to learn a list of vocabulary words, something analogous to verbal rehearsal must have occurred between the child and a teacher or parent (e.g., a teacher helping a class to rehearse information). Thus, internalization is one kind of developmental mechanism for Vygotsky.

It is important to note, however, that children do not merely imitate the actions of a teacher and immediately employ symbols and signs in their problem-solving behavior. Vygotsky (1978, p. 46) argued that " . . . *sign-using activity in children is neither simply invented nor passed down by adults*; rather, it arises from something that is originally not a sign operation and becomes one only after a series of *qualitative* transformations." Thus, Vygotsky is similar to Piaget in his assumption that imitation is mediated by children's current developmental level.

The second answer pertains to concept development. For Vygotskians, one of the primary goals of instruction is to change children's spontaneous concepts into their scientific counterparts. Vygotsky noted, however, that this shift may take many years to accomplish because children do not give up their spontaneous concepts that easily. Using a description quite similar to Piaget's account of assimilation and accommodation, Vygotsky argued that after instruction, spontaneous concepts "grow up" and scientific concepts "grow down."

That is, spontaneous concepts give children an intellectual foothold to which they can partially assimilate a scientific definition. Over time, grappling with a scientific concept causes their spontaneous concepts to become ever more accurate, general, and abstract.

Both the first and second answer to the "learning and knowledge growth" question show the necessity of adult intervention in children's thinking. Vygotsky argued that without adults modeling symbolically-mediated problem-solving or providing instruction on scientific concepts, children's thinking would remain in a lower-level state. Hence, Vygotsky's stance differs from Piaget's in this regard because Piaget suggested that children invent many ideas on their own.

The third answer, which also entails social interaction, appeals to the notion of the **zone of proximal development.** According to Vygotsky, intellectual skills are progressively mastered by children. When they first learn a skill (e.g., reading), they make many errors and rely heavily on teachers for corrective advice. After large amounts of practice and feedback from teachers, however, children ultimately reach a point at which they can perform the skill well on their own. In between the absolute-novice level and the complete-mastery level, there is a point at which a child could perform well if someone were to give him or her just a little help (e.g., a hint). For Vygotsky (1978, p. 86), the zone of proximal development is " . . . the distance between the actual developmental level as determined by independent problem solving and the level of potential development as determined through problem solving under adult guidance or in collaboration with more capable peers."

Teachers and peers foster intellectual growth by providing instruction within a student's zone of proximal development. Some of Vygotsky's followers (e.g., Wood, Bruner, & Ross, 1976) have used the notion of **scaffolding** to describe how teachers and more capable peers lend a hand to students to help them advance to the next level of performance. Scaffolds are those structures that masons climb on to lay higher and higher layers of bricks. When we described Piaget's theory, we used the analogy of children being masons. Whereas Piaget felt that teachers were needed merely to toss bricks to students, Vygotsky implied that without teachers and peers acting as scaffolds, students would be unable to climb up and lay higher levels of knowledge.

Self-Regulation

How do students keep themselves "on track" and adapt to the demands of the classroom? Vygotksy answered this question by describing three aspects of the language function: communicative speech, egocentric speech, and inner speech. **Communicative speech** and **egocentric speech** are both forms of "external" speech that we can hear children using. As the name implies, communicative speech is that form of speech that the child uses in order to communicate with someone else. Egocentric speech, in contrast, is speech to oneself. **Inner speech** is the internalized version of egocentric speech.

Vygotsky argued that the function of egocentric and inner speech is to focus your attention and guide your own behavior. You may find yourself using egocentric speech in situations such as when you are going to the store and ask a friend if he or she needs anything. When you are at the store, you engage in egocentric speech when you say, "Let's see, what did she want me to pick up?" Or, when you are first learning something (e.g., driving a stick shift car), you might say "O.K., to back up you push it this way." Vygotsky found that children used egocentric speech the most when they were performing a hard task and adults were not present to help.

Educational Applications

Vygotsky's theory has four main educational implications:

1. Teachers should act as "scaffolds" in which they provide just enough guidance so as to help children make progress on their own. For example, instead of intrusively telling a child how to solve a problem step-by-step, a teacher should do things such as start problems and ask children to finish them, or give hints that help students discover a solution on their own.

2. Instruction should always be in advance of a child's current level of mastery. That is, teachers should teach within a child's zone of proximal development. If material is presented at or below the mastery level, there will be no growth and children will be bored. If it is presented well beyond the zone, there also will be no growth. This time, however, children will be confused and frustrated.

3. In order for children to internalize a skill, instruction should progress in four phases. In the first phase, teachers should model the skill and give a verbal commentary regarding what they are doing and why. In the second phase, students should try to imitate what the teacher has done (including the verbal commentary). Early on, children will perform poorly, so teachers need to give verbal feedback and correct errors. In the third phase, teachers should progressively "fade" from the scene as children gain more and more mastery over the skill. Palincsar & Brown (1984) used this technique to teach children four reading strategies and were highly successful. They called their approach **reciprocal teaching.** To the standard Vygotskian approach, they added the element of teachers and students repeatedly taking turns. Everyone would take a turn "playing the teacher" until everyone reached mastery. That way, students got sufficient practice to internalize the skill and they also got to see the teacher model expert behavior multiple times.

4. Children need to be repeatedly confronted with scientific conceptions in order for their spontaneous concepts to become more accurate and general. According to Vygotksy, all fields (i.e., math, science, social studies, the arts, etc.) have scientific concepts, not just science so this implication is true for all subject areas.

Relation to Neuroscience

Vygotsky had very little to say about neuroscientific matters. Although he did discuss the construct of maturation in the context of explaining the difference between development and learning (Vygotsky, 1978), it is not clear from this discussion how he construed maturation. In particular, his writings do not indicate whether he believed in an unfolding of ideas or in an account that was more similar to Piaget's interactionist views. He was, however, a "species chauvinist" in the sense that he argued that human cognition is radically different than cognition in lower species. His views on evolution suggest that he would agree with the idea that the expanded neocortex of humans (in the frontal areas) provides certain abilities that animals lack (i.e., language, planning, etc.).

Connectionist Theories

The connectionist paradigm came into prominence during the mid-1980s. It is similar to Information Processing theory in its grounding in computer science, but different in several important respects. These differences will become apparent when we answer the five questions.

The Nature of Knowledge

Connectionists like to create computer models of a person's knowledge in some domain (Klahr & MacWhinney, 1998). Because these models are intentionally designed to be "brain-style" in their basic architecture (Rumelhart, 1989), connectionists often refer to them as **artificial neural networks (ANNs).** The architecture of an ANN has the following features. First, there are *units* that correspond to individual pieces of some represented idea or process. They are depicted in Figure 2.5 as ovals. Units can be turned on or activated in a manner analogous to the way neurons can be activated. Most notably, units have a threshold for being turned on by incoming activation. Moreover, most ANNs include three types of units: (a) *input units* which may be directly stimulated by environmental stimuli or the outputs of prior systems of units; (b) *output units* which represent the choices or decisions made by a network (e.g., the letter B has been perceived, not the letter E); and (c) *hidden units* which are inserted between input and output units by programmers because they are needed for complex computations.

The second feature of ANNs are *connections,* which are hypothetical links among sets of units (represented by lines in Figure 2.5). Connections can be either excitatory or inhibitory. The excitatory connections (indicated by lines with arrowheads) are such that

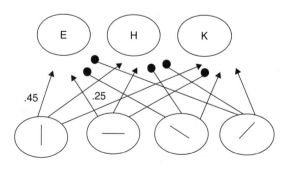

FIGURE 2.5   A Connectionist Model of Letter Recognition

they allow a high level of activation to spread from one unit to another. In effect, each unit gets turned on in succession as activation spreads along excitatory connections. The opposite happens with inhibitory connections (indicated by lines with dots on the ends). Here, the activation from one unit has the effect of dampening the level of activation of the next one in line or turning it off. A second aspect of connections worth noting is that connections from a number of prior units often converge on the same unit (e.g., those from bottom units for horizontal and vertical lines converging on the top unit for the letter E in Figure 2.5). When this occurs, the activation from the prior units is assumed to be additive. The way one represents the amount of activation that can spread from one unit to the next is to assign a numerical weight to each connection (e.g., .45 and .25 as shown in Figure 2.5; other weights are not shown to highlight these two). The threshold for activating a unit is also some numerical value (e.g., .65 for the E unit). When the combination of weights from several prior units exceeds the threshold value for a given unit (e.g., .45 + .25 > .65), the prior units can collectively turn on a subsequent unit. Each of the prior units could not, however, activate the subsequent unit by itself (because, for example, .45 is less than .65). The ANN shown in Figure 2.5 suggests that when an "E" is an input, the system turns on the unit for E and turns off the units for other letters. Hence, the output would be "E."

Although a connectionist ANN seems to be similar to other node-link structures described in this chapter, it is different in several important respects. Whereas the nodes in Schema theory or Information Processing theory refer to full-blown symbolic concepts (e.g., "animal"), those in connectionist models refer to atomic, particularistic elements of these concepts (e.g., a portion of a letter or a primitive meaning element of a concept). Moreover, ANNs do not represent conceptual relations in nodes or even single links. Instead, knowledge is in the *pattern of connections* among sets of units (Klahr & MacWhinney, 1998; Rumelhart, 1989). For example, to say that a child has knowledge of the letter E is to say that he or she has the network of units and connections among these units that allow him or her to recognize an E when it occurs.

Learning and Knowledge Growth

ANNs are designed to perform certain tasks such as recognize letters or make inferences. They perform these tasks by taking an input (e.g., a string of letters) and providing an appropriate output (e.g., deciding that the string of letters is the word HAT). A connectionist modeler sets the goal of creating an ANN that is highly successful. Typically, this means that the outputs are in line with the inputs (e.g., HAT is the input and the ANN says the word is HAT). To create a highly successful ANN, one has to have the right combinations of units that are connected to each other with properly weighted excitatory and inhibitory connections. To make their job really challenging, connectionists set all weights at a fixed value at the beginning of a simulation and then train the ANN to make better and better guesses over time. Training in this case means changing the weights on some or all connections (e.g., changing weights of .5, .5., and .5 into .45, .35, and .20). The ANN does the changing of the weights on its own using some *learning rule* that is built into it (e.g., "if the output is wrong, decrease all weights by .05"). Thus, in a connectionist system, the developmental mechanism consists of a combination of feedback and a learning rule. Given that all weights in a system typically change a little at a time and most units are connected to several others in a tightly woven system, it often takes a great deal of time and hundreds of learning trials to train an ANN until it makes very few errors. Hence, change tends to be very conservative in a connectionist system.

Self-Regulation

Although the connectionist perspective is very behavioristic and associationistic in its orientation, it is curiously similar to Piaget's perspective in the expectation that change tends to occur gradually. This similarity has prompted some to suggest that Piaget's notion of equilibration can be modeled in an ANN. When the pattern of connections changes for the better (i.e., fewer errors occur), one could even call this change a form of accommodation and auto-regulation. Note, however, that there is no conscious agent regulating him- or herself as Information Processing theorists and Vygotskians suggest.

Educational Applications

Although connectionists believe that their approach applies to all kinds of problems in various domains, relatively few educational researchers have used this perspective to study school-related learning (Bereiter, 1985). In recent years, however, this situation has begun to change in the field of reading research (e.g., Adams, 1990; McClelland & Rumelhart, 1981; Metsala, Stanovich, & Brown, 1998). Simulations have shown that the growth curves for ANNs for word recognition are similar to those for beginning readers. In addition, these simulations make many of the same errors as young children. Finally, some researchers have applied connectionists' models to reading disabilities. It remains to be seen whether researchers who study math, writing, science, and social studies will make similar use of this approach in upcoming years.

As for instructional implications, one could say that a connectionist teacher would be very similar to a Thorndikean teacher in his or her emphasis on repetition and feedback.

Relation to Neuroscience

Given the fact that ANNs are intentionally designed to perform "brain-style" computation, connectionist models are clearly compatible with neuroscientific approaches to learning and cognition. Of all the theories described in this chapter, in fact, connectionism has the closest affinity (Byrnes & Fox, 1998).

Conclusions

The six theories in this chapter clearly differ in terms of their stance regarding repetition, meaningful learning, self-regulation, and neuroscience. In addition, they all seem to have unique things to say about the best way to teach children. Nevertheless, it is possible to distill several themes that are common to some or all of the approaches. First, all six theories emphasized the role of practice and repetition. For Thorndike, Information Processing theorists, and connectionists, practice is thought to increase or modify the strength of associative bonds. For Piaget, Schema theorists, and Vygotsky, however, practice helps students internalize skills and form meaningful abstractions. Thus, the suggestion that practice is somehow inimical to meaningful learning is unfounded. Second, three theories emphasized the constructive nature of learning (Piaget, Schema theory, Vygotsky). That is, children interpret reality and instruction; they do not merely internalize as veridical copies. Third, two theories emphasized the importance of goal-directed learning (Piaget, Information Processing theory) while two others emphasized the conservative and slow nature of knowledge change (Piaget, connectionism). In general, then, it may well be possible in the future to combine these theories in a coherent way.

3

Memory

Summary

1. The major components of the human memory system include sensory buffers, rehearsal systems, records, cues, working memory, and permanent memory.

2. The process of creating permanent memories or records is encoding; encoding can involve simple repetition or elaboration. When experiences are elaborated, they are processed more deeply.

3. Brain research generally supports the distinctions between (a) working and permanent memory; (b) declarative, procedural, conceptual, and episodic memory; and (c) implicit and explicit memory; brain research may also explain the effects of emotion and stress on memory.

4. Memories can be easy to retrieve (high strength) or hard to retrieve (low strength); practice can greatly affect the strength of a record.

5. There are three main ways to retrieve a memory: recall, recognition, and inferential reconstruction.

6. There are three main views of forgetting: decay theory, interference theory, and loss of retrieval cues theory; decay theory places a heavy emphasis on the passage of time and lack of practice; the other two place greater emphasis on the strength of the connection between cues and stored memories.

7. Various memory strategies work because they involve practice, the imposition of meaningful relations, and visual imagery; people use strategies only when they realize the need for and value of these strategies.

8. Younger children remember far less than older children and adults because the former: (a) use strategies less, (b) are less likely to see the need for strategies, (c) have less knowledge, and (d) process information less quickly than the latter.

Although a primary focus of the previous chapter was learning (i.e., how information gets into our minds), we often touched upon issues involving memory (i.e., how we remember what we learned). In this chapter, we will focus mostly on memory, though we will often touch upon issues involving learning as well. It turns out that learning and memory are inextricably intertwined because what we remember about some information is often a function of how we learned that information in the first place (Brown, Bransford, Ferrara, & Campione, 1983).

The present chapter is divided into five sections. In the first, the components of the human memory system are described. The goal of the first section is to give you a sense of how we are able to retain information in memory. In the second section, you will learn about the opposite of retention, namely, forgetting. In the third section, you will learn about factors that increase the chances that you will remember information (i.e., use of memory strategies). In the fourth section, you will learn about the development of memory from infancy to adulthood. In the fifth and final section, the instructional implications of memory research will be drawn.

The Nature of Human Memory

The human memory system is described below in two steps. First we will consider the basic components of this system and then we will consider the main processes that occur within these components.

Components of the Memory System

The question, "How does our memory work?" is analogous to the question, "How does a car engine work?" The most helpful answer to either question is one which describes the parts of the system (e.g., "The engine consists of a battery, carburetor, . . . "). The key elements of our memory system include: sensory buffers, rehearsal systems, records, cues, working memory, and permanent memory. Let's examine each of these components in turn.

Sensory Buffers. When we experience something (e.g., go to a party, attend a lecture, read a book, etc.), our sensory detectors (located in our eyes, ears, noses, tongues, and skin) and the perceptual systems corresponding to these detectors (located in our brains) register this stimulation, interpret it, and retain it for a very brief period of time. The visual system, for example, retains (or "echoes") visual patterns for only about 1 second and the auditory system retains speech-like patterns for only about 2–3 seconds (Anderson, 1990, 1995). To get a sense of this phenomenon, look at the matrix of numbers below, close your eyes, and say as many as you can remember seeing:

2	9	3	7
5	1	6	4
8	2	5	3

If you are like most people, you probably registered all of the numbers in the matrix but were unable to name them all because the image of the matrix seemed to fade in about 1 second.

The sensory buffer is useful in that it retains stimulation long enough that your mind can interpret it (e.g., "I see a cat"; "I hear a song I know"), but it would not be very good if we could only retain our experiences for 1 second. At the very least, students would retain nothing from lectures and would fail every exam they take! Fortunately, our memory system includes other components and processes besides sensory buffers.

Rehearsal Systems. If someone told you a phone number and you could not write it down, what would you do? If you are like most people, you would probably say the number over and over to yourself. In doing so, you are using a particular sensory system as a rehearsal system (Anderson, 1995). Based on the work of Alan Baddeley (e.g., Baddeley, 1990), it was once said that we had two distinct rehearsal systems: one for rehearsing verbal information (called the **phonological loop**) and a second system for rehearsing visual or spatial information (called the **visuo-spatial sketch pad**). Whereas scientists still make the distinction between the phonological loop and the visuo-spatial sketch pad (see below), a recent study suggests that we only actively rehearse or maintain information in the phonological loop (Washburn & Astur, 1998). It would seem that people (and rhesus monkeys too) are able to retain information in the visuo-spatial sketch pad without active rehearsal.

At one time, moreover, we used to think that the phonological loop had a fixed capacity of between five and nine units (e.g., "the magic number seven"; Miller, 1956). Thus, if someone has a "span" of, say, seven units and she heard someone call out six letters (one at a time), she could recall all six of them. Similarly, if this person heard someone call out twelve letters, she would probably fail to remember about five of them. These days, we recognize that it is not the number of items per se that influences what we recall, it is how many we can **rehearse** before the sensory trace for each item fades that matters. For example, since we can say "wit, sum, harm, bag, top" in 2 seconds, we could recall all five of these words if they were called out. However, we typically cannot say "university, opportunity, expository, participation, auditorium" in 2 seconds, so we would probably only recall about two or three of these words (Baddeley, 1990). Interestingly, this word length effect was recently replicated in a study of hearing-impaired individuals who used sign language. Some signs take a longer time to perform than others. Participants recalled fewer items when lists contained time-consuming signs than when lists contained shorter signs (Wilson & Emmorey, 1998).

Baddeley likens the process of rehearsal to that of a circus performer spinning plates. Each time we rehearse, we "spin the plate" for that item of information to keep it going. If we have many items (e.g., twelve) or items that take a lot of time to "spin" (e.g., five-syllable words), the "plates" for those items will stop before we can keep them going. A plate stopping is analogous to a sensory trace fading.

Records. The prominent cognitive psychologist John Anderson uses the term "record" to refer to a mental representation of an item of information that is permanently stored in memory (Anderson, 1995). In Anderson's view, when we say that someone "knows" a lot of things, we are really saying that he or she has many records in his or her memory. Many readers of this book have records for such things as their middle name, the town in which they were born, what the answer to "2 + 2" is, and so on.

Over the years, researchers have learned three important things about records. First, as noted in Chapters 1 and 2, people have records corresponding to four types of knowledge: declarative, procedural, conceptual, and episodic (Anderson, 1995; Byrnes, 1999; Squire, 1987). Your *declarative knowledge* or "knowing that" is a compilation of all of the facts you know. Very often, declarative knowledge can be stated in the form of *propositions* and, as such, some researchers contend that our records for declarative knowledge are propositional in nature (e.g., Kintsch, 1974). A proposition is an assertion that can be either true or false (e.g., "Harrisburg is the capital of Pennsylvania [true]"; "There are three cups in a quart [false]"). Many behavioral studies have suggested that declarative knowledge exists in the form of associative networks. In such networks, there are central notions (e.g., bird) that are connected associatively to facts that people know about the central notion (e.g., can fly; lays eggs; etc.).

Your *procedural knowledge* or "knowing how to" is a compilation of all the skills you know and habits you have formed. You probably have records for tying your shoes, performing arithmetic, riding a bike, using a word-processing package, frying an egg, and so forth. Unlike declarative knowledge in which ideas seem to be interconnected in a network, studies have suggested that procedures do not seem to form an associative network among themselves (Anderson, 1993). They do seemed to be associated, however, to cues in the environment (e.g., seeing a fraction causes one to retrieve a procedure for adding them).

Your *conceptual knowledge,* or "knowing why" is a form of representation that reflects your understanding of your declarative and procedural knowledge (Byrnes, 1999). If you can give an accurate answer (that makes sense to you) of why certain declarative facts are true or why procedures work as they do, you have conceptual knowledge. It is one thing to know facts (e.g., diamonds are hard) and another to know why a fact is true (e.g., why diamonds are hard). Similarly, it is one thing to know which procedure to use in a particular instance (e.g., the least common denominator method in the case of adding fractions) and quite another to know why this procedure should be used. In brief, conceptual knowledge helps a student understand what is going on. At this writing, it is not clear whether this form of knowledge is stored as a distinct kind of record or whether it is stored in the form of relations among records.

Your *episodic knowledge* might be called "knowing when and where" because it represents (a) where you were when something happened to you (e.g., your first kiss) and (b) when this event took place in your life (e.g., in the summer of 1990). This personalized and historical quality of episodic knowledge is the reason why is it also called *autobiographical memory* (Shimamura, 1995). One important feature of episodic memory is the ability to remember the *source of the information* in your memory. Obviously, knowing some fact (e.g., that President Clinton's middle name is Jefferson) is different than knowing how you came to know this fact (e.g., reading it in the newspaper, hearing it on TV, being told by a friend, etc.).

The foregoing analysis of record types represents an elaboration of an earlier trichotomy that was proposed by psychologist Endel Tulving in the early 1980s: semantic versus procedural versus episodic (Tulving, 1983). In the earlier account, semantic memory referred to declarative and conceptual knowledge associated with language skills (e.g., reading, writing, comprehending). Procedural and episodic memory referred to the same sorts of things described above. As noted in Chapter 2, the distinctions among the four kinds of knowledge maps onto the claim of Schema theorists that there are two kinds of schemata: those for types of objects (e.g., animal, furniture, vehicles, etc.), and those for events (e.g., birthday parties, restaurant trips, etc.).

Besides assuming that there are four types of knowledge in memory (declarative, procedural, conceptual, and episodic), the second thing that psychologists have proposed is that records can be stored in two types of *codes* or formats: visual or verbal (Anderson, 1995; Paivio, 1971). For example, your declarative knowledge that German Shepherds have pointy ears could be stored as a mental image of what these dogs look like, or stored as the factual proposition "German Shepherds have pointy ears." Similarly, your procedural knowledge of how to fry an egg might be stored as a non-verbal sequence of imagined actions or as a verbalized set of instructions (e.g., "First, turn on the burner. Next, put butter in the pan . . . "). When people interpret language and create a mental image of a situation or set of relationships, they effectively change a verbally coded message into a visually coded representation. In the literature, the latter are called **situation models** (Zwaan & Radvansky, 1998) or **mental models** (e.g., Johnson-Laird, Savary, & Bucciarelli, 2000).

Third, psychologists have developed two constructs to explain why people have an easier time remembering some things instead of others: strength and activation level (Anderson, 1995). The *strength* of a record is the degree to which it can be retrieved from memory and made available to consciousness. High-strength records are well-learned facts, procedures, explanations or personal experiences that come easily to mind when you try to remember them (e.g., your first name; how to tie your shoe). Low-strength records are facts or procedures that you have not learned as well and are difficult to recall (e.g., remembering certain presidents or dates; remembering how to factor an equation). Many studies have shown that the amount of *practice* that you engage in affects the strength of a record. Generally speaking, skills or facts that are practiced regularly attain higher levels of strength than skills or facts that are not practiced to the same degree.

The *activation level* of a record corresponds to its current degree of availability. Making a record sufficiently active to the point that you can think about it is analogous to using a fishing pole to lift a fish close enough to the surface that you can see it. This analogy implies that records need to attain a certain threshold value of activity in order for you to have the experience of remembering the information contained in these records.

Records that are in a high state of activation are, then, conscious and available. Records that are in a low state of activation are not quite conscious or available (Anderson, 1995). Readers familiar with word processing packages know how documents can be retrieved from a floppy diskette or hard drive. Most packages require an author to highlight the title of a document and then click on it with a mouse to retrieve it. When the document comes up on the screen, it has (metaphorically) been made "available" for inspection and revision. Hence, it has been put in a high state of "activation." When it is just sitting there on the diskette, it is in a low state of "activation." The human mind is such that when you metaphorically click on a representation to retrieve a memory (e.g., Who wrote *"Death of a Salesman"*?), sometimes the memory record comes "up" on your mental "screen" and sometimes it does not. High strength items come up quickly and right away. Low strength items do not.

Putting strength and activation together, then, we can say that whereas activation level has to do with the current state of a record, strength has to do with the potential to be activated. High strength records are easier to make highly active (i.e., available to consciousness) than low strength records. Any knowledge that can be made available to consciousness and be verbally described is called *explicit knowledge.* Because explicit knowledge is available to consciousness, people are aware of any changes that happen to it. Unconscious knowledge that cannot be articulated is called *implicit knowledge.* An example is the collection of grammatical rules that people use to process and produce language (see Chapter 6). Because implicit knowledge is not available to consciousness, people are unaware of any changes that occur to it.

Psychologists can, however, test for changes in implicit memory using a variety of techniques. One common approach involves the phenomenon known as *priming.* Priming refers to the increased ability to identify or detect a stimulus as a result of its recent presentation (Squire & Knowlton, 1995). Studies suggest that when a given record is activated, the activation of this record seems to "spread" to other records associated with it or connected to it in a knowledge network. For example, consider the case in which someone has records associated in the following way: the record for "Lincoln" is associated to the records for "President," "Civil War," and "big expensive car." When he or she hears the word "Lincoln," two things happen. First, the activation level of the record for "Lincoln" increases. Second, some of the activation of the "Lincoln" record spreads to the other three records. The results of many behavioral studies suggest that activation spreads throughout an associative network of records and becomes weaker the farther it travels along the network.

Prior exposure to a stimulus (e.g., seeing the word "Lincoln") is said to **prime** the record for that stimulus (i.e., raise its activation level) such that it becomes more easily activated the next time. This facilitation is evident when one uses a two-phase fragment completion task. During the first phase, a list of words is presented (e.g., *Lincoln, banana, moose,* etc.). During the second phase, word stems are shown (e.g., L I _ _ _ _ _) and participants are asked to complete the stems. People are far more likely to complete the stems with words they saw during the first phase (e.g., complete L I _ _ _ _ _ with Lincoln) than people not exposed to these words. What is interesting is that people exposed to the words during the first phase do not remember seeing them. Hence, priming reflects a form of implicit (unconscious) knowledge change (Squire & Knowlton, 1995).

Before moving on, it is important to note that many of the distinctions described in this section have been hotly debated. For example, some psychologists and computer scientists have argued against the distinction between declarative and procedural knowledge because it has been shown that many skills can be simulated using procedure-only computer systems (see Winograd, 1975). Others have had problems with the implicit versus explicit distinction (Schacter, 1989), the semantic-procedural-episodic trichotomy (Tulving, 1984), and the visual versus verbal code distinction (Pylyshyn, 1981). To resolve many of these controversies, psychologists have recently turned to the neurosciences. In particular, the usual tactic has been to look for so-called **double dissociations** in brain-injured individuals. A double dissociation exists when damage to one part of the brain causes one kind of problem (e.g., inability to recall certain procedures) while damage to another part of the brain causes a rather different problem (e.g., inability to recall certain facts). After reviewing many case studies of brain-injured patients, Squire and Knowlton (1995) created

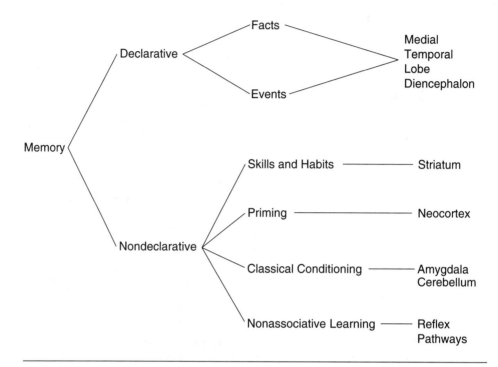

FIGURE 3.1 *A Taxonomy of Brain Locations for Different Kinds of Memory*

the taxonomy shown in Figure 3.1. As can be seen, these authors argue that structures in the medial temporal lobe of the cerebral cortex (i.e., the hippocampus, entorhinal cortex, parahippocampal cortex, and perirhinal cortex) and several other sub-cortical structures (e.g., the thalamus) seem to be important for declarative (explicit) memory. As for non-declarative (implicit) memory, double dissociation studies suggest that the striatum is a particularly important structure for the acquisition of sensori-motor skills and habits. The striatum is one of several sub-cortical structures that collectively comprise the *basal ganglia* (located beneath the cortex near structures such as the thalamus and amygdala). Priming, another form of non-declarative memory, is said to take place between neural circuits that are located in the cortex itself. Classically-conditioned emotional reactions are said to be mediated by the amygdala (located along the inner, lower side of the temporal lobe), while classically-conditioned muscular reactions are said to be mediated by the cerebellum. The final kind of non-declarative memory, non-associative learning, is said to be linked to reflex pathways located mainly in the spinal cord. Thus, combined with the findings of standard psychological experiments, these neuroscientific findings suggest that many of the distinctions in this chapter are well founded.

Cues. Cues are things in the environment or items in a rehearsal system that are connected to records. More specifically, cues can cause records to shift from being in a state of low activation to a state of higher activation. If the level of activation is high enough, the record is available to consciousness. For example, if you read the question, "Who wrote 'Death of a Salesman?' " each of the words in this question (e.g., "death," "salesman") could serve as a cue if it is associated with the record of the author. Or, an additional cue might be the prompt "Arthur _____ wrote 'Death of a Salesman.' "

When you (a) read the question, (b) recode it into an internal representation, or (c) repeat it to yourself, the cues are no longer in the environment, but are now items in a rehearsal system. Using our fishing analogy again, cues are like the rod, reel, and bait. When we "cast" cues, they sometimes help us pull up a record and make it highly active. Using our word processing analogy, perceiving a cue is like clicking on a file icon to retrieve a document.

Working Memory and Permanent Memory. Working memory is a concept used to refer to any information that is currently available for working on a problem (Anderson, 1995). Thus, items in the sensory buffers or rehearsal systems are in working memory as are permanent records that are in a highly active state. Working memory is a concept that has replaced the notion of short term memory in contemporary cognitive psychology. Baddeley and Logie (1999) suggest that working memory is principally involved in tasks such as comprehending and mentally representing the immediate environment, retaining information about immediate past experiences, supporting the acquisition of new knowledge, solving problems, and formulating, relating, and acting on current goals.

We have already seen how information in sensory buffers can fade within a few seconds. Moreover, there is no guarantee that information in a rehearsal system will be turned into a permanent record (see "Main Processes" section that follows). In addition, records that are in a highly active state can easily return to a state of low activation if a person is distracted or stops thinking about the idea. It is for this reason that working memory is considered to be a form of *transient* memory (Anderson, 1995).

In contrast, permanent memory pertains to our storehouse of records. At one time, we used to call permanent memory "long term memory" and call working memory "short term memory" based on several classic models of memory (e.g., Atkinson & Shiffrin, 1968). These models have proven to be somewhat incorrect and misleading, so many cognitive psychologists no longer use the terms associated with them. Records are thought to be embodied in the brain in the form of neural assemblies or stable patterns of interconnections among neurons (Squire, 1987).

In the previous section on records, we saw how permanent memory can be subdivided into different kinds of representations. In the present section, it is useful to describe several of the subdivisions of working memory. The first subdivision was discussed earlier in the section entitled "Rehearsal Systems" (i.e., the phonological loop and the visuo-spatial sketch pad). These two components of working memory were originally proposed to explain findings from psychological experiments. In recent years, however, their existence has been corroborated in research using neuro-imaging techniques. In particular, whereas tasks requiring spatial working memory activate regions of the right hemisphere, tasks requiring verbal working memory activate regions of the left hemisphere (Smith, Jonides, & Koeppe, 1996). The second subdivision of working memory pertains to the difference between a short-term "buffer" that temporarily holds information and a "processing space" that is utilized when information in working memory is operated on (Halford, Mayberry, O'Hare, &

Grant, 1994). To understand this distinction, it is helpful to consider the following analogy. When people are engaged in a home repair project, they usually need some space to do their work (e.g., a corner of their basement, garage, or tool shed). This part of your home is like your memory's "processing space." Note that materials cannot be stored in the processing space of your home because you would be unable to move about and do your project. Hence, there is also a need for space that temporarily holds materials until they can be worked on (e.g., a room or closet adjacent to the room for working on projects). The latter is like the buffer.

The visuo-spatial and verbal components of working memory are said to be "slave" systems to a **central executive** which is thought to be responsible for (a) managing the flow of information in and out of the two slave systems through selective attention and (b) planning, monitoring, and retrieving information about specific operations to be used in a particular task. Moreover, it is thought to off-load some of its own short term functions to the slave systems in order to free its own capacity for performing more complex tasks (Baddeley & Logie, 1999).

Summary.   The main components of the human memory system include sensory buffers, rehearsal systems, records, cues, working memory, and permanent memory. Returning to the car example, these components are analogous to engine parts such as carburetor, battery, and so on. Having described the main parts of our memory "engine," we can now examine important processes that take place within these parts.

Main Processes of the Memory System

Memory processes can be organized into two main types: those for forming permanent records and those for retrieving permanent records. Let's examine each of these two types of processes in turn.

Forming Permanent Records.   Researchers have examined three main processes related to getting information into permanent memory: encoding, rehearsal, and elaboration. **Encoding** is the general term for the process of taking sensory information and transforming it into a permanent record. Said another way, encoding is the process of forming a mental representation of something we experience (Anderson, 1995; Newell & Simon, 1972; Siegler, 1998). Rather than being photographic or complete, encoding is viewed by theorists from a variety of perspectives as being **selective** and **interpretive.** By selective, it is meant that records only include certain aspects of an experience. By interpretive, it is meant that our orientation toward stimulation determines how we encode it. A good example of this phenomenon is how viewers of a presidential debate often think that their candidate won the debate. Here, there is a tendency to encode the times when their candidate made a good come-back, and not encode the times in which the candidate stumbled. In effect, you see what you want to see.

Rehearsal is a process that we already described when we examined rehearsal systems. It is the process of repeating or "re-experiencing" some stimulation over and over. Thus, repeating a phone number over and over is an example of rehearsal. There is a large body of literature supporting the claim that repetition and practice determine the strength of a record. In fact, researchers recently revealed the existence of the **power law of learning** (Anderson, 1995; Newell & Rosenbloom, 1981) that has the general form:

Strength = Practice^{b}

When strength is indexed by the amount of time needed to retrieve an answer (T), one study found that the actual equation was $T = 1.40P^{-.24}$ (Anderson, 1995). This exponential equation (with a negative exponent) means that learners improve their recall the most during the first few study trials. After that point, they can still increase the strength of a record, but the increases will not be as much. For example, if a student studies the material for a test for ten straight days, he or she might recall only 40 percent of the material if tested after the first study day, but 80–90 percent of the material if tested after the second study day. Between the third and tenth days, he or she might increase from 90–95 percent, but note how the increase during the last eight days of 5 percent is much less than the 40–50 percent increase between the first and second days.

The fairly straightfoward implication of the power law of learning is that teachers should do whatever they can to increase the strength of permanent records through practice. By increasing strength, a record becomes more easily accessed.

The third process related to forming a record, **elaborating** pertains to the process of "going beyond the information given" and embellishing a raw experience with additional details. For example, if you read the sentence, "The boy was crying," you could encode the sentence in a fairly impoverished way or embellish your encoding somewhat. We can represent the impoverished encoding using the graphic convention:

Boy

|

Crying

Or, we could ask ourselves questions such as "Who is this boy?" "Why is he crying?" As will be explained more fully in the chapters on reading (Chapters 5 and 6), the minds of skilled readers usually ask such questions automatically. When they do, readers make inferences such as "it is a little boy who fell." Such an inference would modify the impoverished encoding to be:

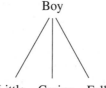

Boy

Little   Crying   Fell

As we saw in the previous chapter in the section on Schema Theory, such embellishments may make it hard for someone to remember what they actually saw and what they inferred. Thus, a reader might falsely recognize the sentence "The little boy was crying because he fell" as the one they read earlier.

Some researchers have put the notions of encoding and elaborating together to form the construct of **depth of processing** (Anderson, 1995; Craik & Lockhart, 1972). In this view, any experience can be encoded "shallowly" or "deeply." To see this, imagine that you are in class listening to someone with a very unusual accent. When they say something like, "Einstein may have been dyslexic," you may pay little attention to the meaning of this sentence and focus mostly on the person's strange way of pronouncing the words. If so, you have processed this sentence shallowly. On the other hand, if you try to understand the meaning of the sentence, make inferences, and relate the information to what you already know, you have processed it more deeply. Studies show that students have better retention of material when they process information deeply (e.g., Benton, Glover, Monkowski, & Shaughnessy, 1983; McDaniel, Einstein, Dunay, & Cobb, 1986).

To get students to process information deeply, teachers can ask questions that get them to think more about it. For example, after reading the Second Amendment of the Constitution ("A well regulated militia, being necessary to the security of a free State, the right of the people to keep and bear arms, shall not be infringed"), a teacher could ask a question that requires students to process the information either shallowly (e.g., "What right does the Constitution provide regarding guns?") or more deeply (e.g., "Why did the authors of the Constitution think it was necessary to give people the right to bear arms?").

Retrieving Records from Permanent Memory.   Creating permanent records by way of encoding, rehearsal, or elaboration is not all there is to remembering information. Even after you get information into memory, you still have the task of getting it out. To get a sense of this problem, note that putting an important paper in your desk drawer is not the only thing you have to do to be able to find it later. Putting it in the drawer is only helpful if (a) doing this helps you remember where it is (e.g., because you always put papers there) and (b) the paper is easy to find once you start looking in the drawer. If you randomly toss it into a disorganized mass of other papers, it may take you a while to find it. If we think of our minds as being similar to a desk drawer, we would have similar difficulty retrieving a record if care was not taken with respect to storing an experience.

There are three main ways we retrieve information from permanent memory: recall, recognition, and inferential reconstruction. **Recall** is the process that is involved when you are presented with a limited number of cues and you try to retrieve information associated with these cues (Flavell, Miller, & Miller, 1993). For example, if on a test a student is asked, "Who was the third president of the United States?," the cues "third" and "president" could prompt him to retrieve the name "Thomas Jefferson" from permanent memory. Similarly, someone's face might serve as a cue for his or her name. Note that the desired information (e.g., the words Thomas Jefferson) are not present in the situation.

Recognition is the process involved when you see, hear, smell, touch, or taste something and have the feeling that you encountered this sight, sound, smell, feeling, or taste before. In this case, you are matching a stored representation of something to the real thing in the world (Flavell et al., 1993). For example, a student might have the fact that Thomas

Jefferson was the third president of the United States stored as a permanent record. When presented with the item "Thomas Jefferson was the third president" on a true-false test, she recognizes this fact as being true. Similarly, you have permanent records for many familiar faces. When you see a person that you know, you match that person's face to the stored representation and recognize him or her. Unlike recall in which cues activate something merely associated with it, in recognition, cues directly match records. In either case, however, most current models assume that the probability of recalling or recognizing something is a function of the strength of the association between cues and records (Raaijmakers & Shiffrin, 1992).

The third retrieval process, **inferential reconstruction,** is used when your cues cause you to retrieve only a few fragments of a more complete record. Upon retrieving these fragments, you build up a plausible story around the fragments that seems to be a close approximation to the original record (Anderson, 1995). To get a sense of this, think of a TV show that you have not seen in many years and try to recall the plot (e.g., "Frosty the Snowman"). If you tried to tell the story to a friend who has not seen it, what would you say? Now think of a show that you saw last week and try to recall its plot. Notice the difference between the two memories. The latter is probably more complete and more similar to the experience of watching the show.

Forgetting

What happens to our memories as time passes? Why is our memory of some things better than our memory of others? Answers to these questions center around the notion of forgetting. After many years of experimentation, three views of forgetting have been proposed: Decay theory, Interference Theory, and the Loss of Retrieval Cues view. Let's examine each of these views next.

Decay Theory

Decay theory is the oldest view of forgetting and one which is quite consistent with the view of the average person on the street (Anderson, 1995). The main premise of this view is that the strength of a record weakens over time if no further practice ensues or if it has not been activated for some time. To get a sense of this notion, let's use the convention that the strength of a record is the probability that it can be recalled. For example, if there is a 40 percent chance that you will give the right answer to the question "What is the square root of 256?" let's say that the strength of the answer "16" is .40. The decay view suggests that a record that starts out with a strength of 1.0 would ultimately weaken to .80, then .60, then .40, and so on with the passage of time.

If our personal computers followed a similar law of decay, a document that we have written and tried to retrieve would be less likely to come up on screen as each day passes. But, of course, a document comes up right away no matter how long it has resided on a floppy diskette (assuming no damage has occurred), so computers do not follow the law of decay.

Research has shown that, indeed, the passage of time does seem to affect the retrievability of a record in a strikingly regular way. Across many different types of memories (e.g., for nonsense syllables, TV shows, factual sentences, etc.), studies show that most of what you forget is lost very early in the game. You continue to forget additional information after this point, but the rate of loss slows. This general trend has been called the **power law of forgetting** (Anderson, 1995). For example, one study showed that people remember 80 percent of canceled TV shows 1 year after they are canceled. Between the first and eighth year after cancellation, retention drops somewhat quickly from 80 percent to about 58 percent (a 22 percent loss). Between the eighth and fifteenth year, however, retention drops only 3 percent further (from 58 percent down to 55 percent) (Squire, 1989).

So the passage of time is an important factor in retrievability. But it has also been found that the amount of practice affects forgetting as well. As we already learned, practice affects the initial strength of a record. Research has shown that, at any point in time, people who have engaged in more practice show a greater likelihood of retrieving a memory than people who have not practiced as much. Nevertheless, even people who practice a lot show the exact same rate of forgetting as people who practice less (Anderson, 1995). So, for example, if Person A practiced something 50 times, she might show a drop from 80 percent correct to about 50 percent right away (a change of 30 percent) and then level off to 45 percent over time (a change of 5 percent further). If Person B practiced something 100 times, he might go from 100 percent correct down to 70 percent (a change of 30 percent) and level off at 65 percent (a change of 5 percent further). Thus, the amount of change is the same, but at each point Person B would recall more than Person A. Schooler and Anderson (1997) put the two factors of time and practice together in the same schematic function:

$$\text{Latency} = A + B * T^d$$

Here, *Latency* is the index of strength and refers to the time to respond with an answer. The *A* is simply a constant, the *B* is the amount of latency that can be reduced by practice, the *T* is the time between presentation and testing, and the exponent *d* reflects the decay rate. To accurately predict latencies, it is necessary to assume that the strength of a memory trace for an item starts to decay each time it is presented again. Each new occurrence, in turn, creates a new decay function with its own decay trajectories. To know what the strength is at any given time, it has been argued that one has to sum parameters across these decay functions (Anderson, Fincham, & Douglas, 1999).

Using somewhat different assumptions than Anderson and colleagues, Rubin, Hinton, and Wenzel (1999) tried to fit over one hundred functions to data from different memory experiments. They found that the best fitting equation for both recall and recognition was:

$$y = a_1 e^{-t/T1} + a_2 e^{-t/T2} + a_3.$$

Here, the *y* is an index of strength (e.g., probability of recall), the *a*'s are multiplicative constants (with values such as .92, .32, and .10, respectively), the lower case *t*'s are measures of time since presentation, and the upper case *T*'s are trial-related fixed values (the number of trials that intervened between study and test). They further argue that the first term (i.e., $a_1 e^{-t/T1}$) describes working memory and the remaining two terms describe long term memory.

If we apply the basic premises of such modeling attempts to classroom settings, we can see that much of the material that children learn early in an academic year will continually lose strength over the course of the year. To minimize the loss, it would be important to have students engage in considerable practice of the early material. A related implication is that children need to engage in practice over the summer to avoid losses between successive years. Middle class children presumably do so given that they show less loss of information over the summer than inner city children (Entwisle & Alexander, 1992).

What is interesting about the power law of forgetting is that our minds seem to be naturally equipped to retain only those events that repeat on a regular basis. That is, our minds seem to be saying, "This event keeps happening, so I better remember it; that event has not happened for some time and did not repeat very much when it did—I better forget it." Researchers have found that there is a strong correlation between the frequency with which things occur in the environment (e.g., the number of times a person's name is mentioned on a daily basis in the newspaper) and the likelihood that people can recall this information (Anderson & Schooler, 1991).

Interference Theory

Although time and practice do seem to affect how much we forget, these factors are not the whole story. Sometimes an **interference** relationship can develop between information already in memory and information that we are just learning. When newly learned information causes students to have trouble remembering old information, that is called "retroactive" interference. For example, first and second graders spend a lot of time learning the fact that 3 + 4 = 7. When they learn a new multiplication fact in third grade such as 3 × 4 = 12, the new associative relation between 3, 4, and 12 may interfere with the old associative relation between 3, 4, and 7. Thus, when asked, "What is 3 + 4?" they may answer "12." In this case, the 3 and 4 are acting as retrieval cues which activate the record for 12 instead of the record for 7. To overcome this problem, students need to form a four-way association between 3, 4, × and 12 as well as between 3, 4, + and 7.

When old information interferes with retention of new information, that is called **proactive** interference. An example of proactive interference would be the case of a third grader responding "7" when asked "What is 3 × 4?" Another example would be an adult giving an old phone number when asked his or her new number. In the latter case, the phrase "phone number" is a retrieval cue that is associated with both numbers, but is associated more strongly with the old number than it is with the new number.

At this point it is worth noting that from the standpoint of both Decay Theory and Interference Theory, forgetting is not seen as information *evaporating* out of memory. Instead, both views consider forgetting to be a problem of pulling up information that is still there (i.e., activating a record to a high enough level). Where these views differ is in how they explain *why* a record fails to attain a high enough level of activation.

To illustrate the decay view, let's assume that retrieval cues increase the probability of recall. For example, if the record for Truman is at .50 strength, assume that the words in the question, "Who was president after Roosevelt?" temporarily increase the strength of Truman by .30 to .80. If the *threshold* of remembering is .70, then the question would easily evoke the answer. However, if the strength of the record for Truman has dissipated to just .30, then the cues in the question might only increase the strength to .60, which falls short of the .70 threshold.

To illustrate the interference view, let's again consider the Truman example, but assume that the cue *Roosevelt* is associated to both the record Taft and the record Truman. Research suggests that a given cue can only send a fixed amount of activation across a set of records (Anderson, 1995). If we split the .30 increase in strength among Taft and Truman (giving .15 to each) and assume that Truman is again at .50 strength normally, then its strength temporarily increases to .65 by the question. Note, however, that if the threshold is .70, we once again get a memory failure. Thus, we can still have trouble activating a record even when it is at high strength if the cues we give are associated to many other records.

Loss of Retrieval Cues

The third explanation of forgetting involves the weakening of associations among retrieval cues and records (Anderson, 1995; Tulving & Psotka, 1971). Sometimes we see a face out of context and have the curious feeling that we know that person. For example, the author of this book might see one of his students at the grocery store. When this student is currently in one of his classes, the student's face is still strongly associated to the classroom context and other things such as his or her name. So, the present author can ask himself, "Is this one of my students?", imagine his classes, and then "see" the student in one class. These cues together help him then recall the student's name. However, when he sees a student from many years ago, the associations among the face, classroom, names, and so forth weaken to the point that he is not even sure that the familiar face is a student he has had!

You have also probably had the experience of trying to remember something in the middle of taking a test. Sometimes contextual cues such as the place you wrote something in your notes can serve as a retrieval cue to help you remember. Although such contextual (episodic) cues may help you right after studying, they will lose their association to information over time. When asked the same test question many months later, you probably will be unable to recall the information.

As was the case for the decay and interference views, the "loss of retrieval cues" view also assumes that forgetting is the problem of activating a record that is still *there* in memory. Again, though, it differs from the other views in terms of how it explains retrieval problems. To illustrate the latter view, let's return to our Truman example. Whereas the words President and Roosevelt were said to temporarily increase strength by .30, let's assume that these cues lose their activating potency over time. Instead of increasing strength by .30, an old cue might only increase strength by .10. Thus, a record at .50 would only be increased to .60, which falls short of the .70 threshold we have been assuming. The discerning reader will recognize that the "loss of retrieval cues" view is simply a decay theory that focuses on a dissipating association between cues and records (rather than a view that focuses on the dissipating strength of a record).

Factors Related to Enhanced Memory

At this point, you should have a good sense of the nature of retention and forgetting. In what follows, we will examine some factors that have been linked to enhanced memory. In the first section on memory strategies, we will examine some things that students can do to help themselves remember information better. As we will see, certain memory strategies work because they exploit the properties of memory that were described in the last two sections of this chapter. Although students use many different strategies, we will focus on five that have received the most attention from researchers: rehearsal, organization, elaboration, the method of loci, and the keyword method. After describing the five strategies, we will next explore a component of the memory system which plays an important role in whether or not we use strategies: metamemory. In the third section, we will examine the role of stress and emotion in memory.

Memory Strategies

Rehearsal.   As mentioned earlier, rehearsal is the strategy of repeating information over and over. At one time, it was thought that rehearsal was absolutely necessary for long term retention; that is, it was thought that repetition would inevitably increase the strength of a record and that records could not attain a high degree of strength without repetition (Anderson, 1995; Atkinson & Shiffrin, 1968). However, many studies have shown that repetition does not always increase the strength of a record and that sometimes people learn after a single exposure to information. Thus, it is best to say that repetition and practice are important for better retention, but they are not the only route to success.

Why does repetition work? As mentioned earlier, it seems that our minds are naturally sensitive to the statistical properties of the environment. We are built to remember things that we are likely to encounter again and to forget rare events. Consistent with this claim is the work which has examined **spacing** effects (Anderson, 1995). One way to study material is to engage in **distributed practice** in which you spread out your studying over time (e.g., one third of the material over each of three days). A second way to study is to "cram" (i.e., study everything at once just before an exam). Research shows that people who engage in distributed practice show better long-term retention of material than people who cram. However, the relative value of one method over the other depends on how much time will elapse between when you finish studying and when the test will occur. If you study once per week for four weeks and a week intervenes between the day you stop studying, say, October 1, and the test day, say, October 8, you will remember more than a student who crams on October 1 and studies no more. However, if you stop on October 1 and a "crammer" studies on October 7, the "crammer" will do better! So, if you want to do well on a test and remember the material long after the test, it is best to combine distributed practice with studying intensively the night before.

Two other findings that have relevance for studying are those that pertain to "primacy" and "recency" effects. When studying, it is common for students to study material in the order that it appears in their notes (i.e., material in the first class studied first; material in the second class studied second, etc.) Research shows that when people study material in this way, they tend to remember the material at the beginning and end of the sequence, and tend to forget the material in the middle (Greene, 1986). The obvious implication of this work is that the material in your notes should be studied in a variety of orders to even out primacy and recency effects across all of the material.

Organization. Organization is the strategy of arranging to-be-remembered material into subgroups and hierarchies of subgroups. To get a sense of this strategy, how would you study the following items?:

> carrot, truck, cake, broccoli, bike, bus, ice cream, peas
> train, potato, candy, pudding, plane, squash, soda

Instead of rehearsing them as a single set of fifteen items, you probably would form three groups of five items (e.g., "veggies," "vehicles," and "sweet stuff") and rehearse them in groups. Then, at the test time, you can use the labels of these groups as retrieval cues (e.g., "o.k., there were five veggies . . . ").

If a teacher presents students with an unordered array of material to study, then it is highly sensible for students to impose some organization on this material. Doing so has two main advantages. First, students will encode the material in a more elaborative way than would be the case with simple rehearsal. Figure 3.2 illustrates the node-link schema corresponding to the encoding for the list of items above. Notice how all ideas are interconnected and how a person has to use his or her existing knowledge of categories to form these groups. Second, the student gives himself or herself additional retrieval cues to recall the material later (i.e., the category labels) (Anderson, 1990; 1995).

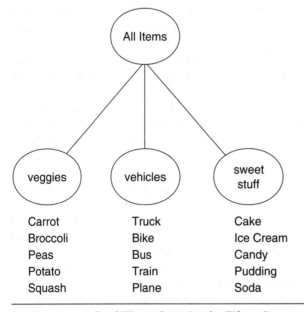

FIGURE 3.2 *A Good Way to Organize the Fifteen Items*

But even when teachers present material in a highly organized way, the organization strategy comes into play because students can use the teacher's organization to help themselves elaboratively encode the material and use their teacher's headings and groupings as retrieval cues. For example, if a biology teacher uses the grouping "endocrine glands" to discuss all of the endocrine glands in the body all at once, students can use this label to help themselves recall all of the endocrine glands at the test.

It is interesting, however, that when students create their *own* organization, they often show better recall than when teachers give an organization to students. This finding has been called the **generation effect** (McDaniel, Waddill, & Einstein, 1988). A recent study showed that the generation effect begins within a few milliseconds of study, but most of the benefits occur later. Overall, the data suggest that the generation effect results from the continuous strengthening of memory traces over time (Smith & Healy, 1998). Teachers have to decide whether or not their students are capable of imposing the right organization on material before letting them construct such an organization. If students lack the necessary background knowledge or have many misconceptions, they are likely to impose an incorrect grouping on the material. Thus, they will remember a lot, but what they remember will be wrong!

Having said that, it is useful at this point to discuss the issue of the intention to learn. A large number of studies have shown that as long as students encode material in an elaborative way, they will show good memory of the material even if they are not trying to remember the material (Anderson, 1995). That is, if you compare (a) people who are told they are in a memory experiment and who encode material elaboratively to (b) people who are unaware they are in an experiment and who nevertheless are made to process information deeply, you find that the intention to learn does not matter. The reason why there is a generation effect in many experiments is not because people are trying to remember as much as they usually do given unorganized, impoverished ideas to work with, but because they are successful at linking up new information with information they already know.

Elaboration.   Elaboration is the general term for imposing meaning of any kind on material. We just learned that organization is one form of elaboration, but the prototypical example of elaboration comes from experiments involving paired-associates learning. If you were presented with the following list of word pairs and told that your job is to learn the pairs, what would you do?

> cat-ribbon
> elephant-pin
> giraffe-scissors
> monkey-sewing machine

Most people tend to form mental images that link one term to another. For example, you may have imagined the cat wearing the ribbon or the elephant getting stuck by the pin. Either way, this interactive imagery has been found to be highly effective for learning the pairs (Weinstein & Mayer, 1986). Whereas it may seem at first that you have never had to engage in such paired associate learning, consider the fact the pairing of states with their capitals is paired associate learning. So is the pairing of faces with names, and so on. Elaboration is useful because it creates meaningful relations when none exists.

There are three reasons why elaboration works as a strategy. First, as the name implies, elaboration involves the creation of an elaborative encoding of the material. Second, when students are free to make up their own images, we have the generation effect (moreover, the image serves as an additional retrieval cue for either word). Third, we have learned from "dual code" theory that we are naturally equipped to retain visual information more easily than verbal information (without active maintenance in the case of visual information). By taking the purely verbal input and linking it to images, we are drawing on one of our natural strengths.

Method of Loci.   The method of loci involves linking up a familiar routine with a series of items that you are trying to learn. Typically, researchers ask students to take a list of facts and mentally "attach" each fact to a route that is very familiar to them. For example, students who have driven to school the same way everyday for four years are highly familiar with this route and can imagine it easily. When given a list of, say, twenty facts to learn for a test, students can divide their route into twenty landmarks along the way (e.g., their neighbor's house, the grocery store on the corner, the church on the next corner, etc.). Then, they can imagine each fact plastered on each of the landmarks. When test time comes, they merely think about their route and the material can be "read" off this image.

The method of loci works for a variety of reasons. Once again, we have elaborative encoding of the material. In addition, students are exploiting their natural capacity to remember visual material better than verbal material. Third, in selecting which route to use and which landmarks, we have the generation effect again. Fourth, the fixed sequence of events imposes an organization on material that may not have an organization. Fifth, each landmark or its label can serve as an additional retrieval cue.

The Keyword Method.   The keyword method is particularly useful for learning verbal material such as new vocabulary words. In this approach, a student takes a new word and finds a portion that may be a familiar-sounding, easy-to-imagine term within the word. For example, with the word "caterwaul" a student might identify both "cat" and "wall" (notice that homonyms can be used). When it is learned that "caterwaul" means a noisy fight, the student can imagine two cats fighting and screeching on a wall. Or, with the spanish word "carta" (meaning "letter") a student could see the term "cart" and imagine a letter being transported by a shopping cart. Research shows that the keyword approach can be highly effective for vocabulary and other similar tasks (Pressley, Levin, & Delaney, 1982).

Let's use a little constructivist learning here. Why is the keyword method effective? The reader should be able at this point to say why, given what has been said about the other approaches.

Metamemory

Of the five strategies previously described, which do you think would be most effective for studying for a test? Do you use any of these strategies? Would you be more likely to use a particular strategy (e.g., organization) for an essay test than for a multiple choice test? The answers that you give to these questions derive from your metamemory. The term metamemory refers to a person's knowledge and beliefs about how his or her memory works (Flavell, Miller, & Miller, 1993). Perhaps the two most important aspects of metamemory concern: (a) the recognition that your memory is not flawless and (b) knowledge of what strategies to use in particular circumstances.

Strategies are things that you do to avoid forgetting something important. But in order to use a strategy, you have to first recognize that there is some likelihood that you might forget something unless you engage in a strategy. At an even more basic level, strategy-users are people who recognize that they sometimes forget. In contrast to good rememberers who know when they are likely to forget something (e.g., they say "I'd better write that down"), poor rememberers think that they never forget. As a consequence, poor rememberers never use strategies and forget a great deal (though they do not recognize this!).

Besides recognizing that they forget, good rememberers know which strategies are effective for them and which are not. For example, a good student might discover that the method of loci never works for her but the keyword method does. Upon learning this, she stops using the method of loci. Similarly, a good student might also recognize that rehearsal works well for learning lists of facts, but that various imagery techniques work better for remembering textbook material. Thus, this student would flexibly shift from rehearsal to imagery as his tasks changed from learning lists to reading textbooks.

A third important aspect of metamemory concerns note-taking. Instead of writing down everything that a teacher says, most students write down things that they think they might forget by test time. Good students are adept at writing down notes in such a way that they can use the notes as effective study aides. Poor students, in contrast, misjudge their memory abilities. As a result, they either take too few or too many notes. It is important to note, however, that there is not a perfect correlation between metamemory accuracy and performance. Some very good students are sometimes way off in their estimates of how well they know the material for a test. It is just that, on average, the gap between what you think you know and what you do know is smaller for good students (Cull & Zechmeister, 1994).

Now that you have learned about the components of the memory system (e.g., records, encoding, strategies, etc.), you probably have a different view of memory than the one you had before you read this chapter. If so, that means that your metamemory beliefs might have changed. If your beliefs have changed, you might be likely to use strategies you never used before because you now understand why they might be effective.

Effects of Stress and Emotion on Memory

Of course, we often remember things without using strategies or having metacognitive insight into the need to remember these things. For example, readers of this book can probably identify personal experiences that seem to be permanently "burned" into their memories. For example, most people remember where they were when they heard about the *Challenger* disaster (or Kennedy assassination in the case of Baby Boomers). These experiences stand out in people's minds because of the unusual level of detail that is retained. Why do we remember so much about these experiences?

One possibility is that we tend to be fully engaged in such emotionally-charged situations. In other words, nearly all of our attentional resources are devoted to encoding the event. Another possibility is that we tend to replay the event over and over in our minds and also repeatedly discuss details with friends (thereby making use of rehearsal mechanisms). A third possibility is that we create very elaborate encodings of these situations because they evoke so many thoughts.

There are, of course, neuroscientific explanations of the flashbulb phenomenon as well. In particular, neuroscientists have long been interested in the anatomical basis of stress-related effects on memory (Cahill & McGaugh, 1998; Robbins & Everitt, 1995). Beginning with Yerkes and Dodson (1908), it has been found that animals seem to learn more when they are in a state of moderate arousal than when they are in a state of either low arousal or high arousal (an inverted U-shaped learning curve). Over the years, neuroscientists have advanced a number of proposals regarding the neuroscientific basis of this phenomenon. Recent proposals have emphasized the roles of hormones released in the periphery as well as distinct tracts of neurons in the brain.

Regarding the first proposal, the adrenal glands (situated on the top of the kidneys) release both epinephrine ("adrenaline") and norepinephrine during stressful situations. Among other things, the former acts to dilate the pupils, increase heart rates, and constrict blood vessels. Neither hormone, however, crosses the blood-brain barrier, so it was generally assumed that neither could play a significant role in the stress modulation of memory. However, recent studies show that the standard effects of stress on memory can be eliminated by administering substances that block the action of these two adrenomedullary hormones (Cahill & McGaugh, 1998). Thus, epinephrine and norepinephrine must play some sort of role. One proposal that has gained empirical support in recent years is the idea that epinephrine affects memory through its modulation of glucose levels in the blood. Glucose levels have also been found to be linked to learning in an inverted U-shaped manner (i.e., medium levels promote more learning than low or high levels), and the level of epinephrine in the blood affects the level of glucose in the blood (Cahill & McGaugh, 1998). An alternative is to assume that it is another adrenal hormone besides epinephrine and norepinephrine that is responsible for stress-related effects on memory (e.g. cortisol). The hippocampus has receptors for cortisol and this substance has been found to cause memory problems when it is acutely administered (Sapolsky, 1999; Schmidt, Fox, Goldberg, Smith, & Schulkin, 1999).

Regarding the second proposal, dopaminergic (DA) neurons that connect the amygdala to the frontal lobes have been found to be activated under stressful situations (Cahill & McGaugh, 1998). The amygdala is thought to be an important structure for negative emotions such as fear and anger, and the frontal lobes are important for working memory (Smith et al., 1996), so the idea that dopaminergic neurons might be involved appears to have some merit.

The Development of Memory

Few people would dispute the claim that older children, adolescents, and adults all seem to remember better than younger children. The question remains, however, as to why memory improves with age. In this section, we will attempt to answer this question by first examining age trends in memory performance and then considering possible explanations of these age trends. The section closes with a brief consideration of the developmental research on the role of stress in memory.

Age Trends in Memory Performance

In the present section, the goal is to provide answers to the following question: Which aspects of the human memory system change with age? In what follows, the answers to this question are organized in a manner consistent with the earlier description of the human memory system.

Changes in Components. The first way to think about age changes is to consider whether the components of the memory system (e.g., the sensory buffers or working memory) change over time. We know that young infants (e.g., four-month-olds) probably have the ability to retain sensory traces in their rehearsal systems because they demonstrate the phenomenon known as **habituation** (Bjorklund, 1999). Here, an infant observes the repeated presentation of some stimulus (e.g., a picture of his or her mother) for a certain number of trials. At some point, a different stimulus is introduced to see if the infant notices the difference. This procedure exploits an infant's inborn tendency to attend to novelty and changes in the environment. On the first trial, the screen changes from being blank to having a picture on it. Infants shift their eyes to this new stimulus and scan it for a few sections (the so-called **orienting response**). With each new presentation, however, the infant looks less and less, as if they know that they have seen the stimulus before. This monotonic reduction in responding is called habituation. When a different picture is presented, infants either give a new orienting response (indicating that they know it is different) or continued habituation (indicating that they cannot see the difference). These and related findings from other modalities suggest that infants can retain information briefly in their sensory buffers. However, we still know very little about (a) the capacity of an infant's sensory buffers and (b) how long information is retained in these buffers.

As for the verbal rehearsal system and the two components of working memory (i.e., the phonological loop and the visuo-spatial sketch pad), children would obviously not have the verbal component until they develop language skills (between the ages of one and five). Of course, having this component available for use as a rehearsal system and actually using it in this way are two separate things (as we shall see when we talk about strategies). As for the visuo-spatial sketch pad, the vast majority of studies have focused on children older than six, though a few have examined this component in four-year-olds in standard sorts of tasks (e.g., Luciana & Nelson, 1998), and also in infants using variants of Piaget's "A-not-B" task (Schwartz & Reznick, 1999; Smith, Thelen, Titzer, & McLin, 1999). In the latter (which was originally designed to be a measure of object permanence), one successively hides an object in two locations. Even nine-month-olds can perform well on this task under certain conditions, so it would appear that the spatial component of working memory comes "on line" earlier than the verbal component. Nevertheless, performance on both verbal and spatial working memory tasks continues to improve through adolescence. In a later section, we will consider whether this improvement reflects increases in the capacity of working memory or other developmental changes.

As for cues and permanent memory, we once again see that even infants seem to be able to associate certain stimuli (e.g., the appearance of a mobile for a crib; their mother's face, etc.) with long term representations (Bjorklund, 1999; Rovee-Collier, Hartshorn, DiRubbo, 1999), though they need occasional reminders to maintain these representations for more than a few weeks or months. Thus, one can say that an infant has the capacity for permanent memory. However, there is little reason to suspect that infants have records corresponding to declarative knowledge, conceptual knowledge, or episodic knowledge. Moreover, their preverbal status suggests that they do not store representations in the verbal code. Overall, then, most studies suggest that infants are limited to the implicit form of procedural knowledge (e.g., conditioned responses and sensori-motor schemes). How do we know they even have the latter? Two kinds of findings support the claim that infants have implicit knowledge of procedures. First, their sensori-motor performance improves over time. Second, there is evidence that these procedures can be primed (Hildreth & Rovee-Collier, 1999). After infancy, there is substantial growth in procedural knowledge and in the remaining kinds of knowledge as well (see Chapters 2, 4, 8, 9, 10; Nelson, 1986).

Changes in the Processes.   Two questions have dominated the developmental work on recognition and recall: (a) When do children first show evidence of recognition and recall? and (b) How do these memory processes change with age? With respect to the first question, studies show that even infants are capable of recognition and recall. To test the former, researchers have relied on the habituation technique described earlier. When infants look less and less at the same stimulus, they show that they recognize it. Beyond infancy, researchers have only found small age differences in recognition skills (Kail, 1990).

Unlike recognition memory which emerges early and changes very little with age, recall ability does not seem to emerge until the end of an infant's first year. Moreover, there are rather substantial age changes in the ability to recall information (Bjorklund, 1999). As implied earlier in this chapter, recall is the ability to think about something that was encountered before but is no longer present. Defined in this way, a student of Piaget's theory will see that the classic object permanence task is really a recall task. In the object permanence task, infants are shown an attractive stimulus and then watch the stimulus being placed under a blanket. Children who know that the stimulus still exists when out of view and who move the blanket to retrieve the stimulus have object permanence (Piaget, 1952). But doing so is a far cry from being able to remember all of the material contained in six chapters or even recall a set of twenty pictures. Children older than ten recall far more information in such situations than younger children. To explain these and the other age trends described above, we need to discuss some of the proposed developmental mechanisms of memory.

Explaining the Age Trends

Theoretically, it is useful to make a distinction between proximal causes of the age trends in memory (i.e., characteristics of children that cause memory increases) and more distal causes (i.e., characteristics of children, contexts of the larger culture that sometimes precipitate the proximal causes). Let's examine each of these types of causes in turn.

Proximal Causes.   As noted before, older children and adults perform better than younger children on working memory tasks and recall tasks. Why is this the case? Three explanations have been provided over the years. The first pertains to **strategy use.** In the earlier section on strategies and metamemory, we saw that strategies improve memory when they function to increase the strength of a record (e.g., rehearsal), promote more elaborate encodings of stimuli (e.g., organization, elaboration), or link up verbal material with imagery (method of loci, keyword method). Developmental researchers who have examined memory have asked, "When do children first use strategies such as rehearsal, organization, or elaboration?"

The results of many studies reveal that children progressively acquire such strategies between the first grade and high school levels (Flavell et al., 1993; Kail, 1990; Ornstein & Naus, 1985). The acquisition of any given strategy can be seen to roughly follow four phases (Flavell et al., 1993):

1. *Strategy not available phase:* At first, children do not use a strategy spontaneously and cannot be taught it very well.
2. *Production deficiency phase:* Children still do not use a strategy spontaneously but can be taught it; when they use it, their performance improves. However, they need to be prompted to use the strategy after they are taught it.
3. *Utilization deficiency:* Children start to spontaneously use a strategy without prompting but accrue little or no benefit from doing so. They have to devote so much attention to using the strategy that they have few resources left for concentrating on the material.
4. *Mature strategy use:* Children spontaneously use a strategy and do so very well. There is no need to prompt them to use it and their recall is substantially higher than children in the "strategy not available," "production deficiency," or "utilization deficiency" phases.

Besides saying that all strategies seem to be acquired in four phases, a second way to summarize the developmental research on strategies is to say that older "Mature Strategy Users" often execute a strategy more effectively than younger "Mature Strategy Users." To illustrate, take the case of rehearsal. When eight-year-olds hear ten items read one-by-one (e.g., "cat . . . tree . . . truck . . . fence," etc.), many are likely to rehearse only the most current item (i.e., the one just said by the experimenter). In contrast, a thirteen-year-old would be likely to engage in the more effective **cumulative** rehearsal in which all prior items are rehearsed as a group. The schematic below illustrates the difference between cumulative and non-cumulative rehearsal:

EXPERIMENTER says: "cat . . . tree . . . truck . . . etc."

8-YEAR-OLD says: "cat,cat,cat . . . tree,tree,tree . . . truck,truck,truck . . . etc."

13-YEAR-OLD says: "cat,cat,cat . . . cat-tree,cat-tree,cat-tree . . . cat-tree-truck, cat-tree-truck,cat-tree-truck . . . etc."

Finally, research suggests that certain strategies are acquired before others. In particular, children seem to acquire rehearsal between the ages of six to eight, organization between the ages of eight to ten, and elaboration between the ages of ten to thirteen. When a child increases his or her repertoire of strategies, he or she can use multiple strategies to study the same information. For example, a child may take a group of twenty pictures and first sort them into five categories (i.e., use organization). Then, she may rehearse them by group. Finally, she may use some form of imagery which links each of the four items in a group together (i.e., use elaboration).

Thus, there is development within terms of (a) the tendency to use a strategy, (b) how well a given strategy is executed, and (c) how many strategies are used in combination. The net result is that older children tend to recall far more information than younger children. However, it is important to add the qualifier ". . .when children are asked to internalize a large body of information on their own." Children learn a great deal between birth and age five. For example, they store thousands of new words in their long-term memories (see Chapter 6). How could this be if they are not using strategies and such poor rememberers? The key to understanding this apparent paradox is to return to an earlier point made about strategies. It does not matter who is doing the repetition and elaborating as long as *someone* is doing so. During the preschool years, parents and teachers often create repetitive and meaningful environments for children. One study, for example, found that the amount of language input from parents predicted growth in vocabulary (Huttenlocher, Levine, & Vevea, 1998). When children are in school, however, they are asked to structure their own environments to learn new material. It is here when strategy use is most beneficial and required.

Besides strategy use, a second proposed proximal cause of memory growth is **knowledge.** Earlier in this chapter, we learned that someone would be more likely to remember a sentence (e.g., "Fred shot Bill") if he or she elaborated this sentence with an inference (e.g., "Bill had an affair with Fred's wife"). A little reflection shows that an individual cannot elaborate on an encoding in this way unless he or she has a certain amount of knowledge. For the sentence above, for example, the person would have to have stored knowledge of the things that prompt people to commit murder. In addition, knowledge helps an individual to create chunks or meaningful groupings of individual bits of information. That way, attention can be allocated to fewer items in a shorter time frame (Chi, Glaser, & Farr, 1988).

Most of the chapters in this book document the many ways in which children gain knowledge with age. Given this pervasive trend, it would be reasonable to assume that older children would be more likely to form elaborative encodings than younger children because the former have more knowledge than the latter. This assumption has been born out in many studies (Flavell et al., 1993).

In a classic study (Paris, 1975), for example, children read passages such as the following:

> Linda was playing with her new doll in front of her big red house. Suddenly, she heard a strange sound coming from under the porch. It was the flapping of wings. Linda wanted to help so much, but she did not know what to do. She ran inside the house and grabbed a shoe box from the closet. Then Linda looked inside her desk until she found eight sheets of yellow paper. She cut up the paper into little pieces and put them in the bottom of the box. Linda gently picked up the helpless creature and took it with her. Her teacher knew what to do.

When asked a question such as "Did Linda find a frog?," older children were more likely than younger children to say "No" because they were more likely to infer that the creature was a bird. Notice how the word "bird" is never stated above. Paris (1975) and many others have shown that inference making such as this helps children remember the content of the passage better because they create more elaborative encodings of the information.

The third alleged proximal cause of memory development is **speed of processing.** To see the importance of speed in memory, let's return to our "plate spinning" metaphor for working memory. Someone who takes a lot of time to spin each plate could only keep, say, three plates spinning simultaneously. If we added a few more plates, some would stop spinning before he could get to the new plates. In contrast, someone who spins plates quickly and who runs fast could keep many more plates spinning at once.

As noted earlier, it is important to perform operations quickly before the information in working memory fades. To see this, try solving the following problem:

Look at the following list of 7 numbers. Then look away and add them all up in your head:

7   2   5   6   1   4   7

If you are someone who normally can rehearse a maximum of seven numbers, being asked to add them up as well causes you to not pay attention to some before they fade. Notice how you might be able to perform this task better if you were extremely fast at adding.

Researchers have shown that across a variety of tasks and mental operations, older children can perform these tasks faster than younger children (Kail, 1991, 1996). Thus, it can be assumed that when older children and younger children are placed in the same situation requiring the same skills, the former would be able to remember more than the latter because the former can simultaneously pay attention to more things than the latter.

Distal Causes.   The previous section suggests that older children recall more than younger children because the former (a) are more likely to use strategies, (b) have more knowledge, and (c) process information faster than the latter. The distal causes emerge when we ask, Why are the former more likely to use strategies, have knowledge, and process information faster than the latter?

As for strategy use, two explanations can be proposed. One appeals to the construct of metamemory and the other appeals to cultural influences. In the previous section on metamemory, we learned that people are likely to use strategies if they (a) recognize that they sometimes forget and (b) know a lot about strategies (e.g., which strategies to use in which contexts). If so, then it would be expected that age differences in strategy use reflect age differences in metamemory. Research generally has supported this hypothesis. In particular, younger children often think they have better memories than they actually have (Kreutzer, Leonard, & Flavell, 1975; Schneider, 1985). Moreover, although preschool children show some insight into the relative effectiveness of protostrategies and comprehend basic ideas about studying (e.g., studying ten items would be harder than studying five items), older children clearly have more insight about the nature and effectiveness of strategies such as rehearsal, organization, or elaboration (Flavell et al., 1993). However, as noted earlier, the link between metamemory and strategy use is far from perfect, so metamemory changes cannot be the whole story (Bjorklund, 1999).

A second way to explain developmental increases in strategy use is to appeal to changing cultural and contextual demands. Most schools are structured such that children tend to get more homework and difficult assignments with age. Whereas parents and teachers remember things for young children, older children are expected to remember things on their own. Moreover, when forgetting occurs in older children, it tends to have increasingly negative consequences. The intelligent behavior in such situations is to use a strategy, so it is interesting that strategy use is correlated with intelligence (Byrnes, 1995).

Culture has also been linked to the development of autobiographical memory. Children who live in cultures that emphasize discussion of past experiences tend to have more elaborate event representations and detailed episodic memories than children who live in cultures that do not emphasize discussion of past experiences (Bjorklund, 1999).

So far we have seen that cultural demands and changes in metamemory beget strategy use, which, in turn, begets enhanced recall. We next have to consider distal causes of knowledge change (which has also been linked to enhanced recall). Here, we can again turn to children's exposure to repetitive and meaningful environments. Such experiences can broaden knowledge even when strategies are not used. When strategies are used in school, knowledge grows at an even faster rate.

As for speed of processing, two distal causes can be proposed. One of the hallmarks of expertise is the ability to perform domain-relevant operations quickly (see Chapter 4). Experts are fast because they have engaged in endless hours of practice and have extensive knowledge. If we assume that children increase in various forms of expertise with age (e.g., reading skills, sports skills, etc.), they would be expected to process information more quickly with age as well. However, large cross-domain correlations in speed of processing argue against the expertise explanation (Kail, 1996). An alternative explanation of developmental changes in speed of processing is to appeal to changes in neuronal myelination that occur between birth and adolescence (Byrnes, in press; Kail, 1996). Neurons fire one hundred times faster when they acquire a myelin sheath along their axons.

Developmental Research on the Role of Stress in Memory

Over the past ten years, a large body of research has accumulated on the role of stress in children's memory. Some of this work emanates from considerations of children's reliability as witnesses in criminal cases, while others have made use of naturally-occurring stressful situations such as hospitalizations. Whereas the former work suggests that young children are less reliable as witnesses than older children (in laboratory simulations), the latter work shows that even preschoolers can have surprisingly accurate and detailed memories (Bjorklund, 1999). As noted earlier, it is not clear whether such stress-related enhancements are due to attentional, emotional, or physiological processes.

Instructional Implications

A reasonable way of stating the instructional implications of memory research is to provide the following list of suggestions:

1. *Teachers should view their job as helping students to form permanent records of the information that is presented in class.* To accomplish this goal, teachers primarily need to (a) maximize the number of opportunities that students have to practice newly-learned material (to increase strength), and (b) promote elaborative encoding of the material (through "why" questioning, use of imagery, and other techniques). Research on stress-related enhancements suggests that memory might also be improved by creating environments that foster increased, though moderate, levels of emotional responding (see Chapter 5).

2. *When creating tests, teachers should provide sufficient cues in their questions to maximize the chances that students will retrieve the information.* One way to do this is to arrange questions to follow the same order that material was presented in class. That way, students can use various episodic cues (e.g., where something was located in their notes; things that happened that day in class) to help them recall something. Another way is to use examples that are highly similar to those presented in class.

3. *Teachers should use multiple methods to promote "deep" processing of the material.* In addition to asking "why" questions, other methods include asking students to solve problems with the information or apply it to the real world in some other way (e.g., after giving the definition of "republic," send students to the library to find examples of republics in the world). In addition, teachers should explicitly teach students about the nature of memory (to alter their metamemories) and also teach them how to engage in rehearsal, organization, elaboration, and other strategies that promote long-term retention. The developmental work, however, suggests that strategy instruction would be most beneficial when children are in the "production deficiency" stage (because less advanced children could not learn the strategy and more advanced students already use the strategy). Of course, younger children in the "mature strategy use" phase for a strategy could always be taught how to use a strategy more efficiently (e.g., shown how to engage in cumulative rehearsal).

4. Because all information seems to be susceptible to the power law of forgetting, spacing effects, and interference effects, *teachers should ameliorate the effects of forgetting through increased distributed practice and occasional reminders of information throughout a school year.* The more things repeat, the less likely they are to be forgotten. The more things are spaced, the less likely they will interfere with each other. Interference can also be minimized through increased practice and elaborative strategies that help information link up with imagery.

4

Higher-Order Thinking and Problem-Solving

Summary

1. Theories of higher-order thinking take either a developmental or definitional focus. Developmental theories assume that (a) there is a continuum of thinking ranging from lower forms to higher forms and (b) students have to master the lower forms of thought before they are capable of the higher forms. In contrast, definitional theories assume that students at all levels can engage in higher order thought.

2. Adjectives that the Developmental theorists use to describe higher-order thinking include "abstract," "logical," "self-regulated," "conscious," and "symbolic." These theorists suggest that higher-order thought is evident when students engage in cognitive processes such as classification, hypothesis-testing, analysis, synthesis, and evaluation.

3. Definitional theories share a common emphasis on non-routine, intelligent problem-solving. Among other things, intelligent problem-solving involves (a) knowing what exactly is at issue, (b) a reflective analysis of one's options, (c) implementation of the best option, (d) an evaluation of outcomes, and (e) avoidance of reasoning biases.

4. Discussions of higher-order thinking and transfer usually go hand in hand. Students rarely transfer what they learn in school to real-world settings. Transfer is more likely if students can (a) partially decontextualize skills and develop conditional knowledge about their application, (b) cast their knowledge in the form of principles, (c) develop a conceptual understanding of procedures, and (d) approach their learning in a mindful way.

Observations of classrooms show that most teachers seem to fall into one of two camps: (a) those who emphasize fact-learning over thinking and (b) those who emphasize thinking over fact-learning. Historically, there have been times when many teachers have fallen into the first camp and times when the opposite was true. Let's call the former time an "emphasis on facts phase" in our history. We can call the other periods of time an "emphasis on thinking phase." It turns out that there have been far more "emphasis on facts phases" than "emphasis on thinking phases" in our history. Moreover, the former phases have lasted considerably longer than the latter. As a result, we can safely say that an emphasis on facts is the "norm" for the United States (Newmann, 1990) and the emphasis on thinking represents an occasional deviation from this norm.

What causes schools to occasionally shift toward emphasizing thinking? The main catalyst seems to be public dissatisfaction with the standard approach of emphasizing facts. More specifically, increases in dissatisfaction seem to occur right after some major technological advance has taken place (e.g., the Soviets launched the "Sputnik" satellite; computers became commonplace in the work world; etc.). Technological advances made the workplace much more complex than it had been up to that point and many people started noticing that workers did not deal with the increased complexity very well. Soon after, many people started complaining that "I wish our graduates could think better!"

If enough influential people complain (e.g, the secretary of education, the president, business executives), school systems ultimately respond by altering the curriculum to focus more on thinking. After the curricular changes are put in place, however, schools usually lapse back into the standard approach of emphasizing facts over thinking. When some new technological advance takes place, the cycle begins again.

An examination of our recent history shows that after a brief interlude in the 1960s in which we emphasized thinking, we lapsed back into a mode of emphasizing fact-learning again. Not surprisingly, many people have started calling for reform again. Leaders in the field of teacher education have heard the most recent calls for reform and have responded in two ways. First, researchers and other experts have proposed "standards" for specific content areas such as math or science (e.g., National Council of Teachers of Mathematics, 1998). These standards almost always suggest that thinking should take precedence over fact-learning. Second, school systems have used these standards to alter the curriculum to foster so-called "higher-order thinking."

Most school systems, however, have defined "higher-order thinking" in their own way. As a result, there is no standard curriculum for promoting thinking skills and there are a large number of distinct definitions of higher-order thinking floating around classrooms (Cuban, 1984; Newmann, 1990). Given this somewhat confusing state of affairs, the primary goal of the present chapter is to clarify the nature of higher-order thinking. More specifically, the discussion shall center around the following questions: What is higher-order thinking and how can it be fostered?

These questions are answered in the four sections of this chapter. In the first section, you will learn about theories of higher-order thinking that place it within a developmental framework (Developmental Approaches). In the second section, you will learn about approaches that define higher-order thinking but do not place it within a developmental framework (Definitional Approaches). In the third section, the research on the transfer of skills is summarized. In the fourth and final section, the instructional implications of the research on higher-order thinking are drawn.

Developmental Approaches

In the present book, the term **developmental approach** refers to any perspective that assumes a progression of thought from lower forms to higher forms with experience. Advocates of such approaches generally assume that it would be unwise to expose young children to the same higher-order thinking curriculums that older children are exposed to because the former would often be frustrated and confused. In what follows, we shall examine four accounts that imply that higher order thinking is a culmination of earlier achievements: (a) Piaget's approach, (b) Vygotsky's approach, (c) Bloom's approach, and (d) the Novice-Expert approach.

Piaget's Approach

There are two overarching assumptions of Piaget's theory that can be used to characterize his view on higher-order thinking: (a) Thinking becomes increasingly *abstract* with development and (b) Thinking becomes increasingly *logical* with development. For Piaget, higher-order thinking is abstract and logical. Let's examine this definition further by "unpacking" the two assumptions above.

Assumption 1.   By "abstract," Piaget meant "removed from immediate perception and action" (Piaget, 1965; Piaget & Inhelder, 1969). Thinking that is closely tied to perception or action is lower-order thinking (e.g., sensori-motor or preoperational thought). Thinking that is less tied to perception and action is higher-order thinking (e.g., concrete and formal operational thought). Moreover, as a child moves between one level of thought and the next, his or her thinking becomes more abstract because each stage transition produces thinking that is one step further removed from immediate perception and action. Thus, preoperational thought is more abstract than sensori-motor thought because the former is one step removed from immediate perception. Similarly, concrete operational thinking is more abstract than preoperational thinking because it is two steps removed from immediate perception, and formal operational thought is more abstract than concrete operational thought because it is three steps removed (Overton & Byrnes, 1991).

When children reach the concrete operations level for some content area, they are capable of reasoning with symbols that do not resemble their real-world referents. For example, the symbol "3" does not resemble a collection of three objects and the word "animal" does not look like any particular animal. In freeing the mind from *particular* concrete referents, children can think about the symbols themselves. Thus, although the symbol "3" can refer to a set of three apples or three trucks, one can ignore *which* objects it refers to in, say, judging that when one takes away one object from any set of three objects, one is always left with two objects (no matter what those objects are). Then, when children reach the formal operations level, symbols can stand for *sets of symbols.* For example, "X" can stand for "3" or "4" or whatever.

In order to be ultimately capable of abstract reasoning, Piaget argued that children need to interact with objects or actual content (see Chapter 2). For example, preoperational children need to count actual sets of objects and form many sets of three things in order for their minds to create structures which help them comprehend symbols such as "3." In particular, through the process of "reflective abstraction," children's minds abstract across sets of object-oriented actions to form schematic representations of set size. Similarly, they need to work on many sets of arithmetic problems (e.g., 3 + 4 = 7) before their minds will abstract a schema that would promote an understanding of algebraic formulas (e.g., x + y = z). In essence, experiences with objects, arithmetic sentences, and so forth are the "grist" for the schema-abstraction "mill." Thus, Piaget would not argue that nothing should be done to promote abstract thinking until children reach a certain age. Abstract thinking will not "emerge" on its own without ample experiences.

Assumption 2.   By "logical," Piaget meant that thinking literally conforms to the canons of logic. Long before Piaget did his experiments, philosophers devised laws and theorems that were argued to be universal "truths." One such theorem was the assertion that "If A > B and B > C, then A > C." Piaget was well-versed in logic and was quite surprised to see that seven-year-olds could make such transitive inferences long before students are exposed to the idea of transitivity in logic or math courses. Whereas a preoperational child would have to examine each item mentioned in a transitive statement in order to reach the correct conclusion (e.g., look at all three of a set of colored sticks that increase in size to know that the first stick is larger than the third), concrete operational children would know the answer without actually comparing the first and third item (e.g., the first and third stick).

In addition to transitive inferences, concrete operational thought conforms to logical analyses in two other ways. First, philosophers have claimed that logical thinking requires that things be classified in such a way that valid inductive and deductive inferences can be drawn. To insure the validity of categorical inferences, it is important to have correct definitions of categories such as "squares" or "mammals." The definition of "squares" is correct if it properly includes all of the things that are squares and properly excludes all of the things that are not squares. According to a classical perspective in philosophy, the best way to create correct definitions is to use lists of "necessary and sufficient" attributes (Smith, 1989). For squares, for example, the necessary and sufficient attributes are that the thing have (a) four sides, (b) equal sides, and (c) 90-degree angles. Anything that has all three attributes is a square and anything that lacks one or more of these attributes is not a square. Inhelder and Piaget (1964) argued that whereas preoperational children categorize things together if they merely look similar (e.g., a trout and a whale are both fish), concrete operational children categorize things using necessary and sufficient criteria. Thus, once again concrete operational thought is more logical than preoperational thought.

The third way that concrete operational thought is more logical pertains to the notions of negation and reversibility. Concrete operational children connect categories and operations to their opposites. For example, all of the things that are "dogs" are grouped together with all other animals that are not dogs through the superordinate category of "animals." This hierarchical grouping allows a child to fully comprehend class-inclusion relations (e.g., that dogs and cats are both animals). In addition, each mental operation is linked to an opposite operation that "undoes" the former. For example, addition is linked to its opposite, subtraction. By linking things to their opposites, children gain a sense of "logical necessity." That is, they feel that their deductions must be true. Thus, when asked, "If all of the dogs in the world were to die, would there be any animals left?", concrete operational children would say, "Of course! Dogs are not the only kind of animals!"

Formal operational thinking extends the logical aspects of concrete operational thinking in new ways. In the first place, inductive, deductive, and transitive inferences can now be applied to both real things and hypothetical ideas. In addition, children become capable of performing valid experiments because formal operational students examine combinations of variables and use the isolation of variables technique to test their hypotheses (see Chapter 10). Moreover, the abstract quality of formal operational thought helps children to step back from a chain of inferences and judge the validity of these inferences, regardless of the content. For example, consider the syllogism, "All frogs are mammals. Mammals are warm-blooded. Therefore, frogs are warm-blooded." Even though the content of this syllogism is factually incorrect (frogs are not mammals), formal operational thought helps an adolescent or adult ignore this fact and recognize that the conclusion follows if we temporarily assume the truth of the prior premises.

Summary.   Piaget argued that with age and experience, children's thinking becomes increasingly abstract and logical. As a result, they can classify things properly and arrange things in terms of increasing magnitude. Once their knowledge is arranged in this way, children can test hypotheses and draw valid inductive, deductive, and transitive inferences. Although preoperational and sensori-motor children also form hypotheses and draw inferences, these inferences are not always correct or valid. For example, children might infer that a horse is a dog because it has four legs. The main source of their reasoning errors is the fact that their knowledge is: (a) often incorrect, (b) not sufficiently abstract, and (c) not fully interconnected (e.g., ideas connected to their opposites).

Before moving on to Vygotsky's view, it is worth noting that many of the "higher-order thinking" curriculum packages on the market specify that teachers should promote inference-making, hypothesis-testing, and classification skills. Piagetian theory suggests that children at all ages are capable of these operations, but are unlikely to *correctly* apply them to real-world content until they have been able to interact sufficiently with things in the world and form abstractions across their experiences.

Vygotsky's Approach

Vygotsky shared Piaget's belief that there is a progression from lower forms of thought to higher forms of thought with development. However, Vygotsky defined higher-order thinking differently than Piaget. For Vygotsky, a given cognitive activity reflects higher-order thinking when: (a) there is a shift of control from the environment to the individual ("other-regulation" to "self-regulation"), (b) an individual has conscious access to this cognitive activity (i.e., the individual is aware of and can articulate what he or she is doing), (c) the cognitive activity has a social origin, and (d) the individual uses symbols or signs to mediate the cognitive activity (Wertsch, 1985). Let's examine each of these aspects of higher-order thinking in turn.

For any given cognitive process such as memory or attention, "self-regulation" means that students are intentionally using the process to learn something or adapt to the environment. In essence, children control their own memory skills or direct their own attention in the service of some goal (e.g., getting an "A" on a test). "Other-regulation" means that someone else (e.g., a parent) is remembering for children, or that something (e.g., a TV) is controlling their attention. As we learned in Chapter 3, there are developmental differences in the extent to which children intentionally use memory strategies to remember material on their own. We saw that such developmental changes in strategy use produce developmental differences in how much children learn and remember. Vygotsky would characterize these developmental differences by saying that older children are self-regulated and younger children are other-regulated.

The second aspect of higher-order thinking, that is, conscious access, is a logical prerequisite to the former one regarding control. It is not possible to control some process unless one can consciously think about the activities which subserve this process (e.g., memory strategies). Researchers have shown that when children are in the process of mastering a cognitive activity such as language, memory, or attention, there is a point at which they can perform the activity well but are unable to consciously reflect on what they are doing (Piaget, 1981; Karmiloff-Smith, 1984). After a period of successful execution of the activity, however, children ultimately become able to reflect on what they are doing. For Vygotsky, the activity is only higher-order thinking when it becomes accessible to consciousness.

The third requirement that a skill has to have a social origin is a hallmark of the Vygotskian perspective. Vygotsky believed that the best forms of human thought are passed on generation-by-generation through interchanges between more competent individuals (e.g., parents and teachers) and less competent individuals (e.g., children). More specifically, skills that become internalized in a child (e.g., using the strategy of rehearsal) start off as a form of social interaction between competent and less competent members of society (e.g., a mother rehearsing something with her child).

A good illustration of how cognitive activities can have a social origin is the form of instruction known as *reciprocal teaching* (Palinscar & Brown, 1984). Reciprocal teaching consists of four steps. In the first step, a teacher creates a small group of children. Then, each person in the group takes turns playing the teacher. On the first day, the teacher models the skill that she wants to teach (e.g., a reading strategy such as summarizing) and describes what she is doing and why. On the second day, one of the children tries to imitate what the teacher did the day before. Early on, children do not perform the skill as well as the teacher, so it is necessary for the teacher to give a lot of verbal feedback and corrections. This process of modeling the skill for the others cycles through the group until all members achieve mastery.

In addition to illustrating how a skill can have a social origin, reciprocal teaching also illustrates the fourth aspect of higher-order thinking: the skill is mediated by symbols and signs. By talking about what one is doing, one's actions become regulated by the most common form of symbol use, namely language. That is, "self-talk" helps you direct your attention and plan your behaviors in such a way that you meet your goals. Moreover, early on in the process, a teacher's verbal feedback can play an important role in children's learning of the skill. In order for children to gain control of the skills, however, it is necessary for teachers to progressively intervene less and less as they see children mastering the skills (a process commonly known as "fading" in educational circles).

Summary. For Vygotsky, any skill is a lower form of thought if (a) something or someone in the environment is totally controlling an actor's performance of the skill, (b) the actor cannot consciously reflect on what he or she is doing, (c) the skill was not acquired through interaction with more competent individuals, and (d) the activity is not mediated by symbol systems such as language. In contrast, the same skill becomes a higher form of thought once the performer controls its execution, has conscious access to it, and uses self-talk to direct his or her performance. For Vygotsky, social interaction and language are keys to shifting a skill from the lower-order version to the higher-order version. As such, preverbal infants and non-human animals are assumed to be incapable of higher-order thought (Vygotsky, 1978).

Bloom's Approach

A number of years ago, Benjamin Bloom and his colleagues devised a hierarchy of instructional objectives that had a profound effect on educational practice (Bloom et al., 1956). Each objective within the hierarchy specifies what a teacher would want his or her students to know and be able to do. By indexing types of knowledge, cognitive processes, and skills within each objective, Bloom et al.'s model is as much a theory of learning and cognition as it is a model of instructional objectives.

As the notion "hierarchy" implies, some types of knowledge are logical prerequisites to others. As a result, Bloom's approach is similar to Piaget's and Vygotsky's approach in the assumption that certain forms of complex thinking are not attainable until other, simpler forms are mastered first.

Bloom's taxonomy describes six levels of knowledge:

1. *The Knowledge Level:* Knowing information in a merely associative or rote-learned way (e.g., knowing your times tables without understanding the process of multiplication; a three-year-old counting to ten in French without knowing what she is doing; etc.);
2. *The Comprehension Level:* Understanding information in a deeper, more elaborative way (e.g., being able to explain an answer and fit it into a "big" picture; getting the main idea of a passage; etc.);
3. *The Application Level:* Taking definitions, formulas, principles, and so forth and using them to identify things in the world or solve real-world problems (e.g., using Piaget's definition of preoperational thinking to identify the level of thought demonstrated by a given child; using the formula "F = ma" to predict the acceleration of a real object that has been dropped from a certain height; etc.);
4. *The Analysis Level:* Breaking complex information down into its component parts and seeing how the parts interrelate (e.g., dividing the Civil War into "key" battles

and relating the battles to each other; identifying and interrelating the major themes of a book; identifying the constituent sounds in a word; etc.);

5. *The Synthesis Level:* Taking a set of components and creating something more complex out of them (e.g., blending separate sounds together to form a word; putting Piaget's theory together with information processing theory; etc.);

6. *The Evaluation Level:* Judging something against a standard of quality (e.g., rating the quality of a painting, play, or novel; arguing that one theory explains some phenomenon better than another theory; explaining why one governmental policy is better than another; etc.).

A little bit of reflection shows that a student could not apply, analyze, synthesize, or evaluate some information before he or she knew and understood the information fairly well. Thus, the first two levels of Bloom's taxonomy are logical prerequisites to the remaining four. Similarly, there are "good" applications of information and there are "poor" applications. Moreover, there are "good" analyses or syntheses and there are "poor" ones. Thus, application, analysis, and synthesis are prerequisites to evaluation.

Given the logical dependency between one level and the next, Bloom's approach suggests that teachers should not attempt to foster higher-order thinking in a group of novices by immediately getting them to think at the highest levels. Rather, instruction should begin with the lower-order skills and move through the higher levels in sequence. It should also be noted that the four higher levels are genuinely higher forms of thought when students perform these processes on information *themselves*. Teachers can apply, analyze, synthesize or evaluate ideas for students in their lectures, but notice how students are passive learners in this process.

The Novice-Expert Approach

Whereas the approaches of Piaget, Vygotsky, and Bloom have been around for some time, the Novice-Expert approach is a somewhat more recent addition to the fields of cognitive development and education. Researchers who espouse the Novice-Expert approach have the goal of identifying the nature of expertise in some area (e.g., math, chess, computers). To reveal the nature of expertise, researchers usually observe experts and novices as they try to solve problems. Then, the problem-solving approaches of novices are compared to those of the experts. The guiding question behind such work is "What is true of experts that is not true of novices?"

Recent summaries of this line of research (e.g., Anderson, 1990; Glaser & Chi, 1988) suggest that there are seven main dimensions of expertise:

1. *Domain-specificity:* At one time, it was thought that chess experts or computer experts were highly skilled and knowledgeable in many domains. In effect, the belief was that experts tend to be very smart. Research shows, however, that there is very little evidence that a person who is highly skilled in one domain (e.g., chess) can transfer this skill to another domain (e.g., math). Think of Michael Jordan in the fields of basketball and baseball. Thus, genuine expertise seems to be limited to a single domain.

2. *Greater Knowledge and Experience:* One of the largest differences between novices and experts is that experts have acquired considerably more knowledge and skills in an area than novices. Thus, given a list of the possible ideas that one could have for an area and some way to inspect the contents of someone's memory, we would find that an expert's memory would contain many more items on the list than a novice's memory. Moreover, by virtue of using skills many times, the expert ends up practicing them to the point that they can be performed quickly and automatically. But it is important to note that experts not only have more knowledge and skills than novices, they also interrelate this information in more complex, elaborate, and abstract ways (Chi et al., 1989).

3. *Meaningful Perception:* When experts and novices look at the same situation, experts tend to see the situation as a meaningful whole and novices tend to see it as a collection of discrete elements. In the earliest demonstration of this phenomenon, chess experts were found to see an arrangement of, say, fifteen chess pieces on a chess board as a single meaningful pattern. Novices, in contrast, saw it as fifteen unrelated units of information. If chess is played repeatedly for many years, certain arrangements will recur many times. Experts recognize the recurrent patterns as ones they have seen before. In an analogous way, expert teachers will recognize recurrent classroom situations, and expert car mechanics will recognize recurrent engine problems.

4. *Reflective, Qualitative Problem Analysis:* Research shows that experts begin their problem-solving attempts with a period in which they pause to understand a problem. Novices, in contrast, do not take the time to analyze a problem very deeply. Instead, they are very quick to "jump right in" and deploy stereotypical responses. For experts, a good portion of the problem-analysis phase consists of trying to recognize the problem, elaborating or imposing constraints on possible solutions, and building a workable mental representation of the problem.

5. *Principled Problem Representation:* An expert's mental representation of a problem is more workable than that of a novice because whereas the expert would understand a problem in a deep (i.e., principled) way, the novice would understand it in a superficial way. For example, a novice might think that two physics problems are similar because both involve an inclined plane. An expert, in contrast, might think they are not very similar because one pertains to Newton's First Law and the other pertains to Newton's Third Law. Similarly, a novice teacher might think that a classroom disturbance is similar to an earlier one simply because the same two students are involved. In contrast, an expert teacher might think that the two situations are dissimilar because one was precipitated by student boredom and the other was precipitated by a student's anger over a grade.

6. *Effective Strategy Construction:* Some studies have found that novices and experts use the same tactics when they solve parts of the problem, but they arrange these tactics in different orders. Thus, once again we have a qualitative difference rather than a quantitative difference.

7. *Post-Analysis Speed and Accuracy:* Although experts spend more time than novices on the analysis phase, they nevertheless are much faster than novices in their execution of problem-solving strategies. Undoubtedly, the former's greater speed derives

from the greater amount of practice that experts have (Anderson, 1990). Moreover, unlike novices who would make many errors if they tried to speed up their responding, experts are found to be quite accurate even when they are given little time to respond.

These seven dimensions of expertise provide two further enhancements to an expert's ability. The first is that experts can make better use of their working memory capacity than novices because of three aspects of their expertise: knowledge, speed, and automaticity (Glaser & Chi, 1988). Recall from Chapter 3 that information fades from working memory if it is not operated on or rehearsed within 2 seconds. A person can rehearse one or two items of information in 2 seconds, but cannot rehearse many items in that much time. But chunking the information in a situation, an expert can rehearse it all more readily. A similar advantage goes with speed. The faster one can process information or perform a skill, the more items one can maintain in working memory. Relatedly, once information is automatized, it no longer requires attentional resources.

The second enhancement is that experts demonstrate greater self-monitoring skills than novices; that is, the former are more likely to know when they are confused or make an error than the latter. This enhanced capacity for self-monitoring appears to accrue from the fact that experts form more accurate mental representations of a problem than novices. These more accurate representations, in turn, derive from experts' greater knowledge and tendency to spend more time analyzing a problem qualitatively.

Research shows that expertise seems to emerge only after an individual gains considerable knowledge and skill in an area and has had sufficient time to practice skills until they are automatic. In fact, several researchers have found that it seems to take about 10 years until someone becomes a "true" expert in an area (Hayes, 1985; Ericsson, 1996; Ericsson & Smith, 1991). However, expertise is only attained in 10 years if (a) an individual engages in a daily regimen of 3.5 hours of deliberate practice (i.e., focused attention, striving toward perfection, a high level of effort, self-imposed challenges) and (b) an individual has access to a coach, parent, mentor, or teacher who gives expert advice and scaffolds during practice sessions (Ericsson, 1996). Given these time and resource constraints, it follows that students should not be asked to "think like experts" from the start of their exposure to an area. For example, Expertise theorists would not expect a third grader who is exposed to math word problems for the first time to be helped by someone saying, "Now, don't jump right in! Take a few minutes to really understand the problem and then do solve it really fast!" In the absence of prior knowledge and problem schemata (see Chapter 9), increased reflection and forced speed may have little benefit.

Summary of Developmental Approaches

Perhaps the best summary of the four developmental approaches would be a recapitulation of the major terms used to describe higher-order thinking so far. For Piaget, the main attributes of higher-order thought are that it is *abstract* and *logical*. The four major cognitive processes include *classification, inference-making* (deductive, inductive, and transitive), *hypothesis-testing,* and *experimentation*. These four processes only reflect higher-order thought when they are applied to knowledge that is abstract and logically organized.

For Vygotsky, higher-order thinking must have a *social origin* and also be *self-regulated, conscious,* and *symbolically mediated.* For Bloom, higher forms of thought involve *understanding, application, analysis, synthesis,* and *evaluation.* For researchers in the Novice-Expert tradition, the central aspects of expertise include *domain-specificity, substantial knowledge and skill, meaningful perception, reflectivity, principled understanding, speed, enhanced memory,* and *enhanced self-monitoring.*

All of the developmental approaches have emphasized the fact that there is a natural progression in thinking from lower forms to higher forms with age or experience. This developmental progression implies that students need to have a certain amount of education, experience, or practice before they can become capable of the highest forms of thought. Hence, each approach implies that it is unwise to ask beginners to engage in the highest forms of thought right away because the tasks that require this type of thought would either be "over their heads" or be performed incorrectly. And yet, each approach also reveals that it is wrong to assume that teachers should do nothing to promote thinking until students reach a certain age.

Definitional Approaches

In this section, we shall examine four approaches to higher-order thinking that define it but do not place it within a developmental framework. That is, there is very little in the following definitions that imply the need to limit higher-order thinking to just those individuals who have progressed sufficiently along a developmental continuum.

Sternberg's Approach

Overview.   In the 1980s, Robert Sternberg proposed an information-processing theory of intelligence (e.g., Sternberg, 1985). Close inspection of Sternberg's theory shows that it is a description of how intelligent people solve problems and acquire information. Soon after his theory was proposed, many people started to ask, "Could I teach my students how to approach problems more intelligently?" In essence, they were asking whether students could be taught how to think better. In many people's minds, there is no real difference between "thinking well" and "higher-order thinking," so Sternberg's theory of intelligence soon became viewed as an approach to higher-order thinking (e.g., Bransford et al., 1986).

Similar to other intelligence theorists who came before him, Sternberg devised his theory in two main steps. In the first step, he identified the key skills and processes involved in intelligent problem-solving and learning. In the second step, he tried to form clusters of skills that seemed to perform similar functions in the mind. In essence, for each skill or process he asked, "What job does this skill or process play in the mind?" Those skills or processes with similar jobs were grouped together to form a single cluster.

Using this approach, Sternberg identified three clusters of skills. He considered each cluster to be a "component" of intelligence. The *metacognitive* component consists mainly of the skills involved in thinking about how to solve a problem before you start. The *per-*

formance component consists of the skills that you use in the midst of solving a problem. The *knowledge acquisition* component is comprised of those skills involved acquiring new information. In what follows, we shall examine these three components in more detail.

The **metacognitive component** consists of skills such as (a) problem definition (i.e., thinking about what you are trying to accomplish and what you are allowed to do), (b) planning (i.e., selecting and ordering a set of problem-solving steps), and (c) allocating attentional resources (i.e., thinking about which things you are going to pay attention to and for how long).

The **performance component** consists of a variety of mental skills and processes that have to do with specific tasks. Each task requires its own key skills and processes. To illustrate, consider analogies such as "Human : Hand :: Animal : (a) Paw, (b) Fur." For Sternberg (1985) analogy problems require the processes of *encoding* (i.e., processing all five terms in the analogy), *inference* (i.e., computing the relation between the first and second terms), *mapping* (i.e., computing the relation between the first and third terms), and *application* (i.e., computing a relation between the third and fourth terms that is parallel to that between the first and second terms). Whereas analogies require encoding, inference, mapping, and application, other tasks require a different set of skills and processes.

The **knowledge acquisition component** consists of three primary processes: selective encoding (i.e., encoding only that information that is relevant to the learning task), selective combination (i.e., taking all of the selectively-encoded information and putting it together in an effective way), and selective comparison (i.e., comparing what you just learned by way of selective encoding to something you already know).

In addition to proposing that intelligence consists of three components, Sternberg also suggests that there are three kinds of intelligence: analytical, creative, and practical (Sternberg, Torff, & Grigorenko, 1998). When these intelligences are infused into instructional practice, the **analytical** type involves "analyzing, judging, evaluating, comparing and contrasting, and critiquing" (Sternberg et al, 1998; p. 374). For example, an activity might focus on three kinds of authority figures: the president, a governor, and a mayor. Students could be asked to compare the powers, privileges, and responsibilities of these individuals. The **creative** type involves "creating, inventing, discovering, imagining, and supposing" (p. 374). An activity requiring creative intelligence might ask students to create their own government agency, justify the need for it, explain how it would be funded, and create an advertisement for it. The **practical** type involves "implementing, using, applying, and seeking relevance" (p. 374). An activity requiring the latter might be group-based brainstorming on how to solve the problem of littering in some community.

Sternberg and colleagues expected that instruction that required the analytical, creative, and practical kinds of intelligences would lead to better performance in school than traditional memory-based instruction for two reasons. First, this triarchic approach would prompt students to encode the information in three different ways (analytically, creatively, and practically). Second, the triarchic approach would allow students who are strong in the analytical, creative, or practical kinds of intelligence to capitalize on their strengths. Results of both a third grade and high school intervention showed that the triarchic approach led to better performance than either an analytical-only or traditional approach (Sternberg et al., 1998).

Higher-Order Thinking.   Sternberg (1985) argued that the metacomponent lies at the heart of intelligence and higher-order thinking because it functions as an "executive"; that is, it coordinates the activities of the performance and knowledge acquisition components. More specifically, the metacomponent is involved in decisions regarding (a) which performance components should accessed and performed in a particular context, (b) when it is time to shift to a new problem-solving solution, and (c) when it is time to learn something new. Thus, if one wanted to foster higher-order thinking, one would attempt to enhance the functioning of the skills that comprise the metacomponent (e.g., planning, problem-definition, monitoring, and allocation of attentional resources).

As indicated in the introduction to this section, there is nothing in Sternberg's theory that suggests that higher-order thinking (as he defines it) could only be found in a group of older, experienced individuals. From what is known about the cognitive abilities of young children, even two-year-olds could approach tasks in the way described by Sternberg.

The IDEAL Problem-Solver Approach

John Bransford and his colleagues have long been interested in the issue of how to teach thinking skills to students. Their thoughtful analysis of many years of research reveals that there are two main components of effective thinking and problem-solving: (a) a set of general problem-solving strategies and (b) specific knowledge that is organized in such a way that it enhances successful performance (Bransford et al., 1986).

General Problem-Solving Strategies.   Bransford and his colleagues use the acronym "IDEAL" to capture the five general strategies that comprise effective thinking and problem-solving: (a) *Identifying* the existence of a problem, (b) *Defining* the nature of the problem, (c) *Exploring* possible solutions to the problem and deciding on the best alternative, (d) *Acting* on this decision by implementing the chosen alternative, and (e) *Looking* at the effects of this decision to see whether the problem was solved. Let's examine each of these five strategies further to see what they mean.

Good thinking begins with the capacity to notice the existence of problems (i.e., **identify** the problem). As implied in the adage "An ounce of prevention is worth a pound of cure," effective problem-solving consists of noticing problems before they get out of hand. People who are highly successful in school, at work, and in their personal lives notice problems early on and work toward solving them soon after they are noticed. Poor thinkers rarely notice problems when they arise. To illustrate, consider how poor readers have been found to be unaware of the fact that they have reading problems (Bransford et al., 1986).

But simply noticing the existence of a problem does not help much in telling the problem-solver how to solve it. Consider how noticing a problem in a personal relationship (e.g., you are fighting with someone all of the time) does not immediately tell you what is wrong and how it should be solved. Similarly, a poor reader might become aware of having trouble reading but not know exactly what is wrong. That brings us to the next step: **defining** the problem.

Problem definition is analogous to a physician's diagnosis of a disease because when you define a problem, you indicate what is causing the problem. In fact, diagnosis is just one form of the general process of problem definition. The key step in diagnosis involves unpacking the question "What is wrong" by thinking about your goals. In most cases, a problem is simply something that is standing in the way of you reaching your goals. With relationships, you might have the goal of interacting harmoniously with your partner as often as possible. Fighting means that you are not meeting this goal. Similarly, a fifth grader might have the goal of getting an "A" on a math test, so encountering some difficult questions on the test is a problem because she may not meet her goal. Good thinking consists of defining and redefining your goals until you have some that help you maximize your success (Sternberg, 1985). Poor thinkers always seem to define the problem incorrectly; that is, they define it in terms of lower-level, non-essential, or overly-constrained goals.

To illustrate, consider the fifth grader who wanted an "A" on her math test. When she encounters the first hard question, she defines her problem (i.e., states her goals) in two ways: (a) I need to get *this* question right in order to get an "A," or (b) I need to get 90 percent of all of the questions right in order to get an "A." If she defines the problem as in "(a)," she may waste a lot of time trying to solve that one problem. In contrast, if she defines it as in "(b)," she might go on to other problems that she can solve.

Our fifth-grader example shows the importance of the problem definition step (the "D" in IDEAL) because notice how strategies relate closely to definitions. Different strategies are considered when one defines problems in different ways (e.g., figuring out the answer to one question vs. figuring out the answers to 90 percent of the questions). Thus, the **explore** step (i.e., the "E" in IDEAL) is very dependent on the prior definition step. But even when two individuals define problems in similar ways, a good thinker engages in exploration differently than a poor thinker. In particular, good thinkers tend to be more reflective and open-minded about possibilities than poor thinkers (Janis, 1989).

Unlike the "identify," "define," and "explore" steps, the "**act**" part of the IDEAL model may not be a step that plays a large role in distinguishing good thinkers from poor thinkers. It is conceivable that good thinkers and poor thinkers can perform the actions that lead to success equally well. Nevertheless, poor thinkers are more likely to fail than good thinkers because only the latter identify, define, and explore effectively. Thus, only the latter *think of* doing the appropriate actions (on their own).

The final crucial step in effective thinking and problem-solving is the "L" in IDEAL. Research shows that good problem-solvers are constantly monitoring their performance. They note when actions lead to success and when they do not. When failure occurs, good thinkers go back to the early steps in the process (e.g., "define" or "explore") to try something else. Poor thinkers have been found to pay little attention to their successes and failures. As a result, they are often unlikely to revise their strategies and **learn** from their mistakes (Bransford et al., 1986).

Domain-Specific Knowledge.   Earlier it was noted that the IDEAL approach specifies that there are two aspects of good thinking: general strategies and domain-specific knowledge. We have already examined the five general strategies, so let's now examine the role of knowledge. Bransford et al. note that good thinking cannot operate in a vacuum. We saw in the section on "Developmental Approaches" that experts are more likely to notice problems and monitor their performance than novices because of the greater knowledge possessed by the former. Moreover, knowledge helps experts appropriately define problems.

Thus, Bransford et al. would agree that having knowledge is a prerequisite to the successful application of the five IDEAL strategies, but they note that students could develop an almost "habit-like" tendency to go through the five steps if teachers of all content areas (e.g., math, science, reading, etc.) used the IDEAL model simultaneously in their classrooms. Moreover, it is possible for students to have sufficient knowledge but nevertheless carry out the IDEAL steps in a suboptimal way. Thus, the IDEAL strategies and knowledge are independent aspects of performance. Perhaps the main difference between the IDEAL approach and the developmental approaches is that an advocate of the IDEAL model might try to promote higher order thinking in young children using topics that they are very familiar with.

Resnick's Approach

Lauren Resnick, an expert on cognition and instruction, was asked by the National Research Council to review the vast literature on higher-order thinking and make recommendations regarding how to foster it in students (Resnick, 1987). She found, as most other reviewers have found, that there are a large number of definitions of higher-order thinking in existence. She quickly recognized that in order to make recommendations regarding how to improve thinking, she would first need to distill a single, unified conception of higher-order thinking from the large number of conceptions that exist. Her attempt at distilling a unified conception generated the following definition:

Higher-order thinking is *non-algorithmic* (i.e., the path of action is not fully specified in advance), *complex* (i.e., there are multiple solutions and the total path is not "visible" from any single vantage point), and *effortful* (i.e., there is considerable mental energy devoted to aspects of problem-solving). Moreover, it involves *nuanced judgments,* the application of *multiple* (sometimes conflicting) *criteria, uncertainty* about what is known, *self-regulation,* and the imposition of *meaning.* In contrast, lower-order thinking is algorithmic, simple, reflex-like, transparent, certain, other-regulated, and associative (rather than meaning-imposing).

Similar to Bransford et al., Resnick recognizes the importance of subject-matter knowledge in the ability to demonstrate higher-order thinking. Nevertheless, she argues that many aspects of good thinking are shared across disciplines and situations. Moreover, she contends that the approach of teaching "basic" skills first and "higher-level" skills second runs counter to the current thinking of subject-matter specialists. That is, she argues that there is no reason why content could not be taught in the midst of solving open-ended, complex problems.

The Actively Open-Minded Thinking Approach

In recent years, a growing number of researchers have adopted a perspective that emphasizes two core aspects of higher-order thought: (a) a competence component that corresponds to a person's *ability* to engage in higher order thinking and (b) a performance component that determines the extent to which an individual actually *makes use* of his or her competence in laboratory or real life situations (e.g., Baron, 1994; Perkins, Jay, & Tishman, 1993; Klaczynski, 1997; Stanovich & West, 1998). Most of the scholars aligned with this perspective suggest that good thinking is manifested, in part, by the dispositional tendency to fight against reasoning errors and personal biases. It is for this reason that this emergent approach is called the "Actively Open-Minded Thinking Perspective" (AOMTP) in the present book. Although several AOMTP researchers have examined age changes in biased thinking (e.g., Klaczynski, 1997), the AOMTP is not strictly a developmental approach because one could adopt a non-development model of the competence component (e.g., the models proposed by Sternberg, Bransford, or Resnick; see above).

In many ways, the AOMTP arose in response to the large number of studies conducted in the 1970s that suggested that the average adult often engages in reasoning that deviates from normative standards of rationality (Stanovich & West, 1998). These normative standards were supplied by logicians and statisticians who represented good thinking in the form of laws and theorems. In some theorems, for example, logicians abstracted the logical form of a very common kind of inference called *modus ponens*. In such inferences, there is a major "if-then" premise (of the form *if p then q*), followed by a minor premise (i.e., *p is true*) and a conclusion (i.e., *q is true*). Examples include "If an animal is a reptile, then it lays eggs; a snake is a reptile; therefore it lays eggs" and "If a person makes a foul shot, his or her team gets one point; a person made a foul shot; therefore his team gets one point." People were shown to deviate from normative standards when researchers began using counterfactual content in their experimental tasks (e.g., "If a plant is a vegetable, it has been cultivated to have edible parts; a rock is a vegetable; therefore it has been cultivated to have edible parts"). Instead of temporarily assuming the premises were true (for the sake of argument) and considering whether the premises would follow if the premises were true, people could not get past the counterfactual content. Content and pre-existing beliefs have also been shown to be a problem when tasks required probabilistic inference and when the results of an experiment had to be evaluated (Baron, 1994; Klaczynski, 1997). Here, participants might use stereotypes to judge the likely culprit in a crime (e.g., the culprit was Black) instead of using objective base rates stated in the problem (e.g., 90 percent of the culprits are White). Or, when an experiment provides data contrary to their views (e.g., murder rates are not lower in states that have the death penalty), they will spend a lot of energy finding flaws in the experiment. When it provides data consistent with their views (e.g., murder rates are lower in states with the death penalty), however, they barely examine the experiment for flaws.

Such studies have generated heated debates among researchers. Some have argued that the frequent departure from normative standards suggests that the human mind is incapable of reasoning rationally (i.e., there is something wrong with our competence). Others have argued that people have the competence but they just do not show it in experiments (i.e., the problem lies in the performance component). A little reflection shows that educators would need to know which of these two claims is correct before they attempt to improve thinking. If the first claim is true, it would be fairly useless to create programs to enhance higher-order thinking. If the latter is true, however, they would need to think about ways to change people's motivations and dispositions for thinking well.

As implied earlier, scholars who advocate the AOMTP think that the primary problem lies in people's tendency to engage in suboptimal reasoning (not in their competence). They have tried to reveal the factors that are predictive of the tendency to engage in rational thought and critical thinking. In one set of studies, for example, Keith Stanovich,

Richard West, and colleagues assessed the competence component by creating a battery of problems that tapped into the ability to draw deductive inferences (e.g., modus ponens), test hypotheses, draw unbiased statistical inferences, and so on (even when the content was contrary to their beliefs). They tried to predict high scores on this composite reasoning battery using indices of intellectual capacity (e.g., SAT scores) and questionnaires that tapped into the dispositional tendency to engage in actively open-minded thinking. By "actively open-minded thinking," they meant the tendency to be reflective (e.g., "If I think longer about a problem I will be more likely to solve it"), the willingness to consider evidence that was contrary to their beliefs (e.g., "People should always consider evidence that goes against their beliefs"), and a willingness to postpone closure (e.g., "There is nothing wrong with being undecided about many issues"). They expected that people would be more likely to reveal reasoning competence if they had more intellectual resources and a tendency toward actively open-minded thinking. Their findings generally supported this expectation (Stanovich & West, 1997, 1998; Sa, West, & Stanovich, 1999) and suggest that intervention programs might well be successful once the competence to reason deductively, critically, statistically, or methodologically is in place.

Summary of Definitional Approaches

The common thread of Sternberg's approach, the IDEAL model, Resnick's approach, and the AOMTP is the conception of good thinking as being flexible, reflective, and unbiased. Contrary to the developmental approaches, the first three definitional approaches suggest that the elements of effective problem solving *can* be fostered early and *should* be fostered across disciplines (the AOMTP is fairly silent on this issue). Nevertheless, the proponents of the definitional approaches also stress that thinking skills operate best when students have acquired sufficient content knowledge and reasoning skills appropriate to a particular context.

Other Approaches

Before moving on to other issues, it is worth pointing out that the developmental and definitional approaches are by no means the only approaches to higher order thinking. Because of space limitations, it was not possible to describe many other approaches that have their followings such as Ennis' model of Critical Thinking (Ennis, 1962), Lipman's Philosophy for Children program (Lipman, 1985), and the CoRT program (de Bono, 1983) (see Halpern, 1990; Nickerson, Perkins, & Smith, 1985; Resnick, 1987; Segal, Chipman, & Glaser, 1985, for reviews of these programs).

The Transfer of Skills

The term "transfer" is used to refer to the process of extending knowledge acquired in one context (e.g., the classroom) to other contexts (e.g., the workplace). In many ways, the issue of how to promote thinking in students is very related to the issue of transfer. Why?

It turns out that when employers and others complain that students cannot think, they often mean that students show very little evidence of transfer. More specifically, the observation is that students often fail to *use* the facts they learn in school to help them solve problems outside of school. With a few notable exceptions, the casual observation that people rarely transfer their knowledge has been confirmed many times in laboratory studies (Singly & Anderson, 1989; Brown, Collins, & Duguid, 1989; Salomon & Perkins, 1989).

If students do not transfer what they learn in school to real-world contexts, that means that our education system is failing miserably. Thus, it is imperative to understand the reasons why transfer does or does not happen. In what follows, we shall examine some of these reasons.

Embeddedness in Single Contexts

One reason why a skill may not be transferred is that students often tie it to the single context in which it was learned. For example, children who learn how to solve math problems in the context of seatwork seem to only call on their arithmetic skills during seatwork. If they are moved to another context (e.g., the candy store), they have no idea how to use their math knowledge to solve a problem in that new context (e.g., how much money they need to buy several pieces of candy). Many scholars argue that in order for a skill to be transferred, it has to first become disembedded from the original learning context (Brown, Bransford, Campione, & Ferrara, 1983; Piaget & Inhelder, 1969; Singly & Anderson, 1989; Stanovich & West, 1998; Vygotsky, 1962). The term "decontextualization" refers to the process of progressively severing links between a skill and irrelevant aspects of the learning context until only the link between one's goals and the skill remain (Singly & Anderson, 1989). For example, word-processing skills become decontextualized once a writer realizes that he or she can use essentially any word-processing package on any computer to write the same letter.

Lack of Conditional Knowledge

Although decontextualizing a skill increases the likelihood of transfer, it is not enough. Students also need to know when and where a decontextualized skill would be useful (Brown et al., 1983; Gagne, Yekovich, & Yekovich, 1993; Garner, 1987). One of the best ways of acquiring such *conditional knowledge* is to connect your skills to goals (Brown, 1989; Singly & Anderson, 1989). For example, if the word-processing function "delete" is linked to the goal of eliminating a word, then moving to a different computer will not be a problem if you say to yourself, "I have to delete this word. I wonder how to do it on this computer?"

If people lack conditional knowledge for a skill, then, it probably has something to do with their goals. If, for example, skills were never linked to appropriate goals in the original learning context, there would be no basis for using these skills in the transfer context. In essence, there would be an incompatibility between the goal structures of the two contexts. To illustrate, consider the situation in which the goal of using a skill in the learning context was "to finish my seatwork," but the goal of using the skill in the transfer context was "to know how much money to give the cashier for these four pieces of candy."

Unprincipled Learning

There are two main ways to teach a set of facts. One way is to present each fact as a separate idea that should be learned in a rote way. A second way is to group facts together that represent instances of the same principle. For example, instead of having students learn individual facts such as "the number that comes after 6 is 7" and "the number that comes after 2013 is 2014," we could teach them the general principle that "to arrive at the number that comes after a given number, add 1 to it" (Brophy, 1990; Gage & Berliner, 1991). Similarly, instead of teaching children the separate pronunciations of "cat," "mat," and "hat," you could teach them a principle about many words that end in "at." Studies have shown that whereas transfer rarely happens when a student's knowledge consists of individual facts learned at the rote level, it happens quite often when they know a principle and the principle applies in a new context (Singly & Anderson, 1989).

Lack of Conceptual Knowledge

Many studies have shown that students are more likely to show transfer when they have a deep conceptual understanding of a skill than when they lack this conceptual understanding (e.g., Mayer, 1989; Resnick, 1980). Perhaps the first demonstration of this phenomenon occurred when Gestalt psychologists tried to show how Thorndike's views on rote learning and transfer were incorrect (see Chapter 2 for more on Thorndike). In one study, Wertheimer (1945) used two methods to teach children the "drop-perpendicular" method for computing the area of a parallelogram. One group of children was simply shown how to perform the drop-perpendicular technique (i.e., they learned it by rote). Another group was given an explanation of why the method works in addition to being shown how to do it. The explanation consisted of showing them how one could cut off a triangular portion of a parallelogram and re-attach it at the other end to make a rectangle (as in Figure 4.1). Then, it became clear that the drop-perpendicular approach was simply an extension of the familiar "length × width" rule for finding the area of a rectangle. When children were presented with a parallelogram in an unusual orientation, the no-explanation group performed the drop-perpendicular method in an inappropriate way. The explanation group, in contrast, adjusted the method to fit the new orientation and derived the right answer.

At this point, we can form bridges across several sections of this chapter. You may have noticed a certain similarity between what was said about learning principles and what was said about conceptual understanding. A conceptual understanding often means having knowledge of principles and what they mean. Moreover, when we examined the Novice-Expert research, we saw that experts have a deeper, more principled understanding of problems than novices. Given this difference in knowledge, it would be expected that experts are more likely to show transfer than novices. The research confirms this expectation.

Inaccurate Conceptions of the Mind

In the beginning of this chapter, it was noted that many studies have shown that people do not transfer skills across contexts. In contrast, in the two sections that you just read, you saw that people often *do* transfer skills. What accounts for the differences across studies?

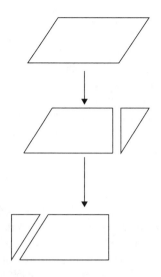

FIGURE 4.1 *A Meaningful Way to Illustrate and Explain the "Drop Perpendicular" Technique*

The main difference seems to be how individuals view the mind. Those individuals who have an accurate conception of how the mind works have been successful in promoting transfer. Those individuals who have an inaccurate conception of how the mind works have not been successful.

To illustrate, consider the early work of E. L. Thorndike on transfer (Thorndike & Woodworth, 1901). Thorndike conducted his studies to disprove an educational approach called the "formal discipline" method. Advocates of the formal discipline method (who still exist today) argue that the mind is composed of a set of "faculties" such as attention and reasoning which could be exercised in the same way one exercises muscles (Singly & Anderson, 1989). These faculties reign over knowledge and can be applied in any situation. Back in Thorndike's day, it was assumed that by taking courses in, say, Latin or logic, faculties such as reasoning could be exercised. The result was that a student would learn how to generally think better after taking such courses. These days, one hears about claims that learning computer programming or chess will sharpen the mind.

Thorndike disagreed strongly with the notion that there are general faculties. He believed that the mind consisted of nothing more than a multitude of stimulus-response bonds. For example, part of your math knowledge would be the associative bond between the stimulus "3 × 3 = ?" and your response "9." The rest of your math knowledge is a variety of other bonds. Thorndike argued that transfer would only happen when there was a great deal of similarity between a learning context and a transfer context. In this "identity of elements" view, similarity consisted of the virtual identity of aspects of the situation (e.g., the same people or objects present) or behavior (the same response was performed). In support of his view (and against the formal discipline view) he showed that transfer only happened when there was a great deal of similarity in situations and responses. Moreover, he (and many others after him) showed that students who take Latin, geometry, and logic courses do not do better in other subject areas than students who do not take such courses. Moreover, there was no evidence that these students thought better than other students.

Thus, Thorndike's studies showed that the notion of "general faculties" is not a correct view of mind. Unfortunately for him, however, many researchers have shown that his view of the mind is not correct either (see Chapter 2). As described in the previous two sections, transfer can occur when people know principles or understand what they are doing. Thorndike's theory made no room for notions such as principles, conceptual knowledge, procedural knowledge, schemata, or expertise. Thus, it now makes sense why he did not observe transfer in his studies.

Lack of Metacognition

There are two meanings of the term "metacognition" that are relevant to discussions of transfer. The first has to do with the notion of *mindfulness* (Salomon & Perkins, 1989). Transfer is more likely when an individual makes a conscious attempt to process a situation in a thoughtful, reflective, and analytical way. One way to be mindful is to ask oneself questions such as "Have I tried to solve a problem like this one before?" (Brown et al., 1983).

A second relevant meaning of "metacognition" pertains to the notion of *learning to learn.* Good learners have a better sense of the nature of learning than poor learners; that is, they have a more accurate "theory of mind" (cf. Wellman, 1992). For example, they recognize that (a) it is normal to be confused sometimes, (b) certain strategies work better in certain situations than others, (c) asking help of an expert can be quite effective, and (d) one's memory is far from fallible. Thus, just as it is important for researchers and teachers to have an accurate view of the mind (see the previous section), it is important for students themselves to have an accurate view of their own minds.

Summary

We have seen that transfer is more likely to occur if students can partially decontextualize skills and develop conditional knowledge about their application. Goals were argued to play a central role in discussions of decontextualization and conditional knowledge. Transfer was also found to be likely if learners cast their knowledge in the form of principles, and also develop a conceptual understanding of procedures and strategies. Finally, transfer is enhanced when students (a) have an accurate conception of the learning process and (b) approach their learning in a mindful way.

Instructional Implications

Having examined eight approaches to higher-order thinking as well as the research on transfer, we are now in a position to examine the instructional implications of all of this work:

1. The developmental approaches of higher-order thinking stress the importance of following a sequence of fostering lower forms of thought before higher forms of thought. Students need considerable experience interacting with concrete content

and solving problems in order to be able to form abstractions and develop mastery over this information. To foster the development of abstractions, teachers can provide many examples and point out the similarities among examples (e.g., present five examples of the same type of word problem and ask students how they are the same; present the government structures of three countries and ask students why they are all democracies). Moreover, they can provide feedback regarding improper classifications and conceptions. To help students gain mastery over skills, they can use methods such as reciprocal teaching. According to developmental views, then, it is not a problem if preschool or early elementary teachers focus mainly on lower-level skills. The problem is that teachers of *older* students never go beyond fact-learning.

2. It is a maxim that students learn what their teachers emphasize in class. Bloom and his colleagues were quite helpful in pointing out the connection between teaching *objectives* and teaching approaches. In particular, if one wants students to know information at the knowledge level, one can simply use a drill and practice approach. In contrast, if one wants students to know information at the comprehension level, they must be taught in ways which help them understand better (e.g., using analogies). Similarly, if teachers want students to be able to apply information, they must show students *how to* apply information and give them multiple opportunities to apply what they know. Students who are just taught facts (e.g., the definition of a "democracy") cannot immediately apply this information (e.g., recognize a democracy when they see one; take a non-democracy and change it into one).

3. Perhaps the main lesson of the theories and research reported in this chapter is that there should be a straightforward connection between school tasks and tasks in the real world. As several prominent researchers have pointed out, the concepts of learning and transfer are very much interrelated (A. Brown et al., 1983; J. S. Brown et al., 1989; Singly & Anderson, 1989). The issue of whether a student will transfer knowledge is an issue of how the skill was learned. If one wants students to be able to use a skill in real world contexts, one should simulate these real world contexts in the classroom. Thus, one should develop real-world problems as content and have students develop solutions to these problems. Moreover, it is important to insure that the goals of the classroom problems are similar to the goals of real-world problems. For example, a town in Maryland has the highest cancer rate in the country. A teacher in Maryland would be better off to use this example to teach the scientific method to students than more remote content (e.g., have them think of reasons for this high cancer rate and set them out to research these possibilities).

4. To foster decontextualization, teachers should have students solve multiple realistic problems that are superficially dissimilar but identical with respect to strategies and goals. Moreover, it should be noted that the goal is not to present skills in a totally decontextualized form (e.g., decoding words on a flashcard or having a separate class on higher-order thinking, decision-making, or study skills). Rather, the goals of decontextualization are to (a) eliminate associations among skills and *irrelevant* aspects of contexts, and (b) form connections between skills and the various contexts to which the skills could be applied. Thus, all skills should be contextualized to a degree. Note that the decontextualization approach is the exact opposite of the one that has been around for some time. Whereas the decontextualization approach goes from

specific situations to general structures, the traditional approach assumes that instruction on general structures (e.g., "the five steps to good decision-making") will work in a top-down manner to specific instances.

5. Whenever content is presented in class, it is helpful if students could be asked to classify things into categories, arrange things along some dimension, make hypotheses, draw inferences, analyze things into their components, and solve problems. These cognitive processes can apply to any subject matter, but once again, it is important that students know and comprehend fundamental information first.

6. Teachers play a vital role in encouraging mindfulness and reflectivity and in promoting an understanding of the learning process. Activities such as allowing a student ample time to think about an answer and rewarding mindfulness would go a long way to increase reflectivity in the classroom. To promote an understanding of the learning process, teachers can use think-aloud to model learning-to-learn strategies, or simply point out to children what they can do to help solve a problem on their own.

7. After reviewing the research on the transfer of critical thinking skills, Halpern (1999) suggests the key ingredients of a successful approach include: (a) a dispositional component to prepare learners for the effortful work of evaluating and critiquing, (b) an instructional component that involves discussion of the processes that one can use to evaluate information critically, (c) a training component that helps students recognize the structural aspects of problems and arguments, and (d) a metacognitive component that includes checking for accuracy and monitoring progress toward the goal.

8. Some of the newest research on higher-order thinking demonstrates the need to take student motivations and pre-existing beliefs into account. Students are more likely to engage in higher-order, critical thinking when they are highly motivated to do so. One of the best ways to engage students in this way is to (a) present compelling lines of argumentation or evidence against their pre-existing biases and (b) give them opportunities to rebut this information in discussion. There is reason to think that a defensive, dogmatic attitude might lessen over time if students were to see that sometimes their opponents engage in an elegant line of reasoning.

In the chapters on reading, writing, math, science, and social studies, you will find case studies of teaching programs that illustrate many of the above principles. Instead of singling out one subject area here (e.g., math) to illustrate how one implements higher-order thinking in the classroom based on these principles, the interested reader can merely turn to the end of each of Chapters 5, 6, 7, 8, 9, and 10 for illustrations. In the meantime, a good Constructivist exercise would be to take a topic that you would want to teach to students and make each of the six guidelines above into a checklist. That is, ask yourself, have students had enough practice with concrete content that they can think abstractly about this content? What do I want them to be able to do? (Recall the facts? Comprehend them? Apply them?). Are my examples and exercises related to real-world tasks? Am I asking them to classify things, arrange things along a dimension, make hypotheses, draw inferences, analyze things into their components, and solve problems? The more you answer "yes" to these questions, the more you will engage your students in higher-order thinking.

5

Motivation

Summary

1. Motivation is a construct used to explain the initiation, direction, and intensity of an individual's behavior.

2. If we want to fully explain students' motivation in a situation, we need to appeal to their (a) goals, (b) knowledge of how to meet these goals, (c) personal standards for what is good enough, (d) beliefs about their abilities and possible emotions, (e) interests, and (f) values.

3. People who are intrinsically motivated engage in a task as an end in itself; people who are extrinsically motivated engage in a task as a means to an end.

4. Because of a variety of factors that conspire together, older children tend to have less achievement motivation for school-related tasks than younger children.

5. Within any classroom, individual differences can be found along any of the aspects of motivation. Students differ in terms of their goals, tendency to monitor, personal standards, ability beliefs, interests, and values. These differences greatly affect how hard students try, how long they persist, and the emotions they feel when confronted with tasks.

6. Teachers and classroom environments can affect student motivation in significant ways. When instruction is meaningful, challenging, and affords a degree of choice, students are more likely to be engaged than when instruction lacks these features. In addition, students are more likely to participate when they establish positive social relationships and feel valued.

For many years now, researchers have argued that children will only succeed in school if they have adequate levels of knowledge AND have adequate levels of motivation. There are, for example, numerous cases of children who have the "skill" to do well in a particular course (e.g., math) but lack the "will" to do so (Paris, Byrnes, & Paris, in press). These children are often called underachievers. Relatedly, there are many cases of children who are not particularly talented but achieve a great deal anyway because they try so hard. These children are often called over-achievers. Collectively, these various skill-will combinations make for important but vexing individual differences in a classroom. When certain children perform poorly in a subject area (e.g., girls in high school math), is it because they lack ability or lack motivation? Before we attempt to explain age trends in specific subject areas in Chapters 6 to 11, then, we first should become familiar with theory and research in the area of motivation.

To get an initial sense of the importance of motivation, answer the following questions:

1. Have you ever received a good grade in a course even though you found the course material to be dull or boring?
2. When you had a chance to take elective courses, why did you choose the ones you did?
3. Why are you reading this book right now?
4. Do you find that you get better grades and have better attendance in courses that you find interesting?

Questions such as these get at the heart of motivation. By the end of this chapter, you will know how they do.

Following the format of many other chapters in this book, we shall examine motivation in four sections. In the first section, motivation will be defined. More specifically, you will learn about the constituent parts of motivation. In the second section, you will learn how these constituent parts develop with age. In the third section, you will learn about individual differences in motivation. In the fourth and final section, the instructional implications of the research on motivation will be drawn.

The Nature of Motivation

Let's begin our discussion of motivation by giving a fairly standard definition: motivation is a construct that is used to explain the initiation, direction, intensity, and persistence of an individual's behavior in a particular situation (Stipek, 1993; Wigfield & Eccles, 1992; Eccles, Wigfield, & Schiefele, 1998). Thus, the notion of motivation is useful for answering questions such as "Why did she start doing that?" (Initiation), "Why did he choose that way of doing it instead of another way?" (Direction), "Why is she trying so hard?" (Intensity), and "Why did he give up so easily?" (Persistence).

This standard definition has been augmented in recent years to include the construct of **engagement** (Eccles et al., 1998; Wigfield & Eccles, 2000). A child who is engaged in a classroom activity is an active, attentive, curious, and willing participant. The opposite would be a disengaged, inattentive, and even resistant student. For obvious reasons, most teachers would love to have a classroom full of engaged students. What does it take to transform this dream into reality?

To answer questions such as these, motivation theorists have identified a large number of constructs. Instead of examining these constructs one by one, we shall examine them in three groupings: Goal-related constructs, knowledge-related constructs, and metacognitive constructs. Then, we gain closure on the description of motivation by considering the importance of social relationships in motivation and by drawing the distinction between intrinsic and extrinsic motivation.

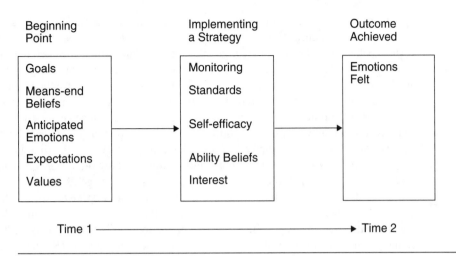

FIGURE 5.1   *Components of Motivation in Temporal Perspective*

To help you understand how all of the parts of motivation fit together, Figure 5.1 is provided. For simplicity, this figure shows a time line ranging from the point at which someone first thinks about what to do, to the point at which he or she experiences the consequences of the course of action he or she has chosen. Each of the parts of motivation (e.g., goals, ability beliefs, etc.) are placed along the time line at a spot which illustrates the role this part plays in motivation.

Goals

In what follows, we shall examine goals in three parts. First, we shall describe the nature of goals and how they relate to student motivation. Then, we shall examine the various types of goals. Finally, we shall see how goals affect student motivation and learning.

The Nature of Goals.   Goals have to do with the *reasons why* people do what they do. More specifically, goals specify something that a person would like to accomplish by engaging in a particular activity (Stipek, 1993; Wentzel, 1991). In specifying how things should turn out ("I would like to get an 'A' in this course"), goals tend to direct or guide behavior (e.g., the goal-setter does things to maximize his or her chances of getting an 'A' like study hard).

In many situations, goals often remain implicit until someone asks questions such as "Why did you go to class?" or "Why are you taking this course?" Answers to such questions usually start with phrases such as "I have to . . ." or "I want to . . ." Regardless of whether you have to do something or want to do something, all goals have to do with personal *desires* (Searle, 1983). Sometimes you have the desire to do what you are told because you have found that circumventing rules can lead to undesirable consequences (e.g., you would get in trouble). Other times you are not trying to avoid problems as much as seek out desirable things (e.g., set a goal of making dinner when you are hungry).

Goals are inherently *cognitive* in that they are mental representations of some future state of affairs (Bandura, 1986). Thus, motivation theorists who espouse goals tend not to be strict behaviorists because they argue that people control their *own* behavior by thinking about some desirable outcome and then performing actions which might bring about this desired outcome. However, goals are not purely cognitive because they typically refer to outcomes that are likely to affect us positively or negatively. The major determinant of the valence of an outcome is the emotional state it might produce (Frijda, 1994). Hence, goal-directed behavior has both cognitive and affective components. Given the "a priori" character of goals, they are shown in Figure 5.1 at the very start of the time line.

Although goals specify how things might turn out, they often start off being somewhat vague. For example, the first time that people set career goals for themselves, they tend to say things like, "I'd like to make a lot of money" or "I'd like to work with people." Such goals are not very helpful or directive since there are several ways to make a good salary and there are many jobs that involve interactions with people. Goals only start directing people in a meaningful way when they become more specific (Klaczynski, Byrnes, & Jacobs, in press).

Types of Goals.   An examination of the research on motivation shows that researchers have proposed four dichotomies and one trichotomy of goal types. The first dichotomy is the "learning versus performance goal" dichotomy (Dweck & Leggett, 1988; Stipek, 1993; Wentzel & Wigfield, 1998). People who have *learning* goals (also called "mastery" or "task" goals) engage in behaviors in order to understand something, gain mastery over a skill, enjoy themselves, or feel competent. In contrast, people who have *performance* goals (also called "ego" goals) engage in behaviors in order to gain the approval of others, look better than others, gain rewards, or avoid criticism.

The second dichotomy of goals pertains to the distinction between proximal and distal goals (Bandura & Schunk, 1981; Schunk, 1991). *Proximal* goals are short-term goals such as "I want to get an 'A' on the test next week." *Distal* goals are long-term goals such as "I want to get a 4.0 by the end of next year." In Information Processing theory terms (e.g., Siegler, 1983), proximal goals can be said to be sub-goals of an overall, superordinate goal. In effect, they seem to be steps along a longer path. Distal goals, in contrast, tend to be of the superordinate variety.

The third dichotomy has to do with the distinction between *academic* and *social* goals (Wentzel, 1991; Wentzel & Wigfield, 1998). Research shows that in addition to having academic goals such as being a successful student, learning new things, understanding things, doing the best you can, and getting things done on time, students also have social goals such as earning approval from others, having fun, making friends, helping others, being dependable, and being responsible.

The fourth dichotomy concerns the distinction between *process* goals and *product* goals (Schunk & Ertmer, 1999). Students who adopt process goals focus on the techniques or strategies that one can use to attain goals. Students who adopt product goals, in contrast, focus on the outcomes of their efforts (e.g., a completed assignment).

In addition to the dichotomies of goals described above, there is also a trichotomy of goals that comes from the work on the Cooperative Learning approach (e.g., Johnson & Johnson, 1987; Slavin, 1990). Advocates of this approach suggest that classrooms can have one of three **goal structures:** individualistic, competitive, and cooperative. When a class-room is arranged in such a way that anyone has the opportunity to get the rewards of the classroom (e.g., good grades), students tend to set the goal of doing as well as they can (an individualistic goal structure). Such students are often indifferent about how well other students do (e.g., "As long as I get my 'A', who cares!"). When only a certain number of students can get the best grade (e.g., just the top ten), students start thinking about doing better than other people in class (not just about doing generally well). Moreover, they want other students to perform poorly. Both of these desires reflect a competitive goal structure. When a classroom is arranged such that the assignment of rewards is based on how well a small group of students perform as a whole, students not only want themselves to do well, but they also want the other students in their own group to do well (a cooperative goal structure).

Effects of Goals on Motivation and Learning.   Researchers have discovered five main ways that goals affect student behavior. As we shall see, three of these outcomes derive from the research on the "learning versus performance goal" dichotomy, one outcome derives from the research on the "proximal versus distal goal" dichotomy, one outcome derives from the "academic versus social goal" dichotomy, and the final one derives from cooperative learning theory.

First, whereas students who have learning goals seek challenging tasks that help them develop their competencies, students with performance goals choose tasks that will make them look competent to others (Dweck, 1986; Nicholls, 1983; Wentzel & Wigfield, 1998). In order to look good all of the time, of course, you need to do things that you are already good at. Thus, students with performance goals would be expected to rarely challenge themselves and to develop expertise in an area at a slower rate than students with learning goals.

Second, whereas students with learning goals see their teacher as a resource or guide, students with performance goals see their teacher as an evaluator who will either reward or punish their behavior (Stipek, 1993). Thus, it would be predicted that students with learning goals would seek help from their teachers more often than students with performance goals. Inasmuch as teachers can be a valuable resource for information and strategies, it would be further expected that students who appropriately seek help would show greater achievement than students who do not (Wentzel, 1991).

Third, goals can affect what students pay attention to in a learning situation. Students who care more about how they look than what they are learning will tend to learn less than students who are mastery-oriented. In support of this claim, research shows that students do not process information at a "deep" level when they are overly concerned about evaluation or looking bad (Graham & Golan, 1991; Nicholls, 1983; Stipek, 1993; Wentzel & Wigfield, 1998).

Fourth, research has found three ways that proximal goals help students more than distal goals: (a) proximal goals provide more frequent and continual feedback, (b) the feedback provided when proximal goals are met gives students a constant sense of progress and mastery (Schunk, 1991), and (c) it is easier to keep proximal goals in mind than distal goals (i.e., students are more likely to forget distal goals).

Fifth, social goals such as being helpful, responsible, and compliant have been found to be strongly related to academic achievement (Wentzel, 1989, 1991). Why should this be the case? It seems that students who know how to get along with others and who are help-ful, responsible, and compliant have more frequent and positive interactions with their teachers and peers. The more interactions one has with teachers and competent peers, the more likely one is to achieve (Vygotsky, 1962; Wentzel, 1991). Of course, not all social goals relate to success in school. For example, students who strongly endorse the goal of having fun in school have been found to have low GPAs (Wentzel, 1989).

Finally, the type of goal structure fostered within individual classrooms has pre-dictable consequences on student learning and achievement. Whereas student achievement is higher when cooperative learning programs have both cooperative and competitive ele-ments (Slavin, 1990), competitive goal structures discourage students from helping each other, set up a "pecking order" in the classroom, and create a situation in which low achiev-ers have little chance of success (Ames, 1986; Johnson & Johnson, 1987). In thinking about the type of classroom they would like to design, teachers have to decide whether the higher achievement fostered by competition outweighs its negative consequences.

Knowledge

Although goals are crucial to "getting the ball rolling," there are several other factors that help you attain your goals. For instance, in addition to knowing what you want (e.g., to be rich), you also need to know how to get what you want (e.g., how to get rich). That brings us to the second key component of motivation: knowledge.

In several contemporary motivational accounts, beliefs related to "how to" knowl-edge have been called *means-end* beliefs (e.g., Skinner, Chapman, & Baltes, 1988). Be-cause means-end beliefs have to do with knowing how to do things to reach certain goals, we can simply say that there is very little difference between means-end beliefs and *pro-cedural knowledge* (See Chapters 3 and 9 for discussions of procedural knowledge). Re-latedly, mean-ends beliefs correspond to beliefs about various kinds of *strategies*. Thus, beliefs about how to add fractions, conduct an experiment, and decode a word are all ex-amples of means-ends beliefs (and procedural knowledge). Examples in the social realm include knowing how to make friends or persuade others.

In support of the hypothesized linkage between goals, strategies, and outcomes, Elliot, McGregor, and Gable (1999) found that college students used different learning strategies depending on whether they had mastery goals, performance goals, or learning-avoidance goals. Learning-avoidance goals pertain to fear of failure and the possibility of negative outcomes. Students who had mastery goals demonstrated greater persistence and effort, and eventually showed better grades. Those with performance-avoidance goals, in contrast, showed more strategic disorganization (e.g., strongly agreeing with items like "I find it difficult to organize my study time effectively"). In a related way, Schunk and Ert-mer (1999) and Zimmerman and Kitsantas (1999) found links between process/product goals, self-regulatory strategies, and performance in a computer course and writing unit, respectively.

So far, then, we have accumulated two possible explanations of someone's behavior. In particular, in response to motivation-related questions such as "Why is she going to graduate school?", we can say such things as "She wants to earn a good salary" (referring to her goals) or "She thinks that getting an M.B.A. will help her get a high-paying job" (referring to her means-ends belief/procedural knowledge). Similarly, we can account for someone's lack of motivation for something (e.g., not finishing high school) by arguing that he or she lacks certain goals or lacks appropriate procedural knowledge.

Metacognitive Processes

The research on motivation reveals that people engage in a variety of monitoring and appraisal activities. Given the self-reflective quality of both monitoring and appraisal (Bandura, 1986), these activities are grouped under the single heading "metacognitive processes" in this book. In what follows, we shall examine three aspects of metacognition related to motivation: (a) monitoring of progress, (b) appraisal of actions, and (c) appraisal of outcomes.

Monitoring of Progress.   Although some goals can be attained quickly with a single action (e.g., scratching one's head to relieve an itch), many other goals involve a series of actions and take some time to fulfill. As a result, it is often necessary to examine how far one has progressed towards one's goals (Bandura, 1986; 1997). To see the utility of occasionally taking stock of one's progress, consider the case of a dieter who sets the goal for himself of losing five pounds by the time he goes to his ten-year college reunion (two months away). After seeing several glowing endorsements by celebrities, he decides to use a popular liquid diet to achieve this goal (a means-end belief). It should be obvious that in order to maximize his goal of losing the five pounds within two months, our dieter should weigh himself occasionally to see whether or not the liquid diet is working. By engaging in monitoring, he could switch diets in sufficient time to lose the weight if he finds out early on that liquid diet is not working (i.e., he could "switch to Plan B").

In a sense, then, humans have the capacity to envision a "path" leading from where they currently are (e.g., five pounds too heavy) to some ultimate goal state (e.g., five pounds lighter). The "path" is a set of intermediate states of affairs that connect the initial state to the goal state (Newell & Simon, 1972). Apparently, this path is a natural consequence of setting a goal and deciding on a particular strategy for attaining the goal. Without this capacity for creating mental paths, we would have no way of knowing how far we have progressed in some endeavor.

Appraisal of Actions.   The use of the term "appraisal" is meant to capture notions such as evaluation and estimation. Thus, when we speak of the appraisal of actions, we are referring to the processes of (a) evaluating actions that have been already performed (e.g., they were performed well; what I am doing is working; I am enjoying myself; etc.) and (b) estimating the likelihood that actions will be performed in a particular way in the future (e.g., it is likely that they will be performed well; it is likely that such-and-such strategy will work; it is likely that I will enjoy myself).

The appraisal of past and future actions often occurs in the midst of monitoring your progress. Whenever you pause to reflect upon your progress, you think about what you have done and whether it is a good idea to continue that course of action. Thus, appraisal is often what we do when we monitor our progress. Having said that, let's now examine four types of beliefs that play an important role in the appraisal process: personal standards, control beliefs, self-efficacy beliefs, and ability beliefs. Then, we shall examine an additional dimension along which we judge actions: interest.

Personal Standards.   Personal standards refer to beliefs about what is "good enough." Recall that when you monitor your progress, you stop and think about how well things are going. In order to form such a judgment, you have to compare your actual progress to some standard (Bandura, 1986). Let's say that you are dieting and you find that you have lost one pound a week for the last three weeks. Is that good enough? Is it too fast? Is it too slow? Or, let's say that you are devoting a certain amount of time and effort to your courses. After getting your midterm exam grades, you might think about whether your grades are good enough. Should you study harder next time or do something different? Thus, standards have to do with issues of quality and often involve considerations of *rate* of change or progress. Obviously, one's standards play an important role in the process of deciding whether to continue a course of action or switch to a new one.

Control Beliefs.   An obvious aspect of goal pursuit is the belief that you have control over outcomes. If a student feels that his or her grade is entirely up to a teacher (and in no way related to his or her own actions), for example, that student would probably not engage in a specific course of action to attain a good grade. Student beliefs about controllability of actions have been found to relate to their motivation levels and achievement (Wentzel & Wigfield, 1998; Eccles et al., 1998). The term *agency belief* refers to the belief that one has control over certain outcomes (Skinner et al., 1988).

Self-efficacy Beliefs.   Self-efficacy pertains to an individual's belief that he or she can succeed on a particular type of task (Bandura, 1986, 1997). In order to feel self-efficacious about something, the individual must first know which actions to perform to do well (a means-end belief) and also how well these actions need to be performed by *anyone*. But self-efficacy has to do with the person's belief that *he* or *she* has the ability to perform these actions well enough to succeed. For example, in the midst of a basketball game, a person might know that he would have to shoot a basketball through the hoop in order to earn the two points that his team needs to win (a means-end belief), but nevertheless believes that he lacks the skill necessary to make that shot under pressure. Bandura's (1986) notion of self-efficacy is quite similar to Skinner et al.'s (1988) notion of *agency beliefs.*

How would self-efficacy beliefs affect the monitoring/appraisal process? Consider our dieting and studying examples again. If our dieter tried extremely hard to lose weight and discovers that he lost three pounds in three weeks, his decision to stay on the liquid diet would be affected by his sense of self-efficacy and by his standards. If he has high self-efficacy about dieting (i.e., he thinks that he has the self-control and pain tolerance needed to diet), and he is dissatisfied with his weight loss, he would be expected to find an even stricter diet. If he has low self-efficacy, however, he would be expected to discontinue dieting altogether.

Similar predictions would be made about studying or pursuing an academic major. Someone with high self-efficacy about his or her ability to study who got disappointing midterm grades would try to find better study habits and expend more effort next time. Someone with low self-efficacy, in contrast, would tend to lose interest in studying. The same could be said for a pre-med student who gets low grades during his or her first semester in college.

In a variety of laboratory studies, researchers have shown that self-efficacy relates to effort, persistence, and quality of problem-solving on tasks (Bandura, 1986, 1997; Bandura & Wood, 1989). In addition, studies of school children show that about 14 percent of the variance in academic achievement is accounted for by self-efficacy (Berry & West, 1993).

Ability-Beliefs.   Ability-beliefs are closely related to, though somewhat distinct from, self-efficacy beliefs. Whereas a self-efficacy belief is a judgment about your ability to be successful on a particular task in a particular situation, an ability-belief is a general sense of your skill in an area or set of areas (Stipek, 1993; Berry & West, 1993; Wentzel & Wigfield, 1998). Thus, whereas an example of a self-efficacy belief would be "I can get an 'A' on that history test tomorrow," an example of an ability-belief would be "I'm pretty good in social studies" or "I'm a very good student."

Most students have a large number of ability-beliefs about school subjects, sports, social relations, and their appearance. Researchers have found that the ability-beliefs that comprise a student's *self-concept* seem to be mentally arranged into a hierarchy. At the top of the hierarchy, there is a general self-concept which is an overall sense of how competent one feels or a general sense of self-worth (e.g., "I feel good about myself"). Just below the general self-concept, beliefs subdivide into academic and non-academic self-concepts (e.g., "I do pretty well in school" versus "I make friends easily"). Then, the academic self-concept is further divided into lower-level beliefs about abilities in specific subjects (e.g., math, science, and English), and the non-academic self-concept is further divided into social, emotional, and physical self-concepts (Marsh, 1989; Harter, 1985). Support for this hierarchical framework comes from studies that show that people who generally feel good about themselves can nevertheless feel that they are not very good in certain things (e.g., math). Similarly, researchers have found a near-zero correlation between verbal and math self-concepts (Feather, 1988; Marsh, 1989).

Recent studies have suggested that the original multidimensional model proposed by Marsh and others needed to be refined further. For example, Lau, Yeung, Jin, & Low (1999) found that the English self-concept could be decomposed into ability beliefs about one's listening skills, speaking skills, reading skills, and writing skills. Other studies revealed the need to expand the number of domains. For example, Marsh, Hey, Roche, and Perry (1997) found that elite athletes had ability beliefs comprised of such traits: beliefs about their athletic skill, aerobic fitness, anaerobic fitness, mental competence, and overall performance. Vispoel (1995) found a similar kind of multidimensionality in the area of artistic skills. Thus, it would seem that students have multidimensional ability beliefs for any relevant skill area.

In most studies in this area, a skill is decomposed into its components and attitudes toward these components are assessed. Another approach consists of looking at different kinds of motivation within a particular domain. To illustrate, Baker and Wigfield (1999) examined the structure of reading motivation in fifth and sixth graders. They found evidence for the following kinds of reading motivation: (a) self-efficacy (e.g., I know I will do well in reading next year), (b) challenge (e.g., I like hard, challenging books), (c) work avoidance (e.g., I don't like reading something when the words are too difficult), (d) curiosity (e.g., I like to read about new things), (e) involvement (e.g., I like mysteries), (e) importance (e.g., It is very important to me to be a good reader), (f) recognition (e.g., I like hearing the teacher say I read well), (g) grades (e.g., I read to improve my grades), (h) competition (e.g., I like being the best at reading), (i) social (e.g., My friends and I like to trade things to read), and (j) compliance (e.g., I read because I have to).

In addition to discovering that people have specific and general beliefs about their abilities in academic subjects, researchers have also found that students develop one of two conceptions of their intelligence. Students who hold an *entity view* of their intelligence believe that (a) intelligence is a fixed capacity that does not increase or decrease over time and (b) smart people learn things effortlessly and rarely make errors. In contrast, students who hold an *incremental view* of their intelligence believe that intelligence is not a fixed capacity. In fact, they feel that each time one learns a new skill, one becomes that much smarter. Moreover, they recognize that when one is learning a new skill, expending effort and making mistakes are all part of the game (Cain & Dweck, 1995; Dweck & Elliot, 1983).

In sum, then, we have very specific beliefs about our abilities in certain areas (e.g., math, sports, social relations) as well as more general conceptions about our overall abilities and intelligence. How do these ability beliefs affect our motivation? It seems that ability beliefs play a role in the appraisal process similar to that played by self-efficacy beliefs. In particular, people who feel good about their ability and who have an incremental view of their intelligence would be expected to expend more effort and persist after failure more often than people with less positive views of their skill or people who hold an entity view of their intelligence.

But in addition to affecting the way people behave "midstream" in their quest for goals, ability beliefs and views of intelligence also affect the initial goals people set for themselves. For example, when given a choice between easy and hard tasks in an area (e.g., science), people who feel more competent about their skill in that area would be more likely to choose the harder task than people with less positive views of their skill. Thus, similar to students who have learning goals (see above), students who have positive views of their ability and who hold an incremental view of their intelligence would be more likely to challenge themselves than students with less positive views of their ability or students with an entity view of their intelligence (Dweck & Elliot, 1983). Thus, Figure 5.1 placed such appraisals midway through the goal-pursuit process, but they could also be placed near the beginning prior to goals.

Interest.   A final factor that plays a role in the process of appraising actions is interest. Interest is conceptualized as a quality of a person-object interaction that can "show itself" in the form of prolonged, relatively effortless attention and feelings of pleasure and concentration (Eccles et al., 1998; Renninger, Hidi, & Krapp, 1991). Thus, interest involves a blending of cognitive processes (i.e., attention) and emotional processes (i.e., feelings of pleasure and enjoyment). Interest has been viewed both as a trait-like tendency of individuals (e.g., having a long-standing interest in science) as well as a property of objects that captures the attention of most people (e.g., a novel that most people find interesting).

Similar to ability beliefs, interest can affect both "early" and "midstream" processes in the motivation system. Early on, interest can affect the choices people make and goals they set for themselves (Wigfield & Eccles, 1992). When people monitor their progress, interest can play a role in judgments of "how things are going." One student might find an activity to be particularly interesting and another might find it to be boring. Interest can affect the degree to which a student persists in an activity, even when the student has high self-efficacy or positive ability beliefs for a skill. For example, a college student who has a "4.0" GPA in engineering and who has positive ability beliefs might nevertheless switch his major to music education because he finds the latter topic to be more interesting than the former.

In addition to predicting choices and persistence in activities, interest has also been linked to deeper processing of information during learning and the use of certain kinds of strategies (Renninger et al., 1991; Alexander & Murphy, 1998). The precise associations between interest, strategy-use, and learning, however, vary according to the amount of knowledge a person has. Students who seem to benefit the most from interest are those who have a moderate amount of knowledge already (as opposed to a high or low amount).

Appraisal of Outcomes. In addition to monitoring their progress and appraising their actions "midstream," people also estimate the likelihood that certain future events will occur and evaluate their performance after their goals have been met. The idea that people think about what will happen next has been implicit in many of the things said so far. For example, when people monitor their progress, they not only think about how well things are going, they also think about how well things will go in the future. Moreover, people with high self-efficacy for a task (e.g., a math problem) believe that although they still might be far from their goal, they can still reach it if they try something else or double their efforts.

In this section, we will examine how people evaluate outcomes both before they occur and after they occur. In particular, we will examine the factors that influence the judgments people make when they ask themselves forward-looking questions such as "What will happen next?", "Why will it happen?", and "How will I feel about it if it does happen?", as well as backward-looking questions such as "What happened?", "Why did it happen?" and "How do I feel about it?". As we shall see, these questions pertain to four additional components of motivation: expectations, causal attributions, values, and emotions.

Expectations. An expectation is a belief about the likelihood of something happening in the future. In theories of motivation and decision-making, the expectations that have received a lot of scrutiny are those pertaining to outcomes (Atkinson, 1964; Eccles et al., 1998; Slovic, 1990). Some examples of expectations for outcomes include statements such as "It probably won't rain today," "It is pretty likely that I will get a 4.0 this semester," and "I think I will find my ideal mate."

When people form judgments about the likelihood that an outcome will happen, they consider both internal and external factors. By internal factors, it is meant such things as (a) how much skill it would take to attain the outcome and whether or not they have the skill and (b) how much effort it would take to reach their goals and whether or not they are likely to expend the necessary effort. By external factors, it is meant those things that are not under the control of the person (e.g., weather patterns, the number of "A" grades given by some teachers, and the number of unmarried, desirable adults that you normally encounter). So, when a person feels that there is only a 20 percent chance that he or she will get a 4.0 this semester, a portion of this estimate could derive from their perceptions of internal factors (e.g., "I have to work really hard to get an 'A' ") and the remainder could derive from their perceptions of external factors (e.g., "I have to take Dr. Jones next semester and he does not give many As").

Causal Attributions.   In contrast to expectations which are forward-looking, causal attributions are initially backward-looking. In particular, causal attributions are made after an outcome has occurred. When someone makes a causal attribution, he or she assigns causality to some factor that seems to be responsible for the outcome (Weiner, 1986). For example, consider the situation in which two students get a "C" on the same test. One student might attribute this outcome to ineffective study strategies and the other might attribute it to poor teaching on the part of the instructor.

When trying to explain achievement-related outcomes, research has shown that people tend to attribute their successes and failures to one of two main factors: ability or effort. For example, when students do poorly on a test, one might say "I'm not very good in math" (attributing the outcome to low ability) and another might say "I didn't try very hard" (attributing the outcome to low effort). But students also have been found to cite bad luck, poor teaching, and a variety of other idiosyncratic factors in explaining why they got the grade they did (Weiner, 1986).

Weiner (1986) argues that causes such as ability and effort vary along three dimensions: stability, controllability, and locus. Whereas stable causes reflect a permanent aspect of a person or situation, unstable causes reflect a transient or variable aspect. Depending on the person, some people might consider their ability to be a stable attribute (if they have a entity view of their intelligence) and effort to be an unstable attribute (if they often apply themselves in a variable way). Other people might view their ability to be an unstable attribute (if they have an incremental view) and effort to be a stable trait (if they consider themselves to be "naturally lazy").

The perceived stability of a cause plays an important role in performance expectations. In particular, if people attribute their performance to a stable cause, it is normal for them to raise their expectations following success and lower their expectations following failure (Weiner, 1986). For example, consider the case of a student who thinks that there is a 60 percent chance that he will get a "B" on a test. If he (a) ends up getting a "C" on the test, (b) attributes his failure to low ability, and (c) believes that ability is a stable trait, he will probably think that he has less than a 60 percent chance of a "B" on the next test. However, if he attributes his failure to a temporary lapse of effort, he might continue to think that he has a 60 percent chance of a "B" on the next test.

In addition to viewing causes as being stable or unstable, students also consider some causes to be controllable (e.g., how hard they try) and other causes to be uncontrollable (e.g., how smart they are). Moreover, some causes of success and failure are believed to be internal (e.g., effort and ability) and others are external (e.g., teacher bias, bad luck, and hard tests).

Values.   In theories of motivation and decision-making, values have to do with the desirable and undesirable aspects of outcomes (Eccles et al., 1998; Feather, 1988; Slovic, 1990;

Wigfield & Eccles, 1992). What makes something desirable or undesirable, of course, depends on the person. For example, whereas some people think that it is important to be rich, others think that it is important to be well-liked.

In a recent analysis, Wigfield and Eccles (1992) argued that there are four different types of values that influence achievement behaviors: *attainment value, intrinsic value, utility value,* and *cost.* Attainment value has to do with whether it is important to do well on the task. To see the attainment value of something, ask yourself questions such as: "Do I care how well I do on this? Is it important to me to do well?" The intrinsic value of a task concerns the enjoyment you would feel if you engaged in the task. To see the intrinsic value of something, ask yourself the following question: "Would I find it to be enjoyable or interesting?" Note that interest seems to play a role when people appraise actions (see above) and when they appraise outcomes. The utility value of a task concerns the relation between the task and future goals. To see the utility value of a task, ask yourself the question, "Will doing this help me meet my goals?" (e.g., will taking this course help me get the job I want?). The cost of a choice concerns all of the negative aspects of performing a task including negative emotions (e.g., embarrassment or anxiety) and the amount of effort needed. To see the cost of something, ask yourself, "What would I lose if I engaged in this task?"

Values affect behavior in the following way: people tend to seek out desirable outcomes and avoid undesirable outcomes. By "desirable," it is meant an outcome judged to be important, interesting, useful, or "low cost" (Wigfield & Eccles, 1992). By "undesirable," it is meant unimportant, uninteresting, useless, or costly outcomes.

Although values are an important reason why people make the choices they do, values alone do not determine achievement behavior. In particular, people only try to attain desirable outcomes if there is a reasonably good chance that they can attain them (Slovic, 1990; Wigfield & Eccles, 1992). For example, whereas most students will tell you that getting an "A" is more desirable than getting a "B," only those students who think that it is possible to get an "A" will try and get it. Thus, *both* expectancies and values affect motivation.

Emotions.   In addition to expectancies, attributions, and values, the final factor that affects how an outcome is appraised is the emotion associated with it. Whereas the attainment of some outcomes is likely to engender "positive" emotions in the person who attains them (e.g., joy, pride, or self-esteem), other outcomes are likely to engender "negative" emotions (e.g., anxiety, guilt, or shame). Clearly, most people want to experience the positive emotions more often than the negative emotions. Thus, we would expect that people would try to attain outcomes which engender positive feelings and avoid those outcomes which engender negative feelings (Frijda, 1994).

Of all the emotions which may affect motivation, there are four that have received the most attention from motivation researchers: anxiety, shame, pride, and self-esteem. Let's examine the two negative emotions first and the two positive emotions second.

Anxiety is a complex emotion that is closely related to fear and worry. Researchers have identified both a self-evaluative component and a somatic/physiological component of anxiety (Wigfield & Eccles, 1989). The self-evaluative component consists of negative cognitions about being able to do well on something (e.g., "I'm afraid I'll probably flunk the exam") and the somatic component involves the actual emotional and bodily reaction associated with thinking about the potential failure. Studies show that the self-evaluative component of anxiety relates more strongly to school performance than the somatic component.

Shame is an emotional response that is engendered when an individual feels responsible for poor behavior (Weiner, 1986). Students are most likely to feel shame when they attribute their failures to low ability. When students attribute their poor performance to low effort, they are more likely to feel guilty than embarrassed.

In sum, then, the two negative emotions come into play when a student is thinking about possible failure in the future or when they are thinking about failures that occurred in the past. As we shall see, the two positive emotions are the consequences of successes rather than failure.

When students feel that they are responsible for their successes through hard work or ability, they are likely to feel *pride.* In a sense, they say "What I did was good and I am entirely responsible for it." *Self-esteem* is a generalized sense of pride and competence that is accrued across many episodes of success.

As mentioned above, emotions play a role in assessments of the desirability of outcomes. Students think that outcomes that engender happiness or pride are more desirable than outcomes that engender anxiety, guilt, or shame. Thus, emotions play a role in decisions regarding which outcomes to go after. In addition, we have seen that some negative emotions play a debilitating role when people are in the middle of trying to attain outcomes. Anxiety can promote maladaptive coping behaviors (e.g., avoiding academic situations; thinking about failure rather than studying properly, etc.) and learned helplessness can foster low levels of effort and persistence.

The Importance of Social Relationships

Earlier it was noted that children have social goals in addition to having academic goals. In addition, it was shown that children who coordinate both kinds of goals do better in school than children who just focus on one kind of goal. Here, we can elaborate on this notion by describing the importance of feeling connected to the classroom and feeling cared for by a teacher (Wentzel & Wigfield, 1998). Recent studies have shown that children who feel that they belong in school and that they are part of something are motivated to do well in school. In other words, to the extent that classrooms foster feelings of belongingness, children emulate the engaged student described earlier in this chapter. Relatedly, there is a high correlation between believing that your teacher cares about you and doing well in school.

Intrinsic versus Extrinsic Motivation

Before moving on to a consideration of developmental and individual differences in motivation, it is important to examine one final issue that, in many ways, captures a lot of what has been said so far: the distinction between intrinsic and extrinsic motivation. People who engage in behaviors to receive praise, gain tangible rewards, or avoid punishment are *extrinsically* motivated (e.g., a fourth grader who works on his science project to win the prize for best project). People who engage in behaviors to feel competent, gain mastery over some skill, or satisfy their curiosity are *intrinsically* motivated (e.g., a fourth grader who continues to work on a science project after the science fair is over to tinker with it further). In effect, when you are intrinsically motivated, you are the one making yourself do something and you are engaging in an activity for that activity's sake (e.g., read for the sake of reading). When you are extrinsically motivated, in contrast, someone else is in control of how you behave. Overall we can say that whereas intrinsic motivation concerns engaging in a task as an end in itself, extrinsic motivation concerns using a task as a means to an end (Deci & Ryan, 1985).

Researchers who have examined intrinsic motivation suggest that people are naturally inclined to seek feelings of competence, gain control over their environment, set challenges for themselves, and satisfy their curiosities (Berlyne, 1966; Deci & Ryan, 1985; Stipek, 1993). That is, no one has to make you want to feel competent and so forth, you just naturally want to. Researchers have found that feelings of competence naturally follow successes, particularly if a student believes she controlled the success. When given a choice of an easy, moderately difficult, or hard task, most people choose the moderately difficult one. Finally, the introduction of novelty, surprise, or events that lack an explanation seem to engender attention and sustained interest.

It is relatively easy to make someone who is intrinsically motivated into someone who is extrinsically motivated. The key factors in this shift are the frequent introduction of external rewards (e.g., prizes, personal recognition) or punishments, as well as the use of competition and social comparison in the classroom (Ames, 1986; Deci & Ryan, 1985).

Given what has been said so far, we can see that learning goals, the incremental view of intelligence, self-efficacy, interest, and values all have to do with intrinsic motivation. In contrast, performance goals, the entity view of intelligence, and the behaviorist notions of reinforcement and punishment have to do with extrinsic motivation.

In recent years, the distinction between intrinsic and extrinsic motivation as well as the data that support this distinction have come under fire (Cameron & Pierce, 1994). Behaviorists would scoff at the idea that people engage in behaviors because these behaviors are intrinsically satisfying. Moreover, they would question the meaning of results that suggest one can dampen intrinsic motivation by supplying an external reward. If a "reward" such as praise or money causes a behavior (e.g., reading) to decrease over time, it is by definition a punishment, not a reinforcer. Another problem for theorists who advocate the intrinsic/extrinsic motivation distinction is that the effects of intended rewards vary according to their type. Across a number of studies, people rewarded with verbal praise or positive feedback show more intrinsic motivation than non-rewarded individuals (as indicated by doing the task even when they are told they can stop). In contrast, those who receive a tangible reward (e.g., money) demonstrate significantly less intrinsic motivation than non-rewarded individuals. These definitional and empirical problems may require revisions in contemporary accounts that emphasize intrinsic motivation, but the matter is highly controversial (see Ryan & Deci, 1996).

Summary

We have seen that motivation constructs can be grouped under three main headings: goals, knowledge, and metacognitive processes. A goal is a future-oriented specification of what someone wants. Knowledge has to do with knowing how to attain goals using procedures or strategies. The metacognitive processes include (a) monitoring of progress, (b) using your beliefs and preferences to appraise ongoing actions, (c) evaluating the likelihood and desirability of outcomes, and (d) explaining why outcomes occurred. In addition, we have found that people can either be intrinsically or extrinsically motivated for an activity. Given this description of the nature of motivation, we would expect to find that motivated individuals would have different goals and knowledge than less motivated individuals, and would also engage in metacognitive processes differently. In the next two sections, we shall examine whether or not this is the case.

The Development of Motivation

So far we have examined the constituent parts of motivation. In this section, we shall examine the literature to see whether there is evidence that these constituent parts change over time. That is, we shall attempt to answer questions such as "Do older students have different goals than younger students?", "Do older students have different means-end beliefs than younger students?", and "Do older students engage in the metacognitive aspects of motivation differently than younger students?"

Goals

Researchers who have examined motivational goals have not made a large number of developmental comparisons. As a result, little is known about developmental trends in the "natural" expression of learning, performance, proximal, distal, academic, or social goals (Eccles et al., 1998). There is, however, some reason to believe that whereas younger children might be more likely to engage in a task for its own sake (i.e., adopt learning goals), older students might be more likely to do so because they believe they should or because they want to get a good grade (i.e., adopt performance goals) (Dweck & Elliot, 1983; Nicholls, 1983). Similarly, there is reason to suspect that whereas social goals might become more important with age, academic goals might become less important with age. If a number of studies were to confirm these expectations, it would mean that students would be less likely to challenge themselves or go after high grades with age.

Although motivation researchers have not compiled extensive evidence in support of the claim that goals change with age, researchers who study other topics have. For example, researchers who study reading comprehension have found that older and younger children have different goals when they read (Paris & Byrnes, 1989; Paris et al., in press). Researchers who study writing have revealed similar findings (Page-Voth & Graham, 1999; Scardamalia & Bereiter, 1986).

Knowledge

Unlike the goals component which concerns the reasons *why* students engage in specific behaviors, the knowledge component has to do with *what* they do. As mentioned in the previous section, older students and younger students often engage in the same behaviors (e.g., read) but do so for different reasons (e.g., "to pronounce words properly" versus "to learn something"). But it is also true that older students could have the same goals as younger students (e.g., get an "A") but nevertheless try to attain these goals in different ways (e.g., using different studying techniques). In the present section, we are concerned with the latter possibility.

As will become clear in Chapters 6 to 11, older students are more likely than younger students to have more accurate and extensive procedural knowledge. In particular, the latter know more math procedures, scientific problem-solving techniques, reading strategies, and writing skills. In addition, we saw in Chapter 3 that they are more likely to know effective memory and study strategies.

Metacognitive Processes

We have seen so far that there are two possible answers to questions of the form "Why are older children doing X and younger children doing Y?" The first would be that older children have different goals than younger children. The second would be that older children have different means-end beliefs than younger children. In this section, we will examine some additional answers that focus on the three subdivisions of metacognitive processes that we examined earlier: monitoring of progress, appraisal of actions, and appraisal of outcomes.

Monitoring of Progress. Research has shown that older children are more likely to monitor their performance than younger children (e.g., Baker & Brown, 1984; Markman, 1981). It turns out that this developmental trend has both positive and negative consequences for younger children. Because they do not monitor how far they have progressed toward a goal, younger children cannot become discouraged by the realization that they have not progressed very far. As a result, it may not matter what their standards are or how highly they think of themselves. All young children would probably continue with the same course of action that they started with. But whereas young children gain something by not being discouraged as often as older children, they lose something in that they will not "fix" a strategy that is not working.

Appraisal of Actions. Very few studies have examined the possibility of developmental differences in personal standards or self-efficacy (Eccles et al., 1998). Bandura (1986) suggests that personal standards become progressively internalized as children interact with parents, peers, and teachers. Both direct instruction and modeling play a role in this internalization process. From this account, we can speculate that older students might be more likely to have standards than younger students. We cannot, however, say whether or not the former have higher standards than the latter.

With respect to self-efficacy, children develop a sense that they have control over successes by virtue of having many experiences in which their actions produced success and proportionately fewer experiences of failure (Bandura, 1986). Given the standard curriculum in which certain skills are re-introduced year after year, one would expect that older children would feel more self-efficacious than younger children when asked to think about the same type of tasks (because the latter have had more practice with these tasks).

In support of this claim, Zimmerman and Martinez-Pons (1990) found that mean levels of self-efficacy for both verbal skills and math skills increased significantly from the fifth to eleventh grades.

If personal standards stay the same over time and more and more children come to believe that they can be successful, it would be predicted that older children as a group would have more motivation than younger children. If standards increase over time, we would expect the levels of motivation of older children to be that much more enhanced. However, if children lower their standards at the same rate that they increase in their sense of self-efficacy, we would expect roughly similar levels of motivation in younger and older students. Clearly, given the complex interactions among goals, standards, and self-efficacy, more developmental research is needed to sort out developmental trends in overall motivation levels.

As for ability beliefs, research has revealed three ways in which these beliefs change over time. First, children's self-concept becomes increasingly differentiated with age. That is, the gap between their academic and non-academic beliefs becomes wider, as does the gap between their math and verbal self-concepts (Marsh, 1989). Concretely, this would mean that whereas younger students would hold themselves in high regard for all subject areas, older students would feel that they are better in some areas than others.

Second, there appears to be a curvilinear trend in which the self-concept declines during preadolescence and early adolescence, levels out in middle adolescence, and then increases in late adolescence and early adulthood (Marsh, 1989). These first two trends would suggest that whereas elementary students would show high levels of motivation and persistence for all subjects, middle school students would show generally less motivation overall. In addition, middle school students would apply themselves only in those subjects for which they have higher ability beliefs. During high school and beyond, motivation levels should return for most subject areas. But again, there is much more to motivation than ability beliefs, so research is needed to examine the patterns.

Third, whereas older students make a clear distinction between effort and ability, younger students seem to think that effort and ability are the same (Nicholls, 1983; Stipek, 1993). Thus, younger students tend to think that someone who is "really smart" is someone who "tries really hard." In contrast, once students acquire an "entity" view of intelligence, they come to believe that smart people do not have to try very hard (i.e., "things come easily to them").

Finally, there are only a few studies that have examined the development of interests over time because researchers have often viewed interest as an individual difference variable rather than a developmental difference variable. In one study, Wigfield et al. (1989) asked first, second, and fourth graders to rate their enjoyment of various school subjects. They found that whereas there were no grade differences in children's liking of math or computers, there were differences in their liking of reading, music, and sports. In particular, both first and second graders liked reading more than fourth graders. The gap in ratings for reading between the first and fourth grades represented about a 15 percent drop. Also, whereas there was a 9 percent decline in children's liking of music over time, there was an 11 percent increase in their liking of sports over time. At all grade levels, children liked computers the best (average rating = 6.3 out of 7) followed by sports (average rating = 6.0), music (average rating = 5.25), reading (average rating = 5.25), and math (average rating = 5.0). Thus, the ratings for math were about 21 percent lower than those for computers.

Because elementary children are not given much choice over the subjects they learn, these age differences would probably affect other aspects of school performance besides course selection such as attention, effort, and persistence. For example, during reading or music lessons, fourth grade teachers would be more likely to find their students having problems with attention and persistence than first grade teachers. Also, the overall average ratings suggest that math would not capture the attention of even the first graders.

In a study involving older students, Wigfield et al. (1991) asked children to rate their liking of social activities, sports, math, and English both before and after they made the transition to junior high school. Whereas students' liking of social activities and English stayed about the same over time, there was a 6 percent drop in interest in sports and a 10 percent drop in interest in math. In addition, there were large differences in what students found interesting. Students rated social activities and sports substantially (i.e., 25 percent) higher than math or English.

Appraisal of Outcomes.   Research shows that young children are generally quite optimistic about things working out in their favor (Stipek, 1993). Part of their optimism stems from how they view their ability, another part derives from their attributions of success and failure, and still another part comes from their inability to differentiate between luck and skill (Nicholls, 1989). If young children hold an incremental view of their intelligence and feel that effort is the key to success, they will tend to be optimistic even after experiencing multiple failures. In particular, after performing poorly, they might say, "Oh well, I'll just have to try harder next time!" Moreover, if luck and skill are not sufficiently differentiated in their minds, they would feel that they have some influence over things that are out of their control (e.g., what will be on a test). Over time, social comparison, feedback from teachers, and other forms of experience inform children about the nature of ability as well as what they can control and what they cannot. As a result, many children will come to feel that they can no longer control success and will lose their initial sense of optimism.

As mentioned earlier, a central component of children's values is the importance they attach to different topics (Wigfield & Eccles, 1992). In their study of first, second, and fourth graders, Wigfield et al. (1989) found that whereas there were no grade differences in the perceived importance of learning math, reading, social skills, or sports, grade differences emerged for learning computers and music. Both computers and music were judged to be less important with age.

In their study of children making the transition to junior high school, Eccles et al. (1989) found that there were significant drops ranging from 3 to 6 percent in the perceived importance of math, sports skills, and social skills between the sixth and seventh grades. The perceived importance of English was found to be lower at the start of the seventh grade but rebounded by the end of that year. Taken together, these two studies show that many subjects lose their value for students between the first and seventh grades.

Finally, in the earlier section on "The Nature of Motivation," we learned that anxiety, learned helplessness, shame, and pride are emotions that play an important role in the motivation system. Here, we shall examine developmental trends in these emotions.

Most theorists assume that students develop test anxiety in response to repeated failure in evaluative situations (Stipek, 1993; Wigfield & Eccles, 1992). Research shows that young students who do poorly on tests do not become anxious right away. Rather, it is not until the end of elementary school that a consistent tendency to be anxious emerges in students.

The key to understanding student anxiety lies in how they define "failure." Most students define a "D" or an "F" as a failure, so "D" students and "F" students would be expected to be more anxious about tests than "B" or "A" students. And yet, students with high ability can also develop test anxiety, especially if they hold unreasonably high standards for themselves (Stipek, 1993). For example, a student who always gets 95 percent correct on tests might nevertheless treat such performances as failures if he or she feels that only 100 percent is good enough.

Personal standards seem to develop from three main sources: (a) parental expectations, (b) teacher behaviors and classroom structure, and (c) social comparisons (MacIver, 1987; Wigfield & Eccles, 1992). When parents and teachers are relatively "transparent" about what they want, when they hold very high standards for performance, and when classrooms are arranged such that it is easy for students to compare their performance to each other, students are more likely to develop anxiety than when the opposite is true.

Besides anxiety, two other emotions or emotion-related states that often emerge in response to repeated failure are shame and learned helplessness. Students who feel that they are responsible for performing poorly are likely to feel ashamed (Covington & Omelich, 1981; Weiner, 1986). Anyone who has experienced shame knows how uncomfortable it is to feel that way. Learned helplessness arises after students come to believe that they have no control over failure and the feelings of shame that are associated with it (i.e., they cannot avoid it).

Pride, of course, is the opposite of shame and is felt when students feel responsible for a successful performance. Both pride and shame emerge during the preschool period soon after children develop a clear sense of self (Stipek, Recchia, & McClintock, 1992). Thus, children enter elementary school with a pre-existing capacity to feel pride when they are successful. Given the age trends for monitoring of performance, conceptions of ability, and internalization of standards, it would be expected that only some students in the later elementary grades would consistently feel pride (i.e., those students who consistently do well on tests). In contrast, it would be expected that the majority of younger students would feel pride for a whole range of behaviors (e.g., being polite, trying hard, etc.).

Besides feeling emotions when they experience success or failure, children also become increasingly sensitive to the emotions expressed by their teachers. For example, whereas children as young as five recognize the link between teacher anger and low effort on the part of students, only students nine years of age and older comprehend the link between teacher pity and low ability attributions (Graham, Doubleday, & Guarino, 1984).

Summary

The overall impression one gets from the developmental literature on motivation is that there are many reasons why older children should show less motivation than younger children (Eccles et al., 1998). First, older children are likely to have different goals than younger children (e.g., social goals versus academic goals). Second, older children are more likely to monitor their performance and gauge it against standards than younger children. Third, students in the period ranging from late elementary school to early high school are more likely to have differentiated conceptions of their abilities as well as an overall lower sense of competence than students in the early elementary years. Fourth, students are more likely to encounter failure with age. Those older students who attribute their poor performance to low ability and who think that failure is unavoidable are likely to have low expectations for future success as well as negative emotional reactions such as anxiety, shame, and learned helplessness. At the very least, these students will not try very hard and will engage in a variety of avoidance behaviors (e.g., truancy). Finally, certain topics have been found to be not very interesting to students even in the first grade (e.g., math) and others that start off interesting become less interesting with age (e.g., reading). This is not to say, of course, that all students become less motivated with age. The most successful students will generally increase in their confidence level with age. The decrease in motivation will probably be limited to the least successful students in a grade.

Considering these overall age trends in motivation, we can now ask, what sorts of developmental mechanisms could explain these trends? The main culprits seem to be (a) personal experiences, (b) repetition, and (c) changing classroom contexts. As noted earlier, success and failure are important sources of information regarding one's competence. With age, children have many opportunities to fail as grading gets harsher, topics become more abstract, and skills become more complex (see Chapters 6 to 11 on the latter two points). If only the top students maintain their high level of performance over time, the average levels of motivation within grades will inevitably fall. With respect to repetition, most subject areas become less interesting the longer one works in these areas. Most adults change their careers several times, so we should not be surprised at children getting a little tired of 12 years of math (or other subjects). With respect to changing classroom context, we shall explore this mechanism further in the instructional implications section at the end of this chapter.

Individual Differences in Motivation

Having described some general trends in the development of motivation, we can now turn our attention to the issue of individual differences. More specifically, we can ask, "Why do some students in a grade have more motivation than other students in that same grade?" As we shall see, individual differences can be found along most dimensions of motivation. Sometimes these differences co-vary with a student's gender or ability level, and sometimes they do not. Notably, very few ethnic differences in motivation have been found (Graham, 1994), so the variable of ethnicity will not be discussed further in this chapter.

Goals

The first way that students differ concerns their goals. In particular, some students in a class have learning goals and others have performance goals (Dweck & Elliot, 1988; Nicholls, 1983). Moreover, some set proximal goals, some set distal goals, and some set no goals at all (Bandura, 1986; Zimmerman & Martinez-Pons, 1990). Finally, some students focus more on their social goals than their academic goals, and others focus more on their academic goals than their social goals (Wentzel, 1989).

Differences among goals do not seem to co-vary with gender, but they are related with achievement levels. In particular, high achievement is associated with having learning goals and setting proximal goals for oneself. In addition, high achievers are adept at coordinating both their academic and social goals. That is, they are not only interested in learning information, they are also interested in working towards cooperative arrangements with their teachers and peers (Wentzel, 1991).

Knowledge

Within any given grade, students differ with respect to their means-end beliefs. For example, memory studies show that students will often disagree about which memory strategies are the most effective (Fabricious & Hagen, 1984). Students also differ in their beliefs about the utility of note-taking, studying, and help-seeking behaviors (Pintrich & DeGroot, 1990; Newman, 1991). As was the case for goals, variations among means-ends beliefs seem to co-vary more with ability level than gender.

So far, then, we have two possible explanations for why one student in a class might be busily working at an assignment while the student seated in front of him or her is not. The engaged student might have different goals, different means-ends beliefs, or both.

Metacognitive Processes

Monitoring.   The main factor that seems to predict which students in a classroom will monitor their progress and which will not is their ability level. Whereas older, high achieving students monitor their progress, their same-aged low achieving and learning disabled peers do not (Baker & Brown, 1984; Paris & Byrnes, 1989).

Appraisal of Actions.   With respect to standards, research shows that whereas some people are "perfectionists," others are "satisficers" (Simon, 1956; Siegler, 1988). Perfectionists set very high standards of performance and only seem to be satisfied when they have performed nearly flawlessly. Satisficers, in contrast, have lower standards than perfectionists and operate on the principle of performing "good enough." Of course, it is possible to be a high achiever and still be a satisficer. For example, consider the situation in which students need to get at least 90 percent of test questions right in order to get an "A." Whereas a perfectionist would only be happy with a 99 or 100, a satisficing student would be content with a 90 or 91. Both students, however, would be given an "A."

With respect to self-efficacy, studies across a variety of domains have revealed that when students in a particular grade are confronted with the same task (e.g., a math or vocabulary task), only some of these students feel highly self-efficacious for that task. Why do some students feel efficacious and others do not? Bandura (1986) suggests that there are four sources of self-efficacy judgments. The first is actual experience with success or failure on that task. Successful people (i.e., high achievers) will tend to feel more efficacious than less successful people (though not always). The second is vicarious experiences in which an individual observes the performance of someone else. Vicarious judgments have their most important effects in those situations in which a student lacks experience on a task and when some other person who has the experience is seen to be similar by the student (e.g., a peer of similar ability). The third is verbal persuasion. Here, the comments of influential others can affect the degree to which an individual feels he or she can control his or her success on a task. The fourth is physiological arousal. Emotional reactions such as anxiety can prompt a student to lose confidence. According to Bandura's (1986) account, individual differences among students in the same classroom could arise from each of these four sources.

It is hard to say at present whether or not there are gender differences in self-efficacy because the results are somewhat mixed (Eccles et al., 1998). In a study of both gifted and non-gifted fifth, eighth, and eleventh graders, Zimmerman and Martinez-Pons (1990) found that boys surpassed girls in their verbal self-efficacy (i.e., their certainty about being able to give the correct definition of words) but not in their mathematical self-efficacy (i.e., their certainty about being able to correctly solve a set of math problems). A study of writing beliefs showed that girls were better writers than boys, but no gender differences in self-efficacy for writing emerged after controlling for writing aptitude (Pajares, Miller, & Johnson, 1999). In a sample of engineering students, Hackett et al. (1992) found no gender-significant differences in school-related and career-related self-efficacy beliefs. These findings can be contrasted with those of Randhawa et al. (1993) and Betz and Hackett (1983) who found that males felt more self-efficacious than females about being able to (a) solve "everyday" math problems, (b) solve math problems at school, and (c) do well in math courses. The difference between the last two studies and the former two appears to be the fact that the students in the Randhawa et al. and Betz and Hackett studies were older than those in Zimmerman and Martinez-Pons (1990) (i.e., had more time to be exposed to failures, vicarious experiences, and verbal persuasion) and contained proportionately fewer talented students than either Zimmerman and Martinez-Pons (1990) or Hackett et al. (1992). Talented students are more successful than non-talented students and are likely to feel more self-efficacious (regardless of their gender). This explanation of the discrepancies among studies is supported by Kelly (1993) who found that achievement was a more powerful predictor of the career self-efficacy perceptions of ninth and eleventh graders than gender.

Research on ability beliefs have revealed a number of gender differences. In particular, studies of students in the first through eleventh grades have shown that whereas boys have more positive beliefs about their math and sports abilities than girls, girls have more positive beliefs about their reading and writing skills (Eccles et al., 1993; Marsh et al., 1984; Marsh, 1989; Wigfield et al., 1991).

At first blush, the findings for ability beliefs seem to contradict those for self-efficacy described above in which few gender differences were found for math-related performance. Viewed in a certain way, however, the two data sets may not be contradictory. In particular, self-efficacy only has to do with a sense that you can be successful. Even if you think you have less ability than someone else, you can nevertheless think that you can be successful (e.g., through hard work). Students may, however, decide that it is not worth the effort to continue a course of actions.

Before moving on to research on interests, it is worth noting that students' *perception* of their abilities seems to play a larger role in their motivation-related behavior than their actual performance. As will be shown in the chapters on reading, writing, and math (Chapters 6, 7, and 8), girls routinely get better grades than boys in all of these subjects. Differences only arise in math during adolescence for SATs and they are not terribly large. Conversely, gender differences favoring girls in verbal skills are extremely small as well. Given their actual performance, then we can say that boys and girls either overestimate their ability or underestimate it. However, girls seem to be more "unrealistic" than boys because the correlations among beliefs and teacher ratings of ability are higher for boys than for girls (Eccles et al., 1989; Harter, 1985).

Turning now to interest, it can be noted that it is, perhaps, the paradigmatic example of an individual-difference variable. Although there are things that nearly all people find interesting (e.g., a car wreck on the side of a highway) or large subgroups of people find interesting (e.g., boys and video games), it is the norm for people to have their own idiosyncratic tastes and preferences (Renninger, 1991). Nevertheless, gender differences in interests are pervasive enough to influence student motivation and, therefore, warrant some discussion. In both younger and older students, the same pattern emerges: whereas no gender difference emerges for interest in math, boys report liking sports more than girls and girls report liking reading and English more than boys (Wigfield et al., 1989; Wigfield et al., 1991). Older girls also report liking social activities more than boys.

Appraisal of Outcomes.   Below the third grade, boys and girls generally do not differ significantly in their expectations for success and failure (Parsons & Ruble, 1977; Stipek & Hoffman, 1980). They begin tasks at an equally high level of optimism and seem equally indifferent to failure experiences. Although slightly older boys and girls also enter tasks with similar levels of optimism, failure seems to affect these older girls more strongly than boys. In particular, whereas boys become only slightly less optimistic after several failures, girls become dramatically less optimistic. Then, when children are nine to eleven years of age, gender differences are apparent even before the task begins, with girls being less optimistic about success than boys.

Within any given classroom, there are individual differences with respect to attributions for success and failure. Some students attribute their performance to their ability (or lack thereof), others attribute it to effort, others attribute it to the ease or difficulty of tests, and still others attribute it to luck (Stipek, 1993; Weiner, 1986).

Beyond these general differences among individuals, a reasonably consistent pattern of gender differences has also been found (Eccles et al., 1998). In particular, girls are less likely than boys to attribute their successes to high ability and more likely than boys to attribute their failures to low ability (Sohn, 1982; Stipek, 1993). These differences in attributions have been argued to underlie the gender differences in expectations described in the previous section. But a number of studies do not fit this pattern, so that data appear to be similar to that reported above for self-efficacy.

As for values, it is common for individuals to disagree about what is important to them. For example, whereas some people think that it is important to be ambitious, others think that it is more important to be honest. Similarly, whereas some people think that it is important to be intellectual and logical, others think that it is more important to be forgiving and helpful (Rokeach, 1973). In the academic realm, studies have shown that individuals disagree about the importance of subjects such as math and English (Feather, 1988; Wigfield & Eccles, 1992).

All of these differences have been hypothesized to affect the choices people make and several studies suggest that they do. For example, Feather (1988) found that having values such as being loving and forgiving predicted the importance that college students placed on English, which in turn predicted their enrollment decisions. Similarly, values related to being clean, obedient, polite, responsible, and self-controlled related to the importance placed on math, which in turn affected enrollment decisions in math-related fields. However, subsequent analyses showed that only math and English values predicted course enrollment when factors such as social class, age, and gender were controlled.

As might be expected from previous sections, gender differences have also been found with respect to values. For example, Feather (1988) found that college men valued math more than college women. The reverse was true for English. When asked to assess the usefulness of math, Betz & Hackett (1983) found that college males rated math higher than females. In a study of first, second, and fourth graders, Eccles et al. (1993) found that whereas boys valued sports activities more than girls, girls valued reading and music more than boys. No gender difference was found for math in these young children.

Finally, given the fact that boys are more likely to attribute their successes to their own ability than girls, it would be expected that boys would be more likely to feel proud after being successful than girls. Conversely, girls should be more likely to feel ashamed or embarrassed after failing than boys because girls are more likely to attribute their failures to low ability than boys. As plausible as these hypotheses may seem, few studies have attempted to verify them. Thus, firm conclusions about gender differences in the expression of pride and shame await future study.

Gender differences have, however, been found for both test anxiety and learned helplessness. In particular, girls are not only more likely to develop test and math anxiety than males (Betz & Hackett, 1983; Wigfield & Eccles, 1989), they are also more likely to show a learned helpless pattern of behavior following a period of prolonged failure (Stipek, 1993; Dweck et al., 1978; Wigfield & Eccles, 1989).

Summary

Within any given classroom, individual differences can be found along any of the aspects of motivation. In particular, students differ in terms of their goals, means-end beliefs, tendency to monitor, standards, self-efficacy, ability beliefs, interests, expectations, and values. Moreover, those who are successful and who view their successes and failures in particular ways tend to experience positive emotions quite often. All other students tend to experience negative emotions quite often.

These overall differences among students also tend to co-vary with a student's gender. In particular, whereas no gender differences have been reported for goals, means-end beliefs, monitoring, and standards (though they may exist), gender differences have been found for the remaining seven constructs. Again, though, the data are not perfectly consistent across studies. Apart from explaining why males and females differ in their choices, levels of persistence and performance in certain activities, these differences mean that school may be a more positive experience for males than females.

Instructional Implications

We shall first examine some general instructional guidelines suggested by the research on motivation. Then, we shall focus on two case studies that can be evaluated in terms of the information in this chapter.

General Guidelines

We shall approach the task of describing general guidelines in two ways. First, we shall examine Ames' (1992) comprehensive proposal that attempts to link classroom structures and experiences to motivation. Second, the literature on motivation will be distilled into a series of heuristics or rules of thumb.

Carol Ames (1992) summarized the literature on the links between classroom structures and motivation in the following way. Classrooms differ with respect to the tasks that children are asked to perform, the amount of authority relegated to students, and the kind of evaluative practices that are implemented. If these dimensions of a classroom are configured in particular ways, students will (a) focus on effort and learning, (b) have high intrinsic interest, (c) attribute their successes to effort and effort-based strategies, (d) employ effective learning and self-regulatory strategies, (e) demonstrate engagement, (f) demonstrate positive affect on high-effort tasks, (g) demonstrate feelings of belongingness, and (h) develop appropriate levels of failure tolerance. What kinds of task, authority, and evaluative structures produce these highly desirable motivation outcomes? In the case of tasks, activities should be meaningful, diverse, and occasionally novel, require short-term self-referenced goals, and require the effective use of learning strategies. With respect to authority, students should be given opportunities to participate in the decision-making and make choices (as opposed to being told what to do and given a single option). Moreover, they should be opportunities to develop responsibility and self-regulation of their behaviors (as opposed to being nagged and threatened). With respect to evaluations, grades should be given to acknowledge individual improvement, progress, effort, and mastery (as opposed to a one-shot attempt to get an absolute number of answers correct). Moreover, only the student, his or her guardian, and the teacher should know of these grades. Finally, teachers should provide opportunities for improvement and encourage the view that mistakes are part of learning.

To this sound list of suggestions, the research described in this chapter suggests that teachers should also:

1. *Help students acquire and coordinate appropriate goals* (e.g., learning goals, proximal goals, social and academic goals).

2. *Empower students with appropriate means-end beliefs* (e.g., not only demonstrate skills but explain why they work).

3. *Provide devices to help them monitor their progress* (e.g., charts and other forms of feedback).

4. *Provide numerous experiences in which children of all skill levels feel successful and competent, but also challenged* (e.g., individualized instruction to just beyond each student's skill level). *Moreover, explicitly point out to students that they controlled successes that just occurred.* Together, such experiences help students develop appropriately high standards, expectations, feelings of self-efficacy, and advantageous attributions.

5. *Adopt and communicate the incremental view of ability to students* (i.e., that intelligence is not fixed but increases as new skills are acquired; errors are normal in the early phases of learning, etc.).

6. *Point out to students the value and importance of learning certain skills using authentic and convincing argumentation* (e.g., why it is important to learn long division or learn about other cultures).

7. *Frequently introduce novelty and information that cries out for explanation.*

Case Studies

Use the aforementioned suggestions and other information in this chapter to evaluate the following case studies.

Case Study 1.   Jacqueline Eccles, Allan Wigfield, and their colleagues have tried to determine why there is a sharp drop in motivation as students make the transition from elementary school to junior high school. In a large-scale study of twelve school districts in Michigan, they identified six differences between elementary classrooms and junior-high classrooms that seem to accelerate the already declining motivation of students (Eccles et al., 1993). First, teachers in junior-high classrooms place greater emphasis on control and discipline and provide fewer opportunities for student choice than teachers in elementary classrooms. Eccles et al. have found that providing students with choices enhances their instrinsic motivation. Second, there are fewer positive or personal teacher-student interactions in junior high than there are in elementary school. Eccles et al. have found that when students perceive there to be less support from their teachers, students tend to value the subjects taught by these teachers less and find the subjects less interesting. Third, teachers in the junior high tend to use whole-class activities, between-class ability grouping, and public evaluation more often than teachers in elementary schools. Moving from small groups to whole classes makes the environment less personal. Between-class ability grouping and public evaluation promote concerns about evaluation and also make competition more likely. Fourth, junior-high teachers feel less efficacious than elementary teachers about their teaching abilities (especially for helping low achieving students do better). Eccles et al. have found that when teachers do not feel efficacious, their students soon acquire low expectations for themselves as well. Fifth, junior-high teachers often assign classwork to first-year students that requires a lower level of cognitive skills than the work these students were assigned a year earlier in elementary school. Sixth, junior-high teachers use a higher standard in grading than elementary teachers (i.e., it is harder to get an "A"). The fifth and sixth factors together can have a disastrous effect when a student gets, say, a "B" for the first time for work on tasks that are perceived as not that challenging! Eccles et al. have found that there is no stronger predictor of students' sense of self-efficacy than the grades they receive. Thus, the harder grading would be expected to produce a new wave of students who suddenly no longer feel efficacious.

This line of research clearly shows that classroom contexts play an important role in student motivation. If you were asked to "fix" this problem in Michigan junior high schools, what would you propose?

Case Study 2.   Diana Cordova and Mark Lepper (1996) tried to enhance children's learning of arithmetic rules through a computerized system that targeted three dimensions of motivation: contextualization, personalization, and the provision of choice. Here, fourth and fifth graders tried to learn the rules related to the order of operations in expressions involving parentheses (e.g., performing operations in parentheses first). To enhance this skill, three versions of a computerized game were created. In one, the context included a screen that merely said "Math Game" (and similar non-descript labels) as well as a number line that ranged from 0 to 50. The first person to move to 50 was declared the winner. During each turn, three numbers between 1 and 5 were randomly generated by the computer. Children had to combine these numbers using any of the four operations (addition, subtraction, multiplication, and division) as well as parentheses. The answer generated was the number of spaces that could be moved. Obviously, children should do what they could to make the largest answer possible. In addition, however, if they landed on any multiple of 10 (e.g., 20 or 30), they automatically moved 10 spaces. Thus, it would sometimes be wise to try and land on a multiple of 10 with a smaller number. The other two contexts were structurally similar, but one placed the game within a context called "Space Quest." Here, points on the number line were replaced with locations such as Planet Earth and Planet Ektar. They were told that Planet Earth was facing the worst energy crisis in history and that their mission was to travel 3 trillion miles to Planet Ektar as quickly as possible to get titanium, a highly powerful source of energy. In the third version, the game was contextualized as a treasure hunt in which they were to play the role of ship captain in search of a hidden treasure on a desert island.

Besides manipulating context in such ways, the versions of the game also included different degrees of control over the type of icons displayed and names of characters, as well as different levels of personalization in which generic information in the game was replaced by personalized information taken from a questionnaire given to children. The authors reported that contextualization, personalization, and choice all produced substantial increases in (a) student motivation (indexed by a questionnaire tapping into their liking the material, likelihood of playing the game after school, and so on), (b) depth of engagement in learning (indexed by the complexity of their strategies and styles of interaction with the options), (c) the amount they learned (indexed by a paper and pencil post-test measure of order-of-operations skill), and (d) their perceived competence (indexed by a questionnaire).

6

Beginning Reading

Summary

1. Although skilled readers process the individual letters in a word, they perceive it as a whole.

2. The connections between written words and their meanings are well-established in a skilled reader's mind.

3. Skilled readers connect the phonemes of their spoken language to written words and syllables.

4. Skilled readers create mental models of what they are reading and use these mental models to form expectations.

5. Skilled readers rely on syntactic cues to create a mental representation of a sentence.

6. The best predictors of early reading success are a child's socio-economic status, knowledge of letters, sentence memory, concepts of print, and phonemic awareness.

7. Children who learn to read the best in the first grade enter first grade already knowing a lot about reading.

8. Children are less likely to rely heavily on context and more likely to decode words quickly and automatically with age.

9. The biggest differences between same-age good and poor readers concern their abilities to (a) recognize words automatically, (b) recognize words rapidly, and (c) recode print items into a phonological representation.

10. Neuroscientific studies suggest that there are specific brain regions associated with orthographic, phonological, semantic, and syntactic processing.

11. Gender differences in beginning reading are fairly small and inconsistent. In contrast, ethnic differences are fairly large and consistent.

At first blush, reading seems to be a fairly simple act of sounding out words. In reality, however, it is a complex collection of skills that take many years to master (Snow, Burns, & Griffin, 1998). To get an initial sense of the kind of mental tasks that skilled readers perform, read the contents of Figure 6.1 in order to answer the following question: "How does the author feel about smoking?"

Finished? Let's now consider some of the things that you did when you tried to answer the preceding question. When you first examined Figure 6.1, you mainly focused your eyes on the words in the table, not the other symbols. When you encountered a line that contained more than one word (e.g., line 2), you read these words from left to right. The fact that you looked for words shows that you know that the *text carries the message*. The fact that you read words from left to right shows that you know the directionality of written English (Clay, 1985). Young, pre-reading children lack such *concepts of print*.

In addition to illustrating print concepts, Figure 6.1 also illustrates certain "levels" of reading (Carver, 1973; Mayer, 1987). For example, when you read the single word "smoked," you recognized this cluster of letters and retrieved ideas associated with it (e.g., smoked salmon). In Carver's (1973) model, this is called "level 1" reading. When you finished reading the first full sentence in line 2, you not only tried to recognize the words and access their meanings, you also integrated all of these meanings into a structural representation of the entire sentence. In Carver's (1973) model, this is called "level 2" reading. When you read the three sentences in line 3, you probably made the inference that "she" and "her" refer to "Mary" and that smoking was the cause of her death. Carver (1973) called this "level 3" reading. Finally, some of you may have also formed the opinion that the author of line 3 was a little extreme in his or her characterization of smoking as the "scourge of mankind." Carver (1973) used the label "level 4" reading to refer to the ability to evaluate or criticize text. Of course, these levels are more in the mind of the theorist than in actual reading because processes at all levels interact to produce meaningful comprehension. Nevertheless, the model is useful for getting a sense of how new skills emerge as one adds complexity to the task of reading.

FIGURE 6.1   *Examples Illustrating "Levels" of Reading*

$$$$$$$$$$$$$$$$$$$$$$

1. smoked

   % %   %%%   % %%%   @@@@@@@

2. Mary smoked three packs of cigarettes a day.

   .... >>>>>>,,,,,,,,,,............

3. Mary smoked three packs of cigarettes a day. After she died, her husband
   sold their Phillip Morris stocks. This was a good thing to do because
   cigarettes are the scourge of mankind.

   ## $ $
   #   ##   #

The goal of the present chapter and the next chapter is to convey the nature and development of reading skills. For expository purposes and considerations of length, we will consider the early phases of reading development in this chapter and some of the later achievements in Chapter 7. In the first section of this chapter, you will first get a sense of what children need to learn in order to become skilled readers (The Nature of Skilled Reading). In the second section, you will learn how reading skills develop (The Development of Reading Skills). In the third section, you will learn how good readers differ from not-so-good readers and consider some of the findings from neuroscientific studies of reading (Individual Differences in Reading Ability). In the fourth section, you will learn how instruction should be designed in order to help young children initially master the fundamental processes of reading ("Instructional Implications").

The Nature of Skilled Reading

In order to know how to help children become good readers, we first need to know what good reading entails. In what follows, the task of defining good reading is approached in two ways. First, we will consider a consensus view of reading that recently emerged from a panel of experts convened by the National Research Council (Snow et al., 1998). Then, we will examine an influential model of proficient reading that emerged approximately 10 years ago (Adams, 1990).

The field of reading research has been continually plagued by deep divisions among camps of researchers who hold diametrically opposed perspectives. Given this history, one would think that it would be impossible to come up with a consensus view of reading that most scholars could agree on. Recently, however, a group of seventeen experts on reading did just that (Snow et al., 1998). Although these experts approach reading from a variety of perspectives, they readily agreed that, at a general level, reading should be defined as "a process of getting meaning from print using knowledge about the written alphabet and about the sound structure of oral language for purposes of achieving understanding" (p. vi). What should be noticed about this definition is the combined emphasis on (a) meaning and understanding (as opposed to an exclusive focus on sounding out words), (b) knowledge of alphabetic characters (as opposed to suggesting that letter knowledge is less important than whole, undifferentiated words), and (c) knowledge of sounds (as opposed to minimizing the role of these sounds). The expert panel in conjunction with a number of reviewers and consultants elaborated on this general definition by suggesting that skilled readers:

- rapidly and automatically identify written words through visual processes, phonological decoding processes, semantic processes, and contextual interpretive processes
- use their general world knowledge and extensive sight vocabulary to comprehend texts literally and draw inferences
- demonstrate the ability to accurately assess and monitor their own understanding
- use a common set of syntactic and inferential processes to comprehend both spoken language and text, as well as text-specific processes to comprehend texts

The second way to understand the nature of skilled reading is to examine contemporary theoretical models of this ability. Although there are a number of such models in existence (Coltheart, Curtis, Atkins, & Haller, 1993), it is most efficient to examine just one of these models for illustrative purposes. The one chosen, that is, Seidenberg and McClelland's (1989) connectionist model, also happens to have made quite an impact on the field (Adams, 1990; Pressley, 1997), though certain kinds of empirical problems caused it to be refined over the years (Brown, 1998). Figure 6.2 depicts the key elements of the original model.

The theory is based on the idea that when people read, they process many different types of information (e.g., letters, word meanings, syntax, etc.). More importantly, the model implies two things: (a) that processing is *divided* among relatively autonomous subsystems that perform their own tasks (indicated by the ovals), and (b) that each subsystem *sends* what it "knows" or has "figured out" to at least one other subsystem (indicated by the arrows). The former point means that readers have many different clues they can use to make sense of a sentence. The latter point means that one processor can send its clues to other processors to help them make sense of their own clues; that is, the processors work *interactively* with one another (Perfetti, 1985). With this in mind, lets examine the jobs performed by the Orthographic, Meaning, Phonological, and Context processors in turn.

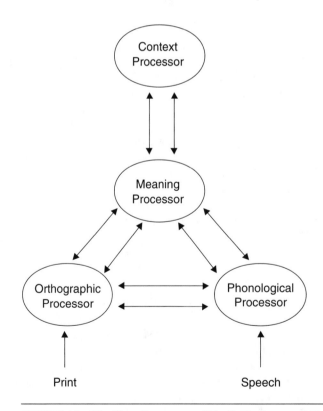

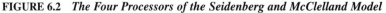

FIGURE 6.2 *The Four Processors of the Seidenberg and McClelland Model*

The Orthographic Processor

Orthographic knowledge consists of knowing the individual symbols of a written language. For example, a child who knows the letters of the English alphabet has orthographic knowledge. The orthographic processor shown in Figure 6.2 can be thought of as a storehouse of orthographic knowledge. More specifically, the orthographic processor has the job of processing and recognizing strings of letters (i.e., words). It accomplishes this feat by means of small "units" that recognize individual letters and parts of letters (McClelland & Rumelhart, 1981; Seidenberg & McClelland, 1989). As noted previously, the system is designed according to Connectionist principles (see Chapter 2 for a description of the Connectionist perspective).

Word recognition occurs when the units for each letter of a word attain a sufficient degree of activation. The main way that each unit becomes activated is through direct perception of the letter it stands for. The second way that units can be activated is through *spreading activation* (see Chapters 2 and 3). A unit can spread its activation to another unit if the units are linked in an associative relationship. Associations form between units when certain letters (e.g., "q") frequently co-occur with other letters (e.g., "u"). Any unit that has been partially activated by spreading activation turns on faster than it would have if the letter were presented alone. In Chapter 3, this process was called *priming*. For example, when someone sees a "q" while scanning a word left to right and then sees a "u" next, the unit for "u" is turned on faster than it would have been if "u" had been perceived alone. Thus, associations and spreading activation promote faster reading.

Any familiar word, then, is really a highly associated pattern of letters and each letter in the word primes the perception of the others. As a result, the entire word is recognized very quickly and automatically as a result of perceiving every one of the letters.

After many years of research using sophisticated technology, we now have a better sense of how the orthographic processor works in skilled readers. Here are some of the findings:

a. Contrary to a common belief held among non-scientists, skilled readers process the individual letters of the words they are reading. They are not aware of this because word recognition has become automatic and subconscious for them. However, skilled readers do not recognize the letters of a word independently of one another. Rather, after many years of reading, associations form between the units for one letter in a word and the units for other letters. As a result, a familiar word is perceived as a whole.

b. The strengths of the association between the units for letters reflect the frequencies with which these letters co-occur in written texts. For example, when the letter "t" occurs as the first letter of a three-letter word, it is extremely likely that the next letter will be an "h" (Adams, 1990). People who read a lot develop mental associations between letters. Once associations form, they allow the activation from the units for one letter to "spread" to the units for another. As a result, skilled readers recognize familiar words very quickly and automatically. In contrast, someone who has never read a book and only knows letters would not recognize words as fast as a skilled reader because no associations have formed among the units for letters. Such a person would, however, recognize isolated letters as fast as a skilled reader.

c. Letter associations also help skilled readers process the proper order of letters in a word (e.g., "THE" versus "HTE") as well as perceive association-preserving pseudowords (e.g., "Mave" and "Teal"). A pseudoword is a made-up word created by researchers. It uses combinations of letters that appear frequently in real words (e.g., the *ave* in Mave).

d. Finally, letter associations also help a reader divide a word into syllables. For example, whereas "dr" is an acceptable combination of letters that maps onto the sounds of spoken English, "dn" is not. As a result, a skilled reader who encounters the word "midnight" would visually divide this word into "mid" and "night." In contrast, skilled readers would not visually divide "address" into "add" and "ress." Moreover, a skilled reader implicitly knows that vowels seem to pull their adjacent consonants into a cluster of association patterns. For example, the "a" in "party" perceptually pulls the "p" and "r" towards itself. This fact combined with the fact that "rt" is an unacceptable spoken combination means that "party" would be divided into "par" and "ty" (Adams, 1990).

It is interesting to note that, historically, written language did not use spacing and punctuation to delineate words (Just & Carpenter, 1987). As a result, readers had to exclusively rely on their orthographic knowledge to make sense of a sentence. To see how this might work, consider the following sentence:

THATTOYWASLOST.

The Meaning Processor

Overview.   Of course, comprehending a sentence requires far more than the ability to determine whether letter strings are orthographically acceptable or familiar. For example, the sentence, "Trat distle quas," contains combinations of letters that appear in real words (e.g., the "tr" in "trat" also appears in "truck" and "tree"), but it is meaningless. Similarly, the sentence "The octogenarian insinuated himself into our organization" would be meaningless to someone who knows she has seen the words "octogenarian" and "insinuated" before, but cannot remember what they mean. Thus, sentence comprehension requires both an Orthographic processor to recognize letter strings and a Meaning processor to access word meanings.

Two views have been proposed regarding how meanings are assigned to words. According to the *Lexical Access* view, entire word meanings are stored in a *lexicon*. The lexicon is simply a mental "dictionary" that organizes word meanings in terms of lists of attributes or schemata (see Chapter 2 for a description of schemata). When a written word is perceived, its meanings are accessed if the resting activation level of these word meanings is high enough (Just & Carpenter, 1987). Moreover, the higher the resting activation level, the faster a word meaning will be retrieved. Word meanings attain a high activation level if the words to which they are attached occur frequently. Thus, the meanings of frequent words are accessed faster than the meanings of infrequent words. For example, whereas common words like "man" might have their meanings accessed in 250 milliseconds, uncommon words like "propensity" might take 750 milliseconds or longer (Carpenter, Miyake, & Just, 1995).

The second view derives from recent *Connectionist* theories (see Chapter 2). According to this view, word meanings are represented in the Meaning processor as associated sets of primitive meaning elements, in the same way that spellings of familiar words are represented in the Orthographic processor as associated sets of letters and parts of letters (Adams, 1990). A person's experience determines which meaning elements get associated and stored for a given word (Hintzman, 1986). For example, a child who hears the word "dog" applied to a specific dog in a specific context might associate the whole experience with the word "dog." The next time she hears the word "dog" applied, however, it might be with a different dog in a different context. According to the Connectionist view, those aspects of the second context that are similar to aspects of the first context (e.g., both dogs had a flea collar) would become associated and stored with the word "dog." Over time, a consistent set of meaning elements would be distilled from these repeated encounters with dogs. Each element would be highly associated with the others and would, therefore, prime one's memory for the others. Moreover, some aspects of the meaning of "dog" would be more central to its meaning and reflect consistent correlations of attributes (e.g., "has fur" and "barks"). Such attributes would be accessed the fastest when the single word "dog" is read. Other meaning elements that are somewhat less central (e.g., "has an owner") would also be accessible but would be accessed more slowly if at all when the word is read in isolation.

As Figure 6.2 shows, the Meaning processor is directly linked to the Orthographic processor. This means that the output of each processor can help the other do its job better. In support of this claim, Whittlesea and Cantwell (1987) found that when a pseudoword is given a meaningful definition, subjects perceived this word faster than they did when it lacked a definition. This improved perceptibility lasted for at least 24 hours, even when the supplied meaning had been forgotten. Thus, the Meaning processor helped the Orthographic processor do its job better. But the reverse can happen as well. As we shall see the section on the development of reading ability, students who frequently read text with new words can dramatically increase the size of their vocabularies. Thus, Orthographic knowledge can improve the capacity of the Meaning processor.

The Phonological Processor

Analogous to the Orthographic and Meaning processors, the Phonological processor consists of units that form associations with each other. In this case, however, the basic units correspond to *phonemes* in the reader's spoken language. Phonemes such as "ba" and "tuh" can be combined into syllables such as "bat" and also into words such as "battle." The auditory representation of a word, syllable, or phoneme is comprised by an activated set of specific units in the Phonological processor (Adams, 1990).

Recent studies suggest that phonemes and larger sound units take on different levels of importance in reading and oral language. In particular, Rebecca Treiman and colleagues have found that many words seem to be represented in terms of an *onset* (e.g., the "tuh" in tap) and a *rime* (e.g., the "ap" in tap), perhaps because certain vowel-final-consonant combinations occur in texts more often than chance (Kessler & Treiman, 1997). Both children and adults make fewer errors and respond faster when they utilize onset-rime information in words (especially rime information). They appear to be less reliant on the more specific connection between graphemes and individual phonemes (Treiman, Mullennix, Bijeljac-Babic, & Richmond-Welty, 1995; Treiman & Zukowski, 1996). In a related way, other studies suggest that the level of the syllable often overrides the level of the phoneme in early writing (Treiman & Tincoff, 1997).

When skilled readers see a written word, they do not have to translate it phonologically in order for its meaning to be accessed. Many studies have shown that meaning can be accessed simply by a visual pattern of letters (Adams, 1990; Seidenberg & McClelland, 1989). And yet, skilled readers often *do* translate words phonologically when they read. Why would people perform some operation when they do not have to? The answer seems to be that the Phonological processor provides a certain degree of redundancy with the information provided by the other processors. This redundancy can be quite helpful when the information provided by the other processors is incomplete, deceptive, or weakly specified (Stanovich, 1980; Adams, 1990).

More specifically, the Phonological processor seems to provide two important services to the overall reading system. In the first place, it provides an alphabetic backup system that may be crucial for maintaining fast and accurate reading (Adams, 1990). This backup system exists mainly because the orthography of written English largely obeys the *alphabetic principle:* written symbols (i.e., graphemes) correspond to spoken sounds (i.e., phonemes). Although this grapheme-phoneme correspondence is not one-to-one or perfectly regular, it is nevertheless fairly predictable (Brown, 1998; Just & Carpenter, 1987; Treiman et al., 1995). As a result, the Phonological processor could provide helpful information in a variety of situations. For example, consider the case in which a reader knows the meaning of a spoken word but has never seen it written down. There would be no direct connection between (a) the units corresponding to the letters of this word in the Orthographic processor and (b) the units corresponding to the meaning of this word in the Meaning processor. There would, however, be a connection between the Phonological processor units and the Meaning processor units for this word. If the word obeys the alphabetic principle fairly well, the person would be able to "sound it out" and hear himself or herself saying the familiar word. This pronunciation, in turn, would access the meaning of the word. Over repeated readings, the two-way association between the Phonological processor units and Meaning processor units for this word would become a three-way association between the Orthographic, Meaning, and Phonological units. The basic premise, then, is that good readers mentally represent the statistical properties of the relations between graphemes and sound patterns that appear in texts (Brown, 1998). Words are read more quickly and accurately if they contain graphemes (e.g., ave) that are consistently related to particular sound patterns (e.g., the rime of gave, save, rave, etc.).

The second service provided by the Phonological processor has to do with readers' memories for what they have just read. In Chapter 3, we discussed that portion of memory known as working memory. Within working memory, research has revealed a "phonological loop" in which verbal information is rehearsed for later processing (Baddeley, 1990). In order to make sense of what they are reading, readers have to take all of the words in a sentence and put them together into a meaningful whole (Caplan & Waters, 1999; Just & Carpenter, 1987). This integration requires a certain degree of memory because when one reads from left to right, only one or two words fall within a reader's visual fixation span. That is, all of the words to the left of a visual fixation point must be retained in working memory. The phonological loop plays a crucial role of keeping a record of all of the words in a sentence in order that all of their meanings can be integrated together. The Phonological processor must be intimately connected to the phonological loop because adults with certain brain injuries show a marked inability to retain words that they just read. One recent proposal based on studies of normal and brain-injured individuals suggests that there may even be a sub-system of working memory that is uniquely specialized for syntactic processing (Caplan & Waters, 1999).

The Context Processor

The Context processor has the job of constructing an on-line, coherent interpretation of text (Adams, 1990). The output of this processor is a mental representation of everything that a reader has read so far. For example, upon reading the sentence, "When the president came in, the reporters all rose," the context may be a mental image of President Clinton walking up to the podium in the White House press room. Whereas some researchers (e.g., Just & Carpenter, 1987) call this image a *referential representation* of the text, others (e.g., van Dijk & Kintsch, 1983) call it a *situation model.* For simplicity and consistency with other chapters, we shall use the latter term.

Semantic, pragmatic, and syntactic knowledge all contribute to the construction of a situation model (Seidenberg & McClelland, 1989). For example, when skilled readers encounter the sentence, "John went to the store to buy a _____," they use their semantic knowledge to access the meanings of all of the words in this sentence. In addition, they use their pragmatic knowledge to expect that "John" will buy something that people usually buy at stores. If the blank were filled in by "savings bond," readers would likely be surprised when their eyes reached the word "savings."

Syntactic knowledge also prompts the reader to form certain expectations about what will occur next (Garrett, 1990; Goodman & Goodman, 1979; Just & Carpenter, 1987). To see how the syntactic "parser" operates, it is useful to describe the notions of grammatical rules and tree structures.

In some circles of linguistics and psychology, language comprehension and production is said to be guided by a set of grammatical rules (Lasnick, 1990). That is, there are certain *types* of sentences and each type can be produced using a specific set of rules. For example, each of the following sentences can be produced by using the same three rules:

1. The fat boy hit the round ball.
2. The girl chewed an apple.
3. A man drew a picture.
4. A woman punched the cop.

These rules are:

R1 Sentence = Noun Phrase + Verb Phrase (i.e., S → NP + VP)
R2 Verb Phrase = Verb + Noun Phrase (i.e., VP → V + NP)
R3 Noun Phrase = Determiner + (optional adjective) + Noun
        (i.e., NP → Det + (adj) + N)

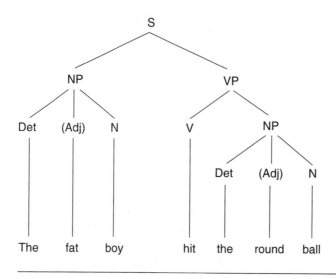

FIGURE 6.3   *A Tree Diagram for the Sentence: The fat boy hit the round ball.*

To depict the hierarchical arrangement of a set of rules, linguists have used so-called "tree structures." Figure 6.3 depicts a tree structure for the three rules presented. By nesting one component (e.g., a determiner) within another (e.g., a noun phrase), the structure shows how the former is part of the latter. It should be noted, however, that other kinds of syntactic theories besides those that entail rules have been proposed (including Connectionist models; Caplan & Waters, 1999). The rule-based ones are presented here for illustrative purposes, but other kinds of models would also provide the basis for grammatical expectations.

Given a specific input sentence and knowledge of grammatical rules, the human mind is thought to build up a particular tree structure for the sentence, component-by-component. For example, upon reading the word "the," the rule for producing noun phrases gets elicited. Implicitly, the mind says "O.K. A noun phrase must be starting." Given that a determiner has already been encountered, Rule 3 sets up the expectation that either an adjective or a noun will be encountered next. When the word "fat" is read next in sentence 1, it is assigned the slot for adjective. Having organized the words "the" and "fat" together, Rule 3 now sets up the expectation that the next word will likely be a noun, and so on. In order for this system to work, written words (e.g., "fat") have to be mentally associated with grammatical classes (e.g., "adjective").

Over the years, various researchers have doubted the existence of a mental "parser," grammatical rules, and grammatical classes. Although these doubters have made some good points, there is considerable evidence that syntactic knowledge is an important aspect of sentence comprehension (regardless of whether the parser relies on rules or others kinds of representations). In the first place, there is the syndrome called *Broca's Aphasia* which results from injury to the Broca's area of the cerebral cortex (located in the left frontal lobe). Individuals who have this disorder are able to comprehend the meanings of individual words, but have trouble with the syntax of sentences (Just & Carpenter, 1987; Caplan & Waters, 1999). For example, they see no difference between the following two sentences:

1. They fed her the dog biscuits.
2. They fed her dog the biscuits.

Although these two sentences have the same words, they have different tree structures and, therefore, different meanings.

In addition, there are many well known "garden-path" sentences such as the following:

3. The old train the young.
4. Since Jay always jogs a mile seems like a short distance to him.
5. The horse raced past the barn fell.

Note that there are no typos in sentences 3 to 5. If you read a few words of each and then said, "Huh?" at some point, that is because your syntax analyzer started to construct one kind of structure until it met a particular word that violated expectations (e.g., the second "the" in 3, and "seems" in 4). A sentence such as "The old train blew its whistle" would probably be more consistent with expectations than sentence 3. In sentence 4, a comma after "jogs" would have helped you create the right tree structure.

Further, there are studies that show how syntax affects both the meaning and pronunciation of a word that is encountered. For example, read the following sentences:

6. John said, "Does are in the park, aren't they?"
7. Tomorrow was the annual one-day fishing contest and fishermen would invade the place. Some of the best bass
   guitarists in the country would come here.

In sentence 6, grammatical rules suggest that "Does" is an auxiliary verb. Instead, it turns out to be the noun referring to female deer. The noun and the auxiliary have different pronunciations and meanings. In sentence 7, grammatical rules and prior context suggest that "bass" is a noun that labels a type of fish. Instead, it turns out to be an adjective in this instance. The noun and adjective have different meanings and pronunciations.

Finally, grammatical relations are evident when a reader encounters ambiguous sentences such as:

8. Visiting relatives can be a nuisance.
9. The burglar saw the cop with binoculars.

Does sentence 8 mean that it can be a bother to go see your relatives or that relatives who come to see you can be a bother? Theoretically, the only way someone could "see" the multiple readings of these sentences is if he or she constructed multiple syntactic structures for each one.

In sum, then, syntactic, pragmatic, and semantic knowledge all contribute to the construction of a situation model. Once in place, this model prompts readers to form expectations about what will occur next in the text. As each new segment of text is encountered, skilled readers interpret what is read in a way that makes it consistent with the current situation model.

The model of proficient reading in Figure 6.2 shows the two-way relationship between the Context processor and the Meaning processor. The model implies that the prior context can influence the meaning assigned to a word and that current meanings influence the construction of a situation model. Thus, when skilled readers process the sentence "John removed the thorn from the rose," they assign a different meaning to "rose" than they would if they read the sentence "The crowd rose to sing the national anthem."

But research has shown that the context-meaning effects are weak relative to the orthography-meaning effects. That is, readers are much better at predicting possible meanings of a word based on its perceived spelling than they are at predicting which word will follow a preceding context (Adams, 1990; Snow et al., 1998). When context-meaning links conflict with orthography-meaning links, the latter win out. Thus, skilled reading consists, first and foremost, of learning the correspondences between written words and their meanings. Context effects occur *after* words are perceived and various possible meanings are accessed. But overall, context, orthography, meanings, and phonology all work in concert to help a reader construct the best possible interpretation of text.

The Development of Skilled Reading

Now that you know what skilled readers do, you have a sense of the "endpoint" of reading development (but, of course, reading always improves a little with continued practice and experience). The beginning point of reading development is that point in a child's life when he or she has no idea what reading involves (e.g., infancy). In this section, we shall examine how children progress from the beginning point to the end point of reading development. The discussion proceeds as follows. In the first part (Emergent Literacy), we will examine a collection of skills that progressively appear prior to the onset of formal reading instruction in first grade. In the second part (Factors Predictive of Reading Success), we will examine the characteristics of preschool children that seem to predict their ability to read well by the end of first grade. In the third part (Explaining Predictive Relations), we will consider explanations of the predictive links between certain factors and reading success, and put the predictors together in a coherent story. In the fourth part (Precocious Readers), we will examine the incidence and causes of precocious reading in preschoolers. In the fifth and final part (Developmental Models), we will consider some general or global trends in the development of reading skills.

Emergent Literacy

Whitehurst and Lonigan (1998, p. 849) suggest that emergent literacy "consists of the skills, knowledge, and attitudes that are presumed to be developmental precursors to conventional forms of reading and writing . . . and the environments that support these developments." The construct of emergent literacy was originally proposed in the 1980s as an alternative to the idea of *reading readiness* that has existed in educational circles since the early 1900s (at least). According to the latter, it is not possible to teach reading to children until they are maturationally "ready" to benefit from this instruction. Some went so far as to use IQ tests to determine when the brain was ready (Morphett & Washburn, 1931). Notwithstanding the merits of this brain-based proposal, a readiness conception implies an all-or-none dichotomy between readers (i.e., first graders who are ready) and non-readers (i.e., preschoolers who are not ready). The emergent literacy conception, in contrast, implies a *continuum* of skills that have their origin well before formal reading instruction begins in first grade (Teale and Sulzby, 1986). Some examples of such skills include knowing that (a) the words in a book tell the story and the pictures are just an accompaniment to the words, (b) one reads words from left to right and lines of words from top to bottom, (c) written words correspond to spoken words, (d) one reads all of the words on a page before reading the words on the next page, (e) pages are read in a specific order from the first to the last page, (f) there is someone (i.e., the author) who had the story in his or her mind and decided to write it down so that children could know the story too, and (g) writing is like speaking because it is a way of communicating ideas (Clay, 1979; Sulzby, 1991; Teale & Sulzby, 1986; Whitehurst & Lonigan, 1998). The advocates of the emergent literacy perspective argue that such ideas are just as important as knowledge of the alphabetic principle for beginning reading.

Whitehurst and Lonigan (1998) elaborated on the original conception of emergent literacy to suggest that it also involves other kinds of skills such as an oral vocabulary, knowledge of syntax, knowledge of letters of the alphabet, metalinguistic knowledge of sounds in words, the alphabetic principle, pretend reading, reading motivation, and verbal processing skills (e.g., rapid naming and verbal working memory). Most of these factors are discussed in the next section, so they will not be described further here.

Predicting Reading Success

Whereas some children enter first grade ready to benefit from formal reading instruction, others do not. This difference, in turn, determines the ease with which children acquire reading skills by the end of first grade. How do the "ready-to-benefit" children differ from the "not-ready-to-benefit" children? Is it possible to predict who will fall into each group using information about children when they are preschoolers? These questions have an obvious practical value for educators and parents. By retracing the steps of the "ready-to-benefit" students, we may figure out how to alter the trajectories of "not-ready-to-benefit" students.

The standard approach to discovering predictive factors is to measure certain characteristics of children when they are preschoolers and see whether these factors are correlated with reading success in the first grade. Correlations can range between −1.0 and +1.0, with numbers closer to −1.0 or +1.0 indicating a stronger predictive relation. If, for example, the number of books in a home is found to correlate $r = .60$ with reading readiness, that means an increase in books is associated with an increase in readiness. However, the fact that the correlation is less than 1.0 means that there may be cases in which there were many books in the home but the child was not ready to read in first grade (and vice versa).

But, as the old adage goes, "correlation does not imply causation." Simply finding a correlation does not mean that one could make all children ready to read by increasing the level of the predictive factor. Continuing the previous example, children's reading readiness would not necessarily go up if the government were to buy lots of books for families that have very few. Other problems with correlational studies include spurious correlations and age changes in the predictive power of certain factors. A **spurious correlation** exists when two variables are linked through some other variable. In effect, the linkage is illusory. To illustrate such a correlation, consider the fact that there is an association between the number of physicians who work in a geographic area and the infant mortality rate in that area (the more doctors there are, the higher the infant death rate). This spurious correlation can be explained as follows. There tend to be more physicians and poor people living in urban areas than in rural areas. The infant mortality rate tends to be much higher among the poor than among the rich, so the infant mortality rate tends to be higher in the cities than elsewhere. Hence, the number of doctors has nothing to do with the infant mortality rate, but a correlation computed between these two factors makes these variables appear to be related somehow. In this case, their apparent linkage is explained by other variables, such as a common geographic area and poverty. Applied to the case of reading success, there are a number of factors that have been found to be correlated with reading success (see below). Before we can understand the differences between ready-to-benefit children and not-ready-to-benefit children, we will first need to determine which of these correlations are real and which are spurious.

Besides spurious correlations, another interpretive problem has to do with the fact that predictive relationships may be more complicated than the "more of X yields more of Y" variety (e.g., more literacy experiences yields more readiness to benefit from instruction). Some activities or skills may be prerequisites for others and fall away in importance as time goes on (de Jong & van der Leij, 1999). The correlation between such prerequisites and later reading scores may be low, but it would be wrong to assume that the factor is not important. Relatedly, some correlations may involve thresholds in which there has to be a minimum level of some experience to have an effect (e.g., you have to read to children at least 10 minutes a day). Any amount over that minimum has no added benefit. When a threshold effect occurs, lower correlations ensue because correlations are only large if an increase in one factor (e.g., minutes read to each day) continues to produce increases in another (e.g., first grade reading test scores) at all levels of the first factor.

With these caveats in mind, we can now look at the list of factors that have found to be correlated with reading success in the first grade in at least two studies. After presenting this list, we will attempt to reduce the number of factors using tests for spurious correlations. Factors are presented in a rank-order, starting with those that (a) have been found to have the highest correlation with being ready to benefit and (b) have the most studies supporting the linkage.

School Readiness.   There are widely-used measures of overall school readiness that tap into a number of component skills such as knowledge of the alphabet, knowledge of numbers, the ability to follow directions, and visual memory for drawings. There are also other more specific measures that are alleged to tap into readiness to read. Five studies found fairly high correlations between overall school readiness measures and first grade reading scores that ranged between .34 and .76. The average correlation across these studies was $r = .62$ (Bolig & Fletcher, 1973; Gordon, 1988; Nagle, 1979; Randel, Fry, & Ralls, 1977). In a related way, twenty-one studies using the more specific reading readiness measures generated an average correlation of $r = .56$ (Snow et al., 1998). Thus, children who had higher readiness scores in preschool showed the highest reading achievement scores at the end of first grade.

Socio-Economic Status (SES).   SES refers to such things as income level and parent education. In their meta-analysis of the correlations between SES and various indices of school achievement, Iverson and Walberg (1982) reported an average correlation of $r = .57$ between SES and reading scores (across eight studies). Other researchers concur that children from higher SES households demonstrate higher levels of reading readiness and emergent literacy than children from lower SES households (Adams, 1990; Bowey, 1995; Baker, Fernandez-Fein, Scher, & Williams, 1998; Snow et al., 1998).

Letter Knowledge.   Starting with Chall (1967) and Bond and Dykstra (1967), a number of studies have shown that children's knowledge of letter names is a very good predictor of their beginning reading achievement (Adams, 1990). Thus, children who enter school knowing that "B" is called "Bee" and "T" is called "Tee" perform better than children who lack this knowledge on end-of-year reading achievement tests in first grade. The correlations tend to hover around $r = .53$ (Snow et al., 1998).

Memory for Stories and Sentences.   Children's ability to repeat sentences or stories that were just read to them is a better predictor of their reading achievement than other kinds of memory measures such as digit span (i.e., repeating a list of numbers that was just called out). Across eleven studies, the median correlation between memory for stories/ sentences and reading achievement was found to be $r = .49$ (Snow et al., 1998).

Concepts of Print.   In the earlier discussion of emergent literacy, we saw that concepts of print involve such things as knowing that one reads from left to right. Across seven studies, the average correlation between measures of concepts of print and reading achievement was found to be $r = .49$ (Snow et al., 1998).

Phonemic Awareness.   Phonemic awareness is the ability to reflect on, manipulate, and discriminate among phonemes. It can be assessed by asking children to delete certain sounds (e.g., "How would *pink* be pronounced if the last sound were eliminated?"), identify the member of a word triad that does not rhyme with the other two (e.g., "dog" in "hat, bat, dog"), tap the number of sounds in a word, and so on. The average correlation between measures of phonemic awareness and reading achievement is $r = .42$ (Adams, 1990; Snow et al., 1998; Tunmer, Herriman, & Nesdale, 1988; Vellutino & Scanlon, 1991).

Language Skills.   Children enter first grade with a variety of oral language abilities. Studies have shown that correlations range between $r = .24$ to $r = .49$, depending on the language skill in question (Hamill & McNutt, 1980; Snow et al., 1998; Vellutino & Scanlon, 1987). Across fifty-nine studies, Snow et al. (1998) report that the average correlation was $r = .38$ between oral language skills and reading achievement in school. Whereas the most predictive language skill was the ability to name a series of pictures ($r = .49$), the least predictive skill was the ability to point to pictures named by the tester ($r = .33$). Thus, it clearly matters whether one uses a measure of receptive vocabulary or productive vocabulary. Researchers have also found that the correlations tend to be higher when one uses an aggregate score of language abilities rather than a single score that represents one ability.

Syntactic Awareness.   Syntactic awareness is the ability to judge the grammatical acceptability of sentences. A child is said to possess syntactic awareness if he or she can tell the difference between an acceptable and unacceptable construction. In most studies, unacceptable constructions are formed by violating word order. For example, a child would be asked to listen to ill-formed sentences such as "Made cookies Mom" or "Why the dog is barking so loudly?" and asked to say whether it is acceptable or not (Bialystok, 1988; Bowey & Patel, 1988; Tunmer et al., 1988). The results of these studies show that the ability to detect grammatical violations as a preschooler tends to correlate about $r = .37$ with first grade reading scores.

Intelligence.   Recall that the readiness construct was partially based on the finding that one could use a child's mental age on an IQ test to predict readiness to read (Adams, 1990; Just & Carpenter, 1987; Stanovich, Cunningham, & Feeman, 1984). While it is true that a child's preschool IQ is correlated with later reading success, this correlation is not as high as the mental age hypothesis would predict. For example, the average correlation between IQ and reading scores for children below the fourth grade is about $r = .45$ (Stanovich, et al., 1984) and the median correlation is $r = .34$ (Stanovich, 1988).

Operativity.   Several studies have shown that concrete operational skills are correlated with first grade reading performance (Arlin, 1981; Tunmer, et al., 1988). The kinds of skills measured in these studies include classification, seriation, and conservation (See Piaget's theory in Chapter 2). The correlations between operativity and reading skills range between .21 and .48 (mean = .33).

Before making too much of any one of these correlations, we need to consider the extent to which they are inflated or even spurious. What we really want to know is whether a predictor remains a strong predictor after one controls for other variables. There are two approaches to test for the unique predictive value of a factor. One approach, called regression, can be illustrated with the following example. Imagine that we gave just two measures to 10 five-year-olds: an IQ test and a measure of their letter knowledge. Then, we came back a year later and measured their reading skills in first grade. The fictional table below shows how the data turned out:

Name	IQ at 5	Letters at 5	First Grade Reading
Matt	High*	High*	Very Good
Ryan	High	High	Poor
Steven	High	Low*	Poor
Chris	Low	Low	Very Good
Tom	High*	High*	Very Good
Kristen	Low*	Low*	Poor
Tiffany	High	High	Poor
Julia	High*	High*	Very Good
Tara	High	Low*	Poor
Amanda	High*	High*	Very Good

If IQ is a good predictor, then every child who has a high IQ at five years of age should be a good reader by the end of first grade (see the data in the top row for Matt). Conversely, every low IQ child should be a poor reader by the end of first grade (like Kristen). The table shows that IQ is not a perfect predictor because only five of ten children show the pattern (Note: children fitting the pattern have an asterisk next to their IQ outcome). Nevertheless, these data would probably generate a correlation of about $r = .30$. As for letter knowledge, a perfect correlation would ensue if every child with high letter knowledge at five was a good reader at the end of first grade and every child with low letter knowledge was a poor reader at the end of first grade. The table again shows that letter knowledge is not a perfect predictor, but seven out of ten children fit the pattern. This fictional data for letter knowledge might generate a correlation of $r = .60$. Comparing the data across the two factors, it is better to know someone's letter knowledge because it predicts success or failure better than IQ. If we had no other information but IQ, however, we would see that it correctly predicts some of the children. But you should also see that when you know both IQ scores and letter knowledge scores, IQ scores add very little new information. The same four children who fit the IQ pattern (Tom, Kristen, Julia, and Amanda) also fit the letter knowledge pattern. So, knowing the IQs for these four children is redundant information. Note further that we pick up three additional children by knowing their letter knowledge (which would have been missed by using just IQ). Finally, note that IQ is highly correlated with letter knowledge (those high on one are high on the other). If we entered these data in a procedure called regression, the procedure would tell us which factors are unique, non-redundant factors and which are merely correlated with the better predictors. In this case, it would say letter knowledge is a unique predictor and that IQ adds no new information beyond letter knowledge.

A second way to discriminate between authentic predictors and spurious predictors is to use partial correlations instead of raw correlations. When a partial correlation is computed, one sees whether the original correlation maintains its numerical value when the effects of other variables that might be involved are mathematically eliminated. For example, let's say that the correlation between letter knowledge and reading achievement is $r = .53$. If this correlation shrinks down to a figure close to zero (e.g., $r = .05$) when the effects of IQ are subtracted out in a partial equation computation, it is probably a spurious correlation. However, if it stays roughly the same size after the effects due to IQ are subtracted out (e.g., $r = .46$), then it is probably not spurious (at least with respect to the variable of IQ).

What happens when regression and partial correlation approaches are applied to the list of nine predictors above? The best way to answer this question would be to assess all nine factors in the same set of preschool children and see how well they read in first grade. Unfortunately, researchers have generally not taken such a comprehensive approach to date. They have, however, assessed three or four of the nine factors in the same study. As might be expected from the size of the correlations reported above, these studies show that SES, letter knowledge, sentence memory, concepts of print, and phonemic awareness all retain their predictive power even when one subtracts out the effects of other variables. In contrast, factors such as receptive vocabulary, syntactic awareness, IQ, and operativity all lose their predictive powers when one controls for one or more of the six factors that are unique predictors (e.g., phonemic awareness and letter knowledge). It is also worth noting that the school readiness and reading readiness measures contain many items tapping into such things as letter knowledge.

Explaining Predictive Relations

How can we explain the fact that SES, letter knowledge, sentence memory, concepts of print, and phonemic awareness all retain their predictive power after the effects of other variables are controlled? The first thing to note is that some of these correlations may still be illusory even though they retain their value after statistical techniques are applied. The only way to know for sure whether a correlation reflects a causal relation between a predictor and outcome is to experimentally manipulate the predictor to see if changes then occur in the outcome variable. The second thing to note is that some of the predictors may be proximally related to reading achievement (e.g., letter knowledge) while others are more distally related (e.g., SES). As noted in Chapter 3, proximal causes are usually answers to the first "Why" question one asks (e.g., Question 1: Why are some children ready to read at the start of first grade? Answer: They have knowledge of letters). In contrast, distal causes are usually answers to the second or third "Why" questions that follow the first one (e.g., Question 2: Why do some children have more knowledge of letters when they start first grade? Answer: They have well-educated parents who taught them letter names).

Our first task, then, is to consider whether any training studies have been conducted to demonstrate a causal relation between the six unique predictors and reading achievement. It is not really feasible to manipulate SES (i.e., it is not ethical to randomly give a high paying job and college education to the parents of children in one group and not give the same things to children in another group) or sentence memory (this may be a fairly stable individual difference trait), so we need to determine whether researchers have tried to teach letter knowledge, concepts of print, or phonemic awareness to preschool children. With respect to letter knowledge, early studies suggested that reading scores do not improve when one provides direct instruction on letter names to preschoolers. However, these studies have been criticized for being too short in duration and for using symbols other than real letters. Later studies that addressed these concerns showed that letter knowledge is both a prerequisite to later skills and a bridge to phonetic decoding (Adams, 1990). With respect to phonemic awareness, a recent meta-analysis of thirty-four training studies showed that interventions designed to increase phonemic awareness regularly lead to substantially enhanced reading skills (Bus & van Ijzendoorn, 1999). As for concepts of print, no experimental investigations seem to have been conducted at this writing (though there are many studies looking at the natural correlates of concepts of print such as preschool curriculum and style of mother-child interaction).

Hence, there is good reason to suspect that letter knowledge and phonemic awareness are causally related to children's ability to benefit from formal reading in first grade. Why might this be the case? With respect to letter knowledge, some have argued that simply knowing letter names is not enough (Adams, 1990). Children who learn to read well are also *fast* and *accurate* in their letter naming; that is, they are highly familiar with this information. As a result, they are free to use their attentional resources to think about other things. In addition, six-year-olds who are fluent in letter names must differ in important ways from six-year-olds who are not. Fluency only comes from lots of repetition. Someone (e.g., a parent or preschool teacher) must present letter names to children in daily interactions and this same person might also engender a budding "emergent literacy" in them as well (Goodman, 1991).

A second possibility is that children who know letter names may use this information to discover the alphabetic principle (Adams, 1990; Treiman, Tincoff, & Richmond-Welty, 1996). In particular, many letter names sound as if a letter is pronounced. For example, the name of "B" is "Bee" and it is pronounced "Buh." Children may exploit this similarity to induce symbol-sound correspondences. Thus, the key to the process may not be letter names per se, but the recognition of the connection between letter names, pronunciations, and the alphabetic principle (i.e., that there is a systematic correspondence between letters and sounds). Rebecca Treiman and colleagues have provided considerable support for the idea that letter names help children come to appreciate the alphabetic principle (Treiman et al., 1996; Treiman, Weatherston, & Berch, 1994). To illustrate one key finding, many preschoolers spell words that start with "w" using "y." The name of "y" is "wei" and this name is close to the "wuh" sound made at the beginning of words like "woman."

The story for phonemic awareness is similar. Children cannot appreciate the alphabetic principle until they can "hear" the component sounds of words and map these sounds onto letters and groups of letters (i.e., graphemes). Early in the preschool period, children cannot say which words rhyme and whether a string of words all start with the name initial sound. To be able to perform these tasks and map sounds onto print, two things have to occur. First, children need to have segmented mental representations of words (Metsala, 1999). In such representations, a sound of a word is stored as an interconnected pattern of component sounds. At first, the phonetic representation of a word is stored as an undifferentiated whole (e.g., bat as "bat"). Over time, it subdivides into components (e.g., bat as "b + at"). The primary factor thought to precipitate these changes is the acquisition of new vocabulary words, especially words that have onsets or rimes that are similar to already-stored words (Metsala & Walley, 1998). For example, when a child already has "bat" stored, her learning of the words "cat," "hat," and "rat" could prompt all these words to be stored as segmented representations with different onsets but a common rime. The second thing that has to occur is that children have to be able to consciously reflect on these segmented representations. In development, many skills start out at the implicit, nonconscious level but eventually become accessible to consciousness (Karmiloff-Smith, 1995).

In sum, then, we now know that training can produce enhancements of letter knowledge and phonemic awareness. Given the paucity of training studies for concepts of print, it is not yet known whether this factor is also causally related or simply a correlate. Whereas future studies can resolve this issue, we may never know the true causal status of SES or sentence memory because these factors cannot be experimentally manipulated.

Nevertheless, the information as a whole permits the following tentative explanation of the differences between "ready-to-benefit" and "not-ready-to-benefit" children. Here, we can appeal to the distinction between proximal causes and distal causes that was alluded to earlier. The three proximal causes of group differences include sentence/story memory, letter knowledge, and phonemic awareness. Children in the ready-to-benefit group have greater sentence/story memory, letter knowledge, and phonemic awareness than children in the not-ready-to-benefit group. Why? Children in the former group have an extensive productive vocabulary that contains numerous segmented representations of words as well as the ability to consciously reflect on these representations. In addition, they have had extensive practice recognizing letters, writing letters, and trying out invented spellings. Further, they have had many stories read to them, causing them to create mental schemata for stories, which in turn helps them to remember stories (See Chapter 2 for more on Schema theory; and Chapter 7 for more on story schemata). They have also been spoken to a great deal and asked to express themselves on numerous occasions. Why would only the ready-to-benefit group have an extensive productive vocabulary, practice with letters, stories read to them, and regular conversational encounters? Because they come from high SES homes. Children who come from high SES homes tend to (a) be exposed to numerous books, (b) have parents who have advanced language skills and who intentionally expose them to letters and writing, and (c) attend high-quality preschools and kindergartens which further engage children in language games (e.g., rhymes and songs) and emergent literacy activities (Snow et al., 1998).

Further evidence of the role of SES comes from several additional sources. Studies of disadvantaged children show that these children have considerable difficulty "hearing" the individual sounds in words as first graders (Adams, 1990; Wallach, Wallach, Dozier, & Kaplan, 1977). One could interpret this finding as evidence that there is a higher incidence of reading disability in disadvantaged children than in advantaged children, or that these children have not had the relevant formative experiences described above. The latter seems more likely, given the success of various tutoring programs that have brought many disadvantaged children "up to speed' in a matter of months (Vellutino, Scanlon, Sipay, Small, et al., 1996). Relatedly, studies suggest that middle-class parents often read to their preschoolers about 10 minutes a day. By the time these children reach their sixth birthday, then, they will have been exposed to 300 hours of book reading (Adams, 1990). Children in low-income homes that do not emphasize reading, in contrast, might accumulate only about 40 hours or less of book reading by the time they are six years old (Heath, 1983; Teale, 1986). Note that the average child receives about 360 hours of reading instruction in first grade (Adams, 1990), which might be enough to get a low SES child, by the end of first grade, up to the point a high SES child was at the *start* of first grade.

Overall, then, we see that the research on skilled readers squares nicely with the research on predictive factors and that it is easy to develop activities to promote important prerequisite skills. The curious thing about the research on predictive factors, however, is the fact that skills such as phonemic awareness and syntactic awareness are not only prerequisites for learning to read, they also seem to *improve* after a child learns to read! That is, children who have been reading for several years (e.g., third graders) show more phonemic awareness and syntactic awareness than children who are just starting to read (Adams, 1990; Stanovich, 1986; Snow et al., 1998). Moreover, having phonemic awareness, syntactic awareness, and insight into the alphabetic principle is a large part of what it means to know how to read. Thus, the research seems to say that children learn to read well in the first grade only if they already know much about reading when they enter first grade (Adams, 1990; Goodman, 1991)! The lesson to be learned from these studies is that reading skills tend to "snowball" over time.

Precocious Readers

It is common for teachers and parents to report that most preschoolers vigorously resist being taught to read. In addition, experimental and informal attempts to teach young children how to read have generally failed when children are below the age of five (Feitelson, Tehori, & Levinberg-Green, 1982; Fowler, 1971). There are, however, documented cases of precocious readers who ranged in age from two to five when they began reading (Fowler, 1971; Goldstein, 1976; Jackson, 1992), as well as a few experimental programs that have been seemingly successful with four- and five-year-olds (Feitelson et al., 1982; Fowler, 1971). If we combine this evidence with the fact that it is often straightforward to teach (non-disabled) working class and middle class six-year-olds to read (Snow et al., 1998), the data as a whole can be interpreted in two ways. According to the reading readiness view, there is a neurological basis to being ready and willing to read. According to a motivational view, the age trends reflect normative trends in reading motivation.

With regard to the reading readiness view, it was noted earlier that well-controlled studies have found that age alone is not a very good predictor of responsiveness to reading instruction when factors related to knowledge and experience are taken into account (Adams, 1990; Bryant, MacLean, Bradley, & Crossland, 1990; Stanovich & Siegel, 1994). Early studies (e.g., Fowler, 1971; Morphett & Washburn, 1931) showed that it was a child's *mental age,* not his or her chronological age that mattered (e.g., a two-year-old who could answer five-year-old questions on an IQ test could learn to read better than a five-year-old who could only answer four-year-old questions). Moreover, mental age and intelligence were soon replaced in later studies with better predictors such as letter knowledge and phonemic awareness. Children are clearly not born with knowledge of letters and they need to acquire a substantial productive vocabulary (through experience) in order to create the segmented, phonetic representations of spoken words that were described earlier (Metsala, 1999). Segmented representations, in turn, are required for creating links between graphemes and phonemes. Thus, a lack of receptivity to instruction could reflect a lack of exposure to relevant information. Similarly, it is no coincidence that precocious readers usually come from affluent, well-educated homes and that four-year-olds who learn to read have unusually high levels of letter knowledge for four-year-olds (e.g., Fowler, 1971).

Thus, it would appear that age constraints on reading instruction reflect the fact that it takes time for children to acquire important kinds of knowledge (i.e., knowledge of letter names and segmented phonetic representations of words). This knowledge, however, must be embodied in the form of neural assemblies (i.e., clusters of neural groups that have formed synaptic connections with each other). In order for neural assemblies to form, there has to be a sufficient number of neurons located in certain regions of the brain that have matured to the point that they can form synaptic connections with neighbors. Studies of brain development suggest that only the neurons in the frontal lobe continue to develop substantially beyond infancy (Byrnes, in press), so the primary temporal constraint related to maturation may well be the time it takes for synapses to form after repeated encounters with the same kind of stimulation (e.g., the sight of a given letter). Conversely, it is possible that skills like phonemic awareness and decoding are subtended by areas in the frontal lobes (Shaywitz, Shaywitz, Pugh, Fulbright, Constable, et al., 1998). If these areas take some time to finish their development, there may be two kinds of factors that explain why it is hard to teach children below the age of four to read: (a) experiential factors (e.g., insufficient exposure to letters and spoken words) and (b) maturational factors (e.g., continued development of frontal brain regions). But again, we cannot discount the potentially important role of motivation. Children who read early have an unusually strong desire to read as preschoolers.

Developmental Models and Trends

In the previous section, we examined reading development from infancy to the point at which children enter the first grade. In this section, we shall extend this analysis somewhat. In particular, this section begins with a description of some general developmental trends in performance. Then, a developmental model of early decoding skill is described.

The general developmental trends can be understood with reference to the model of proficient reading described earlier. In the earliest phases of reading development, children have very little orthographic knowledge but considerable knowledge of meaning-sound relations (i.e., oral vocabulary). Moreover, as mentioned earlier, successful readers also enter first grade with phonemic awareness, syntactic skills, and knowledge of the alphabetic principle. Early reading development consists of putting all of this entering knowledge together with written words; that is, it can be characterized as the progressive acquisition of letter-sound correspondences as well as letter-meaning correspondences.

Because word recognition is slow and effortful at the start, beginning readers rely heavily on prior context to help them guess words rather than read them phonetically. With lots of repeated practice, word recognition eventually becomes automatic, thereby indicating that the connections between words and meanings are firmly established. Whereas prior context and the pronunciations of words are still involved in reading, they are no longer essential for the beginning reader. Rather, they now serve as backup systems to the primary links between the Orthographic and Meaning processors. Thus, children rely more on letter-meaning connections and *less* on prior context and pronunciations with age (Adams, 1990; Snow et al., 1998; Stanovich, 1988). Furthermore, children who enter first grade with phonemic awareness and syntactic awareness dramatically increase these skills as they read more and more. Finally, rapid, efficient word recognition allows readers to attend to meaning more closely and to develop a variety of comprehension strategies (see Chapter 7; Stanovich, 1986).

In addition to these general trends, early reading development can also be cast in terms of Ehri's (1995) phase model. To begin with, Ehri notes that mature readers have at least four ways to read words. For unfamiliar words, they can use **decoding** (i.e., transforming graphemes into phonemes and blending the phonemes into pronunciations), **read-**

ing by analogy (i.e., using already-known sight words to pronounce new words that share letter clusters), and **reading by predicting** (i.e., making educated guesses about words based on context clues or initial letters). For familiar words, however, they tend to use **sight reading** because it is fast and automatic. The goal is to become a reader who shifts from relying mostly on the first three approaches to relying primarily on sight reading. When readers acquire an extensive sight vocabulary, they can allocate most of their cognitive resources to tasks such as accessing word meanings and creating mental models. Sight vocabularies are acquired through extensive reading and repeated exposure to the same words. In effect, connections form between printed words, their meanings, spellings, and pronunciations. When automatic, the sight of a word triggers rapid retrieval of the latter four kinds of information (Ehri, 1995).

After conducting numerous longitudinal studies with young children from the preschool period to fluent reading in the third grade, Ehri suggests that the connection-forming process proceeds through four phases: pre-alphabetic, partial alphabetic, full alphabetic, and consolidated alphabetic. The term "alphabetic" is used to denote the fact that (a) words consist of letters and (b) letters function as symbols for phoneme and phoneme blends in words. During the **pre-alphabetic phase,** "beginners remember how to read sight words by forming connections between selected visual attributes of words and their pronunciations or meanings and storing these associations in memory (p. 118)." For example, they may see the tail of the letter "g" in "dog" and associate it with real dogs, or see the two humps in "m" and associate "camel" with real camels. This phase is called pre-alphabetic because children are not really focusing on letters and their association to phonemes. This is also the phase when children engage in reading environmental print such as stop signs and fast-food symbols. During the **partial alphabetic phase,** "beginners remember how to read sight words by forming partial alphabetic connections between only some of the letters in written words and sounds detected in their pronunciations (p. 119)." For example, they might recognize the "s" and "n" of "spoon," associate these two letters with their names (not their sounds) and retrieve the word spoon based on prior encounters (e.g., the last few times "s" and "n" co-occurred this way, the word was, in fact, spoon). Relatedly, they might recognize KDN as "garden" because "k" and "g" are articulated using the same region of the mouth. During the **full alphabetic phase,** "beginners remember how to read sight words by forming the complete connections seen in the written forms of words and phonemes detected in their pronunciations (p. 120)." For example, in reading "spoon" a child in this phase would recognize that the five letters correspond to four phonemes and that the double "o" corresponds to the sound "u." Finally, in the **consolidated alphabetic phase,** growth in a child's sight word vocabulary produces fully connected spellings for an increasing number of words. After this occurs, letter patterns that recur across different words become consolidated. For example, the connection between the -at in "bat," "cat," and "hat" and the common rime of these words prompts a consolidation of that pattern. Consolidation of many such patterns helps a reader become facile with multi-letter units that correspond to morphemes, syllables, and subsyllabic units. Studies suggest that second grade may be the time when many children's sight vocabularies are large enough to support the consolidation process (Ehri, 1995).

Individual Differences in Reading Skills

If one looks at the reading skills of children in any grade, one will find that some children read well below average, some read at grade level, and some have above-average ability. In this section, we shall explore some of the variables that might account for such individual differences. The first class of variables relate to cognitive processes and the second class of variables relate to demographic factors.

Good Readers versus Poor Readers

Core Differences.   With respect to cognitive processes, there are a number of ways in which good readers could conceivably differ from poor readers. On the one hand, they could differ in terms of general processing factors such as intelligence, working memory capacity, perceptual ability, rule induction, and metacognition. On the other hand, they could differ in terms of reading-specific processes such as word recognition, use of context, phonemic awareness, and comprehension strategies. It turns out that significant differences have been found between good and poor readers for all of these variables (Stanovich, 1980, 1986, 1988). The question is, however, which of these variables seem to most clearly distinguish good readers from poor readers.

Careful reviews of the literature have revealed three particularly important differences between good and poor readers. First, good readers are better than poor readers at recognizing words automatically (i.e., they do not have to pay attention to the decoding process). When word recognition is automatic, a reader can focus his or her attention on higher-level sentence integration and semantic processing (in the same way a skilled driver can drive a car and have a conversation at the same time). However, automatic recognition is most important in the first and second grades because most high-frequency words are automatized to adult levels by the third grade (Stanovich, 1980). Beginning in the third grade, the second and most important difference between good and poor readers emerges: good readers are able to *rapidly* recognize words and subword units (de Jong & van der Leij, 1999). Speed is important because readers need to be able to operate on information in working memory before it dissipates. The third important difference between good and poor readers concerns the ability to recode print items into a phonological representation (de Jong & van der Leij, 1999). Phonological recoding facilitates reading by (a) providing a redundant pathway for accessing word meaning and (b) providing a more stable code for the information that is held in working memory (Adams, 1990; Stanovich, 1980).

At one time, the ability to use prior context was also thought to be a major difference between good and poor readers. After many years of research, however, this proposal turns out to be incorrect. In fact, poor readers use prior context as much if not more than good readers and are likely to make many substitution errors when they encounter an unfamiliar word (Adams, 1990; Stanovich, 1989). Skilled readers rely much more heavily on direct connections between orthography and meaning than on context. Context only exerts an experimental effect on good readers when the text is artificially doctored or degraded. Thus, whereas good readers rely on context less and less as they get older, poor readers do not show a similar kind of decreasing reliance on context presumably because they have so much trouble recognizing and deciphering a word. Of course, this is not to say that context is irrelevant to good readers. As mentioned earlier, context serves as an important backup system to the connections between text and meanings.

Explaining Core Differences.   Why are good readers better at automatic and fast recognition and pronunciation of words than poor readers? From what we know about the nature of skill acquisition and the formation of associations, it seems clear that good readers have had considerably more practice at recognizing and pronouncing words than poor readers. A likely cause of practice differences could be the fact that children are grouped by reading ability starting in the first grade. Children in higher groups are given more opportunities for practice than children in lower groups and the initial gap between groups widens with age (Stanovich, 1989).

But it would also appear that there are fairly stable individual differences in the core phonological processes of reading ability (Stanovich & Siegel, 1994; Torgesen & Burgess, 1998). One study, for example, showed that the longitudinal correlations between phonological processing abilities in successive years in school ranged from a low of .62 to a high of .95 (mean = .81). Hence, it would appear that children's relative ranking in terms of their phonological processing skills remains fairly constant over time. In further support of this claim, another study of disabled readers showed that children who scored at the tenth percentile for phonological skills at the start of school ended up no higher than the thirtieth percentile by the end of fifth grade, even after being provided with remediation services (Torgesen & Burgess, 1998).

The stability of individual differences and apparent intractability of severe reading problems has led many to wonder whether reading skills have a neuroscientific basis. In what follows, we will look at several lines of neuroscientific research to see what they can tell us. To begin with, studies of brain-injured adults have revealed a number of distinct (but sometimes co-occurring) deficits in their reading skills. At one time, the typical approach was to classify collections of deficits in terms of syndromes (e.g., dyslexia with dysgraphia versus dyslexia without dysgraphia). Since the 1960s, information-processing and other psychological accounts have prompted investigators to subdivide acquired reading problems into two general classes: (a) those related to visually analyzing the attributes of written words (*visual word-form dyslexias*) and (b) those related to presumed later stages of the reading process (*central dyslexias*) (McCarthy & Warrington, 1990).

Visual word-form dyslexias include spelling dyslexia, neglect dyslexia, and attentional dyslexia (McCarthy & Warrington, 1990). *Spelling dyslexia* is manifested in brain-injured adults who read letter by letter (e.g., when they see "Dog" they say "D, O, G spells dog"). Such patients may have normal spelling and writing ability, but cannot read back what they have written down. The tendency to spell is a strategy that patients seem to use to overcompensate for an inability to recognize words as units. In most cases, spelling dyslexics have lesions located near the junctions of the occipital, temporal, and parietal lobes (the left angular gyrus). *Neglect dyslexia* consists of omitting or misreading the initial or terminal parts of words (e.g., "his" when confronted with "this"; "wet" when confronted with "let"; "together" when confronted with "whether"). Case studies reveal that whereas the left (initial) portion of words is neglected when there is damage to the right parietal lobe, the right (terminal) part of words is neglected when there is damage to the left parietal lobe. *Attentional dyslexics* can read individual letters quite well (e.g., "A"), but have significantly more difficulty when they have to read individual letters that are flanked by other letters in the visual field (e.g., the "A" in "K A L"). The few patients who have had attentional dyslexia have had large tumors that occupied posterior regions of the left hemisphere and extended into subcortical structures. The rarity of the disorder makes the precise location of damage difficult to specify at present.

In contrast to visual word-form dyslexias, central dyslexias are thought to include reading processes that occur after the initial visual processing of words (McCarthy & Warrington, 1990). The two major types of central dyslexias include reading by sound (*surface dyslexia* or phonological reading) and reading by sight vocabulary (with a corresponding inability to sound out words). Surface dyslexia is a problem because of the abundance of words that defy the rules of regular letter-sound correspondences (e.g., "yacht," "busy," "sew," etc.). Because of their over-reliance on pronunciation rules, surface dyslexics are likely to pronounce irregular words in predictable ways (e.g. "sew" as "sue") and also pronounce phonologically regular pseudo-words quite well (e.g., "blean"). Anatomically, surface dyslexia has been associated with a wide range of lesion locations, but usually tends to involve damage to the temporal lobes in conjunction with damage to other areas.

The second type of central dyslexia consists of being able to read using one's sight vocabulary but losing the ability to read by sound. In contrast to surface dyslexics, such patients are very poor at reading pseudo-words that obey the spelling-sound rules of their language (e.g., "blean" or "tweal"). In addition, patients with the latter disorder may also have difficulty reading function words (e.g., "if", "for," etc.), grammatical morphemes (e.g., "-ed" or "-ing"), or abstract words (e.g., "idea"), and they sometimes make semantic errors as well. The co-occurrence of pronunciation difficulty and difficulty with abstract words has been called *deep dyslexia*. Case studies of such patients reveal no consistent pattern of localization (Warrington & McCarthy, 1990).

The late Norman Geschwind tried to summarize the literature on acquired dyslexias in the form of the anatomical model presented in Figure 6.4 (e.g., Geschwind & Galaburda, 1987). As can be seen, this model suggests that a written word is first registered in the primary visual areas of the occipital lobe. Activity in the visual areas is then relayed to the angular gyrus, which is thought to play an important role in associating a visual form with a corresponding auditory representation in auditory processing areas (e.g., Wernicke's area). Activity then passes from Wernicke's area to Broca's area by way of a bundle of fibers called the *arcuate fasciculus*. If the person is reading aloud, signals are then sent from Broca's area to the primary motor cortex, which controls the movements of the lips, tongue, and so on.

What can be made of the aforementioned findings on the reading problems of brain-damaged adults? Two conclusions seem warranted. First, reading consists of multiple tasks that are performed in concert. For example, there are processes related to (a) perceiving letters and groups of letters, (b) pronunciation of word and letter strings, (c) syntactic processing related to function words and word endings, (d) semantic processes related to retrieving word meanings, and (e) conceptual processes related to the abstract-concrete continuum. Second, these processes seem to be at least weakly modular and redundant (Kosslyn & Koenig, 1992). That is, dyslexic individuals can read some words at least some of the time despite their problems (e.g., surface dyslexics can read phonologically regular

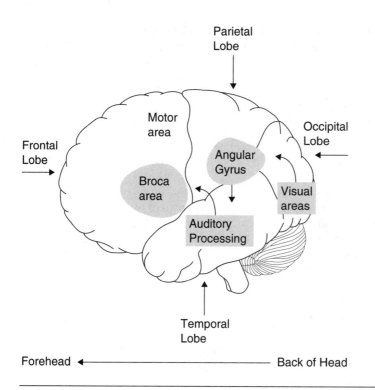

FIGURE 6.4 *Brain Areas Associated with Reading Processes*

words). Moreover, what they can do can overcompensate for what they cannot do (Stanovich & Siegel, 1994).

The findings from studies of dyslexic children (using standard laboratory tasks) and studies of normal adults using PET scans tend to corroborate and extend the findings from studies of brain-injured adults. In particular, a large number of studies have revealed that the vast majority of dyslexic children have the following characteristics: (a) they have a great deal of difficulty pronouncing pseudo-words, (b) they have difficulty on phonological tasks that do not require overt pronunciation, and (c) they show relative strength in orthographic processing skill (Stanovich & Siegel, 1994). Hence, they are more like brain-injured adults who have deep dyslexia than adults who have surface dyslexia.

Given the nature of children's problems, it is not surprising that neuroscientists who study developmental dyslexia have tried to identify morphological abnormalities in areas of the left temporal lobe that seem to be responsible for phonological processing (Hynd et al., 1991). It should be noted, however, that classification systems that are used for acquired dyslexias may not be appropriate for developmental dyslexias (Rayner & Pollatsek, 1989). With acquired dyslexias, there are known sites of brain damage; the existence of damage in developmental dyslexia remains speculative (Reschly & Gresham, 1989). In addition, the practice of superimposing the categories of acquired dyslexia onto individuals with developmental dyslexia can hinder the discovery of the problems and mechanisms that are unique to developmental dyslexia (Raynor & Pollatsek, 1989). Further, it was noted earlier that deep dyslexia has not been associated with damage to particular sites in the brains of adults. If deep dyslexia in adults is, in fact, similar to developmental dyslexia in its manifest symptoms, it is not clear why developmentalists would expect to find abnormalities in particular sites in the brains of children.

Notwithstanding these caveats, Shaywitz and colleagues have recently used MRI technology to determine whether different patterns of brain activity can be observed in the brains of dyslexic children and non-disabled children when they read (e.g., Shaywitz, Shaywitz, Pugh, Fulbright, Constable et al., 1998). Focusing on the regions identified by Geschwind (see Figure 6.4), they found that brain activations differed significantly between the two groups, with dyslexic readers showing relative under-activation in the striate cortex, angular gyrus, and Wernicke's area, and relative over-activation in the Broca area. Whereas these authors suggest that this pattern of activation might be a "signature" for dyslexia, it should be noted that involvement of left frontal areas is also indicative of task difficulty and working memory (Barch, Braver, Nystrom, Forman, Noll, & Cohen, 1997). To show that the aforementioned pattern really is a sign of functional disruption in the reading circuitry, these researchers would need to demonstrate at least two additional things in future studies: (a) that the pattern is not observed in non-dyslexic children who are given a task that is hard for them and (b) that the pattern is not found in non-disabled children who are just beginning to read (who might have as much trouble pronouncing new words as older dyslexic children).

With respect to PET scan studies of normal adults, Posner et al. (1988) and Petersen, Fox, Snyder, and Raichle (1990) have found that passively looking at real words (e.g., "board"), pseudowords (e.g., "floop"), nonwords (e.g., "jvjfc"), and strings of letter-like fonts all activate the same portions of the occipital lobe. However, real words and pseudowords also activate portions of the occipital lobe that are not activated by nonwords and false fonts (the extrastriate cortex). Recall that damage to occipital regions often produces the visual word-form dyslexias that were described earlier. Whereas presentation of real words and being asked to define words activates regions of the left frontal lobe, presentation of pseudowords does not activate these regions. Finally, auditory and phonological processing seem to activate regions of the left temporal and lower parietal cortices, near regions of interest to individuals who study developmental dyslexia.

Collectively, then, a variety of neuroscientific studies have supported the idea that there are specific brain regions associated with orthographic, phonological, semantic, and syntactic processing. Orthographic processing seems to be centered in the primary visual area and extrastriate area. Phonological processing seems to be associated with the superior temporal lobes and the angular gyrus (though Shaywitz and colleagues have also found frontal activation for rhyming tasks). Semantic processing has been associated with two regions in the left hemisphere: the Broca area (frontal lobe) and areas in the medial temporal lobe.

So reading disabilities may reflect some underlying disruption in the normal circuitry for reading. What caused this disruption? At present, it is hard to know because we still do not know for sure whether there is something wrong with a reading disabled child's brain and what the nature of this problem is if the circuitry has been disrupted. A further problem is that there is often slippage in the definition of reading disabled. For example, most school systems assign the label "reading disabled" when there seems to be a discrepancy between a child's intelligence and her or his reading level (i.e., normal IQ but reading two years behind grade level). In recent years, this discrepancy approach has been found to mix together two very different groups of children: those who have an actual reading disability and those who have been dubbed "garden variety" poor readers (Stanovich, 1988). Whereas the latter can be brought up to speed through a short period of intense tutoring (e.g., six weeks), the former cannot (Vellutino, Scanlon, Sipay, Small et al., 1996). Further, comparisons of these two groups show marked differences in their phonological processing skills but no substantial differences in their visual, semantic, or syntactic skills (Vellutino et al., 1996; Stanovich & Siegel, 1994). The key problem here is that the discrepancy approach is not sensitive enough to pick up this phonological core deficit. In addition, use of this approach in longitudinal studies (e.g., Shaywitz et al., 1992), reveals four kinds of children: (a) those who meet the discrepancy criterion at both of two testings (2 percent), (b) those who meet the criterion at the first testing but not the second testing (6 percent), (c) those who are said to be non-disabled at the first testing but reading disabled at the second testing (7 percent), and (d) those found to be non-disabled at both testings (85 percent). If the discrepancy approach were sufficiently accurate, the second group should not appear. After all, a child who catches up after a few years of instruction is probably not really disabled.

In the literature, some researchers have taken pains to make sure that their sample only includes children with authentic reading disabilities. Most others, however, have relied on the discrepancy criteria employed by children's school systems. This difference in definitions makes comparisons across studies difficult. To believe some set of findings (e.g., that dyslexic children demonstrate less blood flow to a certain region of the brain than good readers), we have to believe that the labels applied to children in a given study (i.e., "dyslexic" versus "normal reader") are accurate.

In addition, if the neuroanatomy of reading really is a system of interdependent parts, problems could conceivably arise if something were wrong with any (or several) of the brain regions described above (in the same way that a tight-knit, interdependent baseball team might start to lose if any of its starters were to be injured). Thus, the search for *the* key area of disruption may be misguided. In addition, the idea that there seems to be built-in redundancy in the reading system suggests that more than one area would have to be affected in order for an intractable reading problem to emerge.

With all of these issues of definition and anatomy in mind, we can now examine several recent proposals regarding the etiology of reading disabilities from a more informed perspective. The first proposal arose in response to three sets of findings: (a) a higher incidence of language problems in boys, (b) symmetry or reversed asymmetry in the size of certain brain areas in dyslexic children, and (c) unexpected empirical links between left-handedness, language disorders, and immune disorders (Geschwind & Behan, 1982; Geschwind & Galabura, 1985). To explain all of these findings, Geschwind and colleagues proposed the following. During prenatal development, testosterone levels affect the growth of the left cerebral hemisphere in such a way that an anomalous form of dominance develops. Instead of being right-handed and having language lateralized in the left hemisphere (the most common kind of dominance pattern), affected individuals become left-handed with language lateralized in the right or both hemispheres. This altered physiology, in turn, leads to problems such as developmental dyslexia, impaired language development, and autism. Testosterone levels also affect the thymus, resulting in disorders of the immune system (e.g., allergies, colitis, AIDS).

In early formulations, the elevated level of testosterone was thought to retard the development of the left hemisphere such that it fails to show the typical pattern (in 66 percent of people) of growing larger than the right hemisphere. In later proposals (e.g., Galabura, 1993), however, the suggestion of retarded growth of the left hemisphere was replaced with the idea that something interferes with normal *reductions* in the size of the right hemisphere (e.g., testosterone inhibits the process of cell death). Either way, both proposals were meant to explain the finding mentioned above that 66 percent of dyslexic children tend to have either symmetric brains or reversed asymmetry (right larger than left). The region of particular interest in these studies was the *planum temporale* (located bilaterally at the posterior portion of the superior surface of the temporal lobe). The location of the plana suggested that this region may have something to do with phonological processing, a particular problem for children with dyslexia and language delay.

Although the Geschwind-Behan-Galaburda (GBG) proposal showed some early promise, comprehensive meta-analyses have recently revealed numerous anomalies in the literature (Beaton, 1997; Bryden, McManus, & Bulman-Fleming, 1994). The first problem is that the incidence of reading problems may not be really higher in boys than girls. Boys are simply more likely to be referred for services than girls, reflecting a bias of teachers and other school personnel (Shaywitz, Shaywitz, Fletcher, & Escobar, 1990). Second, studies that have tried to show the three-way relation between left-handedness, immune disorders, and dyslexia have failed to find this relation. Third, the asymmetry of the plana may have more to do with handedness than with language lateralization. Finally, there is no hard evidence that sex hormones affect human brain structure. Problems such as these led Bryden et al. (1994, p. 155) to conclude their review of the literature on the GBG model by saying, "All things considered, we find the evidence to support the [GBG] model lacking and would suggest that psychologists and physicians have more useful things to do than carry out further assessments of the model."

But if the GBG model is incorrect, what else could explain the hard-to-remediate problems of dyslexic children? In other words, if symmetry or reversed symmetry in the plana is not the problem, what is wrong with dyslexic children's reading circuitry and how did it get that way? Several groups of researchers have begun to explore the possibility that reading problems are genetically determined. Studies suggest that 23–65 percent of children who have a parent with dyslexia also have the disorder. The rate among siblings can run as high as 40 percent (Shaywitz, 1996). In a longitudinal study of twins, DeFries, Gillis, and Wadsworth (1993) found that 53.5 percent of identical twins were concordant for reading problems, compared to just 31.5 percent of fraternal twins. Subsequent linkage studies have implicated loci on chromosomes 6 and 15 (Gayan, Smith, Cherny, Cardon et al., 1999).

Although these findings are intriguing, it is important to note that all of the aforementioned studies relied on such things as school records and self-reports to indicate the presence of reading problems within families. It is not clear how many of the children and adults in these studies were truly dyslexic and how many were simply "garden variety" poor readers. Second, estimates of the heritability of reading problems suggest that nongenetic (i.e., environmental) factors account for more than half (56 percent) of the variance

(DeFries et al., 1993). Third, reading problems may not be encoded in a person's genes per se. Instead, there may be a genetic susceptibility to problems in translating genetic instructions into a specific anatomy. Finally, the fact that reading has a genetic component tells us nothing about the nature of the neurological underpinnings of dyslexia. In other words, we still do not know what is wrong with a dyslexic individual's neural circuitry and how it got that way. Moreover, the fact that the concordance rate for reading problems in identical twins is less than 100 percent implies that epigenetic and environmental factors also must be involved.

Gender and Ethnic Differences

Turning now to demographic factors, we can ask whether there are gender or ethnic differences in beginning reading. With respect to gender differences, there is the cultural belief that girls have better verbal abilities than boys. After all, girls talk earlier and tend to be more verbally expressive than boys (Maccoby & Jacklin, 1974; Hyde & Linn, 1988). But do these tendencies translate into an advantage in reading for girls? Surprisingly few studies have addressed this issue. With respect to vocabulary differences, for example, one recent review of studies conducted since the 1960s uncovered only thirteen studies in which gender differences were analyzed (Hyde & Linn, 1988). For children younger than five, the review revealed an average effect-size of .05, which seems to indicate a lack of a gender difference (see Chapter 12 for an explanation of effect-sizes). However, about 40 percent of these studies showed that four-year-old males had slightly larger vocabularies than females and 60 percent showed that four-year-old females had moderately larger vocabularies. Thus, sometimes preschool boys will be found to have better vocabularies and sometimes girls will, but the difference will be small when it is found. For six- to nine-year-olds (i.e., beginning readers), the review revealed just nine studies in which gender differences in vocabulary were examined. Here, the average effect-size was −.31, indicating a moderate advantage for boys. Thus, the cultural view that girls have better vocabularies than boys seems to be wrong.

As for other kinds of emergent literacy skills, the literature is even smaller. Of three studies that examined gender differences in concepts of print in preschoolers and kindergartners, two found gender differences favoring girls (Beach & Robinson, 1992; Rogers, 1987), but one did not (Blatchford et al., 1985). As for letter recognition, only one study was located and this study reported no gender differences (Blatchford et al., 1985). No studies were located that compared boys and girls on their phonemic awareness abilities.

With respect to gender differences in reading comprehension, the review found just two studies of preschoolers and one of these involved disadvantaged children. The effect-sizes for these two studies were .32 and .07, respectively, indicating that female preschoolers have better comprehension skills than preschool boys. For six- to nine-year-old children, the review uncovered six studies yielding an average effect-size of −.14. This average suggests that when children are learning to read, females tend to perform slightly better than males on tests of reading comprehension. However, four out of the six effect-sizes on which this average is based ranged between .01 and .08. Based on such findings, Hyde and Linn (1988) conclude that we should abandon the cultural stereotype regarding gender differences in reading abilities.

A different story emerges when ethnic differences in reading ability are examined. Here, Caucasian students tend to perform substantially better than African-American or Hispanic students. In a study involving first, third, and fifth graders, for example, Stevenson, Chen, & Uttal (1990) found that Caucasian students performed better than African-American and Hispanic students on a non-standardized reading comprehension test in the first grade. By the time these students reached the third grade, the Caucasian students still performed better than the African-American students. For vocabulary, ethnic differences favoring Caucasian students did not emerge until the fifth grade. Over all measures, the effect-sizes ranged from a low of .42 to a high of 1.05 and ethnic differences still remained even after the effects of family income and parental education were removed. In Chapter 12, we shall explore some of the causes and consequences of ethnic differences in reading.

Instructional Implications

Now that we have a sense of the nature and development of skilled reading, we are finally in a position to consider the best ways to teach children how to read. In this section, we first describe some general considerations and then evaluate some current approaches to reading instruction using the information presented in the first three parts of this chapter. After this discussion of current approaches has been completed, you will be asked to evaluate several case studies of approach to beginning reading that are more or less consistent with contemporary theory and research on reading.

General Considerations

As noted in Chapter 1, a powerful way to gain insight into effective instruction is to first chart the developmental trends in some skill and then posit developmental mechanisms that could explain how the child progresses from early levels of the skill to later levels. In this case, how does a child progress from knowing nothing about reading as an infant to having the highly developed and interconnected set of processors shown in Figure 6.2? In other words, how does a child become a fluent reader who can automatically and rapidly decode words, compute syntactic relations, and construct a meaningful situation model? In this chapter, we have seen that the mechanisms include (a) considerable exposure to language and books, (b) drawing children's attention to words, letters in words, and the links between graphemes and phonemes, and (c) extensive practice reading words in context. These activities give children extensive oral language skills, letter knowledge, concepts of print, and phonemic awareness. In effect, the combination of exposure, practice, and effective instruction serve as the developmental mechanism.

Contemporary Approaches

Over the last 30 years (at least), very vigorous debates have been waged about the best way to teach children how to read. These debates have focused on issues such as (a) whether word recognition should be taught via the whole-word ("look-say") approach or the phonics approach, (b) whether basal readers or children's literature should be used to teach reading skills, and (c) whether children's incorrect spelling should be corrected or ignored. Individuals who find themselves on one or the other side of these debates differ in their beliefs about the nature of reading.

On the one hand, there is the *"phonics"* view which emphasizes the systematicity of symbol-sound correspondences. Advocates of this perspective argue that children should be directly taught about the regularities of letter-sound mappings and shown how to identify and blend individual sounds together into a whole word. Moreover, they argue that in order to maximize children's learning of symbol-sound regularities, teachers should explicitly point out these regularities in classroom exercises (Stahl & Miller, 1989). Unfortunately, this assumption has led to the practice of children spending most of their time learning various decoding rules via decontextualized drills instead of using decoding rules while reading meaningful text.

Very often (though not always), teachers who believe in the phonics approach use basal readers. Basal readers contain stories in which the rules for decoding words almost always work for the words in the stories. Moreover, the words are selected from frequency norms to be highly familiar and the sentences containing these words are designed to be short and grammatically simple. The logic behind basal readers is that children will learn to be fluent more quickly by repeatedly reading these artificially-constructed stories.

The phonics approach can be contrasted with the *whole language* view. According to this view, reading instruction should begin in a natural manner using children's own language as a bridge to beginning reading instruction (Stahl & Miller, 1989). At the core of this approach is the idea that children should focus most of their attention on the communicative function of written language rather than its form; that is, children should always be thinking about why the words were written rather than letter-by-letter sound mappings.

With respect to phonics instruction, the whole language view makes four claims. First, advocates suggest that it is nearly impossible to decompose a word down into individual phonemes without losing something in the translation. Each phoneme sounds different when it is part of a word than when it is alone. To see this, try blending the separate sounds for "c," "a," and "r" and compare this blend with the sound made by the whole word. Second, they argue that drills on decoding rules should not be a regular part of every lesson. Rather, decoding help should only be given as needed (e.g., when a child who is reading meaningful text encounters a word he or she cannot decode). Third, advocates argue that there is not a major difference between written and spoken language. Children learn to speak naturally (without explicit instruction on grammar), so they should also learn to read naturally as well (without explicit instruction on decoding rules). Thus, children should be allowed to induce symbol-sound correspondences implicitly as they read the same way that they induce grammatical rules implicitly as they talk to their parents.

In addition, advocates of the whole language view argue that children's literature should be used instead of the artificial stories in (some) basal readers because the latter alter the natural "predictability" of texts. Predictability is important because reading is seen to be a "psycholinguistic guessing game" in which a reader uses prior context, semantics, and syntax to forecast upcoming words. This "guessing game" notion seems to have derived from studies in the 1960s that showed how skilled readers used prior context to help them recognize hard-to-see words.

Furthermore, the whole language view emphasizes children's own writing to help them see that writing, reading, and speaking are all forms of communication. In having children write down their own ideas, they will see that written language is functional from the start. Moreover, writing allows a child to see the cyclic communication pattern that evolves from the germ of an idea: I can think → I can talk about what I think → I can write down what I say → Others can read what I write (which tells them what I think).

Finally, for beginning readers who cannot yet spell or read fluently, whole language teachers often encourage the use of *invented spelling*. The belief is that if teachers focus too much attention on spelling, they teach children to focus more on the form of what they are writing than on the meaning.

Having briefly defined the phonics and whole language methods, we are now in a position to consider how these views are consistent (or not) with the research described in the first three parts of this chapter. Before doing so, however, it is necessary to point out that it is hard to find a teacher who is a "pure" practitioner of either method. Most teachers use elements of both approaches (Adams, 1990; Chall, 1983). Why? The first reason is that the whole language approach gained its initial momentum after many veteran teachers had been using the phonics approach for several years. Rather than abandoning the phonics approach entirely, such teachers merely added certain aspects of the whole language approach to a foundation of phonics instruction. The second reason has to do with experience. Even teachers who are staunch advocates of the whole language approach find that it is often necessary to explicitly teach children how to decode. Thus, the idea that children will acquire knowledge of the symbol-sound correspondences purely by induction has few believers in the classroom.

The third reason is that basal readers have been modified to include more of children's literature than they used to have. To be sure, some of this literature has been "doctored" by substituting familiar, easy-to-decode words for unfamiliar words or words that do not fit the decoding rules. Nevertheless, teachers recognize that one can still follow the basic principles of the whole language approach using the stories in the basal readers.

Thus, it would be hard to find a teacher who practiced the "pure" phonics approach or the "pure" whole language approach. Nevertheless, we can consider which aspects of the extreme versions of these approaches are consistent with the research described earlier.

The primary virtue of the phonics approach is that it focuses attention on individual letters and grapheme-phoneme correspondences. This practice is consistent with the following findings: (a) letter knowledge is an excellent predictor of early reading success, (b) successful readers have phonemic awareness and insight into the alphabetic principle, (c) skilled readers attend to individual letters and letter patterns, (d) skilled readers use phonological information as an important backup system, and (e) good readers primarily differ from poor readers in terms of their ability to rapidly name words and pseudowords out of context. In addition to these findings, we can add that large scale evaluations found that the most successful reading programs always have included explicit phonics instruction (Adams, 1990).

The second set of consistencies derives from the use of basal readers. In particular, basal readers may help readers acquire early skills by organizing specific grapheme-phoneme correspondences together, using familiar words, and using short sentences. By organizing information together, children can identify correspondences more quickly than a natural induction process would allow. By repeating familiar words, children can develop automatic and rapid recognition of those words and thereby be able to attend to the meaning of what they are reading. By using short sentences, children's working memory capacities will not be overloaded. As a result, they will be more likely to construct a meaningful interpretation of a sentence.

What's wrong with the "pure" phonics approach? Several things. In the first place, although the letter-sound connections that develop between the Orthographic and Phonological processors are important, the word-meaning connections that develop between the Orthographic and Meaning processors are much more important. In using isolated drills of letter-sound correspondences, children will not develop the latter type of connections. Second, the largest growth in children's vocabulary occurs when they read new words in context. Because some basal readers rarely introduce unfamiliar words, they stifle children's vocabulary growth. Third, the "pure" phonics approach does not emphasize writing nearly as much as the whole language approach and often does not make an explicit connection between writing and reading.

Turning now to the whole language approach, we can say that its primary virtue lies in the emphasis placed on meaning. As mentioned earlier, there is no substitute for the connections between words and their meanings. Anyone who adheres to the whole language approach will not end up with students who can sound out words well but cannot make sense of what they read. Second, when children's literature is used, children will read new words in context and develop larger vocabularies. Third, when reading-writing connections are emphasized, children will begin to consider authors and what they were trying to convey. Fourth, the Context processor does play an important backup role in the reading process (especially the role of syntax) and the whole language approach emphasizes context far more than the phonics approach.

The final virtue of the whole language approach has to do with its emphasis on invented spelling. Although the whole language theorists are probably right that de-emphasizing correct spelling may help children attend more to the message they want to convey than the form of this message, inventing spelling may play a more important role in helping children gain insight into the alphabetic principle (Adams, 1990). That is, a child can only invent spellings if he or she already knows that letters correspond to sounds.

What's wrong with the "pure" whole language approach? Several things. First, its occasional advocacy of sight-word reading and de-emphasis on phonics instruction is not consistent with the research on the nature and development of skilled reading. Second, the claim that skilled readers use prior context more than less skilled readers has been shown to be incorrect. Prior context is far less important than rapid activation of grapheme-meaning correspondences. Third, the "natural" tendency for children to induce symbol-sound correspondences is only natural for children who enter school with considerable emergent literacy. Children from disadvantaged backgrounds have little knowledge from which to make inductions. Fourth, although invented spelling helps a child gain insight into the alphabetic principle, prolonged invented spelling interferes with the process of forming connections between (proper) spellings, meanings, and pronunciations. A child who always spells "tough" as "tuf" will have difficulty learning to rapidly recognize "tough" when it is encountered in a text. Thus, whereas invented spelling has a place in the context of emergent literacy, it loses its value after insight into the alphabetic principle has been gained.

In sum, then, there are aspects of both approaches that are consistent and inconsistent with the research described earlier. Obviously, the best approach to reading will combine the aspects of both approaches that are consistent with the research. The only remaining lesson of this research has to do with the issues of repetition, practice, and exposure: successful readers have parents who read to them a lot and conversed with them a lot when they were preschoolers. After they learn to read in school, successful readers read a lot in school and out of school. We'll expand on the latter point in Chapter 7.

Case Studies

In what follows, two case studies of instructional approaches to beginning reading will be described. You are asked to use information from the present chapter and Chapters 2 (Theories), 3 (Memory), 4 (Higher-Order Thinking), and 5 (Motivation) to evaluate the strengths and weaknesses of each approach. Moreover, the idea is to think about whether these approaches could serve as powerful developmental mechanisms.

Case 1.   In recent years, "Reading Recovery" has become a very popular program for improving the reading performance of the lowest 10–20 percent of readers in a classroom. It is largely based on the Whole Language approach of Marie Clay (1985) and others. In most school districts, children are placed into the Reading Recovery program if they are identified by their teachers as failing to make sufficient progress after one year of reading instruction (about 10–20 percent of students in some classrooms). Once in the program, children receive one-on-one tutoring until they reach a point at which they can be placed back into standard, small-group reading instruction (i.e., they are "discontinued"). Clay (1985) reports that the method has been highly successful.

As described by Clay (1985), lessons often contain seven activities:

1. rereading books that are familiar to the child;
2. independent reading of a new book that was introduced in the previous lesson; the teacher takes notes on the accuracy of the child's reading (called a "running record");
3. children identifying letters placed a magnetic board (if they still fail to recognize letters);
4. writing of a story (includes phonological awareness training of unfamiliar words in the story);
5. cutting up a story and having the child reassemble it;
6. introducing a new book;
7. reading the new book.

Because it is based on Whole Language philosophy, the Reading Recovery program emphasizes reading connected text, not decontextualized phonics drills. All problem-solving on the part of the child (e.g., how to pronounce a word) is done on-line, as the child reads children's literature.

In a recent study, Iversen and Tunmer (1993) attempted to modify the standard Reading Recovery program to include more systematic phonics instruction than normal to see if this combined approach would be even more effective than the standard approach. After some children had been in Reading Recovery for about fifteen to eighteen lessons and were able to identify at least thirty-five of the fifty-four alphabetic characters used in the third segment of the lesson (see above), they were given instruction on "phonograms." Phonograms are clusters of letters common to groups of words (e.g., "and" for "and," "band," "hand," etc.). Starting with one word (e.g., "and") children were shown how to make one word into another using magnetic letters (e.g., removing the "b" from "band" to make "and"). Each time changes in a word were made, children were asked to say the word and practice changes back and forth.

Iverson and Tunmer compared the performance of children in the standard Reading Recovery program to that of children in the modified program and that of a control group in the regular classroom. They found that children in both of the Reading Recovery programs performed significantly better than children not in these programs on measures of letter recognition, word recognition, print concepts, and phonemic awareness. However, children in the modified program were "discontinued" some fifteen lessons earlier than children in the standard program (i.e., they were remediated faster).

Case 2.   Several years ago, a first grade reading curriculum was devised by a college professor (Patricia Cunningham), a curriculum coordinator (Dorothy Hall), and a first grade teacher (Margaret Defee) at an elementary school in North Carolina (Cunningham, Hall, & Defee, 1991). Their initial strategy was to articulate the major approaches to reading that have been proposed over the last 40 years and distill the sensible aspects of each approach. The result was a year-long curriculum that contained four blocks. The Writing Block began with a 5-minute mini-lesson in which the teacher modeled writing a short piece on an overhead. She thought aloud as she did so, and also modeled invented spelling and writing conventions. Next, children wrote a similar piece and spelled as best they could. After writing three pieces, each child was asked to select the one they wanted to "publish" (i.e., staple it to a folded cover). The teacher worked with each child on revising and editing the selected piece. During the last 5 minutes, children shared their favorite work.

The daily lessons of the second block (i.e., the Basal Block) consisted of children moving from a whole class format (listening to a selection read by the teacher), to a partner format (involving either reading or workbook activities), then back to a whole class format. When in the partner format, one student played the teacher while the other played the student. The basal progressed from six weeks of readiness activities, to four weeks of pre-primer reading, to nine weeks of primer-level reading, to finishing the reader during the last nine weeks of school. Hence, reading became progressively more difficult over time.

During the Real Books block, children were given the freedom to read by themselves or with a partner one of the three kinds of works: trade books (i.e., real books written by children's authors), their own books that they had published, or even stories from their basal.

During the daily lessons of the Working with Words Block, they engaged in two activities: Word Wall and Making Words. In Word Wall, words that appeared in their readings were placed on display on a bulletin board. Five new words were added each week.

Each day, the teacher and selected children called out five words from those on the wall. Each word was then called out and spelled. When words were spelled, each letter was chanted in chorus and children clapped as each letter was read. Next, children tried writing the word themselves, and then tried spelling it aloud using the chant and clap method (to check their spelling). In Making Words, children were given a limited number of letters (e.g., *d, p, s, r, i,* and *e*) and asked to make two-, three-, four-, five- and six-letter words (e.g., *is, red, ride, drips,* and *spider,* respectively).

7

Reading Comprehension

Summary

1. There are both structural aspects and functional aspects of reading comprehension. In terms of structural aspects, comprehension is enhanced when readers have prior knowledge of topics as well as have schemata for narrative and expository texts. In terms of functional aspects, comprehension is enhanced when readers set goals for their reading, construct coherent representations, and employ a variety of reading strategies.

2. With age, children seem to develop both structural and functional competencies that help them process what they are reading. In particular, older children are more likely than younger children to have (a) schematized knowledge of topics, (b) schemata for the different kinds of texts, and (c) knowledge of reading strategies such as inference-making and backtracking.

3. It takes considerable time for schemata to develop on their own. Moreover, older children who are capable of using strategies often do not use them. Instruction which has focused on schemata and strategies has been found to speed up the natural course of events and improve reading comprehension in students.

4. Regular reading has the potential to increase one's reading speed, vocabulary, knowledge, and phonemic awareness. Such changes, in turn, make one a better reader still. In effect, reading skills tend to "snowball" over time.

5. Good readers seem to acquire knowledge, schemata, and strategies faster than same-age peers who are poor readers. Similar to young children, older poor readers have comprehension problems because they lack topic knowledge, schemata, and reading strategies.

In Chapter 6, we examined so-called "beginning reading" and characterized it in terms of Carver's (1973) Levels 1 and 2 (i.e., processing of individual words and sentences). In this chapter, we examine how readers comprehend larger segments of text such as paragraphs (Carver's Level 3). Before proceeding further, however, it should be noted that the distinction between "beginning reading" and "reading comprehension" is somewhat artificial and was made for expository purposes only. Although it has been traditional to characterize the former as "learning to read" and the latter as "reading to learn" (Chall, 1983), this characterization might prompt someone to draw two unwarranted conclusions: (a) that beginning reading never involves the extraction of meaning or information from text and (b) that beginning reading only involves the proper pronunciation of words. Teachers and publishers who have drawn these conclusions have sometimes assumed that young readers do not have to read meaningful text in order to learn how to read (i.e., any text or string of words will do). In contrast, one of the major premises of the Whole Language approach to reading is that any form of reading can, and should be, meaningful (see Chapter 6). The present author shares this view, but notes that certain skills arise in the context of reading full paragraphs and stories that do not arise when single words or sentences are read. The purpose of this chapter is to examine these emergent skills and consider what happens after most children gain fluency in the second and third grades.

In what follows, we shall examine multi-sentence comprehension in four sections. In the first section, the component processes of reading comprehension are described. In the second section, developmental trends in the acquisition of these component processes are presented. In the third section, "good" comprehenders are contrasted with "poor" comprehenders. In the fourth section, the instructional implications of the research on reading comprehension are drawn and several examples of how to implement reading theory in the classroom are presented.

The Nature of Reading Comprehension

A useful way to describe reading comprehension is to first give an overall sense of what it entails, then describe some of its structural aspects, and then describe some of its functional aspects.

Overview

To get an initial sense of what reading comprehension entails, it is helpful to examine the three-way relation between writers, written language, and readers. In the beginning, there are writers who have the goal of creating certain ideas in their reader's minds. To fulfill such a goal, writers ask themselves questions such as, "If I want my readers to have such-and-such thoughts, what words can I use?" Writers choose certain words, phrases, and sentences based on their beliefs about the *conventional* ways to say things and presume that their readers know these conventions. Thus, if the conventional way to state a prediction is to use an "if . . . then" construction and a writer wants her readers to know her prediction, she will use an "if . . . then" construction to make this prediction in print (e.g., "If the economy deteriorates, then Gore will not succeed Clinton as President"). We can say that readers comprehend some written text when they understand what the writer was trying to say (Graesser, Millis, & Zwaan, 1997). In a sense, then, when a reader comprehends a writer, we have a "meeting of minds." Relatedly, we can say that comprehension involves knowing what is going on in some extended portion of text.

In contemporary theories, readers are assumed to achieve this kind of understanding by mentally representing text at five different levels of analysis (Graesser et al., 1997). The first level is called the **surface code** level. Here, readers temporarily store a verbatim trace of some segment of text. How do we know? Studies show that readers can tell the difference between actually presented text and paraphrases, as long as the experimental test items are presented shortly after they read a segment of text. The second level is called the **textbase** level. Here, readers represent the content of text in a stripped-down format that preserves meaning, but not the exact wording or syntax. The textbase may also include a small number of inferences that are generated to create coherence between a pair of successive sentences (see below). The third level, called the **situation model,** "refers to the people, spatial setting, actions, and events" of a mental microworld that is "constructed inferentially through interactions between the explicit text and background world knowledge" (Graesser et al., 1997, p. 167). The fourth level is called the **communication** level. Here, a reader represents the author's communicative intent (e.g., "She is probably telling me this now to throw me off the trail of the killer"). The fifth and final level is called the **text genre** level, because it reflects a reader's ability to categorize texts into different types (e.g., newspaper article, expository text, fiction, and so on). The operation of all five levels is essential for achieving a higher-level or "deep" understanding of text.

One further way to describe comprehension at a general level is to note that textual interpretation is very much a process of creating a **coherent** representation of the ideas contained in a passage or book (Carpenter, Miyake, & Just, 1995; Graesser et al., 1997). Psychologists argue that there are two kinds of coherence: local and global. Local coherence refers to an integrated representation of the ideas contained in a pair of adjacent sentences. Global coherence, in contrast, refers to an integrated representation of ideas that appear across widely dispersed segments of a text (e.g., ideas in the first and last chapters of a book).

Structural Aspects of Comprehension

In Chapters 2 and 3, we learned about cognitive structures called "schemata." A schema was said to be a mental representation of what multiple instances of some type of thing have in common. For example, a schema for a house specifies the things that most houses have in common, and a schema for birthday parties specifies the things that happen at most birthday parties. Besides having schemata for types of objects and events, it has been claimed that skilled readers and writers have schemata for specific types of texts, too. Reading-related schemata are thought to support the ability to create global coherence (Carpenter et al., 1995; Graesser et al., 1997). The two main schemata that have been examined closely are those for *narrative* and *expository* texts, though there are also schemata for genres such as essays. In what follows, we shall see how schemata for specific topics (e.g., houses), narratives, and expository texts help students comprehend and remember what they are reading.

Topic Knowledge. When people read, they bring their existing knowledge to bear on a particular passage. This pre-existing knowledge is often called **background knowledge** or world knowledge by text-processing researchers. A significant portion of this knowledge is said to be represented in the form of schemata. When readers have schematized knowledge for objects and events, they are better able to assimilate the information presented in some text than when they lack this knowledge. In particular, when readers try to process some text, their minds try to find mental "spots" for each successive idea that is expressed in the text. For example, if you are reading a passage that says "Dogs are one of the most common pets," your mind might metaphorically say "I knew that because my 'dog' node is attached to a 'common pet' node by way of an 'is-a' link." But if you next read the line "Dogs were first domesticated by ancient peoples," your mind might say "I didn't know that; let's add that piece of information to my 'dog' schema."

In addition to providing an assimilative base for incoming information, schemata for topics also help readers make inferences when things are not explicitly stated by an author. For example, if you read the line, "The suspect handed Ralphy a bone, . . . " you would probably use your "dog" schema to infer that "Ralphy" is a dog. Similarly, if you were to read the line "Nobody came to Mary's birthday party," you might use your knowledge of people to infer that "Mary" became sad as a result.

This schema-theoretic description of topic or background knowledge has been extended in recent years by considering other forms of declarative and conceptual knowledge that could enhance comprehension. Schemata correspond to an important form of conceptual knowledge (i.e., categorical relations among types of things or events), but there are other kinds of conceptual knowledge that could influence comprehension such as the core principles of some domain (e.g., adaption in the case of biology), causality, temporal relations, spatial relations, mathematical relations, and so on (Guthrie, Cox, Knowles, Buehl, Mazzoni, & Fasulo, 2000). Causality, explanations, and core principles tend not to be modeled via schemata these days. Instead, researchers posit structures such as naive or expert theories in readers' minds, or even connectionist node-link structures (see Chapters 2 and 6 for descriptions of connectionist structures).

Schemata for Narrative Texts.   Authors of narratives attempt to communicate event-based experiences to their readers. In most narratives, there are (a) *characters* who have goals and motives for performing actions, (b) *temporal* and *spatial placements* in which the story takes place, (c) *complications* and *major goals* of main characters, (d) *plots* and *resolutions* of complications, (e) *affect patterns* (i.e., emotional and other responses to the storyline), (f) *points, morals,* and *themes,* and (g) *points of view* and *perspectives* (Graesser, Golding, & Long, 1991).

One tradition within the text processing literature assumes that authors of narratives have schematized knowledge of the above components of a story and rely on this structure to "fill in" the components as he or she writes a particular story (see Chapter 8). It is further assumed that an author does so with the expectation that his or her readers also have this schematized knowledge as well. As each part of a story unfolds, readers rely on their narrative schemata to form expectations as to what will come next. Skilled writers play off these expectations to occasionally surprise readers or "leave them hanging" (as cliffhangers do). Moreover, readers are thought to use their schemata for narratives to help them judge whether or not a story is a good one and also to create a *situation model* of what they have read (see the section "Functional Aspects of Comprehension" that follows or Chapter 6 or Chapter 8 for more on the notion of situation model).

Schemata for Expository Texts.   Whereas the main goal of narratives is to tell a story to entertain readers, the main goal of expository texts is to provide information so that the reader can learn something (Weaver & Kintsch, 1991). Thus, whereas "Snow White" or any of the Harry Potter books are examples of narrative texts, the present textbook or other textbooks in your courses are examples of expository texts.

Just as good writers and readers are thought to have schemata for narrative texts, they are also thought to have schemata for expository texts as well. The two most cited theoretical models of expository schemata are those of Meyer (1985) and Kintsch (1982). In Kintsch's (1982) model, there are three main relations that make up the schemata for expository texts: (a) *general-particular relations* that have to do with identifying, defining, classifying or illustrating things (e.g., "A schema is a mental representation . . . "), (b) *object-object* relations that have to do with comparing or contrasting things (e.g., "Working memory differs from long term memory in that . . . "), and (c) *object-part relations* that have to do with causal relations, how the parts of something are put together, and how the parts work individually and collectively (e.g., "There are three types of memory: short term, working, and long term . . . ").

In Meyer's (1985) model, the ideas in a passage are also said to stand in certain relations to each other. Analyses of many common expository texts show that writers arrange their ideas into five common relations:

1. *collection:* a relation that shows how things are related into a group (e.g., "There are seven types of vehicles on the road today. First, there are . . . ");
2. *causation:* a relation that shows how one event is the antecedent cause of another event (e.g., "The tanker spilled all of its oil into the sea. As a result, the sea life . . . ");
3. *response:* a relation that shows how one idea is a problem and another is a solution to the problem (e.g., "A significant number of homeless people have a substance abuse problem. It should be clear that homelessness will not diminish until increased money goes to treatment of this disorder . . . ");
4. *comparison:* a relation in which the similarities and differences between things are pointed out (e.g., "Piaget and Vygotsky both emphasized egocentric speech; however, Vygotsky viewed it more as . . . ");
5. *description:* a relation in which more information about something is given such as attributes, specifics, manners, or settings (e.g., "Newer oil tankers are safer than they used to be. These days they have power steering and double hulls").

Because these relations pertain to how the ideas are arranged in some text, they are said to make up the **prose structure** of the text. Writers hope that the arrangement of ideas in their readers' minds is the same as the arrangement of ideas in the text.

According to Schema-theoretic models of comprehension, an individual who writes an expository textbook has schematized knowledge of the relations identified by Kintsch (1982) and Meyer (1985) and also knows the conventional ways of communicating these relations. The most common way to prompt readers to recognize a relation is to place sentences close together. When one sentence follows another, skilled readers try to form a connection between them (Carpenter et al., 1995; Graesser et al., 1997). If a writer fears that his or her readers will not make the connection even when sentences are placed in close proximity, he or she can use various *signaling* devices to make the connection explicit. For example, to convey Meyer's (1985) comparison relation, a writer might use the words "In contrast, . . . " To signal causal relations, he or she might use the words "As a result, . . . " Of course, readers do not always need signals to make the connection. Consider the following two passages:

1. "There are two main causes of heart disease. Fatty diets promote the formation of plaque deposits on arteries. Cigarettes enhance the formation of plaque by constricting blood vessels."
2. "There are two main causes of heart disease. First, fatty diets promote the formation of plaque deposits on arteries. Second, cigarettes enhance the formation of plaque by constricting blood vessels."

For most people, the words "First" and "Second" in the second passage are not needed in order to connect the ideas in the three sentences together into Meyer's (1985) "collection" relation. But reading times are enhanced in low-knowledge readers when such devices are used (Graesser et al., 1997).

Over time, it is assumed that readers gain knowledge of the common relations found in expository texts such as collection, causation, response, comparison, and description. In a sense, their minds unconsciously say, "O.K., how is this sentence related to the one(s) that I just read? Is it a causation relation? A comparison?" If the closest sentence does not provide an immediate fit, people read on until they find a sentence that does.

In addition to helping readers form expectations, knowledge of prose structure is thought to help readers comprehend and retain more of what they read (Meyer, 1985; Weaver & Kintsch, 1991). In particular, the five relations identified by Meyer often serve as an author's main point or thesis. Main ideas are connected by one of these five relations and lesser ideas are subsumed beneath this overall relation. People who first encode the main point and then attach additional ideas to the main point demonstrate superior comprehension and memory of the ideas in a passage. People who treat paragraphs as a string of individual ideas show inferior comprehension and memory.

Functional Aspects of Comprehension

In addition to having structural knowledge of topics and the various kinds of texts (e.g., narrative versus expository), readers also need to engage in a variety of on-line processes in order to enhance their reading comprehension (Graesser et al., 1997; Paris, Wasik, & Turner, 1991; Pressley et al., 1994). For descriptive purposes, these processes can be organized into three main clusters: orienting processes, coherence-forming processes, and reading strategies. Let examine each of these clusters in turn.

Orienting Processes.   The first thing that people have to do before they read is orient their cognitive processing toward some textual passage. For example, they need to engage their attentional mechanisms and hopefully motivational components such as interest as well (see Chapter 5 for more on reading motivation). Next, they have to *set a goal* for reading (Pressley et al., 1994). Reading is a *purposeful* activity in that we read things for different reasons (Paris et al., 1991). For example, whereas we usually read a newspaper to find out what is happening in the world, we read spy novels simply to be entertained or take our minds off work. Similarly, sometimes we only want a rough sense of what an author is trying to say, so we only skim the pages for major points. Other times we really want to process everything that an author says so we read every line very carefully (e.g., as when we read a textbook right before a test). Goal-setting is crucial because the goals we set can either enhance or limit what we get from reading. For example, if someone sets the goal of "pronouncing all of the words correctly" but fails to set the goal of "learning something," he or she is unlikely to engage in any of the reading strategies that are described later in this chapter.

Coherence-Forming Processes. Recall that a central goal of reading is to create a coherent mental representation of the ideas in a passage. There are several key processes that facilitate the construction of coherent representations, though *inference-making* is probably the most widely studied of these processes (Graesser et al., 1997; Paris et al., 1991). Readers make inferences in order to (a) elaborate on the meaning of an individual sentence and (b) integrate the meanings of several sentences in a text (Alba & Hasher, 1983). For example, when readers encounter sentences such as, "The man stirred his coffee," many of them elaborate on the ideas presented by inferring that he used a spoon. In addition, when presented with a pair of sentences such as "Joe smoked four packs a day. After he died, his wife sold her Phillip Morris stocks," many readers infer that smoking caused Joe to die. Thus, the two ideas of smoking and dying are integrated together through a causal relation. Moreover, inferences play an important role in the construction of a reader's situation model for the text they are reading. As mentioned above, the principal source of inter- and intra-sentence inferences is readers' knowledge of topics such as "coffee" and "cigarettes." The second source is their knowledge of text structures and genres.

Why do readers make inferences when they read? It seems that a reader's mind is always trying to make sense of what it is encountering. One way of making sense of things is to make the information presented more concrete and specific. So, when people read the sentence above about stirring, their minds naturally ask questions such as, "What kind of thing do people usually use to stir their coffee?" Notice that the inference that a spoon was used is merely probabilistic. People sometimes use whatever is handy such as the handle of a fork.

As to why we make inter-sentence inferences, it is helpful to repeat a point made earlier: It seems that the mind is always asking, "How does this new sentence relate to the sentences that I already read?" When two events occur close in time, it is natural to think that the prior one caused the later one (Bullock et al., 1982; Graesser et al., 1997). For example, by stating the first sentence above about smoking and then the second one about dying right after it, it is natural to assume that smoking killed Joe. Similarly, if one reads "The floor was just mopped. I fell," it is natural to assume that the speaker slipped on the floor. It is possible, however, that smoking did not kill Joe and that the person fell because of something else (e.g., tripping over a bucket). Thus, once again we see that inferences are not necessary conclusions, they are merely probabilistic guesses.

In addition to causal connections, there are a variety of other inter-sentence connections that could be inferred on the basis of one's knowledge. These include inferences regarding (a) the goals and plans that motivate characters' actions, (b) the traits or properties of characters or objects, (c) emotions of characters, (d) the causes of events, (e) the likely consequences of actions, (f) spatial relationships, (g) the global theme or point, and (h) the attitude of the writer (Graesser et al., 1997). Do readers make all of these inferences? It depends on who you ask. Some "minimalist" theorists believe that only causal inferences are made routinely (e.g., McKoon & Ratcliff, 1992). Other more "constructionist" theorists believe that readers usually make inferences related to character goals, inferences as to why certain events occurred, and inferences that establish coherence at the local or global levels (Graesser et al., 1997).

As one further illustration of an inference-based coherence process, note that readers naturally link up a pronoun in a second sentence to a person's name in a first sentence (e.g., "Mary saw the doctor. She said . . . "). Similar to causal inferences, such anaphoric inferences about pronouns are also probabilistic (i.e., The doctor could be a woman). Anaphoric expressions are one kind of class of textual entities called **referring expressions** (Gernsbacher, 1996). Other types include cataphoric expressions that refer to future text elements, and deitic expressions that refer to things in the world. Writers and readers recognize that referring expressions conform to a small set of rules. For example, when a new entity is first introduced in a text, the referring expression usually contains an indefinite determiner (*a* or *an*), a richly specified noun, and a descriptive set of adjectives or prepositional phrases (e.g., *A massive man with a bushy mustache*). The next time this entity appears, however, it usually contains a definite determiner and just the noun (e.g., *the man . . .*).

The final way that coherence is established and maintained is by making use of **inhibition** processes that suppress ideas that are incompatible with the current situation model (Gernsbacher, 1996). When words are read in succession, the multiple meanings of each word are temporarily activated. For example, when people read, "The woman smelled the rose," they temporarily activate meanings such as "thorny flower with soft petals" and "to stand up" when they reach the word *rose*. However, only the former meaning is compatible with the overall meaning of the sentence. To achieve coherence, readers need to suppress or de-activate the inappropriate meanings.

Reading Strategies.   So far, we have seen that readers set goals for reading and engage in processes such as inference-making and inhibition to create a coherent situation model. One further way they enhance their understanding is to apply a number of **reading strategies.** Most theorists argue that a strategy is a deliberate, goal-directed operation that is directed at solving a problem (Bjorklund, 1999). In the case of reading, the "problem" to be solved is achieving a deep and accurate understanding of some text. To say that a strategy is deliberate implies that a reader has some control over it. In other words, he or she intentionally tries to apply it and decides when and where to apply it. The converse would be reading processes that happen automatically or implicitly such as inhibition. Some of the reading strategies that have been investigated include identifying the main idea, summarizing, predicting, monitoring, and backtracking, though there has been some debate as to whether all these processes are under a reader's control (Magliano, Trabasso, & Graesser, 1999; Rosenshine & Meister, 1994). Inference-making has been called a reading strategy too, and there is evidence that it is partially under a reader's control (Magliano et al., 1999). It was discussed in the prior section because it is so central to the coherence-forming processes. Rather than engage in unproductive taxonomic debates regarding which processes are strategies and which are not, it is best to think of strategies and processes being arrayed along a continuum of deliberateness and explicitness, with some being more deliberate and explicit than others. In this section, we shall consider those that are perhaps farther along the deliberateness/explicit continuum than others.

In order to identify the main idea of some passage, readers need to assess the relevance of each idea in the passage and then rank-order ideas in terms of their centrality or importance (van Dijk & Kintsch, 1983). Consider the following paragraph taken from George Lakoff's (1987) book, *Women, Fire, and Dangerous Things:*

> "Most categorization is automatic and unconscious, and if we become aware of it at all, it is only in problematic cases. In moving about the world, we automatically categorize people, animals, and physical objects, both natural and man-made. This sometimes leads to the impression that we just categorize things as they are, that things come in natural kinds, and that our categories of mind naturally fit the kinds of things that are in the world. But a large proportion of our categories are not categories of *things;* they are categories of abstract entities. We categorize events, actions, emotions, spatial relationships, social relationships, and abstract entities of an enormous range: governments, illnesses, and entities in both scientific and folk theories, like electrons and colds. Any adequate account of human thought must provide an accurate theory for *all* our categories, both concrete and abstract" (p. 6).

What is the main idea of this paragraph? Is it contained in the first sentence? The last? The fourth? How do you know? If this were an item from the verbal section of the SAT, one of the questions about this paragraph would ask you which was the main idea. Apart from the practical reality that important standardized tests require the ability to identify the main idea, readers also need this skill in order to construct the prose structure for a text (see the earlier section on "Structural Aspects"). George Lakoff rank-ordered the ideas in his paragraph in a particular way (in his own mind) and he wanted you to get his point about categorization. To say that you comprehended his paragraph is to say that you rank-ordered ideas the same way that he did.

In addition to determining the prose structure of a passage, a second way to identify main ideas is to locate various signals in the text. Sometimes signals are graphic (e.g., italics), sometimes they are lexical (e.g., using the word "essential"), and sometimes they are semantic (e.g., explicit topic sentences). Readers expect that the main idea will occur early in a paragraph, but location is not always a very good predictor. In fact, studies have shown that as few as 25 percent of children's textbooks have main ideas located near the beginning of paragraphs (Garner, 1987). Thus, it may be a better idea to rely on prose structure relations and prior knowledge rather than text signals to find the main idea.

Besides being central to comprehension, an additional reason why identifying the main idea is an important strategy is that it is a prerequisite skill for performing the second important reading strategy: *summarizing.* In order to create a summary, you need to be able to delete unimportant ideas and retain just the "gist" of what is written. The gist, in turn, is comprised mostly of the main ideas.

To see this, consider the five rules for forming a good summary proposed by Brown and Day (1983). The first two rules specify that readers should delete trivial, irrelevant, or redundant information. The third rule suggests that readers should find a superordinate term for members of a category (e.g., "cars" for Buick, Dodge, and Toyota). Rules four and five specify that readers should find and use the main ideas of a passage in their summary. If main ideas are not explicitly provided by an author, readers should construct their own main ideas. Thus, one could not construct a good summary without being able to identify main ideas.

The third important reading strategy is *predicting*. Predicting consists of simply forming expectations regarding what will happen next in a narrative story or anticipating what the author of an expository text will say next. Good writers are skilled at helping readers make predictions and also good at violating expectations in such a way that it is entertaining. To illustrate, consider the following passage taken from the book *Dave Barry Slept Here* written by columnist Dave Barry in 1989:

> "While the United States was struggling to get out of the Depression, the nations of Europe were struggling to overcome the horror and devastation and death of World War I so they could go ahead and have World War II. By the 1930s everybody was just about ready, so Germany, showing the kind of spunky 'can-do' spirit that made it so popular over the years, started invading various surrounding nations. Fortunately these were for the most part *small* nations, but Germany's actions nevertheless alarmed Britain and France, which decided to strike back via the bold and clever strategy of signing agreements with Adolf Hitler" (p. 117).

Dave Barry's sarcasm works well because readers expect him to say one thing and he frequently says another.

The fourth reading strategy is called *comprehension monitoring*. Simply put, comprehension monitoring is the ability to "know when you don't know;" that is, it is the ability to detect a comprehension failure (Markman, 1981). As was discussed in Chapter 6, reading does not consist of simply knowing how to sound out words. Rather, reading consists of extracting meaning from texts. If a portion of a text does not make sense, readers should recognize that the main goal of reading (i.e., extracting meaning) has not been met.

When readers recognize that something that they just read does not make sense, they have two options: (a) they could say, "Oh well! Let's just read on!", or (b) they could decide to do something about their comprehension failure. The latter option brings us to our fifth and final strategy, *backtracking*. Backtracking consists of rereading a portion of a text when a comprehension failure occurs. Garner (1987) suggests that readers backtrack in response to four judgments and beliefs:

1. They do not understand or remember what they just read.
2. They believe that they can find the information needed to resolve the difficulty in the text.
3. The prior material must be scanned to locate the helpful information.
4. Information from several prior sentences may need to be combined and manipulated to resolve the comprehension problem.

Summary

In contemporary reading theories, it is assumed that reading comprehension is greatly aided when readers (a) set goals for understanding, (b) have declarative and conceptual knowledge of the topic, (c) have structural knowledge of the different types of texts (i.e., narrative and expository), and (d) employ a variety of on-line processes such as inference-making, inhibition, identifying the main idea, summarizing, predicting, monitoring, and backtracking. In the next two sections, we shall examine the extent of these structural and functional capabilities in older and younger readers and in more skilled and less skilled readers.

Developmental Trends in Reading Comprehension

To summarize the development of reading comprehension skills, we shall first examine the research concerned with developmental differences in children's schemata, then examine developmental research related to reading strategies, and finally examine research related to the role of extensive reading in the development of reading skills.

Development in Structural Knowledge

In discussing the development of schemata and other kinds of knowledge, one asks questions such as "How do the schemata of younger children differ from those of older children?" and "Do older children have more conceptual knowledge than younger children?" In what follows, we shall attempt to answer such questions by focusing first on the research on the development of knowledge of specific topics, then on the developmental research on schemata for stories, and finally on the research on the development of schemata for expository texts.

Topic Knowledge.   In Chapter 2, we learned that children's knowledge for various topics (e.g., "animals," "fractions," "baseball," etc.) is arranged into schemata. Thus, their knowledge of "birds" might be represented by a node for "bird" connected to a node for "canary" by an "is-a" link, and so on. With age, experience, and increased education, children's schemata for various topics become more and more elaborate. Relatedly, other forms of conceptual and declarative knowledge increase with age as well (Case, 1998). As we will see several times, this increased topic knowledge greatly facilitates children's comprehension.

Story Schemata.   Although several theoretical models of schemata for stories have been proposed over the years (Graesser et al., 1991), the models that have generated the most developmental research are those based on the Story Grammars proposed by Mandler and Johnson (1977) and Stein and Glenn (1979). In Stein and Glenn's (1979) classic account, a Story Grammar is a theoretical description of what most stories have in common. It is not intended to reflect an actual knowledge structure in a young reader's mind. Rather, it is a representation of an *expert's* knowledge of what all stories have in common (Stein,

1982). To get a sense of the formal, abstract character of a Story Grammar, consider the following example: If an adult were to sign up for a writing workshop to learn how to write a book for children, he or she would probably be presented with some form of a Story Grammar by the workshop leader. The workshop leader would say things like, "Any successful story has seven parts. The first part is . . . "

Although children do not start out with a formal, explicit Story Grammar in their minds, it has often been said that they do develop *story schemas* in response to listening to and reading many stories. A story schema contains personalized, implicit knowledge about what most stories have in common (Stein, 1982). Given the personalized nature of story schemas, any two children could develop different story schemas if they listened to very different types of stories during their lives. However, as children read more and more stories and gain increased knowledge about people, their story schemas should become more similar to a formal Story Grammar.

The original Story Grammar proposed by Stein and Glenn (1979) specified that stories have seven main components: (a) a *major setting* that includes the introduction of characters (e.g., "Once upon a time, there was a beautiful young woman called Cinderella . . . "), (b) a *minor setting* that includes a description of the story context (e.g., "She lived in a castle with her stepmother . . . "), (c) *initiating events* that include changes in the environment or things that happen to main characters (e.g., "One day, the prince invited everyone to a ball . . . "), (d) *internal responses* that include the characters' goals, plans, and thoughts that arise in response to the initiating events (e.g., "Cinderella said, 'Oh, I want to go to the ball too!'"), (e) *attempts* that include the character's actions to fulfill the goal (e.g., "So she started to fix an old gown to make it more presentable . . . "), (f) *direct consequences* that specify whether the goal was attained (e.g., "But her stepmother made her clean the castle instead of fixing her gown . . . "), and (g) *reactions* that include the character's feeling or thoughts about the direct consequences (e.g., "When it came time to go to the ball, Cinderella was sad because she could not go . . . "). The first two elements are usually grouped together to form what is called the "Setting" part of a story and the last five elements are grouped together to form what is called the "Episode" part of the story. Hence, prototypical stories contain both a setting and at least one episode.

Research has shown that when stories conform to the canonical structure specified above (i.e., they have all seven of the components arranged in the same order as above), few developmental differences emerge. In particular, even four- and five-year-olds show good recall of the events in a story when it has all of the components outlined in Stein and Glenn's Story Grammar. Older children do, however, recall more information in the story than younger children and also make more inferences than younger children. The majority of these inferences seem to be attempts to fill in category information that was missing in the actual text (Stein, 1982). For example, if the "reaction" portion of a story was missing, older children tend to fill in this component by way of inference. In addition, some studies suggest that whereas children are likely to recall the action elements of a story schema (part of the "attempts" node), adults are more likely to recall internal responses such as a protagonist's goals and the events that initiated these goals (van den Broek, Lorch, & Thurlow, 1996).

When non-canonical stories are used, developmental differences become even more pronounced. For example, when a story is artificially disorganized (e.g., the "initiating event" occurs after the "direct consequence"), older children are more able to recover the canonical structure of the story in their re-tellings than younger children (Stein, 1982). Similarly, when children are given the initial portions of a story and asked to complete it, older children are more likely than younger children to add the components that the Story Grammar would suggest are missing (Eckler & Weininger, 1989). Finally, when presented with stories that are missing some of the components specified in the Story Grammar (e.g., "direct consequences"), older readers (who have well-developed story schemas) are more likely than young readers to say that the story was not a good one (Stein & Policastro, 1984).

Thus, developmental differences are most pronounced when children are asked to comprehend a story that does *not* conform to a Story Grammar. It would seem that a canonical story minimizes the amount of processing that has to be done in order for the story to be comprehended. The argument is that this minimization would only occur if children had something like a story schema in their minds. Since older children tend to have greater processing capacity than younger children, the former can take a non-canonical story and mentally fill in components or re-arrange them to make it into a more canonical story.

In sum, then, story schemas have been thought to play two important roles. First, they minimize the processing that has to occur when a story is read. When presented with a canonical story, readers need not devote all of their mental resources to comprehending the basic facts in the story. Instead, readers can use any additional processing resources to perform other mental tasks such as inference-making (Stein, 1982) and metaphor comprehension (Waggoner, Meese, & Palermo, 1985). Second, story schemas set up expectations as to what will occur next in a story. For example, if the "initiating event" component has just occurred in a story, readers tend to expect that the "internal response" component will be encountered soon. Although older students can make better use of the two roles played by story schemas than younger students, even preschoolers seem to have a rudimentary story schema. In most cases, however, it is necessary to use auxiliary pictures and probing questions to reveal a story schema in children below the age of six (Shapiro & Hudson, 1991).

Many school systems have incorporated the Story Grammar model into their reading curriculum. In fact, it is often the case that teachers frequently ask students to identify the parts of a story that they just read (e.g., "Who can tell me what the setting is? What is the initiating event? etc."). Thus, students learn the parts and then get lots of practice finding the parts in actual stories. If Schema theory is correct that the mind "naturally" abstracts common elements on its own, perhaps this explicit instruction would not be necessary. And yet, at the very least, we would expect that this practice would certainly help students acquire a story schema faster than they would on their own. Research supports this expectation, especially for younger students or students with disabilities (Dimino, Taylor, & Gersten, 1995; Leslie & Allen, 1999; Pressley, Johnson, Symons, McGoldrick, & Kurita, 1989).

Schemata for Expository Texts.   In its purest form, a developmental study of prose structure would take groups of children at two ages and give them well-organized and poorly-organized expository passages to recall (e.g., Danner, 1976). In such a study, one could examine (a) whether older children are more likely than younger children to "use the author's prose structure" to help their recall (i.e., to find the author's main thesis and use it to organize their recall of subordinate ideas), (b) whether older children are less likely than younger children to need explicit text signals to derive the prose structure, and (c) whether older children are more likely than younger children to derive the prose structure in poorly organized passages. All of these findings would support the idea that, with age and increased reading opportunities, children acquire schemata for expository texts.

Unfortunately, such "pure" developmental studies are hard to find. Instead of using multiple age groups, many researchers have used just one age group. In addition, many researchers seemed to be more interested in reading ability than age because when they compared children of two age groups, they usually added reading ability as a variable (e.g., they compared fifth grade, poor comprehenders to third grade, good comprehenders). Further, many researchers provided instruction on how to derive prose structure to see if children's comprehension could be improved. As a result, few of the existing studies can be used to say whether children "naturally" acquire schemata for expository texts simply by reading many of them (as seems to be the case for story schemas).

Nevertheless, the existing research suggests that the derivation of prose structure is often not an easy task for children at any age. Meyer, Brandt, and Bluth (1980), for example, found that when given four well-organized passages to remember, only 22 percent of ninth graders consistently used the strategy of using the author's main thesis to organize their recalls. More than 50 percent of these students failed to use the strategy even once. As a result, even the best readers recalled 70 percent or fewer of the ideas in the passages. Similarly, Zinar (1990) found that fifth graders only recalled about 20–25 percent of the content of short prose passages, suggesting that they too failed to use the prose structure to guide their recall.

This is not to say, however, that children's performance is always so deficient. For example, Garner et al. (1986) found excellent knowledge of prose structure in a group of seventh graders. In particular, 75 percent could provide a meaningful description of a paragraph, 98 percent could exclude topically unrelated sentences from a paragraph, 87 percent knew where to place a topic sentence in a paragraph, and 87 percent could arrange a set of sentences into a cohesive whole. Similarly, Spires, Gallini, and Riggsbee (1992) found that fourth graders in a control group recalled 60 percent or more of the content of expository passages arranged in the form of problem/solution or compare/contrast formats.

The finding that children can perform both extremely well and extremely poorly suggests that something other than schemata for expository texts might be at work. One possible explanation for such variable performance is children's knowledge of the passage topic (Roller, 1990). For very familiar passages, being aware of common formats such as "problem/solution" or "compare/contrast" may add little to one's knowledge of the topic. That is, a reader might show excellent comprehension of a familiar passage even when he or she lacks knowledge of common formats (i.e., lacks a schema for expository passages). For example, a young child who is enthralled by dinosaurs might show very good comprehension of a passage about the extinction of dinosaurs even though this child lacks knowledge of the format in which the ideas are arranged (e.g., "causal" relations). Conversely, a reader may show very poor comprehension of an unfamiliar passage even when he or she knows common formats. For example, an adult who is unfamiliar with computers but familiar with "compare/contrast" formats might show poor comprehension of a passage about the similarities and differences between two kinds of computers.

If both prior knowledge and schemata for expository texts affect comprehension, the effects of schemata for expository texts should be most pronounced when readers are only moderately familiar with a topic. In reviewing the literature on prose structure, Roller (1990) found two findings in support of this notion: (a) presenting disorganized paragraphs has its strongest effects when readers are moderately familiar with the topic and (b) providing instruction of the different types of prose structures (e.g., "problem/solution" and so on) has its strongest effects when readers are moderately familiar with a topic. When readers are either very unfamiliar or very familiar with a topic, these effects are considerably weaker.

In sum, then, there is evidence that children in the later grades have at least implicit knowledge of various prose structures. Whether or not they make use of these structures to aid their comprehension and recall seems to depend on their familiarity with a topic. Because most studies in this area have neither controlled for familiarity nor used a "pure" developmental design, it is hard to say what the "natural" developmental course of schemata for expository texts is. Nevertheless, a number of studies have shown that when children are told about the various types of relations in prose passages and asked to identify these relations (e.g., "Look at this paragraph. Where is a collection relation? How about a cause-effect relation?" etc.), they show improved comprehension. So, just as teaching Story Grammar elements can help improve children's comprehension of stories, so can teaching them the common expository help them comprehend expository passages better. But given the role of familiarity, it would make sense that pointing out expository relations should only be done when the passage contains content that is moderately familiar to students. It would be a waste of time for content that is either highly familiar or highly unfamiliar. One way a teacher could check the familiarity of a topic is to have students generate a group concept map or "web" prior to reading (Guthrie et al., 2000). Here, students would say everything they know about a topic and the teacher would depict this knowledge using a node-link schema on the board.

Development in Functional Aspects of Reading

In what follows, the developmental research on orienting processes, coherence-forming processes, and reading strategies will be described in turn.

Orienting Processes.   Research shows that young children do not set optimal reading goals for themselves. For example, instead of reading something to increase their knowledge about the topic or be entertained, young readers say that the goal of reading is to "pronounce all of the words properly." Other students act as if their goal is to simply "get the assignment done" (Paris et al., 1991; Paris, Byrnes, & Paris, in press). With these goals, students who read all words properly and finish reading an assigned passage will not be bothered if they fail to comprehend what they read. Over time children replace their suboptimal goals with more appropriate ones regarding meaning. Typically, however, this shift takes too many years to complete. It should be clear that teachers need to help students set more appropriate goals for themselves early on in the elementary grades.

Coherence-Forming Processes.   Given the fact that (a) declarative and conceptual knowledge underlies inference-making and (b) declarative and conceptual knowledge increases with age, it should not be surprising to learn that many studies have found that children in the later grades (i.e., fourth, fifth, and sixth grades) are more likely to make inferences than children in the earlier grades (Paris et al., 1991; van den Broek, 1989). For example, when reading the sentence, "The soldier stirred his coffee," older students are more likely than younger students to infer that the soldier used a spoon (Paris, 1978).

But the common finding of developmental differences in inference-making should not imply that younger children are incapable of making inferences. Recent studies have shown that young children demonstrate very good inference-making skills when they are presented with stories about very familiar topics or are given instruction on how to make inferences (Dewitz, Carr, & Patberg, 1987; Paris et al., 1991; Wasik, 1986). Thus, the "natural" course of inference-making can be altered by way of instruction or by using highly familiar content.

One good way of eliciting inferences is to stop in the middle of stories whenever an inference is required and ask questions. For example, when students read the popular "Miss Nelson" stories (about a teacher named Miss Nelson), they need to make the inference that a mean substitute teacher in the story named "Viola Swamp" is really Miss Nelson in disguise. Throughout the book, subtle clues are left to help readers make this connection. Young readers usually miss these clues, so it would be helpful to ask questions such as "What is Viola Swamp's dress doing in Miss Nelson's closet?" Given the centrality of explanations in the comprehension process, "why" questions would also be extremely helpful (Magliano et al., 1999). Over time, repeated questions that require inferences would ultimately help children make inferences on their own. However, since older students seem to make inferences without much prompting, focused instruction on inference-making might be best for kindergartners through fourth graders. The combination of knowledge growth, teacher guidance, and changing goals for reading (see above) should lead to the spontaneous tendency to generate inferences.

Other kinds of coherence-forming processes besides inference-making (e.g., anaphora and inhibition) have received very little attention from developmentalists. At present, for example, there appears to be only one developmental study of the role of inhibition in reading, and this study found that (a) seventh graders demonstrated a greater ability to inhibit distracting information than fifth graders and (b) the ability to inhibit irrelevant information was strongly related to reading comprehension scores (Kipp, Pope, & Digby, 1998). Why age changes in inhibition might occur is still something of a mystery. Some have speculated it has to do with the development of the frontal lobes (Dempster, 1992), but connectionist modeling studies suggest it may have to do with the elaboration of neural nets associated with the reading system (e.g., the addition of inhibitory connections; see Chapter 2).

Reading Strategies.   Children in the elementary grades have difficulty recognizing, recalling, and constructing the main idea in passages (Baumann, 1981; Johnston & Afflerbach, 1985; Paris et al., 1991). Moreover, there is evidence that this skill improves throughout the adolescent and early adult years. Once again, however, the identification of main ideas is more likely when familiar content is used (Sternberg, 1985) and when students are directly taught how to perform this strategy (e.g., Baumann, 1984).

As might be expected given the findings for identifying the main idea, there are clear developmental trends in the ability to provide a good summary. Whereas younger students (e.g., fifth graders) tend to create summaries by simply deleting statements and using the author's words, older students (e.g., high school students) tend to combine and reorganize ideas using their own words (Brown & Day, 1983; Paris et al., 1991; Taylor, 1986).

As was found for both inference-making and identifying the main idea, however, preadolescent children can be taught how to provide a good summary (Brown, Day, & Jones, 1983; Rinehart, Stahl, & Erickson, 1986; Palinscar & Brown, 1984). In the Rinehart et al. (1986) study, for example, children were taught four rules for summarizing over the course of five one-hour lessons: identify the main information, delete trivial information, delete redundant information, and relate main and supporting information. The teacher modeled each strategy and then asked students to practice the modeled strategy. They worked first at the paragraph level, and then moved up to combining paragraph summaries into a single summary for the whole text. When training was over, the researchers found that trained children showed better memory for what they read than untrained children.

With respect to predicting, studies have shown that although many students do not spontaneously make predictions when they read, they can be taught to do so. In support of the claim that good comprehenders make predictions when they read, these studies also show that children's reading comprehension improves after being told how to make predictions (Fielding, Anderson, & Pearson, 1990; Hansen & Pearson, 1983; Palinscar & Brown, 1984; Pearson & Fielding, 1991).

One way to improve student predictions is to have them first look at the cover of a book and make a prediction about what the book will be about after examining the title and cover illustration (Pressley et al., 1994). Then, in the midst of reading the work, children can be asked to stop and make additional predictions as they read. Finally, after the reading is completed, children can be asked to examine their original predictions to see whether they were right or not. Pressley and his colleagues have shown that whereas first graders need a lot of prompting to make such predictions, older students need much less prompting after three years of such instruction.

As noted previously, the essence of reading comprehension is the extraction of meaning; that is, one reads *in order to* gain an understanding of a story or some topic area. If students read a story or an informational passage and do not come away with a good understanding of what they read, that means that they did not attain the central goal of reading (Baker & Brown, 1984; Paris et al., 1991). If it were to be found that many children do not detect their comprehension failures or do not try to fix a comprehension failure when it occurs, that would mean that reading instruction is seriously deficient. To see this, consider an analogy. What would we think about a vocational school that constantly produced car mechanics who could not detect or repair problems with a malfunctioning automobile? Just as the essence of car repair involves knowing the difference between a well-functioning and malfunctioning car (and knowing how to fix the latter), the essence of reading is knowing the difference between adequate and inadequate comprehension (and knowing how to fix the latter).

Unfortunately, many studies have shown that children in the early elementary and middle school years have difficulty detecting their own comprehension failures (Baker &

Brown, 1984; Garner, 1987; Paris et al., 1991). For example, in a classic study, Markman (1979) showed how even sixth graders can fail to detect logical inconsistencies in expository passages. In one passage, several lines pointed out that there is no light at the bottom of the ocean and that it is necessary to have light in order to see colors. After these lines were presented, the very next line stated that fish who live at the bottom of the sea use color to select their food. Even with explicit instructions to find such problems in passages, a sizeable number of sixth graders could not find them. This finding has been replicated many times using similar materials with other age groups (e.g., Baker, 1984).

Overall, the developmental research on monitoring has revealed the following trends: (a) in the elementary grades and somewhat beyond, children often operate on "automatic pilot" when they read and seem oblivious to comprehension difficulties (Duffy & Roehler, 1987); (b) whereas younger readers tend to use a single standard for judging the meaningfulness of what they have read (e.g., problems with a single word), older readers use multiple standards for judging meaningfulness and consistency (Baker, 1984; Garner, 1981); and (c) older students are more likely to construct coherent representations of texts and benefit from instruction that helps them form such representations (Paris et al., 1991).

In her review of the literature, Garner (1987) argued that backtracking develops substantially between the sixth and tenth grades. There are at least three reasons why younger readers tend not to re-read a portion of text: (a) they sometimes think that it is "illegal" to do so, (b) they may not realize that they have a comprehension problem (see the prior paragraph on "monitoring"), and (c) they are often unfamiliar with text structure and cannot, therefore, use text structure to help guide their search for clarifying information. In addition, since many young readers think that the goal of reading is not to construct meaning but to "sound out words properly," they would not be troubled by a comprehension failure (Paris et al., 1991). Thus, if some meaningless portion of a text were sounded-out properly, there is no need to re-read it.

The Role of Extensive Reading

Studies have consistently shown that students who read frequently tend to have higher scores on reading achievement tests than students who read less frequently (e.g., Cipielewski & Stanovich, 1992; Greany, 1980; Greany & Hegarty, 1987; Nell, 1988; Walberg & Tsai, 1984). How should this finding be interpreted? One approach would be to accept the correlation at face value, assume a causal relationship between frequent reading and reading achievement, and infer that a good way to raise test scores is to have students read more often. Another approach, however, would be to examine the evidence more critically before drawing any instructional implications from it. The latter approach is adopted here.

The first way to critically evaluate the link between frequent reading and reading development is to ask, "Is the correlation credible?" As noted in Chapter 6, a good way to assess the credibility of a correlation is to see if it is spurious. Could the correlation between frequent reading and elevated reading scores be due to some other variable that tends to be associated with both frequent reading and high test scores? One obvious "other variable" would be reading ability (Cipielewski & Stanovich, 1992). Motivation theorists recognize that people are more likely to engage in some activity if they feel self-efficacious (see Chapter 5). Moreover, they have shown that talented individuals tend to feel more self-efficacious than their less talented peers. If so, then it would be expected that good readers would tend to read more than poor readers. In addition, good readers, by definition, have higher test scores than poor readers. Hence, it is entirely possible that the correlation between frequent reading and reading achievement is spurious.

As noted earlier, researchers determine whether correlation is spurious by seeing if it maintains its numerical value when the effects of other variables that might be involved are mathematically eliminated. Studies have shown that the correlation between frequent reading and reading achievement does shrink somewhat when the effects of reading ability and other possible factors (e.g., socio-economic status) are subtracted out, but it does not shrink to zero (Anderson, Wilson, & Fielding, 1988; Cipielewski & Stanovich, 1992; Heyns, 1978; Taylor, Frye, & Maruyama, 1990; Walberg & Tsai, 1984). Thus, the correlation between frequent reading and higher test scores does not appear to be spurious.

However, statistics alone cannot determine the meaning of a mathematical relationship or the direction of causality. There has to be a well-regarded theory to lend further support to an assumed connection between two factors. It turns out that there are theoretical grounds for assuming that frequent reading would promote the development of reading skills. However, the links between frequent reading and skill development are more complicated than they would first appear.

Contemporary theories of cognition suggest that one of the best ways to become more proficient in some activity is to practice regularly and extensively (Anderson, 1995; Ericsson & Smith, 1991). In fact, some studies show that a minimum of 4 hours per day of practice is required for someone to attain the highest level of expertise in domains such as tennis, piano, or chess (see Chapter 4). However, research on the so-called "Power Law of Learning" suggests that practice is particularly important during the earliest stages of skill acquisition (see Chapter 3). After a certain point in time, practice provides diminishing returns. To illustrate, consider the case of a first grader who makes pronunciation mistakes about 30 percent of the time in September, but only 15 percent of the time after nine months of regular reading in school (a 50 percent reduction in errors). During the second and third grades, however, she may find that her error rate reduces further from 15 percent to just 10 percent and 8 percent, respectively, after two more years of practice. The latter represent reductions of only 33 percent and 20 percent, respectively, in her error rate. Thus, the notion of diminishing returns suggests that increased practice would be most beneficial to individuals who are in the earliest stages of learning to read (e.g., first through third graders) and least beneficial to individuals who are in the latter stages (e.g., ninth through twelfth graders). If so, then a uniform policy that mandates an increase in reading for all students (e.g., all students should read 15 minutes more per day) would have a greater effect on younger readers than older readers.

In a related way, the idea of diminishing returns suggests that there would be a higher correlation between frequent reading and test scores in younger children (e.g., second and third graders) than in older children (e.g., fifth or sixth graders). It is notable that most of the studies that have investigated the role of frequent reading have focused on children in the fifth grade or older (presumably because many younger children are not yet fluent, independent readers). However, if practice has its strongest effects early in the process, then the correlations generated from studies of fifth graders may underestimate the potential value of frequent reading for younger children.

One further theoretical point relates to so-called "Matthew effects" (Stanovich, 1986). Cognitive psychologists have shown that comprehension of sentence-length constructions requires the ability to process and hold in working memory the meaning of all of the words in the sentence (Just & Carpenter, 1987). As your eyes fixate on each word in a sentence, all preceding words in that sentence must be retained and maintained in working memory before this information fades. If any obstacle to comprehension is encountered before the information starts to fade (about 2 seconds), comprehension processes usually falter (Baddeley, 1990). One such obstacle is the presence of an unfamiliar word. Whereas highly familiar words can be processed in ¼th of a second or less, unfamiliar words can take considerably longer to process. With only 2 seconds to process all of the words, then, unfamiliar words pose quite a problem. However, if a person reads many different types of works and does so on a regular basis, that person tends to convert words that used to be unfamiliar into familiar words (in the same way that unfamiliar faces can become quickly recognized through repeated encounters). Over time, the troublesome words soon become processed nearly as quickly as other words and comprehension problems are no longer disruptive (Perfetti, 1985).

The most significant consequence of this increase in processing speed is that the reader now has better access to the knowledge contained in the texts that he or she is reading. Acquiring more knowledge, in turn, helps the reader make new inferences that further enhance the comprehension process (Pearson & Fielding, 1991). Other benefits of wide reading include (a) the acquisition of new vocabulary words and grammatical constructions that are normally not acquired in conversation (Stanovich & Cunningham, 1992) and (b) enhanced phonemic awareness that can be used in the decoding process (Stanovich, 1986).

Thus, regular reading has the potential to increase one's reading speed, vocabulary, knowledge, and phonemic awareness. Such changes, in turn, make one a better reader still. In effect, reading skills tend to "snowball" over time. This analysis implies that if two individuals were to start out at roughly the same place in the first grade but only one were to read extensively, it would be expected that the extensive reader would show faster growth in reading skills than the less extensive reader. Moreover, if we were to plot their reading scores as a function of time, we would see a widening gap between their respective "learning curves" over time. Stanovich (1986) labeled this phenomenon the "Matthew effect" after the biblical author who makes reference to the rich getting richer (i.e., Matthew).

However, it is important to note that Matthew effects would not be expected to occur if children were to read exactly the same (unchallenging) works again and again. Similarly, little growth would be expected if children were to read new books each time but select books that contain many of the same words and ideas. Thus, researchers would tend to find a higher correlation between extensive reading and reading achievement in a study if they asked questions such as "How many different books did you read last year?" than if they asked "How many minutes do you spend reading each day?" In addition, the idea of Matthew effects suggests that the causal relationship between frequent reading and reading achievement is more appropriately viewed as reciprocal than unidirectional (i.e., frequent reading causes higher achievement, which in turn promotes more frequent reading). But, in general, there does appear to be a solid theoretical basis for assuming that frequent reading would promote higher levels of reading achievement.

So far, then, we have seen that the correlation between frequent reading and reading achievement is probably not spurious and makes sense theoretically. But one further issue relates to the typical size of the correlation. If frequent reading is authentically connected to reading achievement, but the relationship is relatively weak, why should a teacher allocate more instructional time to silent reading (or assign more of it as homework)? Researchers who focus on such issues have approached the idea of magnitude in several ways. One approach consists of assigning the label "small" to correlations in the range of $r = 0$ to .30, "moderate" to correlations between .30 and .80, and "large" to correlations greater than .80 (Cohen, 1992). Then, greater weight is given to correlations in the moderate and large ranges than to correlations in the small range.

Studies show that the correlation between frequent reading and reading achievement typically range between $r = .10$ and $r = .40$ (e.g., Anderson et al., 1988; Cipielewski & Stanovich, 1992; Greany, 1980; Heyns, 1978; Taylor et al., 1990; Walberg & Tsai, 1984). According to the labeling approach above, these correlations would be considered "small" and, perhaps, not given very much consideration in instructional decision-making.

In recent years, however, it has been argued that the conventional labeling approach is not especially helpful when the practical value of some sort of intervention is under consideration. A better approach is to convert the correlation to something called a Binomial Effect Size Display (Rosenthal, 1994). The details of this conversion are less important than the bottom line that so-called "small" correlations (e.g., those found in studies of reading frequency) can be shown to have non-trivial practical implications. For example, let's assume that the average correlation between frequent reading and reading achievement is $r = .24$. Expressed in the form of a Binomial Effect Size Display, a correlation of .24 suggests that an intervention designed to increase reading would tend to produce growth in reading skills in 62 percent of students as opposed to just 38 percent of students who do not increase their reading. At the school level, this difference in success rate would mean that a school of 500 students would show growth in 310 students instead of 190 students (i.e., 120 additional students). At the aggregate level across all of the schools in the United States, this analysis suggests that additional reading would have a noticeable effect that would be clearly worth the effort.

But a reflective practitioner might still wonder why the correlations seem to vary so much across studies. Which of the respective values is closest to the truth? One reason for the variability was alluded to earlier. Some researchers subtracted out the effects of other important variables such as reading ability and socio-economic status, while others did not. Uncorrected, the correlations are closer to $r = .40$. With the corrections, they drop into the range of $r = .10$ to .25.

A second important reason for the variability is the precision and accuracy with which reading frequency has been assessed in each study. If someone asked, "How many books did you read last month?" or "How often do you read books?", you might give a less accurate answer than if you kept a daily journal of your reading for a month. Imprecise measurement tends to lead to smaller correlations than precise measurement, so one would expect that the journal approach would generate higher correlations than the questions approach. Studies generally confirm this expectation. Whereas researchers who used the journal approach have tended to find uncorrected correlations in the .30–.40 range (e.g.,

Anderson et al., 1988; Greany, 1980; Taylor et al., 1990), those using the questionnaire approach have found much smaller correlations (e.g., Walberg & Tsai, 1984).

However, the journal approach is not without its problems. Apart from the fact that it is labor-intensive, there is also the issue of social desirability. People (especially children) may be inclined to report more reading than they actually do in order to make a favorable impression on researchers. In addition, whereas the journal approach taps into current reading habits, it does not assess children's prior reading habits that contributed to their current level of skill. Further, in most studies that utilized the journal approach, researchers chose to focus on the average number of minutes per day spent reading. As noted earlier, the amount of time spent reading may matter less than the type and diversity of books read. To address all of these problems, Keith Stanovich and his colleagues have recently come up with a new technique that taps into a variable called *print exposure* (e.g., Cipielewski & Stanovich, 1992; Stanovich & Cunningham, 1992). In this technique, people are presented with names of authors (e.g., Stephen King), books (e.g., *The Grapes of Wrath*), and magazines (*Cosmopolitan*) and are asked if they recognizes these names. Mixed within the list of actual names are foils (e.g., names of the consulting editors of journals in educational psychology). Note that this measure seems to tap into both the extent of reading *and* the diversity of reading. That is, someone who never reads or who only reads the same three authors would tend to recognize fewer names than someone who reads widely. Also, people who are inclined toward social desirability would tend to check more names, even the foils. Researchers can use the selection of foils to adjust scores down to a more accurate figure.

Aware of the fact that any correlation between print exposure and reading skills might be spurious (e.g., smart people tend to read more and also know more names of authors), Stanovich and colleagues were careful in each of their studies to control for general intelligence (using IQ tests) and aptitude (using various measures of reading comprehension and reading-specific skills such as decoding). Across a series of studies, results showed that print exposure was highly predictive of: (a) college students' orthographic (i.e., spelling) knowledge; (b) children's phonological coding, spelling, vocabulary, verbal fluency, and general knowledge; (c) college students' vocabulary, reading comprehension, knowledge of history and literature, spelling ability, and verbal fluency; (d) children's reading comprehension and reading rate; and (e) college students' and older adults' cultural knowledge (e.g., Stanovich & Cunningham, 1992; Stanovich, West, & Harrison, 1995). On average, the corrected correlations clustered near the value of $r = .28$, suggesting that extensive and diverse reading is associated with growth in reading skills and knowledge. In addition, these studies illustrate how a more precise measurement technique can yield a higher and more accurate indication of the degree of relationship between two factors than less precise techniques.

One final way to address the magnitude question is to consider the likely consequences of increasing reading by a certain amount each day. An interesting aspect of correlational studies is that one can create mathematical formulas that allow one to say how much one factor might increase if the other factor were increased by a certain amount. In the case of reading, several researchers have attempted to determine how much test scores would increase if children were to read a certain amount more. In one study, for example, researchers showed that a unit increase in minutes of book reading would be associated with a 4.9 percentile gain in reading comprehension as measured by a standardized test (Anderson et al., 1988). To illustrate such an increase, a child at the median for book reading in their study (i.e., about 5 minutes per day) would have to increase his or her reading by just 9 minutes more per day (i.e., 13 minutes per day) to show a 4.9 percentile gain. Another interesting aspect of their data was that increases in book reading time produced diminishing returns. For example, a child who went from no reading per day to 6 minutes per day would move from the fortieth percentile for reading comprehension to the sixtieth percentile. In contrast, a comparable 6-minute shift from 6 minutes per day to 12 minutes per day would move a child from the sixtieth percentile to just the sixty-fourth percentile.

Summary

In sum, we now have a good sense of the developmental trends in reading comprehension as well as possible developmental mechanisms (see Chapter 1). With respect to developmental trends, children seem to develop both structural and functional competencies with age that help them process what they are reading. In particular, research shows that older children demonstrate better reading comprehension than younger children because they are more likely than younger children to: (a) have extensive declarative and conceptual knowledge of topics, (b) have structural knowledge of the different kinds of texts (e.g., stories and expository texts), (c) engage in functional processes that enhance comprehension such as inference-making, inhibition, and comprehension monitoring, and (d) have more extensive practice.

  With respect to developmental mechanisms that could explain these age trends, three themes emerge from the research on schemata and strategies. First, it takes considerable time for children to develop schemata and strategies on their own. In the absence of explicit instruction, many middle school and high school students (who have been learning to read for more than five years) fail to make use of schemata and strategies to guide their comprehension. Second, certain kinds of instruction can substantially decrease the amount of time it takes for children to develop schemata and strategies. In particular, a large number of instructional studies have shown that explicit instruction on schemata or strategies can improve the comprehension of even elementary students. Third, children's prior knowledge of a topic can influence the degree to which they use their schemata or strategies to enhance their comprehension. Familiarity can compensate for a lack of knowledge of prose structure and can also enhance the chances that strategies will be deployed. Indeed, several recent studies of poor-reading adults show that people who are very knowledgeable about some topic (e.g., baseball) can show excellent comprehension of a passage on that topic (Recht & Leslie, 1988; Walker, 1987).

Individual Differences in Reading Comprehension

Researchers who have investigated individual differences in reading comprehension have attempted to answer questions such as: (a) Why do certain children obtain higher scores on standardized comprehension tests than other children in the same grade? and (b) Do "good" and "poor" comprehenders in the same grade differ in terms of their schemata for narratives, schemata for expository texts, and reading strategies? The goal of this section is to try to provide answers to these questions.

If the theory presented near the beginning of this chapter is correct (i.e., that adult readers have reading strategies as well as schemata for topics and various types of texts), then it would be expected that (a) "poor" comprehenders would have less knowledge of the structure of stories and prose passages than same-aged "good" comprehenders, and (b) "poor" comprehenders would also be less likely to have or use reading strategies than same-age "good" comprehenders.

For the most part, the research confirms these expectations. For example, in terms of story schemas, Montague, Maddux, and Dereshiwksy (1990) found that when given narratives to recall, normally achieving students from three grades recalled more total ideas and more of the internal responses of characters than same-aged learning-disabled (LD) students. In terms of expository texts, Meyer et al. (1980), Taylor (1980), and McGee (1982), all found that good comprehenders not only recalled more ideas than poor comprehenders, the former were also more likely to organize their recalls in terms of top-level (i.e., superordinate) ideas. Finally, there are a wealth of studies which show how poor comprehenders are less likely to have knowledge of and use reading strategies than good comprehenders (Paris et al., 1991).

More support for the claim that poor comprehenders are deficient in their structural and strategic knowledge comes from a variety of instructional studies. In the case of narratives, Dimino et al. (1990) found that the comprehension level of ninth-grade, poor comprehenders could be improved by teaching them how to identify the main components of a story. Gurney et al. (1990) had similar success with LD students in high school. In the case of expository texts, Geva (1983) and Slater et al. (1985) found that teaching low-ability students how to identify certain text structures improved their comprehension. In the case of reading strategies, it has been shown that poor readers can be successfully taught how to: (a) make inferences (Hansen & Pearson, 1983), (b) identify the main idea (Schunk & Rice, 1989), (c) summarize (Palincsar & Brown, 1984), (d) predict (Fielding et al., 1990), (e) monitor (Miller, Giovenco, & Rentiers, 1987), and (f) backtrack (Garner et al., 1984). One particularly powerful approach to teaching strategies is the approach described in Chapter 2 called Reciprocal Teaching (Rosenshine & Meister, 1994).

Before moving on to the final section on instructional implications, however, it is important to note that while it is true that good and poor readers differ in terms of schemata and strategies, it is best to think of these differences as a *consequence* of earlier reading problems rather than as the primary cause of their later reading problems. As discussed in Chapter 6, the primary variables that distinguish between good and poor readers in the elementary grades are the abilities to (a) recognize words automatically, (b) recognize words quickly, and (c) interrelate graphic representations together with phonemic representations (Stanovich, 1986). Whereas good readers gain mastery over these abilities by the end of the third grade, poor readers do not. As a result, only the former are given multiple opportunities by their teachers to read longer segments of text and only the former have the experiences necessary to acquire higher-level schemata and strategies. Hence, we see the Matthew effect in operation again.

Instructional Implications

A truly Constructivist way to help you translate theory and research about reading comprehension into practice is to provide a set of somewhat general, but not too abstract guidelines as opposed to a set of highly prescriptive and concrete procedures (Pressley et al., 1994). And yet, to the inexperienced, it is often helpful to see examples of research-based instruction to make the application process easier. So, in what follows, we shall end this chapter by first examining some general guidelines and then walk through two case studies of how reading theory can be implemented in the classroom.

General Guidelines

Earlier in this chapter, a summary of the general age trends in comprehension was provided. In that section, it was noted that certain kinds of instruction could serve as powerful developmental mechanisms. Here, we can describe some of the characteristics of effective instruction for reading comprehension. In their review of the research on reading instruction, Pearson and Fielding (1991) summarized the characteristics as follows:

1. Students benefit when their teachers help them to recall, identify, or construct narrative and expository text structures. Successful teachers have used a variety of approaches to help their students identify common relations among ideas. These methods include questioning, modeling, and webbing.
2. Students' comprehension is improved when their teachers draw relationships between their students' background knowledge and the content of their readings. This may be accomplished through (a) evoking appropriate knowledge before reading; (b) asking students to explain, infer, or predict during reading; or (c) asking inferential questions after reading.
3. A crucial aspect of acquiring and using schemata and strategies is the ability to monitor one's comprehension. The only way to detect a common structure across stories or expository passages is to *comprehend* them correctly in the first place (because comprehension entails "seeing" the relationships that the author intended). Moreover, only people who recognize that they have comprehension problems develop and use strategies for overcoming these problems. Studies show that children can be taught how to become more active, discerning, and aware comprehenders.
4. Students can be taught how to discriminate between important and less important information and also how to create succinct summaries. Those students who acquire these skills improve their comprehension considerably.
5. Although the successful approaches have used a variety of methods and focused on a variety of structural skills, they all have the following component in common: they help students *transform* ideas in one form or another. Pearson and Fielding (1991) suggest that this transformation process makes ideas more memorable because they make the author's ideas become the *reader's* ideas.
6. Finally, a new trend emerged in many of the successful instructional studies. In order to transfer reading skills to students so that they use these skills independently,

teachers engaged in a two-phase process of (a) modeling a skill and sharing cognitive "secrets" about this skill as they perform it (i.e., saying what should be done, why it works, when it should be used, etc.) and (b) gradually turning responsibility over to students until they can perform it independently (i.e., "fading").

Case Studies

In what follows, two case studies of instructional approaches to reading comprehension will be described. Use information from the present chapter and Chapters 2 (Theories), 3 (Memory), 4 (Higher-Order Thinking), 5 (Motivation), and 6 (Beginning Reading) to evaluate the strengths and weaknesses of each approach. Moreover, the idea is to think about whether these approaches could serve as powerful developmental mechanisms.

Case Study 1: Project SAIL.   In Montgomery County, Maryland, a program called "SAIL" (Students Achieving Independent Learning) illustrates how reading theory and research can shape instructional practice. The goal of SAIL is to get children to use reading strategies regularly and appropriately. Beginning in the first grade, children are taught how to think aloud, set goals for reading, predict, visualize, make associations between what they are reading and what they know, and summarize what they read. The approach has been used for children of various income levels and ethnic groups.

   Most instruction is carried out in small reading groups. In the early grades, the names of reading strategies are written on cards and spread out in front of children. The teacher selects a card, models the strategy on the card, and explains what she is doing using a think-aloud procedure. For example, to relate what she is reading to what she knows, she may say "this story must be about people who live in Washington, D.C." when she encounters the word "Georgetown" in a story she is reading. She continues this process each time she encounters a word that she can relate to what she knows. After the teacher finishes modeling the strategy, each student in the group takes a turn. With beginners, the teacher has to use a lot of "scaffolding" to elicit adequate strategy use in children (see the section on Vygotsky in Chapter 2). With older students, she no longer needs the cards and she has to use much less prompting because children seem to internalize the strategy after three years of being in the SAIL program.

Case Study 2: Concept-Oriented Reading Instruction (CORI).   In CORI, the instructional framework involves four phases (Guthrie et al., 1996): (a) observe and personalize (e.g., students find a bird's nest and brainstorm in small groups about questions they want to explore with additional observations or reading), (b) search and retrieve (e.g., teaching children how to find the answers they seek), (c) comprehend and integrate the materials retrieved (e.g., teaching and modeling reading strategies such as summarizing and fix-up strategies such as rereading), and (d) communicate to others (e.g., write a report or class-authored book, etc.). These phases continue over and over throughout the school year. The idea is to build connections across subject matters and focus on core principles (e.g., adaptation in the case of science).

8

Writing

Summary

1. Writers rely on four kinds of knowledge when they write: knowledge of topics, knowledge of audiences, knowledge of genres, and knowledge of language. In addition, they set goals for their writing and rely on their critical reading and text production abilities when they generate or revise text.

2. Researchers have tried to link writing skills to specific brain areas.

3. Preschool children seem to pass through three phases in their growing understanding of graphic symbols.

4. Developmental studies show that, with age, children become more knowledgeable about topics, audiences, genres, and language. However, the major change which seems to occur is not so much the acquisition of these forms of knowledge as much as children's ability to consciously reflect on and manipulate this knowledge.

5. Developmental studies also reveal that older children are more likely to create goals for their writing than younger children. This increased focus on goals prompts older children to (a) produce text that is consistent with their goals and (b) revise their writing when it fails to fulfill their goals.

6. Good writers are usually good readers. In addition, good writers are better at manipulating verbal information than poor writers, and also have a larger vocabulary, greater working memory span, and larger repertoire of syntactic constructions than poor writers. Finally, good writers are more likely to plan and revise than poor writers.

7. Research shows that girls tend to be more fluent in their writing than boys and tend to deviate from standard usage less often than boys. In addition, girls are more likely than boys to revise and fulfill the minimum requirement of writing tasks.

8. White students tend to demonstrate higher levels of achievement on writing tests than Black or Hispanic students.

Imagine that you have an instructor who recently gave you a "B" for his course, but you feel that your performance warrants an "A." You think that the reason for the discrepancy is that the instructor just does not like you. When you complain to the dean of the instructor's college, he asks you to follow your university's standard policy for contesting a grade: write an essay in which you explain why you think the grade is unfair and why you should be given an "A." He tells you that the essay will then be read by a committee composed of faculty and students who make recommendations about whether the grade should stand or be changed. In addition, you are told that your instructor will be given a copy of the essay and will be asked to respond to it.

Given such a task, what might your essay say? What would you say first? How would you end the essay? Try writing such an essay now. Stop when you think that you have a version that is good enough to send to the committee.

Finished? Now imagine that your dean is new and made a mistake. He informs you that your instructor will not see the essay and that the committee is supposed to be comprised exclusively of students. Given this new information, would you leave your essay as it is or would you change certain parts? Would you have the same goals for both essays? (i.e., What does your first line accomplish? Your second? etc.)

As we shall see in subsequent sections, this essay example is useful for illustrating the major processes involved in writing. We shall refer back to it often as the components of writing are described, so it might be helpful to be reflective now about what thoughts went through your mind as you were writing it.

In what follows, we shall examine the research on writing in four sections. In the first section, you will learn about what writers know and what they do when they write. In the second section, you will learn about developmental trends in the acquisition of writing knowledge and skills. In the third section, you will learn about individual differences in writing ability. In the final section, you will learn about the instructional implications of the research on writing.

The Nature of Writing

The goal of this section is to provide a reasonably complete answer to the following question: "What are the component processes involved in writing?" The best way to answer this question is to examine current models of writing (e.g., Hayes, 1996; Hayes & Flower, 1986; Scardamalia & Bereiter, 1986) and distill major components from these models. At a global level, these models suggest that there are two kinds of variables that affect the writing process: those that pertain to characteristics of **writing environments** and those that pertain to characteristics of **individual writers** (Hayes, 1996). In what follows, these two types of variables are discussed in turn. Then, we briefly consider some of the neural correlates of writing.

Characteristics of the Writing Environment

When people write, they write in particular contexts or situations. For example, whereas some do their writing on a computer in a secluded cabin in Vermont, others do their writing in the midst of a classroom full of peers using a pencil and paper. Similarly, whereas some are attempting to write to a large popular audience (e.g., a novelist), others may be writing to a single person (e.g., a teacher, a peer, or a pen pal). As a writer moves from one context to another, it is typically the case that the audience, medium (i.e., computer versus paper), and individuals who are present in that context change as well. Such contextual variations are thought to affect the writing process in important ways (Hayes, 1996). With respect to the shift from paper to computer, for example, a meta-analysis of thirty-two studies showed that word processing packages help all writers (especially weaker writers) to produce higher-quality pieces (Bangert-Downs, 1993). Other significant contextual variations include the text that has already been produced and the availability of collaborators. Obviously, the task of adding the last line to a five line paragraph is different than the task of adding the very first line to a blank page. Moreover, studies show that writers continually re-read what they have already written in order to set the stage for the next portion of text (Hayes, 1996). As such, a change in the initial portion would lead to a change in an added portion. In addition, having a collaborator changes the writing process significantly as well. For example, children write very differently when they collaborate with a teacher than when they collaborate with a peer (Daiute, in press).

Characteristics of an Individual Writer

Psychological theories typically explain changes in behavior by appealing to changes in some mental entity. For example, if a person performed Behavior X at one time (e.g., studied really hard) but now performs Behavior Y (e.g., does not study at all), psychologists usually appeal to changes in mental entities such as concepts, values, and beliefs to explain this behavior change (e.g., he no longer believes that studying is effective). Relatedly, psychologists often explain differences in behavior across two individuals (e.g., one studies but the other does not) by appealing to the same sorts of mental entities. To explain variations in the outputs of the writing process (e.g., a well-written essay versus a poorly-written essay), psychologists have appealed to four clusters of person-related variables: (a) motivation factors, (b) forms of knowledge held in long term memory, (c) writing-specific cognitive processes, and (d) components of working memory (Hayes, 1996). Let's examine each of these four kinds of variables in turn.

Motivational Aspects of Writing. People engage in writing for particular reasons. Whereas some write for pleasure, others write because they have been given an assignment by a teacher or an employer. Regardless of whether people write because they want to or have to, it is clear that writing is very **goal-directed** (Hayes, 1996). This analysis suggests that a change in goals would lead to a change in writing output. Notice how a goal such as "I want to write a summary of current research on learning" would lead to a different paper than a goal such as "I want to critically evaluate current theories of learning."

More generally, however, one of the primary aims of education is to produce students who habitually engage in literate activities such as reading and writing (Anderson, Wilson, & Fielding, 1988). Hence, it has been of interest to determine the factors that cause students to regularly engage in writing on their own (Hayes, 1996). Inasmuch as most prolific writers find the writing process intrinsically satisfying, they engage in it as often as possible. Whereas it is relatively easy to get students to write by giving them an assignment, it is quite another to get them to write frequently on their own (or select an occupation because it requires regular writing). In order for students to make the latter kinds of choices, they need to hold positive attitudes toward the writing process and themselves as writers. Moreover, they need to believe that writing affords more benefits than costs. Whereas the tendency to write a particular assignment relates to specific goals, the tendency to write frequently might be called a predisposition to write (Hayes, 1996).

Knowledge Structures in Long-Term Memory.   Of course, a well-written document would not be produced if a person merely had the motivation to write. Such a person also needs certain kinds of writing knowledge and skill. Writing researchers have argued that there are five main types of knowledge that successful writers store in their long-term memories: knowledge of task schemas, knowledge of topics, knowledge of audiences, knowledge of genres, and knowledge of language (Glover, Ronning, & Bruning, 1990; Hayes, 1996; Scardamalia & Bereiter, 1986). Contemporary theories suggest that an alteration in one of these kinds of knowledge (e.g., an absence of topic knowledge in one person versus its presence in another) would lead to outputs that differ in their quality (e.g., one writes a good essay but the other does not).

Task schemas are mental representations of writing tasks that a person regularly encounters. They include global parameters regarding deadlines and length, as well as stored strategies that were successful in the past (e.g., clarifying things with an instructor first, starting at least 3 weeks early, focusing on familiar topics, etc.). As noted in Chapter 3, schemas help people accomplish tasks efficiently. Those who lack schemas need to reinvent the wheel each time they are given a particular task.

As for knowledge of topics, you may have noticed that it is much easier to write a paper when you know a lot about the topic than when you know very little about it. The same is true for even the most skilled writers. Knowledge helps you generate ideas and organize them effectively. To see this, imagine that you were given the assignment of writing an essay on the nature of writing. It should be clear that you would have an easier time writing such a paper after you read this section than before you did (unless you were already familiar with the literature on writing!). As another example, imagine that you were writing the essay regarding an unfair grade for a friend rather than for yourself. If you did not take the class with the friend and experience things the way he or she did, it would be harder to write the essay than if the unfair grade were given to you. Good writers understand the importance of topic knowledge, so they usually do a great deal of research before they attempt to write about an unfamiliar topic. James Michener, for example, usually researched a topic for about three years before he wrote one of his tomes.

However, whereas topic knowledge is necessary for writing a good piece, it is not sufficient. Writers also have to be able to "get inside their reader's minds" in order to be successful. That is, they need to be able to answer questions such as "What do my readers already know? What do they want to hear? How would they probably react to my statements?" In the extreme, writers who fail to understand what their readers know and believe could produce a variety of unwanted responses in their readers. For example, poor writing could make readers feel: (a) confused (if the level is too high), (b) belittled or bored (if the level is too low), or (b) angry (if the author's stance runs contrary to their beliefs). In most cases, readers want to learn something new or form a "connection" with something they read. Readers will not learn anything new if the material is either too familiar or too unfamiliar, and may not have their beliefs confirmed by someone who challenges their opinions. Moreover, readers will gain very little from a piece if they are unable to draw inferences that connect sentences and paragraphs together into a coherent whole (see Chapter 7). When writers egocentrically assume that their readers know what they know, they fail to provide enough clues in the text to support required inferences. Thus, knowing your audience is a key to being a good writer. Note that the element of the task environment related to audience (see above) pertains to who the audience is. Here the issue concerns a writer's knowledge of that audience.

To appreciate the utility of the next kind of knowledge, consider the following question: If someone asked you to write an argumentative essay, a textbook, a story, and a poem, would you know how to write something in each of these genres? As we have seen in Chapter 7, genres have their own distinctive structures that good readers come to know. For example, we saw that stories have a narrative structure involving components such as settings, characters, and outcomes. Given the fact that there are "standard" ways of organizing ideas in specific genres and that readers come to expect this standard format when they read a work in that genre, writers need to stick close to this standard format in order to maximize the chance that their readers will like and comprehend what they have read. Of course, the task of writing something in a particular genre is made easier when a writer has a *schema* for that type of work.

Finally, although having knowledge of topics, audiences, and genres is important to writing well, an absolutely indispensable component of good writing is knowledge of your audience's native language. Writers need to know how to place specific words in specific grammatical constructions in order to convey just the right meaning. That is, writers need to have (a) a good vocabulary, (b) knowledge of grammatical rules, and (c) knowledge of the *pragmatics* of a language (e.g., knowing how to be polite, sarcastic, etc.).

To see how important knowledge of language is, consider the following example: Imagine that a French psychologist who is editing a book on cognitive theories asks an American expert on Piaget's theory to contribute a chapter about Piaget to this volume. The American is told that the readers of this book will be non-English speaking French undergraduates. Even if the American knew a lot about Piaget's theory (i.e., had topic knowledge), had been asked to write chapters many times before (i.e., had a task schema), knew a lot about how French undergraduates think (i.e., had knowledge of the audience), and also had a schema for expository chapters (had knowledge of that genre), it should be obvious that she would be unable to write a good chapter if she were not sufficiently fluent in French.

Writing-Related Cognitive Processes.   In his reformulation of the seminal Hayes and Flower (1980) model, Hayes (1996) suggests that there are three important cognitive processes that help writers translate their knowledge and motivation into action: text interpretation, reflection, and text production. **Text interpretation** refers to a set of processes that are used by a writer to create mental representations of linguistic and graphic inputs. These processes include reading, listening, and scanning graphic images. **Reflection** refers to a set of processes that function to transform one internal representation into another.

Examples include problem-solving, decision-making, and inference-making. These three processes were included as replacements for the planning component in the original 1980 model. **Text production** refers to a set of processes that are used when a writer translates internal representations into written, spoken, or graphic outputs.

This revised model places reading skills at the center of effective writing. However, Hayes (1996) makes a distinction between reading to comprehend and reading to evaluate. As noted in Chapters 6 and 7, readers engage in the following sorts of processes when they read to comprehend: decode words, apply grammatical knowledge, apply semantic and schematized knowledge, draw inferences about instantiations and the author's intentions, and construct a gist. The output of such processes is a representation of text meaning. When people read to evaluate, however, they read with an eye toward problems inherent in the current draft of a document that they have written or someone else has written. Instead of simply decoding words, for example, they also look for spelling errors. Similarly, instead of simply applying grammatical knowledge to form a mental representation of "who did what to whom," they also look for grammatical faults. Components such as semantic knowledge, inference-making, schemata, and consideration of audience needs help writers look for unwarranted inferences, schematic violations, incoherence, and inappropriate tone or complexity.

Thus, to revise a document, writers have to engage in (a) critical reading of what they have written, (b) problem solving and decision-making (i.e., identification of a problem, consideration of alternative ways to fix it, etc.), and (c) text production (i.e., translating these intentions into revised text). These three processes are best coordinated if a writer has a schema for the task of revision. This schema might include a search for common kinds of problems, strategies for locating problems (e.g., not looking at a draft for a few days before returning to it), and so on. In addition, carrying out the three core processes of writing requires the capacity resources afforded by working memory and knowledge resources contained in long term memory.

Using this overall framework, a researcher could explain differences between more experienced and less experienced writers. For example, one study showed that college freshmen tend to focus their revisions at or below the sentence level (e.g., fix spelling or substitute a single word). More experienced writers, in contrast, tended to focus on both local and global problems (Hayes, Flower, Schriver, Stratman, & Carey, 1987). Why might this be the case? One place to look might be a difference in the ability or inclination to detect problems in texts. Conceivably, good writers could be better readers than poor writers. Another place might be working memory differences. A third might be a lack of revision schemata in inexperienced writers. A fourth might be lack of knowledge of good solutions to writing problems that are identified (e.g., "I know it reads sort of choppy but I don't know how to fix it"). A fifth might be differences at the level of production. Good and poor writers might be similar in their ability to read critically and detect problems, but different in their ability to translate their plans into effective text. Studies have shown, for example, that good writers produce segments of sentences that are 53 percent longer than those of poor writers (Hayes, 1996).

Thus, the model is useful for locating numerous possible differences between good and poor writers. Are any of these differences particularly crucial? Hayes (1996) suggests that reading skills are important for reasons other than the fact that they help a writer identify problems in a draft. For example, reading skills help writers gain accurate topic knowledge as they do research. In addition, readers often formulate a representation of the author of some work (including such things as the author's personality traits and political orientation). Collectively, these representations help a writer create and revise documents in ways that are rather different than the methods used by poor readers and writers.

Components of Working Memory.   Kellogg (1996) proposed a model that is similar to that of Hayes (1996) but emphasizes the significance of working memory to a greater extent. In Kellogg's model, the text production process consists of three sub-components: formulation, execution, and monitoring. When in the formulation phase, a writer plans what he or she is going to say then translates this plan into an intention to write down a specific segment of text. When in the execution phase, the motoric and related responses needed to carry out this intention are put into play. Note that this process is relatively straightforward for someone who has been writing long-hand for years or typing for years. For the beginning or disabled writer, however, effortful execution could disrupt the flow of ideas from mind to paper. In other words, a slow writer or typist could forget the exact phrasing that emerged during the formulation phase. During the monitoring phase, the writer reads and edits the text that has been produced. Working memory could affect such processes as well. Kellogg suggests that the key aspect of working memory in this regard is the central executive which allocates some of its resources when the two slave systems are over-taxed (see Chapter 3).

Neuroscientific Basis of Writing

To round out the discussion of writing processes, it is useful to consider the implications of brain research in this area. For over 100 years, clinicians have observed curious deficits in the writing skills of brain-injured adults. Analysis of numerous case studies suggests that handwriting is a complex cognitive and motoric process that consists of a number of component operations (Rapcsak, 1997). When an individual attempts to write a word, for example, he or she first retrieves an abstract representation of letter forms from memory. Next, this information is fed to a motor response program that attempts to carry out the movements necessary to write the word in a particular manner. Success requires that the words are of the right case (lower versus upper), script (block letters versus cursive), size (i.e., all of similar size) and spacing (not too far apart or on top of one another). Studies show that lesions in the left parietal-occipital area (put your finger just behind and above your left ear) cause problems in retrieving the abstract letter forms. Lesions more in the parietal area proper and motor centers of the frontal lobe cause problems in the motor output functions. Motor problems have also been caused by lesions in the same sub-cortical structure affected in Parkinson's disease (the basal ganglia) and in the cerebellum. Of course, the motor and word knowledge systems are part of the larger system of writing described earlier (involving goals, knowledge, and so on). Thus, writing involves multiple areas of the brain that work in concert to produce skilled performance. Given the complexity of this system, " . . . it is perhaps not altogether surprising that writing takes a long time to master and that it remains a fragile skill highly susceptible to disruption by brain damage" (Rapcsak, 1997, p. 166).

The Development of Writing Skills

The developmental research on writing skills is organized as follows. First, we will examine the early emergence of writing during the preschool period. Then, we will consider developmental studies that used the original model of Hayes and Flower (1980) as their guide. For simplicity, the latter studies are grouped according to whether they examined (a) the knowledge needed for writing or (b) writing processes.

Early Writing Skills

Consistent with the literature on emergent literacy (see Chapter 6), a number of studies have shown that children develop conceptions of the writing process well before they are exposed to formal writing instruction in kindergarten and first grade (Brenneman, Massey, Machado, & Gelman, 1996; Gombert & Fayol, 1992; Share & Levin, 1999). To assess what preschoolers know, researchers sometimes dictate words to children and ask them to write these words down. Other times, they may present a picture and ask children to write the word for it. Studies have shown that children progress through a series of approximations to writing between the ages of three and five. For example, they may begin with scribbles, but then progress to wavy lines and pseudo-letters.

After reviewing studies of this sort that were conducted in various countries, Gombert and Fayol (1992) proposed that children progress through three phases in their early writing attempts. In Phase 1 (approximately age three), children produce non-figural graphics such as scribbling and wavy lines. These markings usually obey principles of writing such as unidirectionality and also sometimes have features characteristic of mature writing such as linearity, vertically short traces, and discrete units. Notably, children do not confuse writing with drawing even at this beginning level.

During Phase 2 (between ages three and four), children's writing may consist of strings of circles or pseudo-letters. The distinct characteristic of this phase is the very clear existence of discrete units. These units, however, are used to correspond to verbal dictations in non-phonemic ways. For example, they tend to write longer sequences for words for large things (e.g., an elephant) than for small things (e.g., mouse). Relatedly, they may write these units using the same color as the object (e.g., a red marker for *apple* and a yellow one for *lemon*). Near the end of this phase, however, children may start matching sequence strings to phonemic information (e.g., longer sequences for multi-syllable words).

During Phase 3 (ages four to five), children start to produce writing samples that contain actual letters that children know. In most cases, these letters come from children's own first name but new letters are slowly added. Unlike earlier phases, children no longer attempt to match sequences to dictations in either semantic or phonological ways. The absence of such matching may reflect their having to allocate considerable attention to the task of writing unfamiliar letters (Gombert & Fayol, 1992). With continued practice, however, these matchings reappear, but only in terms of phonological features. For example, they may write KGN for kindergarten. Interestingly, however, many of the oldest children begin refusing to participate, arguing that they do not know how to spell particular words.

Soon thereafter, children enter kindergarten and receive instruction on writing all letters of their native alphabet or idiographies. In first grade and beyond, many also receive instruction in spelling and in the alphabetic principle (see Chapters 6 and 7). Of course, good writing involves more than spelling. As noted earlier, writers set goals, rely on schemata, revise, and so on to draft stories, informative passages, and argumentative essays. In the next two sections, we shall consider children's abilities in these areas during elementary and secondary school.

Further Developments I: Writing Knowledge

Large-scale and small-scale studies have found that children become better writers with age (e.g., Applebee et al., 1990; Greenwald, Persky, Campbell, & Mazzeo, 1999; Scardamalia & Bereiter, 1986). One reason why older students write better is that they have more of the knowledge needed for writing than younger students. As we have seen, writers can have knowledge of such things as topics, genres, audiences, and language. Let's now examine the developmental literature to see whether there are age differences in these forms of knowledge.

Topic Knowledge.   When asked to write a paper on some topic, younger children tend to generate fewer ideas than older children and adults (Scardamalia & Bereiter, 1986). This age difference in the amount of ideas generated derives, in part, from the fact that younger children usually have less topic knowledge than older children and adults. Sometimes age differences are even found within samples of students who are labeled "experts" on some topic. For example, in her study of the effects of knowledge on writing, McCutchen (1986) found that even in a group of children labeled "high knowledge," her high-knowledge eighth graders still had more pertinent knowledge than her high-knowledge fourth or sixth graders. Thus, it is usually safe to assume that for any given topic, older children will know more than younger children. As a result, the latter will have a greater resource of ideas to tap into.

However, studies have also shown that children seem to generate fewer ideas than their knowledge would warrant. In particular, researchers have found that simply prompting children to think of additional ideas causes them to generate many more things to say (Scardamalia et al., 1982; Graham & Harris, 1996). Why do children generate fewer ideas than they are capable of? The first reason seems to be that whereas younger students use a somewhat random method of **associative thinking** to generate ideas, older students use **heuristic search** to guide their generation of ideas (Hayes & Flower, 1986; Scardamalia & Bereiter, 1986).

The difference between associative thinking and heuristic search can best be described by way of an analogy. Imagine that your knowledge is stored in the form of a mental "filing cabinet" and that each piece of your knowledge (e.g., the fact that dogs bark) is a "folder" in the cabinet. Imagine next that if two ideas are highly associated, their folders are connected by way of a fairly strong string. If you pull out one idea (i.e., folder 1), it pulls out the other idea (i.e., folder 2). Ideas that are weakly associated are connected by weak strings. In an associative memory search, you go to a "main" folder for a topic and pull it out. As you do, you find that you pull out all of those ideas that are connected by strong strings, one-by-one, until there are no more folders attached by strings or until some of the weak strings break (leaving their folders behind).

In an heuristic search, in contrast, you first think about *categories* of information and then go to sections of the "cabinet" to pull out an entire set of "folders" for all of the ideas related to specific categories. For example, if you are writing an essay about the status of American education and you are trying to think of things to say, you might locate a section of your mental "cabinet" which groups together "folders" on the problems with the education system. Or, you might think of your ideas as indexed in some way (e.g., metaphorical red dots on folders for things you are good at) and your heuristic search uses this indexing to find specific folders (e.g., "Let's see, let me think of all of the things I'm good at."). Thus, a heuristic memory search is neither random nor purely associative; rather, it is logical and *goal-directed.* Of course, heuristic searches can also be supplemented by associative thinking and such associations help add additional things to say (Scardamalia & Bereiter, 1986).

The second reason why younger students generate fewer ideas than they are capable of is that they tend to retrieve only those ideas at the highest levels of hierarchically-arranged knowledge (McCutchen & Perfetti, 1982; Scardamalia & Bereiter, 1986). When writing about "animals," for example, younger writers might generate ideas immediately connected to the top-level node "animal" and fail to retrieve ideas below that level (e.g., information associated with different types of animals such as dogs and cats). Prompting seems to move them farther down a hierarchy to retrieve more detailed information (e.g., ask them "What can you tell me about different types of animals such as dogs or cats?").

Knowledge of Genres.   In Chapter 7, we learned that extensive reading seems to cause children to acquire schemata for various types of texts (e.g., stories and expository texts). If children do acquire such schemata over time, it would be expected that when they are asked to write something in a particular genre, older children would be more likely than younger children to write something that conforms to the "ideal" structure for that genre.

The literature on story-writing, however, suggests there is a developmental lag between being able to recognize a good story and being able to write one. In particular, even though five- and six-year-olds seem to have good knowledge of the canonical structure of stories (Stein, 1982), studies show that much older students (e.g., fourth, fifth, and eighth graders) sometimes have trouble composing stories that conform to this canonical structure. For example, in the 1990 National Assessment of Educational Progress (NAEP) for writing, 65 percent of fourth graders were found to have an understanding of the basics of story-telling, but only 15 percent were able to write well-developed stories that had both a setting and at least one episode (Applebee et al., 1990). In the 1998 assessment of over 17,000 students, a similar finding emerged (Greenwald et al., 1999). Here, only 38 percent gave a "sufficient" response to story prompts in which they produced a clear but under-developed story with few details. Only 20 percent attained the "skillful" or "excellent" ratings for well-developed, detailed, and coherent stories. It is important to note, however, that students were only given 25 minutes to compose each of their stories.

In a study in which children were given several class periods to compose and potentially revise their stories, Freedman (1987) found that there was development between the fifth and twelfth grades in the degree of realization of the "ideal form" of a story. In the fifth and eighth grades, only 34 percent and 45 percent of children, respectively, wrote stories about true personal experiences that included some setting information and at least one complete episode. When asked to invent a story, however, these percentages rose to 55 percent and 70 percent, respectively. Finally, Langer (1986) found that whereas there were few differences between the stories of eight- and fourteen-year-olds in terms of structure, the stories of the fourteen-year-olds were more elaborate than those of the eight-year-olds. Comparing the NAEP studies with the Freedman and Langer studies, then, we see that the size of the age difference can be large or small depending on the nature of the writing task. But even in the best of circumstances, there still seems to be a lag of three to four years between using schemata to comprehend stories and using them to write stories.

With respect to expository writing, we would expect an even larger developmental lag because of the findings for reading comprehension that show that children seem to comprehend stories better than they comprehend expository texts (see Chapter 7). Several studies support this expectation of relatively poorer performance for expository writing. For example, Langer (1986) found a more marked difference between eight- and fourteen-year-olds for expository writing than for story writing. At both grades, however, performance on the expository task was generally unimpressive. Similarly, in a highly structured task in which students were asked to complete a paragraph that already contained key elements (e.g., topic sentences and signals), Englert, Stewart, and Hiebert (1988) found that whereas sixth graders performed significantly better than third graders in the generation of textually consistent details (40 percent versus 37 percent, respectively) and main ideas (35 percent versus 22 percent, respectively), students at both grade levels tended to perform poorly on both of these expository writing tasks.

In summarizing the 1990 NAEP results for expository writing, Applebee et al. (1990) reported that:

> " . . . about two-thirds of the eleventh graders were able to write from personal experience and supply adequate information for a job application, but only slightly more than half were able to write an adequate newspaper report from given information. . . . For fourth and eighth graders . . . , the simpler and clearer the information provided, the more successful students were in summarizing and presenting it. More complex material required more complex writing strategies, which the majority of students seemed to lack" (p. 25).

Again, the results for the 1998 assessment were similar (Greenwald et al., 1999). Only 38 percent gave "sufficient" responses to informational writing prompts (e.g., designing a TV show). Children in this category used simple sentences that conveyed information in a clear, sequential but sparsely development manner. Only 11 percent received ratings of "skillful" or "excellent."

Over all grades, studies show that children are most successful when they write expository texts in the simple description format (i.e., taking some information and summarizing it). They have much more difficulty writing essays in the "compare/contrast" format or other formats that require them to *analyze* information rather than simply report it (Applebee et al., 1990; Englert et al., 1988). Moreover, their passages need work with respect to organization, development, transitions, and grammatical complexity (Greenwald et al., 1999).

Although most developmental researchers have focused on narrative and expository writing, a few have also examined argumentative writing. Argumentative writing is a form of writing in which an author adopts the goal of convincing his or her readers that a particular point of view is a good one (Applebee et al., 1990; Greenwald et al., 1999). You engaged in argumentative writing when you wrote your essay about deserving an "A." In judging the quality of an argumentative essay, researchers look for the presence of the key elements of a well-structured argument such as claims, data, warrants, recognition of an opposing point of view, and rebuttals (e.g., Knudson, 1992; McCann, 1989). Most developmental studies have shown that children write better argumentative essays with age.

For example, McCann (1989) asked sixth, ninth, and twelfth graders to write argumentative essays and found that the essays of the ninth and twelfth graders not only had more overall quality than those of the sixth graders, they also contained significantly more claims and warrants. No significant grade differences emerged for the use of data to support a claim, however. In a similar study, Knudson (1992) found that fourth and sixth grade students used significantly fewer claims, data, and warrants than tenth and twelfth grade students. Thus, both studies showed that children are more likely with age to include the elements of good arguments.

However, the increased use of such elements does not imply that older students always produce high quality arguments. In particular, the 1990 NAEP for writing showed that only about 20 percent of students in each of the fourth, eighth, and eleventh grades wrote argumentative essays that were judged to be at the "Adequate" level or better (Applebee et al., 1990). On the 1998 assessment, these figures (for the "skillful" or "excellent" levels) were 12 percent (fourth grade), 14 percent (eighth grade), and 22 percent (twelfth grade). These figures should not imply, however, that little development occurred. The raters used more stringent criteria for assigning the highest two levels for the eighth and twelfth graders, and also gave different writing prompts. But overall, most children demonstrated only a basic kind of proficiency in argumentative writing.

In sum, then, most students even in the high school levels have difficulty writing stories, expository reports, and argumentative essays. When development occurs, it is usually in the form of the increased use of key elements of a particular genre, greater cohesion, and provision of details. In the case of stories, older students are more likely than younger students to include both a setting and a major episode in their stories. In the case of expository reports, older students are more likely to use superordinate structures (e.g., main ideas and supportive details) than younger students. In the case of argumentative essays, older students are more likely to use claims, data, and warrants than younger students. Although even elementary students have been found to use some structure in their writing, older students use more structure and tend to elaborate that structure more extensively.

Knowledge of Audiences.   A major difference between writing and having a conversation is that when you have a conversation, you have an actual person to whom you speak. This individual reacts to your statements with facial expressions and also helps keep the conversation going by saying things back to you. When you write, however, you have no one to play these roles for you. As a result, you need to create your own imaginary audience and hypothesize about how these people would probably respond to your statements. Moreover, you need to be able to think objectively about what you have written to see whether someone else might have trouble understanding what you are trying to say. Writing, then, poses greater cognitive demands than having a conversation. If so, then young children may be less effective writers than older children because the former have a harder time creating and writing to an imaginary audience than the latter (Bereiter & Scardamalia, 1982; Knudson, 1992).

In one of the few studies that investigated possible developmental differences in children's knowledge of how audiences affect what is written, Langer (1986) found that both eight- and fourteen-year-olds realized that a text would have to be modified if an audience were to change. However, whereas the younger children said that a shift in audience would mean that there would be different requirements regarding neatness and length, the older children argued that the changes would be reflected in terms of language and form. Obviously, more studies are needed to reveal the existence of other age differences in knowledge of audiences.

Knowledge of Language.   Perfetti and McCutchen (1987, p. 130) define writing competence as "productive control over the grammatical devices of language in the service of some communicative intent." This definition nicely captures the central role played by a writer's knowledge of language. In order to have productive control over one's language and convey exactly what one wants to convey, a writer needs to have a good vocabulary and good command of syntax. Is there evidence that older students have larger vocabularies and greater command of syntax than younger students?

In the case of vocabulary, school children add about 3,000 new words to their vocabularies each year (Adams, 1990). Thus, the notion of "choosing just the right word" is more applicable to older children than younger children since only the former are likely to have the range of words necessary to engage in such a selection process.

In the case of syntax, Loban (1976) and Hunt (1970) found that there is development in syntactic maturity throughout the school years. By "syntactic maturity," it is meant that older children are more likely than younger children to group separate clauses together into single, more complex constructions. For example, instead of writing the three separate sentences in item 1 below, older students are more likely to write the single construction in item 2:

1. Philadelphia has a great baseball team. Philadelphia has a great football team. Philadelphia does not have a good basketball team.
2. Philadelphia has a great baseball team and a great football team, but it does not have a very good basketball team.

Moreover, even nine-year-olds seem to know that item 2 is more acceptable than item 1 when asked which is better. However, these same students could not imitate the constructions such as 1 or 2 when given parallel content (Scardamalia & Bereiter, 1986). Other researchers have found that high school students could not deliberately replicate the very same grammatical errors that they had made on a prior writing assignment. On the 1998 NAEP for writing that included grammatical complexity, grammatical variability, and word choice in its rating scale, only 27 percent of twelfth graders attained the highest two ratings overall (Greenwald et al., 1999). Recall that children needed to write well in a short period of time. Thus, one could summarize such studies by saying that syntactic development during the school years seems to be the progressive attainment of *fluency and conscious control* over complex grammatical constructions.

A final aspect of language knowledge that seems to develop with age is the ability to use cohesive devices. By "cohesive devices," it is meant such things as (a) using pronouns in one sentence to refer back to individuals named in earlier sentences and (b) using the same or related words in several successive sentences. Item 3 illustrates both of these devices. The words that create ties are italicized:

3. Mary was known as a popular girl. *She* was so *popular,* in fact, that *she* was named class president.

A variety of studies have shown that older children are more likely to use cohesive devices than younger children. McCutchen (1986), for example, found differences in coherence between younger (i.e., fourth graders) and older students (i.e., sixth and eighth graders) even when their knowledge of the topic was statistically controlled.

Summary.   Across a variety of studies, older children were found to demonstrate greater knowledge of topics, genres, audiences, and language than younger children. The major change that seems to occur is not so much the acquisition of these forms of knowledge as much as children's ability to consciously reflect on and manipulate this knowledge (Perfetti & McCutchen, 1987; Scardamalia & Bereiter, 1986). In particular, with the exception of knowledge of audiences, children were always found to know more than they demonstrate in writing. In particular, children were found to generate less content than they know, comprehend texts of a particular type (e.g., stories) earlier than they can write texts of that type, and produce or recognize well-formed syntactic constructions before they can write such constructions themselves.

Further Developments II: Writing Processes

In the original 1980 model of Hayes and Flower, writers were said to engage in three main processes: planning, translating, and revising. The questions that have captured the interest of developmental researchers include, "Are older children more likely to carry out these processes than younger children?" and "If so, do older children carry out these processes more effectively?" In what follows, we will examine the developmental literature to see what the answers to these questions are. Note that the revised model of Hayes (1996) that emphasizes such things as social relations, motivation, and reading skills has not received much attention from developmentalists to date.

Planning.   Most developmental studies of writing show that children give very little evidence of explicit planning (Scardamalia & Bereiter, 1986). Although young writers may at times "rehearse" what they will eventually write in the form of partial or full sentences, these notes are probably early drafts of eventual lines rather than plans per se.

Instead of forming goals and writing to these goals, children are more likely to engage in what has been called "knowledge telling" (Scardamalia & Bereiter, 1986). Writers who engage in "knowledge telling" write down everything they know about a topic, in the order that ideas come to mind. Knowledge tellers stop writing when they feel that they have written down everything they know.

Because children do not write from goals and plans, they tend to generate ideas by way of associative thinking rather than heuristic search and often do not organize these ideas in any way. As a result, their stories, essays, and arguments often lack conceptual coherence let alone rhetorical coherence.

Translation.   In the earlier section of the development of writing knowledge, we learned that younger children have smaller vocabularies, a smaller repertoire of syntactic structures and cohesive devices, less fluency, and less conscious control over these language forms than older children. As a result, they are less equipped for translating their personal meanings into precisely interpretable texts. That is, they tend to produce "writer-based" texts rather than "reader-based" texts (Perfetti & McCutchen, 1987). Writer-based prose is "full of idiosyncratic phrases that are loaded with semantic content for the writer—meaning that is not, however, articulated for the reader" (Perfetti & McCutchen, 1987, p. 126). In reader-based prose, in contrast, ideas are well-articulated, there is little in the way of ambiguity, and there is a great deal of inter-sentence cohesion. In fact, the meaning is so well specified that most people who read a segment of the text would come away with the same interpretation of it.

Although few studies have shown that increases in vocabulary and syntax skills with age directly contribute to the production of reader-based prose, several studies have shown that older children are more likely to use a variety of inter-sentence cohesion devices than younger children. Moreover, the tendency to create more cohesive texts seems to increase linearly with age between the third grade and adulthood (Garner et al., 1986; McCutchen, 1986; Wright & Rosenberg, 1993). These findings are reflected in some of the age trends reported in the 1998 NAEP.

Revising.   The literature on developmental trends in revising has revealed four main findings. First, children, adolescents, and inexperienced college students do very little of it (Fitzgerald, 1987; Scardamalia & Bereiter, 1986). Second, when students do revise, the vast majority of changes are superficial rather than conceptual or organizational. That is, students are more likely to focus on specific words, spelling, or grammar than on deeper issues such as goals, plans, and overall intended meanings (Fitzgerald, 1987; Scardamalia & Bereiter, 1986). Third, the main reason why children tend not to revise is that they have trouble detecting problems in the first place (especially in their own writings; Bartlett, 1982). When problems are pointed out to them, children can at times be quite good at making appropriate changes (e.g., Beal, 1990), though some studies have found that the changes do not always improve the quality of the text (Scardamalia & Bereiter, 1986). Fourth, a further constraint on children's revising may be that they lack sufficient memory capacity for dealing with multiple issues of content and quality at the same time. When an adult guides them through revisions in a "scaffolded" way, the quality of revisions improve (Scardamalia & Bereiter, 1986).

Summary.   In sum, then, children not only gain more writing knowledge with age, they also more effectively engage in writing processes as well. Knowledge and processes, of course, play equally important and interactive roles in the development of writing skills. For example, as children gain more knowledge of their language, they are more equipped for performing the process of translation effectively. Similarly, as they gain more knowledge of audiences, they become more skilled at detecting and correcting possible ambiguities in what they have written. Thus, it is best to think of the development of writing ability as the coalescing of knowledge and processes rather than as the acquisition of separate components.

According to Berninger, Mizokawa, and Bragg (1991), there are three types of constraints that affect the rate at which writing knowledge and processes coalesce. First, there are neurodevelopmental constraints that influence young children's writing by affecting the rapid, automatic production of letters and hand movements. These low-level constraints are thought to constrain the so-called transcription process (i.e., writing down symbols) but not the central translation processes (i.e., converting ideas into potential text). After transcription processes have been mastered and automatized, linguistic constraints on words, sentences, and schemata have their effects. Finally, after transcription and translation processes have been sufficiently mastered, cognitive constraints on planning and revising may become evident. Thus, whereas neurodevelopmental constraints have their strongest influence on young writers, older children are influenced mostly by linguistic and cognitive constraints.

So, we know that the core processes and knowledge of writing change with age, but we still do not know much about the developmental mechanisms responsible for these changes. Several likely sources of improvement include (a) writing frequency and practice, (b) extensive reading, and (c) instructional techniques. In particular, practice is likely to engender fluency and the automatization of writing skills. If working memory is freed up to attend to goals and meaning, writing is likely to improve as well. Extensive reading is likely to help because children would be exposed to new vocabulary terms, styles, genres, and syntactic constructions (Stanovich, West, & Harrison, 1995). To make this information explicit, however, children would need to engage in a form of literary criticism. As for instructional techniques, it can be noted here that children historically have not been asked by their teachers to write extensively. Moreover, they tend to get very little feedback on their writing and are rarely asked to revise their work. A more complete discussion of instruction as a developmental mechanism is presented in the final section of this chapter.

Individual Differences in Writing Ability

Having completed our discussion of how older students differ from younger students in their writing ability, we can now move on to the question, "How do individuals of the same age differ from one another?" The research that provides answers to this question can be divided into those studies that have compared skilled writers to less skilled writers and those studies that have revealed the existence of gender and ethnic differences.

Comparisons of Skilled and Less Skilled Writers

The major findings of studies that have compared same-aged good and poor writers are as follows:

1. Although good writers and poor writers do not differ in terms of GPAs, achievement test scores, and short term memory capacity, the former are better at manipulating verbal information than the latter (Benton et al., 1984). In particular, a study of college students showed that when students were asked to (a) reorder strings of letters into alphabetical order, (b) reorder words into a meaningful sentence, or (c) reorder sentences to make a meaningful paragraph, those students who showed good writing ability were faster and more accurate than their peers who wrote less well. Cognitive and educational psychologists have referred to such abilities as being indicative of a large working memory span for verbal information (Kellogg, 1996; McCutchen, Covill, Hoyne, & Mildes, 1994; Ransdell & Levy, 1996).

2. In elementary age children, the mechanics of writing (i.e., handwriting and spelling) contribute significantly to both fluency and overall quality (Graham, Berninger, Abbott, Abbott, & Whitaker, 1997; Greenwald et al., 1999). Good writers are able to write and spell more quickly than poor writers.

3. Good writers tend to be better readers than poor writers (Abbott & Berninger, 1993; Hayes, 1996; Englert et al., 1988; Langer, 1986; Perfetti & McCutchen, 1987). In particular, studies show that there is a high correlation between a student's reading scores and his or her writing scores. Moreover, the same students who use their knowledge of the structure of genres to guide their reading comprehension, also use this knowledge to help them write something in that genre (Wright & Rosenberg, 1993; Scardamalia & Bereiter, 1986). Writing and reading are not, of course, the same, but they do seem to rely on the same central knowledge structures (Perfetti & McCutchen, 1987). But again, there is a difference between reading for comprehension and evaluative reading (see above). Good writers are better at both kinds of reading than poor writers.

4. Just as older writers are more likely than younger writers to use heuristic (i.e., goal-directed) search to retrieve ideas from long term memory, good writers of a particular age group are also more likely to use heuristic search than poor writers of that age group (Scardamalia & Bereiter, 1986) and also likely to engage in incomplete search (Graham & Harris, 1996). When good writers lack knowledge on a particular topic and cannot retrieve information from memory, they may also use their heuristic search methods to delve into the published literature to find what they need (Glover, Ronning, & Bruning, 1990). Few studies, however, have demonstrated this phenomenon. Finally, whereas expert writers usually elaborate on an assignment by building in issues, themes, and constraints, novice writers stick very close to the assignment (Scardamalia & Bereiter, 1986).

5. In terms of language competence, expert writers mainly differ from novice writers in three ways: (a) whereas handwriting, spelling, punctuation, and grammar are largely automatized in the former, these processes are still somewhat effortful in the latter, (b) the former have a larger repertoire of sentence constructions and grammatical

devices than the latter, and (c) good writers add larger segments to their sentential constructions than poor writers (Greenwald et al., 1999; Hayes, 1996; Norris & Bruning, 1988; Perfetti & McCutchen, 1987; Scardamalia & Bereiter, 1986).

6. Whereas good writers spend a great deal of time creating goals and organizing their ideas before they write, poor writers show little evidence of explicit planning and goals. As a result, they tend to "jump right into" the task of writing and their work demonstrates less sophisticated organization (Scardamalia & Bereiter, 1986). Experts are also more likely to comment on how their goals and plans change in the midst of writing.

7. Because expert writers are more likely than novices to create explicit goals and subgoals, the former are more likely to revise than the latter. Why? Deep-level revisions take place when one realizes that a segment of text does not meet the goals set for that segment (Scardamalia & Bereiter, 1986). For example, if you were writing to a friend to tell her that she does something offensive but you had the goal of being polite, you might say in response to reading a draft, "Oh, that's no good. She might be offended by that." In contrast, people who do not write from goals have nothing to compare the text to and will not, therefore, see the need to revise anything. Good writers are also better at revising than poor writers because the former tend to have greater topic knowledge (McCutchen, Francis, & Kerr, 1997), greater executive control over revising (Graham, 1997), and greater sensitivity to their audience (Graham, 1997) than poor writers.

Furthermore, because good writers often change their goals and plans as they write, they will have a tendency to go back over what they have written and delete those portions that do not fit with the new plans and goals. Because poor writers tend not to change goals while writing, they will not engage in such wholesale revisions.

8. Finally, many of the aforementioned differences really concern a difference in *metacognition* between good and poor writers. It is probably incorrect to say that poor writers do not have goals when they write or that they have little knowledge of genres or language. Instead, it is more correct to say that whereas good writers can consciously reflect on and manipulate their goals and knowledge, poor writers do not have the same conscious access to their goals and knowledge (Scardamalia & Bereiter, 1986).

Gender and Ethnic Differences

The literature on gender and ethnic differences in writing is less extensive than that on good and poor writers. Nevertheless, it is still useful to examine the findings of these studies to have a sense of how students of various genders and ethnicities might differ from one another.

Gender Differences.   Studies of school children have revealed gender differences for four aspects of writing: (a) fluency, (b) conformity to standard usage, (c) overall quality, and (d) the tendency to revise. In particular, Berninger and Fuller (1992) investigated whether boys and girls in the early elementary grades differ in their verbal fluency (i.e., speed with which they could name as many examples of something as they could), orthographic fluency (i.e., speed with which they could write the letters of the alphabet in the correct order), and compositional fluency (i.e., speed with which they could write stories and expository compositions). The results showed that whereas boys obtained higher scores for verbal fluency (effect size = .21; see Chapter 12 for an explanation of effect sizes), girls obtained higher scores for orthographic fluency (effect size = −.36) and compositional fluency (effect sizes = −.34 to −.83). Furthermore, of the twenty-eight children who were in the lowest 5 percent of the distribution for compositional fluency, twenty-three (i.e., 82 percent) were boys.

Price and Graves (1980) obtained a similar gender split for the quantity of oral and written language. In particular, whereas boys produced more words in oral language than girls, the former were also twice as likely as the latter to make errors regarding double negatives, verbs, pronouns, and plural inflections in their writing and speech. Price and Graves labeled such errors "deviations from standard usage."

If gender differences in writing were limited to the quantitative differences revealed by Berninger and Fuller (1992) and Price and Graves (1980), there would be no reason to be concerned because the quality of what one writes is usually more important than the quantity. But the 1990 NAEP for writing show that gender differences exist for the quality of writing as well. In particular, at the fourth, eighth, and eleventh grades, girls received higher overall scores than boys (Applebee et al., 1990). On the 1998 NAEP, the findings were very similar. The mean scores at the fourth, eighth, and twelfth grades were 142 (boys) and 158 (girls), 140 (boys) and 160 (girls), and 140 (boys) and 159 (girls), respectively (Greenwald et al., 1999). Thus, girls scores were 11 percent higher at each grade. It should be noted, however, that children were given a fixed period of time to compose and that the average scores of boys and girls were in the middle of the 300 point scale for each grade. Thus, the gender difference may once again reflect differences in fluency. Additional studies need to ascertain whether gender differences would remain or diminish if the time limit were removed.

As to gender differences in the tendency to revise, a small number of studies show that girls tend to engage in more extensive revisions than boys (Fitzgerald, 1987). It is not clear whether we should characterize this difference as one of quantity or quality because the authors do not indicate whether the revisions actually improved what students had written.

Whereas gender differences have been found for four aspects of children's writing, parallel differences have not been reported for college students and professional writers. Instead, researchers have revealed what might be called stylistic and "word choice" differences. For example, some researchers argue that women are more likely than men to use qualifiers (e.g., "kind of"), hedges (e.g., "maybe"), and politeness terms to blunt the force of their assertions (e.g., Lakoff, 1973). Others have argued that there are gender differences in how well men and women write in specific genres because of a purported gender difference in world views (e.g., Flynn, 1988). In particular, a woman's epistemology is said to emphasize connectedness and interpersonal relations (Gilligan, 1982). As a result, they are better suited for writing personal narratives than argumentative essays. Males, in contrast, are thought to view the world in terms of impersonally denoted categories and competition. As a result, they are better suited for writing argumentative essays.

To test these hypotheses about the effects of world views on word choice and competence, Rubin and Greene (1992) asked college students to write a personal narrative and an argumentative essay. Once completed, their compositions were examined for the existence of seventeen categories of terms and structures indicative of specific styles and world views. In contrast to the claim that there are definite male and female "styles," the results showed that there were far more similarities between the genders than differences. In particular, of the seventeen language categories, only five (i.e., 29 percent) revealed significant gender differences.

In sum, then, research with children reveals four trends: (a) girls tend to be more fluent in their writing than boys, (b) girls deviate from standard usage less often than boys, (c) girls are more likely to fulfill the minimum requirements of writing tasks than boys, and (d) girls are more likely to revise extensively than boys. With respect to adults, there is little evidence regarding similar quantitative and qualitative differences in writing. Instead, one finds widespread speculation that males and females have different writing "styles." When empirical tests of stylistic differences have been conducted, however, one finds little evidence that they exist (Rubin & Greene, 1992).

Ethnic Differences.   There is not much that can be said about the extent of ethnic differences in writing ability because so few studies have broken down writing performance by ethnicity. The two exceptions are the 1990 and 1998 NAEPs for writing (Applebee et al., 1990; Greenwald et al., 1999). As can be seen in Figure 8.1 for the 1990 NAEP, White students performed significantly better than Hispanic or Black students at the fourth, eighth, and eleventh grades. In the 1998 NAEP, the percentages of students who performed at least at the basic level were 84–90 percent of White students at each grade, 64–72 percent of Black students at each grade, and 65–72 percent of Hispanic students at each grade. The unfortunate aspect of these data is that it is not at all clear *why* these differences exist and why the gap has not diminished over time. Are White students simply more fluent than minority students (i.e., can they generate more text in a shorter period of time)? Are White students more likely to plan or have greater knowledge of topics, genres, and

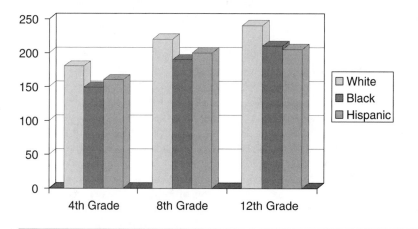

FIGURE 8.1 *Ethnic Differences in Writing*

language? It is essential that we learn the reasons for the performance difference because one cannot create an effective intervention without knowing what causes a discrepancy in the first place. Explanations of ethnic differences in a variety of subjects are provided in Chapter 12.

Instructional Implications

There are two ways to approach the issue of how to teach writing to students. The first way is to propose instructional interventions that would eliminate each of the deficiencies in students' writing ability that have been revealed by research (as described above). Because many of these proposals have not yet been sufficiently verified by research, they should be treated merely as suggestions regarding how we should change the current practice of instruction. The second way to approach instruction is to summarize the results of studies that have compared one form of writing instruction to another. We can then use the research on children's deficiencies to explain why certain approaches seem to be more effective than others. In what follows, research based on each of these two approaches is presented in turn. After examining the implications of these two approaches, we shall conclude this chapter by examining two case studies of writing instruction to see how well they square with contemporary theories of writing, learning, and motivation.

Deficiency-Based Suggestions

Earlier we said that younger students and less-skilled, older students had the following deficiencies that seem to lie at the heart of their writing problems: (a) a lack of explicit knowledge about the structure of specific genres, (b) inadequate knowledge of topics as well as ineffective strategies for retrieving the knowledge they do have, (c) a small vocabulary and a lack of awareness of grammatical structures and devices, (d) a failure to set goals or formulate plans, and (e) a failure to revise in more than a superficial way.

Given these deficiencies, one would expect that the following interventions would improve the quality of students' writing: (a) teaching them about the main elements of a particular genre (e.g., the seven parts of a good story); (b) having them write about highly familiar topics and teaching them how to use heuristic search procedures to access this knowledge; (c) providing instruction on vocabulary, grammatical structures, and cohesion devices; (d) teaching students how to set goals and write to those goals; and (e) teaching them how to revise. Are there studies that tried to see whether these interventions are effective?

In the case of teaching students about specific genres, a variety of authors report that the quality of student writing can be improved if students are taught about the elements of a genre. For example, Taylor and Beach (1984) found that instruction and practice in a hierarchical summary procedure had a positive effect on the expository writing of seventh graders. Similarly, Gambrell and Chasen (1991) and numerous others have found that explicit instruction on the structure of stories positively influenced the narrative writing performance of below-average or disabled elementary and secondary students (Dimino, Taylor, & Gersten, 1995).

In the case of content generation, a number of different interventions have proved successful including (a) having children write on topics about which they have a strong desire to express themselves (Graves, 1975), (b) engaging students in pre-writing activities such as discussions (Boiarsky, 1982), (c) having children list words they might use after they have been assigned a topic (Bereiter & Scardamalia, 1982), (d) having students dictate rather than allocate too much attentional resources to the mechanics of writing (Scardamalia et al., 1982), and (e) prompting students to continue using statements such as "Is there anything else you could say?" (Scardamalia & Bereiter, 1986; Graham & Harris, 1996). But it is important to note that these approaches merely increase the number of ideas that come to mind. They do not teach children how to be self-directed, heuristic searchers.

In the case of teaching children language skills, it is difficult to find studies that show how vocabulary instruction or instruction on cohesive devices improves the quality of writing. But there are studies that show how syntax-based interventions such as "sentence combining" helps students to become more facile writers (Hillocks, 1989). In this technique, students are given separate sentences and asked to combine them into a single, more complex construction.

In the case of instruction designed to increase goal-setting in students, researchers have found two approaches that appear to work: (a) an "ending sentence" task in which students are given a sentence with which their composition must end, and (b) "conferencing" in which teachers help students articulate goals (Scardamalia & Bereiter, 1986). It is important to note, however, that neither approach lets students take responsibility for setting goals themselves. More research is needed in this area.

Finally, in the case of instruction on revision, there are studies that show that the quality of children's revisions can be significantly improved by removing the "executive control" aspect of revision. In particular, if children are walked through a fixed number of revision steps (e.g., stop, evaluate, diagnose, choose a tactic, and carry it out), they are able to revise more effectively than if left to their own devices (Scardamalia & Bereiter, 1986; Graham, 1997). Presumably, with enough practice, these routines could become internalized to the point that students could engage in them without the scaffolded support of their teacher.

In sum, then, most of the interventions that have attempted to remediate deficiencies in students' writing have been at least partially successful. However, a number of studies need to be conducted before firm conclusions can be made in this regard. Ideally it would be useful to know (a) which of these interventions is the most effective, and (b) whether certain interventions should be conducted before others (e.g., goal-setting first, revision second, and so forth).

Comparing Instructional Approaches

The intervention programs described in the previous section were designed to remediate specific deficiencies in students' writing. In most cases, the emphasis was on improving the writing of a single group of students rather than on comparing one instructional approach to another. In the present section, the results of studies that compared specific approaches to the "standard" method of instruction will be described.

Before seeing which approaches are most effective, however, it might be useful to examine what this standard approach is. During any given day, most studies report that students spend very little time writing (Scardamalia & Bereiter, 1986). This finding is surprising given that some teachers believe that drill and practice is the best method for improving writing (Langer, 1986). What we have, then, is the curious finding that the same individuals who feel that practice is important do not provide sufficient opportunities for practice! As noted earlier, if students do not practice writing, two aspects of their competence will take an unnecessarily long time to develop: (a) automaticity in both lower-level and mid-level skills (e.g., transcription and translation), and (b) the acquisition of schemata for particular genres. Moreover, students typically are told what they should write about and are not given assignments in which they can set their own goals. Furthermore, the majority of comments they receive from teachers (if they get any) are about lower-level mechanics such as grammar and spelling. Finally, students are typically not asked to revise a composition after it is turned in (Applebee et al., 1990; Scardamalia & Bereiter, 1986). In sum, then, we should not be surprised to learn that students do not write well because they are not given the type of instruction that could foster the acquisition of writing knowledge and skills.

In a recent review that summarized the results of well-designed studies that compared the standard approach to other approaches, Hillocks (1989) found that the four most effective approaches were the "models" (mean effect size = .22), "sentence-combining" (effect size = .35), "scales" (effect size = .36) and "inquiry" approaches (effect size = .57). The "models" approach consists of presenting students with good examples of writing and helping them to identify the parts or features of the model. As such, there is an emphasis on the product rather than the process of writing. The "sentence-combining" approach consists of teaching students how to combine two or more sentences into a single more complex sentence. In contrast to the models approach, the sentence-combining approach emphasizes the process of writing rather than written products (though students are given feedback about the correctness of their combinatory products). The "scales" approach consists of presenting compositions to students, teaching them how to evaluate the quality of these compositions, and asking them to revise the substandard ones. The emphasis on revision and evaluation makes the "scales" approach distinct from the "models" approach.

As indicated by the fact that it generates the largest effect size when it is contrasted with standard instruction, the "inquiry" approach seems to be more effective than any of the approaches described so far. The "inquiry" approach consists of presenting students with structured data and having them use the data in their writing. Responses to the data can range from simple reporting and describing to generalizing and hypothesizing. It is thought that the use of data probably helps students create plans, organize their thoughts, and circumvent problems associated with content generation.

Taken together, the results for comparative studies suggest that interventions work best when they (a) place a heavy emphasis on writing *processes* such as planning, translation, and revision, (b) use examples of both good and poor writing to gain insight into good *products,* and (c) have students do more of the intellectual work than teachers. Such approaches can be contrasted with approaches in which students passively learn about "good grammar." Hillocks (1989) reports that heavy and exclusive doses of grammar instruction actually engender *poorer* writing than the "standard" approach described earlier (effect size = −.30).

Case Studies

Case 1: Self-Regulated Strategy Development.   A good example of how to translate theory and research about writing into classroom practice is Graham and Harris' Self-Regulated Strategy Development model (Graham & Harris, 1996). In this model, teachers provide writing instruction in six stages:

Stage 1: Develop Background Knowledge. The teacher presents mini-lessons that describe the elements of a particular genre (e.g., the setting and episode of a story) and the criteria for good writing. Students analyze examples of the genre to identify the elements.

Stage 2: Initial Conference. The teacher begins by telling the entire class that she would like to teach them strategies for a particular genre of writing. She asks students to say what they know about that genre (e.g., the parts) and also discusses issues such as goals for learning the strategy and how learning the parts can help someone write better. In addition, students are told the purpose and benefits of strategies as well as when and where to apply them. Finally, she points out that students will be collaborating with each other and that expending effort is necessary before the strategy will be mastered.

Stage 3: Modeling of the Strategy. Students are provided with a chart that lists the strategy steps for producing a particular kind of genre and a mnemonic for remembering questions for the parts of a story. For example, the strategy for writing stories consists of five steps: (1) think of a story you would like to share, (2) let your mind be free, (3) write down the "story part reminder," (4) make notes of your ideas for each part, and (5) write your story. The "story part reminder" is a mnemonic in which the student says "W-W-W, What = 2, How = 2." This mnemonic refers to three questions that start with "who," "when," and "where," respectively (hence, W-W-W), two "what" questions (hence, What = 2), and two "how" questions (hence, How = 2):

> Who is the main character? Who else is in the story?
>
> When does the story take place?
>
> Where does it take place?
>
> What does the main character want to do? What do other characters want to do?
>
> What happens when these characters try to do these things?
>
> How does the story end?
>
> How do the main and other characters feel?

After presenting the strategy, the teacher discusses the parts with them and solicits suggestions for how to carry out certain parts (e.g., freeing your mind).

In the midst of demonstrating the strategy, the teacher thinks aloud regarding how to use the strategy to plan out the parts of a story. As she plans, she uses self-instructions to help her define the problem ("What am I trying to do here?"), plan ("First, I should try to develop the setting"), self-evaluate, self-reinforce, and cope ("Yes, that works pretty well!"). Here, the class discusses the importance of self-instructions and makes notes on things they might say to themselves. With the think-aloud procedure, they notice how the teacher frequently revises plans or parts as she writes.

Stage 4: Memorization of the Strategy and Mnemonic. Students practice the strategy and the mnemonic using whatever approach they want (e.g., alone or with a partner).

Stage 5: Collaborative Practice. As students attempt to use the strategy, the teacher works individually with them to guide them in an unobtrusive, though scaffolded way (e.g., "How's it going? What seems to be the problem? Maybe a different goal for that character would work . . . "). As students work, they are encouraged by the teacher to use goal-setting, self-monitoring, and self-reinforcement procedures.

Stage 6: Independent Performance. Students are encouraged to use the strategy again on a new story. This time, however, they do it largely on their own. Students who do not completely remember the steps of the mnemonic can write them down on the top of a page of paper as a reminder.

Use the information presented in the present chapter and prior chapters (e.g., motivation, memory, reading, etc.) to evaluate this instructional approach.

Case 2: The Process Approach. Starting in the late 1980s, many American schools have adopted Nancie Atwell's (1987) Process Approach to writing instruction. In this approach, teachers have the responsibility of (a) providing ample time for students to write (e.g., at least 3 hours or class periods per week); (b) providing ample materials to support writing (e.g., computers, paper, pencils, resource books, etc.); (c) organizing the classroom in such a way that students can write and revise independently, consult materials, and get feedback from teachers and peers about their writing; and (d) providing non-directive questions and honest, predictable and gentle responses to various drafts of student documents. Atwell assumes that if teachers do their job right, students will take primary responsibility for their own writing and will become habitual writers. Relatedly, they will come to feel that the classroom (called "The Writer's Workshop") is their space (much the same way an artist feels when her studio is arranged to suit her needs and style of painting).

There are three components to instruction that serve different needs. First, there is a mini-lesson on problems that have arisen in previous class periods. For example, if many students are having problems in subject-verb agreement or in punctuation, the mini-lesson might focus on those problems. Alternatively, the focus might be on the difference between showing and telling, or the difference between revising and recopying. Early on, the mini-lessons might even focus on how to function in the workshop (e.g., where the resources are; how to get drafts photocopied for others to read; etc.). Another early and important mini-lesson is the one in which teachers model the process of topic generation and then ask students to search for topics as well. In general, however, the mini-lessons highlight the fact that the problems evident in students' writing are also problems for the teacher and professional writers. Published reports of the self-reported problems encountered by famous authors are particularly helpful.

The second component, Writer's Workshop, is the heart of the writing class that usually consumes about two-thirds of the time allotted. All other components (including the mini-lesson) exist to support what happens in the workshop. The main characteristic of this segment is the fact that writers are "on their own, calling their own shots" (Atwell, 1987, p. 83). Students are told that there are seven rules in the workshop: (a) make corrections by drawing a line through text, not erasing (to allow inspection of changes), (b) write only on one side of the page (to allow cutting and pasting; more easily done with a computer), (c) save all drafts and notes, (d) label and date everything (e.g., Draft #1, Draft #2, Notes, etc.), (e) speak softly when conferring with the teacher or a classmate about his or her writing, and (f) work really hard. During the first workshop, the teacher explains these rules then walks over to an empty chair, puts her head down, and starts writing. Her demeanor suggests that she means business and expects others to follow. Students either start working on a new piece or pick up where they left off on a work in progress. After the teacher writes for 10 minutes, she then walks around the room to meet individually with students. The two primary questions are "Tell me about your piece" and "How's it coming?"

The third component called Group Share fills the last 7–10 minutes of class. Here the teacher and students create a large circle on the floor to discuss their writing. For example, they might audition something new they have written, sharing a technique that seemed to work, asking others for suggested ways to solve a problem, and so on.

Use the information presented in this chapter and previous chapters to evaluate the Process Approach to writing. How well does it seem to instill the knowledge and processes needed for effective writing? How does it deal with the motivational and social aspects of writing? How might it contribute to or ameliorate individual differences in writing skills?

9

Mathematics Learning

Summary

1. Contemporary math educators not only want students to acquire considerable knowledge and skill, they also want students to think like mathematicians. In other words, students should view math as a meaningful goal-directed activity that can help them solve real-world and theoretical problems.

2. Infants seem to show surprising appreciation of set size and simple operations (e.g., addition and subtraction).

3. By the age of four, many preschoolers become proficient counters and also seem to comprehend the unchanging cardinal value of small sets.

4. Between the first and fifth grade, children acquire a range of strategies for solving decontextualized addition and subtraction problems. In addition, they progressively acquire schemata for word problems.

5. In the middle school period, rational numbers and integers pose both conceptual and procedural problems for children.

6. High school students have difficulty understanding the nature of algebraic entities such as variables and functions. They also have trouble (a) performing computations involving formulas and (b) solving algebra word problems.

7. Studies have revealed both gender and ethnic differences in mathematical performance.

8. Mathematically disabled children tend to (a) use less mature strategies, (b) perform the same strategies more slowly, and (c) make calculation errors more often than their non-disabled peers. In addition, they have persistent problems with fact retrieval that do not diminish with training.

Imagine that you have $600 and want to use this money to install a new hardwood floor in your home. The room has the shape and dimensions of that shown in Figure 9.1. The primary issue that concerns you is whether or not the flooring materials will cost more than $600. To find out, you go to a local flooring store and learn four important things: (a) each floor board is 2 feet long by 3 inches wide, (b) each board costs $1.99, (c) boards are only

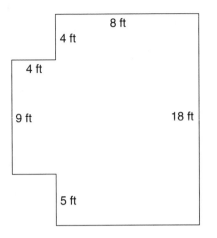

FIGURE 9.1   *The Dimensions of the Room in the Flooring Example*

sold in boxes containing 40 boards each, and (d) you can only get a store credit for the boxes you do not use (not a cash refund). Do you have enough money to install an entire floor?

It should be clear that it would be unwise to simply buy and install as many boards as you can for $600. If it is too little money, you could end up with a half-finished floor. If it is too much money, you could end up with unopened boxes or a store credit that you are unlikely to use. Take some time now to solve the problem.

As students move from the classroom into the world of adults, they confront problems similar to this one on a regular basis. If teachers fail to instill sufficient mathematical competence in their students, it would be extremely hard for students to adapt to the demands of contemporary society. It is for this reason that the primary goal of education has shifted from having students "know math" to having them *use* their math knowledge to solve problems effectively (Carpenter & Lehrer, 1999; National Council of Teachers of Mathematics, 1998). In this chapter, we will examine the nature and development of important math skills. In the first section, we will get a sense of what mathematical proficiency entails. In the second section, we will trace the development of mathematical skills from infancy to adulthood. In the third section, we will examine individual differences in math skills. In the fourth section, we will explore the instructional implications of the research on mathematical thinking.

The Nature of Mathematical Knowledge and Skill

Although end-of-the-year assessments have numerous drawbacks, they do highlight the fact that many children graduate high school with insufficient knowledge of math. Confronted with this evidence every year, school officials and scholars in academia frequently ask themselves the following question: What are we doing wrong? In most cases, discussions around this question eventually lead to discussions around two others: "What should students know and be able to do in math when they graduate high school?" and "What is the best way to instill this knowledge in them?" In recent years, an important outgrowth of such discussions has been the suggestion that students should have the following characteristics when they graduate:

1. *They should think of mathematics as being a meaningful, goal-directed activity that can help them solve problems in a variety of real-world and theoretical contexts.* This conception stands in sharp contrast to the idea that mathematics is nothing more than a catalog of endless, unrelated facts and rote-learned calculation procedures (Romberg & Kaput, 1999).

2. *They should be equipped with the knowledge they need to solve a wide range of problems.* Obviously, it is one thing to have a proper conception of mathematics and quite another to act in accordance with this conception. In order to participate fully in contemporary society, students need a large amount of mathematical knowledge. Recent analyses suggest that three kinds of knowledge are particularly important: declarative, procedural, and conceptual (Byrnes, 1999; English & Halford, 1995).

As noted in Chapter 3, a person's declarative knowledge is his or her knowledge of the facts in some field. In the present case, declarative knowledge would refer to a person's knowledge of math facts (Anderson, 1990). In most people, these facts amount to the answers to various computations (e.g., knowing that 9 is the right answer to 3×3 or that 25 is the square root of 625). Individuals who have considerable math talent usually know a number of math facts that are highly accessible (i.e., it does not take a long time for them to retrieve these facts). However, in recent years, this aspect of mathematical expertise has been downplayed in its importance (especially in the math education community) because people can have considerable knowledge of facts but still lack the ability to solve problems in the classroom or in the real world. In effect, declarative knowledge is thought to be a necessary but not sufficient condition for math talent (Byrnes, 1992).

A *procedure* is a set of operations or actions that is implemented to achieve some goal (Anderson, 1993). Thus, a person who has procedural knowledge in math knows how to achieve certain ends using a series of actions, operations, or steps. Examples include knowing how to: (a) count an array of objects; (b) add, subtract, multiply, or divide whole numbers, fractions, integers, or algebraic symbols; (c) determine the area under a curve; (d) set up and carry out a geometric proof; and (e) use statistics to determine whether a correlation is significantly larger than zero. As implied earlier, regular use of certain procedures on a finite set of mathematical objects (e.g., whole numbers between 1 and 20) yields answers that will ultimately comprise one portion of a person's declarative knowledge base. Moreover, certain forms of procedures have a "syntax" (Hiebert & LeFevre, 1987) in the sense that the steps must be performed in a certain way in order for correct answers to emerge (e.g., lining up the decimal points when adding numbers with decimals using a pencil and paper).

Psychologists and educators further assume that procedures can exist in the mind at different levels of abstraction (Byrnes, 1999). At the lowest level of abstraction, for example, are specific actions or algorithms (e.g., the actions involved in frying an egg or adding two fractions). These actions are specific in the sense that they apply to a limited range of objects and situations. For example, a person would presumably not attempt to crack open a hamburger before frying it or add negative integers with the least common denominator method.

At a somewhat higher level of abstraction are *strategies* and *heuristics*. A strategy is a plan that (a) describes, in outline, how a problem will be approached and (b) includes some specification of the overall goal (e.g., find out what angle X is) and the sub-goals that need to be achieved in order to attain the overall goal (e.g., First I need to find out. . . . Then I have to. . . .). Strategies are more abstract than action-specific procedures because the former may be formulated well before particular methods for attaining each sub-goal are even envisioned. Moreover, the same general strategy may be applied in a variety of situations. A related kind of quasi-general procedural knowledge is called a heuristic or rule of thumb (e.g., "When in doubt, ask the teacher").

So far, then, we have seen that people need to have extensive amounts of declarative and procedural knowledge to be good problem-solvers. Again, however, it is not enough to simply have facts, procedures, strategies, and heuristics stored in long term memory. Mathematical competence involves the ability to call on the right facts, procedures, and strategies at the right time. The third kind of knowledge, *conceptual knowledge,* has been alleged to support this kind of context-sensitive use.

As implied in Chapter 3, people would be expected to develop conceptual knowledge in math as they (a) struggle to understand the *meaning* of mathematical facts and procedures, (b) learn to relate mathematical symbols (e.g., "½") to their referents and construct categories of mathematical entities, and (c) construct cardinal and ordinal representations of mathematical entities (Byrnes, 1992; Case & Okamoto, 1996). Clearly, there is a difference between knowing certain facts and knowing *why* these facts are true. Similarly, there is a difference between knowing how to execute a procedure and knowing why it should be performed in a particular instance (and why it should be executed in a particular way). Individuals with conceptual knowledge understand the meaning and appropriate use of mathematical facts and procedures. Moreover, they relate various mathematical symbols to their referents in appropriate ways (in the same way that literate individuals relate words to their referents). The latter skill requires the construction of mathematical categories and definitions (e.g., *odd number, integer, rational number, integral,* etc.). One particularly important type of categorical representation for math is called a *schema.*

As noted in Chapter 2, schemata are abstract representations of what all instances of something (e.g., word problems that require addition) have in common. Schemata form through repeated encounters with the same kind of problem or situation, especially when analogous or identical solutions are required (Mayer, 1982). When problems are recognized as being of a particular type, their solutions can be immediately retrieved instead of having to be re-invented on the spot.

The final kind of conceptual knowledge refers to the fused, linear representation of the cardinal and ordinal representations of mathematical quantities. **Cardinal** representations describe the amount or extent of a set of objects (i.e., how many objects might be present in a particular situation). When the cardinal representations for various quantities are arranged in increasing magnitude, a student can be said to have an **ordinal** representation of these numbers as well. An example would be a mental line of integer amounts. To assess cardinal and ordinal knowledge, researchers typically present two arrays of objects and ask a person to identify the larger amount. Studies have shown that the fused ordinal-cardinal representation of numbers is particularly important for the acquisition of new procedures and problem-solving skills (Byrnes & Wasik, 1991; Case & Okamoto, 1996; Dehaene, Bossini, & Giraux, 1993).

Thus, conceptual knowledge involves mappings of mental representations to things in the external world (so-called *extension relations*), as well as mappings between multiple representations in the mind (so-called *intension relations*). Together, these relational representations help a student understand and make sense of math facts and procedures (Carpenter & Leher, 1999). By "make sense," it is meant that a child truly understands the big picture when it comes to concepts as well as the likely effects of some procedures. For example, a student with math sense would appreciate what might happen if the 3 in 3 × 4 = 12 were to be replaced by a 4 and how such a change would be different from substituting a 4 for the 3 in 3 + 4 = 7 (Markovits & Sowder, 1994). Hence, the child essentially knows what is going on in math class.

Moreover, the construction of mathematical categories helps a child to avoid inappropriate applications of procedures. For example, a child with conceptual knowledge of fractions would not simply add the numerators and denominators of two fractions together because the two categories of fractions and whole numbers are representationally distinct in their minds (Byrnes, 1992; Byrnes & Wasik, 1991). Each of these categories, in turn, is linked to its own set of procedures. Relatedly, a child who understands the meaning of math symbols (e.g., the 3 in 36 stands for 30) and understands the fact that numbers can be decomposed into base-ten units (e.g., 36 = 30 + 6) is less likely to make procedural errors when adding or subtracting numbers (Carpenter, Franke, Jacobs, Fennema, & Empson, 1997).

Five further benefits of conceptual knowledge include the fact that it (a) fosters the ability to learn procedures in the first place, (b) enhances the ability to retain procedures over time, (c) fosters a high level of intrinsic motivation, (d) supports the ability to solve unfamiliar or non-routine problems, and (e) underlies the ability to invent or reconstruct procedures on one's own (Byrnes, 1992; Carpenter, Fennema, Fuson, Hiebert, Human, Murray, Olivier, & Wearne, 1999; Carpenter et al., 1997; Guthrie, Cox, Knowles, Buehl, Mazzoni, & Fasulo, 2000; Rittle-Johnson & Alibali, 1999). The latter inventive quality of conceptual knowledge is said to be maximized when teachers focus on a few "big ideas" per year as opposed to giving superficial treatment to a wide range of conceptual relations (Carpenter & Lehrer, 1999).

3. *They should demonstrate an efficient and flexible approach to their problem-solving.* Earlier, it was noted that within the category of procedural knowledge there are specific goal-directed actions, number-specific algorithms, generalized strategies, and heuristics. Whereas someone with this repertoire could solve a wide variety of problems, he or she still needs two other kinds of procedural knowledge to be maximally successful in school and in life: estimation skills and graphing (i.e., modeling) skills. Sometimes a problem requires only an approximate solution. For example, an employer may only wish to know the probable month (or even time of year) when a job will be completed, not the exact date.

Or, a homeowner may wish to get only a rough idea of how much a monthly payment would decrease with refinancing, or how much money to bring to the supermarket. In such cases, a skilled individual needs to know how to use math facts, procedures, concepts, and strategies to generate an approximate but still useful solution. For example, consider the case of a third grader who wanted to know the approximate answer to the problem, $25 \times 25 = ?$. She may already know that 20×20 is 400 and that 30×30 is 900. From these two math facts and her ordinal representations of whole numbers (i.e., 25 is midway between 20 and 30), she may deduce that 25×25 is probably somewhere in-between 400 and 900, and perhaps close to the halfway mark of 650 (again using ordinal representations or quick computations to determine the halfway mark). The estimate of 650 is, of course, reasonably close to the correct answer of 625. On important tests like the National Assessment of Educational Progress (NAEP) or the Scholastic Achievement Test (SAT), estimation skills are required for scoring in the highest ranges because most problems have to be solved in 60 seconds or less. Whereas approximate answers can be generated in a few seconds and be compared to possible answers, complete computations often take more than the allotted 60 seconds. Estimation skills are also useful for judging the sensibility of initial answers. Regardless, it should also be clear that one could not be proficient at estimating without having large amounts of declarative, procedural, and conceptual knowledge in math. But again, there are students who have the latter kinds of knowledge but lack the ability or tendency to engage in estimation when it is appropriate to do so.

As for graphing skills, mathematics has often been said to be a discipline that can be used to identify patterns and functional relationships in the world. When data points are presented in a serial fashion or one-by-one, it is often difficult to get an overall sense of what is going on. For example, if a person wanted to get a rough sense of the housing prices in a given neighborhood, he or she could read an unorganized list of prices for the last 100 houses that sold in that neighborhood (one by one), but such an activity would not be very helpful. A better approach would be to make a bar graph or tally sheet to see where most of the prices fall (using prices arranged in increasing order along the bottom of the graph). In a related way, one could create functions for a wide range of phenomena (e.g., growth rates of plants) to get a sense of what is going on (Kaput, 1999). Graphs, charts, and mathematical equations, then, help a person develop a good conceptual understanding of patterns in the data. These aides also reduce the amount of information processing that has to be performed to see the patterns and also greatly facilitate inference-making and problem-solving (Bruner, 1966; Carpenter & Leher, 1999). People with high levels of math ability use graphic aides in a strategic fashion to gain insights into possible solutions. Moreover, they rely on their extensive knowledge to create these models.

4. *They should demonstrate adaptive mathematical behaviors and beliefs.* So far, we have only touched on the knowledge and skills needed to solve problems with mathematics. Ideally, we would also want students to habitually demonstrate the ability and tendency to "mathematize" any situation to their own ends. Being a regular user of mathematics requires that students feel good about this domain and their ability to solve problems that involve mathematics (Romberg & Kaput, 1999). In a highly technological society, moreover, positive attitudes about math are needed to ensure that adequate numbers of individuals choose careers that require high levels of mathematical competence.

The Development of Mathematical Skills

In the previous section, the focus was on the ideal student or a wish list of educators (i.e., Wouldn't it be great if all students had the four characteristics described?). In the present section, we consider the extent to which this ideal ever gets realized in actual children. More specifically, the goal is to chart the development of mathematical skills from infancy to adulthood in four sections: (a) the infancy and preschool periods, (b) the elementary school period, (c) the middle school period, and (d) the high school period. For each period, we shall see different skills being mastered as well as specific topics that cause particular problems for children of that age group.

The Infancy and Preschool Periods

Infancy.   Why would anyone study mathematical thinking in infants or preschoolers? How can children have mathematical ideas before they are exposed to such ideas in school? The main reason why researchers have examined math ideas in very young children is that the concept of "number" has often figured prominently in classical nature-nurture debates. Philosophers and psychologists who are Nativists have argued that infants come into the world equipped with concepts such as number, space, and causality (see Chapter 2). Beginning at birth, infants are said to use these concepts to organize and make sense of their experiences. Nativists believe that if a very young infant could be shown to have a concept of number, that would be pretty strong evidence against non-Nativist views such as Empiricism or Constructivism.

To test the presence of number concepts in young infants, however, researchers have had to be very resourceful. A six-month-old is neither verbal nor adept at pointing. To get around these obstacles, three main methodologies have been used. The first procedure, called *habituation,* involves an infant watching pictures being flashed on a screen. When the same picture is flashed on the screen repeatedly, the infant looks at it less and less (i.e., she habituates to it). The infant, in effect, is saying "I've seen that before. I'm bored!" When a new picture is flashed, however, an infant will look at it for a long time, provided that she can tell the difference between the old and new picture. Let's say that Picture 1 shows two dots and Picture 2 shows three dots. If Picture 1 is flashed fifteen times and Picture 2 is flashed on trial sixteen, a long look on trial sixteen suggests that the infant can tell the difference between "2" and "3," and a short look means that she cannot tell the difference. Researchers have found that even six-month-olds will give longer looks when the set size changes after habituation has occurred (Starkey & Cooper, 1980). However, these findings do not hold up when the set size is larger than three (Strauss & Curtis, 1981).

What do the findings from habituation studies mean? Two interpretations have been offered. The first is that the ability to *subitize* is present very early and seems to be innate. Subitizing is the perception-based ability to rapidly determine the number of objects present without counting them. When there are four or fewer objects in view, most people can immediately "see" (i.e., subitize) how many there are. When there are more than four objects, however, most people have to count them to determine how many there are. The second interpretation of the habituation studies is that the data do not necessarily show that infants can subitize. Rather, the results only show that infants know that *something* differs between the two pictures. One need not infer that infants definitely know that the number of objects differs.

Using the second main technique (which can be called the *surprise* methodology), Wynn (1992) tried to show that five-month-old infants can add and subtract small numbers. The methodology involved four phases. In the first phase, an object (e.g., a teddy bear) was placed on a small stage in front of an infant. In the second phase, a screen rose to hide the teddy. In the third phase, the infant saw a hand holding a second teddy go behind the screen and come out empty. The infant needs to infer that the second teddy was placed next to the first one behind the screen. In the fourth phase, either a "possible" or "impossible" event occurred. In the possible event, the screen was lowered and revealed two teddies. In the impossible event, the screen was lowered and revealed only one teddy (because the other was removed without the infant knowing it). The results showed that infants looked longer at the more surprising impossible event than they did at the possible event, suggesting they were doing some mental addition.

The third main methodology involves a *visual expectation* procedure. Here, an infant sees a picture being flashed two or three times in a row on the left side of a screen. Then, the picture is flashed on the right side. Over time, the infant starts to follow the left-left-right pattern with her eyes. If she fixates at the left side until the second one flashes, then moves her eyes to look for the picture to appear on the right, that seems to suggest that she is counting the ones on the left before looking to the right. Canfield and Smith (1993) found that five-month-olds fixated and shifted their eyes in a manner suggesting that they can count as many as three flashes before shifting their eyes.

What do all of the findings with infants mean? Once again, there are at least two possible interpretations. The first is that the Nativists are right. That is, infants do seem to be born with math concepts (e.g., set size) and procedures (e.g., adding). The second is that infants really do not understand such high-level math ideas. Rather, they are similar to many animal species in that they possess brain structures that are implicitly sensitive to patterns in the environment. Even Skinnerian rats somehow learn that with a "Fixed Ratio 15" schedule of reinforcement, they need to press a bar 15 times before a food pellet is dispensed (Schwartz, 1976). Primitive and not-so-primitive brains can record environmental patterns (e.g., left-left-right) which can signal things like food. What might separate children from rats is that by the time children are five years old, they can abstract, consciously reflect on, and symbolically manipulate numerical patterns in their environment (Geary, 1995). Rats may be limited to non-symbolic, neuron-based pattern detection. Which of the two possible interpretations of the infant data is right? Only additional research and theorizing will tell.

The Preschool Period.   Most of the studies that have examined what preschoolers know have focused on one of two skills: (a) conservation of number and (b) counting. In what follows, the research on these two skills is summarized in turn.

Conservation was a key idea in Piagetian theory and can be defined as the understanding that the amount of something does not change when the objects involved are transformed in someway. In the case of numbers, Piaget (1965) was interested in discovering when children recognize that the *cardinal value* of a set of objects does not change after the objects are simply re-arranged. To truly understand a number, he argued, a child needs to "abstract it" or "decontextualize" it from specific spatial arrangements. In his studies, Piaget found that conservation of number progressed through three phases. In the first phase, children say that two rows of objects only have the same number of objects if the rows look alike. These children do not use counting to verify their claims. Children in the second phase always need to re-count the rows when the objects in them are re-arranged. Children in the third phase immediately realize that (a) the spatial arrangement of objects has no effect on the amount and (b) re-counting is not necessary after a re-arrangement. For Piaget, only the children in the third phase have a "logical" concept of number and only they truly understand the cardinal value of a set.

Although Piaget's finding that most children enter the third phase at around age five or six has been replicated many times (Brainerd, 1978; Fuson, 1988), most contemporary researchers have challenged the claim that preschoolers lack insight into conservation and cardinal value. The most common criticism of Piaget's work is that his tasks underestimate what three- and four-year-old children know. To rectify this presumed underestimation problem, researchers turned to a task that would provide more accurate assessments of early numerical competence: counting.

Counting is a form of procedural knowledge in that it involves performing a sequence of actions in order to achieve a goal. The goal of counting is to determine the numerosity or cardinal value of a set of objects. In essence, counting is an appropriate response to the question, "How many are there?" Although counting is a form of procedural knowledge, children can use it to enrich or inform their conceptual knowledge. For example, earlier we said that the ability to understand that a group of seven objects is a smaller amount than a group of eight objects is a form of conceptual knowledge. In order to form such a judgment, however, a child has to first count the objects in each group. Similarly, counting may ultimately help a child come to understand that the cardinal value of a set of objects does not change when (a) the objects are arranged into a different spatial array (Piaget, 1965) and (b) one counts from left to right rather than right to left (Briars & Siegler, 1984).

Similar to the research on infants' knowledge of number, the research on preschoolers' knowledge of counting is not without its ambiguities. If you ask a two-year-old to count to ten and he does it, does that mean he knows how many ten objects are? How do we know that he has not learned a behavior pattern by rote in the same way that he may have learned "pat-a-cake?" Thus, a child who says the right things may not really know how to count or understand numbers. To avoid misrepresenting what children know, researchers have endeavored to find more decisive ways of measuring counting knowledge in children. The central questions guiding this work are "What does a child need to know in order to count?" and "When do children understand the cardinal value of a set?"

In a seminal work, Gelman and Gallistel (1978) tried to answer these questions by formulating a set of five counting principles. The *one-one* principle reflects the knowledge that each object is assigned one and only one number word. The *stable order* principle involves knowing that number words should always be assigned in the same order (e.g., "one" first, "two" second, etc.). If a child seems to know that the last number assigned indicates the number of objects in the set, he or she is said to know the *cardinal* principle. The *order irrelevance* principle involves knowing that the order in which objects are counted is irrelevant. If a child recognizes that these four principles can be applied to any group of objects, they are said to comprehend the *abstraction* principle.

In judging whether or not a child knows these principles, either a lenient or strict criterion can be used. Consider the case in which you place a row of four chips in front of a child and ask her to tell you how many there are. She says, "One, three, four, nine—there are nine!" You ask her to try again and she says the same thing. Using a lenient criterion, she might be given credit for the one-one, stable order, and cardinal principles because she (a) applies just one word to each chip, (b) always recites the four words in the same order, and (c) uses the last number-word to say how many there are. Using a strict criterion, however, you might say that she should not be given credit for any of the principles because she did not use them correctly to accurately determine how many there are. Of course, the answer to the question "When do children seem to know the five principles?" depends on whether a lenient or strict criterion is used. But the answer also depends on the number of objects in a set. Using lenient scoring and sets of three or fewer objects, some three-year-olds and most four- and five-year-olds are credited with knowledge of the principles. Using the strict scoring and larger sets, only four- and five-year-old children are credited with knowledge.

Gelman and Gallistel's pioneering work was significant because it introduced counting skills overlooked by Piaget and because it revealed knowledge of cardinal value in children younger than five. Since that time, researchers have tried to build on these original findings using various methodologies. For example, some researchers had children comment on the accuracy of a puppet's counting rather than having them count themselves. The puppet's behavior either conformed to or violated the five counting principles. Other researchers simply asked children to give them a certain number of objects (e.g., "Give me four teddies"). Together, these latter studies showed that (a) between the ages of three and four, there is significant improvement in children's knowledge of counting and cardinal value and (b) four- and five-year-olds show considerable, though sometimes imperfect, skill in these areas (Briars & Siegler, 1984; Gelman & Meck, 1983; Ginsburg & Russell, 1981; Wynn, 1990). The difficulty of the task can also be increased by changing the unit of analysis (e.g., asking children to count families of toy animals instead of individual items) and by asking children to match arrays in a sequential pattern (e.g., matching three successive beeps to a picture of three dots). Whereas three- and four-year-olds show some level of skill in the easiest conditions, above-chance performance on harder trials is not apparent until age five (Mix, 1999; Sophian & Kailihiwa, 1998).

So far, we have only examined the studies in which children were asked to count objects or judge the equivalence of two sets. Other researchers have also asked children to count as high as they can, without giving them objects to count. These studies show that even two-year-olds can usually count to three correctly. In the age range of three to four, the average child can count to thirteen without making an error. In the range of five to six, the average child can count to fifty-one without making an error (Fuson & Hall, 1983). Older preschoolers also extend the "one-to-nine" pattern to several decades beyond ten (e.g., 31, 32 . . . 39), but often fail to order the decades correctly. These age trends are generally quite similar across SES groups, but occasionally a study reveals that up to 30 percent of low SES kindergartners cannot count to ten.

Summary.   Given these findings for infants and preschoolers, it should be clear that simplified but developmentally appropriate math instruction could begin by age three for most children. In the absence of counting skills, three-year-olds could be asked to label sets of objects smaller than four using number words. Similarly, they could engage in tasks in which one-to-one correspondences between one set of objects and another are formed (e.g., setting the table for four dolls using four plates). Over time, mismatches and counting could be used to foster an early comprehension of whole numbers (e.g., using counting to figure out why one plate is left over when five plates are used with four dolls).

Returning to the description of mathematical competence presented in the beginning of this chapter, however, it can be said that infants and preschoolers are still a long way from the ideal student who has all four of the characteristics listed. Although they seem to have a rudimentary understanding of certain whole number concepts (e.g., cardinal and ordinal relations of small sets) as well as procedural knowledge of counting, they give little evidence of other forms of declarative, procedural, or conceptual knowledge. This is to be expected given their lack of exposure to the requisite content.

The Elementary School Period

Age trends in math skills during the preschool period are somewhat mysterious given that there is nothing obvious about their lives at home that would explain why there is a shift in numerical skills between the ages of three and four and then again between four and five. From the elementary school period on, however, the developmental sequence of knowledge is not very surprising or mysterious because it largely follows the standard curriculum. That is, children master skills in the same order that these skills are presented in school. But, as we will see, children do not master all skills with equal facility.

In elementary school, children are asked to learn the arithmetic skills of addition, subtraction, multiplication, and division of whole numbers, and also gain some exposure to the application of these operations to fractions as well. In what follows, we shall begin by examining the research on those arithmetic tasks that have been given the most attention from researchers: (a) decontextualized computation problems and (b) word problems. These studies focused on children who were taught in the traditional manner that represents the antithesis of the reforms recommended by the National Council of Teachers of Mathematics (NCTM) in 1989 and 1998 (NCTM, 1998). After describing the trends for such classrooms, we shall look at the findings for children who have spent several years in classrooms reflecting the NCTM standards.

Decontextualized Computation Problems.   Because most of the research on children's computation skills has focused on addition and subtraction, we shall only examine these two operations here. In traditional classrooms that do not reflect NCTM standards, instruction in addition usually begins with single-digit problems that have sums less than ten. Until recently, first graders encountered these problems in the form of decontextualized computation "sentences" such as "$3 + 7 = ?$" Whereas these problems may seem to be "low level" or "easy," they pose quite a challenge to first graders. Why? The first reason is that many first graders are often unfamiliar with the symbolic notation used in these sentences (Resnick, 1987). That is, children have to assign meaning to the "3," "+," and so on. To see the difficulty of this, imagine that you were asked to solve the following problem: "$X^{\#} \backslash\backslash Y^{\#-1} = ?$" What is the answer?

The second reason is that even after the formal sentence is decoded for them by a teacher, children may have no idea how to come up with the answer. To get them started, teachers usually provide explicit instruction in the form of the *count-all* strategy: count out the number of objects indicated by the first number (e.g., put up three fingers), count out the number indicated by the second number (e.g., put up four more fingers), then count all of them (e.g. seven fingers total). Notice how first graders need to come to school being able to count. In most classrooms, children spend several weeks trying to solve addition sentences such as these and then move on to word problems that implicitly embed the same operations in them for the last day or so of a unit (e.g., "John has three apples. Bill gives him four more. How many does he have altogether?").

Before describing age trends in performance on decontextualized sentences, it is first necessary to note that most math educators now feel that the approach of presenting decontextualized sentences first and word problems second is not the best way to go (Carpenter et al., 1999). Why? The first reason is that because counting and addition are forms of procedural knowledge, they should be presented as things children can do to help them solve actual problems. In having children merely mimic a teacher ("Do this first, do this second . . . "), the goal-directed, problem-solving quality of these operations gets lost. The second reason is that children are asked to jump into the symbolic mode well before they may have built up meaningful referents for these symbols (e.g., "3" stands for three objects). That is, they are asked to learn procedures before they have acquired sufficient conceptual knowledge (Hiebert, 1987; Resnick, 1987). In order to avoid these problems, the NCTM recommends reversing the typical sequence of events. That is, they suggest beginning instruction on addition using simple, orally-presented word problems. To build up conceptual referents for symbols, children should be given manipulatives such as poker chips or base-ten blocks. After a good deal of practice with word problems, teachers should then progressively introduce the formal, symbolic mode.

Because this reversed sequence is a relatively recent trend, most of the research that has examined children's single-digit addition and subtraction derives from classrooms in which decontextualized sentences were taught in the traditional way. The primary goal of teachers who use the traditional approach is to move children from a reliance on counting to a reliance on direct retrieval of the answer. To see why, consider how tedious and inefficient the count-all strategy is. With large numbers, it would take a lot of time to come up with the answer and a child would soon run out of fingers and toes! To reach the goal of having students use direct retrieval, most teachers use a lot of repetition. In the first grade, for example, teachers spend a considerable amount of time having their students practice the eighty-one possible pairings of sums involving the numbers one to nine. From the second grade on, teachers re-introduce these pairs, but for fewer and fewer weeks.

Researchers who have studied children's addition strategies have mainly focused on two main questions: (a) What strategies do children use to solve single-digit addition problems? and (b) Do children use specific strategies at specific ages? Regarding the first question, it has not been easy to determine the strategies that children use. Why? In the first place, simple observation often is ambiguous. To see this, imagine that you ask a fifth grader to solve the problem "3 + 4 = ?" After being silent for a few seconds, he says "7." Do you know for sure that he definitely used direct retrieval and did not count? This assessment problem could not be easily overcome by simply asking children to tell you what they did because children often lack conscious access to what they are doing or misreport what they did (Karmiloff-Smith, 1984; Siegler & Jenkins, 1989). To discover what children do, then, researchers have had to resort to a variety of approaches including observation, interviews, and reaction-time experiments (Fuson, 1988; Resnick, 1983). These varied approaches revealed the following strategies:

1. *Count all:* use fingers or other objects to count out the first addend, then the second addend, and then the total (e.g., for 3 + 4, they say "1, 2, 3 . . . 1, 2, 3, 4 . . . 1, 2, 3, 4, 5, 6, 7");
2. *Count on from first:* start the count with the first addend and add on the number indicated by the second addend (e.g., "3 . . . 4, 5, 6, 7").
3. *Count on from second:* start the count with the second addend and add on the number indicated by the first addend (e.g., "4 . . . 5, 6, 7").
4. *Count on from larger* ("Min"): start with the larger of the two addends and add on from there (e.g., "4 . . . 5, 6, 7"). The larger may be either the first or second addend.
5. *Derived facts:* use known facts to construct the answer (e.g., a child might say "3 + 3 = 6, and 4 is one more than 3, so 3 + 4 = 7").
6. *Direct retrieval:* retrieve the answer directly from memory.

A close examination of this list reveals that strategies become increasingly more efficient and dependent on prior knowledge as one moves from the first to the sixth strategy. Also worth noting is the fact that only the count-all and direct retrieval strategies are taught to children. Thus, the remaining strategies seem to be invented by children (Resnick, 1987).

The second question asked by researchers is whether there are age trends in the use of certain addition strategies. Given the standard instructional sequence described earlier, it might be expected that most first graders would use the count-all strategy and most fifth graders would use direct retrieval. It might be further expected that strategies 2–5 (see above) would be used by children in the second, third, and fourth grades. To examine these possibilities, two main approaches have been used. The first, called the *chronometric* approach, involves presenting addition sentences on a computer screen and asking children to give the answer as fast as possible. Then, children's strategies are derived from their reaction times. Although it may seem odd to use reaction times to determine strategy use, the chronometric approach is one way to get around the mismatch between what children say they do and what they actually do. Also, it is clear that the six strategies listed above can be rank-ordered in terms of how long they take to execute.

In line with expectations, the earliest chronometric studies suggested that first graders mostly use the count-all strategy and fifth graders mostly use the "min" and direct retrieval strategies (Ashcraft, 1982; Groen & Parkman, 1972; Siegler & Jenkins, 1989). But researchers soon questioned this conclusion because the chronometric approach did not perfectly account for children's performance. In addition, the approach averages across children and problems, thereby obscuring the fact that (a) children in the same grade may use different strategies and (b) an individual child may use different strategies at different times (Siegler & Jenkins, 1989).

The second approach, called the *microgenetic* approach, was designed to avoid some of the problems of the chronometric approach (Siegler & Jenkins, 1989). In a microgenetic study, an individual child is interviewed and observed for many weeks until he or she discovers a strategy. For example, a child who is taught the count-all strategy might be followed until she invents the count-on strategy on her own. Siegler and his colleagues have found that most children use multiple strategies instead of a single strategy. Moreover, first graders have been found to use direct retrieval for so-called "ties" (e.g., $1 + 1$, $2 + 2$, $3 + 3$, etc.) and fifth graders have been found to use count-all when fatigued or uncertain. Thus, the "one child-one strategy" characterization implied by the chronometric approach appears to be incorrect. The proper characterization of performance seems to be a child deciding among *several* strategies. It is interesting to note that the idea of children using a repertoire of strategies has been found in studies of reform-based classrooms as well (Fuson, Wearne, Hiebert, Murray, Human, Olivier, Carpenter, & Fennema, 1997).

In contrast to the large amount of research conducted with single-digit addition problems, very few studies have examined children's learning of two-digit addition problems such as "$24 + 17 = ?$" One study showed that even first graders can learn to solve two-digit problems that require regrouping when they are given considerable practice learning how to relate the addends to manipulatives (Fuson & Briars, 1990). Using base-ten blocks, children were taught to relate digits in the ones' column of a number (e.g., the "4" in "24") to small, square blocks called "ones" and the digits in the tens' column (e.g., the "2" in "24") to long, rectangular blocks called "tens." Base-ten blocks are such that ten "ones" stuck together in a column is the same length and width as a single "tens" block. The success of Fuson and Briar's study is somewhat surprising given that few people would have thought that first graders could handle the notion of *place value.* Place value misunderstandings are very prevalent in second, third, and fourth graders in traditional classrooms.

As for subtraction, the research on single-digit problems has revealed findings similar to those for single-digit addition sentences. Instruction on subtraction often begins near the end of the first grade and involves children using the "take away" method with fingers or manipulatives. The earliest chronometric and interview studies on subtraction revealed that children seem to use at least three mental counting procedures (Resnick, 1983). In the *decrementing* model, the child starts with the larger number (the minuend) and decrements by one as many times as indicated by the smaller number (the subtrahend). For example, with "$7 - 3$," the child holds up seven fingers and says "6-5-4 . . . 4." This decrementing approach is consistent with what teachers show children. In the *incrementing* model, the child starts with the subtrahend (e.g., 3) and increments it by one until the minuend is reached. For example, she holds up three fingers and says "4-5-6-7 . . . 4" as she progressively adds four fingers to the original three. In the *choice* model, the child decides which of the decrementing or incrementing strategies would produce the answer with the fewest steps. Reaction-time studies suggested that although most primary children use the choice model, many second graders seem to depend on the decrementing model. Using the microgenetic approach, however, Siegler (1989) found that children at all ages rely on multiple strategies when they solve subtraction problems.

In later grades, children progress to two- and three-digit subtraction problems and confront a new set of challenges. Consider several examples:

$$\begin{array}{ll} \text{(a)} \quad 28 & \text{(b)} \quad 24 \\ \quad \underline{-17} & \quad \underline{-17} \end{array}$$

The first issue that children need to deal with is the new vertical "look" of these problems. Additional issues arise when children are asked to solve problems that require regrouping (e.g., example "b" above). The standard algorithm of placing a dash through the left-hand number (e.g., the "2" in 24) in order to add a ten to the right-hand number (e.g., make "4" into "14") usually seems utterly meaningless and mysterious to children. As a result, they often make a number of procedural errors when they try to execute this algorithm.

Brown and Burton (1978) analyzed the types of errors that children make when they try to solve subtraction with regrouping problems. They found that an important source of errors was children's consistent tendency to omit key steps in the general subtraction algorithm. For example, when given a problem such as "205 – 26," children would place a dash through the "0" in "205," change the "5" into a "15," and change the "0" into a "9." However, they would forget to make the "2" into a "1." Thus, they would give the answer of "279," a number larger than either the subtrahend or minuend! Brown and Burton called errors such as these "bugs," because they are like the missing steps in a faulty computer program. Figure 9.2 lists several of the more common subtraction "bugs."

Why are "bugs" so prevalent on regrouping problems? Many experts think that children make these errors because the standard "dashes" algorithm is presented in a meaningless, computational way (Carpenter et al., 1997; Resnick, 1987). As a result, few children understand what they are doing when they place dashes through numbers and decrement them by one. A more meaningful way to present the subtraction algorithm is to expand out minuends and subtrahends into their constituent parts. Consider the problem "205 – 26" again. "205" can be written as "200 + 5" and "26" can be rewritten as "20 + 6." After lining up digits by columns, children can readily see that they cannot take the 6 away from the 5, so they need to regroup the 200 into "190 + 10." That way, the "10" and "5" can be combined into "15." After children become familiar with the expanded format, they will begin to understand why you have to "skip" over the "0" in "205" to borrow the "1" from the "2." Children could also model the problem using Base-ten blocks or other manipulatives (e.g., bundles of sticks).

FIGURE 9.2 *Some of the More Common Subtraction "Bugs"*

1. BORROW/FROM/ZERO

   For problems in which children need to borrow from a 0 (e.g., 205 – 26), they write a "9" above the 0 but do not continue borrowing from the column to the left of 0 (e.g., answer given = 279).

2. SMALLER/FROM/LARGER

   For problems in which a smaller number is above a larger number in a given column (e.g., 217 – 98), children subtract the smaller from larger instead of borrowing (e.g., answer given = 281).

3. DIFF/0 – N = N

   Whenever the top digit in a column is a "0," children write the bottom digit instead of borrowing and subtracting (e.g., 306 – 13 = 313).

From: Brown and Burton (1978).

What is missing in the "dashes" algorithm, then, and is explicit in the expanded format is a meaningful representation of *place value.* The "dashes" algorithm suggests that the "2" in "205" represents a "2," not a "200." Once again we see the hazards of moving too quickly into computational algorithms before children have a sufficient understanding of concepts such as place value. In a recent study, seventh graders were taught to mentally transform numbers in multi-digit subtraction problems into the expanded format. This technique increased the speed and efficiency with which students performed the computations and also enhanced their "number sense" (Markovits & Sowder, 1994).

Word Problems.   When confronted with word problems such as those in Figure 9.3, most children in traditional classrooms have trouble (Carpenter, 1987). Math teachers in these classrooms are initially puzzled by children's difficulty with word problems because there does not seem to be a major difference between, say, the first word problem in Table 9.2 and the decontextualized problem "3 + 5 = ?" What is it about word problems that make them so difficult? Most theorists have tried to answer this question by proposing a set of cognitive operations that need to be performed in order for a problem to be solved. Errors are explained by saying that children failed to perform one or more of these operations correctly. In what follows, we shall examine some of the more central operations.

FIGURE 9.3   *Three Major Semantic Structures of Arithmetic Word Problems*

1. *Change*

   Julia has 3 cookies. Tommy gives her 5 more.
   How many does she have altogether?

   Julia has some cookies. Tommy gives her 5 more. Now Julia has 8. How many did she have to start with?

   Success Rate: First Grade (41–100 percent)[a]
   Fifth Grade (67–100 percent)

2. *Combine*

   Julia has 3 cookies. Tommy has 5 cookies. How many do they have altogether?

   Julia has 3 cookies. Tommy has some cookies too. Together they have 8 cookies. How many does Tommy have?

   Success rate: First Grade (39–88 percent)
   Fifth Grade (72–94 percent)

3. *Compare*

   Julia has 3 cookies. Tommy has 5 cookies. How many does Tommy have more than Julia?

   Julia has 3 cookies. Tommy has 2 more than Julia. How many cookies does Tommy have?

   Success rate: First Grade (6–81 percent)
   Fifth Grade (60–86 percent)

[a]*Note:* Success rates derive from figures provided in Riley et al. (1983) and Morales et al. (1985). Success varies as a function of the placement of the unknown and wording of the question.

One of the first things that a child needs to do in order to solve a word problem is construct an accurate *situation model* (Kintsch & Greeno, 1985). As noted in Chapters 6 and 7, a situation model is a mental representation of the state of affairs described in a text passage. In the case of word problems like those in Figure 9.3, it is a representation of the number of objects that each character has and what happens to each character's objects as the problem progresses. A situation model is "accurate" if it correctly reflects the underlying *semantic structure* of the problem (Carpenter & Moser, 1982; Riley et al., 1983). The notion of semantic structure refers to whether the problem involves increases, decreases, or comparisons of sets (see Figure 9.3 for illustrations of the three most common types). If something interferes with a child's ability to construct an accurate situation model for a word problem, he or she will not be able to solve it.

One factor that interferes with the construction of a situation model is the placement of the unknown in the problem. In "change" problems, for example (see Figure 9.3), the unknown can be in the *start set* (e.g., "Julia has some cookies . . . "), the *change set* (e.g. "Julia has three cookies. Tommy gives her some more . . . ") or the *result set* (e.g., "How many does she have altogether?"). Children have much more difficulty creating a situation model when the unknown is the start set or change set than when it is the result set (Morales, Shute, & Pellegrino, 1985; Riley et al., 1983; Sophian & Vong, 1995).

Young children's difficulty with undefined start sets or change sets has been attributed to their lacking a well-established *part-part-whole* schema for numbers (Resnick, 1983; Riley et al., 1983). With the development of the part-part-whole schema, a given number (the whole) is understood as being made up of multiple combinations of other numbers (the parts). Before the acquisition of a part-part-whole schema, a number such as three is conceptualized as a set of objects whose cardinal value falls between two and four. After the part-part-whole schema develops, however, several things happen. First, a number such as three is now conceptualized as being partitioned into the following combinations: "0 3", "1 2," and "2 1." Second, addition is viewed as being the combination of parts (e.g., $1 + 2 = 3$), subtraction is viewed as the removal of one part from the whole (e.g., $3 - 2 = 1$), and addition and subtraction are viewed as inverse operations (e.g., $3 - 2 = 1$ is the inverse of $1 + 2 = 3$). In contrast, children who lack the part-part-whole schema solve addition and subtraction problems in a linear, "on line" way and fail to see a relationship between expressions such as "$3 + 1 = 4$" and "$1 + 3 = 4$." The reader may note that the part-part-whole schema would be quite useful for understanding the expanded forms of subtraction-with-regrouping problems.

If children lack a part-part-whole schema and try to solve a word problem in a linear way, they will encounter an impasse when an unknown start set or change set is reached. For the fourth problem shown in Figure 9.3, for example, they might say, "Julia has three cookies, so I should hold up three fingers. Tommy has some cookies, so I should hold up. . . . Wait! How many is 'some'?" In contrast, unknown start sets and change sets cause fewer problems for children who have the part-part-whole schema because the unknown is simply seen as a missing element in a three-component schema. In effect, when they are given the fourth problem in Figure 9.3, they might reason, "I know how many Julia has and how many they have altogether, so I need to find out how many Tommy has."

In addition to constructing an accurate situation model, the second thing children need to do in order to solve a word problem is understand what the author of a word problem is asking of them. For the first "compare" problem in Figure 9.3, for example, children may not understand that the question "How many does Julia have more than Tommy?" is asking them to compare Julia's amount to Tommy's amount (Stern, 1993). Performance is often quite poor on compare problems because of this language factor. In a related way, problems arise when the language used (e.g., *more than*) is actually inconsistent with the operation required (e.g., subtraction). When inconsistent language is used, even college students have trouble (Lewis & Mayer, 1987).

After constructing an accurate situation model and determining what is being asked, children are finally in a position to use addition or subtraction to derive the answer. Which operation to perform, of course, will depend on the specific semantic structure of the problem and the placement of the unknown. For example, in "change" problems with an unknown result set (e.g., the first problem in Figure 9.3), addition should be used. In "change" problems with an unknown change set (e.g., the second problem in Figure 9.3), however, subtraction should be used.

Once the barriers to constructing situation models and understanding what is asked are overcome, continued practice is likely to foster the development of (a) *problem schemata* for the various types of word problems, (b) *action schemata* for the solutions to each of these problems (Riley et al., 1983), and (c) associative links between problem schemata and action schemata. The development of such schemata help children come up with correct answers more quickly and efficiently. That is, they would not have to "reinvent the wheel" each time they encounter a problem of a particular type.

Thus, it has been common to explain elementary school children's problems in solving word problems by appealing to (a) their lack of a part-part-whole schema, (b) language or reading barriers that make it difficult to create situation models, and (c) their lack of sufficient practice solving word problems. Although all of these problems could contribute to the observed age trends, it is important to note that even kindergartners have been found to solve both addition and subtraction word problems when an engaging story is used (e.g., a bear who gives objects to friends; a monster who takes objects away) and when the change amount is one (e.g., Sophian & Vong, 1995). Thus, it is possible to find evidence of part-part-schemata in kindergartners.

Concepts and Strategies in Reform Classrooms.   As noted earlier, all of the aforementioned age trends pertained to traditional classrooms that focus very little on concepts and place a heavy emphasis on memorization of calculation algorithms. What happens in classrooms when (a) instruction centers on building conceptual knowledge, (b) emphasis is placed on solving problems from the beginning, (c) children are asked to invent their own strategies for solving these problems, and (d) children are given the opportunity to share their solutions and explain their reasoning to the class? Analysis of four research-based reform classrooms (that have these characteristics) showed that children's problem-solving strategies can be categorized into four types (Fuson, et al., 1997). In the first (*begin-with-one-number methods*), children begin with one number and move up or down by tens and ones. For example, for the problem 38 + 26, a child might reason that 38 + 20 is 58, and 58 + 6 is 64. For the second method (*mixed methods*), a child might add or subtract tens, make a sequence number with the original ones, and then add or subtract other ones. For example, for 38 + 26 the child might add 30 and 20 to make 50; then add 8 to make 58;

then add 6 to make 64. For the third method (*change-both-numbers method*), children change the numbers to make the problem into an easier one. For example, for 38 + 26, the child may add 2 to 38 to make it into 40, and take the same amount away from 26 to make 24. Then he or she would add the 40 and the 24 to get 64. Finally there are *decompose-tens-and-ones* methods in which numbers such as 38 and 26 are decomposed into their constituents (30 + 8, and 20 + 6, respectively). Each of the tens and ones are added or subtracted separately (e.g., 30 + 20 is 50; 8 + 6 is 14; 50 + 14 is 64).

Of note is the fact that none of these strategies emerged in traditional classrooms. Strategies in the latter would only fall into two categories: correct algorithms and buggy algorithms (see above). Thus, reform classrooms tend to produce strategies that are closely linked to conceptual knowledge. In support of this claim, children in these classrooms have been found to have more base-ten conceptual knowledge than children in traditional classrooms, and have also been found to be less likely to demonstrate buggy algorithms (Carpenter et al., 1997).

Other Relevant Findings and Issues.   Whereas most of the research with elementary school children has focused on the strategies that students use with addition and subtraction problems, other studies have investigated such things as children's tendency to encode the parity (i.e., odd/evenness) of numbers in addition to encoding their magnitudes (e.g., Berch, Foley, Hill, & Ryan, 1999), children's performance on multiplication problems (e.g., Baroody, 1999), children's understanding of equivalence problems such as 3 + 2 + 5 = ___ + 5 (e.g., Rittle-Johnson & Alibali, 1999), factors affecting children's selection of strategies in a particular instance (Alibali, 1999; Siegler, 1996), and children's understanding of the inverse relationship between addition and subtraction (e.g., Bryant, Christie, & Rendu, 1999). Collectively, such studies in combination with those described above permit several conclusions to be drawn. First, it is clear that scholars in the fields of mathematics education, developmental psychology, and cognitive psychology approach the domain of mathematics in rather different ways. For example, whereas developmental psychologists try to show what young children (e.g., kindergartners) could do if given considerable contextual supports, mathematics educators try to show what children actually do across several years of instruction in mathematics (on their own). Relatedly, mathematics educators tend to select topics for study that take many years to master (e.g., place value) and begin their observations early in the game. Developmental psychologists, in contrast, sometimes choose topics that can be understood more quickly or acquired in a single session or a few sessions. Cognitive psychologists and developmental psychologists also tend to rely on associationist models of memory (see Chapter 3) to explain error rates and reaction times. Mathematics educators, in contrast, take a more constructivist view in which they trace the slow progressive changes in children's understanding and their invention of strategies.

But this diversity in perspectives has serendipitously produced the second major conclusion: The acquisition of mathematical competencies during the elementary period is multi-faceted and complex. It is good that developmental psychologists have tried to reveal nascent abilities in kindergartners and first graders because we might otherwise get the impression from the mathematics educators' work that young children are incapable of certain math concepts and skills. However, it is also good that mathematics educators focus on the conceptual difficulties faced in real-world classrooms because otherwise we might be puzzled as to why children have trouble (i.e.. If kindergartners can do it, why is it so hard for third graders?). Relatedly, it is important to see that children learn some things quickly and others more slowly in order to develop theories that can account for both kinds of learning. Finally, it is good that cognitive and developmental psychologists have emphasized associations and retrieval because we might have no explanation for errors committed in classrooms that seem to do everything according to NCTM standards. Note, for example, the fact that whereas children in reform classrooms demonstrate buggy algorithms less often than children in traditional classrooms, the former still demonstrate these errors. Successful implementation of strategies not only requires a conceptual understanding of procedures, it also requires storage and retrieval processes that reflect such things as repetition, practice, and interference effects (see Chapter 3). To illustrate this point, it is useful to consider a comment made by a fourth grader who had just participated in a study conducted by the author on the role of conceptual knowledge in procedural learning. When walking back to the classroom after being tested in a post-test (one week after conceptual instruction occurred), he said: "I knew I wasn't supposed to just add the tops and bottoms [of fractions] but I couldn't remember what I was supposed to do instead!" Thus, there is a lot to learn, comprehend, and remember about whole number concepts and procedures during the elementary period. The studies as a whole suggest that teachers can draw on children's nascent abilities to lay a foundation but also should give them ample time to comprehend and practice the major ideas, procedures, and strategies (Carpenter & Lehrer, 1999).

The Middle School Period

By the time they enter middle school, most children are quite proficient in their ability to execute various algorithms for addition, subtraction, multiplication, and division of whole numbers. In reform classrooms, they are also quite skilled at solving problems (even novel ones). But just when things are going so well, teachers introduce ideas such as *rational numbers* (e.g., fractions and decimals) and *integers* (e.g., "+7," "–4"). They are told that a number such as "3" is no longer simply a set of three objects or the product of combinations such as "2 + 1." Now it is described as the rational number "3/1" or the opposite of "–3." It should not be surprising to learn that most children from traditional classrooms find these ideas difficult to grasp. In what follows, we shall try to examine why rational numbers and integers are so hard to understand.

The difficulties children have with rational numbers and integers are both conceptual and procedural (Wearne & Hiebert, 1988). In the case of fractions, children have problems understanding concepts related to *cardinal, ordinal,* and *equivalence* relations (Byrnes & Wasik, 1991; Hiebert & Behr, 1988; Post, Wachsmuth, Lesh, & Behr, 1985). That is, they have trouble (a) relating symbols such as "3/5" to appropriate referents (cardinal relations), (b) understanding that "1/4" is less than "1/3" (ordinal relations), and (c) understanding that "1/2" is the same amount as "3/6" (equivalence relations). Procedurally, they have trouble learning the least common denominator method for adding fractions and the "invert and multiply" procedure for dividing fractions.

With respect to decimals and integers, children again have problems understanding concepts related to cardinal and ordinal relations. For example, they do not understand the role of zeros in decimals and fail to see how ".30" is larger than ".047" (Moss & Case, 1999; Resnick et al., 1989). Similarly, they have trouble relating negative integers to concrete referents and fail to see how "–9" could be less than "2" (Byrnes, 1992). Procedurally, children do not understand (a) why they have to "line up the decimal points" when they add or subtract decimals (Wearne & Hiebert, 1988) or (b) how to compute answers to problems such as "3 + –2" and "–3 – –2" (Byrnes, 1992).

Why do children have such trouble with rational numbers and integers? Three explanations seem plausible. The first is that rational numbers and integers are more abstract than positive whole numbers. Consider how it is easier to conceptualize "5" as "five dollars" than to conceptualize "–5" as "5 dollars in the hole." Similarly, it is easy to relate "3 + 2" to concrete actions (e.g., two children adding their cookies together) but not so easy to relate division of fractions to concrete actions.

The second explanation is that the concepts and procedures related to rational numbers and integers are quite different than those related to positive whole numbers. For example, the procedure for adding "1/3 + 1/2" is nothing like the procedure for adding "3 + 2." Thus, children cannot simply assimilate information about rational numbers and integers to their existing knowledge of whole numbers. They have to create brand new schemata for these new classes of numbers.

Because information about rational numbers and integers is so discrepant from what they know about whole numbers, both Piagetian theory and Vygotskian theory would predict that children would either ignore this new information or distort it to fit with what they already know (see Chapters 2 and 3). Close examination of children's errors suggests that many children seem to distort what they are learning. Consider the case of fractions. Conceptually, a child wants "1/3" to be less than "1/4" because "3" is less than "4." Procedurally, he wants to simply add numerators and denominators (e.g., 1/2 + 1/3 = 2/5) because that is how whole numbers are added. Similar "over-assimilations" or "mis-analogies" exist for decimals and integers (Byrnes, 1992; Byrnes & Wasik, 1991), and have been found when children shift from addition to multiplication (Baroody, 1999).

The third explanation is that many teachers in traditional classrooms spend very little time teaching the conceptual underpinnings of procedures related to rational numbers and integers. Most of the time they teach procedures in a purely computational way (Byrnes, 1992; Hiebert & Behr, 1988; Gearhart, Saxe, Seltzer, Schlackman, Ching, Nasir, Fall, Bennett, Rhine, & Sloan, 1999). As noted earlier, children who lack conceptual knowledge are likely to make many computational errors. In support of this claim, Byrnes (1992), Byrnes and Wasik (1991), and Hecht (1998) found that children who had more conceptual knowledge of fractions and integers prior to instruction learned procedures for adding these numbers better than children with less conceptual knowledge, even after controlling for grades and intellectual ability. Hecht (1998) also showed that conceptual knowledge of fractions predicted performance on fractions word problems as well.

Once again, though, there are studies conducted by developmental psychologists who show that children as young as five can demonstrate some implicit insight into the part-whole reasoning required to understand fractions and proportions (e.g., Sophian,

Garyantes, & Chang, 1997; Sophian & Wood, 1997). But translating this implicit understanding into success on classroom problems involving fractions is another matter. Do these findings suggest that first graders could be brought to understand solutions to problems such as: "Pretend we have half a pizza left after a party that is cut into four pieces. If we cut these pieces up further to give equal-sized pieces to eight children who helped clean up, what fraction of the pizza would each one get?" Probably not. But the findings with young children do suggest that the typical approach of whole numbers first (until third grade) followed by fractions later could be problematic. Perhaps children would be less inclined to make faulty analogies if they learned fractions in parallel with whole numbers. And yet, the order may matter less than the manner in which fractions and other rational numbers are presented to children. When children learn multiple representations of rational numbers (e.g., the relation between ½, 50 percent, and .50, 1 divided by 2, etc.), they do not demonstrate as many conceptual and procedural problems (Moss & Case, 1999).

The High School Period

Although many high school students take courses in algebra, geometry, trigonometry, and calculus, most educational researchers have focused exclusively on a single subject: algebra. As a result, only the research on algebra will be examined here. In what follows, the literature on students' comprehension of algebraic formulae is summarized first and that concerning their understanding of algebra word problems is summarized second.

Algebraic Formulae.   Historically, mathematicians developed algebra to be "generalized arithmetic." That is, its formulae are abstractions across a large class of specific arithmetic "sentences." (Kaput, 1999; Resnick, Cauzinille-Marmeche, & Mathieu, 1987). For example, the expression "X + Y" is a generalization of specific arithmetic sentences such as "2 + 1," "3 + 2," and "9 + 7." One of the first things that children need to grasp in order to understand formulae, then, is the fact that "X" could stand for the "2," "3" or "9" of the three arithmetic sentences. In fact, "X" could stand for any number.

This notion of a *variable* is quite difficult for children to understand at first. In particular, research has shown that they seem to progress through several levels of understanding before they master it. At the lowest level, children immediately assign a number to "X" because they fail to grasp the notion of "unknown value." For example, when asked to "write a number that is three more than X," they first put down a value for X (e.g., 5) and then write one that is three more than the value given for X (e.g., 8). At the second level, they think that "X" stands for a specific number that is not yet known. At the third level, "X" is considered to be a generalized number; that is, it can take on more than one value. At the fourth level, "X" considered to be a variable that not only represents a range of values, but also is linked in a systematic way to a set of values represented by another variable such as "Y" (Herscovics, 1989; Kieran, 1989).

Of course, if students have trouble understanding the notion of variable, they will also have trouble dealing with algebraic expressions. When given an expression such as "X + 3 = Y" and asked "What is the value of Y?" children initially refuse to put the answer "X + 3" because they think that answers have to be a single, determinate value. In addition, children also have trouble combining variables within algebraic expressions. For example, some students do not understand why "7a" is the answer to "2a + 5a" and others make the error of assuming "z" is the answer to "2yz – 2y" (Kieran, 1989).

Why do students make such errors? Four explanations can be offered. First, just as "–5" is more abstract than "5," "X" is more abstract than either of the former two numbers (cf. Resnick et al., 1987). In particular, whereas any negative or positive number can be related to a specific concrete array of objects, variables must be related to an array of possible *numbers*. Second, algebraic operations cannot be easily assimilated to arithmetic operations. For example, although the expression $(3 + 2)^2$ is formally related to the generalization $(a + b)^2$, the "answer" to these two problems would be computed in distinct ways. In particular, few children would solve the former by first forming the expression "(3 + 2)(3 + 2)" and then using the "foil" method to generate "$3^2 + (2)(3*2) + 2^2$." Most would say "5 squared is 25." Third, algebraic operations are usually taught in a non-conceptual, computational way (Wagner & Kieran, 1989). If these first three explanations seem familiar, they should because they were offered earlier when rational numbers and integers were at issue.

The fourth explanation has to do with the notion of *malrules* (Matz, 1982; Resnick et al., 1987). According to this proposal, students construct prototype rules from which they extrapolate new rules. For example, after working with many distributivity problems such as "3*(4 + 2) = 3*4 + 3*2" and "a(b + c) = ab + bc," children form the prototype rule "a # (b @ c) = (a#b) @ (a#c)." Then, when confronted with a problem such as $\sqrt{b + c}$, they think it can be decomposed into $\sqrt{b} + \sqrt{c}$.

Given the cognitive complexity of algebra, it may not be surprising to learn that many high school students perform poorly on the algebra items of large scale national assessments (e.g, Carpenter et al., 1981). For example, when given the equation "W = 17 + 5A" and asked "According to this formula, for each year older someone gets, how much more should he weigh?" only 64 percent of seventeen-year-olds with two years of algebra gave the right answer of "5 pounds more each year." Similarly, when given a table such as that below, only 80 percent of students who had two years of algebra could generate the missing numbers and only about a quarter of those students could generate the equation "y = X + 3" for this table.

X:	6	4	5	8	1
Y:		7	8		4

One way to help improve children's performance in algebra is to help them develop more accurate "mental models" of variables and algebraic operations (Kaput, 1999). One straightforward way to help them acquire a clear sense of functions such as "y = f(x)" is to have them release a ball from different heights and measure how high it bounces. In this way, they can create two columns of drop points (i.e., "x" values) and their corresponding bounce heights (i.e., "y" values). They will see that the height with which something bounces is a function of the height at which it is released. They will also clearly see that there is a very large range of possible heights (eliminating the one value interpretation of variables).

Algebra Word Problems.   Simply put, students have considerable difficulty with algebra word problems (Chaiklin, 1989; Mayer, Larkin, & Kaldane, 1984). In order to understand why this is so, most researchers have engaged in two phases of research. In the first phase, they proposed a model of the cognitive operations responsible for success on algebra word problems. That is, they gave an answer to the question, "What things do you need to do in your head in order to solve an algebra word problem?" In the second phase, they tried to identify the factors which interfere with a student's ability to execute one or more of the necessary operations.

Perhaps the most influential model of performance on algebra word problems is that proposed by Mayer, Larkin, and Kaldane (1984). Mayer et al. contend that students need to engage in four steps when they solve problems such as those in Figure 9.4:

1. First, the problem must be *translated* into a fragmented internal representation. That is, a string of propositional knowns and unknowns must be constructed using linguistic and factual knowledge. For example, for the "astronaut" problem in Figure 9.4, students need to create a string of mental propositions such as "OXYGEN PER ASTRONAUT PER DAY = 2.2," "NUMBER OF ASTRONAUTS = 3," and so on.
2. Second, the fragmented internal representation has to be reorganized into a coherent structure (e.g., "TOTAL OXYGEN = (OXYGEN PER ASTRONAUT PER DAY) × (NUMBER OF ASTRONAUTS) × (NUMBER OF DAYS) . . .)." Once the coherent structure is formed, the problem is *understood.* Mayer et al. believe that schemata for specific types of problems help students reorganize propositions into coherent structures;

FIGURE 9.4   *Examples of Algebra Word Problems*

The Astronaut Problem

An astronaut requires 2.2 pounds of oxygen per day while in space. How many pounds of oxygen are needed for a team of 3 astronauts for 5 days in space?

_____ 13.2   _____ 15.2   _____ 33   _____ 330

The Student-Professor Problem

Write an equation using S and P to represent the following statement: "There are six times as many students as professors at this university." Use S for the number of students and P for the number of professors.

The River Problem

A river steamer travels 36 miles downstream in the same time that it travels 24 miles upstream. The steamer's engine drives in still water at a rate of 12 miles per hour more than the rate of the current. Find the rate of the current.

Examples taken from Mayer et al. (1984).

3. Third, a plan has to be developed for how to generate the answer (e.g., "O.K., first I need to figure out TIME so I can then use this number to figure out the total amount of oxygen . . . "). Students' existing *strategic knowledge* helps them construct an effective plan;

4. Fourth, the plan has to be *executed* using appropriate algorithms (e.g., carry out the computations such as "2.2 × 3 × 5"). The execution phase, of course, requires knowledge of various algorithms.

There are two primary reasons why Mayer at al.'s model has credibility. First, it is based on successful computer simulations of algebra problem solving (e.g., Paige & Simon, 1966). Second, it has received good empirical support in the psychological literature. For example, Mayer (1982) found that when college students tried to make sense of so-called "relational" statements in word problems (e.g., "the rate in still water is 12 mph more than the rate in the current"), they had a strong tendency to misinterpret them as so-called "assignment" statements (e.g., "The rate in still water is 12 mph"). In addition, Clement (1982) found that only 63 percent of college students could write the proper formula for the "student-professor" problem in Figure 9.4. The most common error was to translate "six times as many students" as "6S" and put "6S = P" as their answer. Of course, if students make such errors during the translation phase of problem solving, they will not be able to come up with the right answer.

Additional empirical support for the four step model comes from studies which show the importance of problem schemata. For example, Hinsley, Hayes, and Simon (1977) found that many students demonstrate an immediate recognition of types of problems (e.g., "Oh, that's one of those 'rate' problems"). Students who are familiar with a type of problem will, of course, have a very good idea how to set up a plan for solving it. Other studies show that (a) students have an easier time recalling word problems if these problems are of the type that occur frequently in their algebra textbook (Mayer et al., 1984) and (b) students seem to use their schemata for problems to discriminate between irrelevant and relevant details (Low & Over, 1993).

Summary.   The last four subsections examined the development of mathematical skills from infancy to young adulthood. Three main themes emerged from this research. The first theme is that the more abstract math gets, the more children have conceptual and procedural problems. The second theme is that a number of children's problems seem to derive from the fact that traditional math instruction places far more emphasis on procedural knowledge than it does on conceptual knowledge. As a result, children make many "mindless" computational errors because they do not understand what they are doing. The third theme is that the acquisition of schemata greatly enhances children's understanding of, and success in, math.

As noted in Chapter 1, the key to fixing educational problems is to understand the developmental mechanisms responsible for these age trends. The chapters on theories, memory, and higher-order thinking (i.e., Chapters 2–4) help to explain the problems children face as they encounter increasingly abstract ideas. In addition, they suggest that growth in understanding would generally take a considerable amount of time as children progressively reconstruct their understanding of mathematics (Fuson et al., 1997). Moreover, the chapters show the importance of guided problem-solving in the acquisition of higher-order thinking and also the importance of sustained, deliberate practice in creating high-strength memory traces and the acquisition of mathematical expertise.

Individual Differences in Mathematical Skills

If classrooms were homogeneous such that all students were fairly similar to each other, then math teachers would only have to read the literature on developmental trends in order to know what to expect when teaching a particular age group. But, of course, classrooms are not homogeneous and the differences among students often seem to overwhelm the similarities. Thus, to get a complete picture of the classroom, a teacher needs to know something about developmental differences *and* individual differences.

In examining individual differences in math performance, researchers have asked, "Given this age group, are there subgroups of children who behave differently than others?" Typically, five variables have been used to form and compare subgroups of children within math classes: (a) gender, (b) ethnicity, (c) presence of a disability, (d) strategy preference, and (e) motivation. In what follows, the research on these five variables is described in turn.

Before proceeding, however, it should be noted that in the perspective of this book, the to-be-reported differences on gender and ethnic differences are not the inevitable consequence of education. Rather, many of these differences are symptomatic of an educational system that is not sufficiently sensitive to the needs of subgroups of children. The differences between genders and ethnic groups are merely reported in this chapter. Explanations of why these differences occur can be found in Chapter 12.

Gender Differences

Take a moment to answer the following three questions:

1. Who has more natural ability in math, boys or girls?
2. Who gets better grades in math, boys or girls?
3. Who does better on math achievement tests and experimenter-made math tests, boys or girls?

The consensus among most researchers is that the answer to the first question is "they both have the same," the answer to the second question is "girls," and the answer to the third is "it depends on factors such as age, type of test, and selectivity of the sample" (Halpern, 1992; Hyde, Fennema, & Lamon, 1990; see Chapter 12). Unfortunately, the consensus among average Americans seems to be that the answer is "boys" to all three questions (Eccles et al., 1985). Most people, then, are apparently unfamiliar with the current research on gender differences.

Let's examine the research pertinent to the third question because the data from achievement tests seem to play an important role in the average person's perceptions. Extensive reviews of many studies reveal that boys sometimes perform better than girls, girls sometimes perform better than boys, and sometimes there is no difference between boys and girls. In particular, gender differences favoring boys usually only emerge when the math test requires problem solving (e.g., the Scholastic Aptitude Test or SAT) *and* the students taking this test are either older than fourteen or gifted. Of course, there are exceptions to this general trend. For example, one recent study showed that whereas first grade boys are more likely to use direct retrieval when solving computation problems, girls are likely to use counting strategies (Carr & Jessup, 1997). No differences in achievement were found, however. Another exception would be the findings on the 1992 and 1996 National Assessment of Educational Progress (NAEP) for mathematics. Although the NAEP problems are very similar to those found on the SAT, no gender differences have been found in overall proficiency (Reese, Miller, Mazzeo, & Dossey, 1997).

Gender differences favoring girls are likely to emerge in two situations: (a) when the math test requires computational skill *and* the students are below the age of fifteen or (b) when the math test contains items that require knowing when you have enough information to answer *and* the students are gifted (Becker, 1990). However, few of these differences are large in absolute terms and there are lots of cases in which no gender differences are found (e.g., on tests measuring math concepts; Hyde et al., 1990). Thus, the cultural belief that boys always do better in math is incorrect. The origins and social consequences of faulty beliefs about gender differences are discussed in Chapter 12.

Ethnic Differences

In contrast to gender differences, ethnic differences tend to be large at all grade levels and are found for all three kinds of math tests (computations, concepts, and problem-solving). More specifically, whereas most "effect sizes" for gender differences are .20 or smaller (Hyde et al., 1990), most effect sizes for ethnic differences are .40 or larger (e.g., Stevenson, Chen, & Uttal, 1990; see Chapter 12 for an explanation of "effect size"). Moreover, if a difference exists between ethnic groups on one type of test (e.g., computations), a similar difference exists for other types of tests as well (e.g., problem-solving).

As to the specifics of ethnic differences, several conclusions can be drawn. First, as early as the first grade, White students tend to perform better than African-American or Hispanic students on math achievement tests (Alexander & Entwhistle, 1988; Johnson, 1989; Stevenson et al., 1990). Second, no clear or consistent differences emerge between African-American and Hispanic students; that is, sometimes African-Americans do better than Hispanics (e.g., Stevenson et al., 1990), sometimes Hispanics do better than African-Americans (e.g., College Board, 1988), and sometimes these groups perform about the same (e.g., Gross, 1993). Third, Asian-American students tend to perform better than White students, especially as children move into the middle school and high school years (Gross, 1988; College Board, 1988). On the SATs, for example, whereas the average math score for Asian students is 522, the average for White students is 490. For African-American and Hispanic students, the averages are 384 and 424, respectively. This means that Asian students get approximately thirty out of the sixty SAT items right (50 percent), White students get about twenty-seven right (45 percent), Hispanic students get about nineteen right (32 percent), and African-American students get about fourteen right (23 percent). The findings for the NAEP are very similar (Reese et al., 1997).

A significant factor that seems to contribute to ethnic differences in performance is a student's socio-economic status (SES). In particular, Stevenson et al. (1990) found that performance differences in math between White, African-American, and Hispanic students disappear when one controls for SES. In addition, SAT scores seem to be highly related to family income. For example, for those students whose family income is less than $10,000, the average SAT math score is 418. For those students whose family income falls between $30,000 and $40,000, the average is 473. If family income is $70,000 or more, the average is 523 (College Board, 1988). In terms of percent correct, these SAT scores turn out to be 32 percent, 42 percent, and 50 percent, respectively. We shall examine the role of SES further in Chapter 12.

Before moving on, it is important to note that the largest ethnic differences arise for so-called "formal" mathematics; that is, ethnic groups differ in terms of how well they have learned the curriculum-based math ideas appropriate for their grade level. In contrast, few ethnic or cross-cultural differences arise for the "informal" mathematical ideas that children construct prior to school or outside of school (Ginsburg & Russell, 1981). In Ginsburg and Russell's (1981) study, for example, White and African-American preschoolers differed on only two out of seventeen tasks that tap into informal math ideas (Ginsburg & Russell, 1981). In addition, low SES African-American students performed similarly to middle-class White students on these measures. The fact that ethnic differences emerge by the end of the first grade suggests that school differences may be producing the ethnic differences described earlier.

Students with Mathematical Disabilities

Approximately 6 percent of any classroom will contain children who meet the diagnostic criteria for having a mathematical disability (MD). Analysis of MD children shows that they have both procedural and fact-retrieval deficits. Moreover, these deficits appear to follow different developmental trajectories (Geary, 1993; Geary, Hoard, & Hamson, 1999). In the case of procedural problems, for example, it has been found that MD children usually lag behind their nondisabled peers in the sense that they often (a) use less mature strategies (e.g., "count all" versus "min"), (b) perform the same strategies more slowly, and (c) make calculation errors more often. By the end of second grade, however, the computational skills of MD children approach those of their non-MD peers. In contrast, fact-retrieval deficits tend to persist indefinitely and are resistant to remediation through extensive training. When MD children attempt to recall facts, they tend to recall fewer facts, the retrieval times associated with these facts are very unsystematic, and they make a large number of retrieval errors (Geary, 1993; Geary et al., 1999). These children also show problems in speed of processing, rapid naming of numbers, comparing the relative size of numbers, and working memory (Bull & Johnson, 1999; Geary et al., 1999; McLean & Hitch, 1999). Although MD children have no known history of brain injury, it has been common to look to the neuroscientific literature for possible explanations of their problems. To illustrate this approach, we can briefly examine some of the findings in this area. Studies have either involved brain-injured adults who experienced math problems after their injury or the use of neuroscientific measurement techniques (e.g., EEG recordings).

As for brain-injured adults, two models have been recently proposed to account for the patterns of calculation deficits that have sometimes occurred following brain injuries.

For expository purposes, these theoretical frameworks are called the *McCloskey model* and *Dehaene model,* respectively, though the focal individuals have had several collaborators.

The McCloskey Model.   After conducting a detailed analysis of fourteen case studies of brain-injured adults, Michael McCloskey and colleagues (e.g., McCloskey, Caramazza, & Basili, 1985; McCloskey, Aliminosa, & Sokol, 1991) proposed that calculation abilities can be decomposed into two clusters of functionally autonomous components. The first cluster, which comprise a *number processing system,* includes one set of components for comprehending numbers and another set for producing them. Within each of the comprehension and production sub-systems, moreover, there are distinct components for processing arabic numbers (e.g., *53*) and verbal numbers (e.g., *fifty-three*). All of these components were originally proposed to account for various forms of so-called "double dissociations" that appeared in the focal cases. For example, some of the patients could recognize arabic numbers but could not write them down when asked. Similarly, some could write arabic numbers but not verbal numbers.

The components in the second cluster comprise the *calculation system.* McCloskey et al. argue that these components perform three kinds of processes: (a) comprehension of the signs or words for operations (e.g., ÷, *divided by*), (b) retrieval of arithmetic facts (e.g., that 39 is the answer to 13 × 3), and (c) execution of calculation procedures (e.g., the algorithm for long division). Again, these components were inferred on the basis of certain double dissociations. Some patients, for example, could recognize the signs for operations but could not perform the operations indicated by these signs. Others, however, could perform the operations, but could not retrieve math facts associated with these operations. Moreover, there were individuals who could do some of the operations from the calculation system but could not do others from the number processing system (McCloskey et al., 1991). When the two systems are intact, however, they are thought to be linked via the ability to create abstract representations of the numbers and operations in a problem. This abstract representation is also linked to action systems that are alleged to regulate the implementation of goal-directed procedures.

Beyond such double dissociations, five other interesting aspects of the fourteen cases emerged. The first is that, in most of the patients (64 percent), problems developed after these patients experienced a cerebrovascular accident in the left hemisphere. In two other patients (14 percent), the cerebrovascular accident occurred in the right hemisphere. The remaining patients experienced a closed head injury (14 percent) or anoxia (7 percent). Thus, calculation skills in arithmetic seem to be localized in the left hemisphere, but the data are not completely consistent in this regard.

The second interesting finding was that in all fourteen cases, the calculation deficits were limited to multiplication (i.e., arithmetic skills for addition and subtraction were left largely intact). Thus, these findings suggest that there are brain regions associated with multiplication and other regions associated with arithmetic and subtraction. The third finding was that all patients showed uneven patterns of performance across particular kinds of multiplication problems. For example, some patients could solve all problems except those involving zero (e.g., 3 × 0 or 0 × 4). Others could solve problems with zero when it was the first but not the second multiplicand. Still others had no problem with items involving zeros and ones (e.g., 3 × 0 and 1 × 4), but had problems with all other combinations that had multiplicands between 2 and 9. The fourth was that each person seemed to have problems with their own types of items. Such findings suggest that each fact seems to be stored in its own format. Further analysis showed that many patients forgot the facts associated with all types of problems but could quickly reconstruct the facts for the problems with zero or one because the more abstract rules for these items were spared (e.g., "any number multiplied by 1 is itself"). Thus, there seem to be brain regions that store such abstract rules as well as others for storing other kinds of multiplication algorithms (e.g., how to line things up in columns for problems such as 317×32).

The Dehaene Model.   Dehaene and Cohen (1997) reviewed the neuropsychological literature related to mathematical deficits and proposed a "triple-code" model to account for the myriad of findings. As the name implies, the triple-code model suggests that there are three main representations of numbers: (1) a *visual arabic code* that is localized in the left and right inferior occipital-temporal areas, (2) an *analogical quantity* or *magnitude code* that is localized in the left and right inferior parietal areas, and (3) a *verbal code* that is localized in the left perisylvian areas. The visual arabic code, which subserves multidigit operations, is utilized during the identification of strings of digits, and during judgments of parity (e.g., knowing that numbers that end in 2 are even). The magnitude code, in contrast, is assumed to correspond to distributions of activation on an oriented number line. This code subserves the ability to evaluate proximity (e.g., that 18 is close to 20) and ordinal relations (e.g., that 20 is larger than 18). The verbal code, finally, represents numbers via a parsed sequence of words. It is involved when an individual accesses rote verbal memories of arithmetic facts.

Dehaene and Cohen further suggest that there are two basic routes through which arithmetic problems can be solved. In the direct route, the problem (e.g., 2×9) is first encoded into a verbal representation (e.g., "two times nine is . . . "). The verbal representation, in turn, triggers the rote-learned verbal answer that is stored in memory (e.g., "eighteen"). The latter process is thought to involve a left cortico-subcortical loop through the basal ganglia and thalamus. Hence, the direct route does not require conceptual analysis of any type and is largely devoid of meaning. In contrast, the second route is more indirect and calls on stored semantic knowledge of numbers. When problems are solved by the indirect route, a person recodes the arabic symbols into quantity representations. These quantity representations (thought to be localized in the left and right parietal areas) subserve semantically meaningful operations, such as when one alters a representation of the quantity 5 to make it into a representation of 7 or 3. The results of such manipulations are thought to be transmitted from the left inferior parietal cortex to the left perisylvian language network for naming.

Dehaene and Cohen's model, then, proposes that there are two major sets of brain areas that are critical for calculation: (a) the bilateral inferior parietal areas that are responsible for semantic knowledge about numerical quantities and (b) the left cortico-pallidum-thalamic loop that is involved in the storage of the verbal sequences that correspond to arithmetic facts. The model further assumes that brain lesions would have different effects depending on which of these two areas were damaged. The calculation deficits (or *acalculias*) that arise from damage to the inferior parietal areas should be domain-specific (i.e., damage should only affect number knowledge and not other kinds of knowledge) and be limited to problems that rely heavily on semantic math knowledge such as estimation, comparison, and ordinality (i.e., automatized facts should be uneffected). In contrast, acalculias that arise from damage to the cortico-subcortical loop should be domain-general (i.e., other kinds of rote-learned material besides math facts may be affected as well), and should involve loss of math facts combined with spared semantic skills (e.g., estimation, comparison, and ordinal relations).

Dehaene and Cohen (1997) demonstrated the utility of this model by applying it to two case studies. Whereas one of these patients had a localized inferior parietal lesion in the right hemisphere, the other had a left subcortical infarct. As predicted, the patient with the parietal lesion demonstrated the following double dissociation: he had difficulty considering semantic relations (e.g., comparing two numbers) but could recall automatized math facts. The other patient, in contrast, demonstrated the opposite kind of double dissociation.

It is notable that the two primary deficits of MD children correspond to two of the three component operations of the calculation system proposed by McCloskey and colleagues (see above). The fact-retrieval problem is also consistent with aspects of Dehaene and Cohen's model. The research on which these models are based further suggests that procedural and fact-retrieval problems are particularly likely to arise following lesions to the left hemisphere or the left cortico-subcortical systems. This left hemisphere bias is interesting given the fact that 40 percent of the children who have MD have been found to have a reading disability as well (Geary, 1993). As we saw in Chapter 6, many important reading skills seem to be localized in the left hemisphere.

As for neuro-imaging studies of healthy adults, Dehaene et al. (1996) presented number pairs to eight healthy adults. In one third of the trials, subjects were asked to mentally identify the larger of the two numbers. In another third of trials, they were asked to multiply the two numbers together. In the remaining third of trials, they simply rested with their eyes open. Using PET scans, Dehaene et al. considered the differences in blood flow patterns that were evident when any of the two conditions were compared to each other (e.g., multiplying numbers versus identifying the larger one). Results showed selective increases or decreases in blood flow in a number of brain areas. Notably, the number comparison task " . . . did not yield any significant activations over and above those that . . . are related to stimulus identification and response selection (lateral occipital cortex, precentral gyrus, and [supplementary motor area]) . . . Hence, no critical brain areas for number comparison emerged . . . " (Dehaene et al., 1996, p. 1103). Small activations, however, did emerge in the left and right inferior parietal region, but these activations were not significant (contrary to predictions based on Dehaene and Cohen's model; see above). It is not clear whether the use of PET scans, inadequate control trials, or a small sample size were responsible for these inconclusive results.

Using EEG technology, Dehaene (1996) limited his focus to just number identification and comparison. He attempted to verify a three-stage processing model that suggested that number comparison involved an initial stage of number comprehension (with distinct components for comprehending arabic symbols such as *3* and verbal symbols such as *three*) that was followed by comparative processes that operate on the mental representations that emerge after the symbols are interpreted. Results suggested that arabic digits are initially comprehended bilaterally in posterior occipito-temporal regions. Verbal digits, however, seem to be processed mainly in the left posterior region. As for the second stage of number comparison, activation seemed to occur mainly in the right parieto-occipito-temporal junction. This finding is consistent with the results of a case study reported by Dehaene and Cohen (1997) in which a right parietal lesion caused problems in quantity estimation. Dehaene (1996) concluded his paper by noting that "the right hemisphere appears to possess both the ability to identify a digit and to represent its magnitude relative to other numbers" (p. 64).

In sum, these findings regarding disabled and non-disabled individuals suggest that there are different regions of the brain for storing and processing different kinds of math facts (e.g., addition versus multiplication) and different kinds of math procedures (e.g., subtraction and multiplication). Also, these regions are distinct from those involved in certains of conceptual knowledge (e.g., ordinality). All of these regions tend to be localized near the sides and back of the head in both hemispheres. The fact that MD children also have problems with working memory and related tasks, however, suggests problems in coordinating information from the posterior regions (e.g., the parietal lobe) and the frontal lobes. Notably, the frontal-parietal system has also been found to be activated in other kinds of working memory tasks (see Chapter 3).

Strategy Preferences

As discussed earlier in the section on arithmetic, microgenetic studies have revealed that children possess a range of strategies for solving addition and subtraction problems. What was not mentioned earlier was that this research also revealed subgroups of children who have almost trait-like tendencies to solve problems in characteristic ways. Siegler (1988) labeled these subgroups "perfectionists," "good students," and "not-so-good" students.

When presented with arithmetic sentences (e.g., "3 + 7 = ?"), "perfectionists" tend to use time-consuming counting strategies unless they are highly confident that they could retrieve the answer directly from memory (e.g., 90 percent sure). "Good" students seem to set a lower threshold for confidence than perfectionists (e.g., 70 percent sure), so they count less often and use direct retrieval more often than perfectionists. This preference for efficiency seemed to pay off because "good" students were often correct when they used direct retrieval. "Not-so-good" students were similar to "good" students in their greater reliance on direct retrieval over counting, but the answers they retrieved were often wrong.

If you had to predict which of these subgroups would show the most achievement in math, which one(s) would it be? Perfectionists will almost always be correct because they almost always use a fool-proof method (i.e., counting). Good students should also do well because they seem to know when they should fall back on a fool-proof method. Not-so-good students, in contrast, would probably not do well. In support of these expectations, Siegler (1988) found that perfectionists were at the 84th and 80th percentiles on a standardized math test for computation and problem-solving, respectively. The corresponding figures for good students were 68 (computations) and 80 (problem-solving). For not-so-good students, they were 22 (computations) and 38 (problem-solving).

Motivational Differences

As noted in Chapter 5, motivation is the paradigmatic individual difference variable. Hence, whenever a difference in math achievement occurs between two individuals, it is always reasonable to wonder whether one person was more motivated to learn math than another. A recent meta-analysis of over one hundred studies showed, in fact, that students' attitude toward math tends to correlate about $r = .25$ with their mathematics achievement (Ma & Kishor, 1997). In other words, those with positive attitudes tend to do better than those with more negative attitudes. Conversely, a meta-analysis of twenty-six studies on the relationship between math anxiety and achievement found an average correlation of $r = -.27$. In other words, students who felt more anxious about math tended to perform worse on math assessments. Whereas these correlations do not seem to be very large, note that when they are expressed as binomial effect-size displays (Rosenthal, 1994), they suggest that there is a 25 percent difference in success rates between students who value math and those who do not (e.g., 37.5 percent of those who have negative attitudes do well versus 62.5 percent who have positive attitudes).

Instructional Implications

By way of introduction into the instructional implications of the research on developmental and individual differences in math skills, it is useful to return to the four characteristics of the ideal high school graduate that were presented earlier. The research as a whole provides very little evidence that the average twelfth grader in the United States (a) thinks of mathematics as being a meaningful, goal-directed activity that can help him or her solve problems in a variety of real-world and theoretical contexts, (b) is equipped with the knowledge he or she needs to solve a wide range of problems, (c) demonstrates an efficient and flexible approach to problem-solving, and (d) demonstrates adaptive mathematical behaviors and beliefs (see Chapter 5 for more on age trends in math beliefs and values). It is precisely this state of affairs that has precipitated the 1989 and 1998 standards of the NCTM.

In what follows, we shall first examine some general guidelines for instruction with an eye toward the reforms suggested by the NCTM and the research presented in this chapter. In contemporary Constructivist theory, flexible teaching is assumed to ensue when teachers have a clear understanding of the causes of success and failure in mathematics, not when they are simply armed with "teacher-proof" techniques (see Chapter 1). The guidelines tap into the causes of success and failure implicated earlier in this chapter. After the general guidelines have been presented, we shall examine two case studies of mathematics instruction for your evaluation.

General Guidelines

The research on mathematical thinking suggests the following instructional implications:

1. Preschool experiences should be structured in such a way to enhance children's existing mathematical knowledge, however informal or implicit it may be. In light of the importance of counting in early arithmetic, instruction that (a) prompts children to induce and extend the five counting principles and (b) increases their familiarity with numbers is also encouraged.

2. In line with the recommendations of the NCTM (1989 and 1998), instruction in arithmetic should focus on building children's conceptual referents for symbols using

concrete, goal-directed activities; There should be no chasm between rote computation and problem-solving. All computations should be performed in the service of solving a problem. The emphasis on conceptual understanding holds true for whole numbers, rational numbers, integers, and algebraic expressions. As a further illustration of the NCTM standards, see Figure 9.5.

FIGURE 9.5   *NCTM Standards for Pre-Kindergarten to Grade 12*

Standard 1: Number and Operation

Mathematics instructional programs should foster the development of number and operation sense so that all students (a) understand numbers, ways of representing numbers, relationships among numbers, and number systems, (b) understand the meaning of operations and how they relate to each other, and (c) use computational tools and strategies fluently and estimate appropriately.

Standard 2: Patterns, Functions, and Algebra

Mathematics instructional programs should include attention to patterns, functions, symbols, and models so that all students (a) understand various types of patterns and functional relationships, (b) use symbolic forms to represent and analyze mathematical situations and structures, and (c) use mathematical models and analyze change in both real and abstract contexts.

Standard 3: Geometry and Spatial Sense

Mathematics instructional programs should include attention to geometry and spatial sense so that all students (a) analyze characteristics and properties of two- and three-dimensional geometric objects, (b) select and use different representational systems, including coordinate geometry and graph theory, (c) recognize the usefulness of transformations and symmetry in analyzing mathematical situations, and (d) use visualization and spatial reasoning to solve problems both within and outside of mathematics.

Standard 4: Measurement

Mathematics instructional programs should include attention to measurement so that all students (a) understand attributes, units, and systems of measurement and (b) apply a variety of techniques, tools, and formulas for determining measurements.

Standard 5: Data Analysis, Statistics, and Probability

Mathematics instructional programs should include attention to data analysis, statistics and probability so that all students (a) pose questions and collect, organize, and represent data to answer those questions, (b) interpret data using exploratory data analysis, (c) develop and evaluate inferences, predictions, and arguments that are based on data, and (d) understand and apply basic notions of chance and probability.

Standard 6: Problem-Solving

Mathematics instructional programs should focus on solving problems as part of understanding mathematics so that all students (a) build new mathematical knowledge through their work with problems, (b) develop a disposition to formulate, represent, abstract, and generalize in situations within and outside mathematics.

FIGURE 9.5   *Continued*

Standard 7: Reasoning and Proof

Mathematics instructional programs should focus on learning to reason and construct proofs as part of understanding mathematics so that all students (a) recognize reasoning and proof as essential and powerful parts of mathematics, (b) make and investigate mathematical conjectures, (c) develop and evaluate mathematical arguments and proofs, and (d) select and use various types of reasoning and methods of proof as appropriate.

Standard 8: Communication

Mathematics instructional programs should use communication to foster understanding of mathematics so that all students (a) organize and consolidate their mathematical thinking to communicate with others, (b) express mathematical ideas coherently and clearly to peers, teachers, and others, (c) extend their mathematical knowledge by considering the thinking and strategies of others, and (d) use the language of mathematics as a precise means of mathematical expression.

Standard 9: Connections

Mathematics instructional programs should emphasize connections to foster understanding of mathematics so that all students (a) recognize and use connections among different mathematical ideas, (b) understand how mathematical ideas build on one another to produce a coherent whole, and (c) recognize, use, and learn about mathematics in contexts outside of mathematics.

Standard 10: Representation

Mathematics instructional programs should emphasize mathematical representations to foster understanding of mathematics so that all students (a) create and use representations to organize, record, and communicate mathematical ideas, (b) develop a repertoire of mathematical expressions that can be used purposely, flexibly, and appropriately, and (c) use representations to model and interpret physical, social, and mathematical phenomena.

Adapted from the 1998 discussion draft of the NCTM 2000 Standards (NCTM, 1998).

3. In line with Vygotskian and Piagetian theory (see Chapter 2), instruction should form bridges between children's informal math ideas and the formal mathematics presented in school (Allardice & Ginsburg, 1983; Fuson et al., 1997). Early ethnic differences in school performance may well reflect differences in the way teachers can build such bridges.

4. Instructional activities should promote the acquisition of part-part-whole schemata for numbers as well as the schemata which underlie successful performance on various types of word problems. Generally, this is accomplished by having students solve structurally similar problems and asking them to induce the similarities (Gick & Holyoak, 1983; Sweller & Cooper, 1985).

5. Teachers in the later grades should identify existing differences between subgroups of students and try to tailor instruction to the specific needs of these subgroups. Teachers in the early grades should try to avoid creating performance differences in the first place.

6. Teachers should strive to create as many "perfectionists" and "good students" as possible. High standards for accuracy are likely to promote the former grouping (see Chapter 5 for more on personal standards). Exercises that promote an accurate metacognitive understanding of when you do and do not know an answer is likely to promote the latter grouping.

7. Finally, teachers need to coordinate their multiple emphases on conceptual understanding, problem-solving, and easy-to-access memory traces of mathematical information. By focusing on conceptual understanding and problem-solving, teachers increase the chances that their students will (a) learn procedures in the first place, (b) retain procedures over time, (c) develop intrinsic motivation for solving problems involving math, (d) solve unfamiliar or non-routine problems, and (e) invent or reconstruct procedures on their own. Students also need time to practice their newly acquired strategies in order to supplement the memory enhancements that accrue from inventing procedures and learning them in context (see Chapter 3 for more on the so-called generation effect and the role of practice).

Case Studies

Case Study 1. To illustrate how teachers can translate contemporary theory and research on math learning to practice, we can give more detail to the study of Markovits and Sowder (1994) that was described earlier. These researchers worked closely with a classroom teacher to increase the "number sense" of her seventh grade students using a total of seventy-six lessons that were 5 to 50 minutes in duration. Let's examine a portion of one of these lessons that tried to help students increase their estimation skills.

There were three parts to this lesson. During the first part, the teacher discussed each of seven problems on a worksheet. The first problem on the sheet was "26 + 58 = 84. What happens if you add 1 to 26 and subtract 1 from 58?" The second was "26 × 58 = 1508. What happens if you add 1 to 26 and subtract 1 from 58?" As students discussed these problems, the teacher helped them see and understand how adding or subtracting numbers to operands works differently with addition and multiplication.

During the second part of the lesson, students discussed their homework problems involving estimation. One problem asked them to add four numbers, each of which had three or four digits. The idea of such exercises is that when you estimate, it is important to round up and round down numbers in compensatory ways. If you round up all numbers, the answer will be way off. For example, the answer to "450 + 550 + 650 + 750" is "2400." If you round all numbers up to 500, 600, 700, and 800, respectively, you get the answer 2600, and you are off by 200. In contrast, if you round to get 500, 500, 700, and 700, you get exactly 2400.

In part three of the lesson, students were shown a problem and asked which of three answers would give the closest estimate. For example, given a problem similar to 42 × 73, and the choices 40 × 70, 42 × 70, and 40 × 73, students were led to see that 40 × 70 cannot be the closest because both numbers are rounded down. To decide between the other choices, students were asked to determine how much they would lose in each estimate. With 42 × 70, they come to see that they lose 3 × 42 or 126. With 40 × 73, they lose 2 × 73 or 146. The discussion was then followed with a card game in which students were asked to decide the closest estimates using similar multiplication problems.

Use the information presented earlier in this chapter as well as that presented in the chapters on theories, memory, higher-order thinking, and motivation to evaluate this lesson.

Case Study 2.   In an effort to reduce the conceptual and procedural problems associated with rational numbers, Moss and Case (1999) created the following unit for fourth graders. The visual prop used throughout the unit was a beaker of water. In the early lessons, children were asked to assign numerical values from 1 to 100 to various amounts of water. For example, they might be asked, "If 0 is for completely empty (points to bottom) and 100 is for completely full (points to top), what number should we give this amount (points to halfway mark)?" In effect, the early lessons were intended to instill insight into the idea of percentage. As the lessons progressed, children were encouraged to exploit their intuitive conceptions of fullness, numerical halving, and composition. These conceptions were linked to amounts of water in the beaker and they were encouraged to link visual and motor activities to these conceptions. For example, for numerical halving, they were asked to make a "c" shape with their thumb and index finger and place these digits against the side of the beaker (with the space between digits matching the amount of water in the beaker). After children seemed to understand how percentage values could be computed numerically and coordinated with their visual-motor behaviors, they were then introduced to two-place decimals. Here, they were told that two-place decimals indicate the "percentage of the way between two adjacent whole number distances that an intermediate point lies (e.g., 5.25 is a distance that is 25 percent of the way between 5 and 6). Finally, children were presented with exercises in which fractions, decimals, and percents were used interchangeably.

Evaluate this unit using the information presented in this chapter and the information presented in Chapters 2–5.

10

Scientific Thinking

Summary

1. Scientific knowledge helps students to become better decision-makers, problem-solvers, and critical thinkers.

2. Scientists create theories to explain phenomena. Non-scientists also create theories, but these naive theories often contain misconceptions.

3. Children seem to develop framework theories for psychology, biology, and physics during the preschool period. However, these theories change considerably over time.

4. People develop naive theories in response to their experiences. People who have different experiences usually develop different theories. Moreover, personal theories can be highly idiosyncratic.

5. Science education can be viewed as changing naive theories into their scientific counterparts. In general, theories become more accurate, elaborate, and metacognitive with age.

6. Scientists use their theories to form hypotheses. In addition, they use the "isolation of variables" technique to test their hypotheses. Non-scientists, in contrast, often conduct experiments in which variables are not systematically controlled. Moreover, they usually try to confirm their hypotheses rather than disconfirm them.

7. With age, there is a decrease in the tendency to conduct uncontrolled experiments and seek confirmation of one's hypotheses. Nevertheless, many adolescents and adults engage in imperfect scientific reasoning.

8. Whereas small gender differences have been found on science achievement tests that require knowledge of facts, no gender differences have been found for hypothesis-testing, experimentation, and misconceptions. In contrast, large ethnic differences have been found in science achievement.

Most readers of this book would probably agree that math and reading skills are essential for successful adaptation to the world of adults. In other words, it would almost be impossible for someone to get a high-paying job, manage household finances, and so on without reading and math skills. But next consider the case of science. Could a high school graduate be successful in life if he or she had very little knowledge of the key ideas and methodological strategies of biology, physics, psychology, or chemistry? Why should students learn anything at all about these domains if they do not intend to become scientists when they grow up?

Educators, parents, and policy-makers constantly grapple with such questions. Note that when something is taught during a given class period, that means that something else is *not* being taught. How much time should be devoted to science during a given day or week of the school year? Other important decisions relate to the proper timing of instruction. As noted in Chapter 1, it would be fairly useless to introduce topics in a particular grade when these topics would be beyond the comprehension level of children in that grade. When should science topics first be introduced?

The primary goal of this chapter is to answer these and related questions in four main sections. In the first, questions pertaining to the importance of higher-order thinking skills in science are addressed. In the second, research pertinent to the development of scientific knowledge and skills is reviewed. In the third, individual differences in scientific knowledge and skills are described. In the final section, the instructional implications of the research on scientific thinking are drawn.

The Importance and Nature of Higher-Order Scientific Thinking

The goal of the present section is to give a sense of what it means to be competent in the area of science and why this competence is important for students to have.

Why Include Science in the Curriculum?

Science educators are similar to their colleagues in the areas of mathematics, reading, and writing in their emphasis on expert models of performance (see Chapters 6–9). That is, in response to the question, "What should students know and be able to do in the area of science when they graduate?" science educators assume that students should think and behave like practicing scientists. Notably, the goal here is to get *all* students to think and behave in this way, not just students who want to pursue a science-related career.

What is so special about scientific thinking that educators would want all students to become competent in this regard? The first thing to note is that the primary goal of science is to reveal the causal structure of the world. When we understand what causes what, we can manipulate nature to (a) make desirable things happen and (b) keep undesirable things from happening (as far as possible). It is through science that we have learned how to grow crops in the desert, lose weight but remain healthy, cure life-threatening diseases, teach students better, raise responsible and caring children, and so on. The more students understand about the causal structure of the world, the more they will be equipped to recognize the difference between effective courses of action and ineffective courses of action (e.g., fads). In effect, *science helps students to become better decision-makers and problem-solvers.*

A related point is that there is a fair amount of overlap between the constructs "high-quality scientific thinking" and "critical thinking" (Klaczynski & Narasimham, 1998). Scientists are trained to make use of logical argumentation and credible evidence to draw appropriate conclusions about the causal structure of the world. For example, competent scientists would not draw unwarranted inductive inferences (e.g., "This group of three-year-olds wanted to learn how to read so all three-year-olds probably would"), nor would they accept data at face value. Data is only informative regarding the structure of the world when it is obtained using valid forms of measurement and experimentation. To illustrate, imagine that there was something wrong with the equipment used to measure the temperature of the earth. This equipment might suggest that the earth is heating up or cooling down when its temperature is really staying the same. The government, in turn, may pass laws to correct a problem that does not really exist. As another example, a lot of people became excited about data that seemed to suggest that taking music lessons improves spatial and math ability (e.g., Rauscher, Shaw, Levine, Wright, Dennis, & Newcomb, 1997), until other researchers showed that such data could not be replicated or was due to experimental artifacts (Steele, Bass, & Crook, 1999). In spite of the latter results, people are making a great deal of money from music videos and CDs for children that will have no effect on children's spatial and math skills. It staggers the mind to think of all the programs and policies that have been implemented over the years on the basis of scant or misleading data. To reduce the incidence of flawed decision-making in the future, it is vital that parents, educators, and politicians engage in the kind of reasoning evident in our best scientists.

But in order to get our high school and college graduates to think like competent scientists, we need to answer two important questions: (a) What characteristics of scientists help them to reveal the causal structure of the world? and (b) What is the best way to instill these characteristics in students? In what follows, we will attempt to answer the first of these questions. The second question will be addressed later when we consider the instructional implications of the research on science.

The Characteristics of Competent Scientists

Most scholars agree that the causal structure of the world is relatively opaque (Byrnes, 1998). In other words, it is not always clear why certain actions have the effects that they do. More importantly, it is often the case that actions that seem to be effective are not really effective. Consider two health-related examples to illustrate. Some people take Vitamin C when they feel a cold coming on. If an individual were to compare the people who take Vitamin C to those who do not, that individual would find that both groups get over their colds in the same number of days. The average person does not bother to conduct such an experiment, so those in the Vitamin C group have only the fact that they got over the cold as evidence of the effectiveness of Vitamin C (i.e., they have no idea what would happen if they did not take it). Hence, they are misled into thinking that it works. A related example is the use of antibiotics for young children. In most cases, antibiotics have to be taken for fourteen days before they "work." It is probably the case that many untreated children would get over an ailment in two weeks on their own, but parents would never find this out because they feel like they have to give something to help their children. Of course, the causal structure of relations in areas besides health are also relatively opaque or deceptive. Ever notice how instructional approaches seem to work especially well in schools that are full of high-income children and exceptional teachers? When an approach works, is it because of the children, the teacher, or the fact that the approach is compatible with the design of the mind (see Chapter 1)?

The opaque and deceptive quality of causal relations in the world mean that it can be difficult to get at the "truth." Relatedly, the nature of the world requires that we make use of certain specialized knowledge acquisition devices to uncover the authentic relationship between actions and outcomes. Scientists make use of such devices when they investigate a problem and examine the results of experiments conducted by others (Chen & Klahr, 1999; Kuhn, Garcia-Mila, Zohar, & Anderson, 1995).

What are these devices? Essentially, scientists combine **hypothesis-testing** with sound **measurement** and **experimental techniques.** In other words, they think about the possible antecedent events that could have caused some outcome (e.g., parent input, child intelligence, and teacher behaviors as possible causes of high test scores) and gather data using techniques that simultaneously "rule in" some of these events and "rule out" others. If all goes well, scientists will discover the causes of a particular outcome. But the key here is to understand how to make things go well. A scientist will not discover the causes of an outcome if he or she starts out with hypotheses that are way off base. For example, imagine the case of a scientist who thinks that high test scores are caused by living in a beautiful climate. To begin with a plausible set of hypotheses (that have some chance of being confirmed through data collection), a scientist has to have a reasonably accurate and elaborate **theory.** As will be described more fully later, theories are mental representations that depict the causal relations inherent in some phenomenon (e.g., Action X causes Outcome Y) as well as the **causal mechanisms** that explain how antecedent events (e.g., Action X) produce consequent events (e.g., Outcome Y). But even when a scientist has an accurate theory, he or she could still be misled by data that was collected in a substandard manner. In addition to using a valid form of measurement (e.g., a well-designed questionnaire or task that truly taps into the phenomenon of interest), a scientist needs to use the **isolation of variables** technique. Here one creates comparisons in which everything is the same except for one variable (e.g., students are alike in every respect except that they have different teachers).

In keeping with content of other chapters, then, we can say that there are both structural and functional aspects of good scientific thinking. The structural aspects include a scientist's declarative and conceptual knowledge of the phenomenon in question. As noted in many chapters, declarative knowledge is knowledge of facts in some domain. Conceptual knowledge, in contrast, refers to relationships among key ideas and facts. In the case of science, a person's declarative and conceptual knowledge is embodied in the form of his or her theories. As noted above, causal relations constitute one important kind of conceptual relation in a theory. But theories also involve categorical relations as well (Carey, 1985a; Murphy & Medin, 1985). In particular, it is common for both scientists and non-scientists to group objects together into various categories after they have developed theories to explain the characteristics of these objects. For example, zoologists try to explain the characteristics of animals (e.g., mammary glands) and botanists try to explain the characteristics of plants (e.g., year-round green leaves). After finding adequate explanations of an animal's characteristics, zoologists created taxonomic categories of these animals (e.g., "mammals," "fish," "crustaceans," etc.) and botanists did the same for plants (e.g., "evergreens," "deciduous trees," etc.). All major sciences include such taxonomic categories, but the categories that derive from some theories are not so obvious. For example, psychologists have created categories of children based on what they can do (e.g., "concrete operational" children, "learning disabled" children, etc.).

The functional aspects of scientific thinking include hypothesis-testing and the measurement and experimental techniques described earlier (e.g., isolation of variables). The latter, then, constitute a large portion of a scientist's procedural knowledge. Other kinds of scientific procedural knowledge include (a) the ability to locate and process the findings of others when one lacks personal knowledge of causal relations (i.e., conduct a literature search) and (b) recognize the kinds of outcomes that would count toward confirmation or disconfirmation of one's hypotheses. To illustrate the latter, consider the case of a scientist who creates the following hypothesis: If students have well-educated parents, they will do well in school. This hypothesis would be confirmed by cases in which students have well-educated parents and they do well in school, and disconfirmed by cases in which students have well-educated parents but they do not do well in school. Other cases (e.g., students do not have well-educated parents but do well anyway) are recognized as having no direct bearing on the hypothesis. In order to know the difference between outcomes that confirm or disconfirm, scientists have to have the ability to *consciously reflect* on their theories and make a distinction between their theories and the evidence that could be used to support (or disconfirm) these theories (Kuhn, 1992; Moshman, 1998).

Collectively, the structural and functional aspects of good scientific thinking help a scientist figure out what is really going on much faster than a person without these aspects ever could. But history shows that these aspects of scientific thinking may not be enough to clarify the nature of perplexing phenomena (T. Kuhn, 1962). Scientists are not immune to various kinds of reasoning biases that are regularly found in the general population (Klaczynski & Narasimham, 1998; Stanovich & West, 1998). For example, they tend to give great weight to data that supports their views and tend to dismiss data that is inconsistent with their views. Relatedly, they spend a lot of effort finding flaws in studies that disconfirm their views and very little time assessing the credibility of data that supports their views. Finally, they may possess the personality trait of dogmatism that makes them especially disinclined to change their views despite repeated encounters with disconfirming evidence (Byrnes, 1998). Thus, the fourth important aspect of good scientific thinking (besides high levels of theoretical knowledge, high levels of procedural knowledge, and conscious access to one's theories and evidence) is awareness of the possibility of personal biases and the tendency to overcome these biases through actively open-minded thinking (see Chapter 4 for more on actively open-minded thinking).

The Development of Scientific Knowledge and Skills

Now that we have a better sense of what good scientific thinking entails, we can consider the extent to which students seem to demonstrate this kind of thinking by the time they graduate high school or college. In keeping with the analysis of scientific reasoning described in the previous section, developmental research will be described in three subsections related to (a) structural aspects of scientific thinking, (b) functional aspects of scientific thinking, and (c) reasoning biases.

Development of Structural Aspects of Scientific Thinking

As noted earlier, the structural aspects of scientific thinking largely pertain to a person's theories. As such, we shall in the present section examine age changes in children's theories. The paradigm that is largely responsible for contemporary thinking in this regard is called "Theory Theory" (Wellman & Gelman, 1998). The central premises of this perspective are as follows:

- Children's knowledge in particular domains can be appropriately construed as naive theories.
- These theories are naive in the sense that they are (a) constructed before formal education in the domain occurs and (b) under-developed relative to the theories of practicing scientists.
- Children's naive theories of psychology, biology, and physics are central to their survival and everyday interactions; as such, these theories are especially important to study and likely to emerge very early in development.
- Children's theories are likely to change in a manner analogous to that reported in the philosophy of science and history of science literatures.
- There may be very little correspondence among theories; for example, changes within any given theory may occur independently of changes in others. Thus, in contrast to accounts that emphasize domain-general structures and changes (e.g., Piaget's theory), Theory theorists emphasize domain-specificity.
- To show that a naive theory has emerged at a particular point in development, it is not sufficient to demonstrate that children have a certain amount of declarative knowledge or bits of domain-relevant information; instead, one needs to show that children "(a) divide the world into fundamentally different kinds of 'things'—for example, thoughts versus solid objects, (b) appreciate fundamentally different sorts of causes—for example, processes activated by collisions with solid objects versus processes activated by desires and intentions, (c) appeal to distinctive underlying constructs in their understandings—for example, [mental] states that underpin human behavior versus the atoms and substances out of which solid objects are composed, and (d) create larger systems within which these concepts, causes, and constructs cohere" (Wellman and Gelman, 1998, p. 525).
- Children use their theories to explain outcomes, predict outcomes, and interpret evidence.

From a methodological standpoint, these premises would be investigated in the following sorts of ways. To show that children make ontological distinctions indicative of separate theories (e.g., a thought is not the same kind of thing as a solid object), one can use the inductive projection technique (e.g., Carey, 1985a). Here, an exemplar from a theory-relevant category (e.g., a biological kind such as "dog") is said to have a particular characteristic (e.g., a spleen). Children are then asked whether an exemplar from a category relevant to another theory (e.g., a physical kind like "rock") also has the characteristic (e.g., "A dog has a spleen. Does a rock have a spleen too?").

To show that children enlist different kinds of causes across different naive theories, researchers have often presented some outcome (e.g., the heart pumps blood) and asked children to explain this outcome. The goal is to show that children do not use causal agents from one theory (e.g., beliefs and desires from their naive psychology) to explain outcomes relevant to another naive theory (e.g., saying that the heart wants to pump blood or thinks it's a good idea to pump blood). In other words, the goal is to show that children do not use (a) psychological causes to explain biological or physical outcomes, (b) biological causes to explain psychological or physical outcomes, or (c) physical causes to explain psychological or biological outcomes. Beyond keeping their causes straight, however, children also need to appeal to unobservable entities to explain or predict outcomes. For example, they might appeal to beliefs or desires to explain someone's behavior in a given situation (e.g., "He looked in the cabinet because he wanted the candy and thought it was there").

Finally, to show how theories change in a manner similar to that reported in the philosophy of science literature (e.g., T. Kuhn, 1962), researchers typically present children with evidence contrary to their hypotheses to see how they respond. If children are like most scientists, they will probably dismiss or ignore the evidence at first, then demonstrate the tendency to explain it in a post hoc and incoherent manner, and finally change their theories to conform to the evidence (Gopnik & Wellman, 1992; Karmiloff-Smith, 1984). Some changes in children's theories are so substantial that they are analogous to the scientific revolutions reported in the philosophy of science literature (Carey, 1985a). Thus, theory change should occur over an extended period of time, reflect the tendency towards bias, and involve occasional reorganizations that promote qualitative or even radical changes in understanding.

In the literature on naive theories, these methodological strategies have been used to address the following sorts of questions: (a) When do naive theories of psychology, physics, and biology first emerge in development? and (b) How do the naive theories of young children differ from those of older children and adults? In the next three subsections, answers to these questions are provided for each theory in turn.

Naive Psychology.   Children are assumed to use their naive psychologies to explain, predict, and interpret the behavior of people (including themselves). When naive psychologies are accurate and well-developed, individuals can engage in a variety of adaptive behaviors such as form lasting social relationships, recognize when they are being conned, comprehend narrative stories, and attribute their success and failure to appropriate causes (see Chapter 5 on the latter). At the core of an adult's naive psychology is an epistemology centered on beliefs and desires (Gopnik & Wellman, 1992). That is, adults regularly assume that internal beliefs and desires are causal agents that produce specific behaviors in people. For example, if one person asks another for directions, an on-looker might explain this behavior by saying that the lost individual wanted to find a particular place (a desire) and thought that the person he stopped might know where the location is (a belief). Of course, the naive psychology of the average adult extends well beyond the simple belief-desire network to include many of the same constructs included in the formal psychological theories presented in textbooks (which is why many students complain that psychology is nothing but common sense!). When searching for the earliest signs of naive theories, however, one turns to the fundamental constructs.

Most scholars in this area assume that by age three or four, a rudimentary naive psychology seems to be in place (Wellman & Gelman, 1998). For example, preschoolers seem to know that there is a difference between a picture or mental image of a dog and a real dog. Hence, they make some of the ontological distinctions that Theory-theorists require. Also, they explain a character's behaviors in terms of beliefs and desires and also make predictions from beliefs and desires to behaviors. Furthermore, they seem to recognize that emotions are subjective states that may depend on other mental states such as goals. For example, if told that a character wanted to get to a dance on time but ended up being late, children recognize that the character would probably feel disappointed.

Nevertheless, children demonstrate greater facility on some tasks than others. In addition, they seem to understand the causal role of emotions and desires (around age three) before they understand the causal role of beliefs (around age four or five). The latter difficulty is clearly demonstrated on so-called **false belief** tasks. Here, children are told a story using concrete props such as a doll house and dolls. For example, they might be told about a child who put his candy in one location (e.g., the kitchen counter) and then left. The child's mother comes in and places the candy elsewhere (e.g., a cabinet). The experimental subject is then asked where the character will look for his candy when the character returns. Young children mistakenly believe that the character will look in the new location (e.g., the cabinet). By age four or five, however, children switch to the correct response. Thus, many researchers feel that these and related findings demonstrate one of the major reorganizations that were alluded to earlier.

Other significant developments emerge over time in response to experience and the demands of schooling. For example, children grow in their understanding of cognitive abilities such as memory, reading, and intelligence (see Chapters 3, 5, and 7). In addition, their causal attributions for school-related and relationship failures change as well (Weiner, 1986). Further, they develop more abstract representations of themselves and come to recognize the possibility of having two emotions at once (Harter, 1999). Given that the vast majority of recent studies have focused on the preschool period, it is not clear whether these and other changes reflect major reorganizations in their naive theories. It is also not clear whether young children have explicit access to their naive psychologies and know the difference between their theories and the evidence that can be used to support them. Some studies with college students, for example, suggest that many students at this level fail to differentiate between their psychological theories of some behavior (e.g., recidivism of criminals) and the evidence that can be used to support these theories (Kuhn, 1992).

Naive Physics.   A second kind of knowledge that enhances one's chances of survival is knowledge of the physical world (Wellman & Gelman, 1998; Pinker, 1997). Physical knowledge helps one recognize that objects: (a) are solid entities that continue to exist when out of view, (b) can be molded or reconfigured into tools, (c) travel a certain distance in a given trajectory when tossed, (d) can be interconnected to make shelters, and so on. When do children first provide evidence of such understandings? Piaget (1952) showed that children recognize the permanence of objects by around eight- to twelve-months of age. When he hid a desired object under a blanket, for example, children in this age range tried to retrieve it but children younger than eight months tended not to. Other researchers using different techniques have found that object permanence may be evident as early as five or six months (Baillargeon, Kotovsky, & Needham, 1995). Either way, this concept is present fairly early.

In other studies, researchers wondered when infants seem to recognize constraints on physical causality such as the requirement that objects need to make contact with each other in order for an effect to occur and the requirement that outcomes follow immediately after causes. Once again, studies suggest that by twelve months of age, many children seem to be sensitive to these requirements (Wellman & Gelman, 1998). To test for such knowledge, one might show two videotapes. In one, a billiard ball is shown knocking another aside. In the second, the first billiard ball hits the second, but the second does not move immediately. Infants have been found to look longer at the tape that fails to conform to expectations. In related kinds of experiments, one might give infants a heavy ball and a light ball (that look identical in appearance) and have them see how only the light one can be raised by a paddle. Then, they can be shown films in which the opposite occurs to see how they respond (Schilling & Clifton, 1998).

What happens after infancy? One important development is children's increased reliance on various causal attribution rules to figure out which events caused which outcomes. Early in development, physical knowledge seems to start off as a network of correlations between pairs of environmental events (Keil, 1991). For example, a young child might notice the co-variation between pushing her glass over (Event 1) and her milk splashing to the floor (Event 2). Children seem to use the "co-variance" rule that if one event frequently co-occurs with another, the two events are causally connected (Bullock, Gelman, & Baillargeon, 1982). They also understand the "temporal order" rule which specifies that the second event is caused by the first event. In addition, they are more likely to believe that there is a causal relation between two events if (a) the time gap between the first event and the second is short (the "temporal proximity" rule), and (b) the objects or people involved are close together or make contact (the "spatial proximity" rule) (Shultz, 1982). All of these rules seem to be established by the end of the preschool period.

What is often missing in young children's causal analysis, however, is knowledge of the mechanism responsible for the consistent co-variation. In the absence of knowledge of causal mechanisms, children and adults will attribute causality anyway if what they observe conforms to the causal rules described above (Keil, 1991; Piaget & Garcia, 1974). That is, they seem to form a belief such as "I know that these things are causally related, but I don't yet know how or why" (Keil, 1991; Gelman & Coley, 1991). For example, the author of this book and most people know very little about how a car engine works. Nevertheless, we all still believe that we cause our car to start when we turn the key.

When we learn about mechanisms, our causal beliefs are strengthened considerably. Many teachers, for example, believe that their teaching techniques are effective, but are not quite sure why these techniques are effective. After learning about Piaget's theory or Schema theory, teachers often learn of the mechanisms responsible for their success. This knowledge, in turn, reinforces their original beliefs.

But there are times in which things happen so quickly that we do not have time to consider temporal order, consistent co-occurrence, and so on. In fact, we do not need to experience things ourselves to attribute causality. All we need is information about mechanisms that makes sense to us. Some studies have shown, for example, that knowledge of causal mechanisms can be more important than the four causal rules when children and adolescents form causal judgments (Shultz, 1982; Koslowski & Okagaki, 1986). For example, someone who has never driven a car or turned the key herself might nevertheless come to believe that turning the key starts the car after taking a class which explains how a car engine works.

So early on in development, children use the four causal rules to create mental networks of correlated events. They do not yet know the details of the causal mechanisms involved, but they suspect that there must be *some* mechanism involved. Over time, they invent mechanisms (Piaget & Garcia, 1974) or learn about them in school and add this information to the correlation network. In the absence of instruction, most of the mechanisms that children and adults invent are almost always incorrect. Thus, continued instruction ultimately causes children's and adult's physical theories to change from being "naive" to being "scientific." But as we will see in the section below on misconceptions, many high school students and adults include constructs in their naive theories of physics that are not included in the theories of physics experts.

One way to enhance children's understanding of physical phenomena is to have them build or manipulate physical models of those phenomena. When systems are presented that involve constraints on the movement of elements within these systems (e.g., interlocking gears, models of human joints) or when systems refer to abstract ideas (e.g., the balance of forces, electricity), elementary and middle school children find these systems initially difficult to grasp (Piaget & Garcia, 1974; Penner, Giles, Lehrer, & Schauble, 1997). However, if given the opportunity to build their own models of these systems, manipulate them, form linkages across multiple models, and make predictions, children and adolescents eventually gain insight into the structure of these systems (Frederiksen, White, & Gutwill, 1999; Lehrer & Schauble, 1998; Penner et al., 1997; Raghavan, Sartoris, & Glaser, 1998). Such an approach can be contrasted with the standard lecture-based approach or one that only involves observation of natural phenomena (e.g., lunar phases). Children and college students tend to develop or maintain misconceptions in such situations (Stahly, Krockover, & Shepardson, 1999).

Before moving on, it is important to note that it is still not clear when a naive physics first emerges in development. In contrast to what was found for the domain of naive psychology, researchers have not spent a great deal of time showing that young children make key ontological distinctions for the physical domain (except indirectly from the fact that they distinguish between mental states and physical objects). In addition, they have not shown that preschoolers regularly appeal to unobserved, hypothetical entities to explain physical outcomes or use these entities to make predictions. When preschoolers understand mechanisms, these mechanisms (e.g., dominoes tumbling) are usually observable (e.g., Bullock et al., 1982; Shultz, 1982). Older preschoolers do, however, recognize that objects in different categories (e.g., watches versus animals) have different "insides" that reflect their essences (Wellman & Gelman, 1998). Researchers have also found that children seem to recognize the difference between social laws (you have to obey the speed limit) and physical laws (one solid object cannot pass through another) by age five (Kalish, 1998). However, researchers have not shown that young children systematically refrain from using psychological or biological causes to explain physical outcomes. Some studies, in fact, suggest that children over-extend psychological and biological constructs to the physical domain (e.g., Kelemen, 1999; Solomon & Cassimatis, 1999). In addition, there is very little evidence that young children have conscious access to their naive physics or that they can discriminate between their theories and evidence (Kuhn et al., 1995). Further, preschoolers and elementary-age students sometimes have trouble understanding that actions such as squashing or rolling substances have no effect on the amount of the substance present (Inhelder & Piaget, 1969), but, paradoxically, preschoolers do sometimes recognize that dissolved substances do not really vanish (Au, Sidle, & Rollins, 1993). These studies combined with studies of college students (see below) suggest that the basic framework for a naive theory of physics may be in place by age five, but it continues to develop considerably after the preschool period.

Naive Biology.   Knowledge of the biology domain has been claimed to be adaptive because of its relevance to such things as growing and finding food, avoiding predators, and maintaining physical health (Wellman & Gelman, 1998; Pinker, 1997). As was the case for naive theories of psychology and physics, the question of central importance for a Theory-theorist has been, When in development is there a separate biological domain? At minimum, children would need to (a) make an ontological distinction between animate and inanimate things (Carey, 1985a), (b) realize that " . . . certain entities operate outside the forces of mechanical or belief-desire causation" (Wellman & Gelman, 1998, p. 546), and (c) demonstrate an "understanding of specific biological causal forces such as growth, reproduction, and inheritance" (Wellman & Gelman, 1998, p. 546) before they could be said to have a naive biological theory.

When asked whether certain things are alive, preschoolers attribute life to things such as mechanical monkeys (which older children and adults judge to be inanimate) but fail to attribute life to such things as plants (which older children and adults judge to be animate) (Carey, 1985a; Hatano, Siegler, Richards, & Inagaki, 1993). Thus, they do make ontological distinctions, but not necessarily the same ones as adults. Some researchers have questioned this finding, however, by suggesting that the term *alive* may mean different things to children and adults (Wellman & Gelman, 1998). When asked to imitate a model's actions with toys, even fourteen-month-olds maintain a distinction between things that can sleep or drink (i.e., animals) and things that do not sleep or drink (e.g., vehicles) (Mandler & McDonough, 1996). Also, some studies suggest that three- and four-year-olds recognize that plants and animals both grow (Hickling & Gelman, 1995), that plants can heal by themselves (Backscheider, Shatz, & Gelman, 1993), and that plants can decompose and become repugnant (Springer, Ngyuen, & Samaniego, 1996).

Other early achievements relate to their understanding that (a) biological forces operate outside of mechanical or psychological causation and (b) there are invisible processes responsible for biology-specific phenomena such as genetic inheritance and contamination. Regarding the former, Kalish (1997) found that preschoolers seemed to recognize that they could not eliminate an illness caused by contamination simply by wishing it away (though about 70 percent of three-year-olds and 40 percent of four-year-olds thought they could). Similarly, Inagaki and Hatano (1993) found that around 85 percent of four- and five-year-olds recognized that they had little control over automatic bodily processes such as breathing and digestion. Regarding invisible processes, Springer (1992) found that four- to seven-year-old children will attribute a biological property from a mother animal to her offspring (e.g., the ability to see in the dark) more frequently than they attribute this property to an unrelated, but similar-looking animal from the same species (i.e., about 85 percent of the time versus 70 percent of the time). Children do not show the same pattern when the traits were things that an animal learns or psychological traits. In addition to early insights into invisible aspects of genetics, children also show some insight into invisible processes related to contamination. For example, young children seem to recognize that contact with contaminants is necessary for contamination (Springer & Belk, 1994) and that invisible particles described as germs are responsible for causing illnesses (Kalish, 1996).

Nevertheless, the claim that five-year-olds maintain key ontological distinctions in biology, refrain from mixing causal processes across domains, and refer to invisible particles is rather controversial at present (Solomon & Cassimatis, 1999; Wellman & Gelman, 1998). After reviewing the evidence with respect to contamination, for example, Solomon and Cassimatis (1999, p. 114) argue that:

> "We are persuaded that preschoolers (a) can reject imminent justice explanations as the cause of illness [i.e., illnesses are not punishments for immorality]; (b) understand that contamination can involve the material transfer of particles too small to be seen; (c) understand that ingesting contaminated foods and beverages can make one ill; (d) know that germs can cause illness; and (e) know the fact of contagion from one person to another. But we are not persuaded that preschoolers necessarily integrate these understandings in the service of a coherent biological system of predication and causal explanation."

Across a series of five well-controlled experiments, Solomon and Cassimatis showed that young children did not appreciate the difference between contagious causes of illness (e.g., germs) and non-contagious causes of illness (e.g., poison). Moreover, children did not seem to appreciate germs as being uniquely biological agents. For example, it was not until age ten to eleven where a majority of children said that germs had the same biological properties that people, ants, and trees have (e.g., can eat and have babies).

In addition, it is not until children are in the fourth grade that they seem to refrain from believing in the teleological basis of the properties of animals and objects (Keleman, 1999). Prior to that time, children believe that properties exist for a purpose (e.g., rocks are pointy so that people can use them as tools) (Kelemen, 1999). Furthermore, it is not until the third grade that children realize that a transplant of an animal's brain or insides would lead to changes in the animal's thoughts and memories (Gottfried, Gelman, & Schultz, 1999). Finally, sixth graders and tenth graders have been found to have difficulty understanding the inter-dependence of species in an ecosystem (Palmer, 1997) and tenth graders require a 10-week genetics course to shift from (a) viewing genes as passive particles that are passed from parents to offspring to (b) viewing genes as active particles that control characteristics (Venville & Treagust, 1998). Thus, preschoolers may have nascent insights into biological phenomena, but their naive theories continue to change considerably with experience and education.

Summary of Research on Naive Theories.   Research on children's naive theories of psychology, physics, and biology reveal that preschoolers have much more knowledge than many scholars in the science education community might have thought. Among the researchers who revealed these competencies (i.e., developmental psychologists), the consensus seems to be that (a) the basic outlines of three important naive theories are in place by the time children enter first grade (though the case for biology is still controversial) and (b) each of these theories continues to develop substantially between preschool and adulthood. What researchers have generally not addressed as yet are developments in other naive theories besides psychology, physics, and biology (e.g., economics, chemistry, etc.), and the extent to which children have a metacognitive understanding of their theories and the evidence that could support or refute it. Additional work is needed to examine the claim that children's theories change in a manner analogous to that found in the philosophy of science literature.

One Further Structural Feature: Misconceptions.   Over the past twenty years, the topic of scientific misconceptions has been one of the most popular research topics in science education (though interest seems to be waning somewhat). Studies in this area show that instead of coming to science class with minds that are "blank slates," students come to class with minds that are filled with a variety of informal or intuitive conceptions that do not square with the scientific concepts taught in class. For example, students come to class with their own concepts of "force" or "temperature" that are quite different than the concepts of "force" and "temperature" taught in their science classes (Linn, 1986). The conflict between their informal conceptions and those taught in class causes them to distort or forget the proper conceptualizations. Because students' intuitive concepts deviate from the conceptions endorsed by a larger scientific community, the intuitive concepts are frequently called "misconceptions," though those with a constructivist orientation prefer labels such as "alternative frameworks" (Eylon & Linn, 1988), in deference to the idea that it is not terribly useful to believe in a single correct way to view things.

Before examining the research on misconceptions, it first is helpful to understand how scientific concepts relate to theories. In most instances, a *concept* is a part of a scientific explanation. For example, concepts such as "force" and "gravity" are part of a physicist's explanation for why objects move the way they do. Similarly, "bonding," "molecule," "atom," and "reaction" are part of a chemist's explanation of processes such as corrosion and fermentation. Finally, concepts such as "encoding" and "retrieval" are part of a psychologist's explanation for how people remember. In essence, then, a theory is made up of concepts. Therefore, when we say that a student has a misconception about a concept such as "force," we are also saying that a portion of his or her naive theory of physics deviates from a scientific theory of physics.

To get a flavor of the way intuitive and scientific concepts differ, consider the task presented in Figure 10.1. Imagine that a ball is on top of a cliff and it is kicked off. Which of the three choices shown in Figure 10.1 illustrates the proper trajectory of ball? Do you know why? Although the correct choice is the middle option, many people draw the first

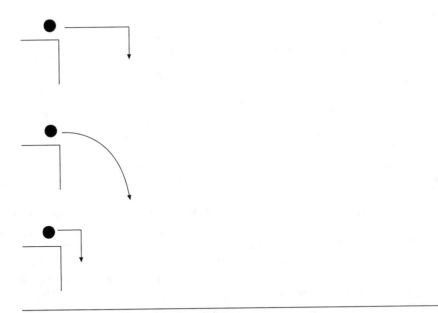

FIGURE 10.1 *Possible Trajectories of the Ball According to Students*

or third option because they fail to realize that only the force of gravity is operating on the ball after it is kicked. It travels in a curved trajectory because of laws having to do with inertia (i.e., an object sent in a particular direction will continue in that direction unless acted on by a force or friction) and vector addition (the vector for straight ahead added to the vector for straight down is a vector in-between).

At present, there are literally hundreds of studies which were conducted to document the extent of misconceptions in students. Most studies reveal a wide range of misconceptions. For example, one study revealed fifty-two different misconceptions regarding atoms and molecules in a sample of twelfth graders (Griffiths & Preston, 1992). Some students believed that a water molecule was as big as a speck of dust and others thought that it became bigger when heated.

It would not be surprising to learn that students have misconceptions before they take a physics or chemistry class. It took brilliant scientists such as Newton many years to develop the proper conception of "force." It is very unlikely that the average fifth grader would invent this concept on his or her own. And yet, standard instruction is not sufficient to eliminate misconceptions. Many studies show that certain misconceptions persist even after students take science classes (e.g., Abraham et al., 1992; BouJaoude, 1992; Clement, 1982; Garnett & Treagust, 1992; McCloskey, 1983).

Why do students have misconceptions? The principal reason seems to be that many science concepts have to do with abstractions or non-observable entities. Consider the concept of density (i.e., mass per unit volume of a substance). By sight and feel, a 12-ounce can of regular Coke and a 12-ounce can of Diet Coke seem to be the same. But if you put both in a tub of water, the Diet Coke floats and the regular Coke sinks. This counterintuitive result occurs because Diet Coke is less dense than water (i.e., less mass per unit volume) and regular Coke is more dense. Students have difficulty with this concept because whereas you can see the can's size and feel its weight, you cannot directly perceive its density. Thus, if a teacher were to use the "Coke" task to elicit student theories, it is likely that many misconceptions about density would be revealed. In fact, any physical phenomenon is likely to reveal misconceptions in younger students because the "true" explanation probably involves abstract mechanisms.

The findings from the studies of misconceptions are significant for several reasons. First, studies show that teachers seem to be unaware that their students have misconceptions (e.g., Abraham et al., 1992). The mismatch between a teacher's perception and a researcher's perception probably arises from the fact that researchers ask children different questions than teachers. In class, many science teachers are most concerned about children learning the proper science "vocabulary" (e.g., what "photosynthesis" means) and usually teach "at" students (Carey, 1986; Roth, 1994). Although a child could get an "A" on a test by learning vocabulary and other facts by rote, such a child would probably not understand the concepts behind this information. Researchers, in contrast, ask questions that require deeper understanding such as "Can a molecule be weighed by a scale?" and "Does a molecule get bigger when it is heated?" If teachers asked such questions and found out that their students did not truly understand what they presented, they would clearly try to modify their teaching. One way to modify things immediately is to spend more time asking questions of students rather than presenting information in a lecture format.

The second reason why misconceptions are significant is that if the concepts that make up a person's theory are inaccurate, then he or she will make a number of inaccurate predictions. Moreover, a person with inaccurate concepts will attempt to control the wrong variables. For example, Newton and his followers espoused the concept of "ether" (a gaseous substance presumed to "fill up" the space between planets and other heavenly bodies). In the late 1800s, researchers finally gave up the idea of "ether" after studies repeatedly failed to find evidence of this substance.

Although there are certain misconceptions that almost all students develop before instruction, there are a variety of other misconceptions than only one or two students in a classroom develop. Thus, studies show a wide range of individual differences in the number and type of misconceptions held by students (Griffiths & Preston, 1992; Heller & Finley, 1992). For example, Griffiths and Preston (1992) found that only six of a total of fifty-two misconceptions were held by more than half of their sample.

Even when a common misconception is revealed, studies show that people differ in terms of how strongly they cling to this misconception. For example, some students are very reluctant to give up the belief that "energy" flows through wires in an electrical circuit. Other students more readily give up this belief after instruction (Heller & Finley, 1992). Each student, then, seems to have "core" beliefs that are held with a high degree of certainty and "peripheral" beliefs that they readily change to defend their core beliefs (Linn, 1986; Kuhn et al., 1988).

At present, it is not at all clear why some misconceptions are held by many students and why some are held by only a few students. We also do not know why some beliefs end up as core beliefs and others end up as peripheral beliefs. The reason for this lack of knowledge is that we still do not have a clear sense of where misconceptions come from. Whereas there is some evidence that textbooks contribute to the problem (Abraham et al., 1992) and other evidence that many teachers have misconceptions (Heller & Finley, 1992), we still need more information on the various sources of misconceptions. Once all of these sources are identified, we can then try to determine how these sources contribute to individual differences.

As for developmental differences, most studies of misconceptions have revealed the faulty beliefs of a single age group and only a handful of studies have considered whether children at different ages hold different misconceptions. As a result, it is difficult to draw developmental conclusions about this research. Perhaps the only conclusion that can be drawn is that misconceptions can be found at virtually all age levels. Most studies, however, have interviewed students either just before or just after they took a science course (e.g., physics). As a result, the majority of studies have interviewed middle school, high school, or college students. There is, then, a need for more developmental research in this area especially using preadolescent students as subjects.

Development of Functional Aspects of Scientific Thinking

Whereas structural aspects of scientific thinking have to do with what people know about scientific concepts, facts, or phenomena, functional aspects have to do with what people do when they try to solve a scientific problem. Two functional aspects of scientific thinking are described next: hypothesis-testing and experimentation techniques.

Hypothesis-Testing.   As noted earlier, hypotheses derive from a person's theory and are predictions about the way things will turn out if the theory is true. A common way to state an hypothesis is to use an "if . . . then" sentence (Piburn, 1990; Ward, Byrnes, & Overton, 1990). For example, someone who believes in Einstein's Theory of Relativity might form the hypothesis that "If an astronaut in space had a watch and someone on Earth had one too, we'd find that the astronaut's watch would run slower." Similarly, someone who believes in Bowlby's theory of infant attachment might form the hypothesis that "If we placed a twelve-month-old in a room with a stranger, she'd start to cry." If things turn out the way a scientist predicts (e.g., the watch in space does run slower), that means that a portion of his theory could well be correct. If things do not turn out as predicted, that means that a portion of his theory may not be correct. Thus, hypothesis-testing is an important way for scientists to know whether or not their theories are correct.

To assess the ability to test hypotheses, the first thing to do is either (a) have students create their own hypotheses or (b) present them with ready-made hypotheses. To get them to create an hypothesis, you could ask them "what would happen if" questions (e.g., "What would happen if you rolled a ball off this table?"). After an hypothesis is created or presented, the next step is to introduce evidence that either does or does not have a bearing on the accuracy of the hypothesis. Once again you could have students gather their own evidence through experimentation and observation (e.g., "Roll the ball off a few times and see if you are right.") or present them with evidence. Finally, you need to have them *evaluate* the evidence; that is, they need to judge whether their prediction was correct or not (e.g., "All right, here's what happened when someone rolled the ball. Was your prediction right?").

Early studies of hypothesis-testing did not attempt to link a person's theories with his or her hypotheses. Instead, people were asked to form hypotheses about arbitrary relations of colors, shapes, or numbers. For example, Bruner, Goodnow, and Austin (1956) presented adults with a shape of a certain color and had them guess whether or not it "fit a rule." After subjects made a guess (e.g. "this red square fits"), they were told if they were right or wrong. If they were told that the shape did fit the rule, they had to form an hypothesis regarding the basis for grouping all shapes that received a "Yes." For example, subjects might be shown a variety of shapes and learn that a red circle, red square, and red triangle all received a "Yes." They might then form the hypothesis that the group consists of "red things." Thus, people were presented with evidence (i.e., the shapes) and then asked to create an hypothesis to account for the evidence.

Figure 10.2 shows two other classic tasks that also involve relations that bear no relation to a person's theories: the "4-card" and "2-4-6" tasks. Presumably, researchers who used all of these tasks were interested in "abstract" or "general" hypothesis testing ability and did not want to facilitate or artificially inflate adults' performance by allowing them to rely on their prior knowledge. What are the "right" ways of behaving on Bruner et al.'s task and the tasks in Figure 10.2? According to philosophers of science (e.g., Popper, 1959), adults in these studies should not have sought evidence which would confirm (i.e., support the truth of) a rule. Rather, they should make sure that no evidence exists that *disconfirms* the rule. In this view, it makes little sense to keep trying to prove an initial hypothesis is

FIGURE 10.2   *Hypothesis Testing Tasks*

The Four Card Task

Rule: If there is a vowel on one side of a card, there is an even number on the other side.

Each of the four cards above has a letter on one side and a number on the other. Which of the four cards would you definitely need to turn over in order to see whether the rule has been broken?

The 2-4-6 Task

I am using a rule to generate three numbers. Your job is to keep giving me three numbers that you think fit the rule I used. When you are sure that you know the rule, tell me what the rule is. O.K. Three numbers that fit the rule are 2, 4, and 6. Now you give me sets of three numbers that fit the same rule. When you are sure you know the rule, tell me what it is.

right by gathering data that supports or confirms this hypothesis because things could continually turn out as you predict for the *wrong reasons*.

To illustrate this point using a meaningful example, suppose you have a theory that Vitamin C helps people fend off colds. To test this theory, you set up the hypothesis "If someone feeling a cold coming on takes Vitamin C, that person will not get the cold." To prove this hypothesis, you ask three people you know who feel like they are getting a cold to take Vitamin C for several days. After letting the Vitamin C have a chance to work, you call your friends to see how things went. You find that all three did not get a cold. You conclude, "You see, I was right!"

What is wrong with this thinking? To show that Vitamin C matters, you should have contacted a larger number of people and followed them for the same amount of time. Some of these people should have taken Vitamin C and some should not have (see below). What you should be looking for is not so much the people who took the Vitamin C and avoided the cold as much as people who took Vitamin C but still got a cold anyway. By trying to prove yourself wrong, you would have found data against your hypothesis. By trying to prove yourself right, you may not have discovered this disconfirming data and would probably not think of other reasons why your friends failed to get colds (e.g., perhaps they really were not coming down with colds). The tendency to only look for confirming cases has been called the **confirmation bias.**

Besides keeping you from thinking of other reasons why the data turned out the way you expected, another problem with the confirmation bias is that even though an hypothesis turns out to be true right now, it could always be proven wrong in the future. Philosophers use the example of swans to illustrate this point. Consider a man named Harry who finds that every swan he has ever seen is white. It would be wrong for him to infer that "All swans are white" because there exists a species of black swans. It just happens that Harry has not encountered black swans yet. Consider next our Vitamin C example again. It is possible that the first three people you contact and give Vitamin C do not get colds, but the next ten who take Vitamin C get the colds anyway. By stopping at the first three, you would have never encountered the last ten.

The confirmation bias has been found in a variety of experiments since the 1950s. Adults and children show a strong tendency to seek confirmation of their favorite hypotheses instead of trying to disconfirm their own or rival hypotheses (Schauble, 1990; Kuhn et al., 1988; Mynatt, Doherty, & Tweney, 1977; Wason, 1983). For example, they choose just the "D" card in the four-card task (see Figure 10.2), or continually generate three numbers that are consistent with a rule in the 2-4-6 task (e.g., 2-4-6, 6-8-10, 12-14-16, etc. for the rule "Even numbers that increase by 2").

According to philosophers of science in the Logical Positivist tradition, this persistent confirmation bias demonstrates that children and adults rarely show high levels of scientific thinking. Others, however, argue that the behavior of children and adults is perfectly appropriate (e.g., Klayman & Ha, 1987; Koslowski & Maqueda, 1993). In the first place, it makes sense to first gather data to see if certain variables (e.g., the thickness of the ozone layer) correlate with certain other variables (e.g., the skin cancer rate). Once this co-variation is established and a theory is developed to explain the relationship, one can then look for data that disconfirms the theory (e.g., historical times when the ozone was even thinner and the cancer rate was less than it is now).

Second, Koslowski and Maqueda argue that scientists often gather data that not only support the causal relation that they favor, but also simultaneously disconfirm other alternative explanations. For example, you might believe that the main causal determinant of a girl's math achievement is her parent's beliefs. In contrast, a rival scientist believes that parent beliefs do not matter, only genes do. To prove that you are right and your rival is wrong, you find pairs of identical twins who are separated at birth. Then, you find a subset of pairs in which one twin was raised by sexist parents and the other was raised by nonsexists. Finally, you discover that parental beliefs are more important than genes because only the twins who have sexist parents differed in math achievement. Koslowski and Maqueda argue that without a certain kind of probing, an outside observer who examines your experiment might think that you are just trying to prove the correctness of your own "parental belief" hypothesis. Thus, Koslowski and Maqueda argue that many of the hypothesis-testing studies need to be re-examined in order to see whether children and adults were not trying to simultaneously confirm their own hypotheses while disconfirming other rival hypotheses.

Notwithstanding these arguments, however, there is evidence that children and adults pay attention to only that data which is consistent with their theory and will distort or ignore evidence that is contrary to their favored theory (Karmiloff-Smith & Inhelder, 1974; Kuhn et al., 1988; Shustack, 1988). This, too, is indicative of a confirmation bias. Lets say that you have the hypothesis that left-handed females are good in math (because their brains are more like a male's brain). Frequently, you meet females with high levels of math ability, but only notice the left-handed ones because being left-handed is more salient than being right-handed. Thus, the left-handed ones stand out and make you think that left-handedness goes with good math ability.

In the midst of conducting experiments with their students, it is very important for teachers to point out disconfirming data to them. In fact, constructing labs so that the data generated in them will disconfirm existing misconceptions should be a central tactic in science classes. It is only through disconfirmation that theories and misconceptions can change.

Besides behaviors related to the confirmation bias, researchers have found other behaviors that seem to conflict with the proposals advanced by philosophers of science. For example, Logical Positivists argue that when evidence is found that suggests that your hypothesis is wrong, you should abandon this hypothesis and create a completely new one. Instead of doing so, however, children, adults, and scientists seem to cling to hypotheses even when disconfirming data arises. People are especially likely to do so if they feel certain that they are correct (Kuhn et al., 1988; Lakatos, 1971). For example, a scientist might observe the radiation coming from a distant planet and come to believe that the planet must have moons. She looks through her telescope, however, and sees no moons. Instead of abandoning her hypothesis, she continually builds stronger and stronger telescopes to find moons.

As was the case for the confirmation bias, the act of clinging to an hypothesis in the face of disconfirming data has been interpreted as being irrational by some scientists and perfectly reasonable by others (Koslowski & Maqueda, 1993; Nisbett & Ross, 1980). Koslowski and Maqueda, for example, argue that although most scientists tend to retain a working hypothesis after encountering data that disconfirms it, they also use the disconfirming data to *modify* rather than discard the hypothesis. Many important and less important discoveries would have been missed had an initial hypothesis been totally abandoned rather than modified. To illustrate, consider our Vitamin C example above. It might be that a person needs to have *both* a specific antibody to cold viruses and take Vitamin C in order to avoid a cold (because Vitamin C speeds up the duplication of the antibody). If someone took Vitamin C and got a cold anyway, it would be wrong to conclude that taking Vitamin C has no effect on colds. Moreover, just as it makes sense to repeat an experiment to make sure a causal relationship exists, it makes sense to repeat an experiment to make sure a causal relationship does *not* exist. Problems arise only when a person clings to an hypothesis after numerous disconfirming cases or modifies it in implausible ways.

As for developmental differences in hypothesis-testing skill, research suggests that adults tend to have more hypothesis-testing skill than children. In particular, adults are more likely than children to (a) know what kind of evidence would support the truth of an hypothesis and what kind of evidence would disconfirm it (Overton, 1990), (b) seek evidence to disconfirm a favored hypothesis (Bruner et al., 1956), and (c) discard or modify an hypothesis on the basis of disconfirming evidence (Dunbar & Klahr, 1989; Koslowski & Maqueda, 1993; Schauble, 1990). Moreover, adults are less likely to demonstrate a confirmation bias than children or young adolescents. This is not to say that all adults engage in appropriate hypothesis-testing. Rather, it is best to say that a greater percentage of adults engage in appropriate hypothesis-testing than children.

In addition, the size of the developmental differences depends on the meaningfulness of the content. Differences are smaller when adults and children have similar amounts of knowledge (Carey, 1985b). Differences are larger when (a) hypotheses refer to arbitrary or abstract relations (e.g., Figure 10.2) or (b) adults have more knowledge in the domain from which hypotheses derive. To illustrate the latter assertion, consider several studies of Dunbar and Klahr (1989). Whereas 95 percent of adults in their first experiment discovered the correct operation of a "repeat" key on a small robot, only 5 percent of eight- to eleven-year-olds in their third experiment did. Adults apparently knew from prior experience with computer programming that numbers in a command like "repeat 5" could refer to line numbers in a list of commands (e.g., "Go to 10" means "go to line 10"). Due to less experience and education, children apparently thought that a number could only refer to the number of times something occurred. Thus, they fixated on interpretations such as "repeat 5" means "perform all actions in a command five times." In general, the more knowledge someone has, the greater number of hypotheses he or she can construct. Because adults tend to have more knowledge than children, they can generate a greater variety of plausible hypotheses. This ability in conjunction with their greater tendency to reject hypotheses in the face of disconfirming evidence means that adults will more often discover the correct relation among the variables under study.

The implication of this finding is that students should either be taught effective hypothesis-testing using moderately familiar material or spend a lot of time becoming familiar with a topic before they begin experimentation. Unfortunately, studies show that labs typically have little to do with the material concurrently presented in lectures or students' texts (Roth, 1994), so it once again makes sense why few students seem to demonstrate high levels of hypothesis-testing skills. When students have been asked to engage in cycles of prediction followed by data collection in biology labs, they showed significant gains in their biological knowledge and attitudes toward science (Lavoie, 1999).

Experimentation Techniques.   In addition to having an accurate theory and setting up plausible hypotheses, good scientific thinking consists of knowing the best ways to gather data to test hypotheses. In most instances, this "best way" is a properly controlled experiment. Why? Consider our Vitamin C example again. Imagine that the real factor that determines whether or not you will succumb to a cold is the existence of a particular antibody in your immune system. If you have this antibody, you will successfully fend off the invading virus. If you lack the antibody (or your immune system is under stress for some reason), you will catch the cold. Lets say that Joe has the antibody and takes Vitamin C for three days. If he fends off the cold, it is really because he had the antibody, not because he took the Vitamin C. Thus, Joe's belief that the Vitamin C helped would be fallacious.

How could Joe have avoided this error? He should have done the following. First, he should take the Vitamin C for this cold and document what happens. He should note whether he was under stress, had another ailment, was eating properly, and getting enough sleep. Second, he should wait until he feels another cold coming on and then repeat the entire procedure except for taking the Vitamin C. If everything is the same except for the presence versus absence of Vitamin C (i.e., he was under similar amounts of stress, slept the same, and so on), then this would constitute a reasonably conclusive test. If he fends off the cold with the Vitamin C, but gets a cold without it, he should conclude that Vitamin C helps. Otherwise, he should believe that Vitamin C does not matter. If Joe ever did conduct such a test, he would find that Vitamin C does not help. Upon learning this, he should search for another factor that determines whether or not he gets sick (e.g., the antibody in his immune system).

As noted earlier, the technique of varying one variable (e.g., Vitamin C) while holding all other variables constant (e.g., the amount of sleep, etc.) has been given various labels including the "isolation of variables scheme" (Inhelder & Piaget, 1958), "separation of variables scheme" (Martorano, 1977) and "controlling variables strategy" (Linn, Clement, & Pulos, 1983). Regardless of the label, this technique is considered a central aspect of good scientific thinking because, as noted earlier, scientists are always striving to distinguish between genuine causal relations and illusory causal relations.

The first wave of developmental research tried to substantiate Inhelder and Piaget's (1958) claim that the isolation of variables scheme does not emerge until age eleven or twelve. What these researchers found was both good news and bad news for Piagetians. The good news was that children below the age of ten seldom controlled variables when given the same tasks that Piaget used (e.g., the pendulum task in which students had to figure out whether variables such as the heaviness of a weight or length of a string affected how fast a pendulum swung). Although adolescents and adults did control variables on these tasks, the bad news was that only about 40 percent of them did (Keating, 1980). Thus, most of the subsequent research in this area did not try to answer the basic question "When does the isolation of variables scheme first emerge in development?" Rather, the question became "Why do so few adolescents and adults control variables and is there anything we can do to improve their performance?"

The research that tried to answer the second question revealed that the performance of adolescents and adults can be greatly affected by (a) the content of the task, (b) the questions asked, and (c) training or feedback (Kuhn et al., 1988; Linn, 1978; Linn et al., 1983;

Linn, Pulos, & Gans, 1981; Stone & Day, 1978). For example, whereas only 40 percent of subjects will control variables when given a pendulum and asked "Which factor affects the rate of oscillation, the weight or the length of string?" 90 percent will control variables when asked to determine which of two types of seeds produces a bigger plant. In addition, multiple-choice questions produce a greater percentage of correct answers than free response questions, especially in older adolescents. Finally, short training sessions or simple forms of feedback can elevate the performance of adolescents and adults up to 90 percent correct.

Most studies have found that the use of different contents and question formats tends to have little effect on the performance of children below the age of ten (Chen & Klahr, 1999; Kuhn et al., 1995). However, it is possible to reveal the isolation of variables scheme in gifted eight-year-olds (Case, 1974) and average ten-year-olds (Chen & Klahr, 1999; Siegler & Liebert, 1975) by using more intensive training, reducing the number of variables to control, and providing feedback on comparisons. For example, after training, gifted eight-year-olds will come to recognize that a comparison between a short thin rod and long fat rod is not "a fair test" of the role of length in the rod's flexibility. Of course, recognizing an unfair test after training and devising a controlled experiment *on one's own* are two separate things. It is not difficult to elicit the latter skill in adolescents and adults, but it is distressing that many tend not to control variables unless prompted to do so. Chen and Klahr (1999) found that explicit, hands-on training in the control of variables strategy combined with experimental probes (i.e., questions about the comparisons made by students) led children to select unconfounded comparisons on about 65 percent of trials on a posttest conducted seven months after training. Their performance was similarly good on transfer problems (e.g., growth of plants) that were unlike the training problems (e.g., balls on ramps). Using a computer-based intervention with adults, Varelas (1997) likewise found that getting students to reflect on or justify their comparisons led to greater transfer of the control of variable strategy.

What all of this research means is that, in everyday contexts, children younger than ten years of age and many adolescents and adults are likely to believe that certain variables (e.g., Vitamin C) are causally related to certain outcomes (e.g., avoiding a cold), when in fact they are not. Students should spontaneously see the need to control variables to rule out deceptive relations, but they tend not to. The prevalence of such faulty and uncritical reasoning can have serious consequences. Consider how a math teacher might see the co-variation between high SAT math scores on one hand and being male on the other. This data might lead him to believe that there is a genetic component to math ability. This belief may in turn cause him to favor boys in his class and treat girls as if they were unintelligent. Had he conducted a properly controlled experiment (or examined the literature to find one), he might find that his behavior towards his female students is unwarranted because his belief in the genetic component is not well-established (see Chapter 12).

Scientific Reasoning Biases

So far we have examined age changes in children's theories and their tendency to engage in appropriate forms of hypothesis-testing and experimentation. In this section, we will examine their tendency to fall prey to various reasoning biases. Recall that reasoning biases add another layer to the process of discovering the authentic causal basis of some phenomenon. That is, even when researchers have a reasonably accurate theory and use appropriate data-collection techniques, they might still distort or ignore the data that emerges.

Studies conducted by Deanna Kuhn and colleagues have found that (a) objective, scientific reasoning improves little between late childhood and early adulthood, (b) pre-existing beliefs interfere with both the development and evaluation of hypotheses, and (c) belief-consistent hypotheses are constructed with the goal of confirmation rather than disconfirmation (Kuhn et al., 1995). Studies conducted by Paul Klaczynski and colleagues have found similar results. For example, middle and late adolescents found more strengths and fewer flaws in studies that provided data in support of their theories (e.g., that music affects behaviors like suicide; that religious upbringing causes positive outcomes) than in studies that provided data that refuted their pre-existing theories (Klaczynski, 1997; Klaczynski & Narasimham, 1998). However, unlike Kuhn and colleagues, Klaczynski and colleagues also found that other elements of scientific reasoning improved over the course of adolescence. This discrepancy among camps of researchers is probably due to the fact that Klaczynski and colleagues used content that was more personally meaningful to their subjects (e.g., music and their own religion).

Overall, however, research suggests that biased reasoning extends well into adulthood. For example, one study showed that college students' religious beliefs affected their stance toward evolutionary theory (Dagher & BouJaoude, 1997). Another found that college students had one of eight reactions to anomalous data: (a) ignore it, (b) reject it, (c) profess uncertainty about its validity, (d) exclude it from the domain covered by the theory, (e) hold it in abeyance, (f) reinterpret it, (g) accept it and make peripheral changes to the theory, and (h) accept it and change the theory more substantially (Chinn & Brewer, 1998). Note that only the last two stances would lead to revisions in a theory if disconfirming data were to be encountered.

Summary of Developmental Differences

Research has shown that children develop framework theories in the areas of psychology, physics, and biology well before they demonstrate the capacity to generate and test hypotheses in an unbiased and appropriate manner. The framework theories, however, continue to develop after the preschool period principally in terms of becoming more elaborate and making use of abstract causal mechanisms to explain various phenomena. Note that "abstract" means something more than unobservable. In this context it means that it could not be easily concretized in a model (e.g., the concept of force in physics). Whereas theories and experimental techniques develop to the point of being fairly productive by late childhood/early adolescence, the existence of reasoning biases and misconceptions continue to restrict the extent to which adolescents and adults can draw appropriate conclusions from scientific evidence. To a large extent, these problems are a function of the standard instructional sequence in science which tends to emphasize facts over experimentation, hypothesis testing, and model building.

Individual Differences in Scientific Thinking

So far, we have examined the nature of higher-order scientific thinking and also considered the development of this competence. In the present section, we consider the various ways students of the same grade level can differ in their scientific reasoning skills. For consistency with previous sections, we will begin by considering individual differences in (a) structural aspects of scientific thinking, (b) functional aspects of scientific thinking, and (c) reasoning biases. In the final subsection, the focus shifts to gender and ethnic differences in achievement data.

Individual Differences in Structural Aspects

To address the issue of individual differences in theories, one can ask two questions: (a) If we focus on just one age group, do all of the people in this age group have similar theories or do some people have different theories than others? and (b) What could cause students in the same grade to develop different theories?

Research has shown that the answer to the second question is straightforward: two peers will have different theories if they have had different personal experiences or different amounts of education in particular topics. To illustrate the first case, consider studies that have shown that women who have had children tend to have different "naive developmental psychologies" than women without children or even their husbands (Holden, 1988). To illustrate the second case, consider that experts have more elaborate and detailed theories than novices. For example, a twenty-six-year-old graduate student in physics will have a vastly different theory of physics than a twenty-six-year-old accountant (Chi, Glaser, & Rees, 1982).

These claims regarding the role of experience and education in theory development have implications for gender differences in theories. Given that females tend to take fewer science classes in high school than males and tend to have fewer informal experiences related to physical sciences, it should not be surprising to learn that males sometimes perform better than females on science achievement tests (Linn & Hyde, 1989; see below). That is, males tend to know more science facts than females (see Chapter 12). Researchers who have studied framework theories have not reported gender differences in young children, however.

One way teachers can elicit and determine individual differences in the naive beliefs of students is to present them with a phenomenon that requires an explanation (e.g., why a twelve-ounce can of regular Coke sinks in a bucket of water when a twelve-ounce can of Diet Coke does not). Then, they can ask small groups of students to devise a theory of the phenomenon. Teachers will find that nearly every group will come with a theory that differs from those of other groups. Discussion can then ensue about how to decide which (if any) of these theories is consistent with the current opinions of practicing scientists.

Individual Differences in Functional Aspects

Studies show that there are always individuals in the later grades who demonstrate appropriate hypothesis-testing behaviors; that is, they try to (a) disconfirm rather than confirm their hypotheses, (b) take into account all evidence, not just that which is consistent with their views, and (c) modify or discard hypotheses when disconfirming data accumulates. Such people tend to be in the minority, but they clearly differ from individuals who demonstrate all of the biases described above. At present, we lack an explanation of why some people perform as they should and why some do not. Increased education seems to co-vary with higher levels of performance (e.g., Kuhn et al., 1988; Kuhn, 1992), but it is not at all clear why only *some* of the individuals with the same education demonstrate high levels of performance. It would be quite valuable to discover how certain individuals are able to take advantage of their education so that we could know how to elevate the performance of those who do not.

A second type of individual difference has emerged in studies conducted by David Klahr and his associates (e.g., Klahr & Dunbar, 1988; Dunbar & Klahr, 1989). These researchers discovered that adults adopted one of two approaches when they hypothesized about the behavior of a small robot. The robot walked forward, turned, and made noises depending on which buttons on a control pad were pushed. For example, the "→" button told it to turn a certain number of degrees and the "hold" button told it to do nothing for a certain period of time. If someone pressed the sequence, "→ 15, hold 50, fire 2" the robot would turn right, pause for 50 seconds, and then fire two shots. After learning how several buttons worked, subjects were asked to discover how the "repeat" button worked. Consider, for example, what might happen if the command "repeat 2" were added to the string of three commands above. Most people initially thought that the command "repeat 2" meant "do the three-action sequence twice." In reality, it meant "do the last two actions again."

About one third of Klahr and Dunbar's subjects tested the first erroneous hypothesis until they encountered several instances of disconfirming data. After realizing that they needed a new hypothesis, they consulted their knowledge for other hypotheses and then engaged in new experiments. These subjects (who Klahr and Dunbar called "theorists") seemed to say, "Huh! I guess the 2 doesn't mean do the whole thing 2 times. But what else could the 2 stand for? Maybe it stands for the second command. Maybe it stands for the last 2 commands. . . ."

Klahr and Dunbar called the remaining two thirds of subjects "experimenters." Unlike the "theorists," "experimenters" did not discover the correct rule by relying on their knowledge. Rather, after realizing that their initial hypothesis was wrong, they first conducted a number of experiments and then induced an hypothesis that was consistent with the behavior of the robot.

The difference in style between "theorists" and "experimenters" did not result in one group having more success than the other. All but one or two adults discovered how the "repeat" key worked. Instead, the difference between groups was manifested in how *efficient* they were in discovering how the "repeat" button worked. It took the "experimenters" twice as much time to discover the correct function because they conducted twice as many experiments as "theorists."

As for strategies such as control of variables, two factors have been found to produce individual differences in this regard. The first is an individual's pre-existing theories. When presented with a situation in which four or five variables could produce an outcome, people do not tend to control all of these presented variables. Instead, they use their pre-existing theories to decide which variables *could* relate to an outcome and then control just those variables (Linn & Swiney, 1981; Kuhn et al., 1988; Schauble, 1990). People who have different theories would then control different variables. For example, pretend that you and a friend are asked to decide which of the following variables affects the gas mileage of a car: (a) how fast it is driven, (b) how heavy it is, (c) the type of muffler it has, and (d) its color. In conducting an experiment, you might think of controlling the first two variables while ignoring the other two. For example, to test the role of weight, you compare the gas mileage of a heavy car that is driven at 30 miles per hour to a light car driven at the same speed (ignoring the color and type of muffler on each). You might do so because you think that a car's color and muffler have no effect on its gas mileage. You would be right in the case of color, but wrong in the case of the muffler. Your friend, in contrast, might know that mufflers relate to gas mileage so she controlled mufflers in her tests.

The second individual difference variable concerns the way people process visual information. Some people can appropriately perceive a certain visual stimulus even when other stimuli surrounding the stimulus are distracting. Such individuals are called "field independent." Individuals who cannot perceive the focal stimulus because they cannot overcome the distracting information are called "field dependent." Research has shown that field independent subjects are more likely to control variables than field dependent subjects, presumably because only the former perceive and control variables that have less obvious or subtle effects (Linn, 1978; Linn, Pulos, & Gans, 1981).

As for gender differences in functional aspects of scientific reasoning, essentially no differences have emerged between males and females in their tendency to test hypotheses or control variables in particular ways (Kuhn & Brannock, 1977; Meehan, 1984; Roberge & Flexer, 1979). Overton and Meehan (1982), however, found that females who were identified as "learned helpless" performed worse than non-helpless males and females on an isolation of variables task.

Individual Differences in Reasoning Biases

In every study of reasoning biases, there are individuals who exhibit the normative trends towards self-motivated reasoning as well as others who tend to deviate from these trends. Hence, there clearly are individual differences in the tendencies to be biased or dogmatic. In a series of studies, Keith Stanovich and colleagues have tried to reveal the factors that are predictive of the tendency to engage in rational thought and critical thinking. College students were given a battery of problems that tapped into the ability to draw deductive inferences, test hypotheses, draw unbiased statistical inferences, and so on (even when the content was contrary to their beliefs). They tried to predict high scores on this composite reasoning battery using indices of intellectual capacity (e.g., SAT scores) and questionnaires that tapped into the dispositional tendency to engage in actively open-minded thinking. By "actively open-minded thinking," they meant the tendency to be reflective (e.g., "If I think longer about a problem I will be more likely to solve it"), the willingness to consider evidence that was contrary to their beliefs (e.g., "People should always consider evidence that goes against their beliefs"), and a willingness to postpone closure (e.g., "There is nothing wrong with being undecided about many issues"). They expected that people would be more likely to reveal reasoning competence if they had more intellectual resources and a tendency toward actively open-minded thinking. Their findings generally supported this expectation (Stanovich & West, 1997, 1998; Sa, West, & Stanovich, 1999).

Gender and Ethnic Differences in Achievement Data

In 1996, the National Center for Educational Statistics administered the most recent National Assessment of Educational Progress (NAEP) for Science. The 1996 NAEP had multiple-choice questions that assessed students' knowledge of important facts and concepts, constructed-response questions that explored students' ability to explain or reason about scientific information, and hands-on tasks that probed students' abilities to make observations or evaluate experimental results (O'Sullivan, Reese, & Mazzeo, 1997). Based on these responses, students were assigned to one of four proficiency levels: advanced, proficient, basic, and below basic. Results for a large, nationally representative sample of children in the fourth, eighth, and twelfth grades showed that there were no gender differences at the fourth or eighth grades. At the twelfth grade, however, a significant difference emerged. Whereas the percentages falling into the top three levels of proficiency for males were 4 percent (advanced), 25 percent (proficient), 60 percent (basic), the corresponding percentages for females were 1 percent (advanced), 17 percent (proficient), and 55 percent (basic). Translated into scores ranging between 0 and 300, the average scores for twelfth-grade males and females were 152 and 148, respectively. Such differences are fairly small in absolute terms, but are statistically significant given the large sample size.

When Black, White, and Hispanic students are compared, however, the differences are much larger. Here, the percentages falling into the three main categories were 3 percent (advanced), 27 percent (proficient), and 68 percent (basic) for twelfth-grade White students; 0.1 percent (advanced), 4 percent (proficient) and 23 percent (basic) for twelfth-grade Black students; and 0.8 percent (advanced), 7 percent (proficient), and 33 percent (basic) for twelfth-grade Hispanic students. Translated into proficiency scores, the findings are as follows: 159 (twelfth-grade White), 124 (twelfth-grade Black), and 130 (twelfth-grade Hispanic). In contrast to what was found for gender differences, large ethnic differences were found at the fourth and eighth grade as well.

Implications for Teaching

As noted earlier, one of the goals of education is to instill in all students the kinds of scientific knowledge and skills they will need to be successful in the world of adults. In other words, we want our high school graduates to have (a) reasonably accurate and elaborate domain-specific theories, (b) effective knowledge-acquisition devices (i.e., hypothesis-testing, control of variables), (c) the disposition toward actively open-minded and critical thinking, and (d) explicit (metacognitive) awareness of their theories, knowledge-acquisition strategies, and biases. The preceding review of developmental and individual differences in science shows that we are a long way away from meeting this goal. Children graduate with a fair amount of factual knowledge, but they have relatively few accurate conceptual understandings and harbor many misconceptions. Moreover, they tend not to be very critical about scientific results unless these challenge beliefs that are dear to their hearts and often accept theories without much evidence. Furthermore, White students tend to demonstrate substantially more scientific knowledge than minority students.

Cast in a problem-solving framework, these trends represent the problem that has to be fixed. What we need to consider in this section are strategies than can be used to move us closer to more desirable outcomes. Before we can consider better ways to do things, however, we need to first reflect on what we are doing now, because the present approach is obviously not working. At present, the standard approach to science instruction is to have students passively accept a large amount of scientific facts and vocabulary terms (Carey, 1986; Hogan, 1999). For the most part, widespread science instruction begins in the fourth or fifth grade and occurs three or more times per week in grades four through eight. In high school, science instruction intensifies with about 55 percent of high school students taking at least seven semesters of science (O'Sullivan et al., 1997). Whereas the focus in eighth grade tends to be earth science and physical science, 75–100 percent of high school students report taking biology and chemistry, while another 40–50 percent report taking earth science, space science, or physics. As for teacher training and resources, O'Sullivan et al. (1997) report that

- 60 percent of fourth and eighth graders were taught by teachers whose highest degree was a bachelor's degree; 16 percent and 62 percent of these teachers reported holding an undergraduate or graduate degree in science or a minor in science (or science education), respectively; 25 percent of fourth-grade teachers and 75 percent of eighth-grade teachers reported that they were certified to teach in the area of science;
- 60–65 percent of fourth and eighth grade teachers reported that they had all or most of the resources they needed to teach science, though only 40–50 percent reported having access to one or more computers in their classrooms.

Stated in these terms, alternative strategies for improving science education might be to start intensive science education earlier than the fifth grade (Metz, 1995, but see Kuhn, 1997); diversify the kinds of scientific domains beyond earth science, biology, and chemistry; increase the science education of elementary and middle school teachers; and provide more resources for teachers so they could do more hands-on exploration and hypothesis-testing work. Beyond these macro-level changes, however, there are other considerations that derive from the research presented earlier as well as proposals suggested by the National Research Council. Let's examine these general guidelines next and then focus on two case studies at the end of the chapter.

General Guidelines

As noted above, in many science classrooms, teachers have the goal of having their students master a series of facts and a specific scientific vocabulary. Little attempt is made to get children to think and act like scientists (Carey, 1986; Linn & Songer, 1993; Roth, 1994). In taking a content mastery approach, teachers convey the idea to children that scientific knowledge is fixed and absolute rather than constantly changing. Many educators argue that this approach to science instruction is the reason why students demonstrate confirmation biases, fail to spontaneously conduct controlled experiments, and hold many misconceptions. It is clear, then, that science education is in need of reform.

One promising way to reform science education is to move from the content mastery model of instruction to an *apprenticeship* model of instruction (Brown, Collins, & Duguid, 1989; Linn & Songer, 1993; Roth, 1994). The primary goal of the apprenticeship model is to have students progressively internalize the beliefs and practices of working scientists. Ideally, the apprentice model should begin as soon as science instruction begins. Instead of mastering facts, students would observe scientific phenomena, propose explanations of these phenomena, and conduct controlled experiments to see if their theories are correct. In this way, laboratory exercises would not be totally divorced from everyday classroom lectures. Instead, labs would be at the *center* of instruction.

The role of teachers in the apprenticeship model is to help children construct experiments and point out how the data generated from experiments either support or contradict children's current theories. Teachers would not present vocabulary in isolation, but would present scientific terms in the context of conversing with children about scientific phenomena or the results of experiments. That way, children would acquire a scientific vocabulary in the same way that they acquire other words in their natural language. If any lecturing is done, it would be historical in nature, pointing out how some of the misconceptions held by students were held by scientists many years ago (e.g., the "impetus" conception of force). Historical perspectives would also allow children to see that scientific knowledge is constantly changing.

In addition to these general implications, the research on scientific thinking has more specific instructional implications:

1. Teachers need to acknowledge the fact that their students have naive theories. Education should have the effect of changing students' naive theories into the theories of professionals in a given domain. One of the best ways of affecting this change is to help children acquire a more accurate understanding of various theoretical mechanisms. Instruction should, therefore, focus directly on mechanisms.

2. Confirmation and preservation biases are fairly natural tendencies or "habits of mind" when students test hypotheses. These biases can be overcome if teachers repeatedly point out how to avoid them when experimental data is interpreted in class. But it should be noted that instruction that is limited to helping students avoid biases will not help students become better hypothesis-testers. Even if they avoid biases, students still need to have an accurate theory if they want to be successful at predicting outcomes.

3. With respect to experimentation, elementary students should be taught how to control variables in the manner of Case (1974), Siegler and Liebert (1975), and Chen and Klahr (1999); that is, they should have multiple experiences designing "fair tests." Due to information processing limitations (see Chapter 2), these tests should involve only two variables in the early grades. By the time these students enter middle school or high school, they probably will not need training or feedback to conduct a controlled experiment with two or more variables.

4. With respect to misconceptions, the main strategy should be to diagnose, confront, and remediate them. Teachers who are unaware of misconceptions and who simply lecture about science topics will not reduce or eliminate misconceptions in their students.

One promising strategy for remediating misconceptions is the use of "bridging" analogies (Brown, 1992). Bridging analogies were devised for cases in which the gap between an idea that you want your students to understand and those ideas that they already understand is too large to make a connection. To get a sense of this phenomenon, try to answer the following two questions: (a) When you put a book on a table, does the table exert a force on the book? and (b) When you press down on a spring with your hand, does the spring exert a force back on your hand? You may know that the answer to both questions is "Yes," but only really believe it is for the second one. Often teachers try to use examples like the one with the spring to help students understand the one about the book. However, the gap between the situations is too large for students to see a connection.

The logic behind bridging analogies is to progressively modify an example that students already understand (e.g., the spring example) until you have transformed it into the example that you want them to understand (e.g, the book example). For example, you could first ask the question about the spring. Then, you could ask, "If you put a book on a spring, does the spring exert a force back on the book?" Next, you could ask, "If you put the book on a flexible board suspended over two sawhorses, would the board exert a force back on the book?" And finally, you would present them with the example of a book on a table. Brown (1992) found that this approach greatly reduced misconceptions in high school students about the concept of force.

A second approach to remediating misconceptions is to help learners become dissatisfied with their existing conceptions and find new, more accurate concepts to be intelligible, plausible, and fruitful (Stofflett, 1994). To make new concepts more intelligible, it is important to make analogies to what students already know and understand. To make them more plausible, learners have to find it potentially believable and consistent with their experiences (experiences they are not thinking of). To be fruitful, learners have to recognize how new practical applications or experiments can arise from the new conceptions.

Beyond these recommendations that derive from contemporary theory and research on science learning, there are also the recommendations embodied in the 1996 National Science Teaching Standards proposed by the National Research Council (NRC). Figure 10.3 lists these standards. Note that they include a discussion of hands-on inquiry learning, modeling of appropriate scientific behaviors and attitudes by the teacher, extended discourse to create communities of learners, and regular assessment to see how things are going. Hence, the standards are largely consistent with contemporary theory and research in science learning. On the surface, then, classrooms that follow the reforms suggested by the NRC would be expected to demonstrate higher achievement than traditional classrooms. One recent study of achievement data for tenth graders showed this to be the case, but only for White students. In fact, the gap between ethnic groups was found to be larger in reform classrooms than in standard classrooms (Von Secker & Lissitz, 1999). Thus, something other than the reforms may be needed to eliminate ethnic differences in science.

In all, there is a great deal that needs to be done in science classrooms in order for children to ultimately think and behave as scientists. Although achievement tests and many

FIGURE 10.3   *The 1996 National Science Teaching Standards*

All standards begin with "Teachers of science . . . "

Standard A: plan an inquiry-based science program for their students. In doing this teachers (a) develop a framework of yearlong and short-term goals for their students, (b) select science curricula to meet the interests, knowledge, understanding, abilities, and experiences of students, (c) select teaching and assessment strategies that support the development of student understanding and nurture a community of science learners, and (d) work together as colleagues within and across disciplines and grade levels.

Standard B: guide and facilitate learning. In doing this, teachers (a) focus and support inquiries while interacting with students, (b) orchestrate discourse among students about scientific ideas, (c) challenge students to accept and share responsibility for their own learning, (d) recognize and respond to student diversity and encourage all students to participate fully in science learning, and (e) encourage and model the skills of scientific inquiry, as well as the curiosity, openness to new ideas and data, and skepticism that characterize science.

Standard C: engage in ongoing assessment of their teaching and of student learning. In doing this, teachers (a) use multiple methods and systematically gather data about student understanding and ability, (b) analyze assessment data to guide teaching, (c) guide students in self-assessments, (d) use student data, observations of teaching, and interactions with colleagues to reflect on and improve teaching practice and also to report student achievement and opportunities to learn to students teachers, parents, policy-makers, and the general public.

Standard D: design and manage learning environments that provide students with the time, space, and resources needed for learning science. In doing this, teachers (a) structure the time available so that students are able to engage in extended investigations, (b) create a setting for student work that is flexible and supportive of science inquiry, (c) ensure a safe working environment, (d) make the available science tools, media, and technological resources available to students, (e) identify and use resources outside of school, and (f) engage students in the learning environment.

Standard E: develop communities of learners that reflect the intellectual rigor of scientific inquiry and the attitudes and social values conducive to science learning. In doing this, teachers (a) display and demand respect for the diverse ideas, skills, and experiences of all students, (b) enable students to have a significant voice in decisions about the content and context of their work and require students to take responsibility for the learning of all members of the community, (c) nurture collaboration among students, (d) structure and facilitate ongoing formal and informal discussion based on a shared understanding of rules of scientific discourse, and (e) model and emphasize the skills, attitudes, and values of scientific inquiry.

Standard F: actively participate in the ongoing planning and development of the school science program. In doing this, teachers (a) plan and develop the school science program, (b) participate in the decisions concerning the allocation of time and other resources to the science program, and (c) participate fully in planning and implementing professional growth and development strategies for themselves and their colleagues.

Adapted from the National Research Council (1996). *National Science Education Standards.* Washington, D.C.: National Academy Press.

studies reveal flaws in students' thinking, a number of studies show that students can reveal scientific competence given sufficient amounts of advanced education. The emphasis now is on having students demonstrate proficiency well before they reach graduate school.

Case Studies

Case Study 1. Students in a study conduced by Hewson and Hewson (1983) were mostly Black ninth graders from Soweto, South Africa, who held many misconceptions about mass, volume, and density. Hewson and Hewson wanted students to become dissatisfied with their misconceptions and find the correct conceptions to be more intelligible, plausible, and fruitful. At the point at which instruction began, students had been taught the proper conception two times in previous years but still held on to the misconceptions.

There were three major segments to the instructional sequence. In the first part, the authors identified students' existing conceptions of, and misconceptions about, mass, volume, and density. Once identified, the goal was to have them eliminate the misconceptions and replace them with correct conceptions.

For example, many students defined "density" as the packing of particles of different materials. Through discussion, the teacher had students exchange this definition for the definition that density involves both the packing of particles *and* the mass of the packed particles. Through workbook exercises, students also came to differentiate their idea that density is simply "crowdedness" into the idea that density involves the number of objects **per unit area.** In order for this differentiation and exchange of ideas to take place, the discussion and worksheet had to make the new ideas intelligible and plausible (e.g., by helping students envision the definition using metaphors such as the number of boxes in a room). Following these experiences, two discussions and three experiments were conducted. In the discussions, students were told about the facts that (a) density is the mass of something per unit volume (e.g., grams per cubic centimeter), (b) all matter has density, and (c) all matter has mass and volume. Through experiments, students came to characterize the relative density of objects (that one object is more dense than another) and that it is the density of an object and not its weight or volume that determines whether or not it will float. The floating experiments helped students see that something that is lighter may nevertheless sink while something that is heavier may nevertheless float. In showing these contradictions, students became dissatisfied with their misconceptions and came to see how the correct conception was more fruitful (i.e., applicable to more cases).

Use the information in the present chapter (including the Standards in Figure 10.3) and in the chapters on theories, memory, higher-order thinking, and motivation to evaluate this instructional approach.

Case Study 2. The late Ann Brown and her colleagues developed an instructional approach called "Communities of Learners" that they implemented in inner-city second-grade and sixth-grade classrooms (Brown & Campione, 1994). There are six core aspects to the approach. First, content is regularly introduced using the Reciprocal Teaching method described in Chapters 2 and 4. In addition to modeling and taking turns demonstrating comprehension strategies such as summarizing and predicting, teachers and students also modeled explanation, argument, and discussion forms. Second, they made use of a modified version of the jigsaw method of cooperative learning. Here, students were assigned curriculum themes (e.g., changing animal populations) that were divided into about five sub-topics (e.g., extinct, endangered, artificial, assisted, and urbanized). Students then formed separate research groups, each of which focused on one of the sub-topics (e.g., a group of four students might focus on extinction). After researching the topic, students prepared teaching materials using commercially available computer software. Then, they regrouped into reciprocal teaching seminars with the goal of re-assembling and integrating each fifth of the information. All children in a given group were expert on one portion of the topic, taught this information to others, and prepared questions for a test (that covered the entire unit) that all students would take. In dividing and distributing expertise in this manner, each student took responsibility for the material and taught from strength.

To foster cohesion and predictability, class periods have several ritualistic and familiar participant structures. For example, students regularly form into three groups. One group might be composing on the computer, one might be conducting research using various kinds of media, and the third might be working with the teacher in some way (e.g., editing manuscripts or discussing progress). Another familiar routine is the reciprocal teaching seminars described above. A third is an activity called "crosstalk" that was invented by the students. Here, the members of one expertise group report on their progress to the others. Students from other groups get to ask questions to clarify matters or extend their understanding. One final recurrent activity is the benchmark lesson in which the teacher or an outside expert models processes such as thinking skills, self-reflection, introducing new information, and stressing higher-order relations. Brown and colleagues argued that the ritualistic, repetitive nature of these routines allowed children to make the transition from one participant structure to another effortlessly and also helped them understand their roles in these structures.

Three other features of the approach are also noteworthy. First, the goal was to establish a "community of discourse" in which " . . . constructive discussion, questioning, and criticism are the mode rather than the exception" (Brown & Campione, 1994, p. 236). Second, there are "multiple zones of proximal development" that provide children at different levels of readiness to learn certain topics in a unit various pathways to gain understanding. With teachers and various peers presenting information and modeling activities in different ways, there are many opportunities for information to be presented just beyond (but not too far above) children's current level of understanding. Finally, there are phenomena called "seeding," "migration," and "appropriation of ideas" by Brown and colleagues. Here, the metaphor is that teachers create multiple zones of proximal development by "seeding" ideas that migrate around the groups. For example, the teacher might set out a thought experiment such as the question, "Could a cheetah change from a meat diet to a vegetable diet and survive?" By struggling to understand core principles in a unit and talking about them, students are thought to "appropriate them" rather than internalize them as meaningless facts. That is, they take on a personalized meaning that incorporates the shared understanding of the construct that was developed within the culture of the classroom.

Use the information in the present chapter (including the Standards in Figure 10.3) and in the chapters on theories, memory, higher-order thinking, and motivation to evaluate this instructional approach.

11

Social Studies Learning

Summary

1. The primary goals of social studies education are to help students (a) become knowledgeable and active citizens, (b) get in touch with their personal identities and values, and (c) develop a sensitivity to other cultures and values. Some of the core disciplines that comprise the social studies include history, geography, economics, and civics.

2. History educators want students to (a) know the chronology of significant events, (b) understand why these events occurred, and (c) understand why these events were significant. Moreover, they want students to understand that historians interpret and reconstruct events using partial evidence. Research shows that although these tasks are progressively mastered by children as they move through school, many students do not attain high levels of historical understanding by the time they graduate high school.

3. Among other things, geography educators want students to be able to interpret maps, locate major natural resources, and understand the factors related to the movement of peoples. Research shows that although geographic skills increase with age, most twelfth graders only possess basic knowledge.

4. Economics educators want students to be able to comprehend important concepts such as *profit, scarcity, supply,* and *demand.* Research shows that children seem to pass through various levels of understanding of these concepts.

5. As far as civics is concerned, national tests show that students do not gain mastery over knowledge of government and individual rights of citizens until they are in the twelfth grade.

6. Many social studies educators argue that children's performance on social studies assessments would improve if we did not wait until the fourth or fifth grade to teach social studies ideas in meaningful ways.

7. Gender differences in social studies knowledge are fairly small and inconsistent. Ethnic differences, in contrast, are rather large and consistent at all age levels.

Over the years, four important questions have sparked a number of debates within the field of social studies: (a) Which disciplines make up the social studies? (b) Why should students learn social studies? (c) When should social studies instruction begin? and (d) What is the best way to teach social studies? (Armento, 1986; Brophy, 1990; Brophy & VanSledright, 1997). With respect to the first question, some experts limit the selection to just geography, civics, and political science. Others, however, want to include history, psychology, and sociology as well. Thus, it can be very difficult to propose a definition of "the social studies" that everyone will agree with. Nevertheless, it is not a good idea to begin a chapter with only a vague sense of what it will be about. Therefore, let's propose a reasonable definition to gain some initial clarity: the social studies consist of an interrelated set of topics related to the history, environment, economics, lifestyles, and governments of peoples who live in this and other regions of the world.

As to the second question regarding the purpose of teaching social studies, most experts agree that the content of social studies classes should help students do at least three things: (a) become knowledgeable and active citizens, (b) get in touch with their personal identities and values, and (c) develop a sensitivity to other cultures and values (Brophy, 1990).

To see the importance of such knowledge and values, consider what would happen if we never instilled them in students. Without an informed and active electorate, government officials would be free to do as they please. Moreover, many of the most important changes in society would not have taken place if it were not for volunteer citizen groups (e.g., the civil rights movement). Furthermore, without knowledge of other cultures and values, students might develop or retain biases against certain ethnic or religious groups and be inclined to impose their values on others. Without knowledge of their own ancestral origins, students might never feel a sense of pride in their own ethnic and national identities.

To be able to answer the third and fourth question above, we need to delve into the literature on developmental and individual differences in social studies knowledge. In what follows, we shall examine this literature in four sections. In the first, the essential skills of social studies expertise are explored. In the second, the development of this expertise is at issue. In the third, we shall explore individual differences in social studies learning. In the fourth and final section, we shall explore the instructional implications of all of this work.

Expertise in the Social Studies

As is evident in many chapters of this book, many educational reforms are based on the premise that students should be encouraged to emulate professionals in specific fields. For example, we learned in Chapter 9 that math educators want students to be able to think like mathematicians by the time they leave the twelfth grade. Similarly, in Chapter 10 we saw that science educators want students to think and act like practicing scientists, and in Chapter 8 we saw that language arts scholars want students to emulate professional writers. Although many experts in the field of social studies education also argue that the goal of social studies instruction is to get students to think and act like social scientists, others argue instead that curricular decisions in the social studies should be guided more by the needs of students and society (Brophy, 1990). By emphasizing *citizen education,* the goal of social studies education becomes one of helping students make appropriate and informed *decisions* about public-policy issues.

Nearly all Americans live in a community and many of them are parents. As a result, most need to be well-informed about a great variety of issues that could affect them. For example, consider some issues that Americans have been grappling with for many years:

1. Should there be a national heath plan that guarantees health insurance to all Americans?
2. Should America send troops to help a democratic ally that has fallen prey to a military coup?
3. Should we eliminate a 4-cents-a-gallon tax on gasoline because we no longer have a national deficit?
4. Should we allow prayer in public schools?
5. Should we impose fines on people who pollute?
6. Should there be a constitutional amendment to prohibit flag burning?
7. Is there still a need for affirmative action?

Take some time now to provide a reasoned answer to each of these questions.

It should be clear that taking an appropriate stance on any of these issues requires considerable knowledge on your part. Individuals who are ignorant of certain facts (e.g., the number of American soldiers, other soldiers, and civilians who would be killed in an invasion) might adopt a stance that they would later regret.

But effective decision-making involves *values* in addition to knowledge (Slovic, 1990). To see this, imagine the situation in which a congressman holds a "town hall" meeting to get input from his constituents about invading a foreign country to restore democracy there. Imagine next that two of his constituents are both armed with the same information: 350 Americans would probably lose their lives during the invasion. If one constituent believes that no loss of life is justifiable, he might urge the congressman to vote against the invasion. If the other believes that 500 lives are expendable if the lives of one million people would be better off, she might urge the congressman to vote for the invasion. Thus, people who have the same knowledge but different values will choose different options.

Social studies educators hope that by teaching students about the history, economics, lifestyles, and governments of this and other countries, students will have the knowledge they need to make informed decisions about public-policy issues. In many private and public schools, there is also an emphasis on instilling certain values in students as well (e.g., love of country; respect for others). Some schools, however, do not try to instill values as much as help students get in touch with the values they already have (Brophy, 1990). Note that social studies has historically been the place where patriotism (or, more cynically, nationalist propaganda) occurs and also locus of character education. A little reflection shows why curricular decisions related to the role of social studies are often very heated and value-laden.

When can students understand the facts they need to be good citizens and decision-makers? Do certain groups gain more social studies knowledge than others? We shall address these questions in the next two sections.

The Development of Social Studies Knowledge and Skills

In what follows, we shall examine the development of social studies knowledge by looking at age trends within four of the disciplines that comprise the social studies: history, geography, economics, and civics.

History

It is safe to say that we not only want our students to know certain historical facts, we also want them to *comprehend* the significance of these facts (Brophy, 1990). For example, in addition to simply knowing *that* the Boston Tea Party occurred, we want students to (a) understand *why* it occurred, (b) understand *why* it was a significant event (according to historians), and (c) know its place in the chronology of significant events in American history.

What does it take to understand historical events in this way? Three cognitive abilities seem to be indispensable. The first is the ability to order events in time. The second is the ability to understand causal relations among events. The third is the ability to recognize that historians do not merely record reality, they *interpret* it and are selective in what they choose to interpret. Lets examine the development of these sub-skills further. After doing so, we shall examine age trends in performance on national assessments of history knowledge.

Concepts of Time.   Clearly, we would be fighting a losing battle if we tried to teach history to students who could neither understand the difference between the past and the present nor mentally arrange past events into a sequence. Fortunately for elementary school teachers, considerable development occurs in these abilities during the preschool period. Beginning about two years of age, children's language suggests that they distinguish between things that are happening now and things that happened earlier (Friedman, 1990; Nelson, 1991). Moreover, two-year-olds can imitate a sequence of events as long as the sequence is familiar to them and involves just two actions. By the age of four, these event representations develop into extended, multiple-sequence "scripts" (e.g., a "lunchtime script," see Chapter 2 or Nelson, 1986).

However, whereas young children can comprehend the difference between the past and present and also arrange events into short sequences, William Friedman, an expert on children's concept of time notes that (1990, p. 93):

> " . . . their sense of past and future probably differs markedly from our own . . . lacking both knowledge of long-scale patterns and of conventional frameworks . . . young children undoubtedly experience a far less differentiated past. Probably past events can only be located within islands of structure . . . without any appreciation of where the islands lie relative to one another."

It should also be noted that children's early successes with respect to temporal notions derive from their own activities. It is more difficult to conceptualize a series of events that happened to someone else than to recall a series of events in which you participated.

In reviewing the extant research, Friedman (1990) argues that whereas older preschoolers can represent a span that extends about 24 hours into the past, most six- and seven-year-olds can correctly order sets of cards that represent seasons or holidays, suggesting that they can comprehend annual patterns. Moreover, they can order the days of the week and months of the year. Between eight years of age and adolescence, children's conceptualizations of temporal patterns increase in span and uniformity. Adolescents are also more likely than younger children to comprehend the conventional quality of time (e.g., understanding daylight savings time).

It would appear, then, that whereas attempts to teach a "timeline" of historical events clearly would not be successful for preschoolers, it would also not be successful for children in the early elementary grades. This assumption seems to be endorsed by most school districts because many have limited social studies instruction to the "expanding communities" framework for children in the fourth grade and below (Brophy & VanSledright, 1997; Brophy, VanSledright, & Bredin, 1992; Wyner & Farquhar, 1991). In this framework, instruction focuses on the self in kindergarten, the family in the first grade, the neighborhood in the second grade, the community in the third grade, and the state in the fourth grade. A systematic focus on American History and Western Civilization usually does not start until the fifth grade or later. For young children, then, "history" becomes their own personal history (i.e., they focus on events that have happened to them and on their family tree) and progressively shifts toward the history of their neighborhood, community, and state. This expanding communities framework was based on the Piagetian ideas that young children tend to be concrete and view things best from their own perspective.

And yet, it is a truism that children often learn what they are taught. Many researchers are rejecting the idea of waiting to teach American and Western history until the fifth grade because they question the Piagetian research on which this delay was originally based (Levstik & Pappas, 1987). Some reviewers contend that when earlier instruction has been tried, it has met with some success (Alleman & Rosean, 1991). Moreover, the research that shows that children become more facile with clocks and calendars with age makes sense given the fact that children are exposed to these instruments in school. In a study to directly test what children could do, Levstik and Barton (1996) asked children in kindergarten to grade six to place nine pictures drawn from nine different historical periods (e.g., the Colonial period, the late nineteenth century, the 1960s) into chronological order. Although there was sizable agreement across grades in the orders generated, children used different strategies for ordering pictures. For example, whereas the youngest children could make broad distinctions (e.g., today versus recent past versus remote past), older children used clues such as clothing to make finer distinctions. It was not until the third grade that dates took on any significance and not until the fifth or sixth grades that dates were associated with historical periods (e.g., the Colonial period). The fact that children in this study came from traditional "expanding communities" schools suggests that teachers could make greater headway with timelines than one would think.

One way to help children acquire an earlier understanding of history is to have them play-act a series of historical events in the proper order. By engaging in the behaviors themselves, children might get a better sense of motives and could also develop "scripts" for the events. However, given that the formation of scripts requires a certain amount of consistency and repetition, perhaps children could repeat the same play-act sequence several years in a row (e.g., kindergarten, first, and second grade). But as Case (1998) and others have noted (Brophy & VanSledright, 1997), script-like knowledge needs to be fused with children's naive psychologies in order for them to develop a *narrative* understanding of history. Such an understanding would give them the temporal-causal insight needed to make better sense of the sterile timeline that is typical in the standard curriculum. In addition, by introducing the narrative approach, teachers can make use of fictionalized historical texts that bring history alive for children and make it seem more interesting (Brophy & VanSledright, 1997).

Causal Notions.   As several researchers have noted, the essence of a comprehensive historical perspective is being able to understanding *why* certain events took place and *how* these events affected the course of history (Brophy & VanSledright, 1997; Hallden, 1986; McKeown & Beck, 1990). We know from research that infants and preschoolers can comprehend simple causal relations (see Chapter 10), but does that mean that somewhat older students can understand why events such as the Boston Tea Party occurred and what effect such events had on subsequent events in American history?

At a minimum, students would need to understand abstract concepts such as "taxation" and "representation" in order to understand why the Boston Tea Party occurred (McKeown & Beck, 1990). Moreover, they would need to understand the motivations and belief-systems of significant individuals as well as comprehend significant aspects of group behaviors and processes. Hence, they would need to understand causal principles of psychology, philosophy, sociology, and political science (because these sciences explain the behaviors of individuals and groups). Given the abstract and sophisticated nature of these principles, it should not be surprising to learn that, despite the best efforts of teachers, students often simplify the causes of events down to the level of the personal motives of individuals (Hallden, 1986). Moreover, given the absence of causal explanations in many history textbooks, it also should not be surprising to learn that students' historical knowledge is often characterized by simple associations and unconnected structures (McKeown & Beck, 1990).

One way to test students' causal understanding is to have them engage in *counterfactual reasoning.* Someone who can engage in counterfactual reasoning can envision what would have happened if certain events did *not* occur. To see how this works, try answering the following questions:

1. Would there have been a Protestant Reformation if the Catholic Church had given a divorce to Henry VIII and rectified the problems identified by Martin Luther?
2. Would the United States have pulled out of Vietnam if President Kennedy had not been assassinated?

According to Piagetian theory, children cannot engage in counterfactual reasoning until they are ten or eleven years old (see Chapter 2). We know that Piaget underestimated the abilities of young children sometimes, so it remains to be seen whether research would show that younger children could not engage in counterfactual reasoning under some circumstances. But, of course, in order to understand what would happen if something did not occur, you first need to understand why things happened as they did. Since we just argued that this is not an easy task for students, perhaps counterfactual reasoning would be hard for elementary students as well.

Historians as Interpreters and Evidence Gatherers. Besides constructing mental timelines and understanding causal relations, a third obstacle to understanding history is the ability to understand that historians are people who have pet theories and biases that cause them to look at events in interpretative ways. Several studies have shown that young children think that there is only one "reality" that we all see in the same way (Kuhn, Amsel, & O'Loughlin, 1988). When told about two historians who witnessed the same event (e.g., the same battle in the Civil War), young children often think that the historians would necessarily record the events in the same way. As an adult, you have a better sense of how these accounts could differ. In particular, you would clearly recognize how an historian from a conservative southern United States university could see things differently than an historian from a liberal northern United States university.

Although above-average fifth graders have a rudimentary sense of the notion of the possibility of biased interpretations (Brophy et al., 1992), a fully mature conception of multiple interpretations may not be evident until students are college age and beyond (Kuhn et al., 1988). Thus, most elementary students take all information presented in history classes as immutable "facts." Once again, though, children's perceptions may be due to the fact that textbooks and teachers may present historical information in this way (VanSledright & Kelly, 1998). If so, then perhaps instruction could foster an earlier appreciation of multiple perspectives than has been found to date. One strategy might be to have children form teams and ask them to create a seasonal display (e.g., for Thanksgiving). After telling them that the team with the best display wins, you then appoint two judges, one from each team to rate the display. Children will soon learn that observers can be biased.

One final aspect of historical understanding is the notion that historians reconstruct history using a variety of sources that vary in their validity. To get a sense of this process, imagine you were an historian who was asked to determine how slaves *really* felt about being slaves or being given their emancipation. What kinds of evidence would you attempt to find? How about letters written from one slave owner to another? If the former were to say in his letters that his slaves were very content and it is not clear why the [Civil] war was being fought, would that be credible evidence? How about evidence in local records related to the frequency with which slaves attempted to escape? Could a certain number of attempts be clear evidence that slaves were happy or unhappy? Whereas professional historians look to the credibility of the evidence used to draw certain historical interpretations (Rouet, Favart, Britt, & Perfetti, 1997; Wineburg, 1991), children in the elementary and middle grades show little insight into the evidence collection process (VanSledright & Kelly, 1998). Again, though, their lack of insight may be due to the manner in which historical claims are presented as unquestioned facts by teachers and textbooks. Studies with college-level non-historians show that students can create coherent mental models out of several sources (Rouet, Britt, Mason, & Perfetti, 1996). It is not clear when this ability would be evident prior to college, however.

Age Trends on National Assessments. In 1988, the National Center for Educational Statistics conducted a large-scale study of the history knowledge of fourth, eighth, and twelfth graders (i.e., the National Assessment of Educational Progress or NAEP for history). From the items used on this test, researchers derived four levels of performance. Figure 11.1 describes the four levels and Figure 11.2 shows the percentage students who scored at these levels. As can be seen, whereas nearly all students at all ages knew simple historical facts (Level 200), very few seemed to understand basic historical terms and relationships (Level 300), and fewer still could interpret historical information and ideas (Level 350). The largest shifts in knowledge occurred between the fourth and eighth grades for Level 250 knowledge (which includes a conception of timelines), and between the eighth and twelfth grades for Level 300 knowledge (which includes a beginning comprehension of causal relationships). The authors of a summary report for this study concluded that although factual knowledge clearly increases with age, " . . . the assessment results indicate that across the grades, most students have a limited grasp of United States history"

FIGURE 11.1   *Levels of Understanding on the 1988 NAEP for History*

Level 200: Knows Simple Historical Facts

Students at this level know some historical facts of the type learned from everyday experiences. For example, they can identify a few national holidays and patriotic symbols. They can read simple timelines, graphs, charts, and maps.

Level 250: Knows Beginning Historical Information and has Rudimentary Interpretive Skills

Students at this level know a greater number and variety of historical facts of the type commonly learned from historical studies. For example, they can identify a number of historical figures, events, and terms. They are developing a sense of chronology and can interpret timelines, maps, and graphs.

Level 300: Understands Basic Historical Terms and Relationships

Students at this level have a broad knowledge of historical terms, facts, regions, and ideas. They have a general sense of chronology and can recognize characterizations of particular time periods in history. These students have some knowledge of the content of primary texts in United States political and constitutional history, such as the Declaration of Independence and the Constitution. They are familiar with certain historically significant economic and social developments and have some awareness of different social and cultural groups. These students are beginning to comprehend the historical significance of domestic governmental policies and also the international context of United States history. They show an emerging understanding of causal relationships.

Level 350: Interprets Historical Information and Ideas

Students at this level are developing a detailed understanding of historical vocabulary, facts, regions, and ideas. They are familiar with a wider array of texts such as the Articles of Confederation and Federalist Papers. They are aware of the religious diversity of the United States and recognize the continuing tension between democratic principles and social realities such as poverty and discrimination. They have a rudimentary understanding of the history of United States foreign policy and are beginning to relate social science concepts (e.g., price theory and separation of powers) to historical themes and can evaluate causal relationships.

Source: David C. Hammock et al. (1990), *The U.S. History Report Card.* Princeton, NJ: National Assessment of Educational Progress.

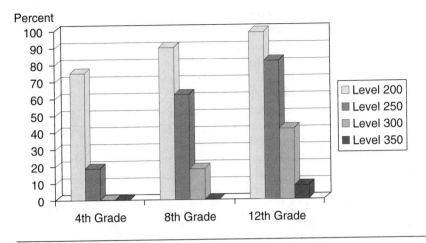

FIGURE 11.2 *Age Trends on the 1998 NAEP for History*

(Hammock et al., 1990, p. 10). What is not clear at present is whether the poor performance of younger students reflects the fact that they are conceptually incapable of the reasoning required at Levels 300 and 350 or that they were taught in inappropriate ways (e.g., they were never asked to think at higher levels).

In 1994, the NAEP for history was re-administered using a somewhat different theoretical and assessment framework. Based on the recommendations of over fifty professional historians, educators, administrators, and researchers, the new framework stressed the idea that children should show understandings related to four themes (Beatty, Reese, Persky, & Carr, 1996): (a) change and continuity in American democracy: ideas, institutions, practices, and controversies (e.g., issues related to the Civil War, the civil rights movement, etc.); (b) the gathering and interactions of peoples, cultures, and ideas (e.g., migration patterns, roles of religion in conflicts, changing roles of men and women); (c) economic and technological changes and their relation to society, ideas, and the environment (e.g., the shift from being a rural, agricultural economy to an industrial economy); and (d) the changing role of America in the world (i.e., understanding the factors that have shaped American foreign policy). Items were created for each theme and the test was given to a large, representative sample of fourth, eighth, and twelfth graders.

After the data was collected, children's performance was categorized into three levels: Basic (denotes partial mastery of prerequisite knowledge and skills that are fundamental for proficient work at each grade), Proficient (i.e., solid performance reflecting competency over challenging subject-matter knowledge, application of such knowledge to real-world situations, and analytical skills appropriate to the subject matter), and Advanced (signifies superior performance). Note that what constitutes Basic, Proficient, and Advanced varies according to grade level. For example, the Proficient level for grade four corresponds to abilities such as identifying and commenting on the significance of many historical people and events, interpreting information in texts, maps, and timelines, and recognizing the role of invention and technological change in history. At the eighth-grade level, however, these abilities are extended to include the ability to understand the connections between historical events and their historical context. Moreover, eighth graders also need to show an understanding of the benefits and challenges inherent in the diversity of America. Finally, they need to be able to communicate ideas about historical themes citing evidence from primary and secondary sources to support their conclusions. At the twelfth-grade level, the skills mentioned in the eighth grade level need to be extended further to include in-depth understanding of the inter-connectedness of historical events and the ways in which political, economic, geographic, social, religious, technological, and ideological factors conspire to shape history.

The results showed that at the fourth-grade level, 47 percent of children were at the Basic level, 15 percent were at the Proficient level, and 2 percent were at the Advanced level. At the eighth-grade level, the percentages were 46 percent (Basic), 13 percent (Proficient), and 1 percent (Advanced). At the twelfth-grade level, the figures were 32 percent (Basic), 10 percent (Proficient), and 1 percent (Advanced). These findings suggest, then, that most children in the fourth and eighth grades performed at or above the Basic level, but nearly 40 percent of children did not make the standards for Basic understanding. The results for twelfth graders are even more disappointing: a staggering 57 percent performed below the Basic level. Compared to the 1988 NAEP, the 1994 results suggest that educators have not managed to elevate children above a rudimentary understanding of facts, famous historical figures, and simple timelines by the time they graduate high school.

Geography

Geography texts present a variety of topics that can be grouped under the headings "geographical skills" (e.g., map reading), "human geography" (e.g., location of major cultural groups) and "physical geography" (e.g., location of the world's natural resources) (Farrell & Cirrincione, 1989). Many teachers, however, consider the topics having to do with map skills and locations as being the most important to cover (see Figure 11.3). It is useful, therefore, to examine the literature to see if there are developmental trends in children's learning of the latter topics.

Map Skills.   In order to comprehend the meaning of a map, students need to be able to do at least three things: (a) recognize and differentiate among cartographic or pictographic symbols (e.g., see the difference between the "star" for the capital of a state and a "dot" for other cities in the state), (b) understand that these symbols refer to real, three-dimensional counterparts (e.g., actual cities), and (c) project the spatial arrangement of symbols on the map (e.g., the symbol for Pennsylvania is above that for Maryland) onto the real physical world (e.g., recognize that the state of Pennsylvania is north of the state of Maryland) (Bluestein & Acredolo, 1979; Liben & Downs, 1993). In addition, students need to be able to use the map even when it is not aligned to their own perspective (as is the case with "you are here" maps found in shopping malls).

Studies show that many preschoolers possess rudimentary map reading skills. For example, when a two-dimensional drawing of room is used to show children where a teddy bear is hidden, 50 percent of three-year-olds and nearly all four- and five-year-olds can use

FIGURE 11.3   *Geography Topics Judged Most Important by Social Studies Teachers*

Topic	Rating
1. Map interpretation	4.32
2. Location of major land forms and bodies of water	4.30
3. Global interdependence	4.29
4. Location and distribution of natural resources	4.24
5. Finding places on maps and atlases	4.23
6. Conservation of natural resources	4.17
7. Location of major cultural regions	4.15
8. Location and distribution of major cultural groups	4.14
9. Location and characteristics of major global political divisions	4.11
10. Relations between political decisions and land use	4.06

Adapted from Farrell, R. T. & Cirrincione, J. M. (1989). The content of Geography curriculum—a teachers perspective. *Social Education, 53,* 105–108; Rating scale ranged from "not very important" (1) to "very important" (5).

the map to find the bear (Bluestein & Acredolo, 1979; Presson, 1982). However, when a more complex map of a classroom is used and they need to indicate on the map the location of a person in the room, five-year-olds indicate the correct location about 43 percent of the time. Success rates increase to 65 percent and then again to 85 percent by the first and second grades, respectively (Liben & Downs, 1993). In addition, whereas rotating the map 180-degrees away from the child's perspective has no effect on children's performance in the fifth and sixth grades, performance drops considerably for younger children.

Thus, even young children can understand that a map "stands for" an actual set of locations and that they can use the map to find a particular location. Despite this early prowess, however, map skills continue to improve throughout the middle childhood period. In particular, children become more able to deal with unaligned maps, maps of places they have never been, and maps which use abstract symbols that do not resemble their real-world counterparts (Liben & Downs, 1993).

An important contributor to this increasing skill is the development of spatial abilities that were originally identified by Piaget. In particular, studies show a consistent correlation between success on Piagetian spatial tasks and map reading tasks (Liben & Downs, 1993; Muir, 1985). But in the Piagetian perspective, skills are constructed through experience. It is possible that by increasing map use in schools (e.g., to find a "treasure" hidden in the school yard) that children will become more facile. To help with comprehending more difficult aspects of maps, these exercises should substitute abstract symbols for realistic symbols (e.g., a star for a drawing of a tree, a square for a swing set) and use misaligned maps to teach children how to mentally rotate their perspective.

Identifying Locations.   As might be expected from the increasing emphasis on social studies with age, older children can identify locations on a map of the world better than young children. In one study of about 2,800 students, Herman, Hawkins, Barron, and Berryman (1988) found that the percentages of correct placements of ten countries were 30 percent for fourth graders, 40 percent for fifth graders, and 44 percent for sixth graders. Children at all grades were most successful locating Mexico (43 percent, 63 percent, 63 percent correct, respectively) and least successful at locating Venezuela (18 percent, 31 percent, and 34 percent correct, respectively). In a study of college freshman, Cross (1987) found that students showed an overall success rate of only 39 percent for the locations of the following eleven countries: China, Cuba, Great Britain, El Salvador, Ethiopia, India, Iran, Lebanon, Poland, South Africa, and the Soviet Union. Students were most successful in identifying the Soviet Union (73 percent) and Cuba (65 percent) and least successful in identifying Lebanon (11 percent) and Poland (12 percent). Overall, then, the data suggests that whereas there is improvement with age in location skills, performance is mediocre at best even in college students. Such findings for location skills are consistent with the findings of the 1988 National Assessment of Educational Progress (NAEP) for geography which showed that twelfth graders score about 300 on a scale that ranges from 0 to 500 (Digest of Educational Statistics, 1990). These findings are intriguing in light of the fact that teachers think it is very important to teach children how to identify locations (Farrell & Cirrincione, 1989).

In 1994, the NAEP for geography was re-administered and utilized the following three-part framework. First, the architects of the framework (i.e., geography experts and others) assumed that children should know geography "as it relates to places on Earth, to spatial patterns on Earth's surface, and to physical and human processes that shape such spatial patterns (Persky, Reese, O'Sullivan, Lazer, Moore, & Shakrani, 1996, p. 4). In addition to such space and place knowledge, the assessment examined children's knowledge of environment and society. Here, students needed to show insight into the "nature, scale, and ramifications of . . . environmental transformations" caused by human intervention (Persky et al., 1996, p. 4). Finally, the Spatial Dynamics and Connections subscale focused on such things as knowledge that the world's resources are unevenly distributed and this situation contributes to migration patterns, trade patterns, and international conflicts.

Again, performance was scaled into Basic, Proficient, and Advanced levels for each grade. At the fourth grade, for example, a Proficient student should be able to locate places on maps, create their own maps from descriptions, use a fundamental geographic vocabulary appropriately, and illustrate how people "depend on, adapt to, and modify the environment" (Persky et al., 1996). At the eighth and twelfth grades, these skills need to be extended to more in-depth analysis and use of multiple sources to construct reasonable interpretations. Results showed the following percentages for children in the fourth grade: 45 percent Basic, 19 percent Proficient, and 3 percent Advanced. The corresponding percentages for eighth and twelfth graders were 39 percent Basic, 24 percent Proficient, 4 percent Advanced, and 41 percent Basic, 25 percent Proficient, and 2 percent Advanced. Similar to what was found for the 1994 NAEP for history, then, most children scored near the basic level, but 30 percent did not even make that level. Thus, many American students have only a rudimentary grasp of geographic knowledge and skills.

One could dismiss all of these findings by saying, "Who cares! Only airline pilots need to know where places are!" However, locations are an important aspect of understanding world events. For example, Poland's unfortunate history relates to the fact that it is a neighbor to both Germany and Russia. In one sense, locations can only be learned through repetition. But there are a variety of memory strategies that could improve retention (e.g., imagery, see Chapter 3) as well as incentives that improve motivation. Have you ever noticed that you learn locations and use a map better when you want to go somewhere? (e.g., drive several states away for a spring break vacation). But issues related to uneven resources and the effects of humans on the environment are not easily understood through simple role playing and repetition.

Economics

As noted above, in any given society there are people who have certain wants and needs (e.g., thirst, hunger, movement) and resources that can be used to fulfill these needs (e.g., water, food, and transportation). Economics is the study of how people try to balance their personal needs with limited and shared resources (Sunal, 1991). In trying to describe this situation and explain how the balance is struck, economists have created concepts such as "scarcity," "monetary value," "profit," "consumption," "production," and "economic inequality." Educational and developmental researchers have tried to determine when children can comprehend such abstract concepts and the functional relationships between these constructs (e.g., supply and demand).

In most studies, researchers used Piagetian methods to assess economic understanding. In particular, it has been common to use concrete stimuli to elicit responses (e.g., play money in a pretend shop) and then propose stages in children's economic conceptions (Schug, 1987; Sunal, 1991).

Although the number and details of the stages vary by concept, several common age trends emerge across studies. In the early grades, children possess a very limited understanding of economic notions. For example, young children think that everyone usually gets what he or she needs and that shopkeepers do not sell items at a higher price than they bought them for. Moreover, any exchange of money at a store is seen as merely a ritualistic behavior (Sunal, 1991).

With age, children acquire a progressively more accurate understanding of concepts such as "scarcity" and "profit," but do not integrate ideas into a system of related notions. For example, students may not realize that shops exist because we have needs and that shopkeepers earn a living (i.e., make a profit) by helping us meet our needs. Ultimately, concepts become integrated into a system such that by adolescence, students seem to understand basic economics ideas in the manner described by economists (Schug, 1987).

As with other social studies domains, a number of experts recently have called into question the idea that younger children are incapable of understanding basic economics notions. Most have argued that young children lack insight into certain ideas because they lack experience. When children engage in school-based "mini-economies," for example, they show a greater understanding than the stage-like accounts suggest (Schug & Walstad, 1991). Relatedly, use of alternative methodologies has also been found to produce some forms of economic insight in younger children. For example, Siegler and Thompson (1998) presented four- to ten-year-olds with stories about children who operated a lemonade stand.

At issue was children's understanding of the relevance of five variables to the number of cups of lemonade that would be sold on a given day: (a) demand (i.e., more people seeking lemonade would increase sales), (b) supply (i.e., competition from other stands would decrease sales), (c) motivation (i.e., strength of the person's desire to sell lemonade), (d) morality (i.e., the ethics of the person in unrelated situations), and (e) color of the cups used. Across three experiments, results showed that even preschoolers understood the effect of demand. By age seven, children also seemed to understand the effects of supply. It was not until age nine, however, that children demonstrated a consistent ability to explain how motivation and morality might influence sales.

Civics

In order to be able to participate in a democracy, students need to learn about the responsibilities of government (e.g., national defense, education of children, etc.), the responsibilities and rights of individuals (e.g., voting and freedom of speech), and the interrelations between citizens and their government. Civics educators strive to instill this knowledge in students. Are they successful?

Unfortunately, most studies suggest that the answer to this question is "no." For example, some small-scale studies show that students have at best a superficial understanding of civics "facts" and also have serious misconceptions of how our government works (Patrick & Hoge, 1991). National assessments show that whereas students do acquire more civics knowledge with age, even twelfth graders lack sufficient knowledge to fully participate in a democracy. For example, the 1988 NAEP for civics showed that the percentage of students who understand (a) governmental responsibilities, (b) the relations among citizens and government, and (c) individual rights were 10 percent, 61 percent, and 89 percent, for fourth, eighth, and twelfth graders, respectively. The corresponding percentages for understanding the structures, functions, and powers of the American government as defined in the Constitution were 0 percent, 13 percent, and 49 percent, respectively (Digest of Educational Statistics, 1990).

In the 1998 NAEP for civics, the results were comparable but the findings are somewhat distinct due to changes in the test. In this more recent NAEP, the focus was on five kinds of knowledge that students should be able to demonstrate: (a) civic life, politics, and government; (b) foundations of the American political system; (c) how the government established by the Constitution represents the purposes, values, and principles of American democracy; (d) the relationship of the United States to other nations and world affairs; and (e) the roles of citizens in American democracy (Lutkus, Weiss, Campbell, Mazzeo, and Lazer, 1999). To score at the Proficient level, a fourth grader would have to be able to answer questions such as "Which of the following is the most important reason why the United States trades with other countries: (a) people get a chance to travel, (b) it helps people get things they need, (c) it helps us learn about other cultures, and (d) we can learn other languages." An eighth grader, however, would have to answer questions such as one in which a quote from former Chief Justice Earl Warren ends by saying "In that way we [i.e., the Supreme Court] are making the law aren't we?" Students are then asked,

"Some people are troubled by the role of the Court as described by Chief Justice Warren. Which argument could they effectively use against it?

    a. It is dangerous to give nonelected officials such as judges so much power in the government.

    b. The Supreme Court makes it too difficult for the federal government to exercise its power over the states.

    c. Supreme Court judges are the members of society most capable of making decisions about public policy.

    d. The main task of the Supreme Court is to rewrite the Constitution to respond to modern problems."

At the twelfth grade level, an item representative of the Proficient level might be like the following that begins with a quote: " 'Absolute arbitrary power, or governing without settled laws, can neither of them be consistent with the ends of society and government,' said John Locke. List two ways the American system of government is designed to prevent 'absolute arbitrary power' and 'governing without settled laws.' "

Results showed that at the fourth grade, the percentages falling into the Basic, Proficient, and Advanced levels were 46 percent, 21 percent, and 2 percent, respectively. The corresponding percentages for the eighth and twelfth grades were 48 percent (Basic), 21 percent (Proficient), and 2 percent (Advanced), and 39 percent (Basic), 22 percent (Proficient), and 4 percent (Advanced), respectively. Thus, only one in five students in each grade level is demonstrating a solid performance indicative of the kinds of civics understanding we would want to see in students.

Summary of Developmental Trends

Two themes emerge from the research that has examined age trends in children's learning of history, geography, economics, and civics. The first is that whereas factual knowledge in these subjects increases between the fourth and twelfth grades, many students leave high school with only a superficial understanding of important social studies concepts. The second is that the poor performance of younger students may be due to two factors: (a) their lack of experience with the core topics in each domain (i.e., they are only taught a few basic ideas in the elementary years) and (b) the abstract nature of the constructs involved. If these findings are combined with attitudinal indices suggesting that most students find topics in history, geography, economics, and civics to be fairly boring (Beatty et al., 1996; Lutkus et al., 1999; Persky et al., 1996), there seems to be something fundamentally wrong with the way students learn social studies. There must be some way to enhance students' conceptual knowledge of these core ideas especially in older children and early adolescents.

It might be added that all of the developmental research described above only shows how much knowledge students have acquired (or have not acquired). It does not tell us whether twelfth graders who have acquired knowledge make better decisions about public-policy issues than students with less knowledge. It also does not indicate whether knowledgeable twelfth graders are more likely to be active citizens than less knowledgeable twelfth graders. Given that making decisions and being an active citizen are the two major goals of social studies education, additional research needs to be done to see if these goals have been met. Most Americans do not participate beyond voting (Ferguson, 1991), so clearly a lot needs to be changed.

Individual Differences in Social Studies Knowledge

Having discussed global age trends, we next turn to the issue of how same-aged individuals differ from one another. Research has revealed four variables associated with individual differences in social studies knowledge and skill: gender, SES, ethnicity, and expertise. Let's examine the research on these four variables in turn.

Gender Differences

History and Geography.   Figure 11.4 displays the average scores of twelfth-grade males and females on the 1988 NAEP exams for history and geography. As can be seen, whereas males performed better than females on both assessments, the differences are not terribly large. In the case of history, for example, the male score is only 2 percent higher than the female mean. For geography, the male mean is only 5 percent higher. On the 1994 NAEPs for history and geography, males scored 1 percent and 2.5 percent higher than females, respectively.

The 2- to 5-percent difference on the NAEP geography exam is consistent with the findings of Herman et al. (1988) for location skills. In particular, the percentages of boys and girls in the fourth-sixth grades who could correctly locate countries were 40 percent and 35 percent, respectively. For comparison purposes, it might be helpful to note that the male score on the math subtest of the SAT is typically 10 percent higher than the female score (see Chapter 12). It is also worth noting that the geography assessments rely heavily on spatial skills. It remains to be seen why no gender differences emerged on the NAEP for geography but did emerge on other kinds of spatial tests (Hyde, Fennema, & Lamon, 1990).

The one exception to the typically small gender difference in performance is Cross' (1987) study of the location skills of students attending a satellite campus of the Univer-

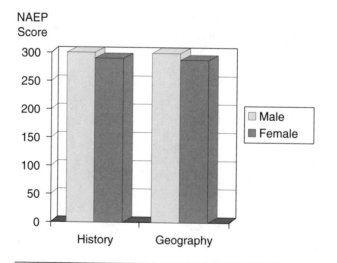

FIGURE 11.4   *Gender Differences in 12th Graders*

sity of Wisconsin. In this study, the percentages of correct locations identified were 48 percent for males and 31 percent for females. What is particularly troubling about this latter finding is the fact that many of the females in this study were education majors.

Economics.   Reviews of research on economics learning show that there are consistent, though small, gender differences at the elementary, secondary, and college levels (Schug & Walstad, 1991). Most of the studies that showed gender differences, however, involved multiple choice tests. When essay tests were used, females performed better than males.

Civics.   The story for civics is similar to what has been said so far for history, geography, and economics: when there is a difference favoring males, it is not terribly large. Figure 11.5 shows gender differences for two components of the 1988 NAEP exam for civics: (a) understanding the nature of our political institutions and (b) understanding specific government structures and functions. As can be seen, whereas females performed slightly better on the items comprising the former component of the test (2 percent higher), males performed better on the items comprising the latter component (Digest of Education, 1990). Note, though, that by the 1996 NAEP, the gender differences were reversed at the eighth and twelfth grades. The female scores were 3 percent higher than the male means at both grade levels (i.e., means of 148 and 152, for males and females, respectively).

Summary.   For history, geography, economics, and civics, there has been a tendency for males to perform better on assessments than females. The size of the gender gap does not appear to be age-related (i.e., it is the same size from about the fourth grade on), but it is usually small at all ages. In addition, there is some suggestion that females can be more knowledgeable than males for certain types of social studies information and also perform better when they have a chance to exercise their writing skills. Finally, the 1996 NAEP for geography showed that females performed better than males at the oldest two grades.

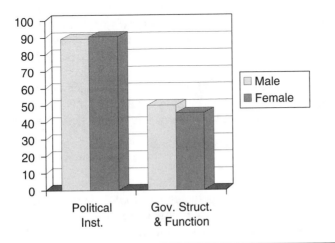

FIGURE 11.5   *Gender Differences on the 1988 NAEP Civics*

Socio-Economic Status (SES)

In many of the studies described earlier in this chapter, researchers examined the relation between a student's socio-economic status (SES) and his or her performance. In assigning students to various SES levels, researchers often created a composite index based on their household characteristics as well as the income, education level, and occupation of their parents. It has generally been found that students from lower SES levels perform more poorly than students from higher SES levels.

For example, in their study of the location skills of fourth, fifth, and sixth graders, Herman et al. (1988) found that high- and middle-SES students correctly identified more countries than low-SES students (percents correct = 45 percent, 42 percent, and 32 percent, for high, middle, and low SES groups, respectively). Similarly, the 1988 NAEP for geography showed that the scores of twelfth graders varied by their parents' level of education and the amount of reading materials in their home. For example, if students had parents who graduated college or provided four types of reading materials in the home, they scored around 300 on the exam. In contrast, if their parents were high school dropouts or provided two or fewer types of reading materials, students scored about 270 on the exam (Digest of Educational Statistics, 1990). For the 1994 NAEP for geography, the gap between children of college graduates and children of high school graduates was still 20 points or a 7 percent difference (Persky et al., 1996).

For the 1988 NAEP for history, the findings were quite similar. At each of the fourth, eighth, and twelfth grades, students scored about ten points higher for each successive level of education that their parents attained. At the twelfth grade, for example, the average score for children of high school dropouts was 274. If their parents were high school graduates, the average score was 285. When their parents attended some college or graduated college, the scores were 297 and 306, respectively (Hammock et al., 1990). The findings for the 1994 NAEP for history were nearly identical to those for the 1998 NAEP (Beatty et al., 1996).

Summary.   In contrast to gender, then, SES seems to be a powerful determinant of performance on social studies assessments. If children come from homes in which their parents are educated, make a good income, and provide numerous reading materials, results show that they perform better on national assessments and tests than children who come from lower SES homes. At present, however, it is not clear whether these home factors are causally responsible for success on social studies tests or whether the differences reflect differences in the quality of education received by children in different SES groups. After all, children from more affluent homes often have access to the best education available.

Ethnic Differences

As might be expected from the fact that SES often co-varies with ethnicity, differences in performance among ethnic groups mirror those found for SES levels. In particular, the average scores of White, Hispanic, and Black twelfth graders on the 1988 geography NAEP were 301, 272, and 258, respectively (Digest of Educational Statistics, 1990). Thus, White students had scores that were 11 percent and 17 percent higher, respectively. On the 1994 assessment, the gaps were somewhat smaller at 9 percent and 13 percent, respectively. For the 1988 history NAEP, the average scores of White, Hispanic, and Black twelfth graders were 301, 274, and 274, respectively. Thus, the scores of White students were 10 percent higher than the scores of Hispanic and Black students. On the 1994 history NAEP, the findings were nearly identical. Thus, the gaps are rather large for geography and history and do not appear to be getting any smaller.

As for civics, the conclusions are essentially the same. At all grade levels on the 1998 assessment, the percentage of White students who demonstrated an understanding of political institutions and governmental functions was always about twenty points higher than the percentages for Black and Hispanic students who demonstrated such an understanding. In comparison to the 2- to 7-percent difference between males and females, then, the discrepancy between White students and minority students for the civics NAEP is three to ten times larger. Once again, the findings for the 1998 NAEP revealed that the scores of twelfth grade White students were 20 percent higher than those of Black or Hispanic students. If the overall findings suggest that something is wrong with the way we teach social studies (see above), these unnecessarily large ethnic gaps add fuel to the fire.

Novice-Expert Differences

As discussed in Chapter 4, differences between novices and experts become apparent when they are asked to solve domain-specific problems. James Voss and his colleagues have used this problem-solving approach to reveal expertise-related differences on political science problems (e.g., Voss, Tyler, & Yengo, 1983).

One of the problems they have used is the following. Try solving it now in order to get a better understanding of the results of this work:

"Assume you are the head of the Soviet Ministry of Agriculture and assume that crop productivity has been low over the past several years. You now have the responsibility of increasing crop production. How would you go about doing this?"

This example is representative of many problems in the social science area in that the "problem" is an undesirable state of affairs that needs to be improved or eliminated. In such cases, it is common for people to identify the cause of the undesirable state of affairs and propose solving the problem by eliminating the cause. Voss and his colleagues refer to this strategy as the "Identify and Eliminate Causes" (IEC) solution.

Voss et al. (1983) have found that whereas both experts and novices use the IEC strategy to propose solutions to the "crop productivity" problem and other problems, they go about it in different ways. In particular, experts did not immediately identify causes of a problem. Rather, they first embellished what they had been told by thinking about aspects of the former Soviet agricultural system that would interfere with the implementation of most solutions. Voss et al. called these perceived interferences "constraints." To illustrate how experts build in constraints before they even begin to entertain causes, consider the beginning of one expert's response:

> "I think that as minister of agriculture, one has to start out with the realization that there are certain kinds of special agricultural constraints within which you are going to work. The first one, the most obvious one, is that by almost every count only ten percent of the land

in the Soviet Union is arable. . . . And secondly, even in that arable ten percent of the total land surface, you will still have climate problems over which you have no direct control. Okay, so that is sort of the overall parameter in which we are working" (p. 215).

This expert went on to add several other constraints as well.

In contrast, novices rarely mentioned constraints. Instead, they engaged in a strategy of simply citing causes and proposing solutions based on these causes. For example, one novice proposed a total of twelve causes and twelve distinct solutions. For each cause that the novice identified (e.g., outdated farm machinery), he or she proposed a solution that would eliminate that cause (e.g., providing new machinery to the workers).

Besides the recognition of constraints, a second difference between experts and novices was the abstractness of the proposed causes. Whereas novices proposed specific and concrete causes, experts proposed more abstract causes. For example, instead of blaming low productivity on outdated machinery, one expert attributed the problem to inadequate technology at many levels of production (e.g., machinery, irrigation, fertilization, computerization, etc.).

The third major difference concerned the tendency of experts to spend most of their time justifying one or two solutions rather than spending their time rattling off many solutions. The tendency of experts to justify their solutions may be due to the fact that they were *social* scientists. Unlike the fields of physics or mathematics in which problems can be said to have a single, agreed-upon solution, problems in the social sciences often have no definitive solution. Moreover, there is no clear way to assess whether a solution has "worked." Take the crop productivity problem, for example. If a solution is implemented, how far does productivity have to rise in order for the solution to be thought of as effective? Clearly, there could be disagreements about an acceptable level. The social scientists in Voss et al.'s study may have been very used to arguing about hard-to-implement and hard-to-evaluation solutions.

The three differences between novices and experts seem to derive from two main sources: (a) experts' greater knowledge and (b) experts' greater experience practicing in the discipline. Knowledge helped experts think of constraints as well as data that could be used to bolster claims. Moreover, knowledge helped experts to group causes together into more abstract categories. Experience in researching and writing about political issues helped them recognize the complexities of solutions (i.e., nothing is simple or perfect) and the need to justify their proposals (because the readers of their work often challenged what the experts have written).

In support of these claims, Voss and his colleagues found that social scientists who were not experts on the Soviet Union nevertheless built in constraints and tried to justify their solutions the same way that Soviet experts did. Professional chemists, on the other hand, gave responses similar to those of novices. Thus, this data suggests that helping novices to think like experts requires more than coursework. Whereas traditional coursework will increase knowledge, it will not promote the development of a generalized problem-solving *approach* to issues (e.g., "think about constraints and remember to justify your solutions"). To attain this goal, students would need lots of practice thinking through hypothetical problems.

Instructional Implications

In what follows, we shall examine the instructional implications of the research on social studies learning in two ways. First, we shall examine several general guidelines for how to approach social studies instruction. Then, we shall examine several case studies to see how well they conform to the principles described in the general guidelines and information presented in other chapters.

General Guidelines

The results of the research on developmental and individual differences in social studies learning suggest that something is seriously wrong with the way students are taught social studies. Even when we are talking about twelfth graders or groups within a grade who are performing better than others (e.g., males or Whites), performance is only mediocre at best.

Why do students perform so poorly? Experts suggest that there are two main causes: (a) an emphasis on fact-learning over comprehension, application, and decision-making in the classroom (Brophy, 1990; Brophy & VanSledright, 1997) and (b) the use of textbooks that include unnecessary detail and do not provide explanations of events and issues (McKeown & Beck, 1990). These two deficiencies in the classroom suggest the first two instructional implications:

1. In teaching social studies, it is more important to stress major principles and generalizations and focus on a few illustrative examples than to give shallow coverage to a large number of facts. Using examples of history and geography, for example, Brophy (1990, p. 404) suggests,

"[teachers should] emphasize the basic economic, social, or political forces that have shaped [a country's] development (not just a chronology of noteworthy events), linking these to discipline based concepts, generalizations, and principles (such as colonization and modernization). Similarly, in focusing more specifically on [a country's] geography, [teachers should] stress the relationships between its climate and natural resources, its economy, and its location and power vis-a-vis other countries as determinants of its past history and current status, not just descriptive and statistical facts."

Of course, in emphasizing higher-order thinking over shallow coverage, students will not necessarily perform better on national assessments because most require recall of facts. We would still have many seventeen-year-olds, then, not knowing the dates of the Civil War. And yet, we would possibly have a more impressive group of seventeen-year-olds who could recognize a current event (e.g., an invasion of a country) as another example of a general principle that they learned in class. Moreover, we might have a larger percentage of active citizens.

If it is desirous to have students recall factual information, there are techniques such as "elaborative interrogation" that have been found to be more effective for geographic facts than other approaches (e.g., Martin & Pressley, 1991). Using this technique, one asks students *why* some fact is true (e.g., "Why is Saskatchewan the province which produces the most apples in Canada?") instead of asking them to learn the fact by rote. Wood et al. (1993) found elaborative interrogation to be effective for even preschoolers and elementary students.

2. If teachers will be placing an increased emphasis on explanation, comprehension, application, and generalization, textbooks have to be altered to be in synchrony with this new approach. Current textbooks are rife with facts (often inaccurate or irrelevant) and low on causal explanation. Relatedly, there is clearly room for alternative kinds of texts such as historical novels (with children as the main characters) and use of newspapers and other documents from a given era (Brophy & VanSledright, 1997). Students find these materials much more interesting and engaging.

The remaining instructional implications derive from the outcomes of the research on developmental and individual differences:

3. Theories and research on cognitive development suggest that certain concepts (e.g., a timeline of events, abstract causal relations, etc.) might be too difficult for younger elementary students to comprehend. And yet, children have cognitive capacities that teachers can exploit to help them gain at least partial insight into these difficult ideas. For example, children can form mental "scripts" of common activities by repeatedly engaging in these activities. They should be able to form scripts for historical events in the same way. The formation of such scripts through plays and so forth would be more effective in helping children develop a timeline of events than verbal description. Also, young children are quite capable of analogical reasoning (Brown, 1989) and teachers can rely on analogies to help children grasp somewhat foreign or difficult ideas. For example, teachers can have students relate and compare their own family experience to that of other families in this and other countries. Finally, simulated experiences such as "mini-economies" and "mini-governments" can go a long way in helping students understand their real-life counterparts. In sum, then, the standard "expanding communities" framework could be augmented with all of these activities (some say this framework should be replaced).

4. The research on individual differences suggest that the most troublesome findings pertain to low SES and minority students. The fact that SES co-varies with success on achievement tests could mean that a great deal of social studies knowledge is acquired outside of school, or that high SES children attend more effective schools than low SES children (or both). If only the former is true, three things could be tried. First, it would be important to create extra-curricular activities for low SES students (e.g., after school, summer or weekend "academies"). Second, large scale parent education efforts could begin. Third, perhaps watching educational TV programs might be required of students (e.g., "Carmen Sandiego").

If the second possibility is true, it is essential that deficiencies in schools that serve low SES students be identified. If the principals and teaching staff need professional development (e.g., learn about new teaching techniques), efforts should begin in that regard. It is often the case that there is a wide gap between academia and classroom practice. One important step would be to have scholars in colleges of education around the country collaborate with faculty in struggling communities.

5. Finally, the proposal mentioned in the first implication about improving comprehension could be augmented by asking students to solve hypothetical problems. Teachers could provide mild criticism of solutions offered to students and instruct them on how to provide justifications for their tentative ideas. In this way, students would emulate practicing social scientists and potentially develop a scripted approach to thinking about problems in the social studies.

Case Studies

Examine the following case studies to see how well they conform to the information presented in this chapter and other chapters.

Case Study 1.   If indeed we want students to use social studies knowledge to make decisions and solve problems, then it makes sense to ask them to learn social studies facts to make decisions and solve problems. An interesting way to achieve this goal is illustrated by the ICONS project created by Judith Torney-Purta and her colleagues at the University of Maryland. Students who participate in ICONS are placed into teams and asked to pretend that they are the foreign ministers of various countries. For example, some students take on the role of being the foreign ministers of France, some form a Russian team, and some form a Brazilian team. Then, each team is asked to represent their country in a simulated international conference in which they are confronted with contemporary world problems. During one conference, for example, students were asked to develop a consensual policy about how to coerce South Africa into abandoning its apartheid policy as well as think about how to solve Mexico's foreign debt problem of the early 1990s. At other conferences, students delved into issues such as global warming and the war in Bosnia.

To be able to effectively participate in this process, students had to learn a great deal about the country they were trying to represent. For example, students who formed a South African team had to learn about the origins of apartheid and why some South Africans supported this policy. Similarly, students who formed the Russian teams had to learn enough about Russia to say how its foreign ministers would respond to the problem of apartheid. Thus, they learned facts about these countries not to simply know the facts, but to know how to formulate a national policy.

Each team was supervised by teachers who served more as resources than directive authoritarians. That is, they collected appropriate reading materials and helped students locate information that the students learned they would need. They also coordinated within-teams' discussions about a country's response, once enough information about a country and the issue at hand was collected. In trying to reach a consensus, students learned a great deal about effective forms of negotiation and compromise. Teachers played a role in teaching students how to solicit opinions and operate on the principles of democracy.

After each team forged a proposed way to deal with a problem, they sat down at a networked computer terminal and conferred with other countries via computer messages. That is, teams were always in different rooms and very often they were from different schools in the states of Maryland and Pennsylvania.

As a result of the ICONS experience, students were substantially more conversant about foreign countries and contemporary issues than students who learned the same material using the standard lecture format. In addition, students were motivated to learn the material and construct their own understanding of it through readings, discussions, and inter-group arguments.

Case Study 2.   Bruce VanSledright, a former high school teacher and current Associate Professor at the University of Maryland, took the unusual step (for a college professor) of teaching two units of American history in a fifth-grade classroom over a period of three months. Instead of asking students to memorize a series of facts or famous battles, he asked students to regularly engage in tasks such as figure out what happened during the Boston Massacre, who did the shooting, and why. Students were given various kinds of documents to help them explore such questions including testimonies given by eyewitnesses, newspaper stories, and sketches drawn of the events at that time. He wanted to see how students would react to the task of mimicking historians and also wanted to see if he could deepen their understanding of the significant historical events that transpired in the Colonial period.

Case Study 3.   Mrs. Linda Fowler of Friends School in Baltimore utilized the following approach in her third-grade social studies class. As part of a unit on Colonial America, children prepared for a play in which the main characters were folk heros such as John Henry, Molly Pitcher, and Paul Bunyan. The play followed the unit on Colonial America and was preceded by readings and discussions of tall tales. Some of the books used were *John Henry* by Julius Lester, *Swamp Angel* by Anne Isaacs, and *Paul Bunyan* by Stephen Kellogg. In the play, the story of each folk hero was told by way of songs and short skits. Different groups of children participated in each skit, thereby becoming especially familiar with particular characters. However, they also gained information about all of the other characters as well.

12

Explaining Gender and Ethnic Differences

Summary

1. To make comparisons across studies of gender or ethnic differences easier to interpret, we can use either percentages or effect sizes.

2. Studies show that females perform a lot better than males on writing tests, a little better on reading comprehension tests, and slightly better on some civics tests. Whereas the reading and writing differences are apparent in elementary school, the civics difference does not appear until high school. Males, in contrast, do a little better than females on math problem-solving tests and slightly better on history and geography. All of these differences emerge in adolescence. Hence, the largest differences are found for writing fluency and quality at all age levels (favoring females) and for math problem-solving during adolescence (favoring males, especially among students with academic talent).

3. There are four categories of theories that have been proposed to explain gender differences in cognitive performance: (a) genetic/physiological views, (b) socialization views, (c) differential experience views, and (d) cognitive process views. Each of these theories has its shortcomings.

4. The findings for ethnic differences are quite consistent across subject areas: White students perform substantially better than both Hispanic and African-American students; Hispanic students perform slightly better than African-American students.

5. There are three main explanations of ethnic differences in cognitive performance: (a) the cognitive deficit view, (b) the contextual view, and (c) the cultural incongruity view. Each of these views has its shortcomings.

6. The seven theories of gender or ethnic differences provide clues as to how to eliminate these differences. However, the fact that all of these theories have problems means that theory-based attempts to eliminate gender or ethnic differences will often fail.

In Chapters 5 through 11, you were told about a variety of performance differences between subgroups of children in the same grade (e.g., males versus females), but you were not told **why** these subgroups may have differed. In the present chapter, you are provided with possible explanations of these differences. For the sake of brevity, however, we shall limit the focus to just two types of individual differences that were reported in nearly every chapter: gender differences and ethnic differences.

This chapter is organized as follows. In the first section, we shall define a key construct that has been used to quantify the size of gender and ethnic differences: an effect size. In the second section, we shall examine and evaluate explanations of gender differences in cognitive performance. In the third section, we shall examine and evaluate explanations of ethnic differences. In the final section, the instructional implications of the work on gender and ethnic differences will be drawn.

Effect Sizes

If you were given the assignment of finding all of the studies in which gender differences were found for cognitive skills, you would find a large number of studies. If asked, "On average, how large is the difference between men and women?" you would immediately recognize that this question is hard to answer because the authors of these studies all seemed to use a different test. For example, in one study, researchers may have given a twenty-item spatial test to men and women and found that, on average, men got fifteen right and women got ten right. Another study might have given a sixty-item math test (e.g., the SAT-math) to men and women and found that, on average, men got twenty-eight right and women got twenty-two right. Is the five-item difference on the spatial test big or small? How about the six-item difference on the SAT? Which of these differences is bigger?

The main reason why these questions are hard to answer is that the differences are not on the same scale. One way to put all of the differences on the same scale is to convert everything to percents-correct. For example, for the spatial test, we would say that men got 75 percent correct and women got 50 percent correct. For the math test, we would say that men got 47 percent correct and women got 37 percent correct. Once scores were converted in this way, we could find the average size of the difference in percents-correct. The average of a 25 percent difference (i.e., 75 percent minus 50 percent) and a 10 percent difference (i.e., 47 percent minus 37 percent) is a 17.5 percent difference.

The reader will note that in this book, individual differences were often reported in terms of a difference in percents-correct. Although this practice solves our problem of putting things on the same scale, it does not tell us whether an average difference is big or not. Since there does not appear to be any existing conventions in this regard, we shall have to devise our own metric. To do so, we can use a classroom analogy as a guide. In many courses, students who get 90 percent correct or greater on a test get an "A." Those who get 80 percent to 89 percent, get a "B," and so on. Within this system, then, a 10 percent difference is a whole letter grade (e.g., an "A" versus a "B"). If so, then a 5 percent difference would be half of a letter grade (e.g., an "A" versus and "A+"). Let's say that any difference in scores of 10 percent or greater is fairly substantial. Anything 5 percent or less is fairly small and inconsequential because the scores would probably be the same letter grade.

Of course, the suggestion that a 10 percent difference is fairly substantial can be backed up in other ways as well. For example, the average height of men is around 5 feet, 11 inches. The average height of females is around 5 feet, 4 inches. This is a 10 percent difference in height and is clearly noticeable. It is also significant in the sense that such a difference would have practical consequences (e.g., reaching things, fitting into compact cars, sports skills, and so on).

Besides converting scores to percents-correct, a second way to put everything on the same scale is to convert mean differences to **effect sizes.** To create an effect size, you need to compute the **mean** (i.e., average) score on some test for each of the two groups as well as the **standard deviation** for scores on that test. In a very rough sense, a standard deviation can be thought of as the average amount that a person's score differs from the group score. If we use the formula (found in any basic statistics book) for determining the standard deviation for females on the SAT and find that it is, say, 118, then we can say that most women who took the SAT got a score that differed, on average, about 118 points from the group mean of 453 points. So, for example, Mary Jones may have received a 603 (+150), Sarah Parker may have received a score of 335 (−118), Marsha Fensterbach may have received a score of 557 (+104) and Julia Smith may have received a score of 353 (−100). On average, these women differed about 118 points from the female mean of 453 (because the average of 150, 118, 104, and 100 is 118).

After we find the means for the two groups of interest (e.g., men and women) and compute the pooled standard deviation (across groups), we then use the formula, "(Mean$_1$ − Mean$_2$)/standard deviation" to find the effect size. For our SAT example, if the male mean is 500, the female mean is 453, and the standard deviation is 118, then we have an effect size of (500−453)/118, or .40. What this value of .40 means is that the groups differ by four-tenths of a standard deviation. Had the male mean been 571 and the female mean been 453, then we would say that they differed by one full standard deviation (i.e., (571−553)/118 = 1.0). Effect sizes can either be positive or negative and can be sometimes larger than 2.0.

Why would anyone go to the trouble of computing effect sizes when percents-correct seem to work just as well? The reason is that effect sizes can tell us many things that a difference in percents-correct cannot. In the first place, standard deviations help us see on some test who is performing in the average range, who is performing above average, and who is performing below average. In particular, if you take the mean score for a group and create a range of scores starting from one standard deviation below that mean and ending at one standard deviation above it, you will often find that 68 percent of people fall within this range of scores. Using our SAT example again for women (i.e., a mean of 453 and a standard deviation of 118), we would find that 68 percent of the women in this study scored between 335 (−118) and 571 (+118). The remaining 32 percent would split evenly into either the 0–334 range (i.e., below average) or the 572–800 range (i.e., above average).

From this perspective, we can say that any woman whose SAT score is one standard deviation or higher above the mean is doing quite well relative to her peers. In fact, her score is probably better than 84 percent of her peers (i.e., the 68 percent in the average range added to the 16 percent in the below average range). Analogously, if we find an effect size of 1.0, that tells us that the people in the higher group (e.g., males) who scored right at their mean are performing better than 84 percent of the lower group! In other words, with an effect size of 1.0, someone in the higher group who is average relative to his or her own group is well above average relative to the comparison group. It is for this reason that effect sizes are thought to be big when they get closer to 1.0. The closer they are to zero, the smaller they are thought to be. For example, our hypothetical effect size of .40 for SATs is closer to zero than it is to 1.0, so we might call it "smallish" or "moderately-sized," (depending on our bias, perhaps).

The other thing effect sizes tell us is the degree of overlap between two "bell-shaped" distributions of scores. When we get an effect size of 0, that not only indicates that means for the comparison groups are identical (e.g., (500–500)/118), it also tells us that the two distributions of scores for the groups completely overlap and lay on top of each other. To get a pictorial sense of this notion, take a look at Figure 12.1. The one figure illustrates the

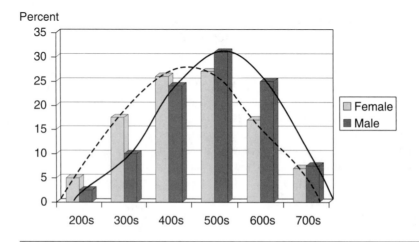

FIGURE 12.1a *Actual Distribution for SAT-Math Scores*

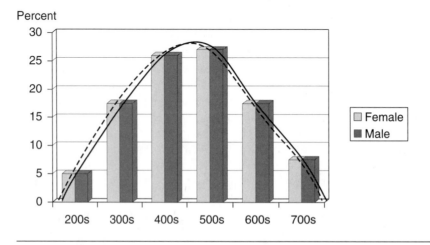

FIGURE 12.1b *SAT Distributions If Effect Size Were Zero*

usual 47-point difference in, and distribution of, SAT scores (Digest of Educational Statistics, 1993) and the other hypothetical one illustrates how the distributions would overlap if the male and female means and distributions were the same.

Because effect sizes are more informative than percents-correct, they have been used as often as possible in this book. Percents-correct have only been used when pertinent information has not been provided by the authors of the reviewed study (e.g., standard deviations). Either way, we shall use the convention that a large difference approaches a "1.0" effect size or a difference of 10 percent or greater in scores.

Explaining Gender Differences

Because it is difficult to remember all of the specifics of the gender differences reported in previous chapters, we shall begin with a summary and partial expansion of the findings. Then, we shall examine explanations of these differences.

Summary of Gender Differences

Reading.   The average effect size for seven studies of early reading (first to third graders) is $d = -.18$ (favoring females; not quite one-fifth of a standard deviation). For reading comprehension in older students, the 1990 National Assessment of Educational Progress (NAEP) found that nine-, thirteen-, and seventeen-year-old females obtained scores that were 3 percent to 5 percent higher than those of males. The findings for the 1998 NAEP were identical: a 3 percent difference at the fourth grade and a 5 percent difference at the eighth and twelfth grades. On the SAT-verbal, females scored slightly higher than males for many years. In recent years, however, males have scored about eight points (i.e., 4 percent) higher. The SAT involves vocabulary and verbal reasoning in addition to reading comprehension. With the exception of the SAT, then, females tend to perform better than males. Some suggest that the size of this difference is so small, however, it is hardly worth talking about (e.g., Hyde & Linn, 1988). Put in analogous terms for height, a 5 percent difference would be like females being 5 feet 7 inches and males being 5 feet 4 inches. Would such a 3-inch difference be even noticeable? Is it practically significant? For example, would the 5 feet 7 inches person be able to do things the 5 feet 4 inches person could not (and vice versa)?

Writing.   In the elementary grades, moderate (−.30s) to fairly large (−.80s) effect sizes (favoring girls) have been found for both orthographic fluency and compositional fluency. In addition, one study found that 82 percent of the students in the lowest 5 percent of the distribution for compositional fluency were boys. In the 1990 NAEP for writing, fourth-, eighth-, and eleventh-grade girls received scores that were 9 percent to 11 percent higher than boys. On the 1998 NAEP, the differences were even larger at 11 percent (fourth), 14 percent (eighth), and 14 percent (twelfth). Thus, females tend to perform considerably better than boys on writing. Note that a 14 percent difference in height would be like the difference between someone who was 5 feet 4 inches and someone who was 6 feet 1 inch.

Math. No gender differences are typically found for preadolescent students (e.g., $d = -.07$ for five- to fourteen-year-olds), except when mathematically precocious students are studied ($d = .41$). At around age fifteen, a small to moderate difference appears when problem-solving is at issue ($d = .29$), especially when college-bound students are under investigation. No gender differences are found for older teenagers in studies of math concepts and computational skills, however (*d's* of 0 and $-.07$). The average effect size for all types of math tests and ages of $d = .20$ (favoring boys) is similar in size to that for reading comprehension (favoring girls). The largest effect size for average students occurs for the SAT-math ($d = .40$). Since 1967, there has been a 47-point (i.e., 10 percent) difference in SAT-math scores favoring males. However, females consistently tend to obtain higher grades in math courses than males at all grade levels (*d's* ranging from $-.09$ to $-.35$; Kimball, 1989). Also, on the 1992 and 1996 NAEP for mathematics, no significant differences emerged at all grade levels (Reese, Miller, Mazzeo, & Dossey, 1997). The means for the 1996 NAEP, for example, were 226 (males) and 222 (females) for fourth graders, 272 (males) and 272 (females) for eighth graders, and 305 (males) and 303 (females) for twelfth graders. Note that many of the items used on the NAEP are similar to those used on the SAT, so the discrepancy between the two tests is somewhat puzzling. Either way, gender differences in math are spotty rather than consistent across all kinds of math, all age levels, and all talent levels.

Science. Males have been found to perform better than females on some science achievement tests. For example, the 1990 NAEP for science showed that whereas the difference between genders amounted to less than 1 percent in nine-year-olds, it increased to 3 percent in thirteen-year-olds, and 5 percent by the end of high school (favoring males). On the 1996 NAEP, the findings were pretty much the same except that the difference at the twelfth grade was only 3 percent. Such differences are half to one-third as large as those found for math and can be considered fairly small.

Social Studies. NAEP results show that males scores are about 2 percent to 5 percent higher than females on tests of history and geography. On the 1990 NAEP for civics, however, females performed slightly better on one section of the test and males performed better on the other. Moreover, on the 1996 NAEP, females scored 3 percent better overall than males at both the eighth and twelfth grades. Collectively, then, the evidence is not consistent. Sometimes males do a little better and sometimes females do a little better. Overall, though, the differences are very small.

Summary. In sum, then, females perform a lot better than males on writing tests, a little better on reading comprehension tests, and slightly better on some civics tests. Whereas the reading and writing differences are apparent in elementary school, the civics difference does not appear until high school. Males, in contrast, do a little better than females on math and slightly better on history and geography. All of these differences emerge in adolescence. Hence, the largest differences are found for writing fluency and quality at all age levels (favoring females) and for math problem-solving during adolescence (favoring males, especially among students with academic talent). The other differences are considerably smaller and suggest that the distributions of scores for the genders largely overlap.

Theories of Gender Differences

Now that we know **how** the genders differ in the different subject areas, and **when** these differences start to emerge, we can begin to address the issue of **why** these differences emerge as they do. Four categories of theories have been proposed to explain the origin of gender differences in cognition: (a) genetic/physiological views, (b) socialization views, (c) differential experience views, and (d) cognitive process views. Let's examine and evaluate proposals within each of these categories in turn.

Genetic/Physiological Views.   Over the last hundred years, neuroscientists have attempted to discover the nature of the brain's morphology and how this morphology relates to human performance. Although there are clear disagreements about the specifics of what we now know (Byrnes, in press; Halpern, 1992; Kosslyn & Koenig, 1992; Squire, 1987), there is nevertheless an emerging consensus about how structures in the brain are arranged and function. This consensus can be summarized as follows:

1. Different types of information (e.g., visual, verbal) seem to be processed and stored in different regions of the brain; that is, there is a certain degree of **localization** of function and storage. Some functions seem to cluster, more or less, to different hemispheres of the brain (left or right). This left-right clustering is called **lateralization.**
2. Although specific regions of the brain seem to handle specific tasks (e.g., pattern recognition), any complex skill (e.g., overall vision) involves a whole series of these regions. It is for this reason that damage to one processing area may have little overall effect on function. To make an analogy, automobiles are assembled in different stages in different regions of a factory (or even different factories). If one region or factory shuts down (e.g., the one responsible for painting), it still may be possible to produce a car that works reasonably well. Of course, certain regions of the brain are crucial to overall functioning and damage to these regions may produce an obvious deficit.
3. Despite the localization and lateralization of functions, the brain is nevertheless highly interconnected. Almost any region connects and communicates with any other. Thus, we can say that a certain region **mainly** performs certain tasks, but we cannot say that it only does that task or that no other region participates in the task.

Researchers who adopt the physiological view all assume that there is an optimal morphology for high-level performance. For example, some assume that having a highly lateralized brain is better than a brain that spreads tasks out over both hemispheres. Researchers differ, however, in terms of their beliefs about which mechanisms are responsible for achieving this optimal morphology. Some researchers appeal to genetics and suggest that male genes specify a different brain morphology than female genes. Using a building metaphor, one would say that the female architecture is based on a flawed set of blueprints in the case of math, but the male blueprint is flawed in the case of writing. These geneticists would explain the male superiority in math and the female superiority in writing to differences in brain organization and function.

Others start with genes but suggest that hormones are the agents that directly alter the brain. Research with rats show that male and female hormones alter the morphology of brain structures such as the hypothalamus and corpus callosum. At present, there is no research with humans that demonstrates similar, unequivocal differences in brain structure. There are merely suggestive independent pieces of evidence that have been strung together by some into speculative theories.

For example, consider the account proposed by researchers such as Camilla Benbow and Beth Casey to explain gender differences in math (e.g., Benbow, 1988; Casey, Pezaris, & Nuttall, 1992). These researchers sought a physiological account that would emphasize the right hemisphere. They found what they needed in the work of the late Norman Geschwind and colleagues on the anatomical basis of dyslexia. As noted in Chapter 6, Geschwind et al. proposed a model to explain three sets of findings: (a) a higher incidence of language problems in boys than in girls, (b) symmetry or reversed asymmetry in the size of certain brain areas in dyslexic children, and (c) unexpected empirical links between left-handedness, language disorders, and immune disorders (Geschwind & Behan, 1982; Geschwind & Galabura, 1985). To explain all of these findings, Geschwind and colleagues proposed the following. During prenatal development, testosterone levels affect the growth of the left cerebral hemisphere in such a way that an anomalous form of dominance develops. Instead of being right-handed and having language lateralized in the left hemisphere, affected individuals become left-handed with language lateralized in the right or both hemispheres. This altered physiology, in turn, leads to problems such as developmental dyslexia, impaired language development, and autism. Testosterone levels also affect the thymus, resulting in disorders of the immune system (e.g., allergies, colitis). To explain asymmetries in the size of the left and right hemispheres, Geschwind and colleagues suggested the testosterone may either retard the growth of the left hemisphere or interfere with normal reductions in the right.

This proposal seemed promising because of the claim that some individuals might be born with atypical dominance and a larger-than-normal right hemisphere (Benbow, 1988). The reasoning was that

> "The right hemisphere is traditionally considered specialized for non-verbal tasks and the left for verbal, although these differences may not be qualitative but quantitative. Mathematical reasoning ability, especially in contrast to computational ability, may be more strongly under the influence of the right hemisphere" (Benbow, 1988, p. 180).

To test these speculations, Benbow and colleagues considered whether gifted children were more likely than non-gifted children to be left-handed and have immune disorders (e.g., allergies). To assess handedness, Benbow and colleagues gave the Edinburgh Handedness Inventory (Oldfield, 1971) to two kinds of children who were drawn from their sample of over 100,000 gifted students: (a) an extremely precocious group of seventh-grade children ($N = 303$) who scored above 700 on the SAT-math or above 630 on the SAT-verbal, and (b) a less precocious group who scored closer to 500 on the SAT-math ($N = 127$). Whereas the norms for Edinburgh Handedness Inventory suggest that 8 percent of Scottish adults use their left hands occasionally or often to perform everyday tasks, 13 percent of children who were extremely precocious for math and 10 percent of the less precocious group were left-handed in this way (Benbow, 1986). Whereas the incidence of left-handedness was found to be significantly higher in the extremely precocious children than in the Scottish adults ($p < .04$), two other comparisons revealed no significant differences: (a) less precocious children versus the Scottish adults and (b) extremely precocious children versus less precocious children.

As for gender differences in the extent of left-handedness in extremely precocious students, Benbow (1988) reports that more males (16 percent) than females (11 percent) were left-handed in the study ($p < .05$, using an unspecified test). However, the present author applied the standard test for comparing frequencies (i.e., the chi-square test) to Benbow's (1986) data and found that the difference between 16 percent and 11 percent is not significant ($p = .17$). In addition, the key difference between mathematically precocious males (14 percent) and mathematically precocious females (6 percent) was also not significant ($p = .33$).

With respect to immune disorders, Benbow (1988) reports that students with extremely high mathematical ability are twice as likely to have allergies as children in the general population (53 percent versus 25 percent). A comparison between extremely precocious males (53 percent) and females (54 percent), however, showed no significant difference in the incidence of allergies.

Thus, the preliminary findings based on handedness and allergies were not terribly supportive of the idea of greater right hemisphere involvement in gifted children, in general, and gifted males, in particular. It could be argued, however, that these studies really do not test the right-hemisphere proposal directly because indices such as handedness and allergies are fairly imprecise. A more direct approach would be to look at patterns of activation in the right and left hemisphere using either neuro-imaging or gross electrical recording techniques. In their review of the literature using the latter, O'Boyle and Gill (1998) report that gifted adolescents appear to engage their right hemispheres more than non-gifted adolescents when they listen to auditory stimuli or process facial expressions. In addition, gifted adolescents show a pattern of resting neural activation that is similar to that of college students and significantly different from non-gifted adolescents (i.e., greater activation in the frontal and occipital lobes).

Finally, comparisons of gifted males and females have revealed gender differences with respect to the involvement of the right hemisphere for the processing of faces and mental rotation (more involvement for males), but not for verbal stimuli. In addition, figures presented in Alexander, O'Boyle, and Benbow (1996) also suggest greater resting activations in the parietal and possibly frontal lobes in gifted males than in gifted females, but these specific comparisons were not reported in the text. The one study that had the potential to consider whether greater right hemisphere involvement was associated with higher SAT-math scores (i.e., O'Boyle & Benbow, 1990) failed to report this correlation because the authors expressed concerns over a restricted range problem with the SAT-math scores (i.e., most students scored over 500). The authors did report a correlation of $r = -.29$ between laterality scores and total SAT scores (i.e., greater bias to process faces in the right hemisphere corresponded to higher SAT scores).

Whereas Benbow and colleagues suggested that the right hemisphere is associated with math skill in some unspecified way, Casey and colleagues suggest the link has to do with spatial ability (Casey, Nuttall, Pezaris, & Benbow, 1995). This idea seemed reasonable because there are rather substantial gender differences in spatial skills such as mental rotation (d's on the order of .7 to 1.5). Math is often alleged to require spatial skills (e.g., to imagine solutions), so Casey and colleagues wanted to see if (a) spatial ability would predict performance on the SAT-math (controlling for other factors) and (b) gender differences on the SAT-math would disappear once one controlled for spatial ability. As for the first hypothesis, Casey et al. (1995) found that spatial ability did predict SAT-math scores after one controlled for SAT-verbal scores (an average of 9 percent of the variance in four female age groups and 8 percent in four male age groups). However, verbal skills explained two to three times as much variance as spatial skills (26 percent in females and 15 percent in males). In another study of eighth graders, spatial ability only predicted math skills for non-right-handed females. It did not predict math skills for right-handed females, right-handed males, or left-handed males (Casey et al., 1992). As for the second prediction, Casey et al. (1995) found that the significant difference in SAT-math scores can be eliminated when one controls for spatial ability. However, whereas such an effect was found for college students and high ability high school students, it was not found for precocious students.

Thus, the evidence as a whole does not lend powerful support to the idea that talented individuals, in general, and gifted males, in particular, are better in math because they tend to engage their right hemispheres more than other individuals. In addition, there are other reasons to have serious doubts about this right-hemisphere proposal. First, most neuroscientists assume that the frontal lobes are the most likely sites of higher-order reasoning (Luria, 1973). More posterior regions of the right hemisphere could be associated with certain aspects of conceptual knowledge in math or certain types of spatial reasoning (but not all), but these regions are also active when working memory and attention are engaged (see Chapter 3). Thus, even if evidence suddenly did accumulate that suggested that extremely talented mathematicians engage their right hemispheres more than less talented individuals, this difference could reflect the former's greater reliance on math concepts, spatial skills, or working memory. These capacities may relate to the kind of reasoning required to do well on the SAT, but the core processes of problem comprehension and strategic planning are likely to be associated with the frontal lobes.

Second, speculations about size differences in the right hemisphere between genders have not been born out in brain scan studies or autopsies (Byrnes, in press). These studies have shown that the average female brain tends to be 9 percent smaller overall. The difference is not limited to the right hemisphere. Note that females are also 10 percent shorter, so the difference in brain size is inconsequential when one corrects for body mass.

Third, it is not at all clear why a theory designed to account for reading disabilities (i.e., the model of Geschwind and colleagues) would even be appropriate for explaining high levels of math *talent*. If the Geschwind model really did apply, one would expect to find reading disabilities in many of the extremely precocious children or people with high spatial ability. In fact, however, most of these children have a great deal of verbal ability in addition to having considerable math ability (Benbow, 1986, 1988). Fourth, in Chapter 6, it was noted that there is very little evidence in support of the proposals of Geschwind and colleagues.

Fifth, many studies have shown that experience can alter brain morphology (Byrnes, in press). So, if the genders do in fact differ in brain morphology (and that is still a big "if"), it is not clear whether this difference has arisen due to genes, hormones, or experience. Sixth, males and females may have the same morphology but use different strategies when they solve tasks (Byrnes & Takahira, 1993; Halpern, 1992). These strategies might show up as different regions of the brain "firing" when problem-solving is underway, but such a difference in activity does not mean that male and female brains are "naturally" more or less lateralized (or better organized, etc.). If all students are taught to use the same strategy, then the same regions of the brain would probably be active in all students.

Finally, perhaps the biggest problem with the existing physiological views is that they do not provide a comprehensive story that can account for the *entire pattern* of gender differences across content areas (e.g., large differences in writing favoring females at all ages, occasional smallish differences in math problem solving, no real differences in social studies). Some theorists have proposed evolutionary accounts to explain such patterns, but note that a key feature of these accounts is a presumed link between spatial ability and math (e.g., Geary, 1998). We just saw that this link was fairly tenuous in the studies of Casey et al. Other studies have found no correlation at all (e.g., Fennema & Sherman, 1977). Critics of the spatial view have also argued that it is not clear that spatial skills would even be required to solve SAT items (e.g., Royer, Tronsky, Chan, Jackson, & Marchant, 1999).

Socialization Views.   The polar opposite of the genetic/physiological category is the Socialization view. Researchers who adopt this view assume that gender differences in cognitive performance arise from the values inherent in a society or particular group that are transmitted to students by their family, peers, and teachers (Eccles, 1983; Halpern, 1992; Parsons, Kaczala, & Meece, 1982). Certain domains (e.g., math and science) are stereotyped as "male" domains and others (e.g., reading and writing) are stereotyped as "female" domains. Such stereotypes are likely to affect the achievement-related beliefs of students in a variety of ways. In the first place, girls would be less likely to find math interesting or important than boys, and would be more likely to form low expectations for how well they will perform in math than boys. In addition, girls would be less likely to (a) try hard in math classes, (b) believe they have high math ability, (c) pursue math-related careers, and (d) take the additional math courses required for such careers. Further, gender biases in teachers would prompt them to expect more of boys and interact with them more during math class.

Many studies have supported these predictions (Eccles, Wigfield, & Schiefele, 1998; Leder, 1992). In fact, as reviewed in Chapter 5, gender differences in beliefs can be found as early as the first grade. Thus, it is clear that students and teachers do seem to internalize cultural values. The question is, however, whether gender differences in beliefs are causally responsible for the gender differences in achievement found for reading, writing, math, science, and social studies.

What is needed to support such an assertion is a comprehensive theory that links beliefs to those behaviors which serve as intermediaries to successful performance on achievement tests. For example, one theory might be that interest promotes active, engaged listening in class (rather than passive listening coupled with "spacing out"). Moreover, prior to taking classroom tests, students who value math and believe that they have talent in math will study harder and more effectively than students who do not. Over time, the former students will gain more expertise in a subject area than the latter students. Then, when students are not forced to take certain classes anymore (e.g., math in high school), only the interested and self-efficacious student will take electives in that domain. These additional classes, in turn, would promote still greater knowledge and skill. With greater knowledge and skill, students can perform quite well on achievement tests.

Such an account could effectively explain the gender differences reported earlier. Perhaps girls like to read and write more than boys. Perhaps boys like math, science, and social studies better. All of this sounds reasonable, but it remains to be tested directly. There is, however, indirect evidence than can be gleaned from cross-cultural studies. If the socialization view is right and the genetic view wrong, then there should be a positive correlation between the strength of gender biases in a culture and the size of the gender gap in certain subject areas. For example, in cultures that espouse the idea that math is a male subject, the gender gap in math achievement should be largest. In cultures that take a less biased stance, however, the gender gap in math achievement should be small or non-existent. One study of math performance in eighth graders in nineteen countries showed just such a correlation. If gender differences were entirely genetic, the gap should not vary this way and there should be no countries in which males and females perform the same. In fact, however, Takahira (1995) and Byrnes, Li, and Shaoying (1997) found no gender differences in performance on SAT-math items in Japanese and Chinese high school students, respectively. Interestingly, they used SAT items that produced the largest gender differences in American students in these studies.

Although the foregoing arguments and evidence seem compelling, the Socialization view runs into its own problems. In the first place, it is hard to find a study that demonstrates the longitudinal relations between interest, type of engagement, amount of studying, and so forth described above. Instead, we have only piecemeal, often low (i.e., .30), correlations between one or two variables from cross-sectional studies. Second, we have the fact that girls routinely get better grades than boys in subjects such as math and science. Girls think that math is more difficult than boys and value it less (Parsons et al., 1982; Wigfield et al., 1989), so why are girls trying so hard to get better grades? If we assume that good grades mean that they are learning something, girls must be acquiring a considerable amount of skill over time, are they not? Third, studies of mathematically precocious students show no gender differences in beliefs, yet thirteen-year-old precocious boys perform significantly better than thirteen-year-old precocious girls on the SAT (Benbow, 1988). Fourth, whereas gender differences in beliefs can be found in the first grade, some gender differences in achievement test performance do not occur until adolescence. Fifth, whereas the correlation between cultural values and math performance holds up when children are in the eighth grade, they do not hold up when children in the same countries are in the twelfth grade (Hanna, Kundinger, & Larouche, 1992). Also, in the Third International Mathematics and Science Study (TIMSS) conducted in 1995, twelfth-grade males outperformed twelfth-grade females in twelve out of sixteen countries. The pervasiveness of the differences would be difficult to explain from the standpoint of socialization theories (unless one could demonstrate that Sweden, France, Germany, Canada, Lithuania, Russia, Switzerland, Czech Republic, Austria, United States, and Denmark are more sexist than Greece, Cyprus, Australia, Italy, and Slovenia). Finally, the socialization view could not easily accommodate the lack of gender differences in studies of Japanese or Chinese students because gender biases (favoring males) exist in these countries too (Byrnes et al., 1997).

Differential Experience Views.   One of the first versions of the Differential Experience view to appear in the literature was the Differential Coursework account that was originally proposed by researchers such as Fennema and Sherman (1977) and Pallas and Alexander (1983). Pallas and Alexander (1983) showed that taking courses such as algebra, geometry, and calculus was a good predictor of success on the SAT. This predictive relation makes sense in light of the fact that the SAT requires knowledge of arithmetic, algebra, and geometry (but not calculus). In addition, Pallas and Alexander showed that the usual 47-point gender difference could be statistically reduced to 13 points when prior coursework is controlled. In a related vein, Byrnes and Takahira (1993, 1994) found that knowledge of arithmetic, algebra, and geometry topics was a good predictor of success on SAT items. Typically, one gets such knowledge by way of courses.

In one sense, the Differential Coursework view can be thought of as a subtheme of the Socialization view. Recall that the Socialization view predicts differential coursework on the part of high school boys and girls. And yet the former is distinct from the latter because the former merely says that coursework matters. It does not specify why students chose the courses they did.

Despite the empirical support it receives from Pallas and Alexander and Byrnes and Takahira, the Differential Coursework view has its problems. In the first place, the gender difference in math and science starts either just before (i.e., age thirteen) or right after girls and boys start taking different classes (i.e., age fifteen). For coursework to have an effect, one would think that several years of different course-taking has to pass. Second, performance on calculus courses predicts success on the SAT, but calculus material is not part of this test. So perhaps course-taking is a proxy variable for math talent. Third, gender differences in reading and writing occur from the beginning of schooling, not after boys and girls have taken different courses for years. Fourth, the 1986 NAEP for science showed that a similar number of males and females took biology (i.e., 88 percent, 89 percent, respectively) and chemistry courses (i.e., 44 percent, 40 percent, respectively) in high school. Taking the latter two courses did improve student scores considerably, but it improved the scores of **both** males and females to the same extent. For example, the scores of males who took chemistry were 16 percent higher than the scores of males who did not take chemistry. The exact same 16 percent improvement was found for females. Hence, one could not explain the 5 percent gender gap in NAEP science scores in eleventh graders by saying that males took more science courses or that they were helped more by these courses than females. Fifth, Linn and Kessel (1996) found that even when boys and girls in a large sample in Maryland took exactly the same courses from the same teachers, an effect size of $d = .40$ was still found for the SAT-math. Finally, gifted thirteen-year-olds who have not attended high school still show the usual gender difference in SAT performance.

Of course, one could revise the Differential Coursework view so as to accommodate many of these problems. Using the category label "Differential Experience" view, for example, one could say that knowledge and skill can be acquired either in school or out of school. Moreover, formal courses may be less important than experiences within specific courses. For example, perhaps boys and girls receive different amounts of reading and writing experiences in the preschool years. Similarly, perhaps gifted children receive more instruction in algebra and geometry in elementary school than the average seventh graders get (which they clearly do and the latter do receive some instruction in algebra and geometry). Finally, perhaps boys and girls have different amounts of informal exposure to science in their home lives. In support of the latter claim, Figure 12.2 shows the percent of

FIGURE 12.2   Percentages of Students Engaging in Science-Related Activities

	Grade		
	3	*7*	*11*
Have you ever used a:			
Yardstick			
male	68	—	—
female	67	—	—
Scale to weigh			
male	67	—	—
female	72	—	—
Magnifying Glass			
male	68	—	—
female	71	—	—
Microscope			
male	**51**	92	98
female	**37**	90	97
Telescope			
male	**58**	**80**	**85**
female	**45**	**64**	**71**
Barometer			
male	—	**30**	**51**
female	—	**20**	**41**
Electricity Meter			
male	—	**31**	**49**
female	—	**10**	**17**

Note: Data from the 1986 NAEP for Science; blank entries mean that students in the age group were not asked about those instruments. The largest differences appear in bold.

boys and girls who had informal experience with scientific instruments. Males clearly had more experience with some of these instruments than females. In fact, the percentage gap in use of instruments far exceeds the 5-percent gap on NAEP science scores. Nevertheless, before the value of the Differential Experience view can be fully assessed, additional studies need to be conducted that carefully document experience differences such as these and trace their effects.

Cognitive Process Views.   All of the views presented so far have included either "proximal" or "distal" variables in their explanation of gender differences. By "proximal," it is meant that explanatory variables are closely connected to performance in space or time. By "distal," it is meant that explanatory variables are somewhat removed from actual performance. For example, in a chain of events such as,

$$genes \rightarrow hormones \rightarrow lateralization \rightarrow SAT \; performance,$$

the variable "genes" would be viewed as somewhat "distal" because it is at least three steps removed from performance. In contrast, given the chain of events depicting the Differential Coursework view,

$$beliefs \rightarrow coursework \rightarrow SAT \; performance,$$

the variable "coursework" would be considered to be "proximal" because it is just one step removed. Beliefs, in turn, would be more distally related.

The Cognitive Process view involves variables that are even more "proximal" than those of the Differential Coursework view because the former's variables would be inserted between the "coursework" and "SAT performance" steps in the second chain above. Researchers who have adopted the Cognitive Process view have tried to identify the key processes responsible for success on an achievement test. After delineating these processes, they try to determine which processes seem to clearly differentiate the two groups of interest (usually high scorers and low scorers).

To illustrate, Byrnes and Takahira (1993, 1994) used the Cognitive Process approach to explain success on SAT items. They argue that students have to successfully execute the following processes in order to perform well on the SAT:

a. *define the problem* (i.e., determine what the author of the item wants him or her to do),
b. *access prior knowledge* (i.e., retrieve item-specific concepts and procedures from long term memory),
c. *assemble an effective strategy* (i.e., arrange prior concepts and procedures into an effective sequence of problem-solving steps),
d. *perform computations without error* (i.e., solve for unknowns using arithmetic and algebra),
e. avoid being seduced by *misleading alternatives,* and
f. carry out operations "(a)" to "(e)" *quickly enough* that each problem can be solved in one minute or less.

After identifying the key processes in this way, Byrnes and Takahira (1993) tried to see whether males performed any of these processes better than females. More specifically, they used a statistical procedure called "regression" to see which processes predict success (see a reader-friendly description of regression in Chapter 6). In this procedure, a computer program determines which variables predict success and which do not and includes predictive variables into an algebraic equation. Variables that are included in the equation are unique predictors in the sense that they are not confounded with other variables. Byrnes and Takahira asked the computer which of the following variables were good predictors: (a) prior knowledge of specific arithmetic, algebra, and geometry concepts and procedures, (b) the strategies subjects used to solve individual problems, (c) their math grade point average, and (d) the student's gender. What they found was that whereas prior knowledge and strategies were unique and strong predictors of success on the SAT (explaining 50 percent of the variance), the variable "gender" was not. In other words, success was more a function of one's knowledge skill than one's gender (because some successful students were knowledgeable and strategic females and some unsuccessful students were unknowledgeable and unstrategic males). In follow-up studies, Byrnes and Takahira (1994), Takahira (1995), and Byrnes et al. (1997) found further support for the model in American, Japanese, and Chinese students, respectively.

The value of the Cognitive Process approach is that the findings immediately suggest the causes of failure in the group that is performing less well (e.g., they are using suboptimal strategies or lack prior knowledge). Once these causes have been identified, a training program can be implemented to improve performance (e.g., training them to use better strategies).

Like the other approaches, however, the Cognitive Process approach has its problems. The main defect is that it fails to specify **why** males and females may differ on the processes identified. For example, it does not tell us why females have less knowledge, or use suboptimal strategies, or fall prey to misleading alternatives. Of course, one way to solve this problem is to combine the Socialization, Differential Experience, and Cognitive Process views. In other words, cultural values determine the experiences students have. Experiences, in turn, promote the acquisition of key cognitive processes. A more elaborate account still would somehow weave in physiological processes. Try to create your own synthesis of these views too see how the synthetic view could answer the question of why males and females differ with respect to specific variables.

Explaining Ethnic Differences

Similar to the section of gender differences, we shall first refresh our memories about the nature of ethnic differences in cognitive performance and then examine explanations of these differences. Of principal concern in this chapter are the differences among White, African-American, and Hispanic students because these differences have been most often reported in the studies described in earlier chapters (presumably because the latter two groups are the largest minority groups in the United States).

Summary of Ethnic Differences

Reading.   For early reading, one study revealed effect sizes ranging from −.42 to −1.05 (favoring White students). This same study showed that ethnic differences remained even after the effects of SES were statistically controlled. Using a large sample of nine-, thirteen-, and seventeen-year-olds, the 1990 NAEP for reading found that the reading scores of White students were 8 to 15 percent higher than those of same-age minority students. Within minority students, the scores of Hispanic students were 1 to 4 percent higher than those of African-American students. On the 1998 NAEP, the scores of twelfth grade White students were 8 percent higher than those of Hispanic students, and the scores of Hispanic students were 2 percent higher than those of Black students.

Writing.   The 1990 NAEP for writing revealed ethnic differences that were as large or larger than those found for reading. In particular, the scores of White students were 7 to 20 percent higher than the scores of African-American and Hispanic students. Hispanic students scored 4 to 9 percent higher than African-American students. On the 1996 NAEP, the scores of twelfth grade White students were 16 percent higher than the scores of Black and Hispanic students.

Math.   Studies have found that most effect sizes are −.40 or larger beginning in the first grade for both computation and problem-solving measures. For the SAT-math, the scores of Asian students are 5 percent higher than those of White students, 18 percent higher than those of Hispanic students, and 27 percent higher than those of African-American students. The scores of White students are 13 percent higher than those of Hispanic students and 22 percent higher than those of African-American students. On the 1996 NAEP, scores of White students were 8 percent higher than scores of Hispanic students; scores of Hispanic students were 2.5 percent higher than those of Black students.

Science.   The 1986 NAEP for science showed that the scores of White students were 17 percent to 20 percent higher than those of African-American students, and 14 to 16 percent higher than those of Hispanic students. The scores of Hispanic students were about 3 to 5 percent higher than those of African-American students. On the 1996 NAEP, the scores of twelfth grade White students were 22 percent higher than those of Hispanic students; the scores of Hispanic students were 5 percent higher than the scores of Black students.

Social Studies.   On each of the geography, history, and civics NAEPs, conducted in the last 10 years, the scores of White students ranged between 10 and 20 percent higher than those of African-American and Hispanic students. Scores of students in the latter two groups are essentially the same.

Summary.   In sum, then, the findings are quite consistent across subject areas: White students perform substantially better than both African-American and Hispanic students, and

Hispanics perform slightly better than African-American students. Unlike gender differences that sometimes appear early and sometimes appear later, ethnic differences are large at all grade levels. If we assume that the gender difference of 10 percent on the SAT-math is large enough to cause concern, we clearly should be concerned about ethnic differences because most of the White-Minority differences are 10 percent or larger. In what follows, we shall examine possible explanations of these large differences.

Theories of Ethnic Differences

There are three main explanations of ethnic differences in cognitive performance. In this book, they are called: (a) the Cognitive Deficit views, (b) the Contextual views, and (c) the Cultural Incongruity views. Let's examine and evaluate each of these views in turn.

The Cognitive Deficit Views.   From the perspective of Cognitive Deficit view, minority children are thought to possess hard-wired (i.e., physiologically based) deficiencies in reasoning and analytical ability that are difficult to overcome (Ginsburg & Russell, 1981). Researchers who espouse the Cognitive Deficit view fall into one of two camps depending on their beliefs about what causes presumed hard-wired differences: geneticists (e.g., Jensen, 1969; Herrnstein & Murray, 1994) and environmentalists (e.g., Hunt, 1964; Pollit et al., 1993).

Whereas the genetic view is self-explanatory (i.e., genes specify a suboptimal morphology), the environmental position needs further explication. Instead of assuming that genes produce different brain morphologies, these researchers assume that all ethnic groups probably start out with the same morphology (or potential for the same morphology) early in development but that factors such as prenatal insult, postnatal nutrition, and postnatal impoverishment change the initially healthy morphologies of minority children into a suboptimal variety.

To bolster their claims, these researchers appeal to four sets of findings (see Byrnes, in press). First, there is the well-established fact that growth in the size of brain neurons begins prenatally and continues postnatally. Second, they appeal to studies with animals that suggest that nutrition can have a powerful effect on the rate and extent of neuronal growth. Third, they cite studies that show how brain cells need to be stimulated in the first few years of life in order for vital functions to emerge (e.g., vision) and how enriched environments can actually alter brain physiology. Finally, they appeal to studies that show that children begin life with three times as many brain cells and synaptic connections than they need. Over time, excess cells are preprogrammed to die and redundant connections become "pruned" in the absence of stimulation. Environmentalists speculate that too few cells are produced, too many cells die, and too many connections are pruned in under-nourished and under-stimulated infants.

Why would minority children be more likely affected by prenatal insult and less likely to receive adequate nutrition and stimulation? It turns out that a large proportion of mothers who live in poverty or who have a drug dependency are of an ethnic minority. The children of these mothers become part of national samples of students who take national assessments and are thought by environmentalists to pull the overall mean of minority students down.

Because of their differences about the cause of ultimate brain differences, the geneticists and environmentalists also disagree about the effectiveness and utility of intervention programs. The geneticists would argue that no intervention would eliminate ethnic differences because students start off with different brain morphologies (even before they experience the environment). In contrast, the environmentalists would argue that certain types of interventions would work (e.g., enriched nutrition and enhanced stimulation during the first two years of life). If interventions begin too late (e.g., after age three), however, the environmentalists would also agree that little could be done to eliminate ethnic differences.

Having described both of the Cognitive Deficit views, we are now in a position to evaluate the overall approach. Four points can be made. First, at present, we cannot specify the optimal brain morphology for performance, so we obviously cannot say what a suboptimal morphology would look like. In other words, we could not "see" the difference if we examined the brains of White and minority children because we do not know what we are looking for. This is a serious problem because there is no way to verify the physiological claims that lie at the heart of this approach. Second, achievement tests scores co-vary considerably with the SES of parents. In the case of reading, for example, NAEP scores increase by ten to twenty points for each education or income level surpassed by students' parents. Poorer, less-educated parents may not only provide less adequate nutrition and stimulation during infancy (supporting the Cognitive Deficit camp), but, as we said in Chapter 6, they also read considerably less to their children than richer, better-educated parents (supporting other views we will describe later). Since both things are true of a large subgroup of minority families, we cannot know which factor has caused the ethnic differences in reading performance. However, one could select out high-income minority children and compare them to high-income White children to see what happens to the performance gap. Third, a number of studies have shown that the performance of minority children **can** be substantially elevated using tutoring, cooperative learning, and other approaches (Slavin, Karweit, & Wasik, 1994). This improvement would seem to be impossible if there were some unalterable physiological deficit interfering with success.

Contextual Views.   Researchers who espouse the Contextualist view place very little emphasis on physiological differences. Instead, they assume that skill development is entirely a function of **opportunity** and **emphasis** (Laboratory of Comparative Human Cognition, 1983). In particular, they argue that highly skilled students come from cultures that (a) provide multiple opportunities for learning these skills and (b) place a high value on these skills. In other words, you learn what your culture wants you to learn.

How do cultures provide opportunities for learning? Consider the fact that parents decide how their preschool children will spend their time. If preschool children are awake 14 hours a day, their parents could allow them to watch TV or play alone for 10 of these hours and spend the rest of the time eating. Conversely, parents could verbally interact with them for 5 hours (e.g., joint play, conversations, joint reading), place them in preschool programs for 3 hours, and allow them to watch educational TV programs for 4 hours. Studies clearly show that parents differ in how much time they let their children engage in various activities (Adams, 1990).

After children enter school, cultures have their effects once again (Stevenson & Lee, 1990). School boards and other officials decide which subjects are taught in school and for how long. Subjects that are thought to be more important (e.g., math, reading) are given more time than subjects that are thought to be less important (e.g., music, the arts). Note that in the America 2000 proposal for reforming American schools, the only subjects that are referred to are science and math. It is clear that the United States values certain subjects more than others.

Thus, powerful individuals in a culture (e.g., parents, teachers, and the people they respond to) play an important role in the **selection, arrangement,** and **duration** of contexts. From the perspective of the Contextual view, ethnic differences in most of the subject areas derive from the fact that powerful individuals in the ethnic subcultures select different contexts, arrange them differently, or allow them to last for different amounts of time. For example, for economic and other reasons, middle- and upper-class White children are probably the largest consumers of books and make up the largest percentage of students in elite private preschool programs. In addition, there may be differences in the degree of emphasis placed on different subjects among schools that have different populations (e.g., largely White versus largely minority schools).

Thus, the ethnic differences in school readiness and actual performance in school are to be expected given differences in the types of contexts experienced by White and minority students. But it should be noted that the fact that White students tend to have more formal school-related knowledge by the time they graduate high school than minority students does not mean that minority students are somehow completely unknowledgeable or unskilled. On the contrary, the Contextualists would suggest that minority students acquire a variety of skills that are valued within their own sub-culture (e.g., story-telling, monetary skills) that often are not valued within the traditional classroom. It is for this reason that the Contextualists often prefer the label "Cognitive Difference" to "Cognitive Deficit" to explain ethnic differences in cognition (Ginsburg & Russell, 1981). The notion of "Cognitive Difference" is meant to imply that all ethnic groups know a lot, but they know different things. It so happens that White students know more things that are valued by the powers-that-be in the larger culture (e.g., government officials and school boards).

How would ethnic differences be eliminated? According to the Contextual view, we would have to homogenize the selection, arrangement, and duration of contexts across White, African-American, and Hispanic subcultures. Because such an experimental intervention has not been carried out, this proposal is speculative. Whereas programs such as Head Start were designed to eliminate contextual differences, it is not at all clear whether a Head Start classroom functions the same way that a middle class family would or could. Thus, we currently cannot evaluate the Contextual view since many studies have to be conducted to test some of its claims. Of the few studies that bear on the claims, some pose problems for the Contextual view because White and minority parents do not seem to differ in terms of their goals and values about education (Stevenson, Chen, & Uttal, 1990). Thus, differences may not have to do so much with *what* parents want for their children and what they value, as much as *knowing how* and *being able to* accomplish these things.

Cultural Incongruity Views.   The Cultural Incongruity view is related in many ways to the Contextual view in terms of its basic assumptions. For example, Cultural Incongruity theorists emphasize the importance of cultural beliefs and practices in shaping ethnic differences. Moreover, they do not place much stock in the physiological explanation of ethnic differences. Where the two views differ is in terms of explaining how cultural differences lead to performance differences.

Whereas the Contextual view emphasizes ethnic differences in values and exposure to certain contexts, the Cultural Incongruity view emphasizes ethnic differences in **communication patterns** and **participation structures** as well as the incompatibility between the ways these patterns and structures are manifested at home and the way they are manifested at school. Studies show differences, for example, between the way White, Native American, African-American, Hispanic, and Hawaiian children communicate and interact with their parents. The nature of turn-taking, wait-time for answers to questions, and so forth differs among ethnic groups (Gay, 1991). In traditional classrooms, one person talks at a time and is given about one second to answer a question. This pattern is similar to the way people communicate in White homes. A child who comes from an environment in which many people talk at once and people are given several seconds to answer a question would find the traditional classroom difficult to cope with.

In support of this view are the studies that show how student performance significantly improves after teachers are taught how to communicate, ask questions, and structure participation in a way which is more compatible with the way these activities are carried out in their students' homes (e.g., Boggs et al., 1985). Unlike the Contextual view which seems to imply a homogenizing of parent and student values to eliminate differences, the Cultural Incongruity view places the onus on teachers to change and allow for diversity.

Because this approach is still in its infancy, it is hard to say how it will ultimately be evaluated. Only time will tell. Two potential criticisms of this approach are that (a) it seems to work best for classrooms in which all children are of one ethnicity and the teacher is of a different ethnicity (what about classrooms that contain mixtures of ethnicities?), and (b) students would not learn the communication patterns and participation structures that predominate in the Anglo-dominated work world.

Instructional Implications

In what follows, we shall explore the instructional implications of the research on gender and ethnic differences in two sections. In the first, some general guidelines are proposed. In the second, you will be asked to evaluate two case studies using the information presented in this book.

General Guidelines

There are several themes that cut across the work on gender differences and ethnic differences. For example, physiological and environmental explanations have been offered for each type of difference. Within the environmental explanations, the notion of values has played a prominent role. With these similarities in mind, we can simplify the instructional implications somewhat by considering gender and ethnic differences together:

1. Research has revealed a range of differences between genders and between ethnic groups. Some of these differences are small, some are moderate, and some are large. For practical reasons, we should devote most of our time and energy to dealing just with the moderate and large differences (Hyde & Linn, 1988). In this book, we have characterized moderate or large differences as being at least a 10 percent difference in percents-correct, and an effect size that is .40 or larger. In the case of gender, then, we should try to do something about the gender difference in writing found at all age levels and the gender difference found for math problem-solving in gifted samples and average students older than fifteen. We should not be troubled by the small differences in reading, early math, science, or social studies. In the case of ethnicity, large differences exist for all subject areas. Hence, much of our resources should be devoted to remediating the pervasive differences between White, African-American, and Hispanic students.

2. The various explanations of individual differences described earlier provide a number of suggestions for how to eliminate gender and ethnic differences. For example,

(a) The environmental version of the Cognitive Deficiency view would suggest that nutrition and stimulation programs should be targeted at low-income children.

(b) The Socialization view of gender differences and the Contextual view of ethnic differences suggest the creation of societal mechanisms that foster the adoption of the same values in all students, parents, and teachers. These mechanisms might include presentations in the media (e.g., atypical role models such as female or African-American engineers on TV shows), parent education programs, and workshops for teachers.

(c) The Differential Experience view of gender differences and the Contextual view of ethnic differences would suggest making the same learning contexts available to both genders and all ethnicities. This would mean, for example, making sure that young girls are candidates for a math program for gifted students as well as finding scholarship funds for minority children to attend prestigious preschool programs.

(d) The Cognitive Process view would suggest that school systems should engage in a two-step remediation program. During the first phase, the cognitive source of failure on achievement tests can be identified (e.g., insufficient conceptual and procedural knowledge). During the second phase, training programs should be designed which target the deficiencies identified during the first phase.

(e) Finally, the Cultural Incongruity view would suggest teacher workshops and other professional development experiences that inform teachers about the communication patterns and participation structures of their students' home lives.

Case Studies

Case Study 1. In a public high school in rural northern Maine (N = 750 students), one section of College Algebra I was designated to be all female. After a computer system assigned both males and females to this section, the males were all moved from this section to other mixed sex classes. This procedure was followed for four successive years until a sample of 77 girls was created. The students in this intervention group were compared to 52 girls who took the regular mixed-sex section of College Algebra I. The researchers (i.e., Wood & Brown, 1997) then considered whether the intervention group differed from the non-intervention group on several key variables. Comparison of their course-taking patterns in math and science revealed no significant differences between the intervention and non-intervention groups. Similarly, no differences emerged in students' grades in such classes. The researchers concluded that single sex classes do not promote higher achievement in girls.

Case Study 2.   Dr. Saundra Nettles of the University of Maryland has developed a partnership with the staff at Stanton Elementary school in southeast Washington, D.C. All of the students are African American, and the median household income for the school catchment area is $12,000. Nearly all of the students are in the free lunch program.

Stanton is designated a Comer school, which means that it works to create a caring, supportive environment with high expectations for student success. In response to calls to improve academic skills in its students, Stanton developed a multi-point plan that emphasized: (a) improved writing, problem-solving, and higher-order thinking, (b) heightened parent and community involvement, and (c) enhanced professional staff development to reflect emerging reforms. In addition to using Title I funds to help realize these goals, the staff at Stanton forged a number of school/community partnerships (e.g., mentoring and tutoring from volunteers from local businesses). Despite the fact that students regularly experience a number of stressful life events (e.g., witnessing violent crimes), a large percentage were recently found to perform at or near the national averages on the reading and math scales of the Stanford Achievement tests.

References

Abbott, R. D. & Berninger, V. W. (1993). Structural equation modeling of relationships among developmental skills and writing skills in primary- and intermediate-grade writers. *Journal of Educational Psychology, 85,* 478–508.

Abraham, M. R., Grzybowski, E. B., Renner, J. W., & Marek, E. A. (1992). Understandings and misunderstandings of eighth graders of five chemistry concepts found in textbooks. *Journal of Research in Science Teaching, 29,* 105–120.

Adams, M. J. (1990). *Beginning to read: Thinking and learning about print.* Cambridge, MA: MIT Press.

Alba, J. W. & Hasher, L. (1983). Is memory schematic? *Psychological Bulletin, 93,* 203–231.

Alexander, J. E., O'Boyle, M. W., & Benbow, C. P. (1996). Developmentally advanced EEG alpha power in gifted male and female adolescents. *International Journal of Psychophysiology, 23,* 25–31.

Alexander, K. L. & Entwistle, D. R. (1988). Achievement during the first two years of school: Patterns and processes. *Monographs of the society for research in child development* (No. 218).

Alexander, P. A. & Murphy, P. K. (1998). Profiling the differences in students' knowledge, interest, and strategic processing. *Journal of Educational Psychology, 90,* 435–447.

Alibali, M. W. (1999). How children change their minds: Strategy change can be gradual or abrupt. *Developmental Psychology, 35,* 127–145.

Allardice, B. S. & Ginsburg, H. P. (1983). Children's psychological difficulties in mathematics. In H. P. Ginsburg (Ed.), *The development of mathematical thinking* (pp. 319–353). New York: Academic Press.

Alleman, J. E. & Rosean, C. L. (1991). The cognitive, social-emotional, and moral development of students: Basis for elementary and middle school social studies. In J. P. Shaver (Ed.), *Handbook of research on social studies teaching and learning* (pp. 121–133). New York: MacMillan.

Ames, C. (1986). Effective motivation: The contribution of the learning environment. In R. S. Feldman (Ed.), *The social psychology of education.* Cambridge, MA: Cambridge University Press.

Ames, C. (1992). Classrooms: Goals, structures, and student motivation. *Journal of Educational Psychology, 84,* 261–271.

Anderson, J. R. (1983). *The architecture of cognition.* Cambridge, MA: Cambridge University Press.

Anderson, J. R. (1990). *Cognitive psychology and its implications* (2nd edition). New York: Freeman.

Anderson, J. R. (1993). Problem solving and learning. *American Psychologist, 48,* 35–44.

Anderson, J. R. (1995). *Learning and memory: An integrated approach.* New York: Wiley.

Anderson, J. R., Fincham, J. M., & Douglas, S. (1999). Practice and retention: A unifying analysis. *Journal of Experimental Psychology: Learning, memory, and cognition, 25,* 1120–1136.

Anderson, J. R. & Schooler, L. J. (1991). Reflections on the environment in memory. *Psychological Science, 2,* 396–408.

Anderson, R. C., Wilson, P. T., & Fielding, L. G. (1988). Growth in reading and how children spend their time outside of school. *Reading Research Quarterly, 23,* 285–303.

Applebee, A. N., Langer, J. A., Mullis, I. V. S., and Jenkins, L. B. (1990). *The writing report card, 1984–1988: Findings from the national assessment of educational progress.* Princeton, NJ: ETS.

Arlin, P. (1981). Piagetian tasks as predictors of reading and math readiness. *Journal of Educational Psychology, 73,* 712–721.

Armento, B. (1986). Research on teaching social studies. In M. C. Wittrock (Ed.), *Handbook of research on teaching* (pp. 942–951). New York: MacMillan.

Ashcraft, M. H. (1982). The development of mental arithmetic: A chronometric approach. *Developmental Review, 2,* 213–236.

Atkinson, J. W. (1964). *An introduction to motivation.* Princeton, NJ: Van Nostrand.

Atkinson, R. C. & Shiffrin, R. M. (1968). Human memory: A proposed system and its control processes.

In K. W. Spence & J. T. Spence (Eds.), *The psychology of learning and motivation: Advances in research and theory* (Vol. 2). New York: Academic Press.

Atwell, N. (1987). *In the middle: Writing, reading, and learning with adolescents*. Portsmouth, NH: Heinemann.

Au, T. K. F., Sidle, A. L., & Rollins, K. B. (1993). Developing an intuitive understanding of conservation and contamination—invisible particles as a plausible mechanism. *Developmental Psychology, 29,* 286–299.

Backscheider, A. G., Shatz, M., & Gelman, S. A. (1993). Preschoolers' ability to distinguish living kinds as a function of regrowth. *Child Development, 64,* 1242–1257.

Baddeley, A. D. (1990). *Human memory: Theory and practice*. Boston: Allyn & Bacon.

Baddeley, A. D., & Logie, R. H. (1999). Working memory: The multiple-component model. In A. Miyake & P. Shah (Eds.), *Models of working memory: Mechanisms of active maintenance and executive control.* (pp. 28–61). New York, NY, USA: Cambridge University Press.

Baillargeon, R., Kotovsky, L., & Needham, A. (1995). The acquisition of physical knowledge in infancy. In D. Sperber & D. Premack (Eds.), *Causal cognition: A multidisciplinary debate* (pp. 79–116). New York: Clarendon Press/Oxford University Press.

Baker, D. & Piburn, M. D. (1990). Teachers perceptions of the effects of a scientific literacy course on subsequent learning in biology. *Journal of Research in Science Teaching, 27,* 477–491.

Baker, L. (1984). Spontaneous versus instructed use of multiple standards for evaluating comprehension: Effects of age, reading proficiency, and type of standard. *Journal of Experimental Child Psychology, 38,* 289–311.

Baker, L. & Brown, A. L. (1984). Metacognitive skills and reading. In P. D. Pearson, M. Kamil, R. Barr, & P. Mosenthal (Eds.), *Handbook of reading research* (Vol. 1, pp. 353–394). White Plains, NY: Longman.

Baker, L., Fernandez-Fein, S., Scher, D., & Williams, H. (1998). Home experiences related to the development of word recognition. In J. L. Metsala & L. C. Ehri (Eds.), *Word recognition in beginning literacy* (pp. 263–287). Mahwah, NJ: Erlbaum.

Baker, L. & Wigfield, A. (1999). Dimensions of children's motivation for reading and their relations to reading activity and reading achievement. *Reading Research Quarterly, 34,* 452–477.

Bandura, A. (1986). *Social foundations of thought and action: A social cognitive theory.* Englewood Cliffs, NJ: Prentice-Hall.

Bandura, A. (1997). *Self-efficacy: The exercise of control.* New York: W. H. Freeman.

Bandura, A. & Schunk, D. (1981). Cultivating competence, self-efficacy, and intrinsic interest through proximal self-motivation. *Journal of Personality and Social Psychology, 41,* 586–598.

Bandura, A. & Wood, R. (1989). Effect of perceived controllability and performance standards on self-regulation of complex decision making. *Journal of Personality and Social Psychology, 56,* 805–814.

Bangert-Downs, R. L. (1993). The word processor as an instructional tool: A meta-analysis of word processing in writing instruction. *Review of Educational Research, 63,* 69–93.

Barch, D. M., Braver, T. S., Nystrom, L. E., Forman, S. D., Noll, D. C., & Cohen, J. D. (1997). Dissociating working memory from task difficulty in human prefrontal cortex. *Neuropsychologia, 35,* 1373–1380.

Baroody, A. J. (1999). The roles of estimation and the commutativity principle in the development of third graders' mental multiplication. *Journal of Experimental Child Psychology, 74,* 157–193.

Baron, J. (1994). *Thinking and deciding* (2nd edition). Cambridge: Cambridge University Press.

Bartlett, E. (1982). *Children's difficulties in establishing consistent voice and space/time dimensions in narrative text.* Paper presented at the meeting of the American Educational Research Association.

Barwise, J. (1989). *The situation in logic.* Stanford, CA: Center for the Study of Language and Information.

Baumann, J. F. (1981). Effect of ideational prominence on children's reading comprehension of expository prose. *Journal of Reading Behavior, 13,* 49–56.

Baumann, J. F. (1984). The effectiveness of a direct instruction paradigm for teaching main idea comprehension. *Reading Research Quarterly, 20,* 93–115.

Beach, S. A. & Robinson, R. J. (1992). Gender and grade level differences in the development of concepts about print. *Reading Psychology, 13,* 309–328.

Beal, C. R. (1990). The development of text evaluation and revision skills. *Child Development, 61,* 247–258.

Beaton, A. (1997). The relation of planum temporale asymmetry and morphology of the corpus callosum to handedness, gender, and dyslexia: A review of the evidence. *Brain and Language, 60,* 255–322.

Beatty, A. S., Reese, C. M., Perksy, H. R., & Carr, P. (1996). *The NAEP 1994 U.S. History Report Card for the nation and the states.* Washington, D.C.: U.S. Department of Education, Office of

Educational Research and Improvement, National Center for Educational Statistics.

Becker, B. J. (1990). Item characteristics and gender differences on the SAT-M for mathematically able youths. *American Educational Research Journal, 27,* 65–87.

Belfiore, P. J. & Hornyak, R. S. (1998). Operant theory and application to self-monitoring in adolescents. In D. H. Schunk & B. J. Zimmerman (Eds.), *Self-Regulated Learning: From Teaching to Self-Reflective Practice* (pp. 184–202). New York: Guilford Press.

Benbow, C. P. (1986). Physiological correlates of extreme intellectual precocity. *Neuropsychologia, 24,* 719–725.

Benbow, C. P. (1988). Sex differences in mathematical reasoning ability in intellectually talented preadolescents: Their nature, effects, and possible causes. *Behavioral and Brain Science, 11,* 169–232.

Benton, S. L., Glover, J. A., Kraft, R. G., & Plake, B. S. (1984). Cognitive capacity differences among writers. *Journal of Educational Psychology, 76,* 820–834.

Benton, S. L., Glover, J. A., Monkowski, P. G., & Shaughnessy, M. (1983). Decision difficulty and recall of prose. *Journal of Educational Psychology, 75,* 727–742.

Berch, D. B., Foley, E. J., Hill, R. J., & Ryan, P. M. (1999). Extracting parity and magnitude from arabic numerals: Developmental changes in number processing and mental representation. *Journal of Experimental Child Psychology, 74,* 286–308.

Bereiter, C. (1985). Toward a solution of the learning paradox. *Review of Educational Research, 55,* 201–226.

Bereiter, C. & Scardamalia, M. (1982). From conversation to composition: The role of instruction in a developmental process. In R. Glaser (Ed.), *Advances in Instructional Psychology* (Vol. 2, 1–64). Hillsdale, NJ: Erlbaum.

Berlyne, D. (1966). Curiosity and exploration. *Science, 153,* 25–33.

Berninger, V. W., Mizokowa, D., & Bragg, R. (1991). Theory-based diagnosis and remediation of writing disabilities. *Journal of School Psychology, 29,* 57–79.

Berninger, V. W. & Fuller, F. (1992). Gender differences in orthographic, verbal, and compositional fluency: Implications for assessing writing disabilities in primary grade children. *Journal of School Psychology, 30,* 363–382.

Berry, J. M. & West, R. L. (1993). Cognitive self-efficacy in relation to personal mastery and goal setting across the life span. *International Journal of Behavioral Development, 16,* 351–379.

Betz, N. E. & Hackett, G. (1983). The relationship of mathematics self-efficacy expectations to the selection of science-based college majors. *Journal of Vocational Behavior, 23,* 329–345.

Bialystok, E. (1988). Aspects of linguistic awareness in reading comprehension. *Applied Psycholinguistics, 9,* 123–139.

Bjorklund, D. F. (1999). *Children's thinking: Developmental function and individual differences* (3rd edition). Belmont, CA: Wadsworth.

Blatchford, P. et al. (1985), Educational achievement in the infant school: The influence of ethnic origin, gender and home on entry skills. *Educational Research, 27,* 52–60.

Block, N. (1990). The computer model of the mind. In D. N. Osherson & E. E. Smith (Eds.), *Thinking* (pp. 245–289). Cambridge, MA: MIT Press.

Bloom, B. S., Englehart, M. B., Furst, E. J., Hill, W. H., & Krathwohl, O. R. (1956). *Taxonomy of educational objectives: The classification of educational goals. Handbook 1: The cognitive domain.* New York: Longman.

Bluestein, N. & Acredolo, L. (1979). Developmental changes in map-reading skills. *Child Development, 50,* 691–697.

Boggs, S. T., Watson-Gegeo, K., & McMillan, G. (1985). *Speaking, relating and learning: A study of Hawaiian children at home and at school.* Norwood, NJ: Ablex.

Boiarsky, C. (1982). Prewriting is the essence of writing. *English Journal, 71,* 44–47.

Bolig, J. R. & Fletcher, G. O. (1973). The MRT vs. ratings of kindergarten teachers as predictors of success in first grade. *Educational Leadership, 30,* 637–640.

Bond, G. L. & Dykstra, R. (1967). The cooperative research program in first-grade reading instruction. *Reading Research Quarterly, 2,* 10–141.

Bornstein, M. H. (1989). Stability in early mental development: From attention and information processing in infancy to language and cognition in childhood. In M. H. Bornstein & N. A. Krasnegor (Eds.), *Stability and continuity in mental development: Behavioral and biological perspectives.* Hillsdale, NJ: Erlbaum.

BouJaoude, S. B. (1992). The relationship between students' learning strategies and the change in their misunderstandings during a high school chemistry course. *Journal of Research in Science Teaching, 29,* 687–699.

Bower, G. H., Black, J. B., & Turner, T. J. (1979). Scripts in memory for text. *Cognitive Psychology, 11,* 177–220.

Bowey, J. A. (1995). Socioeconomic status differences in preschool phonological sensitivity and first-grade reading achievement. *Journal of Educational Psychology, 87,* 476–487.

Bowey, J. A. & Patel, R. K. (1988). Metalinguistic ability and early reading achievement. *Applied Psycholinguistics, 9,* 367–383.

Brainerd, C. J. (1978). The stage question in cognitive-developmental theory. *Brain and Behavioral Science, 2,* 173–213.

Bransford, J., Sherwood, R., Vye, N., & Rieser, J. (1986). Teaching thinking and problem-solving. *American Psychologist, 41,* 1078–1089.

Brenneman, K., Massey, C., Machado, S. F., & Gelman, R. (1996). Young children's plans differ for writing and drawing. *Cognitive Development, 11,* 397–420.

Briars, D. & Siegler, R. S. (1984). A featural analysis of preschoolers' counting knowledge. *Developmental Psychology, 20,* 607–618.

Brophy, J. (1990). Teaching social studies for understanding and higher-order applications. *Elementary School Journal, 90,* 351–417.

Brophy, J. & VanSledright, B. (1997). *Teaching and learning history in elementary schools.* New York: Teachers College Press.

Brophy, J., Van Sledwright, B., & Bredin, N. (1992). Fifth graders' ideas about history expressed before and after their introduction to the subject. *Theory and Research in Social Education, 4,* 440–489.

Brown, A. L. (1989). Analogical reasoning and transfer: What develops? In S. Vosniadou & A. Ortony (Eds.), *Similarity and analogical reasoning* (pp. 369–412). Cambridge: Cambridge University Press.

Brown, A. L. & Campione, J. C. (1994). Guided discovery in a community of learners. In K. McGilly (Ed), *Classroom lessons: Integrating cognitive theory and classroom practice* (pp. 229–270). Cambridge, MA: The MIT Press.

Brown, A. L. & Day, J. D. (1983). Macrorules for summarizing texts: The development of expertise. *Journal of Verbal Learning and Verbal Behavior, 22,* 1–14.

Brown, A. L., Day, J. D., & Jones, R. (1983). The development of plans for summarizing texts. *Child Development, 54,* 968–979.

Brown, A. L., Bransford, J. D., Ferrara, R. A., & Campione, J. C. (1983). Learning, remembering, and understanding. In J. H. Flavell & E. M. Markman (Eds.), *Handbook of Child Psychology: Vol. 3. Cognitive Development* (pp. 263–340). New York: Wiley.

Brown, D. E. (1992). Using examples and analogies to remediate misconceptions in physics: Factors influencing conceptual change. *Journal of Research in Science Teaching, 29,* 17–34.

Brown, G. D. A. (1998). The endpoint of skilled word recognition: The ROAR model. In J. L. Metsala & L. C. Ehri (Eds.), *Word recognition in beginning literacy* (pp. 121–138). Mahwah, NJ: Erlbaum.

Brown, J. S. & Burton, R. B. (1978). Diagnostic models for procedural bugs in basic mathematical skills. *Cognitive Science, 2,* 155–192.

Brown, J. S., Collins, A., & Duguid, P. (1989). Situated cognition and the culture of learning. *Educational Researcher, 18,* 32–42.

Bruner, J. S. (1966). *Toward a theory of instruction.* Cambridge, MA; Belknap Press of Harvard University Press.

Bruner, J. S., Goodnow, J. J., & Austin, G. A. (1956). *A study of thinking.* New York: John Wiley.

Bryant, P., Christie, C., & Rendu, A. (1999). Children's understanding of the relation between addition and subtraction: Inversion, identity, and decomposition. *Journal of Experimental Child Psychology, 74,* 194–212.

Bryant, P. E., MacLean, M., Bradley, L., & Crossland, J. (1990). Rhyme and alliteration, phoneme detection, and learning to read. *Developmental Psychology, 26,* 429–438.

Bryden, M. P., McManus, I. C., & Bulman-Fleming (1994). Evaluating the empirical support for the Geschwind-Behan-Galaburda model of cerebral lateralization. *Brain and Cognition, 26,* 103–167.

Bull, R. & Johnston, R. S. (1999). Children's arithmetical difficulties: Contributions from processing speed, item identification, and short-term memory. *Journal of Experimental Child Psychology, 65,* 1–24.

Bullock, M., Gelman, R., & Baillargeon, R. (1982). The development of causal reasoning. In W. J. Friedman (Ed.), *The developmental psychology of time.* New York: Academic Press.

Bus, A. G. & van Ijzendoorn, M. H. (1999). Phonological awareness and early reading: A meta-analysis of experimental training studies. *Journal of Educational Psychology, 91,* 403–414.

Byrnes, J. P. (1992a). Categorizing and combining theories of cognitive development and learning. *Educational Psychology Review, 4,* 309–343.

Byrnes, J. P. (1992b). The conceptual basis of procedural learning. *Cognitive Development, 7,* 235–257.

Byrnes, J. P. (1995). Domain-specificity and the logic of using general ability as an independent variable or covariate. *Merill-Palmer Quarterly, 41,* 1–24.

Byrnes, J. P. (1998). *The nature and development of decision-making: A self-regulation model.* Mahwah, NJ: Erlbaum.

Byrnes, J. P. (1999). The nature and development of mental representation: Forging a synthesis of competing approaches. In I. E. Sigel (Ed.), *Development of mental representation: Theories and applications* (pp. 273–294).

Byrnes, J. P. (in press). *Minds, brains, and education: Understanding the psychological and educational relevance of neuroscientific research.* New York: Guilford.

Byrnes, J. P. & Fox, N. A. (1998). The educational relevance of research in cognitive neuroscience. *Educational Psychology Review, 10,* 297–342.

Byrnes, J. P., Li, H., & Shaoying, X. (1997). Gender differences on the math subtest of the scholastic aptitude test may be culture-specific. *Educational Studies in Mathematics, 34,* 49–66.

Byrnes, J. P. & Takahira, S. (1993). Explaining gender differences on SAT-math items. *Developmental Psychology, 29,* 805–810.

Byrnes, J. P. & Takahira, S. (1994). Why some students perform well and others perform poorly on SAT-math items. *Contemporary Educational Psychology, 19,* 63–78.

Byrnes, J. P. & Wasik, B. A. (1991). Role of conceptual knowledge in mathematical procedural learning. *Developmental Psychology, 27,* 777–786.

Cahill, L. & McGaugh, J. L. (1998). Modulation of memory storage. In L. R. Squire & S. M. Kosslyn (Eds.), *Findings and current opinion in cognitive neuroscience* (pp. 85–90). Cambridge, MA: MIT Press.

Cain, K. M. & Dweck, C. S. (1995). The relation between motivational patterns and achievement cognitions through the elementary school years. *Merrill-Palmer Quarterly, 41,* 25–52.

Calfee, R. & Drum, P. (1986). Research on teaching reading. *Handbook of Research on Teaching* (3rd Edition, pp. 804–849). New York: Holt, Rinehart & Winston.

Cameron, J. & Pierce, W. (1994). Reinforcement, reward, and intrinsic motivation: A meta-analysis. *Review of Educational Research, 64,* 363–423.

Canfield, R. L. & Smith, E. G. (1993). *Counting in early infancy: Number-based expectations.* Presented at the Meeting of the Society for Research in Child Development, New Orleans, LA.

Caplan, D. & Waters, G. S. (1999). Verbal working memory and sentence comprehension. *Behavioral and Brain Sciences, 22,* 77–126.

Carey, S. (1985a). *Conceptual change in childhood.* Cambridge, MA: MIT Press.

Carey, S. (1985b). Are children fundamentally different thinkers and learners than adults? In S. F. Chipman, J. W. Segal, & R. Glaser (Eds.), *Thinking and learning skills* (vol. 2). Mahwah, NJ: Erlbaum.

Carey, S. (1986). Cognitive science and science education. *American Psychologist, 41,* 1123–1130.

Carpenter, P. A., Miyake, A., & Just, M. A. (1995). Language comprehension: Sentence and discourse processing. *Annual Review of Psychology, 46,* 91–120.

Carpenter, T. P. (1987). Conceptual knowledge as a foundation for procedural knowledge. In J. Hiebert (Ed.), *Conceptual and procedural knowledge: The case of mathematics* (pp. 113–132). Hillsdale, NJ: Erlbaum.

Carpenter, T. P., Corbitt, M. K., Kepner, H. S., Lindquist, M. M., & Reys, R. E. (1981). *Results from the second mathematics assessment of the National Assessment of Educational Progress.* Reston, VA: National Council of Teachers of Mathematics.

Carpenter, T. P., Fennema, E., Fuson, K., Hiebert, J., Human, P., Murray, H., Olivier, A., & Wearne, D. (1999). Learning basic number concepts and skills as problem-solving. In E. Fennema & T. A. Romberg (Eds.), *Mathematics classrooms that promote understanding* (pp. 45–62). Mahwah, NJ: Erlbaum.

Carpenter, T. P., Franke, M. L., Jacobs, V. R., Fennema, E., & Empson, S. B. (1997). A longitudinal study of invention and understanding in children's multidigit addition and subtraction. *Journal for Research in Mathematics Education, 29,* 3–20.

Carpenter, T. P. & Lehrer, R. (1999). Teaching and learning mathematics with understanding. In E. Fennema & T. A. Romberg (Eds.), *Mathematics classrooms that promote understanding* (pp. 19–32). Mahwah, NJ: Erlbaum.

Carpenter, T. P. & Moser, J. M. (1982). The development of addition and subtraction. In R. Lesh & M. Landau (Eds.), *Acquisition of mathematical concepts and processes* (pp. 42–68). New York: Academic Press.

Carr, M. & Jessup, D. L. (1997). Gender differences in first-grade mathematics strategy use: Social and metacognitive influences. *Journal of Educational Psychology, 89,* 318–328.

Carver, R. P. (1973). Reading as reasoning: Implications for measurement. In W. H. MacGinitie (Ed.), *Assessment problems in reading.* Newark, DE: International Reading Association.

Case, R. (1974). Structures and strictures: Some functional limitations on the course of cognitive growth. *Cognitive Psychology, 6,* 544–573.

Case, R. (1998). The development of conceptual structures. In W. Damon (series ed.), D. Kuhn, & R. S. Siegler (volume eds.), *Handbook of child psychology. Volume 2. Cognition, perception, and action* (pp. 745–800). New York: Wiley.

Case, R. & Okamoto, Y. (1996). The role of central conceptual structures in the development of children's thought. *Monographs of the Society for Research in Child Development, 61* (serial no. 246).

Casey, M. B., Nuttall, R., Pezaris, E., & Benbow, C. P. (1995). The influence of spatial ability on gender differences in mathematics college entrance test scores across diverse samples. *Developmental Psychology, 31,* 697–705.

Casey, M. B., Pezaris, E., & Nuttall, R. L. (1992). Spatial ability as a predictor of math achievement: The importance of sex and handedness patterns. *Neuropsychologia, 30,* 35–45.

Chaiklin, S. (1989). Cognitive studies of algebra problem solving and learning. In S. Wagner & C. Kieran (Eds.), *Research issues in the learning and teaching of algebra* (pp. 93–114). Reston, VA: National Council of Teachers of Mathematics.

Chall, J. S. (1967). *Learning to read: The great debate.* New York: McGraw Hill.

Chall, J. S. (1983). *Stages of reading development.* New York: McGraw Hill.

Chen, Z. & Klahr, D. (1999). All other things being equal: Acquisition and transfer of the control of variables strategy. *Child Development, 70,* 1098–1120.

Chi, M. T. H., Glaser, R., & Farr, M. J. (1988). *The nature of expertise.* Mahwah, NJ: Erlbaum.

Chi, M. T. H., Glaser, R., & Rees, E. (1982). Expertise in problem-solving. In R. Sternberg (Ed.), *Advances in the psychology of human intelligence* (Vol. 1). Hillsdale, NJ: Erlbaum.

Chi, M. T. H., Hutchinson, J. E., & Robin, A. F. (1989). How inferences about novel domain-related concepts can be constrained by structured knowledge. *Merrill-Palmer Quarterly, 35,* 27–62.

Chinn, C. A. & Brewer, W. F. (1998). An empirical test of a taxonomy of responses to anomalous data in science. *Journal of Research in Science Teaching, 35,* 623–654.

Cipielewski, J. & Stanovich, K. E. (1992). Predicting growth in reading ability from children's exposure to print. *Journal of Experimental Child Psychology, 54,* 74–89.

Clay, M. (1985). *The early detection of reading difficulties.* Auckland, New Zealand: Heinemann.

Clement, J. (1982). Algebra word problem solutions: Thought processes underlying a common misconception. *Journal for Research in Mathematics Education, 13,* 16–30.

Cobb, P., Yackel, E., & Wood, T. (1992). A constructivist alternative to the representational view of mind in mathematics education. *Journal for Research in Mathematics Education, 23,* 2–33.

Cohen, J. (1992). A power primer. *Psychological Bulletin, 112,* 155–159.

College Entrance Examination Board (1988). *1988 profile of SAT and achievement test takers.* New York: Author.

Collins, A. M. & Loftus, E. F. (1975). A spreading-activation theory of semantic processing. *Psychological Review, 82,* 407–428.

Coltheart, M., Curtis, B., Atkins, P., & Haller, M. (1993). Models of reading aloud: Dual-route and parallel-distributed-processing approaches. *Psychological Review, 100,* 589–608.

Cordova, D. L. & Lepper, M. R. (1996). Intrinsic motivation and the process of learning: Beneficial effects of contextualization, personalization, and choice. *Journal of Educational Psychology, 88,* 715–730.

Covington, M. & Omelich, C. (1981). As failures mount: Affective and cognitive consequences of ability demotion in the classroom. *Journal of Educational Psychology, 73,* 796–808.

Craik, F. I. M. & Lockhart, R. S. (1972). Levels of processing: A framework for memory research. *Journal of Verbal Learning and Verbal Behavior, 11,* 671–684.

Cross, J. A. (1987). Factors associated with students' place location knowledge. *Journal of Geography, 86,* 59–63.

Cuban, L. (1984). Policy and research dilemmas in the teaching of reasoning: Unplanned designs. *Review of Educational Research, 54,* 655–681.

Cull, W. L. & Zechmeister, E. B. (1994). The learning ability paradox in adult metamemory research: Where are the metamemory differences between good and poor learners? *Memory & Cognition, 22,* 249–257.

Cunningham, P. M., Hall, D. P., & Defee, M. (1991). Non-ability grouped multilevel instruction: A year in a first grade classroom. *Reading Teacher, 44,* 566–571.

Dagher, Z. R. & BouJaoude, S. (1997). Scientific views and religious beliefs of college students: The case of biological evolution. *Journal of Research in Science Teaching, 34,* 429–445.

Daiute, C. (in press). Social relational knowing in writing development. In E. Amsel & J. P. Byrnes (Eds.), *Language, literacy, and cognitive development.* Mahwah, NJ: Erlbaum.

Danner, F. (1976). Children's understanding of intersentence organization in the recall of short descriptive passages. *Journal of Educational Psychology, 68,* 174–183.

de Bono, E. (1983). The direct teaching of thinking as a skill. *Phi Delta Kappan, 64,* 703–708.

Deci, E. & Ryan, R. (1985). *Intrinsic motivation and self-determination in human behavior.* New York: Plenum Press.

DeFries, J. C., Gillis, J. J., & Wadsworth, S. J. (1993). Genes and genders: A twin study of reading disability. In A. M. Galaburda (Ed.), *Dyslexia and development: Neurobiological development of extraordinary brains* (pp. 187–204). Cambridge, MA: Harvard University Press.

Dehaene, S. (1996). The organization of brain activations in number comparison: Event-related potentials and the additive factors method. *Journal of Cognitive Neuroscience, 8,* 47–68.

Dehaene, S., Bossini, S., & Giraux, P. (1993). The mental representation of parity and number magnitude. *Journal of Experimental Psychology: General, 122,* 371–396.

Dehaene, S. & Cohen, L. (1997). Cerebral pathways for calculation: Double dissociation between rote verbal and quantitative knowledge of arithmetic. *Cortex, 33,* 219–250.

Dehaene, S., Tzourio, N., Frak, V., Raynaud, L., Cohen, L., Mehler, J., & Mazoyer, B. (1996). Cerebral activations during number multiplication and comparison: A PET study. *Neuropsychologia, 34,* 1097–1106.

Dempster, F. N. (1992). The rise and fall of the inhibitory mechanism: Toward a unified theory of cognitive development and aging. *Developmental Review, 12,* 45–75.

Dewitz, P., Carr, E., & Patberg, J. P. (1987). Effects of inference training on comprehension and comprehension monitoring. *Reading Research Quarterly, 22,* 99–121.

Department of Education (1990). *Digest of Educational Statistics.* Washington, D.C.: Author.

Dimino, J., Gersten, R., Carnine, D., & Blake, G. (1990). Story grammar: An approach for promoting at-risk secondary students' comprehension of literature. *The Elementary School Journal, 91,* 19–32.

Dimino, J. A., Taylor, R. M., & Gersten, R. M. (1995). Synthesis of the research on story grammar as a means to increase comprehension. *Reading and writing quarterly: Overcoming learning difficulties, 11,* 53–72.

Duffy, G. & Roehler, L. (1987). Improving classroom reading instruction through the use of responsive elaboration. *Reading Teacher, 40,* 514–521.

Dunbar, K. & Klahr, D. (1989). Developmental differences in scientific discovery processes. In D. Klahr & K. Kotovsky (Eds.), *Complex information processing: The impact of Herbert A. Simon.* Hillsdale, NJ: Erlbaum.

Durkin, D. (1979). What classroom observations reveal about reading comprehension instruction. *Reading Research Quarterly, 14,* 481–533.

Dweck, C. (1986). Motivational processes affecting learning. *American Psychologist, 41,* 1040–1048.

Dweck, C., Davidson, W., Nelson, S., & Enna, B. (1978). Sex differences in learned helplessness II: The contingencies of evaluative feedback in the classroom, and III: An experimental analysis. *Developmental Psychology, 14,* 268–276.

Dweck, C. & Elliot, E. (1983). Achievement motivation. In P. H. Mussen (Ed.), *Handbook of Child Psychology, Vol. IV: Socialization, Personality, and Social Development* (pp. 643–691). New York: John Wiley.

Dweck, C. & Leggett, E. (1988). A social-cognitive approach to motivation and personality. *Psychological Review, 95,* 256–273.

Eccles, J. (1983). Expectancies, values, and academic behavior. In J. T. Spence (Ed.), *Achievement and achievement motives: Psychological and sociological approaches* (pp. 77–146). San Francisco: Freeman.

Eccles, J., Adler, T. F., Futterman, R., Goff, S. B., Kaczala, C. M., Meece, J. L., & Midgley, C. (1985). Self-perceptions, task perceptions, socializing influences, and the decision to enroll in mathematics. In S. F. Chipman, L. R. Brush, and D. M. Wilson (Eds.), *Women and mathematics: Balancing the equation* (pp. 95–121). Hillsdale, NJ: Erlbaum.

Eccles, J. S., Midgley, C., Wigfield, A., Flanagan, C., Buchanan, C. M., Reuman, D., & MacIver, D. (1993). *American Psychologist, 48,* 90–116.

Eccles, J. S., Wigfield, A., Flanagan, C., Miller, C., Reuman, D., & Yee, D. (1989). Self-perceptions, domain values, and self-esteem: Relations and changes at early adolescence. *Journal of Personality, 57,* 283–310.

Eccles, J. S., Wigfield, A., & Schiefele, U. (1998). Motivation to succeed. In W. Damon (series ed.), N. Eisenberg (volume ed.), *Handbook of child psychology: Vol. 3. Social, emotional, and personality development* (5th edition, pp. 1018–1095). New York: Wiley.

Eckler, J. A. & Weininger, O. (1989). Structural parallels between pretend play and narratives. *Developmental Psychology, 25,* 736–743.

Ehri, L. C. (1995). Phases of development in learning to read words by sight. *Journal of Research in Reading, 18,* 116–125.

Elliot, A. J., McGregor, H. A., & Gable, S. (1999). Achievement goals, study strategies, and exam performance: A mediational analysis. *Journal of Educational Psychology, 91,* 549–563.

Englert, C. S., Stewart, S. R., & Hiebert, E. H. (1988). Young writer's use of text structure in expository text generation. *Journal of Educational Psychology, 80,* 143–151.

English, L. D. & Halford, G. S. (1995). *Mathematics education: Models and processes.* Mahwah, NJ: Erlbaum.

Ennis, R. H. (1962). A concept of critical thinking. *Harvard Educational Review, 32,* 81–111.

Entwisle, D. R. & Alexander, K. L. (1992). Summer setback: Race, poverty, school composition, and mathematics achievement in the first two years of school. *American Sociological Review, 57,* 72–84.

Ericsson, K. A. (1996). *The road to excellence: The acquisition of expert performance in the arts, science, sports, and games.* Mahwah, NJ: Erlbaum.

Ericsson, K. A. & Smith, J. (1991). *Toward a general theory of expertise: Prospects and limits.* Cambridge: Cambridge University Press.

Eylon, B. & Linn, M. C. (1988). Learning and instruction: An examination of four research perspectives. *Review of Educational Research, 58,* 251–301.

Fabricius, W. V. & Hagen, J. W. (1984). The use of causal attributions about free recall performance to assess metamemory and predict strategic memory behavior in young children. *Developmental Psychology, 20,* 975–987.

Farrell, R. T. & Cirrincione, J. M. (1989). The content of the geography curriculum—teachers perspective. *Social Education, 53,* 105–108.

Feather, N. T. (1988). Values, expectancies, and course enrollment: Testing the role of personal values within an expectancy-valence framework. *Journal of Educational Psychology, 80,* 381–391.

Feitelson, D., Tehori, B. Z., & Levinberg-Green, D. (1982). How effective is early instruction in reading? Experimental Evidence. *Merrill-Palmer Quarterly, 28,* 485–494.

Fennema, E. & Sherman, J. (1977). Sex-related differences in mathematics achievement, spatial visualization and affective factors. *American Educational Research Journal, 14,* 51–71.

Ferguson, P. (1991). Impacts on social and political participation. In J. P. Shaver (Ed.), *Handbook of Research on Social Studies Teaching and Learning.* New York: Macmillan.

Fielding, L. G., Anderson, R. C., & Pearson, P. D. (1990). *How discussion questions influence children's story understanding* (tech. rep. No 490). Urbana: University of Illinois, Center for the Study of Reading.

Fitzgerald, J. (1987). Research on revision in writing. *Review of Educational Research, 57,* 481–506.

Flavell, J. H., Miller, P. H., & Miller, S. A. (1993). *Cognitive Development* (3rd edition). Englewood Cliffs, NJ: Prentice Hall.

Flynn, E. (1988). Composing as a woman. *College Composition and Communication, 39,* 423–435.

Fowler, W. (1971). A developmental learning strategy for early reading in a laboratory nursery school. *Interchange, 2,* 106–124.

Frederiksen, J. R., White, B. Y., & Gutwill, J. (1999). Dynamic mental models in learning science: The importance of constructing derivational linkages among models. *Journal of Research in Science Teaching, 36,* 806–836.

Freedman, A. (1987). Development in story writing. *Applied Psycholinguistics, 8,* 153–170.

Friedman, W. (1990). *About time: Inventing the fourth dimension.* Cambridge, MA: MIT Press.

Frijda, N. (1994). Emotions are functional, most of the time. In P. Ekman & R. J. Davidson (Eds.), *The nature of emotion* (pp. 112–122). New York: Oxford University Press.

Fuson, K. C. (1988). *Children's counting and concepts of number.* New York: Springer-Verlag.

Fuson, K. C. & Briars, D. J. (1990). Using a base-ten blocks learning/teaching approach for first- and second-grade place-value and multidigit addition and subtraction. *Journal for Research in Mathematics Education, 21,* 180–206.

Fuson, K. C. & Hall, J. W. (1983). The acquisition of early word meanings: A conceptual analysis and review. In H. P. Ginsburg (Ed.), *Children's mathematical thinking.* New York: Academic Press.

Fuson, K. C., Wearne, D., Hiebert, J. C., Murray, H. G., Human, P. G., Olivier, A. I., Carpenter, T. P., & Fennema, E. (1997). Children's conceptual structures for multidigit numbers and methods of multidigit addition and subtraction. *Journal for Research in Mathematics Education, 28,* 130–162.

Gage, N. L. & Berliner, D. C. (1991). *Educational Psychology* (5th edition). Boston: Houghton Mifflin.

Gagne, E. D., Yekovich, C. W., & Yekovich, F. R. (1993). *The cognitive psychology of school learning.* New York: Harper Collins.

Galabura, A. M. (1993). *Dyslexia and development: Neurobiological aspects of extra-ordinary brains.* Cambridge, MA: Harvard University Press.

Gambrell, L. B. & Chasen, S. P. (1991). Explicit story instruction and the narrative writing of fourth- and fifth-grade below-average readers. *Reading Research and Instruction, 31,* 54–62.

Gardner, H. (1983). *Frames of mind.* New York: Basic Books.

Garner, R. (1987). Strategies for reading and studying expository texts. *Educational Psychologist, 22,* 299–312.

Garner, R., Alexander, P., Slater, W., Hare, V. C., Smith, T., & Reis, R. (1986). Children's knowledge of structural properties of expository text. *Journal of Educational Psychology, 78,* 411–416.

Garner, R., Hare, V. C., Alexander, P., Haynes, J., & Winograd, P. (1984). Inducing the use of a text lookback strategy among unsuccessful readers. *American Educational Research Journal, 21,* 789–798.

Garnett, P. J. & Treagust, D. F. (1992). Conceptual difficulties experienced by senior high school students of electrochemistry: Electrochemical (galvanic) and electrolytic cells. *Journal of Research in Science Teaching, 29,* 1079–1099.

Garrett, M. F. (1990). Sentence processing. In D. N. Osherson & H. Lasnik (Eds.), *An invitation to cognitive science, Vol. 1: Language* (pp. 133–175). Cambridge, MA: MIT Press.

Gay, G. (1991). Culturally diverse students and social studies. In J. P. Shaver (Ed.), *Handbook of research on social studies teaching and learning* (pp. 144–156). New York: Macmillan.

Gayan, J., Smith, S. D., Cherny, S. S., Cardon, L. R., Fulker, D. W., Brower, A. M., Olson, R. K., Pennington, B. F., & DeFries, J. C. (1999). Quantitative-trait locus for specific language and reading deficits. *American Journal of Human Genetics, 64,* 157–164.

Gearheart, M., Saxe, G. B., Seltzer, M., Schlackman, J., Ching, C. C., Nasir, N., Fall, R., Bennett, T., Rhine, S., & Sloan, T. F. (1999). Opportunities to learn fractions in elementary mathematics classrooms. *Journal for Research in Mathematics Education, 30,* 286–315.

Geary, D. C. (1993). Mathematical disabilities: Cognitive, neuropsychological, and genetic components. *Psychological Bulletin, 114,* 345–362.

Geary, D. C. (1995). Reflections of evolution and culture in children's cognition: Implications for mathematical development and instruction. *American Psychologist, 50,* 24–37.

Geary, D. C. (1998). *Male, female: The evolution of human sex differences.* Washington, D.C.: American Psychological Association.

Geary, D. C., Hoard, M. K., & Hamson, C. O. (1999). Numerical and arithmetical cognition: Patterns of functions and deficits in children at risk for a mathematical disability. *Journal of Experimental Child Psychology, 74,* 213–239.

Gelman, R. & Baillargeon, R. (1983). A review of some Piagetian concepts. In P. H. Mussen (Ed.), *Handbook of child psychology: Vol. 3. Cognitive development* (4th edition, pp. 167–230).

Gelman, R. & Gallistel, C. R. (1978). *The child's understanding of numbers.* Cambridge, MA: Harvard University Press.

Gelman, R. & Meck, E. (1983). Preschoolers' counting: Principles before skill. *Cognition, 13,* 343–359.

Gelman, S. A. & Coley, J. D. (1991). Language and categorization: The acquisition of natural kind terms. In S. A. Gelman & J. P. Byrnes (Eds.), *Perspectives on language and thought: Interrelations in development* (pp. 146–196). Cambridge: Cambridge University Press.

Gernsbacher, M. A. (1996). The Structure-Building Framework: What it is, what it might also be, and why. In B. K. Britton & A. C. Graesser, (Eds.), *Models of understanding text.* (pp. 289–311). Mahwah, NJ, USA: Lawrence Erlbaum Associates.

Geschwind, N. & Behan, P. (1982). Left-handedness: Association with immune disease, migraine, and developmental learning disorder. *Proceedings of the National Academy of Sciences, 79,* 5097–5100.

Geschwind, N. & Galabura, A. M. (1985). Cerebral lateralization: Biological mechanisms, associations, and pathology I: A hypothesis and a program for research. *Archives of Neurology, 42,* 428–459.

Geschwind, N. & Galaburda, A. M. (1987). *Cerebral lateralization.* Cambridge, MA: MIT Press.

Geva, E. (1983). Facilitating reading comprehension through flowcharting. *Reading Research Quarterly, 18,* 383–405.

Gick, M. L. & Holyoak, K. J. (1983). Schema induction and analogical transfer. *Cognitive Psychology, 15,* 1–38.

Gilligan, C. (1982). *In a different voice: Psychological theory and women's development.* Cambridge, MA: Harvard University Press.

Ginsburg, H. & Russell, R. L. (1981). Social class and racial influences on early mathematical thinking. *Monographs of the Society for Research in Child Development, 46* (No. 193).

Glaser, R. & Chi, M. T. H. (1988). Overview. In M. T. H. Chi, R. Glaser, & M. Farr (Eds.), *The nature of expertise.* Hillsdale, NJ: Erlbaum.

Glover, J. A., Ronning, R. R., & Bruning, R. H. (1990). *Cognitive Psychology for Teachers.* New York: Macmillan.

Goldstein, D. M. (1976). Cognitive-linguistic functioning and learning to read in preschoolers. *Journal of Educational Psychology, 68,* 680–688.

Gombert, J. E. & Fayol, M. (1992). Writing in preliterate children. *Learning and Instruction, 2,* 23–41.

Goodman, Y. M. (1991). Comments in "Beginning to read: A critique by literacy professionals and a response by Marilyn Jager Adams." *The Reading Teacher, 44,* 375.

Goodman, K. S. & Goodman, Y. (1979). Learning to read is natural. In L. B. Resnick & R. A. Weaver (Eds.), *Theory and practice of early reading* (pp. 51–94). Hillsdale, NJ: Lawrence Erlbaum.

Gopnik, A. & Wellman, H. M. (1992). Why the child's theory of mind really is a theory. *Mind & Language, 7,* 145–171.

Gordon, Roberta R. (1988). Increasing efficiency and effectiveness in predicting second grade achievement using a kindergarten screening battery. *Journal of Educational Research, 81,* 238–244.

Gottfried, G. M., Gelman, S. A., & Schultz, J. (1999). Children's understanding of the brain: From early essentialism to biological theory. *Cognitive Development, 14,* 147–174.

Graesser, A., Golding, J. M., & Long, D. L. (1991). Narrative representation and comprehension. In R. Barr, M. L. Kamil, P. Mosenthal, & P. D. Pearson (Eds.), *Handbook of reading research, Vol II* (pp. 171–205). New York: Longman.

Graesser, A. C., Millis, K. K., & Zwaan, R. A. (1997). Discourse comprehension. *Annual Review of Psychology, 48,* 163–189.

Graham, S. (1994). Motivation in African-Americans. *Review of Educational Research, 64,* 55–117.

Graham, S. (1997). Executive control in the revising of students with learning and writing difficulties. *Journal of Educational Psychology, 89,* 223–234.

Graham, S., Berninger, V. W., Abbott, R. D., Abbott, S. P., & Whitaker, D. (1997). Role of mechanics in composing of elementary school students: A new methodological approach. *Journal of Educational Psychology, 89,* 170–182.

Graham, S., Doubleday, C., & Guarino, P. (1984). The development of relations between perceived controllability and the emotions of pity, anger, and guilt. *Child Development, 55,* 561–565.

Graham, S. & Golan, S. (1991). Motivational influences on cognition: Task involvement, ego involvement, and depth of information processing. *Journal of Educational Psychology, 83,* 187–194.

Graham, S. & Harris, K. R. (1996). Self-regulation and strategy instruction for students who find writing and learning challenging. In C. M. Levy & S. Ransdell (Eds.), *The science of writing: Theories, methods, individual differences, and applications* (pp. 347–360). Mahwah, NJ; Erlbaum.

Graves, D. H. (1975). An examination of the writing processes of seven-year-old children. *Research in the Teaching of English, 9,* 227–241.

Greany, V. (1980). Factors related to amount and time of leisure reading. *Reading Research Quarterly, 15,* 337–357.

Greany, V. & Hegarty, M. (1987). Correlates of leisure-time reading. *Journal of Research in Reading, 10,* 3–20.

Greene, R. L. (1986). Sources of recency effects in free recall. *Psychological Bulletin, 99,* 221–228.

Greenwald, E. A., Perksy, H. R., Campbell, J. R., & Mazzeo, J. (1999). *The NAEP 1998 writing report card for the nation and the states.* Washington, D.C.: U.S. Department of Education, Office of Educational Research and Improvement, National Center for Educational Statistics.

Griffiths, A. K. & Preston, K. P. (1992). Grade-12 students' misconceptions relating to fundamental characteristics of atoms and molecules. *Journal of Research in Science Teaching, 29,* 611–628.

Groen, G. J. & Parkman, J. M. (1972). A chronometric analysis of simple addition. *Psychological Review, 79,* 329–343.

Gross, S. (1993). Early mathematics performance and achievement: Results of a study within a large suburban school system. *Journal of Negro Education, 62,* 269–287.

Gurney, D., Gersten, R., Dimino, J., & Carnine, D. (1990). Story grammar: Effective literature instruction for high school students with learning disabilities. *Journal of Learning Disabilities, 23,* 335–348.

Guthrie, J. T., Cox, K. E., Knowles, K. T., Buehl, M., Mazzoni, S. A., & Fasulo, L. (2000). Building toward coherent instruction. In L. Baker, M. J. Dreher, & J. T. Guthrie (Eds.), *Engaging young readers: Promoting achievement and motivation* (pp. 209–236). New York: Guilford.

Guthrie, J. T., Van Meter, P., McCann, A. D., Wigfield, A., Bennett, L., Poundstone, C. C., Rice, M. E., Faisbisch, F. M., Hunt, B., & Mitchell, A. M. (1996). Growth of literacy engagement: Changes in motivations and strategies during concept-oriented reading instruction. *Reading Research Quarterly, 31,* 306–332.

Hackett, G., Betz, N. E., Casas, J. M., & Rocha-Singh, I. A. (1992). Gender, ethnicity, and social cognitive factors predicting the academic achievement of students in engineering. *Journal of Counseling Psychology, 39,* 527–538.

Halford, G. S., Mayberry, M. T., O'Hare, A. W., & Grant, P. (1994). The development of memory and processing capacity. *Child Development, 65,* 1338–1356.

Hallden, O. (1986). Learning history. *Oxford Review of Education, 12,* 53–66.

Halpern, D. F. (1990). *Thought and knowledge: An introduction to critical thinking* (2nd Edition). Hillsdale, NJ: Erlbaum.

Halpern, D. F. (1992). *Sex differences in cognitive abilities* (2nd edition). Hillsdale, NJ: Erlbaum.

Halpern, D. F. (1999). Teaching critical thinking for transfer across domains. *American Psychologist, 53,* 449–455.

Hamill, D. D. & McNutt, G. (1980). Language abilities and reading: A review of the literature on their relationship. *Elementary School Journal, 80,* 268–277.

Hammock, D. C. et al. (1990). *The U.S. History Report Card.* Princeton, NJ: National Assessment of Educational Progress.

Hanna, G., Kundinger, E., & Larouche, C. (1992). Mathematical achievement of grade 12 girls in fifteen countries. In L. Burton (Ed.), *Gender and mathematics: An international perspective* (pp. 86–97). London: Cassell.

Hansen, J. & Pearson, P. D. (1983). An instructional study: Improving the inferential comprehension of good and poor fourth-grade readers. *Journal of Educational Psychology, 75,* 821–829.

Harter, S. (1985). Competence as a dimension of self-evaluation: Toward a comprehensive model of self-worth. In R. L. Leahy (Ed.), *The development of the self* (pp. 55–121).

Harter, S. (1999). *The construction of the self: A developmental perspective.* New York, NY: The Guilford Press.

Hatano, G., Siegler, R. S., Richards, D. D., & Inagaki, K. (1993). The development of biological knowledge: A multi-national study. *Cognitive Development, 8,* 47–62.

Hayes, J. R. (1985). Three problems in teaching general skills. In J. Segal, S. Chipman, & R. Glaser (Eds.), *Thinking and learning, Vol. 2.* Hillsdale, NJ: Erlbaum.

Hayes, J. R. (1996). A new framework for understanding cognition and affect in writing. In C. M. Levy & S. Ransdell (Eds.), *The science of writing: Theories, methods, individual differences, and applications* (pp. 1–27). Mahwah, NJ: Erlbaum.

Hayes, J. R. & Flower, L. S. (1980). Identifying the organization of writing processes. In L. Gregg & E. R. Steinberg (Eds.), *Cognitive processes in writing* (pp. 3–30). Hillsdale, NJ: Lawrence Erlbaum.

Hayes, J. R. & Flower, L. S. (1986). Writing research and the writer. *American Psychologist, 41,* 1106–1113.

Hayes, J. R., Flower, L. S., Schriver, K. S., Stratman, J., & Carey, L. (1987). Cognitive processes in revision. In S. Rosenberg (Ed.), *Advances in psycholiguistics. Vol. 2.* Reading, writing, and language

processing (pp. 176–240). New York: Cambridge Univ. press.

Heath, S. B. (1983). *Ways with words: Language, life and work in communities and classrooms.* Cambridge: Cambridge University Press.

Hecht, S. A. (1998). Toward an information processing account of individual differences in fractions skills. *Journal of Educational Psychology, 90,* 545–559.

Heller, P. M. & Finley, F. N. (1992). Variable uses of alternative conceptions: A case study in current electricity. *Journal of Research in Science Teaching, 29,* 259–275.

Herman, W. L., Barron, M., Hawkins, M. L., & Berryman, C. (1988). World place location skills of elementary school students. *Journal of Educational Research, 81,* 374–376.

Herrnstein, R. J. & Murray, C. (1994). *The bell curve: Intelligence and class structure in American life.* New York: The Free Press.

Herscovics, N. (1989). Cognitive obstacles encountered in the learning of algreba. In S. Wagner & C. Kieran (Eds.), *Research issues in the learning and teaching of algebra* (pp. 60–86). Reston, VA: National Council of Teachers of Mathematics.

Hewson, M. G. & Hewson, P. W. (1983). Effect of instruction using students' prior knowledge and conceptual change strategies on science learning. *Journal of Research in Science Teaching, 20,* 731–743.

Heyns, B. (1978). *Summer learning and the effects of schooling.* New York: Academic Press.

Hickling, A. K. & Gelman, S. A. (1995). How does your garden grow? Early conceptualization of seeds and their place in plant growth cycle. *Child Development, 66,* 856–876.

Hiebert, J. (1987). *Conceptual and procedural knowledge: The case of mathematics.* Hillsdale, NJ: Erlbaum.

Hiebert, J. & Behr, M. (1988). *Number concepts and operations in the middle grades.* Hillsdale, NJ: Erlbaum.

Hiebert, J. & LeFevre, P. (1987). Conceptual and procedural knowledge in mathematics: An introductory analysis. In J. Hiebert (Ed.), *Conceptual and procedural knowledge in mathematics* (pp. 1–27). Hillsdale, NJ: Lawrence Erlbaum.

Hildreth, K. & Rovee-Collier, C. (1999). Decreases in the response latency to priming over the first year of life. *Developmental Psychobiology, 35,* 276–290.

Hillocks, G. (1989). Synthesis of research on teaching writing. *Educational Leadership, 44,* 71–82.

Hinsley, D. A., Hayes, J. R., & Simon, H. A. (1977). From words to equations: Meaning and representation in algebra word problems. In P. A. Carpenter & M. A. Just (Eds.), *Cognitive processes in comprehension.* Hillsdale, NJ: Erlbaum.

Hintzman, D. L. (1986). "Schema abstraction" in a multiple-trace memory model. *Psychological Review, 93,* 411–428.

Hogan, K. (1999). Thinking aloud together: A test of an intervention to foster students' collaborative scientific reasoning. *Journal of Research in Science Teaching, 36,* 1085–1109.

Holden, G. W. (1988). Adults thinking about a childrearing problem: Effects of experience, parental status, and gender. *Child Development, 59,* 1623–1632.

Hunt, J. M. (1964). *Intelligence and experience.* New York: Ronald Press.

Hunt, K. W. (1970). Syntactic maturity in school children and adults. *Monographs of the Society for Research in Child Development, 35* (No. 134).

Huttenlocher, J., Levine, S., & Vevea, J. (1998). Environmental input and cognitive growth: A study using time-period comparisons. *Child Development, 69,* 1012–1029.

Hynd, G. W., Marshall, R., & Gonzales, J. (1991). Learning disabilities and presumed central nervous system dysfunction. *Learning Disability Quarterly, 14,* 283–296.

Hyde, J. S., Fennema, E., & Lamon, S. J. (1990). Gender differences in mathematical performance: A meta-analysis. *Psychological Bulletin, 107,* 139–155.

Hyde, J. S. & Linn, M. C. (1988). Gender differences in verbal ability: A meta-analysis. *Psychological Bulletin, 104,* 53–69.

Inagaki, K. & Hatano, G. (1993). Young children's understanding of the mind-body distinction. *Child Development, 64,* 1534–1549.

Inhelder, B. & Piaget, J. (1958). *The growth of logical thinking from childhood to adolescence.* New York: Basic Books.

Inhelder, B. & Piaget, J. (1964). *The early growth of logic in the child.* New York: Basic Books.

Inhelder, B. & Piaget, J. (1969). *The psychology of the child.* New York: Basic Books.

Iverson, B. K. & Walberg, H. J. (1982). Home environment and school learning: A qualitative synthesis. *Journal of Experimental Education, 50,* 144–151.

Iverson, S. & Tunmer, W. E. (1993). Phonological processing skills and the reading recovery program. *Journal of Educational Psychology, 85,* 112–126.

Jackson, N. E. (1992). Precocious reading of English: Origins, structure, and predictive significance. In P. S. Klein & A. J. Tannenbaum (Eds.), *To be young and gifted.* Norwood, NJ: Ablex Publishing.

Janis, I. L. (1989). *Crucial decisions.* New York: The Free Press.

Jensen, A. R. (1969). How much can we boost IQ and scholastic achievement? *Harvard Educational Review, 39,* 1–123.

Jensen, A. R. (1987). The *g* factor beyond factor analysis. In R. R. Roning, J. A. Glover, J. C. Conoley, & J. C. Witt (Eds.), *The influence of cognitive psychology on testing.* Hillsdale, NJ: Erlbaum.

Johnson, D. W. & Johnson, R. T. (1987). *Learning together and alone.* Englewood Cliffs, NJ: Prentice-Hall.

Johnson, M. L. (1989). Minority differences in mathematics. In M. M. Lindquist (Ed.), *Results from the fourth mathematics assessment of the national assessment of educational progress* (pp. 135–148). Reston, VA: National Council of Teachers of Mathematics.

Johnson-Laird, P. N., Savary, F., & Bucciarelli, M. (2000). Strategies and tactics in reasoning. In W. Schaeken, & G. De Vooght (Eds.), *Deductive reasoning and strategies.* (pp. 209–240). Mahwah, NJ: Erlbaum.

Johnston, P. & Afflerbach, P. (1985). The process of constructing main ideas from text. *Cognition and Instruction, 2,* 207–232.

de Jong, P. F. & van der Leij, A. (1999). Specific contributions of phonological abilities to early reading acquisition: Results from a Dutch latent variable longitudinal study. *Journal of Educational Psychology, 91,* 450–476.

Just, M. A. & Carpenter, P. A. (1987). *The psychology of reading and language comprehension.* Boston: Allyn & Bacon.

Kail, R. V. (1990). *The development of memory* (3rd edition). New York: W. H. Freeman.

Kail, R. V. (1991). Developmental changes in speed of processing during childhood and adolescence. *Psychological Bulletin, 109,* 490–501.

Kail, R. V. (1996). Nature and consequences of developmental change in speed of processing. *Swiss Journal of Psychology, 55,* 133–138.

Kalish, C. (1996). Preschoolers' understanding of germs as invisible mechanisms. *Cognitive Development, 11,* 83–106.

Kalish, C. (1997). Preschoolers' understanding of mental and bodily reactions to contamination: What you don't know can hurt you, but cannot sadden you. *Developmental Psychology, 33,* 79–91.

Kalish, C. (1998). Reasons and causes: Children's understanding of conformity to social and physical laws. *Child Development, 69,* 706–720.

Kaput, J. J. (1999). Teaching and learning a new algebra. In E. Fennema & T. A. Romberg (Eds.), *Mathematics classrooms that promote understanding* (pp. 133–156). Mahwah, NJ: Erlbaum.

Karmiloff-Smith, A. (1984). Children's problem-solving. In M. E. Lamb, A. L. Brown, & B. Rogoff (Eds.), *Advances in developmental psychology* (Vol. 3, pp. 39–90). Hillsdale, NJ: Erlbaum.

Karmiloff-Smith, A. (1995). *Beyond modularity: A developmental perspective on cognitive science.* Cambridge, MA: MIT Press.

Karmiloff-Smith, A. & Inhelder, B. (1974). If you want to get ahead, get a theory. *Cognition, 3,* 195–212.

Keating, D. P. (1980). Thinking processes in adolescence. In J. Adelson (Ed.), *Handbook of adolescent psychology* (pp. 211–246). New York: Wiley.

Keil, F. C. (1991). Theories, concepts, and the acquisition of word meaning. In S. A. Gelman & J. P. Byrnes (Eds.), *Perspective on language and thought: Interrelations in development* (pp. 197–223). Cambridge: Cambridge University Press.

Kelemen, D. (1999). Why are rocks pointy? Children's preference for teleological explanations of the natural world. *Developmental Psychology, 35,* 1440–1452.

Kellogg, R. T. (1996). A model of working memory in writing. In C. M. Levy & S. Ransdell (Eds.), *The science of writing: Theories, methods, individual differences, and applications* (pp. 57–72). Mahwah, NJ: Erlbaum.

Kelly, K. R. (1993). The relation of gender and academic achievement to career self-efficacy and interests. *Gifted Child Quarterly, 37,* 59–64.

Kessler, B. & Treiman, R. (1997). Syllable structure and the distribution of phonemes in English syllables. *Journal of Memory and Language, 37,* 295–311.

Kieran, C. (1989). The early learning of algebra: A structural perspective. In S. Wagner & C. Kieran (Eds.), *Research issues in the learning and teaching of algebra* (pp. 33–56). Reston, VA: National Council of Teachers of Mathematics.

Kimball, M. M. (1989). A new perspective on women's math achievement. *Psychological Bulletin, 105,* 198–214.

Kintsch, W. (1974). *The representation of meaning in memory.* Hillsdale, NJ: Erlbaum.

Kintsch, W. (1982). Text representations. In W. Otto & S. White (Eds.), *Reading expository material* (pp. 87–102). New York: Academic Press.

Kintsch, W. & Greeno, J. G. (1985). Understanding and solving arithmetic word problems. *Psychological Review, 92,* 109–129.

Kipp, K., Pope, S., & Digby, S. E. (1998). The development of cognitive inhibition in a reading comprehension task. *European Review of Applied Psychology, 48,* 19–25.

Klaczynski, P. A. (1997). Bias in adolescents' everyday reasoning and its relationship with intellectual ability, personal theories, and self-serving motivation. *Developmental Psychology, 33,* 273–283.

Klaczynski, P. A., Byrnes, J. P., & Jacobs, J. E. (in press). Introduction to the special issue on decision-making. *Journal of Applied Developmental Psychology.*

Klaczynski, P. A. & Narasimham, G. (1998). Development of scientific reasoning biases: Cognitive versus ego-protective explanations. *Developmental Psychology, 34,* 175–187.

Klahr, D. & Dunbar, K. (1988). Dual space search during scientific reasoning. *Cognitive Science, 12,* 1–48.

Klahr, D. & MacWhinney, B. (1998). Information processing. In W. Damon (series ed.), D. Kuhn & R. S. Siegler (volume eds.), *Handbook of child psychology: Vol. 2. Cognition, perception and language* (pp. 631–678). New York: Wiley.

Klayman, J. & Ha, Y. (1987). Confirmation, disconfirmation, and information in hypothesis testing. *Psychological Review, 94,* 211–228.

Knudson, R. E. (1992). The development of written argumentation: An analysis and comparison of argumentative writing at four grade levels. *Child Study Journal, 22,* 167–181.

Koslowski, B. & Maqueda, M. (1993). What is confirmation bias and when do people actually have it? *Merrill-Palmer Quarterly, 39,* 104–130.

Koslowski, B. & Okagaki, L. (1986). Non-Humean indices of causation in problem-solving situations: Causal mechanism, analogous effects, and the status of rival alternative accounts. *Child Development, 57,* 1100–1108.

Kosslyn, S. M. & Koenig, O. (1992). *Wet mind: the new cognitive neuroscience.* New York: Free Press.

Kreutzer, M. A., Leonard, C., & Flavell, J. H. (1975). An interview study of children's knowledge about memory. *Monographs of the Society for Research in Child Development, 40* (No. 159).

Kuhn, D. (1992). Piaget's child as scientist. In H. Beilin & P. Pufall (Eds.), *Piaget's theory: Prospects and possibilities* (pp. 185–210). Hillsdale, NJ: Erlbaum.

Kuhn, D. (1997). Constraints or guideposts? Developmental psychology and science education. *Review of Educational Research, 67,* 141–150.

Kuhn, D., Amsel, E., & O'Loughlin, M. (1988). *The development of scientific thinking skills.* New York: Academic Press.

Kuhn, D. & Brannock, J. (1977). Development of the isolation of variable scheme in experimental and 'natural experience' contexts. *Developmental Psychology, 13,* 9–14.

Kuhn, D., Garcia-Mila, M., Zohar, A., & Anderson, C. (1995). Strategies of knowledge acquisition.

Monographs of the Society for Research in Child Development, 60 (4, serial no. 245).

Kuhn, T. S. (1962). *The structure of scientific revolutions.* Chicago, IL: University of Chicago Press.

Laboratory of Comparative Human Cognition (1983). Culture and cognitive development. In P. H. Mussen (Ed.), *Handbook of child psychology* (Vol. 4, *History, theory, and methods,* pp. 296–355). New York: Wiley.

Lakatos, I. (1971). Falsification and the methodology of scientific research programmes. In I. Lakatos & A. Musgrave (Eds.), *Criticism and the growth of knowledge* (pp. 91–180). Cambridge: Cambridge University Press.

Lakoff, G. (1987). *Women, fire, and dangerous things: What categories reveal about the mind.* Chicago: University of Chicago Press.

Lakoff, R. (1973). Language and women's place. *Language and Society, 2,* 45–79.

Langer, J. A. (1986). *Children's reading and writing: Structures and strategies.* Norwood, NJ: Ablex.

Lasnick, H. (1990). Syntax. In D. N. Osherson & H. Lasnik (Eds.), *An invitation to cognitive science* (Vol. 1: *Language,* pp. 5–22). Cambridge, MA: MIT Press.

Lau, I. C., Yeung, A. S., Jin, P., & Low, R. (1999). Toward a hierarchical, multidimensional English self-concept. *Journal of Educational Psychology, 91,* 747–755.

Lavoie, D. R. (1999). Effects of emphasizing hypothetico-predictive reasoning within the science learning cycle on high school student's process skills and conceptual understandings in biology. *Journal of Research in Science Teaching, 36,* 1127–1147.

Leder, G. C. (1992). Mathematics and gender: Changing perspectives. In D. A. Grouws (Ed.), *Handbook of research on mathematical teaching and learning* (pp. 597–624). New York: Macmillan.

Lehrer, R. & Schauble, L. (1998). Reasoning about structure and function: Children's conceptions of gears. *Journal of Research in Science Teaching, 35,* 3–25.

Leslie, L. & Allen, L. (1999). Factors that predict success in an early literacy intervention project. *Reading Research Quarterly, 34,* 404–424.

Levstik, L. S. & Barton, K. (1996). They still use some of their past: Historical salience in elementary children's chronological thinking. *Journal of Curriculum Studies, 28,* 531–576.

Levstik, L. S. & Pappas, C. C. (1987). Exploring the development of historical understanding. *Journal of Research and Development in Education, 21,* 1–15.

Lewis, A. B. & Mayer, R. E. (1987). Students' miscomprehension of relational statements in arithmetic word problems. *Journal of Educational Psychology, 79,* 363–371.

Liben, L. S. & Downs, R. M. (1993). Understanding person-space-map relations: Cartographic and developmental perspectives. *Developmental Psychology, 29,* 739–752.

Liberman, I. Y., Shankweiler, D., Fischer, F. W., & Carter, B. (1974). Explicit syllable and phoneme segmentation in the young child. *Journal of Experimental Child Psychology, 18,* 201–212.

Linn, M. C. (1978). Influence of cognitive style and training on tasks requiring formal thought. *Child Development, 49,* 874–877.

Linn, M. C. (1986). Science. In R. F. Dillon & R. J. Sternberg (Eds.), *Cognition and instruction* (pp. 155–204). New York: Academic Press.

Linn, M. C., Clement, C., & Pulos, S. (1983). Is it formal if it's not physics? (The influence of content on formal reasoning). *Journal of Research in Science Teaching, 20,* 755–770.

Linn, M. C. & Hyde, J. S. (1989). Gender, mathematics, and science. *Educational Researcher, 18,* 17–27.

Linn, M. C. & Kessel, C. (1996). Success in mathematics: Increasing talent and gender diversity among college majors. *CBMS Issues in Mathematics Education, 6,* 101–144.

Linn, M. C., Pulos, S., & Gans, A. (1981). Correlates of formal reasoning: Content and problem effects. *Journal of Research in Science Teaching, 18,* 435–447.

Linn, M. C. & Songer, N. B. (1993). How do students make sense of science? *Merrill-Palmer Quarterly, 39,* 47–73.

Linn, M. C. & Swiney, J. (1981). Individual differences in formal thought: Role of expectations and aptitudes. *Journal of Educational Psychology, 73,* 274–286.

Lipman, M. (1985). Thinking skills fostered by philosophy for children. In J. W. Segal, S. F. Chipman, & R. Glaser (Eds.), *Thinking and learning skills: Vol. 1: Relating instruction to research.* Hillsdale, NJ: Erlbaum.

Loban, D. W. (1976). *Language development: Kindergarten through grade twelve* (Research Report No. 18). Urbana, IL: National Council of Teachers of English.

Low, R. & Over, R. (1993). Gender differences in solution of algebraic word problems containing irrelevant information. *Journal of Educational Psychology, 85,* 331–339.

Luciana, M. & Nelson, C. A. (1998). The functional emergence of prefrontally-guided working memory systems in four- to eight-year-old children. *Neuropsychologia, 36,* 273–293.

Luria, A. R. (1973). *The working brain*. New York: Basic Books.

Lutkus, A. D., Weiss, A. R., Campbell, J. R., Mazzeo, J., & Lazer, S. (1999). *The NAEP 1998 Civics Report Card for the Nation*. Washington, D.C.: U.S. Department of Education, Office of Educational Research and Improvement, National Center for Educational Statistics.

Ma, X. & Kishor, N. (1997). Assessing the relationship between attitude toward mathematics and achievement in mathematics: A meta-analysis. *Journal for Research in Mathematics Education, 28,* 26–47.

Maccoby, E. & Jacklin, C. N. (1974). *The psychology of sex differences*. Stanford, CA: Stanford University Press.

MacIver, D. (1987). Classroom factors and student characteristics predicting students' use of achievement standards during ability self-assessment. *Child Development, 58,* 1258–1271.

Magliano, J. P., Trabasso, T., & Graesser, A. C. (1999). Strategic processing during comprehension. *Journal of Educational Psychology, 91,* 615–629.

Mandler, J. M. & Johnson, N. S. (1977). Remembrance of things parsed: Story structure and recall. *Cognitive Psychology, 9,* 111–151.

Mandler, J. M. & McDonough, L. (1996). Drinking and driving don't mix: Inductive generalization in infancy. *Cognition, 59,* 307–335.

Markman, E. M. (1979). Realizing that you don't understand: Elementary school children's awareness of inconsistencies. *Child Development, 50,* 643–655.

Markman, E. M. (1981). Comprehension monitoring. In W. P. Dickson (Ed.), *Children's oral communication skills*. New York: Academic Press.

Markovits, Z. & Sowder, J. (1994). Developing number sense: An intervention study in grade 7. *Journal for Research in Mathematics Education, 25,* 4–29.

Marr, D. (1982). *Vision: A computational investigation into the human representation and processing of visual information*. San Francisco: W. H. Freeman.

Marsh, H. W. (1989). Age and sex effects in multiple dimensions of self-concept: Preadolescence to early adulthood. *Journal of Educational Psychology, 81,* 417–430.

Marsh, H. W., Barnes, J., Cairns, L., & Tidman, M. (1984). The self-description questionnaire (SDQ): Age effects in the structure and level of self-concept for preadolescent children. *Journal of Educational Psychology, 76,* 940–956.

Marsh, H. W., Hey, J., Roche, L. A., & Perry, C. (1997). Structure of physical self-concept: Elite athletes and physical education students. *Journal of Educational Psychology, 89,* 369–380.

Martin, V. L. & Pressley, M. (1991). Elaborative-interrogation effects depend on the nature of the question. *Journal of Educational Psychology, 83,* 113–119.

Martorano, S. C. (1977). A developmental analysis of performance on Piaget's formal operations tasks. *Developmental Psychology, 13,* 666–672.

Matz, M. (1982). Towards a process model for high school algebra errors. In D. Sleeman & J. S. Brown (Eds.), *Intelligent tutoring systems* (pp. 25–50). New York: Academic Press.

Mayer, R. E. (1979). Twenty years of research on advance organizers: Assimilation theory is still the best predictor of results. *Instructional Science, 8,* 133–167.

Mayer, R. E. (1982). Memory for algebra story problem. *Journal of Educational Psychology, 74,* 199–216.

Mayer, R. E. (1987). *Educational Psychology*. Boston: Little Brown.

Mayer, R. E. (1989). Models for understanding. *Review of Educational Research, 59,* 43–64.

Mayer, R. E., Larkin, J. H., & Kaldane, J. B. (1984). A cognitive analysis of mathematical problem-solving ability. In R. J. Sternberg (Ed.), *Advances in the psychology of human intelligence* (pp. 231–273). Hillsdale, NJ: Erlbaum.

McCann, T. M. (1989). Student argumentative writing knowledge and ability at three grade levels. *Research in the Teaching of English, 23,* 62–72.

McCarthy, R. A. & Warrington, E. K. (1990). *Cognitive neuropsychology: A clinical introduction*. San Diego: Academic Press.

McClelland, J. L. & Rumelhart, D. E. (1981). An interactive model of context effects in letter perception: I: An account of the basic findings. *Psychological Review, 88,* 375–407.

McCloskey, M. (1983). Naive theories of motion. In D. Gentner & A. L. Stevens (Eds.), *Mental Models* (pp. 299–324). Hillsdale, NJ: Erlbaum.

McCloskey, M., Aliminosa, D., & Sokol, S. M. (1991). Facts, rules, and procedures in normal calculation: Evidence from multiple single-patient studies of impaired arithmetic fact retrieval. *Brain and Cognition, 17,* 154–203.

McCloskey, M., Caramazza, A., & Basili, A. (1985). Cognitive mechanisms in number processing and calculation: Evidence from dyscalculia. *Brain and Cognition, 4,* 171–196.

McCutchen, D. (1986). Domain knowledge and linguistic knowledge in the development of writing ability. *Journal of Memory and Language, 25,* 431–444.

McCutchen, D., Covill, A., Hoyne, S. H., & Mildes, K. (1994). Individual differences in writing: Implications of translating fluency. *Journal of Educational Psychology, 86,* 256–266.

McCutchen, D., Francis, M., & Kerr, S. (1997). Revising for meaning: Effects of knowledge and strategy. *Journal of Educational Psychology, 89,* 667–676.

McCutchen, D. & Perfetti, C. A. (1982). Coherence and connectedness in the development of discourse production. *Text, 2,* 113–139.

McDaniel, M. A., Einstein, G. O., Dunay, P. K., & Cobb, R. S. (1986). Encoding difficulty and memory: Toward a unifying theory. *Journal of Memory and Language, 25,* 645–656.

McDaniel, M. A., Waddill, P. J., & Einstein, G. O. (1988). A contextual account of the generation effect: A three factor theory. *Journal of Memory and Language, 27,* 521–536.

McGee, L. M. (1982). Awareness of text structure: Effects on children's recall of expository text. *Reading Research Quarterly, 17,* 581–591.

McKeown, M. G. & Beck, I. L. (1990). The assessment and charactertization of young learners' knowledge of a topic in history. *American Educational Research Journal, 27,* 688–726.

McKeown, M. G., Beck, I. L., Omanson, R. C., & Perfetti, C. A. (1983). The effects of long-term vocabulary instruction on reading comprehension: A replication. *Journal of Reading Behavior, 15,* 3–18.

McKoon, G. & Ratcliff, R. (1992). Inference during reading. *Psychological Review, 99,* 440–466.

McLean, J. F. & Hitch, G. J. (1999). Working memory impairments in children with specific arithmetic learning difficulties. *Journal of Experimental Child Psychology, 74,* 240–260.

Meehan, A. M. (1984). A meta-analysis of sex differences in formal operational thought. *Child Development, 55,* 1110–1124.

Metsala, J. L. (1999). Young children's phonological awareness and nonword repetition as a function of vocabulary development. *Journal of Educational Psychology, 91,* 3–19.

Metsala, J. L., Stanovich, K. E., & Brown, D. A. (1998). Regularity effects and the phonological deficit model of reading disabilities: A meta-analytic review. *Journal of Educational Psychology, 90,* 279–293.

Metsala, J. L. & Walley, A. C. (1998). Spoken vocabulary growth and the segmental restructuring of lexical representations: Precursors to phonemic awareness and early reading ability. In J. L. Metsala & L. C. Ehri (Eds.), *Word recognition in beginning literacy* (pp. 89–120). Mahwah, NJ: Erlbaum.

Metz, K. (1995). Reassessment of developmental constraints on children's science instruction. *Review of Educational Research, 65,* 93–127.

Meyer, B. J. F. (1985). Prose analysis: Purposes, procedures, and problems. In B. K. Britton & J. B. Black (Eds.), *Understanding expository text* (pp. 11–66). Hillsdale, NJ: Erlbaum.

Meyer, B. J. F., Brandt, D. M., & Bluth, G. J. (1980). Use of top-level structure in text: Key for reading comprehension of ninth-grade students. *Reading Research Quarterly, 16,* 73–103.

Miller, G. A. (1956). The magical number seven, plus or minus two: Some limits on our capacity for processing information. *Psychological Review, 63,* 81–97.

Miller, G. E., Giovenco, A., & Rentiers, K. A. (1987). Fostering comprehension monitoring in below average readers through self-instruction training. *Journal of Reading Behavior, 19,* 303–317.

Mix, K. S. (1999). Preschoolers' recognition of numerical equivalence. *Journal of Experimental Child Psychology, 74,* 309–332.

Montague, M., Maddux, C. D., & Dereshiwsky, M. I. (1990). Story grammar and comprehension and production of narrative prose by students with learning disabilities. *Journal of Learning Disabilities, 23,* 190–197.

Morales, R. V., Shute, V. J., & Pelligrino, J. W. (1985). Developmental differences in understanding and solving simple mathematics word problems. *Cognition and Instruction, 2,* 59–89.

Morphett, M. & Washburn, C. (1931). When should children begin to read? *Elementary School Journal, 31,* 496–503.

Moshman, D. (1998). Cognitive development beyond childhood. In W. Damon (series ed.), D. Kuhn & R. S. Siegler (volume eds.), *Handbook of child psychology: Vol. 2. Cognition, perception and language* (pp. 997–1016). New York: Wiley.

Moss, J. & Case, R. (1999). Developing children's understanding of the rational numbers: A new model and an experimental curriculum. *Journal for Research in Mathematics Education, 30,* 122–147.

Muir, S. P. (1985). Understanding and improving students' map reading skills. *The Elementary School Journal, 86,* 207–216.

Murphy, G. L. & Medin, D. L. (1985). The role of theories in conceptual coherence. *Psychological Review, 92,* 289–316.

Mynatt, C. R., Doherty, M. E., & Tweney, R. D. (1977). Confirmation bias in a simulated research environment: An experimental study of scientific influence. *Quarterly Journal of Experimental Psychology, 29,* 85–95.

Nagle, R. J. (1979). The predictive validity of the metropolitan readiness tests, 1976 edition. *Educational and Psychological Measurement, 39,* 1043–1045.

Nagy, W., Herman, P., & Anderson, R. (1985). Learning words from context. *Reading Research Quarterly, 20,* 233–253.

National Council of Teachers of Mathematics (1989). *Curriculum and evaluation standards for school mathematics.* Reston, VA: Author.

National Council of Teachers of Mathematics (1998). *Principles and standards for school mathematics: Discussion draft.* Reston, VA: Author.

Neisser, U. (1967). *Cognitive psychology.* New York: Appleton-Century-Crofts.

Nell, V. (1988). The psychology of reading for pleasure: Needs and gratification. *Reading Research Quarterly, 23,* 6–50.

Nelson, K. (1986). *Event knowledge: Structure and function in development.* Hillsdale, NJ: Erlbaum.

Nelson, K. (1991). The matter of time: Interdependencies between language and thought in development. In S. A. Gelman & J. P. Byrnes (Eds.), *Perspectives on language and thought: Interrelations in development* (pp. 278–318). Cambridge: Cambridge University Press.

Newell, A. & Rosenbloom, P. S. (1981). Mechanisms of skills acquisition and the law of practice. In J. R. Anderson (Ed.), *Cognitive skills and their acquisition.* Hillsdale, NJ: Erlbaum.

Newell, A. & Simon, H. A. (1972). *Human problem solving.* Englewood Cliffs, NJ: Prentice-Hall.

Newman, R. (1991). Goals and self-regulated learning: What motivates children to seek academic help? In M. Maehr & P. Pintrich (Eds.), *Advances in motivation and achievement, Vol. 7* (pp. 151–183). Greenwich, CT: JAI Press.

Newmann, F. M. (1990). Higher order thinking in teaching social studies: A rationale for the assessment for classroom thoughtfulness. *Journal of Curriculum Studies, 22,* 41–56.

Nicholls, J. (1983). Conceptions of ability and achievement motivation: A theory and its implications for education. In S. Paris, G. Olson, & H. Stevenson (Eds.), *Learning and motivation in the classroom* (pp. 211–237). Hillsdale, NJ: Erlbaum.

Nickerson, R. S., Perkins, D. N., & Smith, E. E. (1985). *The teaching of thinking.* Hillsdale, NJ: Erlbaum.

Nisbett, R. E. & Ross, L. (1980). *Human inference: Strategies and shortcomings of social judgment.* Englewood Cliffs, NJ: Prentice Hall.

Norris, J. A. & Bruning, R. H. (1988). Cohesion in the narratives of good and poor readers. *Journal of Speech and Hearing Disorders, 53,* 416–424.

O'Boyle, M. W. & Benbow, C. P. (1990). Enhanced right hemisphere involvement during cognitive processing may relate to intellectual precocity. *Neuropsychologia, 28,* 211–216.

O'Boyle, M. W. & Gill, H. S. (1998). On the relevance of research findings in cognitive neuroscience to educational practice. *Educational Psychology Review, 10,* 397–410.

Oldfield, R. C. (1971). The assessment and analysis of handedness: The Edinburgh inventory. *Neuropsychologia, 9,* 97–113.

Ornstein, P. A. & Naus, M. J. (1985). Effects of the knowledge base on children's memory strategies. In H. W. Reese (Ed.), *Advances in child development and behavior* (Vol. 19). New York: Academic Press.

O'Sullivan, C. Y., Reese, C. M., & Mazzeo, J. (1997). *The NAEP 1996 Science report card for the nation and the states.* Washington, D.C.: U.S. Department of Education, Office of Educational Research and Improvement, National Center for Educational Statistics.

Overton, W. F. (1990). Competence and procedures: Constraints on the development of logical reasoning. In W. F. Overton (Ed.), *Reasoning, necessity and logic: Developmental perspectives* (pp. 1–32). Hillsdale, NJ: Erlbaum.

Overton, W. F. & Byrnes, J. P. (1991). Cognitive development. In R. M. Lerner, A. C. Petersen, & J. Brooks-Gunn (Eds.), *Encyclopedia of adolescence* (Vol. 1 pp. 151–156). New York: Garland Publishing.

Overton, W. F. & Meehan, A. M. (1982). Individual differences in formal operational thought: Sex role and learned helplessness. *Child Development, 53,* 1536–1543.

Page-Voth, V. & Graham, S. (1999). Effects of goal setting and strategy use on the writing performance and self-efficacy of students with writing and learning problems. *Journal of Educational Psychology, 91,* 230–240.

Paige, J. M. & Simon, H. A. (1966). Cognitive processes in solving algebra word problems. In B. Kleinmuntz (Ed.), *Problem-solving: Research, method, and theory.* New York: Wiley.

Paivio, A. (1971). *Imagery and verbal processes.* New York: Holt, Rinehart & Winston.

Pajares, F., Miller, M. D., & Johnson, M. J. (1999). Gender differences in writing self-beliefs of elementary school students. *Journal of Educational Psychology, 91,* 50–61.

Palincsar, A. M. & Brown, A. L. (1984). Reciprocal teaching of comprehension-fostering and comprehension-monitoring activities. *Cognition and Instruction, 1,* 117–175.

Pallas, A. M. & Alexander, K. L. (1983). Sex differences in quantitative SAT performance: New evidence on the differential coursework hypothesis. *American Educational Research Journal, 20,* 165–182.

Palmer, D. H. (1997). Students' application of the concept of interdependence to the issue of preservation of species: Observations on the ability to generalize. *Journal of Research in Science Teaching, 34,* 837–850.

Paris, S. G. (1975). Integration and inference in children's comprehension and memory. In F. Restle, R. Shiffrin, J. Castellan, H. Lindman, & D. Pisoni (Eds.), *Cognitive theory* (Vol. 1). Hillsdale, NJ: Erlbaum.

Paris, S. G. (1978). Coordination of means and goals in the development of mnemonic skills. In P. A. Ornstein (Ed.), *Memory development in children.* Hillsdale, NJ: Erlbaum.

Paris, S. G. & Byrnes, J. P. (1989). The constructivist approach to self-regulation and learning in the classroom. In B. J. Zimmerman & D. H. Schunk (Eds.), *Self-regulated learning and academic achievement: Theory, research, and practice.* New York: Springer Verlag.

Paris, S. G., Byrnes, J. P., & Paris, A. H. (in press). Constructing theories, identities, and actions of self-regulated learners. In B. Zimmerman & D. Schunk (Eds.). *Self-regulated learning: Theories, research, practice* (2nd edition). New York: Guilford.

Paris, S. G., Wasik, B. A., & Turner, J. C. (1991). The development of strategic readers. In R. Barr, M. L. Kamil, P. B. Mosenthal, & P. D. Pearson (Eds.), *Handbook of reading research, Vol. II* (pp. 609–640). New York: Longman.

Parsons, J., Kaczala, C., & Meece, J. (1982). Socialization of achievement attitudes and beliefs: Classroom influences. *Child Development, 53,* 322–339.

Parsons, J. E. & Ruble, D. N. (1977). The development of achievement-related expectancies. *Child Development, 48,* 1075–1079.

Patrick, J. J. & Hoge, J. D. (1991). Teaching government, civics, and the law. In J. P. Shaver (Ed.), *Handbook of social studies teaching and learning* (pp. 427–436). New York: MacMillan.

Pearson, P. D. & Fielding, L. (1991). Comprehension instruction. In M. Barr, M. L. Kamil, P. B. Mosenthal, & P. D. Pearson (Eds.), *Handbook of reading research, Vol. II* (pp. 815–861). New York: Longman.

Penner, D. E., Giles, N. D., Lehrer, R., & Schauble, L. (1997). Building functional models: Designing an elbow. *Journal of Research in Science Teaching, 34,* 125–143.

Perfetti, C. A. (1985). *Reading ability.* New York: Oxford University Press.

Perfetti, C. A. & McCutchen, D. (1987). Schooled language competence: Linguistic abilities in reading and writing. In S. Rosenberg (Ed.), *Advances in applied psycholinguistics* (pp. 105–141). Cambridge: Cambridge University Press.

Perkins, D. N., Jay, E., & Tishman, S. (1993). Beyond abilities: A dispositional theory of thinking. *Merrill-Palmer Quarterly, 39,* 1–21.

Persky, H. R., Reese, C. M., O'Sullivan, C. Y., Lazer, S., Moore, J., & Shakrani, S. (1996). *The 1994 NAEP geography report card for the nation and the states.* Washington, D.C.: U.S. Department of Education, Office of Educational Research and Improvement, National Center for Educational Statistics.

Peterson, P. L., Fennema, E., Carpenter, T. P., & Loef, M. (1989). Teacher's pedagogical content beliefs in mathematics. *Cognition and instruction, 6,* 1–40.

Petersen, S. E., Fox, P. T., Snyder, A. Z., & Raichle, M. E. (1990). Activation of extrastriate and frontal cortical areas by visual words and word-like stimuli. *Science, 240,* 1041–1044.

Piaget, J. (1952). *The origins of intelligence in children.* New York: International Universities Press.

Piaget, J. (1962). *Play, dreams, and imitation in childhood.* New York: Norton.

Piaget, J. (1965). *The child's conception of number.* New York: Norton.

Piaget, J. (1969). *The child's conception of time.* New York: Basic Books.

Piaget, J. (1970). *Structuralism.* New York: Harper & Row.

Piaget, J. (1976). *The grasp of consciousness.* Cambridge, MA: Harvard University Press.

Piaget, J. (1980). *Experiments in contradiction.* Chicago: University of Chicago Press.

Piaget, J. (1983). Piaget's theory. In P. H. Mussen (Ed.), *Handbook of child psychology: Vol. 1. History, theory, methods* (pp. 103–128).

Piaget, J. & Garcia, R. (1974). *Understanding causality.* New York: Basic Books.

Piaget, J. & Inhelder, B. (1969). *The psychology of the child.* New York: Basic Books.

Piburn, M. (1990). Reasoning about logical propositions and success in science. *Journal of Research in Science Teaching, 27,* 887–900.

Pinker, S. (1997). *How the mind works.* New York: Norton.

Pintrich, P. R. & DeGroot, E. V. (1990). Motivational and self-regulated learning components of classroom academic performance. *Journal of Educational Psychology, 82,* 33–40.

Pirie, S. & Kieren, T. (1992). Creating constructivist environments and constructing creative mathematics. *Educational Studies in Mathematics, 23,* 505–528.

Pollitt, E., Gorman, K. S., Engle, P. L., Martorell, R., & Rivera, J. (1993). Early supplemental feeding and cognition: Effects over two decades. *Monographs of the Society for Research in Child Development, 58* (No. 235).

Popper, K. R. (1959). *The logic of scientific discovery.* London: Hutchinson.

Posner, M. I., Peterson, S. E., Fox, P. T., & Raichle, M. E. (1988). Localization of cognitive operations in the human brain. *Science, 240,* 1627–1631.

Post, T. R., Wachsmuth, I., Lesh, R., & Behr, M. J. (1985). Order and equivalence of rational numbers: A cognitive analysis. *Journal for Research in Mathematics Education, 16,* 18–36.

Pressley, M. (1997). The cognitive science of reading: Comments. *Contemporary Educational Psychology, 22,* 247–259.

Pressley, M., Almasi, J., Schuder, T., Bergman, J., Hite, S., El-Dinary, P. B., & Brown, R. (1994). Transactional instruction of comprehension strategies: The Montgomery County Maryland SAIL program. *Reading and Writing Quarterly, 10,* 5–19.

Pressley, M., Borkowski, J. G., & Schneider, W. (1987). Cognitive strategies: Good strategy users coordinate metacognition and knowledge. In R. Vasta & G. Whitehurst (Eds.), *Annals of child development* (Vol. 5, pp. 89–129). Greenwich, CT: JAI.

Pressley, M., Johnson, C. J., Symons, S., McGoldrick, J. A., & Kurita, J. A. (1989). Strategies that improve children's memory and comprehension of text. *Elementary School Journal, 90,* 3–32.

Pressley, M., Levin, J., & Delaney, H. D. (1982). The mnemonic keyword method. *Review of Educational Research, 52,* 61–92.

Presson, C. C. (1982). The development of map-reading skills. *Child Development, 53,* 196–199.

Price, G. B. & Graves, R. L. (1980). Sex differences in syntax and usage in oral and written language. *Research in the Teaching of English, 14,* 147–153.

Pylyshyn, Z. W. (1981). The imagery debate: Analogue media versus tacit knowledge. *Psychological Review, 88,* 16–45.

Pylyshyn, Z. W. (1989). Computing in cognitive science. In M. I. Posner (Ed.), *Foundations of Cognitive Science* (pp. 49–92). Cambridge, MA: MIT Press.

Raaijmakers, J. G. W. & Shiffrin, R. M. (1992). Models for recall and recognition. *Annual Review of Psychology, 43,* 205–234.

Raghavan, K., Sartoris, M. L., & Glaser, R. (1998). Why does it go up? The impact of the MARS curriculum as revealed through changes in student explanations of a helium balloon. *Journal of Research in Science Teaching, 35,* 547–567.

Randhawa, B. S., Beamer, J. E., & Lundberg, I. (1993). Role of mathematics self-efficacy in the structural model of mathematics achievement. *Journal of Educational Psychology, 85,* 41–48.

Randel, M. A., Fry, M. A., & Ralls, E. M. (1977). Two readiness measures as predictors of first and third grade reading achievement. *Psychology in the Schools, 14,* 37–40.

Ransdell, S. & Levy, C. M. (1996). Working memory constraints on writing quality and fluency. In C. M. Levy & S. Ransdell (Eds.), *The science of writing: Theories, methods, individual differences, and applications* (pp. 93–106). Mahwah, NJ: Erlbaum.

Rapcsak, S. Z. (1997). Disorders of writing. In L. J. Gonzalez Rothi & K. M. Heilman (Eds.), *Apraxia: The neuropsychology of action* (pp. 149–172). London: Taylor & Francis.

Raynor, K. & Pollatsek, A. (1989). *The psychology of reading.* Englewood Cliffs, NJ: Prentice-Hall.

Rauscher, F. H., Shaw, G. L., Levine, L. J., Wright, E. L., Dennis, W. R., & Newcomb, R. L. (1997). Music training causes long-term enhancement of preschool children's spatial-temporal reasoning. *Neurological Research, 19,* 2–8.

Recht, D. R. & Leslie, L. (1988). Effect of prior knowledge on good and poor readers' memory of text. *Journal of Educational Psychology, 80,* 16–20.

Reese, C. M., Miller, K. E., Mazzeo, J., & Dossey, J. A. (1997). *The NAEP 1996 mathematics report card for the nation and the states.* Washington, D.C.: U.S. Department of Education, Office of Educational Research and Improvement, National Center for Educational Statistics.

Renninger, K. A. (1991). Individual interest and development: Implications for theory and practice. In K. A. Renninger, S. Hidi, & A. Krapp (Eds.), *The role of interest in learning and development* (pp. 361–396). Hillsdale, NJ: Erlbaum.

Renninger, K. A., Hidi, S., & Krapp, A. (1991). *The role of interest in learning and development.* Hillsdale, NJ: Erlbaum.

Reschly, D. J. & Gresham, F. M. (1989). Current neuropsychological diagnosis of learning problems: A leap of faith. In C. R. Reynolds & E. Fletcher-Janzen (Eds.), *Handbook of clinical child neuropsychology* (pp. 503–519). New York: Plenum.

Resnick, L. B. (1980). The role of invention in the development of mathematical competence. In R. H. Kluwe & H. Spada (Eds.), *Developmental models of thinking* (pp. 213–244). New York: Academic Press.

Resnick, L. B. (1983). A developmental theory of number understanding. In H. P. Ginsburg (Ed.), *The development of mathematical thinking* (pp. 109–151). New York: Academic Press.

Resnick, L. B. (1987a). Constructing knowledge in school. In L. S. Liben (Ed.), *Development and learning: Conflict or congruence?* (pp. 19–50). Hillsdale, NJ: Erlbaum.

Resnick, L. B. (1987b). *Education and learning to think.* Washington, D.C.: National Academy Press.

Resnick, L. B., Nesher, P., Leonard, F., Magone, M., Omanson, S., & Peled, I. (1989). Conceptual bases of arithmetic errors: The case of decimal fractions. *Journal for Research in Mathematics Education, 20,* 8–27.

Resnick, L. B., Cauzinille-Marmeche, E., & Mathieu, J. (1987). Understanding algebra. In J. A. Sloboda & D. Rogers (Eds.), *Cognitive processes in mathematics.* Oxford: Oxford University Press.

Resnick, L. B. & Omanson, S. F. (1987). Learning to understand arithmetic. In R. Glaser (Ed.), *Advances in instructional psychology* (Vol. 3, pp. 41–95). Hillsdale, NJ: Erlbaum.

Riley, M. S., Greeno, J. G., & Heller, J. I. (1983). Development of children's problem-solving ability in arithmetic. In H. P. Ginsburg (Ed.), *The development of mathematical thinking* (pp. 62–71). New York: Academic Press.

Rinehart, S. D., Stahl, S. A., & Erickson, L. G. (1986). Some effects of summarization training on reading and studying. *Reading Research Quarterly, 21,* 422–438.

Rittle-Johnson, B. & Alibali, M. W. (1999). Conceptual and procedural knowledge of mathematics: Does one lead to the other? *Journal of Educational Psychology, 91,* 175–189.

Robbins, T. W. & Everitt, B. J. (1995). Arousal systems and attention. In M. S. Gazzaniga (Ed.), *The cognitive neurosciences* (pp. 703–720). Cambridge, MA: MIT Press.

Roberge, J. J. & Flexer, B. K. (1979). Further examination of formal operational reasoning abilities. *Child Development, 50,* 478–484.

Rogers, C. S. (1987). *Kindergarten children's concepts about print.* Unpublished doctoral dissertation. University of Maryland, College Park.

Rokeach, M. (1973). *The nature of human values.* New York: Free Press.

Roller, C. M. (1990). The interaction between knowledge and structure variables in the processing of expository prose. *Reading Research Quarterly, 25,* 80–89.

Romberg, T. A. & Kaput, J. J. (1999). Mathematics worth teaching, mathematics worth understanding. In E. Fennema & T. A. Romberg (Eds.), *Mathematics classrooms that promote understanding* (pp. 1–18). Mahwah, NJ: Erlbaum.

Rosenshine, B. & Meister, C. (1994). Reciprocal teaching: A review of the research. *Review of Educational Research, 64,* 479–530.

Rosenthal, R. (1994). Parametric measures of effect size. In H. Cooper, & L. V. Hedges (Eds.), *The handbook of research synthesis* (pp. 231–244). New York: Russell Sage Foundation.

Roser, N. & Juel, C. (1982). Effects of vocabulary instruction on reading comprehension. In J. Niles & L. Harris (Eds.), *New Inquiries in reading research and instruction* (pp. 110–118). Rochester, NY: National Reading Conference.

Roth, W. M. (1994). Experimenting in a constructivist high school physics laboratory. *Journal of Research in Science Teaching, 31,* 197–223.

Rouet, J. F., Britt, M. A., Mason, R. A., & Perfetti, C. A. (1996). Using multiple sources of evidence to reason about history. *Journal of Educational Psychology, 88,* 478–493.

Rouet, J. F., Favart, M., Britt, M. A., & Perfetti, C. A. (1997). Studying and using multiple documents in history: Effects of discipline expertise. *Cognition and Instruction, 15,* 85–106.

Rovee-Collier, C., Hartshorn, K., & DiRubbo, M. (1999). Long-term maintenance of infant memory. *Developmental Psychobiology, 35,* 91–102.

Royer, J. M., Tronsky, L. N., Chan, Y., Jackson, S. J., & Marchant, H. (1999). Math-fact retrieval and the cognitive mechanism underlying gender differences in math test performance. *Contemporary Educational Psychology, 24,* 181–266.

Rubin, D. C., Hinton, S., & Wenzel, A. (1999). The precise time course of retention. *Journal of Experimental Psychology: Learning, Memory, and Cognition, 25,* 1161–1176.

Rubin, D. L. & Greene, K. (1992). Gender-typical style in written language. *Research in the Teaching of English, 26,* 7–40.

Rumelhart, D. E. (1984). Schemata and the cognitive system. In R. S. Wyler & T. K. Srull (Eds.), *Handbook of social cognition* (Vol. 1, pp. 161–188). Hillsdale, NJ: Erlbaum.

Rumelhart, D. E. (1989). The architecture of min: A connectionist approach. In M. I. Posner (Ed.), *Foundations of cognitive science* (pp. 133–160). Cambridge, MA: MIT Press.

Ryan, R. M. & Deci, E. L. (1996). When paradigms clash: Comments on Cameron and Pierce's claim that rewards to not undermine intrinsic motivation. *Review of Educational Research. 66,* 33–38.

Sa, W. C., West, R. F., & Stanovich, K. E. (1999). The domain specificity and generality of belief bias: Searching for a generalizable critical thinking skill. *Journal of Educational Psychology, 91,* 497–510.

Salomon, G. & Perkins, D. N. (1989). Rocky roads to transfer: Rethinking mechanisms of a neglected phenomenon. *Educational Psychologist, 24,* 113–142.

Sapolsky, R. M. (1999). Glucocorticoids, stress, and their adverse neurological effects: Relevance to aging. *Experimental Gerontology, 34,* 721–732.

Scardamalia, M. & Bereiter, C. (1986). Research on written composition. In M. C. Wittrock (Ed.), *Handbook of research on teaching* (3rd edition, pp. 778–803). New York: Macmillan.

Scardamalia, M., Bereiter, C., & Goelman, H. (1982). The role of production factors in writing ability. In M. Nystrand (Ed.), *What writers know: The language, process, and structure of written discourse.* New York: Academic Press.

Schacter, D. L. (1989). Memory. In M. I. Posner (Ed.), *Foundations of cognitive science* (pp. 683–726). Cambridge, MA: MIT Press.

Schauble, L. (1990). Belief revision in children: The role of prior knowledge and strategies for generating evidence. *Journal of Experimental Child Psychology, 49,* 31–57.

Schilling, T. H. & Clifton, R. K. (1998). Nine-month-old infants learn about physical events in a single session: Implications for infants understanding of physical phenomena. *Cognitive Development, 13,* 165–184.

Schooler, L. J. & Anderson, J. R. (1997). The role of process in the rational analysis of memory. *Cognitive Psychology, 32,* 219–250.

Schmidt, L., Fox, N. A., Goldberg, M. C., Smith, C. C., & Schulkin, J. (1999). Effects of acute prednisone administration on memory, attention and emotion in healthy human adults. *Psychoneuroendocrinology, 24,* 461–483.

Schneider, W. (1985). Developmental trends in the metamemory-memory behavior relationship: An integrative review. In D. L. Forrest-Pressley, G. E. MacKinnon, & T. G. Waller (Eds.), *Cognition, metacognition, and performance.* New York: Academic Press.

Schug, M. C. (1987). Children's understanding of economics. *Elementary School Journal, 87,* 507–518.

Schug, M. C. & Walstad, W. B. (1991). Teaching and learning economics. In J. P. Shaver (Ed.), *Handbook of research on social studies teaching and learning* (pp. 411–419). New York: Macmillan.

Schunk, D. (1991). Goal-setting and self-evaluation: A social-cognitive perspective on self-regulation. In M. Maehr & P. Pintrich (Eds.), *Advances in moti-*

vation and achievement (Vol. 7, pp. 85–113). Greenwich, CT: JAI Press.

Schunk, D. & Rice, J. (1989). Learning goals and children's reading comprehension. *Journal of Reading Behavior, 21,* 279–293.

Schunk, D. H. & Ertmer, P. A. (1999). Self-regulatory processes during computer skill acquisition: Goal and self-evaluative influences. *Journal of Educational Psychology, 91,* 251–260.

Schwartz, B. (1976). *Psychology of learning and behavior* (2nd edition). New York: W. W. Norton.

Schwartz, B. B. & Reznick, J. S. (1999). Measuring infant spatial working memory using a modified delayed-response procedure. *Memory, 7,* 1–17.

Searle, J. (1983). *Intentionality.* Cambridge: Cambridge University Press.

Seidenberg, M. S. & McClelland, J. L. (1989). A distributed, developmental model of word recognition and naming. *Psychological Review, 96,* 523–568.

Segal, J. W., Chipman, S. F., & Glaser, R. (1985). *Thinking and learning skills* (Vols. 1 and 2). Hillsdale, NJ: Erlbaum.

Shapiro, L. R. & Hudson, J. A. (1991). Tell me a make-believe story: Coherence and cohesion in young children's picture-elicited narratives. *Developmental Psychology, 27,* 960–974.

Share, D. & Levin, I. (1999). Learning to read and write in Hebrew. In M. Harris & G. Hatano (Eds.), *Learning to read and write: A cross-linguistic perspective* (pp. 89–111). New York: Cambridge University Press.

Shaywitz, S. E. (1996). Dyslexia. *Scientific American, 94,* 98–104.

Shaywitz, S. E., Shaywitz, B., Fletcher, J. M., & Escobar, M. D. (1990). Prevalence of reading disability in boys and girls. *Journal of the American Medical Association, 264,* 998–1005.

Shaywitz, S. E., Escobar, M. D., Shaywitz, B. A., Fletcher, J. M., & Makuch, R. (1992). Evidence that dyslexia may represent the lower tail of a normal distribution of reading ability. *The New England Journal of Medicine, 326,* 144–150.

Shaywitz, S. E., Shaywitz, B., Pugh, K. R., Fulbright, R. K., Constable, R. T., Mencl, W. E., Shankweiler, D. P., Liberman, A. M., Skudlarksi, P., Fletcher, J. M., Katz, L., Marchione, K. E., Lacadie, C., Gatenby, C., & Gore, J. C. (1998). Functional disruption in the organization of the brain for reading in dyslexia. *Proceedings of the National Academy of Science, 95,* 2636–2641.

Shimamura, A. P. (1995). Memory and frontal lobe function. In M. S. Gazzaniga (Ed.), *The cognitive neu-*

rosciences (pp. 803–813). Cambridge MA: MIT Press.

Shultz, T. R. (1982). Rules of causal attribution. *Monographs of the society for research in child development, 47* (No. 194).

Shustack, M. (1988). Causal thinking. In R. Sternberg & E. E. Smith (Eds.), *The psychology of human thought*. Cambridge, MA: MIT Press.

Siegler, R. S. (1983). Information processing approaches to cognitive development. In P. H. Mussen (Ed.), *Handbook of child psychology: Vol. 1: History, theory, and methods*. New York: Wiley.

Siegler, R. S. (1988). Individual differences in strategy choices: Good students, not-so-good students and perfectionists. *Child Development, 59,* 833–851.

Siegler, R. S. (1989). Hazards of mental chronometry: An example from children's subtraction. *Journal of Educational Psychology, 81,* 497–506.

Siegler, R. S. (1991). *Children's thinking* (2nd Edition). Englewood Cliffs, NJ: Prentice Hall.

Siegler, R. S. (1996). *Emerging minds: The process of change in children's thinking*. New York: Oxford University Press.

Siegler, R. S. (1998). *Children's thinking* (3rd edition). Englewood Cliffs, NJ: Prentice Hall.

Siegler, R. S. & Jenkins, E. A. (1989). *How children discover new strategies*. Hillsdale, NJ: Erlbaum.

Siegler, R. S. & Liebert, R. M. (1975). Acquisition of formal reasoning by 10- and 13-year-olds: Designing a factorial experiment. *Developmental Psychology, 11,* 401–402.

Siegler, R. S. & Thompson, D. R. (1998). "Hey, would you like a nice cold cup of lemonade on this hot day": Children's understanding of economic causation. *Developmental Psychology, 34,* 146–160.

Simon, H. A. (1956). Rational choice and the structure of the environment. *Psychological Review, 63,* 129–138.

Singly, M. K. & Anderson, J. R. (1989). *The transfer of cognitive skill*. Cambridge, MA: Harvard University Press.

Skinner, B. F. (1974). *About behaviorism*. New York: Knofp.

Skinner, E., Chapman, M., & Baltes, P. (1988). Control, means-ends, and agency beliefs. A new conceptualization and its measurement during childhood. *Journal of Personality and Social Psychology, 54,* 117–133.

Slater, W. H., Graves, M. F., & Piche, G. L. (1985). Effects of structural organizers on ninth-grade students' comprehension and recall of four patterns of expository text. *Reading Research Quarterly, 20,* 189–202.

Slavin, R. (1990). *Cooperative learning: Theory, research, practice*. Englewood Cliffs, NJ: Prentice-Hall.

Slavin, R. E., Karweit, N. L., & Wasik, B. A. (1994). *Preventing early school failure: Research, theory, and practice*. Boston: Allyn & Bacon.

Slovic, P. (1990). Choice. In D. N. Osherson & E. E. Smith (Eds.), *Thinking*. Cambridge, MA: MIT Press.

Smith, E. E. (1989). Concepts and induction. In M. I. Posner (Ed.), *Foundations of cognitive science* (pp. 501–526). Cambridge, MA: MIT Press.

Smith, E. E., Jonides, J., & Koeppe, R. A. (1996). Dissociating verbal and spatial working memory using PET. *Cerebral Cortex, 6,* 11–20.

Smith, E. E. & Medin, D. L. (1981). *Categories and concepts*. Cambridge, MA: Harvard University Press.

Smith, L. B., Thelen, E., Titzer, R., & McLin, D. (1999). Knowing in the context of acting: The task dynamics of the A-not-B error. *Psychological Review, 106,* 235–260.

Smith, R. W. & Healy, A. F. (1998). The time-course of the generation effect. *Memory and Cognition, 26,* 135–142.

Snow, C. E., Burns, M. S., & Griffin, P. (1998). *Preventing reading difficulties in young children*. Washington, D.C.: National Academy Press.

Snow, R. E. (1994). A person-situation interaction theory of intelligence in outline. In A. Demetriou & A. Efklides (Eds.), *Intelligence, mind, and reasoning: Structure and development* (pp. 11–28). Amsterdam: North-Holland.

Sohn, D. (1982). Sex differences in achievement self-attributions: An effect size analysis. *Sex Roles, 8,* 345–357.

Solomon, G. E. A. & Cassimatis, N. L. (1999). On facts and conceptual systems: Young children's integration of their understandings of germs and contagion. *Developmental Psychology, 35,* 113–126.

Sophian, C., Garyantes, D., & Chang, C. (1997). When three is less than two: Early developments in children's understanding of fractional quantities. *Developmental Psychology, 33,* 731–744.

Sophian, C. & Kailihiwa, C. (1998). The relation between conceptual understanding of mathematical equivalence and procedures for solving units of counting: Developmental changes. *Cognitive Development, 13,* 561–585.

Sophian, C. & Vong, K. I. (1995). The parts and wholes of arithmetic story problems: Developing knowledge in the preschool years. *Cognition and Instruction, 13,* 469–477.

Sophian, C. & Wood, A. (1997). Proportional reasoning in young children: The parts and the whole of it. *Journal of Educational Psychology, 89,* 309–317.

Spires, H. A., Gallini, J., & Riggsbee, J. (1992). Effects of schema-based and text structure-based cues on expository prose comprehension in fourth graders. *Journal of Experimental Education, 60,* 307–320.

Springer, K. (1992). Children's awareness of the biological implications of kinship. *Child Development, 63,* 950–959.

Springer, K. & Belk, A. (1994). The role of physical contact and association in early contamination sensitivity. *Developmental Psychology, 30,* 864–868.

Springer, K., Ngyuen, T., & Samaniego, R. (1996). Early understanding of age- and environment-related noxiousness in biological kinds: Evidence for a naive theory. *Cognitive Development, 11,* 65–82.

Squire, L. R. (1987). *Memory and brain.* Oxford: Oxford University Press.

Squire, L. R. (1989). On the course of forgetting in very long term memory. *Journal of Experimental Psychology: Learning, memory, and cognition, 15,* 241–245.

Squire, L. R. & Knowlton, B. J. (1995). Memory, hippocampus, and brain systems. In M. S. Gazzaniga (Ed.), *The cognitive neurosciences* (pp. 825–837). Cambridge, MA: MIT Press.

Stahl, S. A. & Miller, P. D. (1989). Whole language and language experience approaches to beginning reading: A quantitative research synthesis. *Review of Educational Research, 59,* 87–116.

Stahly, L. L., Krockover, G. H., & Shepardson, D. P. (1999). Third grade students' ideas about the lunar phases. *Journal of Research in Science Teaching, 36,* 159–177.

Stanovich, K. E. (1980). Toward an interactive-compensatory model of individual differences in the development of reading fluency. *Reading Research Quarterly, 16,* 32–65.

Stanovich, K. E. (1986). Matthew effects in reading: Some consequences of individual differences in the acquisition of literacy. *Reading Research Quarterly, 21,* 360–407.

Stanovich, K. E. (1988). Explaining the differences between the dyslexic and the garden-variety poor reader: The phonological-core variable-difference model. *Journal of Learning Disabilities, 21,* 590–604, 612.

Stanovich, K. E. & Cunningham, A. E. (1992). Studying the consequences of literacy within a literate society: The cognitive correlates of print exposure. *Memory and Cognition, 20,* 51–68.

Stanovich, K. E., Cunningham, A. E., & Feeman, D. J. (1984). Intelligence, cognitive skills, and early

reading progress. *Reading Research Quarterly, 29,* 278–303.

Stanovich, K. E. & Siegel, L. S. (1994). Phenotypic performance profile of children with reading disabilities: A regression-based test of the phonological-core variable-difference model. *Journal of Educational Psychology, 86,* 24–53.

Stanovich, K. E. & West, R. F. (1997). Reasoning independently of prior belief and individual differences in actively open-minded thinking. *Journal of Educational Psychology, 89,* 342–357.

Stanovich, K. E. & West, R. F. (1998). Individual differences in rational thought. *Journal of Experimental Psychology: General, 127,* 161–188.

Stanovich, K. E., West, R. F., & Harrison, M. R. (1995). Knowledge growth and maintenance across the lifespan: The role of print exposure. *Developmental Psychology, 31,* 811–826.

Starkey, P. & Cooper, R. G. (1980). Perception of numbers by human infants. *Science, 210,* 1033–1035.

Steele, K. M., Bass, K. E., & Crook, M. D. (1999). The mystery of the Mozart effect: Failure to replicate. *Psychological Science, 10,* 366–369.

Stein, N. L. (1982). What's in a story: Interpreting the interpretations of story grammars. *Discourse Processes, 5,* 319–335.

Stein, N. L. & Glenn, C. G. (1979). An analysis of story comprehension in elementary school children. In R. O. Freedle (Ed.), *New directions in discourse processing.* Norwood, NJ: Ablex.

Stein, N. L. & Policastro, T. (1984). The story: A comparison between children's and teacher's viewpoints. In H. Mandel, N. L. Stein, & T. Trabasso (Eds.), *Learning and comprehension of text.* Hillsdale, NJ: Erlbaum.

Stern, E. (1993). What makes certain arithmetic problems involving the comparison of sets so difficult for children? *Journal of Educational Psychology, 85,* 7–23.

Sternberg, R. J. (1985). *Beyond IQ: A triarchic theory of human intelligence.* Cambridge: Cambridge University Press.

Sternberg, R. J., Torff, B., & Grigorenko, E. L. (1998). Teaching triarchically improves school achievement. *Journal of Educational Psychology, 90,* 374–384.

Stevenson, H. W., Chen, C., & Uttal, D. H. (1990). Beliefs and achievement: A study of black, white, and hispanic children. *Child Development, 61,* 508–523.

Stevenson, H. W. & Lee, S. Y. (1990). Contexts of achievement. *Monographs of the Society for Research in Child Development, 55* (No. 221).

Stipek, D. J. (1993). *Motivation to learn: From theory to practice* (2nd edition). Boston: Allyn & Bacon.

Stipek, D. & Hoffman, J. (1980). Children's achievement-related expectancies as a function of academic performance histories and sex. *Journal of Educational Psychology, 72,* 861–865.

Stipek, D., Recchia, S., & McClintock, S. (1992). Self-evaluation in young children. *Monographs of the Society for Research in Child Development, 57* (No. 226).

Stofflett, R. T. (1994). The accommodation of science pedagogical knowledge: The application of conceptual change constructs to teacher education. *Journal of Research in Science Teaching, 31,* 787–810.

Stone, C. A. & Day, M. C. (1978). Levels of availability of a formal operations strategy. *Child Development, 49,* 1054–1065.

Strauss, M. S. & Curtis, L. E. (1981). Infant perception of numerosity. *Child Development, 60,* 521–538.

Sulzby, E. (1991). Assessment of emergent literacy: Storybook reading. *The reading teacher, 44,* 498–500.

Sunal, C. S. (1991). *Early childhood social studies.* Columbus, OH: Merrill.

Sweller, J. & Cooper, G. A. (1985). The use of examples as a substitute for problem solving in learning algebra. *Cognition and Instruction, 2,* 59–89.

Takahira, S. (1995). *Cross-cultural study on variables influencing gender differences in mathematics performance.* Unpublished doctoral dissertation, University of Maryland, College Park.

Taylor, B. M. (1980). Children's memory for expository text after reading. *Reading Research Quarterly, 25,* 399–411.

Taylor, B. M. (1986). Summary writing by young children. *Reading Research Quarterly, 21,* 193–208.

Taylor, B. M. & Beach, R. W. (1984). The effects of text structure in the recall of expository material. *Reading Research Quarterly, 25,* 79–89.

Taylor, B. M., Frye, B. J., & Maruyama, G. M. (1990). Time spent reading and reading growth. *American Educational Research Journal, 27,* 351–362.

Teale, W. H. (1986). Home background and young children's literacy development. In W. H. Teale & E. Sulzby (Eds.), *Emergent Literacy* (pp. 173–206). Norwood, NJ: Ablex.

Teale, W. H. & Sulzby, E. (1986). *Emergent literacy.* Norwood, NJ: Ablex.

Thorndike, E. L. (1913). *Educational Psychology.* New York: Teachers College Press.

Thorndike, E. L. & Woodworth, R. S. (1901). The influence of improvement in one mental function upon the efficiency of other functions. *Psychological Review, 8,* 247–261.

Torgesen, J. K. & Burgess, S. R. (1998). Consistency of reading-related phonological processes throughout early childhood: Evidence from longitudinal-correlational and instructional studies. In J. L. Metsala & L. C. Ehri (Eds.), *Word recognition in beginning literacy* (pp. 161–188). Mahwah, NJ: Erlbaum.

Treiman, R., Mullennix, J., Bijeljac-Babic, R., & Richmond-Welty, E. D. (1995). The special role of rimes in the description, use, and acquisition of English orthography. *Journal of Experimental Psychology: General, 124,* 107–136.

Treiman, R. & Tincoff, R. (1997). The fragility of the alphabetic principle: Children's knowledge of letter names can cause them to spell syllabically rather than alphabetically. *Journal of Experimental Child Psychology, 64,* 425–451.

Treiman, R., Tincoff, R., & Richmond-Welty, E. D. (1996). Letter names help children to connect print to speech. *Developmental Psychology, 32,* 505–514.

Treiman, R., Weatherston, S., & Berch, D. (1994). The role of letter names in children's learning of phoneme-grapheme relations. *Applied Psycholinguistics, 15,* 97–122.

Treiman, R. & Zukowski, A. (1996). Children's sensitivity to syllables, onsets, rimes, and phonemes. *Journal of Experimental Child Psychology, 61,* 193–215.

Tulving, E. (1983). *Elements of episodic memory.* New York: Oxford University Press.

Tulving. E. (1984). How many memory systems are there? *American Psychologist, 40,* 385–398.

Tulving, E. & Psotka, J. (1971). Retroactive inhibition in free recall: Inaccessibility of information available in the memory store. *Journal of Experimental Psychology, 87,* 1–8.

Tunmer, W. E., Herriman, M. L., & Nesdale, A. R. (1988). Metalinguistic abilities and beginning reading. *Reading Research Quarterly, 23,* 134–158.

Van den Broek, P. (1989). Causal reasoning and inference making in judging the importance of story statements. *Child Development, 60,* 286–297.

Van den Broek, P., Lorch, E. P., & Thurlow, R. (1996). Children's and adults' memory for television stories: The role of causal factors, story-grammar categories, and hierarchical level. *Child Development, 67,* 3010–3028.

van Dijk, T. A. & Kintsch, W. (1983). *Strategies of discourse comprehension.* New York: Academic Press.

VanSledright, B. A. & Kelly, C. (1998). Reading American history: The influence of multiple sources on six fifth graders. *Elementary School Journal, 98,* 239–265.

Varelas, M. (1997). Third and fourth graders' conceptions of repeated trials and best representatives in science experiments. *Journal of Research in Science Teaching, 34,* 853–872.

Vellutino, F. R. & Scanlon, D. M. (1987). Phonological coding, phonological awareness, and reading ability:

Evidence from a longitudinal and experimental study. *Merrill-Palmer Quarterly, 33,* 321–363.

Vellutino, F. R. & Scanlon, D. M. (1991). The preeminence of phonologically based skills in learning to read. In S. A. Brady & D. P. Shankweiler (Eds.), *Phonological processes in literacy.* Hillsdale, NJ: Erlbaum.

Vellutino, F. R., Scanlon, D. M., Sipay, E. R., Small, S. G. et al. (1996). Cognitive profiles of difficult-to-remediate and readily remediated poor readers: Early intervention as a vehicle for distinguishing between cognitive and experiential deficits as basic causes of specific reading disability. *Journal of Educational Psychology, 88,* 601–638.

Venville, G. J. & Treagust, D. F. (1998). Exploring conceptual change in genetics using a multidimensional interpretive framework. *Journal of Research in Science Teaching, 35,* 1031–1055.

Vispoel, (1995). Self-concept in artistic domains: An extension of the Shavelson, Hubner, and Stanton (1976) model. *Journal of Educational Psychology, 87,* 134–153.

Von Seeker, C. E. & Lissitz, R. W. (1999). Estimating the impact of instructional practices on student achievement in science. *Journal of Research in Science Teaching, 36,* 1110–1126.

Voss, J. F., Tyler, S. W., & Yengo, L. A. (1983). Individual differences in the solving of social science problems. In R. F. Dillon & R. R. Schmeck (Eds.), *Individual differences in cognition* (Vol. 1, pp. 205–232). New York: Academic Press.

Vye, N. J., Delclos, V. R., Burns, M. S., & Bransford, J. D. (1988). Teaching thinking and problem-solving: Instructional issues. In R. J. Sternberg & E. E. Smith (Eds.), *The psychology of human thought* (pp. 337–365). Cambridge: Cambridge University Press.

Vygotsky, L. S. (1962). *Thought and language.* Cambridge, MA: MIT Press.

Vygotsky, L. S. (1978). *Mind in society.* Cambridge, MA: Harvard University Press.

Waggoner, J. E., Meece, R., & Palermo, D. (1985). Grasping the meaning of metaphor: Story recall and comprehension. *Child Development, 56,* 1156–1166.

Wagner, S. & Kieran, C. (1989). *Research issues in the learning and teaching of algebra.* Reston, VA: National Council of Teachers of Mathematics.

Walberg, H. J. & Tsai, S. (1984). Reading achievement and diminishing returns to time. *Journal of Educational Psychology, 76,* 442–451.

Walker, C. H. (1987). Relative importance of domain knowledge and overall aptitude on acquisition of domain-related information. *Cognition and Instruction, 4,* 25–42.

Wallach, M. A. & Wallach, L. (1979). Helping disadvantaged children learn to read by teaching them phoneme identification skills. In L. A. Resnick & P. A. Weaver (Eds.), *Theory and practice of early reading* (Vol. 3, pp. 227–259). Hillsdale, NJ: Erlbaum.

Wallach, L., Wallach, M. A., Dozier, M. G., & Kaplan, N. E. (1977). Poor children learning to read do not have trouble with auditory discrimination but do have trouble with phoneme recognition. *Journal of Educational Psychology, 69,* 36–39.

Ward, S. L., Byrnes, J. P., & Overton, W. F. (1990). Organization of knowledge and conditional reasoning. *Journal of Educational Psychology, 82,* 832–837.

Wasik, B. A. (1986). *Familiarity of content and inference making in young children.* Unpublished doctoral dissertation, Temple University.

Washburn, D. A. & Astur, R. S. (1998). Nonverbal working memory of humans and monkeys: Rehearsal in the sketchpad? *Memory and Cognition, 26,* 277–286.

Wason, P. C. (1983). Realism and rationality in the selection task. In J. St. B. T. Evans (Ed.), *Thinking and reasoning: Psychological approaches* (pp. 44–75). London: Routledge & Kegan Paul.

Wearne, D. & Hiebert, J. (1988). Constructing and using meaning for mathematical symbols: The case of decimal fractions. In J. Hiebert & M. Behr (Eds.), *Number concepts and operations in the middle grades* (pp. 220–235). Reston, VA: National Council of Teachers of Mathematics.

Weaver, C. A. & Kintsch, W. (1991). Expository text. In R. Barr, M. L. Kamil, P. Mosenthal, & P. D. Pearson (Eds.), *Handbook of reading research* (Vol. II, pp. 230–245). New York: Longman.

Weiner, B. (1986). *An attribution theory of motivation and emotion.* New York: Springer-Verlag.

Weinstein, C. E. & Mayer, R. E. (1986). The teaching of learning strategies. In M. C. Wittrock (Ed.), *Handbook of research on teaching* (3rd edition). New York: Macmillan.

Wellman, H. M. (1992). *The child's theory of mind.* Cambridge, MA: MIT Press.

Wellman, H. M. & Gelman, S. A. (1998). Knowledge acquisition in foundational domains. In W. Damon (series ed.), D. Kuhn, & R. S. Siegler (volume eds.), *Handbook of child psychology. Vol. 2. Cognition, perception, and language* (pp. 523–567). New York: Wiley.

Wentzel, K. R. (1989). Adolescent classroom goals, standards for performance, and academic achievement: An interactionist perspective. *Journal of Educational Psychology, 81,* 131–142.

Wentzel, K. R. (1991). Social and academic goals at school: Motivation and achievement in context. In

M. Maehr & P. Pintrich (Eds.), *Advances in motivation and achievement, volume 7* (pp. 185–212). Greenwich, CT: JAI.

Wentzel, K. R. & Wigfield, A. (1998). Academic and social motivational influences on students' academic performance. *Educational Psychology Review, 10,* 155–175.

Wertheimer, M. (1945). *Productive thinking.* New York: Harper & Brothers.

Wertsch, J. V. (1985). *Vygotsky and the social formation of mind.* Cambridge, MA: Harvard University Press.

Whitehurst, G. J., Falco, F. L., Lonigan, C. J., Fischel, J. E., DeBaryshe, B. D., Valdez-Menchaca, M. C., & Caulfield, M. (1988). Accelerating language development through picturebook reading. *Developmental Psychology, 24,* 552–559.

Whitehurst, G. J. & Lonigan, C. J. (1998). Child development and emergent literacy. *Child Development, 69,* 848–872.

Whittlesea, B. W. A. & Cantwell, A. L. (1987). Enduring influence of the purpose of experiences: Encoding-retrieval interactions in word and pseudoword perception. *Memory and Cognition, 15,* 465–472.

Wigfield, A. & Eccles, J. S. (1989). Test anxiety in elementary and secondary school students. *Educational Psychologist, 24,* 159–183.

Wigfield, A. & Eccles, J. S. (1992). The development of achievement task values: A theoretical analysis. *Developmental Review, 12,* 265–310.

Wigfield, A. W. & Eccles, J. S. (2000). Expectancy-value theory of achievement motivation. *Contemporary Educational Psychology, 25,* 68–81.

Wigfield, A., Eccles, J., Harold-Goldsmith, R., Blumenfeld, P., Yoon, K. S., & Friedman-Doan, C. (1989). Gender and age differences in children's achievement self-perceptions during elementary school. Paper presented at the biennial meeting of the Society for Research in Child Development, Kansas City, April.

Wigfield, A. W., Eccles, J., MacIver, D., Reuman, D., & Midgley, C. (1991). Transitions at early adolescence: Changes in children's domain-specific self-perceptions and general self-esteem across the transition to junior high school. *Developmental Psychology, 27,* 552–565.

Wilson, M. & Emmorey, K. (1998). A "word length effect" for sign language: Further evidence for the role of language in structuring working memory. *Memory and Cognition, 26,* 584–590.

Wineburg, S. S. (1991). Historical problem solving: A study of the cognitive processes used in the evaluation of documentary and pictorial evidence. *Journal of Educational Psychology, 83,* 73–87.

Winograd, T. (1975). Frame representations and the declarative/ procedural controversy. In D. G. Bobrow & A. Collins (Eds.), *Representation and understanding: Studies in cognitive science* (pp. 185–210). New York: Academic Press.

Wood, B. S. & Brown, L. A. (1997). Participation in an all-female Algebra I class: Effects on high school math and science course selection. *Journal of Women and Minorities in Science and Engineering, 3,* 265–277.

Wood, D., Bruner, J. S., & Ross, G. (1976). The role of tutoring in problem-solving. *Journal of Child Psychology and Psychiatry, 17,* 89–100.

Wood, E., Miller, G., Symons, S., Canough, T., & Yedlicka, J. (1993). Effects of elaborative interrogation on young learners' recall of facts. *Elementary School Journal, 94,* 245–254.

Wright, R. E. & Rosenberg, S. (1993). Knowledge of text coherence and expository writing: A developmental study. *Journal of Educational Psychology, 85,* 152–158.

Wyner, N. B. & Farquhar, E. (1991). Cognitive, emotional, and social development: Early childhood social studies. In J. P. Shaver (Ed.), *Handbook of research on social studies teaching and learning* (pp. 109–120). New York: Macmillan.

Wynn, K. (1990). Children's understanding of counting. *Cognition, 36,* 155–193.

Wynn, K. (1992). Addition and subtraction by human infants. *Nature, 358,* 749–750.

Yerkes, R. M. & Dodson, J. D. (1908). The relation of strength of stimulus to rapidity of habit-formation. *Journal of Comparative Neurology and Psychology, 18,* 459–482.

Zimmerman, B. J. & Kitsantas, A. (1999). Acquiring writing revision skill: Shifting from process to outcome self-regulatory goals. *Journal of Educational Psychology, 91,* 241–250.

Zimmerman, B. J. & Martinez-Pons, M. (1990). Student differences in self-regulated learning: Relating grade, sex, and giftedness to self-efficacy and strategy use. *Journal of Educational Psychology, 82,* 51–59.

Zinar, S. (1990). Fifth graders' recall of propositional content and causal relationships from expository prose. *Journal of Reading Behavior, 22,* 181–199.

Zwaan, R. A. & Radvansky, G. A. (1998). Situation models in language comprehension and memory. *Psychological Bulletin, 123,* 162–185.

Index